HUMAN
RIGHTS
WATCH

WORLD REPORT

2014

EVENTS OF 2013

Front cover photo: **Syria** – *Two boys stand in a school building damaged by government shelling in Aleppo on February 7, 2013.*
© 2013 Nish Nalbandian/Redux

Back cover photo: **South Sudan** – *A young, unmarried girl stands amid a herd of cattle outside Bor, Jonglei State. Cattle carry significant social, economic, and cultural importance for South Sudan's pastoralist ethnic groups, which use cows for dowry payments—a key driver of child marriage, February 2013.*
© 2013 Brent Stirton/Reportage by Getty Images for Human Rights Watch

Cover and book design by Rafael Jiménez

www.hrw.org

Human Rights Watch defends the rights of people worldwide. We scrupulously investigate abuses, expose the facts widely, and pressure those with power to respect rights and secure justice. Human Rights Watch is an independent, international organization that works as part of a vibrant movement to uphold human dignity and advance the cause of human rights for all.

Human Rights Watch began in 1978 with the founding of its Europe and Central Asia division (then known as Helsinki Watch). Today, it also includes divisions covering Africa; the Americas; Asia; and the Middle East and North Africa; a United States program; thematic divisions or programs on arms; business and human rights; children's rights; disability rights; health and human rights; international justice; lesbian, gay, bisexual, and transgender rights, refugees, terrorism/counterterrorism; and women's rights; and an emergencies program. It maintains offices in Amsterdam, Beirut, Berlin, Brussels, Cairo, Chicago, Geneva, Johannesburg, London, Los Angeles, Moscow, New York, Paris, São Paolo, San Francisco, Sydney, Tokyo, Toronto, Washington DC, and Zurich, and field presences in 20 other locations globally. Human Rights Watch is an independent, nongovernmental organization, supported by contributions from private individuals and foundations worldwide. It accepts no government funds, directly or indirectly.

HUMAN RIGHTS WATCH

The staff includes Kenneth Roth, Executive Director; Michele Alexander, Deputy Executive Director, Development and Global Initiatives; Carroll Bogert, Deputy Executive Director, External Relations; Iain Levine, Deputy Executive Director, Program; Chuck Lustig, Deputy Executive Director, Operations; Walid Ayoub, Information Technology Director; Pierre Bairin, Media Director; Clive Baldwin, Senior Legal Advisor; Emma Daly, Communications Director; Alan Feldstein, Associate General Counsel; Barbara Guglielmo, Acting Operations Director; Peggy Hicks, Global Advocacy Director; Babatunde Olugboji, Deputy Program Director; Dinah PoKempner, General Counsel; om Porteous, Deputy Program Director; Aisling Reidy, Senior Legal Advisor; James Ross, Legal and Policy Director; Joseph Saunders, Deputy Program Director; Frances Sinha, Global Human Resources Director; and Minky Worden, Director of Global Initiatives.

The division directors of Human Rights Watch are Brad Adams, Asia; Joseph Amon, Health and Human Rights; Daniel Bekele, Africa; John Biaggi, International Film Festival; Peter Bouckaert, Emergencies; Richard Dicker, International Justice; Bill Frelick, Refugees; Arvind Ganesan, Business and Human Rights; Liesl Gerntholtz, Women's Rights; Steve Goose, Arms; Alison Parker, United States; Graeme Reid, Lesbian, Gay, Bisexual, and Transgender Rights; José Miguel Vivanco, Americas; Shantha Rau Barriga, Disability Rights; Zama Coursen-Neff, Children's Rights; Sarah Leah Whitson, Middle East and North Africa; and Hugh Williamson, Europe and Central Asia.

The advocacy directors of Human Rights Watch are Philippe Bolopion, United Nations–New York; Maria Laura Canineu, Brazil; Juliette De Rivero, United Nations–Geneva; Kanae Doi, Japan; Jean-Marie Fardeau, Paris; Meenakshi Ganguly, South Asia; Lotte Leicht, European Union; Tiseke Kasambala, Southern Africa; Sarah Margon (acting), Washington DC; David Mepham, UK; and Wenzel Michalski, Berlin.

Table of Contents

Foreword

World Report 2014 is Human Rights Watch's 24th annual review of human rights practices around the globe. It summarizes key human rights issues in more than 90 countries and territories worldwide, drawing on events from the end of 2012 through November 2013.

The book is divided into three main parts: an essay section, photo essays, and country-specific chapters.

Reflecting on the "Rights Struggles of 2013," Executive Director Kenneth Roth highlights three main themes. In Syria, the slaughter of civilians continued with only a weak international response, straining the "Responsibility to Protect," or R2P, doctrine, which commits world governments to respond to imminent or ongoing mass atrocities. Elsewhere, governments are engaged in what Roth calls "abusive majoritarianism"—expressing outward commitment to democracy while in reality using the real or perceived preferences of the majority to limit dissent and suppress minorities. And in the United States, new disclosures about the use of dragnet surveillance and targeted drone killings have fueled debate about the tactics of counterterrorism. But Roth sees encouraging signs. The R2P doctrine appears to be holding up enough to provide at least some help in several African countries facing mass atrocities, including the Central African Republic, South Sudan, and the Democratic Republic of Congo; public reaction has been strong against what Roth calls "feigned democracy"; and the US government faces increased pressure to change current counterterrorism practices. In addition, he notes improvements in the machinery that helps to defend human rights, including the United Nations Human Rights Council. The year 2013, he concludes, may have had "more than enough suffering," but it also featured a "vigorous movement fighting back."

Next, Maria McFarland Sánchez-Moreno charts Human Rights Watch's evolving approach to current global policies aimed at curbing drug use and the multi-billion dollar illegal drug trade ("The Human Rights Case for Drug Reform"). For many years, Human Rights Watch documented widespread abuses that governments committed in the name of combatting drugs. But research in several countries led us to the increasing conviction that, when it came to personal use and possession of drugs, the criminalization of drugs was not only ineffective and corrosive of

institutions, but also inconsistent with personal autonomy and the right to privacy. In 2013, Human Rights Watch adopted a policy calling on governments to
decriminalize all personal use and possession of drugs, and to adopt alternative
policies on the drug trade—a "new course" that McFarland argues is vital to avoiding the crippling human costs of the current approach to drug control.

More than a decade ago, world governments established eight Millennium
Development Goals (MDGs)—including commitments to reduce child and maternal
mortality and achieve universal primary education—all to be achieved by 2015. In
"Putting Development to Rights," David Mepham argues that despite real progress
in some areas, the neglect of human rights in the MDGs has diminished and distorted development efforts, with many people excluded or unable to benefit from
development programs. More worrying still, many people have been harmed by
economic policies carried out in the name of development. Mepham suggests that
the current UN-led process to establish successor goals to the MDGs provides a
crucial opportunity to broaden our understanding of development and fully integrate human rights into development policy and practice. Doing so, he says, will
help promote more just and inclusive development, and improve the lives of millions of the world's poorest and most marginalized people.

After 2013's flood of revelations about pervasive US online surveillance, Dinah
PoKempner pushes back against those who argue that we must simply live with it
because public expectations of privacy have eroded ("The Right Whose Time Has
Come (Again)"). Privacy, she says, is a crucial "gateway" to almost every other
right, and "nothing less than the shelter in which we work out what we think and
who we are." Putting the vulnerability that many people feel as lives migrate
online into historical and legal perspective, she describes legal efforts from the
end of the nineteenth century to address technological developments seen as
menacing people's private lives. Once again, she says, technology is evolving and
the law must catch up.

The photo essays that follow highlight three underreported human rights crises:
child marriage in South Sudan, the impact of the 2014 Sochi Olympics on human
rights in Russia, and the growing human rights and humanitarian tragedy in the
Central African Republic.

The rest of the volume consists of individual country entries, each of which identifies significant human rights issues, examines the freedom of local human rights defenders to conduct their work, and surveys the response of key international actors, such as the UN, the European Union, the US, and various regional and international organizations and institutions.

The report reflects extensive investigative work that Human Rights Watch staff undertook in 2013, usually in close partnership with human rights activists in the country in question. It also reflects the work of our advocacy team, which monitors policy developments and strives to persuade governments and international institutions to curb abuses and promote human rights. Human Rights Watch publications, issued throughout the year, contain more detailed accounts of many of the issues addressed in the brief summaries in this volume. They can be found on the Human Rights Watch website, www.hrw.org.

As in past years, this report does not include a chapter on every country where Human Rights Watch works, nor does it discuss every issue of importance. The absence of a particular country or issue often simply reflects staffing limitations and should not be taken as commentary on the significance of the problem. There are many serious human rights violations that Human Rights Watch simply lacks the capacity to address.

The factors we considered in determining the focus of our work in 2013 (and hence the content of this volume) include the number of people affected and the severity of abuse, access to the country and the availability of information about it, the susceptibility of abusive forces to influence, and the importance of addressing certain thematic concerns and of reinforcing the work of local rights organizations.

The *World Report* does not have separate chapters addressing our thematic work but instead incorporates such material directly into the country entries. Please consult the Human Rights Watch website for more detailed treatment of our work on children's rights, women's rights, arms and military issues, business and human rights, health and human rights, disability rights, international justice, terrorism and counterterrorism, refugees and displaced people, and lesbian, gay, bisexual, and transgender people's rights, and for information about our international film festivals.

Rights Struggles of 2013:
Stopping Mass Atrocities, Majority Bullying, and Abusive Counterterrorism

By Kenneth Roth

Looking back at human rights developments in 2013, several themes stand out. The unchecked slaughter of civilians in Syria elicited global horror and outrage, but not enough to convince world leaders to exert the pressure needed to stop it. That has led some to lament the demise of the much-vaunted "Responsibility to Protect" doctrine, which world governments adopted less than a decade ago to protect people facing mass atrocities. Yet it turned out to be too soon to draft the epitaph for R2P, as it is known, because toward the end of the year it showed renewed vitality in several African countries facing the threat of large-scale atrocities: Central African Republic, South Sudan, and the Democratic Republic of Congo.

Democracy took a battering in several countries, but not because those in power openly abandoned it. Many leaders still feel great pressure to pay lip service to democratic rule. But a number of relatively new governments, including in Egypt and Burma, settled for the most superficial forms—only elections, or their own divining of majoritarian preferences—without regard to the limits on majorities that are essential to any real democracy. This abusive majoritarianism lay behind governmental efforts to suppress peaceful dissent, restrict minorities, and enforce narrow visions of cultural propriety. Yet in none of these cases did the public take this abuse of democracy sitting down.

Since September 11, 2001, efforts to combat terrorism have also spawned human rights abuses. The past year saw intensified public discussion about two particular counterterrorism programs used by the United States: global mass electronic surveillance and targeted killings by aerial drones. For years, Washington had avoided giving clear legal justifications for these programs by hiding behind the asserted needs of secrecy. That strategy was undermined by whistleblower Edward Snowden's revelations about the surveillance program, as well as by on-the-ground reporting of civilian casualties in the targeted-killing program. Both now face intense public scrutiny.

In the midst of all this upheaval, there were also important advances in the international machinery that helps to defend human rights. After a slow and disappointing start, the United Nations Human Rights Council seemed to come onto its own, most recently with significant pressure applied to North Korea and Sri Lanka. And two new multinational treaties give hope for some of the world's most marginalized people: domestic workers and artisanal miners poisoned by the unregulated use of mercury.

Responsibility to Protect: Pummeled but Still Potent

In 2005, the world's governments made an historic pledge that if a national government failed to stop mass atrocities, they would step in. The international community has since invoked the R2P doctrine successfully to spare lives, most notably in Kenya in 2007-2008 and Côte d'Ivoire in 2011. However, many governments criticized the doctrine after NATO's 2011 military intervention in Libya, where NATO was widely perceived to have moved beyond the protection of civilians to regime change. The reaction poisoned the global debate about how to respond to mass atrocities in Syria. The utter failure to stop the slaughter of Syrian civilians has raised concerns that the doctrine is now unraveling. Yet that damning shortcoming should not obscure several cases in 2013 in which R2P showed considerable vibrancy. In the Central African Republic and South Sudan, the African Union (AU) and UN Security Council moved quickly to deploy peacekeeping troops in an effort to prevent the slaughter of civilians on religious and ethnic grounds. And in eastern Democratic Republic of Congo, international pressure succeeded in convincing Rwanda to stop its military support for the latest in a succession of rebel groups committing atrocities in this long-suffering region.

Syria

Syria was by far the deadliest armed conflict of 2013. Now in its third year, the uprising-turned-civil war stood out for the ruthlessness of the government's military strategy. Rather than targeting only opposing combatants, as international humanitarian law requires, the government indiscriminately attacked civilians in areas held by the armed opposition. One of its apparent aims appeared to be to drive away as many civilians as possible so rebel forces would not deploy among them or live off a functioning economy. It also used collective punishment to turn people against the opposition and to send a message to all Syrians that life will be miserable if they let the opposition prevail where they live.

The most outrageous example of this strategy was the August 21 sarin attack on Ghouta, an opposition-held suburb of Damascus, which evidence strongly suggests was carried out by government forces. Hundreds of civilians were killed that night, including many children in their pajamas. Local monitoring groups report that roughly 5,000 individuals are being killed by conventional weapons each month, many the result of laws-of-war violations, with civilians constituting some 35 percent of the deaths. Opposition forces have also been responsible for atrocities, and concern about their conduct has grown as Islamist extremists, some linked to Al-Qaeda, gain ascendancy in their ranks. But the vast majority of civilian deaths result from government attacks. Syrian troops have used ballistic missiles, rockets, artillery shells, cluster bombs, incendiary weapons, fuel-air explosives, barrel bombs, and regular aerial bombardment, as well as chemical weapons to indiscriminately attack populated areas in opposition-held territory and sometimes to target functioning bakeries, medical facilities, schools, and other civilian structures.

Government forces have also massacred civilians and fighters in their custody, and horror stories have emerged about the fate of the countless individuals who have been arbitrarily detained, tortured, and in some cases killed in Syrian detention facilities. As Syria's population has become increasingly displaced (approximately 2.3 million outside Syria and 6.5 million within) and needy (an estimated 10 million depend on humanitarian aid), the government has erected countless obstacles to delivering humanitarian supplies to civilians in opposition-held territory, despite a UN Security Council presidential statement in October that urged these barriers be lifted.

The international community's response to this slaughter and suffering has been painfully narrow. Amid questions about whether US President Barack Obama would enforce his declared "red line" over the use of chemical weapons and his threat to use military force, the United States and Russia brokered an agreement in September according to which Syria is to surrender those weapons. Reports indicate Syria is largely cooperating. But the accord addresses the method responsible for a small fraction of the civilians killed in the conflict. Insufficient pressure is being put on Syria to stop killing civilians by conventional means, and to permit

3

humanitarian access to besieged towns and cross-border humanitarian assistance as the easiest and surest way to reach many of those in need in opposition-held areas.

In recent months, international efforts to address the Syria conflict have focused mainly on peace talks known as Geneva II. But while the likelihood of reaching a political accommodation among the warring factions anytime soon is remote, the fear of doing anything that might dissuade Damascus from participating in Geneva II has become the latest excuse for not putting real pressure on Syria to stop killing civilians by conventional means and to permit the free flow of humanitarian aid. The US has also been reluctant to pressure Russia—as Syria's primary backer, the government with the greatest influence over Damascus—because of other priorities, most recently ensuring its help in implementing the chemical-weapons deal to avoid renewed calls for the military action that President Obama was so eager to avoid. Iran's support for Syrian President Bashar al-Assad has been overshadowed by negotiations over its nuclear capacity. The consequence is diplomatic complacency about the Syrian government's largely unimpeded, murderous strategy for Syrian civilians.

What pressure might help to curb the slaughter? Western and Arab governments so far have been unwilling to deploy more aggressive banking sanctions of the sort that have proven so powerful elsewhere. Russia has been unwilling to countenance the UN Security Council referring Syria to the International Criminal Court (ICC), imposing an arms embargo, or even condemning government atrocities. In the case of the ICC, Washington also has not publicly backed a role for the court, apparently guided partly by a desire to avoid the unlikely possibility that Israeli officials would be prosecuted for transferring people to the relatively static settlements on the Israeli-occupied Golan Heights. (The expanding West Bank settlements are a different matter, but a Syrian referral would not confer ICC jurisdiction there).

Governments in the region have also been unhelpful. Lebanon, Iraq, and Egypt have reportedly refused to enforce Arab League sanctions, sending oil to keep Syria's killing machine running. Gulf countries, including Saudi Arabia and Qatar, have reportedly armed and funded extremist groups that have been responsible for repeated atrocities, and along with Kuwait, have closed their eyes to funding by their citizens. Iran and Hezbollah continue to back the Syrian government.

The international community seems all too willing to let the killing of Syrian civilians continue. Some governments reinforce their apathy by promoting the narrative of ruthless combatants killing each other, whether the Syrian military, Hezbollah, or jihadists. Arab governments, particularly in the Gulf, see the conflict mainly through the prism of Sunni-Shia relations, and a simmering conflict between Saudi Arabia and Iran over regional hegemony. But to a horrifyingly large extent, this is a war on civilians. Urgency, rather than complacency, should be the order of the day.

Central African Republic and South Sudan

Despite this failure in Syria, the final months of 2013 showed that the R2P doctrine still retained considerable force. When mass slaughter on religious grounds broke out in the Central African Republic, France and the AU sent troops to reinforce overwhelmed AU peacekeepers, the US contributed more than US$100 million, and the UN began preparing for its own, much-needed peacekeeping mission. Much more remains to be done to pull the country back from the brink, but the international community has demonstrated a greater acceptance of its responsibility to act.

In mid-December, in neighboring South Sudan, hundreds were killed as a political conflict degenerated into the ethnic targeting of civilians and a wider civil war. Within days, the UN Security Council approved an additional 5,500 peacekeepers for the country. That may not be enough to stop the mass killing or stabilize the dire situation, but the swift response suggests that, at least in the right circumstances, the R2P doctrine is still a force to be reckoned with.

Notably, the intervention in each case was as much about stopping the slaughter of civilians by government troops and militias as by rebel forces—one of the most controversial challenges for the R2P doctrine.

Rwanda and the Democratic Republic of Congo

The international community also mounted an effective international response in eastern Congo, where Rwanda has long supported a succession of abusive rebel groups, contributing to the massive loss of life over the past two decades. President Paul Kagame typically got away with this because of a combination of the international community's guilt at not having stopped the 1994 genocide in Rwanda and admiration for the economic progress that the country has made under his leadership.

Things began to change in June 2012, when Human Rights Watch and a group of UN experts uncovered compelling evidence that Rwanda was providing extensive military support to the M23 rebel group in eastern Congo despite its record of atrocities. For the first time, Western powers, including Rwanda's most important backers, the US and Britain, began to publicly criticize the government and even suspended some assistance. Rwanda flatly denied supporting the M23, undermining the government's credibility and reconfirming the importance of pressuring it to stop.

At first the pressure succeeded in forcing the M23 to pull back from Goma, the area's largest city, but this was not enough to stop the M23 from preying on the people of the region. The UN Security Council responded by significantly bolstering the military capacity of peacekeeping troops deployed in eastern Congo. Then, when the M23 launched an offensive in October 2013 with ongoing Rwandan military support, US Secretary of State John Kerry and British Foreign Secretary William Hague phoned Kagame and told him to stop. This time, the combination of pressure and firepower seemed to work. Deprived of Rwandan military support and facing intensified pressure from the reinforced UN peacekeeping force, the M23 crumbled within days. Other armed groups, as well as the Congolese army, are still responsible for attacks on civilians, but eastern Congo is at the time of writing apparently free of the predations of a Rwandan-backed armed group for the first time in years.

Abusive Majoritarianism

Democracy has three essential components: periodic elections, the rule of law, and respect for the human rights of all. Many dictatorships fear allowing anything like free and fair elections. But authoritarian governments have also learned that it is possible to adopt the form but not the substance of democracy, permitting elections, often controlled, but nothing more. This feigned democracy rejects basic principles, such as that governments must be accountable under the rule of the law, limited by the human rights that protect minorities, and committed to allowing free and continuous public debate.

In the past year, many relatively new governments pursued this abusive majoritarianism, showing more enthusiasm for representing a majority—sometimes determined by elections, sometimes by their own convenient assessment—than for respecting the basic rights within which a democracy is supposed to function. Some leaders also seemed to adopt a conveniently narrow vision of democracy in which all that matters is a vote on election day, not public debate the rest of the year. Resenting the give and take of ordinary politics, they tried to suppress the public protests and criticism in the press and on social media that are also a staple of any meaningful democracy.

The most glaring example was in **Egypt**. First, the Muslim Brotherhood government of President Mohammed Morsy ruled in a manner that left secular and minority groups fearing exclusion in an Islamist-dominated government. Then, in the wake of Morsy's ouster by the army in July, the military-dominated government of Gen. Abdel Fattah al-Sisi launched the worst repression that Egypt has known in decades, including by killing hundreds of Muslim Brotherhood protesters.

Despite Morsy's narrow win in the 2012 presidential contest—a 25 percent plurality in the first round, and a bare majority of 51.7 percent in the second—he governed as if the rights of the minority were of little concern. He convened a constituent assembly that many felt gave an inadequate role to non-Brotherhood representatives, and rammed through a constitution, endorsed by referendum, which many feared would privilege an Islamist interpretation to the detriment of basic rights, especially for women and religious minorities. He temporarily gave himself exceptional powers to stand above judicial review "on sovereign matters." And in a misguided effort to buy good will, he made little effort to end the impunity that the security forces enjoyed, despite their long record of killing, torture, and arbitrary detention. Indeed, the military was granted even greater autonomy under Morsy than it ever enjoyed under President Hosni Mubarak, a former general.

When millions of Egyptians took to the streets in June 2013 to demand new elections, the military read the protests as license to overthrow Morsy, claiming to speak for the majority without even the benefit of an election. It then proceeded to disregard basic rights far more blatantly than Morsy ever dared. It drafted a constitution that, while promising some greater protection for the rights of women and religious minorities, retained military trials for civilians and expanded the shield protecting the military from civilian oversight. And despite this constitutional exercise, the military acted as if unconstrained by any rights at all.

The military-dominated authorities used excessive lethal force to break up Muslim Brotherhood sit-in protests in Cairo, indiscriminately and in some cases deliberately killing up to 1,000 people. They rounded up thousands of Muslim Brotherhood leaders and rank-and-file members and detained them, sometimes without acknowledging their detention, frequently on trumped-up or no charges. They officially designated the Muslim Brotherhood a terrorist organization, exposing its members to criminal sanctions and even the death penalty, and seizing its assets. They also froze the assets of affiliated medical centers and threatened to take over Brotherhood mosques and replace their preachers.

The government adopted a law banning demonstrations without official permission, which it showed no inclination to grant. It deepened the military's autonomy beyond anything Mubarak had ever allowed and worse even than Morsy's permissive approach. And despite many liberals misguidedly backing these measures, it began turning its repressive attention to the secular activists who had been at the forefront of the original Tahrir Square movement three years earlier. For the second time since the fall of Mubarak in February 2011, a government is in power with little apparent inclination to limit itself by respecting basic rights.

Tunisia offered proof that Egypt could have taken a different path. In 2011 elections to the National Constituent Assembly, Tunisia's first free elections, the Islamist Nahdha party won a plurality of the vote, well ahead of others. Despite a stalled economy and political polarization, the major political parties across the spectrum negotiated compromises that preserve important rights. In the draft constitution, they removed provisions referring to the "complementary" role of women, which could undermine gender equality, and criminalizing attacks on "sacred values," a vague provision that could be used to penalize peaceful expression. A draft law on "immunization of the revolution" was abandoned to avoid excluding people from political life who have no history of criminal conduct merely because of their past political affiliations.

The hubris of claiming to speak for a majority without regard for rights could be found in other countries as well. In **Turkey**, Prime Minister Recep Tayyip Erdogan has repeatedly won a parliamentary majority, but his method of ruling has seemed increasingly autocratic as he shows less willingness to listen to opponents, critics, or rivals. The tipping point was Erdogan's plan to replace one of the few parks in central Istanbul with a shopping-mall complex. The police's violent dispersal of a small sit-in against the project in May triggered a much larger occupation of the park and mass protests in other cities. Erdogan treated the demonstrations as a personal affront, repeatedly deploying the police to break them up. The police used excessive force, including deliberately firing teargas canisters at protesters, leading to deaths and serious injuries. Even once the protests subsided, Erdogan and his circle continued to exert strong pressure on media organizations that they saw as too sympathetic to their political opponents. And while strongly supportive of the police in their handling of the demonstrations, Erdogan was quick to demote dozens of officers and even a prosecutor whose investigations threatened to implicate government ministers and his own son in a corruption scandal.

In **Burma**, the government of President Thein Sein has committed itself to reform, but major questions remain about its willingness to allow open political competition, including by letting opposition leader Aung San Sui Kyi run for president. The government has been particularly disappointing in its response to violence by Buddhist extremists against ethnic Rohingya and other Muslims, with security forces often standing aside as mobs attack and doing little to bring the perpetrators to justice. It also has done nothing to prosecute security force personnel for war crimes committed in the context of the various ethnic-based civil wars along the country's periphery.

Aung San Suu Kyi has been disappointing as well. Aware that the army will determine her ability to run for president, she has refrained from criticizing its abuses. And because the vulnerable and stateless Rohingya are so unpopular in Burma, she has refused to come to their verbal defense as they have been violently attacked. The Nobel laureate defends her stance by saying that she was always a politician and remains so. The world was apparently mistaken to assume that as a revered victim of rights abuse she would also be a principled defender of rights.

In **Thailand**, the government of Prime Minister Yingluck Shinawatra took advantage of its electoral majority to seek a broad amnesty both for people involved in violent abuse and, not incidentally, her elder brother, former prime minister Thaksin Shinawatra, who has been living in exile since 2006 to avoid corruption charges. This overplaying of her parliamentary majority sparked widespread street protests. Many in the opposition, however, seemed virtually to solicit a military coup, opposing new elections out of fear that, yet again, they would lose. That appeared to breach the principle that, even though elections are no excuse to abuse rights, they are a prerequisite for democratic rule.

In **Kenya,** the government of President Uhuru Kenyatta and his deputy, William Ruto, has used its narrow electoral victory—50.07 percent of the vote, barely avoiding a runoff—to deploy all the resources of the state toward stopping their prosecution by the International Criminal Court for their alleged leadership roles in the 2007-08 post-election violence. Ruto himself, as well as Kenyatta's support- ers, fought efforts to create a special tribunal in Kenya to address the violence, betting that the ICC would never get involved. They bet wrong.

Now that the ICC has charged the two, they have been decrying its so-called inter- ference in their ability to govern, particularly since the Islamist armed group Al- Shabaab's October attack on a Nairobi shopping mall, and what they portray as the ICC's exclusive focus on African suspects—which also happens to be a focus on African victims. But the alternative they offer is not national prosecution but impunity. Their unstated and wrongful assumption is that their electoral victory is sufficient to extinguish the right to justice for the victims of the electoral violence and their families. Although its efforts failed to orchestrate a mass withdrawal of African states from the ICC, Kenya has succeeded in enlisting the African Union on behalf of its quest for impunity. One can only hope that other African leaders pri- oritize African victims over the powerful who prey upon them.

In **Russia,** President Vladimir Putin was clearly shaken in 2011 and 2012 by the large protests in opposition to his party's parliamentary victory in a reportedly fraudulent election and his own return to the Kremlin. Since then, the government has taken various steps to prevent the opposition from mounting further chal- lenge, including limiting protests, punishing dissent, and trying to force critical nongovernmental groups (NGOs) that receive foreign funding to wear the discred- iting label of "foreign agent." The Kremlin has also pandered to its conservative political base through a series of abusive measures such as banning homosexual "propaganda" (ostensibly to protect children), and imposing punitive, dispropor- tionate charges on activists from the punk band Pussy Riot and the environmental group Greenpeace. Apparently to avoid international criticism as February 2014's Sochi Winter Olympics approached, Putin then amnestied or pardoned many of

Russia's highest-profile prisoners. But the effect was largely to highlight the arbitrariness of his rule as the crackdown on government critics continued, drawing new victims into the revolving doors of Russia's politicized justice system.

In **Ukraine**, when President Viktor Yanukovych's decision to eschew closer ties with the European Union met with mass protests in Kiev, the authorities largely let the protests proceed. But when episodes of police brutality against protesters and journalists reporting on the protests sparked wider demonstrations across Ukraine, the authorities promised to bring officials responsible for the violence to account. So far, they have mainly tried to intimidate protesters who complained about stalled investigations.

In **Venezuela**, after Nicolás Maduro was declared the winner of the April presidential election, the results of which were disputed by the opposition, state security forces beat and arbitrarily detained supporters of his opponent, Henrique Capriles, who staged anti-government rallies. Some of those arrested reported being asked, "Who is your president?" and being beaten if they did not respond "Nicolás Maduro," yet public prosecutors failed to investigate credible allegations of abuse. When Capriles called for a peaceful demonstration in the capital, Maduro said he would not allow it to take place, vowing to respond to such "fascism" with an "iron fist" and attributing responsibility for all post-election violence to Capriles. Days after the election, while the opposition was calling for a recount, the president of the National Assembly—who belongs to Maduro's party—refused to give fellow legislators the right to speak until they individually recognized Maduro's victory. Maduro's minister of housing threatened to fire any employee critical of the government. In November, at Maduro's behest, members of his party passed legislation granting him sweeping power to govern by decree. The government has continued to intimidate and sanction media outlets critical of its policies, and has impeded human rights defenders with funding restrictions and the threat of prosecution.

In **China**, the government will not even risk elections for senior officials but claims to speak for the majority based on the self-appointed leadership of the Communist Party. The new government of President Xi Jinping introduced some modest reforms—abolishing "re-education through labor" but not other methods of detaining people without trial, and easing the conditions in which some Chinese couples can have a second child, but not ending altogether the use of official coercion and surveillance in such personal matters. However, the government continued its predecessor's intolerance toward organized dissent, and even retaliated against journalists who work for media companies that took up such sensitive topics as the enormous unexplained wealth of Chinese leaders and their families. Nobel Laureate Liu Xiaobo remains in prison serving an 11-year sentence for advocating democracy, and his wife, Liu Xia, remains under unlawful house arrest.

China seemed most worried about the new threat to its monopoly over public conversation posed by the rise of social media. China's "Great Firewall," built to block access to the Internet outside the country, is worthless for preventing conversation among Chinese that social media sites like Sina Weibo now permit. And with China having an estimated 400 million social media users and growing, the government is having a hard time keeping up, despite its proliferation of censors. Social media have given the Chinese people new opportunities to spotlight official misconduct, and at times the government has had no choice but to be responsive.

Beyond elections, abusive majoritarianism comes in **cultural** forms as well. Whether it is Saudi Arabia or Afghanistan restricting the rights of women, or Uganda or Russia undermining the rights of gays and lesbians, abusive leaders often speak in terms of a dominant or traditional culture, as if that justifies abusing those who differ from it or fomenting discrimination against them. Typically these leaders pretend that alternatives to their tradition are imposed from the outside, as if all homosexuals in their country were imported or all women who oppose discrimination are transplants. In fact, the only imposition going on is by the dominant elites of those countries against those who dare to differ or stand up for their rights. No one insists that any particular women must reject gender stereotypes or that particular gays or lesbians must abide by their own sexuality rather than the government's preconceptions. But if they choose to do so, anti-discrimination obligations make it their choice, not that of the government. The international community gets involved when a government denies that choice, not to impose any particular choice.

National Security: An Excuse for Violating Rights

Since beginning his second term in January 2013, President Obama has done little to alter his disappointing record on national security issues. To his credit, upon taking office he banned torture and closed CIA detention centers where suspects were forcibly disappeared for months or years—two of the most shameful practices of the Bush administration in response to the September 11, 2001 attacks. Yet he has refused to prosecute anyone for those abuses. He also has stymied efforts to investigate them and provide redress for victims.

In addition, Obama has done little to fulfill his promise to close the Guantanamo Bay detention center and has continued to try suspects before fundamentally flawed military commissions despite their dismal record. In two important areas— targeted killing, often by drones, and mass government electronic surveillance— he has built on and expanded his predecessor's programs.

With respect to **drones**, the Obama administration has not followed its own stated policies or made clear what legal framework it believes governs specific strikes. Though formally eschewing the Bush administration's "global war on terrorism," the Obama administration has asserted that it is in an armed conflict with the Taliban, Al-Qaeda, and "associated forces" with no geographic boundaries. It has engaged in targeted killings in Pakistan, Yemen, and Somalia, saying it is at war with these armed groups or claiming national self-defense.

But given the at-most sporadic violence involving the United States in many of these places, it is far from clear that the more permissive laws of war even apply. And even if they do, civilians have been killed unlawfully under that legal framework without any US inquiry or known compensation to the victims or their families. The separate and more restrictive body of international human rights law allows the use of lethal force as well but in far more narrow circumstances: only if absolutely necessary to meet an imminent lethal threat. That would make even more of the deaths caused by drones unlawful.

In a May speech, Obama suggested that the use of the rules of war should end at some unspecified time, and outlined policies governing drone attacks to limit civilian casualties that are in many respects closer to human rights law than the laws-of-war rules that the CIA and military claim to follow. But it is far from clear that these announced policies are being followed. Civilians continue to be killed, and the Obama administration refuses to take public responsibility for carrying out all but a few attacks.

The US government seems to feel no urgency to demonstrate the lawfulness of its use of drones for attacks because for the moment it stands nearly alone in using them. But that will certainly change, and Washington will undoubtedly rue the precedents it has set of enabling governments to label anyone deemed to be a threat as a "combatant" subject to attack under the laws of war, rather than abiding by the more protective standards of human rights law.

Because of the disclosures of whistleblower Edward Snowden, the world is now aware of the virtually unchecked **mass electronic surveillance** that the US government and certain allies, most notably Britain, is conducting. No one questions that national security sometimes requires governments to use targeted surveillance after making an evidentiary showing. But the US government's mass surveillance without such limits has largely eradicated the right to privacy in a modern world that virtually requires electronic communication.

To justify this conduct, the US government has invoked a series of legal assumptions that do not withstand serious scrutiny, even though most have been ratified by a secret and deferential Foreign Intelligence Surveillance Court that hears only the government's arguments. For example, the government feels free to collect metadata about potentially all phone calls in the US because, under woefully outdated rules, no one is said to have any legitimate expectation of privacy when it comes to this information because they share it with the phone company. Despite a huge percentage of the world's Internet and phone communications passing through the United States, the government has adopted the policy that non-Americans outside the country have no recognized privacy interest in even the content of their communications. And the government conveniently claims that the right to privacy is not implicated when it collects communications, only when it examines them—as if it would be okay for the government to collect and store a video stream from peoples' bedrooms so long as it purports not watch the video until it comes up with some compelling reason.

Global outrage at this trampling on the right to privacy offers some promise of change. Brazil and Germany, for example, sponsored a unanimously adopted UN General Assembly resolution demanding further study of the violation of privacy "in the context of domestic and extraterritorial surveillance … including on a mass scale"—a welcome development, as there is little transparency about the kind of surveillance that governments other than the United States and its immediate allies have undertaken. But for all the protests, there is disturbingly little willingness by any rights-abiding government to shelter Snowden as a whistleblower from US efforts to prosecute him under the US Espionage Act. Sadly, this has allowed Russia, which granted temporary asylum to Snowden, to recast itself as a champion of privacy rights.

To his credit, Obama appointed a reform panel that recommended 46 policy amendments—a strong starting point for reform. It called for an end to the government's bulk metadata collection, greater privacy protection for non-Americans, and increased transparency, among other things. But it is unclear whether any of these recommendations will be acted on. Moreover, there is a danger that in response to the US government's overreaching, other governments, some with poor rights records, will force user data to stay within their own borders, setting up the potential for increased Internet censorship.

Enhanced Human Rights Machinery

The defense of human rights depends on many elements: a vibrant movement of activists and NGOs, a general public that believes in the importance of basic rights, and governments that are committed to upholding these principles. In addition, an international architecture has emerged to bolster this defense. Two developments strengthened that architecture over the past year: the UN Human Rights Council in Geneva is increasingly living up to its promise as the leading multilateral institution devoted to the protection of rights, and two new treaties were adopted that should help protect some of society's most vulnerable members.

Greater Hope for the UN Human Rights Council

Over the past year the council continued to show promise after a dismal beginning. The council was established in 2006 to replace the UN Human Rights Commission, which had lost credibility as repressive governments flocked to it in an effort to use their votes to avoid censure. The council has tighter membership standards, but for its first few years was little better than its predecessor.

In recent years, however, the council has come into its own. One important factor was the Obama administration's decision to join it after the Bush administration had shunned it. Other governments have also played an important role, including Mexico, Switzerland, Chile, Botswana, Brazil, Argentina, Mauritius, Benin, Maldives, Costa Rica, and a number of EU states. Together they successfully bridged the political divides and overcame the apathy that often blocked effective action. Even traditionally more reluctant countries, such as Nigeria and Thailand, were persuaded to play productive roles.

The positive results were most visible with Sri Lanka. In 2009, when some 40,000 civilians were killed in the waning months of the conflict with the Tamil Tigers, the council's initial reaction was to congratulate the government on its victory. But for the past two years, the council has pressured Sri Lanka to honor its pledge to investigate war crimes by both sides and to bring those responsible to account. Similarly in March 2013, among other useful steps, the council established a commission of inquiry to collect evidence of North Korea's crimes against humanity—the first step toward possibly prosecuting those responsible.

These and others such steps show that a pro-rights majority exists on the council, despite the election at the end of 2013 of several countries such as China, Cuba, Russia, and Saudi Arabia that historically have been hostile to human rights enforcement. With proper diplomatic efforts, this majority can be mobilized to respond to the most severe human rights crises.

Two New Treaties to Protect Rights

The tens of millions of women and girls laboring as cleaners and caregivers in people's homes are among the world's most vulnerable workers. Working in isolation and historically excluded from basic protections afforded most other workers under national labor laws, they are at high risk of economic exploitation, physical and sexual abuse, and trafficking. Many governments have been reluctant to legislate working conditions in the home, and employers have often pushed the myth that these workers are treated like members of the family.

That should begin to change with the International Labour Organization's **Domestic Workers Convention**, which took effect in September. It entitles domestic workers to protection from abuse and harassment as well as key labor rights such as a weekly day off, limits on hours of work, and a minimum wage. Domestic workers, trade unions, migrants groups, and human rights activists have leveraged the convention to advocate for national reforms. In the two years since the convention was adopted, dozens of countries have embraced important reforms, including comprehensive legislation in the Philippines and Argentina and new protections in Brazil's constitution. There is still a long way to go, but increasingly domestic workers' second-tier status under national labor laws is coming to an end.

The world also took a step forward toward realizing the right to the highest attainable standard of health by addressing the danger of **mercury** poisoning. Much of the world's artisanal gold mining uses mercury to separate gold from ore. Mercury is toxic, and particularly harmful to children. Exposure can cause life-long physical and mental disability. A treaty adopted in October requires governments to eliminate the most dangerous uses of mercury in mining and promote alternative forms of gold processing that do not require the metal.

Conclusion

Despite the year's turmoil year, with numerous atrocities in some countries and deepening repression in others, 2013 also featured a vigorous movement fighting back. In several cases there were victories to savor. More often there was a struggle that, if not immediately victorious, at least raised the cost of abuse—a strategy that, over time, tends to mitigate human rights violations.

The Responsibility to Protect doctrine was certainly strained, at an unspeakable price for the people of Syria, but it retained enough vitality to provide a modicum of assistance to people facing mass atrocities in several African countries. A notable number of leaders opted to govern under a convenient assessment of majority preferences without respecting the rights that allow all elements of society to participate in the political process or to live secure from governmental abuse. But as the public protested, this stratagem did not bring leaders the legitimacy they sought. And as the perennial problem of human rights abuse in the name of counterterrorism centered on mass electronic surveillance and targeted killings by drones, the traditional efforts to avoid legal challenges by hiding behind the secrecy of national security were clearly failing. So while the year certainly had more than enough suffering, it also held out promise that steps were being taken to curtail these rights abuses.

Kenneth Roth is the executive director of Human Rights Watch.

The Human Rights Case for Drug Reform
How Drug Criminalization Destroys Lives, Feeds Abuses, and Subverts the Rule of Law

By Maria McFarland Sánchez-Moreno

Nearly every country in the world plays a part—as producer, consumer, or transit point—in the multibillion-dollar illicit drug trade that supplies more than 150 million people every year and keeps on growing.

To combat this trade, many countries over recent decades have launched so-called "wars on drugs" that entail crackdowns on participants large and small in the drug business, including harsh penalties for users.

Human Rights Watch has long documented the widespread human rights abuses resulting from this approach: in the United States, the devastation that disproportionate prison sentences for drug offenses have wrought on individuals and their families and disturbing racial disparities in drug law enforcement; in Mexico, the killings committed in the name of combatting drugs; in Canada, the US, and Russia, how fear of criminal law enforcement deters people who use drugs from accessing necessary health services, exposing them to violence, discrimination, and illness; in Afghanistan and Colombia, how narcotics production has fueled armed groups opposed or allied to the government; in India, Ukraine, and Senegal, how cancer patients suffer severe pain due to drug control regulations that render morphine inaccessible; and in China, Vietnam, and Cambodia, the "drug rehabilitation centers" where people are subjected to torture, forced labor, and sexual abuse.

But there was a growing sense within Human Rights Watch that this approach did not go far enough—that the problem did not lie merely with ill-considered policies or their abusive execution. Rather, the criminalization of drugs itself seemed to be inherently problematic. Especially when it came to personal possession and use, imposing the full force of the criminal justice system to arrest, prosecute, and incarcerate appeared contrary to the human rights to privacy and personal autonomy that underlie many rights.

Heavy emphasis on enforcing criminal prohibitions on drug production and distribution was also dramatically enhancing the profitability of illicit drug markets and fueling the growth and operations of groups that commit atrocities, corrupt authorities, and undermine democracy and the rule of law in many countries.

In my own work as Human Rights Watch's Colombia researcher from 2004 to 2010, it was clear that the illicit drug market was a major factor in the country's long-running war involving left-wing guerrilla groups, right-wing paramilitary groups, and security forces.

Certainly, Colombia's staggering levels of abuse—massacres, killings, rape, threats, and kidnappings that displaced more than 3 million people—had roots that went beyond the drug trade and predated the explosion in the cocaine market in the 1970s. But most armed groups in Colombia in some way benefitted from the illicit trade. The paramilitaries, in particular, were among Colombia's biggest drug lords. Often, they threatened or killed people living on land they wanted to control for coca production or as drug transportation corridors. Illicit drug profits helped pay for their weapons and uniforms, wages for their "soldiers," and bribes for public officials to evade justice for their crimes.

So it became increasingly difficult—as we documented the atrocities, called for justice, and pressed the US to enforce human rights conditions on its assistance (the US provided Colombia more than US$5 billion in mostly military aid in 2000-2010)—to ignore that many of the abuses we advocated to end would inevitably continue in some form unless US and global drug policy itself changed.

My later work on US policy towards such countries as Afghanistan and Mexico, and on the US criminal justice system, only strengthened my view—which others at Human Rights Watch shared—that drug criminalization was inherently inconsistent with human rights.

After much discussion, the organization in 2013 adopted a policy calling on governments to decriminalize all personal use and possession of drugs. We also urged them to consider—and eventually adopt—alternative policies on the drug trade to reduce the enormous human rights costs of current approaches.

Change is urgent, as our research consistently shows.

Medellín: The More Things Change, the More They Stay the Same

Alex Pulgarín knew a lot about the power that the illicit drug trade gave to criminals—and the damage it could inflict.

When I interviewed him in 2007, he was a fresh-faced 30-year-old with an easy smile who looked younger than his age but spoke with the confidence of a seasoned player in the complicated politics of his city, Medellín, a major hub for Colombia's cocaine trade.

As a child in the 1980s, Alex witnessed the bloody "war" the infamous Medellín cocaine kingpin Pablo Escobar waged against Colombia's government in a bid to secure a ban on extraditions to the US. The car bombings, airplane hijackings, and frequent assassinations that Escobar ordered garnered Medellín the label, "murder capital of the world."

So many rejoiced when Colombian security forces, with US backing, killed Escobar in 1993. But the bloodletting didn't end there. As the world turned its attention elsewhere, others discreetly filled his shoes.

One of them was Diego Murillo, also known as "Berna," a former Escobar rival who in the 1990s went on to build his own drug trafficking empire in Medellín, forging close ties with the paramilitaries. As a teenager in a low-income neighborhood, Alex saw his peers get swept into a seemingly endless cycle of brutality and death as Berna and others battled for control over the city.

But when I interviewed Alex, city officials were claiming that Medellín had turned a corner. The government and paramilitaries had announced a "peace deal," and hundreds of young men had turned in weapons at "demobilization" ceremonies, signing up for government stipends. Former paramilitary leaders received reduced prison sentences. Homicide rates were near their lowest in years.

Among those who supposedly demobilized was Berna. Several of his henchmen formed the Democracy Corporation, a group with the ostensible mission of working with the city to help demobilized paramilitaries get education and jobs and reintegrate into society.

But Alex told a different story. The corporation, he said, was a front for organized crime, still under Berna's control. The government's backing gave the corporation a veneer of legality, allowing it to exert political influence while retaining its ruthless dominance over much of the city. "Peace with a knife to your throat," as Alex called it.

A Democracy Corporation leader, Antonio Lopez ("Job"), had ordered his accomplices to kill demobilized individuals who disobeyed him—especially "coordinators," point people for the demobilized in each neighborhood. Others confirmed what Alex said: the apparent peace that Medellín was experiencing was not due to Berna's demobilization, but rather the result of his monopoly over crime in the city after he defeated most competing groups. And he was retaining that control in part through the Democracy Corporation.

While Alex knew many people in the world of local crime, he had taken a different path. He had become an activist, joined the left-leaning Democratic Pole party, and won a spot on his neighborhood action council. Respected and well-liked, he dreamed of running for higher office.

But Alex was now in Job's sights. A few months earlier, Job had asked him to run for the Medellín City Council as the Democracy Corporation's candidate, trying to capitalize on Alex's popularity. Alex would get a car, armed guards, and a stipend if he agreed. He refused.

Instead, he began reporting what he knew to police and prosecutors, recording his calls with coordinators who were being threatened and sharing them with the authorities. He spoke during community meetings with international agencies and the Catholic Church. "Aren't you afraid you'll get killed?" I asked when we met. He brushed off the question.

Two years later, in 2009, it looked like Alex might emerge unscathed. Berna had been extradited to the US, where he pled guilty to cocaine trafficking charges and received a 31-year sentence from a federal court in New York City. Job had been gunned down, reportedly by rivals, in an upscale restaurant near Medellín. And Alex testified in a trial against another Democracy Corporation member, John William López, or Memín. Several witnesses were murdered during the trial, but Memín was convicted of forcibly interfering with elections, conspiracy, and forced displacement.

But it is hard to escape the grasp of Colombia's criminal networks. That December, armed men—Memín associates—accosted Alex on the street and shot him several times in broad daylight. He died at the scene.

A Resilient and Lucrative Global Market

Profits from the illicit drug trade in Colombia have not only fueled the country's conflict but have also enabled criminals to buy off or intimidate public officials. More than 100 Colombian congress members and countless other officials have been investigated in recent years for alleged collusion with paramilitaries. In Medellín, new groups with shadowy leadership structures have replaced Berna's organization, much as Berna's had replaced Escobar's. Violence—often via threats and displacement—is pervasive.

These problems extend well beyond Colombia. In many countries illicit drug profits are an enormous motivator and funding source for groups that commit atrocities, corrupt authorities, and undermine democracy and the rule of law.

Indeed, according to the United Nations Office on Drugs and Crime (UNODC), illicit drugs constitute the largest income source for transnational crime and may account for one-fifth of all crime proceeds. The UNODC also estimated the value of the 2003 global illicit drugs market to be $322 billion at retail—higher than the gross domestic product of 88 percent of the world's countries at the time.

Afghanistan, for example, produces around 90 percent of the world's opium (along with cannabis). In 2009, the late Richard Holbrooke, then-US special representative for Afghanistan and Pakistan, decried how enforcing drug policies—particularly US efforts to eradicate poppy (a crucial crop for many impoverished Afghan farmers)—drove people "into the arms of the Taliban." But that has only been part of the picture. The illegal opium market has dramatically distorted the country's power structure, bankrolling armed groups such as the Taliban and local warlords responsible for numerous atrocities. It also fuels rampant corruption, making efforts to apprehend and prosecute those implicated in these crimes extraordinarily difficult.

Meanwhile, in Mexico the homicide rate has exploded, with at least 80,000 people killed in the country's "war on drugs" since 2007 (El Salvador, Honduras, and Guatemala face similar problems). The US has provided more than $2 billion in funding to Mexico to combat drugs during that time. Yet the Mexican security forces deployed in the country's "war on drugs" have themselves often been involved in torture, extrajudicial killings, and other abuses.

Tougher Enforcement?

The US, Russia, and other countries, with UNODC support, have argued the answer to the exploding violence and corruption around illicit drug markets is to vastly expand enforcement. For decades, they have poured billions of dollars into combatting drugs (some estimate at least $100 billion a year). With varying degrees of lawfulness they have pursued, surveilled, killed, extradited, prosecuted, and imprisoned kingpins and low-level dealers alike. They have fumigated crops, paid farmers to grow other crops, and interdicted shipments.

Yet, as the Global Commission on Drug Policy—a group of former presidents, senior UN officials, and prominent public figures—stated in its June 2011 report, these vast expenditures have "clearly failed to effectively curtail supply or consumption. Apparent victories in eliminating one source or trafficking organization are negated almost instantly by the emergence of other sources and traffickers."

Indeed, as pressure increases in one place, the drug trade often shifts accordingly. My native country, Peru, recently replaced Colombia as the world's largest producer of coca, according to UNODC—the same position it occupied in the 1980s.

In turn, "tough" enforcement has created its own nightmare for human rights protection. Thailand's 2003 "war on drugs" resulted in some 2,800 extrajudicial killings by state security forces in its first three months. In Canada, Kazakhstan, Bangladesh, and Ukraine, police have violently mistreated people who use drugs. In Tanzania, police and quasi-official vigilante groups brutally beat people who inject drugs. Russia's policies have resulted in mass incarceration, often in environments that pose high risk of HIV transmission, and detention of drug offenders without trial.

In countries such as Singapore and Malaysia, drug offenders face the death penalty. Iran imposes a mandatory death sentence for various drug offenses. Other countries impose grossly disproportionate punishment in drug cases. The US, for example, has the world's largest reported incarcerated population (2.2 million people in adult prisons and jails), in significant part due to harsh sentences for drug offenses. Nearly a quarter of all prisoners—498,600 in 2011—including nearly half of federal inmates, were serving time for mostly low-level drug offenses. Some of those convicted, and many of those arrested, have done nothing more than use drugs, yet they will suffer the consequences of their conviction or arrest record for the rest of their lives. For immigrants, convictions, even for nonviolent offenses, can mean deportation and separation from their families.

US drug law enforcement is also marred by deep, discriminatory racial disparities. Although whites and blacks use and sell drugs at comparable rates in the US, blacks are arrested on drug charges at more than three times the rate of whites and are imprisoned for drug convictions at ten times the white rate.

The Harms of (Criminalizing) Drug Use

Proponents of criminalization of drug use often argue that it is necessary to protect individuals' health and keep people from harming themselves or others.

It is legitimate for governments to address societal harms that may result from drug abuse. But policymakers too easily attribute social problems—domestic abuse, unemployment, or violence—to illicit drug use, when causes are more complex.

Imprisoning people who use drugs does little to protect their health: prisoners often find that drug treatment—as we found in New York—is not available. Recidivism of drug offenders is common.

Instead, criminalization often compounds existing harms. Fear of law enforcement can drive people who use drugs underground, deterring them from accessing health services and increasing the risk they face of violence, discrimination, and serious illness, as our research in Canada, the US, and Russia has shown. Outside Africa, one-third of HIV infections are attributable to contaminated injection equipment. But police enforcement of drug prohibitions is a barrier to providing sterile syringes, and incarceration makes it harder to treat and care for those already living with HIV.

Aggressive laws and enforcement also contribute to the stigmatization and abusive treatment of people who use drugs. Poor public education around drugs and their risks means that, in many countries, there is little understanding about the real harms that may flow from drug abuse, much less how to prevent or treat them.

The Pitfalls of Involuntary Treatment

While criminalization is deeply problematic, extrajudicial systems of drug control can also be extremely abusive. Thailand, for example, detains people who use drugs without trial for extended periods in locked "treatment facilities." In China, the 2008 Anti-Drug Law allows officials to detain people who use drugs for up to six years with no trial or judicial oversight.

In Cambodia, Laos, and Vietnam, people who use drugs are held in government-run centers where they are often mistreated in the name of "treatment." In Vietnam, detainees are used as forced labor to process cashews or manufacture clothes for export. In Cambodia, they are subjected to brutal punishments, including torture. In 2013, four years after we first reported on this issue, we found that individuals held in these drug detention centers are still being beaten, thrashed with rubber water hoses, forced to stand in septic water pits, and sexually abused. Lack of due process protections also renders these facilities convenient places to detain people whom Cambodian authorities consider "undesirable"— including homeless people and street children—in sporadic crackdowns often occurring before visits of foreign dignitaries.

A Human Rights Approach to Drug Control

To ensure their drug policies are in line with international human rights standards, governments should:

- **Decriminalize personal use and possession of drugs for personal use.**
  Laws criminalizing drug use are inconsistent with respect for human autonomy and privacy rights. Governments may limit these rights if necessary for a legitimate purpose, such as preventing harm to others. But like other private behavior that some may view as immoral (such as consensual homosexual conduct among adults), there is no legitimate basis for criminalization. Nor is criminalization necessary to protect people who use drugs: Governments have many non-penal measures to encourage people to make good choices around drugs, including offering substance abuse treatment and social support. Governments can also criminalize negligent or dangerous behavior (such as driving under the influence) to regulate harmful conduct by individuals who use drugs, without criminalizing drug use itself.

• **Reduce criminal regulation of drug production and distribution.**
Criminalization of the drug trade carries enormous human rights costs, dramatically enhancing the profitability of illicit drug markets and fueling the
growth and operations of groups responsible for large-scale violence and
corruption. Finding alternative ways to regulate production and distribution
and cutting into illicit drug profits would allow governments to weaken the
influence of such groups and reduce the various abuses—killings, disproportionate sentencing, torture, and barriers to access to health care—that governments often commit in the name of fighting drugs.

• **Ground approaches to treatment and care in human rights, avoiding abusive
administrative sanctions and ensuring patients have access to needed
medications.**
Governments should close drug detention centers where people are held in
violation of international law and expand access to voluntary, community-
based drug treatment with the involvement of competent nongovernmental
organizations. They should also ensure that anyone with a legitimate medical need for controlled medications like morphine or methadone has adequate access to them.

Many alternatives to current policies have yet to be tested (except with
respect to alcohol). So governments should assess proposed solutions carefully to reduce the risk they could lead to new problems or human rights concerns.

Yet, there are some models to consider: Some governments have decriminalized personal use and possession of illicit drugs or resisted enforcing certain
prohibitions. In Portugal, in conjunction with comprehensive harm-reduction
strategies, decriminalization had positive results; rather than substantially
increasing, drug consumption reportedly dropped in some categories—as did
recidivism and HIV infection. Researchers have also developed theoretical
models for potential systems of drug regulation with varying ways of handling licensing, privatization versus state monopoly control of supply, taxation, public health education, the protection of children, and treatment. And
some jurisdictions are beginning to put these models into practice.

A Changing Landscape

The pendulum is starting to swing on drug policy, with Mexico, Guatemala, and Colombia calling for a review of the global drug control regime. "As long as the flow of resources from drugs and weapons to criminal organizations [is] not stopped," they said in a 2012 joint statement decrying the failure of current prohibitionist strategies, "they will continue to threaten our societies and governments."

In a study in 2013 on the effectiveness of current policies, the Organization of American States opened up a discussion about their costs and outlined, without endorsing, various possible scenarios for future development—including decriminalization.

In December, Uruguay approved a law legalizing marijuana and establishing a regulated system of production and distribution for the drug, though a compulsory treatment bill was also pending at time of writing.

Change is slowly happening in the US, too. Attorney General Eric Holder in 2013 issued guidance for federal prosecutors that would allow US states to legalize marijuana, noting that a regulated market may further federal priorities of combatting organized crime. Washington State and Colorado are legalizing the possession, production, and distribution of marijuana for recreational use; 20 other states have legalized medical marijuana.

Several UN agencies and special rapporteurs have called for drug detention centers to close immediately. The United Nations Children's Fund (UNICEF) called for all children to be removed from Cambodia's centers; still, one in 10 people held in Cambodia's centers today is a child.

Indeed, progress has been limited and fragile. Criminalization remains the tool of choice for drug control in most countries, where there is often little debate around harsh and counterproductive policies. Meanwhile, the devastating costs of the current approach—in lives lost to violence, people subjected to long prison terms, barriers to health, harm to families and communities, and damage to the rule of law—keep mounting. It is time to chart a new course.

Maria McFarland Sánchez-Moreno is deputy director of the US Division.

Putting Development to Rights:
Integrating Rights into a Post-2015 Agenda
By David Mepham

Before Tunisia's popular uprising erupted in late 2010, many in the international community saw the country as a development success story. Economic growth was close to 4 percent, 9 in 10 children went to primary school, and life expectancy was an impressive 75 years.

But for many Tunisians this progress was clearly not enough: higher incomes and better access to services did not compensate for the ills and costs of corruption, repression, inequality, and powerlessness. Nor did it satisfy aspirations for greater justice, freedom, and dignity. In January 2011, popular protests ousted Zine el-Abidine Ben Ali from the presidency after 23 years in power.

While Tunisia's struggle for rights-respecting democracy continues, its recent experience exposes the narrowness and inadequacy of many existing approaches to development. It also provides a compelling case for development to be reframed more broadly, not just as higher income (important as this is), but as the creation of conditions in which people everywhere can get an education, visit a doctor, and drink clean water, and also express themselves freely, be protected by a fair and accessible justice system, participate in decision-making, and live free of abuse and discrimination. These are some of the basic economic, social, cultural, civil, and political rights that governments are obligated to honor but deny to hundreds of millions of people.

Many of those who are most impoverished belong to society's most marginalized and vulnerable social groups—women, children, people with disabilities, ethnic minorities, people infected with HIV—who often lack the power, social or legal standing, or access to decision-making that allows them to challenge their disadvantaged status or improve their circumstances.

For the most part, development policy and programs have ignored the critical interdependence of economic and social rights with civil and political rights, and so have failed to challenge systemic patterns of discrimination and disadvantage that keep people in poverty. As a result, many poor people have been excluded, or have failed to benefit, from development programs. More disturbingly still, people have been harmed by abusive policies carried out in the name of development: forced from their land to make way for large commercial investors, compelled to toil long days for low pay in dangerous and exploitative conditions, or exposed to life-threatening pollution from poorly regulated industries.

Development can also be unsustainable, achieved at considerable cost to the environment —including carbon emissions, soil erosion, pollution, depletion of fresh water supplies, over-fishing, or damage to biodiversity—which then damage people's rights, including those to life, health, safe food, and clean water.

More than a decade ago, in 2001, world governments set about addressing such problems by agreeing on eight Millennium Development Goals (MDGs). Set for achievement by 2015, they included halving the proportion of people suffering from extreme hunger, reducing child and maternal mortality, and achieving universal primary education.

With this date fast approaching, a United Nations-led process is under way to agree on successor goals. This is a crucial opportunity to change the daily reality for millions of people currently overlooked, disadvantaged, or damaged by development efforts. Despite growing civil society support for rooting development in human rights standards, many governments, especially authoritarian ones, remain hostile to them, and will seek to minimize and marginalize the role of rights in any new international agreement.

To counter this threat and build wider international support for rights, it is essential and urgent to show how their fuller integration can contribute to improved development outcomes—promoting a form of development that is more inclusive, just, transparent, participatory, and accountable, precisely because it is rights-respecting.

An Unfulfilled Vision

The UN Millennium Declaration of 2000 was strong on human rights and democratic principles. World governments endorsed it in September 2000, asserting that freedom, equality, solidarity, and tolerance were fundamental values. Making progress on development, they said, depended on "good governance within each country," adding that they would "spare no effort" to promote democracy, strengthen the rule of law, and respect internationally recognized human rights and fundamental freedoms.

Strong words. But the Millennium Declaration's vision, and the important principles it contained, never found their way into the new Millennium Development Goals (MDGs), which emerged from a UN working group in early 2001 and soon became the dominant framework for international development cooperation.

While drawn from the Millennium Declaration, the MDGs were far more circumscribed. They prioritized an important set of economic and social issues, which were seen as less political and easier to measure, such as child and maternal mortality and access to primary education. These issues were defined in technical terms rather than as a set of rights obligations. Nor did the MDGs set any goals or targets related to political freedom or democratic participation, equality for ethnic minorities or people with disabilities, freedom from violence and abuse in the family and community, freedom of expression, or rights to peaceful protest and assembly.

Despite these limitations, the MDGs have contributed to real progress for many people. They have embodied and helped generate substantial international consensus about the focus of development cooperation. And in many countries they have facilitated higher levels of public investment in health and education, contributing to significant increases in school enrolment rates and big reductions in child mortality over the last decade. Since 1990, for example, child mortality has almost halved globally, plummeting from 12 million to 6.6 million in 2012, while the number of primary school-age children out of school has fallen from 102 million in 1990 to 69 million in 2012.

But the neglect of human rights by many governments, donors, international institutions, and the MDG framework has been a serious missed opportunity, which has greatly diminished development efforts and had other harmful consequences for poor and marginalized people, as elaborated below.

Unequal Development

Even before the MDG framework was established, many governments were unwilling or unable to address discrimination and exclusion in their development strategies and their broader social and economic policies. Authoritarian governments were obviously reluctant to empower restless minorities or disadvantaged groups that might threaten their grip on power, and were generally unwilling to address sensitive issues around ethnic or religious conflict. Such governments also often refuse to accept that women, girls, indigenous people, or other marginalized social groups deserve equal status under the law.

But development donors and international institutions like the World Bank also shied away from the more complex and politicized approach to development implied by an explicit emphasis on rights. The MDGs, with their stress on measuring development in terms of average or aggregate achievement of particular goals, for example on child and maternal mortality, did little to change these calculations and meant that marginalized communities continued to be overlooked.

Indeed, because it is often more difficult or expensive to assist poor and marginalized communities, the MDG framework may have actually worked against them, incentivising a focus on people who are easier to reach and assist, such as those living in cities rather than far-flung rural areas.

Nowhere is unequal development better documented and more visible than in the widespread and systematic discrimination against women and girls. Most development organizations have identified gender discrimination as a major obstacle to inclusive development and there is a growing international consensus on the need to tackle it. For example, the World Bank, the European Commission, and the United Kingdom's Department for International Development (DFID) have all made strong statements on the importance of combating gender inequality and empowering women and girls. As the World Bank's Chief Economist Justin Yifu Lin put it in 2012, "Blocking women and girls from getting the skills to succeed in a globalized world is not only wrong but economically harmful. Sharing the fruits of growth equally between men and women is essential to meeting key development goals."

Nonetheless, development agencies often underreport or fail to address properly many forms of gender discrimination. In Bangladesh, for example, where considerable progress has been made (at the aggregate level) towards some MDGs, Human Rights Watch has documented entrenched discrimination in the country's Muslim, Hindu, and Christian laws governing marriage, separation, and divorce. These often trap women or girls in abusive marriages or drive them into poverty when marriages fall apart, contributing to homelessness, reduced incomes, hunger, and ill-health.

Our 2012 report *"Will I Get My Dues Before I Die?,"* for example, documented the disastrous consequences of this discrimination for Shefali S., a Muslim woman who was abandoned by her abusive husband while pregnant and, according to the country's laws, not entitled to maintenance from 90 days after notice of divorce. Without income, she was plunged into poverty and dependence, and was forced to live with her in-laws who beat her.

Many of the 1 billion people with disabilities worldwide—80 percent live in the developing world—also experience unequal development. Human Rights Watch's research on education in Nepal and China has documented widespread discrimination against children with disabilities, who are much less likely to be in school than other children. This is despite the fact that both countries are state parties to the UN Convention on the Rights of the Child (CRC), which affirms the right to education, and to the UN Convention on the Rights of Persons with Disabilities (CRPD).

Our 2011 report, Futures Stolen, documented how in one school in the far west of Nepal, a 16-year-old boy had to crawl to his classroom due to lack of ramps, and—unable to use the toilet by himself, and unaided by teachers—was forced to wait until he got home, or have another child run home to fetch his mother to assist him. Other children, afraid to sit near him, left him isolated in a corner. These patterns of discrimination are replicated across the world and explain why people with disabilities are disproportionately represented among the world's poor people. And yet, the MDGs make no reference whatsoever to disability.

In our 2008 report *A Question of Life or Death*, we similarly documented barriers to treatment for women and children in Kenya living with HIV, violating their right to health. Mothers and children suffered discrimination, abuse, and abandonment by husbands and relatives, and many lived in precarious conditions after being kicked out of their homes. In addition, HIV policies prioritized HIV care for adults, and HIV care for children was not widely available. Many children died as a result.

Ethnic and religious minorities also often experience serious discrimination, sometimes rooted in basic prejudice towards them on the part of other groups; at other times linked to hostility towards the political or separatist agendas of partic-ular ethnic groups. This discrimination can worsen levels of poverty and prevent these groups from benefiting from development opportunities. The London-based Overseas Development Institute (ODI) suggested in a recent report that two-thirds of the world's poorest people live in households headed by a member of an ethnic minority, with these families more likely to be sick, illiterate, and malnourished.

Abusive Development

The neglect of human rights in many development strategies and programs, as well as in the MDGs, has another serious, adverse consequence. Incongruous as it may sound—especially to those who view development as a uniformly benign process—large numbers of poor, vulnerable, and marginalized people around the world are harmed by policies carried out in the name of development. These abu-sive patterns occur because basic rights—including the right to consultation, par-ticipation, fair treatment, to join with others in a trade union, and to just and accessible legal processes—are missing.

In China, for example, the government maintains that its development progress is extraordinarily successful. Income poverty has indeed fallen very rapidly in recent years, with the UN estimating a decline in extreme poverty from 60 to 12 percent from 1990 to 2010. But the record is decidedly less impressive if development is defined, as it should be, to include freedom from fear, violence, ill-health, life-threatening environmental pollution, and abusive employment practices, as well as the opportunity to be protected from abuse, or seek remedy for abuse, through a fair and accessible justice system.

In our 2011 report, *My Children Have Been Poisoned,* Human Rights Watch docu-mented the devastating effects of lead poisoning on children who could no longer talk or walk, had stopped eating, or were constantly sick. This poisoning epidemic in four provinces—Shaanxi, Henan, Hunan, and Yunnan—is rooted in tension between the Chinese government's goals for economic growth and its stated com-mitments and international obligations to protect its citizens' health and well-being. Without institutions to protect their rights and hold local officials account-able for abuses, hundreds of thousands of Chinese children have had their right to health violated and have suffered appallingly, including from reading and learning disabilities, behavioural problems, comas, and convulsions. Some have even died.

Aspects of Ethiopia's development model have similar problems. The country has made commendable progress in relation to the MDGs on health and education, but other elements of its development strategy have led to serious rights abuses. Our 2012 report "Waiting Here for Death," documented rights violations linked to the "villagization" resettlement program in Gambella region. Ethiopia's government justifies the program in development terms, and says it is voluntary. Some 1.5 million people in five regions are being relocated to new villages with the stated aim of giving them better infrastructure and services. But our research into the first year of the program in one of those regions found people were forced to move against their will and that government security forces beat and abused some who objected. Moreover, new villages often lacked promised services and adequate land for farming needs, resulting in hunger, and even starvation.

Our 2012 report *What Will Happen if Hunger Comes?* also documented that the Ethiopian government is forcibly displacing indigenous peoples from southern Ethiopia's Lower Omo Valley to make way for large-scale sugar plantations. The cost of this development to indigenous groups is massive: their farms are being cleared, prime grazing land is being lost, and livelihoods are being decimated. While failing to meaningfully consult, obtain their free, prior, and informed consent, compensate, or discuss with these affected communities, and recognize their rights to land, the Ethiopian government has used harassment, violence, and arbitrary arrests to impose its development plans.

Workers are particularly vulnerable to abusive development. They include the more than 50 million domestic workers worldwide, most of them women and girls, who are employed as cooks, cleaners, and nannies. In many countries, such workers lack basic legal rights and protection. Yet their work provides essential services to households and enables the economic activity of others. Human Rights Watch's research over 10 years, in countries as diverse as Indonesia, Saudi Arabia, Morocco, Guinea, and El Salvador, has exposed many examples of abuse, including employers insisting on extremely long working hours; withholding or providing low wages; confiscating passports; and subjecting workers to beatings, verbal abuse, and sexual violence.

Similarly, millions of migrant workers in more visible sectors of the economy, like construction, suffer abuses. Ironically, these are often most egregious in the context of hugely expensive and high-profile construction projects intended to showcase economic achievements and encourage investment and tourism. In our 2012 report, Building a Better World Cup, Human Rights Watch documented pervasive abuses against migrants as they build sleek hotels, state-of-the-art infrastructure, and other glossy construction projects in Qatar linked to the 2022 World Cup. Abuses include arbitrary wage deductions, lack of access to medical care, and dangerous working conditions. A recent investigation by the UK's Guardian newspaper found that 44 Nepalese workers died from work-related accidents in Qatar between June and August 2013, more than half of them from heart attacks, heart failure, or workplace accidents.

Human Rights Watch has also exposed the terrible abuses and right to health violations—including fevers, nausea, and skin conditions that leave fingers corroded to stumps, and flesh prematurely aged, discolored, and itchy—that many thousands of people suffer while working in tanneries in and around Hazaribagh, a neighbourhood of Bangladesh's capital, Dhaka. Our 2012 report, *Toxic Tanneries*, shows that these abuses are occurring in what is the backbone of the country's lucrative leather industry. The tanneries employ some 15,000 people—some as young as seven-years-old—and export millions of dollars' worth of leather goods to around 70 countries worldwide. Our 2013 report on Tanzania *Toxic Toil* documented similar abuses in Tanzania, especially affecting young children working in small-scale gold mines. Many are exposed to toxic mercury and vulnerable to mercury poisoning.

Rights-Respecting Development

Making rights integral to a post-2015 global development framework would have a number of clear benefits, not least by:

- **Ensuring focus on the poorest and most marginalized communities**. The MDGs include global targets for percentage reductions of child and maternal mortality and hunger. By contrast, a rights approach to development would need to set universal goals for providing effective and accessible healthcare and nutrition for all women and children, including the poorest and most disadvantaged, alongside specific targets for reducing disparities between social groups and improving the conditions of the worst off. Progress would be greatly aided and incentivised by disaggregating national and international data, making it possible to measure policy impact on different social, income, and age groups.

- **Prompting action to address root causes of poverty**—such as inequality, discrimination, and exclusion—by requiring legal and policy reforms and challenging patterns of abuse, as well as harmful cultural practices like child marriage. Governments and donors should be obliged in a new development framework to bring their policies and practices into line with international standards on non-discrimination and equality. Concerted action is also needed to tackle formal, informal, and cultural barriers that prevent women, ethnic minorities, people with disabilities, and indigenous peoples in particular from owning and having equal access to land, property, assets, and credit; inheriting and transferring property; and accessing education and health services.

- **Making people agents and not subjects of development** by emphasising empowerment, participation, transparency, the rule of law, and access to justice. A rights approach requires that poor people are fully consulted about development projects or programs that affect them. Indigenous peoples, for example, have the right to give or withhold consent to development projects on their traditional lands before they are approved and after receiving all relevant information. Such safeguards would help prevent the kind of abusive, environmentally harmful patterns of development already cited. But abusive development also occurs in places like China because basic civil and political freedoms are not respected more generally and because the legal system is politicized and discriminatory. Commitments to civil and political rights should be integral to the post-2015 development agenda, including to freedom of speech, assembly, and association, the ability of people to participate in free elections, and access to fair and effective justice systems. Transparency and free flow of information are critical too, creating space for informed debate about use of the national budget, exposing mistakes and environmental harm, and allowing communities to mobilize for social change and redress for abuse and malpractice.

- **Tackling corruption**. Each year, senior government officials or powerful private individuals steal hundreds of millions of dollars that were intended to benefit the poor through development programs in health, education, nutrition, or water. In our 2013 report on Uganda, *Letting the Big Fish Swim*, Human Rights Watch documented a lack of political will to address corruption and the harmful consequences of this. Ugandan anti-corruption institutions have been crippled by political interference, as well as harassment and threats to prosecutors, investigators, and witnesses. Most recently, US$12.7 million in donor funds was discovered to have been embezzled from Uganda's Office of the Prime Minister. This money had been earmarked to help rebuild northern Uganda, ravaged by a 20-year war, and to help development in Karamoja, Uganda's poorest region. Rights-respecting development would help to tackle corruption of this kind by emphasizing budget transparency, freedom of information, and free media; strengthening efforts to prosecute those responsible for corrupt practices, including the highest ranking members of the government; and supporting anticorruption civil society organizations.

- **Bringing rights standards into the work of business and international institutions**. In the debate about the post-2015 development agenda, there has been little discussion about the responsibilities of either the private sector or international financial institutions to protect, respect, and fulfil rights. Over the years, Human Rights Watch has documented many cases of corporate complicity with human rights violations, including a Canadian mining company using forced labor, via a local contractor, in Eritrea; out-of-control mining operations fuelling corruption and abuse in India; and sexual violence by private security guards employed by a Canadian company in Papua New Guinea. Governments should introduce mandatory requirements for corporations to report publicly on human rights, and the social and environmental impact of their work. Similarly, international financial institutions such as the World Bank, which influence development in many countries by providing millions of dollars-worth of development assistance and loans, should have to respect human rights in all their work and be held accountable if they fail to do so, as set out in our 2013 report, *Abuse Free Development*.

- **Strengthening accountability**. Accountability is fundamental to rights-respecting development: rights are of limited value if no one is charged with guaranteeing them or if citizens whose rights are denied have no opportunity to seek redress or remedy. The post-2015 development agenda should therefore require all those involved in development—governments and international bilateral donors, international financial institutions, the business sector, private foundations, and NGOs—to be more accountable and transparent about implementing their commitments and the impact their policies have on the rights of the poor, including through feedback and complaints mechanisms and regular reporting at the local, national, and global level.

- **Affirming the universality of the global development agenda**. Low income is not an excuse for governments of poor countries to abuse their citizens' rights, and many developing country governments have scope to make different choices about how they allocate national resources. Still, low income and limited capacity can make it harder for well-intentioned governments to meet their rights obligations. A post-2015 development agenda should therefore place two important obligations on the world's wealthier governments:

  - To do no harm, by ensuring that existing policies and practices do not directly or indirectly contribute to human rights violations, unequal development, or abusive development elsewhere, through policies on trade, tax, investment, intellectual property, arms sales, and transfers of surveillance technology. These governments have an obligation to respect and protect human rights and to remedy any violations.

  - To proactively help to advance rights-respecting development in other countries, including through support for inclusive development in areas like health, education, nutrition, and sanitation, as well as support for the rule of law, and police, justice, and security sector reform.

Bringing Rights to the Fore

How human rights issues will be dealt with in any new post-2015 development agreement remains unclear. Support for rights emerged as a priority among civil society participants in the UN-sponsored global consultations on post-2015, and there were strong references to human rights in the reports of the High Level Panel

39

of Eminent Persons on the post-2015 Development Agenda and the UN secretary general's report on the same topic in June 2013.

But many governments remain hostile. With the process now at the stage of inter-governmental negotiations, we can anticipate serious efforts to marginalize the role of rights or chip away at progress that has been made. Some will no doubt continue to invoke the tired old argument that poor people care mainly about material improvements and that wider human rights entitlements, like freedom of speech and association or access to justice, are not necessary to secure these.

But this position has been thoroughly discredited, not least by ordinary peoples' own actions and expressed preferences. Across the globe, people are striving not only for economic improvement, but also for an end to indignity and injustice, for their voices to be heard, and for the opportunity to shape their future.

As UN Secretary General Ban Ki-moon stated in July 2013, "Upholding human rights and freeing people from fear and want are inseparable." A post-2015 development agenda that embraces this essential truth will help promote development that is more inclusive and just, and advances basic rights and freedoms for allSome of the most powerful and sophisticated actors on the world stage are companies, not governments. In 2011 alone, oil and gas behemoth ExxonMobil generated revenues of US$467 billion—the size of Norway's entire economy. Walmart, the world's third-largest employer with more than 2 million workers, has a workforce that trails only the militaries of the United States and China in size.

David Mepham is UK director at Human Rights Watch.

The Right Whose Time Has Come (Again)

Privacy in the Age of Surveillance

By Dinah PoKempner

Technology has invaded the sacred precincts of private life, and unwarranted exposure has imperiled our security, dignity, and most basic values. The law must rise to the occasion and protect our rights.

Does this sound familiar?

So argued Samuel Warren and Louis Brandeis in their 1890 *Harvard Law Review* article announcing "The Right to Privacy." We are again at such a juncture. The technological developments they saw as menacing—photography and the rise of the mass circulation press—appear rather quaint to us now. But the harms to emotional, psychological, and even physical security from unwanted exposure seem just as vivid in our digital age.

Our renewed sense of vulnerability comes as almost all aspects of daily social life migrate online. At the same time, corporations and governments have acquired frightening abilities to amass and search these endless digital records, giving them the power to "know" us in extraordinary detail.

In a world where we share our lives on social media and trade immense amounts of personal information for the ease and convenience of online living, some have questioned whether privacy is a relevant concept. It is not just relevant, but crucial.

Indeed, privacy is a gateway right that affects our ability to exercise almost every other right, not least our freedom to speak and associate with those we choose, make political choices, practice our religious beliefs, seek medical help, access education, figure out whom we love, and create our family life. It is nothing less than the shelter in which we work out what we think and who we are; a fulcrum of our autonomy as individuals.

The importance of privacy, a right we often take for granted, was thrown into sharp relief in 2013 by the steady stream of revelations from United States government files released by former National Security Agency (NSA) contractor Edward

Snowden, and published in the *Guardian* and other major newspapers around the world. These revelations, supported by highly classified documents, showed the US, the UK, and other governments engaged in global indiscriminate data interception, largely unchecked by any meaningful legal constraint or oversight, without regard for the rights of millions of people who were not suspected of wrongdoing.

The promise of the digital age is the effortless, borderless ability to share information. That is its threat as well. As the world's information moves into cyberspace, surveillance capabilities have grown commensurately. The US now leads in ability for global data capture, but other nations and actors are likely to catch up, and some already insist that more data be kept within their reach. In the end, there will be no safe haven if privacy is seen as a strictly domestic issue, subject to many carve-outs and lax or non-existent oversight.

Human Rights Watch weighed in repeatedly throughout 2013 on the human rights implications of Snowden's revelations of mass surveillance, and the need to protect whistleblowers. This essay looks at how the law of privacy developed, and where it needs to reach today so that privacy is globally respected by all governments, for all people. Global mass surveillance poses a threat to human rights and democracy, and once again, the law must rise to the challenge.

A Concept Develops: The "Right to be Let Alone"

Many countries have long recognized the values that underlie the legal right to privacy—honor, reputation, and the sanctity of home and family life. But it was in the United States that private rights of action to defend privacy crystallized in the wake of Warren and Brandeis' call.

Judge Cooley in 1882 described privacy as "the right to be let alone." Tort law over the next century allowed people—many of them celebrities or people trying to avoid celebrity—to obtain remedies against unwanted public disclosure or nonconsensual exploitation of private information. The developing legal doctrine, aimed at shielding reputation and honor, quickly conflicted with press freedom and the public's right to information—most notably when newspapers sought to cover issues of general public interest that might include embarrassing information about public figures.

The law as it developed in the US was deferential to freedom of speech concerns, in practice allowing media-wide latitude; in Europe, there was greater emphasis on protecting reputational rights and shielding personal information.

Privacy as a limit on government intrusion gained ground in the wake of World War II and the rise of modern surveillance states. The Third Reich had relied heavily on census data to persecute, while many Communist states developed elaborate surveillance and data collection systems to monitor their populations and suppress dissent—restrictions that continue today in China, Vietnam, North Korea, Turkmenistan, and Cuba.

After World War II, the right to privacy made its way into many international human rights instruments and national constitutions, often phrased as freedom from interference with "privacy, family, home or correspondence," and the more traditional freedom from attacks on "honour and reputation."

Privacy has never been considered an absolute right. In international law it can be derogated, or restricted, when a grave public emergency threatens the nation's life. Even then, the emergency must be officially proclaimed, and restrictions not greater than the threat requires, nondiscriminatory, and consistent with international law, including respect for human rights.

If there is no such emergency, intrusions on privacy, family, home, and correspondence may not be arbitrary and must be embodied in laws that create clear expectations as to how and when they will likely be applied. These laws must aim to protect a legitimate interest in a democratic society, such as public safety or national security, be necessary and proportional to that end, and subject to judicial safeguards and remedies. These basic principles are common to most modern judicial consideration of various aspects of privacy.

Mind the Gap: New Technology and "Reasonable" Expectations

An important aspect of the law of privacy developed from the regulation of government search and seizure, generally in the context of criminal investigation. As the law developed, judicially authorized warrants for official searches became a common requirement, and some legal systems treated unauthorized searches as a a crime. The notion of "correspondence" broadened to include new technologies, such as telephones, with laws regulating when authorities could use wiretaps.

Yet protecting privacy has often lagged behind technological change. In the 1928 *Olmstead* case, the Supreme Court held that an unauthorized wiretap introduced as evidence in a criminal trial did not violate the constitutional right of the people "to be secure in their persons, houses, papers and effects." In 1967, the court reversed course, determining a person has "reasonable expectation of privacy" when talking in a public phone booth. This bit of common sense developed into a doctrine for when to limit government power to conduct warrantless searches. While the home has generally remained inviolable in US law, what is outside the home or in public view (trash at the curb, a car backseat) is not.

But even judicial doctrine as to when expectation of privacy is "reasonable" has often not kept pace with rapid technological shifts or even popular expectations. Brandeis, later a Supreme Court justice, foresaw this problem in his famous *Olmstead* dissent when he predicted: "Ways may someday be developed by which the Government, without removing papers from secret drawers, can reproduce them in court, and by which it will be enabled to expose to a jury the most intimate occurrences of the home." He added: "Can it be that the Constitution affords no protection against such invasions of individual security?"

Brandeis' concern is fully justified in our age of mass data interception. Wiretaps eventually needed warrants, but surveillance metastasized in the 21st century under new laws that set lax standards for many types of digital information.

Privacy: Secrecy or Self-Determination?

The "reasonable expectation" doctrine led US law to conclude that many types of business records were not protected from search without warrant, based on the rationale that an individual shared the information willingly with a third party and could not object if it became known.

But the objection has often been raised that sharing some personal information with a corporation does not mean there is an expectation it will be divulged to the government; on the contrary, we usually expect some discretion and confidentiality in our business transactions. Nor is it entirely accurate to say that sharing personal information via business records is entirely "voluntary," given how many necessary transactions of modern life require considerable disclosure.

US law has grown to equate "privacy" of communications with "secrecy," an approach "ill-suited to the digital age," in the recent words of Justice Sonia Sotomayor. The law in Europe took a different path. Germany, which recognizes a constitutional right of "personality," or the protection of one's integrity and capacity for self-development, led the way. In 1983, its Constitutional Court annulled the national census law, announcing "informational self-determination" as a fundamental democratic right.

Key to the European approach was the belief that individuals have a right to access and correct their data held by various institutions, and ultimately have a right to determine its use and disposal. An interlocking system of regional guidelines and standards emerged, albeit subject to national variation in legislation and application.[19] In contrast, US data privacy law is a welter of difficult-to-navigate state laws or laws governing particular industry sectors that are often focused on data breach and fraud rather than on informational self-determination.

Still, the European approach is not beyond criticism: it has required businesses to retain data for significant periods beyond their own needs so the government may have access, and makes oversight of government access subject to varying national standards. As data accumulation has moved from centralized storage to global "cloud" computing that involves more jurisdictions, actors, and laws, maintaining control over one's personal data has become more complicated as well.

Anonymity as the Ultimate Data Protection

One of the surest ways to control personal data—withholding one's real identity when communicating—found acceptance more readily in the US than elsewhere, not least because many of the nation's founders published revolutionary manifestos under pseudonyms.

While anonymity has never been considered an absolute or stand-alone right, the US Supreme Court has long recognized it to be part of speech that is entitled to a high level of protection, in part, as Justice Stevens wrote in 1995, because it can encourage speech. "Anonymity," he asserted, "...provides a way for a writer who may be personally unpopular to ensure that readers will not prejudge her message simply because they do not like its proponent."

Anonymity is increasingly precious—and imperilled—amid the growing quantity of information online and advances in aggregating and searching databases, and is critical for people to be able to share ideas publicly without fear of retaliation or persecution.

 In April 2013, the UN special rapporteur on the promotion and protection of the right to freedom of opinion, Frank LaRue, wrote of the "chilling effect" that restrictions on anonymity had on the free expression of information and ideas. He pointed out that when corporate actors exploit real name registration requirements to amass and mine personal data, they assume a serious responsibility to protect the privacy and security of such information.

Physical Privacy: Autonomy, Security, and Identity

As the law of search and seizure shows, understanding privacy in the physical world can influence its application to the virtual world. The strand of law protecting a person's intimate bodily attributes and decisions—including whether to choose marriage, abortion, start a family, or accept medical treatment—describes privacy as a way to assert one's physical autonomy and preferred identity, not as isolation or secrecy. As such, it holds relevance for protecting autonomy and identity in cyberspace as well.

A key decision related to physical privacy is the 1994 case of *Nicholas Toonen v. Australia*. The Human Rights Committee, the treaty body that interprets the International Covenant on Civil and Political Rights (ICCPR), repudiated Tasmania's criminal law of sodomy declaring "it is undisputed that adult consensual sexual activity in private is covered by the concept of 'privacy.'" *Toonen* rejected the rationale that the law was to prevent the spread of HIV/AIDS, and argued it was not a reasonable or proportionate means to that end, and more likely to drive a vulnerable population underground.

In *Goodwin v. U.K.*, the European Court of Human Rights in 2002 similarly emphasized the many adversities post-operative transsexuals suffer when they cannot change the sex on their birth certificate, including denying their right to marry, employment discrimination, and the denial of social benefits. The court focused on privacy in the sense of "the right to establish details of their identity as individual human beings" and concluded that transsexuals were entitled to "personal development and physical and moral security in the full sense enjoyed by others in society."

The logic of *Toonen and Goodwin* informs two recent foci of Human Rights Watch's privacy-related work: our call for decriminalizing simple drug use and possession (see the essay *The Human Rights Case for Drug Reform* in this volume), and our push for decriminalizing voluntary sex work by adults.

Both drug use and even voluntary sex work can pose serious risks to health and safety (including heightened risk for HIV/AIDS), but driving participants into the shadows is usually highly counterproductive to efforts to treat, mitigate, or prevent harm. Criminalization in both cases can cause or exacerbate a host of ancillary human rights violations, including exposure to violence from private actors, police abuse, discriminatory law enforcement, and vulnerability to blackmail, control, and abuse by criminals. These severe and common consequences, and the strong personal interest that people have in making decisions about their own bodies, mean it is unreasonable and disproportionate for the state to use criminal punishment to discourage either practice.

These approaches to physical self-determination are directly relevant to online privacy too. The physical and the virtual world are of course connected; our offline choices about friends, work, sexual identity, and religious or political beliefs are reflected in our online data and communications. Unwanted exposure of our private information can undermine the physical and moral security that the *Goodwin* decision emphasized is a key aim of privacy, and prevents us from developing a personal identity sheltered from coercion—considerations that underlie the creation of data privacy laws in the first place.

Surveillance's "Golden Age"

Two important developments have transformed the debate on privacy and ushered in what some have termed a "golden age of surveillance."

The first was the shift of almost every aspect of social, economic, and political relations online, so that disruption to, or surveillance of, online activity can potentially harm or be used to harm almost every human right—whether civil, political, economic, social, or cultural.

The second development is the enormous advance in our ability to store, search, collate and analyze data with minimal effort and cost. This has serious implications for collecting and retaining data, providing enormous incentive to amass information at a time when much of our lives is exposed through online data. Moreover, governments like that of the US have devoted considerable resources to ensuring our data is always accessible, including seeking backdoors into technology and collection points, and cracking strong encryption.

Concerns about the privacy of online communications and digital information were strong even before Edward Snowden began disclosing in June 2013 the massive and global extent of surveillance by the US National Security Agency. But since then, intense debate has raged as to whether mass surveillance is ever justified, and whether privacy can actually be effectively protected against governments and corporations bent on espionage.

Once again, we find that law and the courts have not kept pace.

Legal Loopholes for Surveillance

Though a crime in most legal systems, espionage is not banned in international law, and most governments practice it to some degree. But as the birthplace of the Internet, home to major related industries, and with most global online communications running through its territory or facilities, the US is uniquely placed to conduct global surveillance. Consequently, it is worth examining the loopholes it has knit into its legal doctrines that give it a relatively free hand in capturing bulk data.

The first big loophole is that the US does not extend Constitutional rights to foreigners abroad, whether protection from "unreasonable" search, privacy, or freedom of speech (including anonymous speech). Nor does the US recognize extraterritorial application of its obligations under the International Covenant on Civil and Political Rights. Instead, US law authorizes warrantless surveillance of foreign intelligence so long as the secret Foreign Intelligence Surveillance Court (FISC) approves measures to "target" collection of "foreign intelligence" information and "minimize" the incidental collection of the communications of US citizens or residents. While foreigners have no protection against data collection, there are many exceptions for US persons that allow the government to retain their data as well—including encrypted communications and attorney-client communications.

Another big loophole is that the US considers "metadata," or the information about each message—such as date, time, location, sender, recipient—to be business records that are disclosed to third parties, and so entitled to a far lower standard of protection than substantive conversation, under both constitutional doctrine and section 215 of the PATRIOT Act. This type of data can provide an incredibly detailed portrait of anyone's movements, interlocutors, transactions, and concerns over time.

These two exceptions give enormous scope for bulk surveillance, but the government has also applied elastic interpretations to the law's already generous terms. Orders for "targeting" foreign intelligence do not need to specify particular investigations or persons, just general objectives; and such "targeted" surveillance means having just "51% confidence"—a hair better than a coin toss—that the people whose data is collected are foreigners abroad. The FISC determined that *all* metadata records from major US telephone companies such as Verizon could be "relevant" to intelligence or espionage investigations, an interpretation that begs the meaning of "relevant."

Another major loophole to both international and domestic legal obligations is intelligence sharing arrangements that let states avoid particular legal strictures on their own data collection activities. This appears to have been the case with US cooperation with the UK.

The present-day data collection practices of European states, including those collaborating with the NSA, have yet to be tested under the European Convention on Human Rights, but the case of *Klass v. Germany* suggests more demanding scrutiny could eventuate. There, the European Court of Human Rights emphasized that for surveillance to respect the right to privacy, there must be "adequate and effective guarantees against abuse" and that in view of the danger secret surveillance poses to democracy, states may not, "in the name of the struggle against espionage and terrorism, adopt whatever measures they deem appropriate."

The US Congress is percolating with legislative proposals to reform the legal structure that enables mass surveillance, though none so far would protect the privacy rights of foreign persons located outside US territory. But a world of globalized communications and surveillance needs universal standards that are not too readily evaded or bent. Unless the development of privacy as a legal right catches up to fill these gaps, the right may well become obsolete.

Global Communications, Global Obligations

What should be done?

Some argue we must simply live with the reality of pervasive online surveillance, and that public expectation of privacy has eroded. But this is neither accurate nor dispositive. Our understanding of privacy has in fact grown far beyond "a right to be left alone" into a right of personal self-determination, embracing the right to choose whom we share our personal details with and what identity we project to various communities. When applied to the digital world, privacy gives us some boundaries against unwanted monitors, and with it the essential freedom for personal development and independent thought.

While global surveillance will require a complex and global response, the US bears a particular burden, as a leader in both cyber-technology and mass surveillance, to rein in the serious overreach Edward Snowden brought to light. Among the steps Human Rights Watch has emphasized are requiring judicial warrant protection for metadata, recognizing that privacy is breached when data is collected (and not just when viewed or used), revamping the FISA court to make it a more adversarial and transparent body to check the NSA, and protecting whistleblowers who reveal rights-violating national security practices.

We must also recognize that the duty to protect rights in a world of globalized communication cannot stop at territorial borders. International law of the twentieth century assumed that a state's primary obligation is to ensure rights to all people in its territory or under its jurisdiction or effective control. This makes sense, as generally one state cannot secure rights for people abroad without violating another country's sovereignty. But there are circumstances when a government must carry its human rights obligations beyond its national borders—such as when its police or military abroad capture an individual. What about when it captures the communications of millions of people at home and abroad?

Arguably, collecting and banking mass personal data over time confers such power to track, analyze, and expose people's lives that it should be thought of as a form of "effective control." Some of us may not care about who sees our Facebook postings, but the security and human dignity of many people all over the world depends on the ability to limit who knows about their political preferences, sexual orientation, religious affiliation, and more.

Intentionally damaging acts, such as blackmailing, drone targeting, and coercion depend on discovering personal details; even when information is carelessly handled or misconstrued, terrible harms may result. A state that, without reasonable cause, appropriates in bulk the communications data of another state's inhabitants is damaging their security, autonomy, and exercise of their rights. At minimum, governments should apply the same legal protections to all persons whose privacy they breach as they do to their own citizens.

The several bills before the US Congress seek to address some of the abuses involved in NSA bulk surveillance, though none compel the US to protect the privacy of foreigners abroad. European governments, quick to condemn NSA excesses, have failed so far to carry out effective reviews of their own policies of mass surveillance at home or abroad, including the extent to which they have collaborated in, or benefitted from, US data collection.

It will take time to move the debate towards recognizing a global duty for states with extraterritorial surveillance capability to respect the privacy of all within their reach, but several encouraging signs suggest this will happen. In 2009, for example, Special Rapporteur on Human Rights and Counter-Terrorism Martin Scheinin called for developing soft law on data privacy and surveillance. In 2013, Special Rapporteur LaRue endorsed the need for the Human Rights Committee to update its General Comment on the right to privacy.

Two sets of principles that civil society expert groups recently issued may provide a basis for increasing consensus around standards: the Global Principles on National Security and the Right to Information ("The Tshwane Principles"), endorsed by the Parliamentary Assembly of the Council of Europe; and the International Principles on the Application of Human Rights to Communications Surveillance. These largely collect and restate general principles related to the right to privacy, transparency, and regulating surveillance in international law.

Most recently, Brazil and Germany in November 2013 introduced a UN General Assembly resolution that aims to create consensus against privacy abuses in digital surveillance both at home and abroad. The resolution calls for continuing reporting on mass surveillance and the right to privacy, including the implications of extraterritorial surveillance. Mirroring these efforts to articulate new standards are demands from civil society actors to reform government surveillance practices, ranging from a statement from major internet companies to a petition addressed to world leaders by 562 well-known authors in 80 countries. These developments can strengthen international legal consensus and tip the balance of power back to individuals.

The year 2013 may well come to be viewed as a watershed when people around the world stood up to reassert their right to privacy. But this can only happen if these debates produce global standards and enforceable domestic laws with teeth. We cannot wait for individuals like Edward Snowden to blow the whistle, but must demand thorough investigation into the full extent of government and corporate data collection and analysis. States should commit to transparent and public review of their practices and laws in order to maximize—not trade off—privacy, security, and technical innovation that can enhance and further our lives and rights as human beings.

The right to privacy is not just about leaving people alone; it is about empowering them to connect, speak, think, and live on their own terms, without arbitrary state interference. The technological revolution is upon us, and we must do our best to help the law catch up—again.

Dinah PoKempner is general counsel at Human Rights Watch.

WORLD REPORT 2014

PHOTO ESSAYS

The photo essays that follow highlight three underreported
human rights crises: child marriage in South Sudan,
the impact of the 2014 Sochi Olympics on human rights
in Russia, and the human rights and humanitarian tragedy in
the Central African Republic.

CHILD MARRIAGE
SOUTH SUDAN
BY BRENT STIRTON/REPORTAGE BY GETTY IMAGES FOR HUMAN RIGHTS WATCH

Almost half of all South Sudanese women and girls between ages 15 and 19 are married, some as young as age 12. Many families in South Sudan see child marriage as a means of accessing cattle, money, and other gifts by transferring wealth through the traditional payment of dowries. An egregious violation of women and girls' human rights, child marriage in South Sudan exacerbates the country's high levels of poverty, low levels of literacy, pronounced gender gaps in education, and soaring rates of maternal mortality—currently among the highest in the world.

Helen, 16, stands beside her husband, Jade, 50, outside their home in a village near Juba, South Sudan. Helen was married at 15 and said she would have chosen school over marriage, but her family was could not afford school fees. She was in labor for five days before having a cesarean section. Her son is now 8 months old.

Kansuk, Central Equatoria State, February 2013

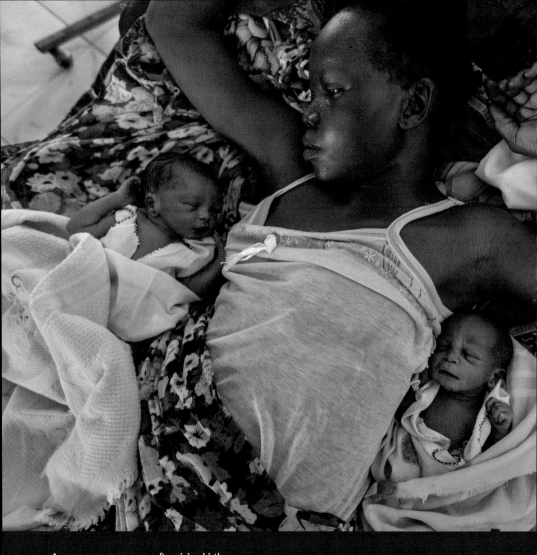

A young woman recovers after giving birth to twins in Bor Hospital in Jonglei State. She was married at the age of 12 and had her first child at the age of 15, enduring a five-day labor. She is now 20 and these are her 4th and 5th children.

Akuot's father died when she was a young child. Her uncle tried to force her into marriage, even though she and her mother protested. Now 16, Akuot resisted the marriage and ran away, determined to continue her education. Her uncle and male cousins caught her, dragged her back to their village, and beat her for three days while keeping her locked inside without food or water.

A pregnant student stands in a classroom at the Juba Day Secondary School. The school administration does not permit students who become pregnant to remain in regular classes, but the teachers union offers evening sessions for pregnant girls and young mothers to continue their education.

Juba, Central Equatoria State, February 2013.

Cattle rest in the countryside near the town of Bor. In pastoralist communities, dowry is largely paid in cattle, while agriculturalist communities combine money with cattle or other livestock. Customary practices attach great social and economic importance to dowry payment, and a husband's consequent rights over his wife.

Bor, Jonglei State, February 2013

In February and March 2014, Russia will host the Winter Olympic and Paralympic Games in the Black Sea city of Sochi. For Russia's leaders, the Olympics are an opportunity to showcase their ability to organize major events and burnish the country's international image, and Sochi has been transformed with gleaming new Olympic venues. But this change has come at a cost to many Sochi residents, some of whom have been displaced for Olympic construction and have lost their homes without compensation. It has also affected workers, including migrant workers who are helping to build key Olympic venues, some of whom have been exploited and abused. Activists and journalists seeking to criticize or document Olympics-related abuse have faced pressure, harassment, and in some cases, arrest and prosecution.

A woman points towards the Caucasus Mountains in the Black Sea city of Sochi, Russia, which will host the 2014 Winter Olympic and Paralympic Games in February and March respectively.

PEOPLE AND POWER
THE 2014 SOCHI OLYMPICS
BY BRENT STIRTON/REPORTAGE BY GETTY IMAGES FOR HUMAN RIGHTS WATCH

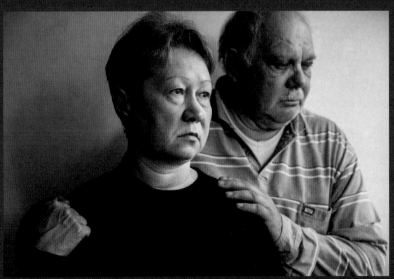

(opposite page, above) Migrant workers from Tajikistan on a construction site in Krasnaya Polyana, Sochi. Thousands of workers from outside Russia and from other parts of Russia have come have come to Sochi to work in construction that is underway ahead of the 2014 Winter Olympic and Paralympic Games.

(opposite page, below) Alexander Mzokov, 59, and his wife, Natalia, who lived with their sons Yuri and Evgenii and eight of their relatives in a three-story home in Sochi, learned in April 2012 that the authorities would demolish their home of 13 years to make way for a road providing infrastructure for the 2014 Winter Olympic and Paralympic Games in Sochi. Although the Mzokovs had full legal title to the house and the land on which it stood, the authorities sued them for constructing an "illegal structure," and on appeal won a court order to demolish the house without providing them fair compensation. The house was demolished on October 4, 2012.

(above) Members of the Sochi branch of the Russian Geographical Society conducting field research in the Caucasus Mountains in Sochi. The Society's Sochi branch has frequently publicized information about the potential environmental impacts of Olympic construction. Numerous activists and journalists in Sochi have faced harassment, pressure, and threats after criticizing Olympics-related human rights abuses and other concerns.

Residents of Kudepsta, Sochi, protest the proposed construction in their mountain village of what was projected to be the world's largest natural gas power station. The plant was to be part of infrastructure development in Sochi ahead of the 2014 Winter Olympic and Paralympic Games. Before environmental review and other legally required procedures were completed, workers built a bridge, felled trees, and erected a large fence at the power plant site. Residents painted "No to the Kudepsta power station!" on the bridge. Residents fear pollution, property devaluation, and devastation of the landscape and the town's appeal as a tourist destination.

UNFOLDING TRAGEDY
THE CENTRAL AFRICAN REPUBLIC

BY MARCUS BLEASDALE/VII FOR HUMAN RIGHTS WATCH

In September 2013, the Central African Republic's human rights and humanitarian situation took a sharp turn for the worse. After months of brutality by the predominantly Muslim Seleka ("alliance") forces, which had overthrown the government of President François Bozizé in March, the mainly Christian militias known as the anti-balaka ("anti-machete") began to organize counterattacks. The anti-balaka, which began as local self-defense groups under Bozizé, have targeted Muslim communities and committed numerous abuses. Michel Djotodia, the Seleka leader who in August was officially sworn in as president until 2015 elections, announced in September the Seleka were being dissolved. However, the ex-Seleka fighters continued their string of abuses across the country.

FOMAC peacekeepers confiscate machetes from people who fled into the FOMAC compound to escape fighting between anti-balaka militias and former Seleka forces.

Displaced people find shelter in a disused factory at the Christian mission in Bossangoa. Tens of thousands of people have been displaced by the fighting between Seleka and anti-balaka forces.

(above) Captain Wilson, from the Republic of Congo, stands in the FOMAC peacekeeping compound. When heavy clashes erupted in Bossangoa in December 2013, the captain rallied his peacekeeping troops with remarkable speed, deploying them around town to safeguard tens of thousands of displaced people sheltering in the Catholic church and other sites.

(left) Residents of Bossangoa, Central African Republic, lie on the ground of the compound of FOMAC, the regional peacekeeping Multinational Force of Central Africa, on December 5, 2013. The residents had fled from gunfire from anti-balaka forces. FOMAC troops tried to protect people from anti-balaka attacks in the town, which lies 300 kilometers (190 miles) north of the capital, Bangui.

Anti-balaka fighters have recruited and armed children in villages surrounding Bossangoa.

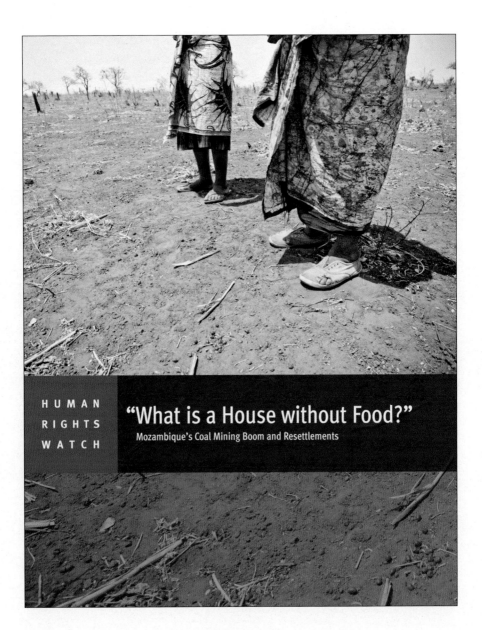

HUMAN
RIGHTS
WATCH

"What is a House without Food?"

Mozambique's Coal Mining Boom and Resettlements

WORLD REPORT
2014

AFRICA

Angola

José Eduardo Dos Santos, Angola's president for the past 34 years, secured another five-year term in the August 2012 elections. Although the polls consolidated the control of the ruling Popular Movement for the Liberation of Angola (MPLA), the authorities intensified repressive measures to restrict freedom of expression, association, and assembly in 2013.

The government has pursued numerous criminal defamation lawsuits against outspoken journalists and activists, while continuing to use police abuse, arbitrary arrests, and intimidation to prevent peaceful anti-government protests, strikes, and other gatherings from taking place. The government also resumed mass forced evictions of informal settlements in 2013 and launched a new initiative to remove street traders in the capital, Luanda. Both measures affect Angola's poorest communities and have been conducted with brutality.

Freedom of Expression

Freedom of expression is severely restricted in Angola due to limited independent media, self-censorship, and government repression. Only 3 percent of the Angolan population has access to the Internet and social media, which are the main channels for commenting on government policies.

The authorities use criminal defamation laws to silence and intimidate journalists and bloggers. On July 5, bloggers José Gama and Lucas Pedro were charged with "abuse of press freedom" and defamation for articles published on the news website www.club-k.net, which is hosted outside of Angola. Brought by Angola's attorney general and the criminal investigation police director, the lawsuits are based on articles published between January and May that accused the attorney general of corruption and criminal investigation police officers of torture.

Between March and July, Rafael Marques, an investigative journalist and human rights defender who won the Transparency International Integrity Award in 2013, was charged with defamation in 11 criminal lawsuits. The plaintiffs are high-ranking generals, their business associates, and three private companies that operate in the diamond-rich Lunda Norte province. Marques accused the plaintiffs of involvement in torture, rape, and killings in a book he published in Portugal in 2011. Angola's Attorney General's office shelved a complaint filed by Marques against the generals and business associates in 2012, and has failed to investigate the allegations. Marques has regularly experienced threats, harassment, and pervasive surveillance, including apparently targeted hacker attacks on his computer and blog.

On June 11, Domingos da Cruz, journalist of the private weekly *Folha 8*, was charged with "instigation of collective disobedience" according to a 1978 law on crimes against the security of the state. The law was revoked and replaced by a new law in 2010. The charges were based on an opinion piece that da Cruz published in 2009. A court acquitted him on September 9, arguing the law had been revoked.

Right To Peaceful Assembly

Despite constitutional protection for freedom of assembly, since 2011 the authorities have responded to peaceful anti-government protests organized by youth groups and others in Luanda and elsewhere with excessive force, arbitrary arrests, unfair trials, harassment, and intimidation of participants, journalists, and observers. The state-owned media, controlled by the ruling party, present the protests as a threat to peace. Protest organizers and participants were also targeted by surveillance and harassment and occasionally by violent attacks and abduction by security agents in 2013.

On December 22 in 2012, and March 30, May 27, and September 19 in 2013, police used excessive force to disperse peaceful youth protests in Luanda, arbitrarily detaining protesters and in several cases threatening journalists. Most protesters were released the same day without charges. However, 22-year-old Emiliano Catumbela, who was arrested on May 27, was charged with bodily harm, and later charged with attempted assassination of a police commander. He was denied access to his lawyers for several days and said he was beaten and tortured in custody. On June 25, he was released without charges.

On September 12, police arrested 17-year-old Manuel Chivonde Nito Alves, a youth activist and protest organizer, when he collected t-shirts produced for a protest planned for September 19. He was charged with "outrage" against the president based on the t-shirt slogan which called President Dos Santos a "disgusting dictator." "Outrage" against the president is considered a crime against the security of the state under Angolan law since 2010. He was conditionally released on November 8 to await trial, after being jailed arbitrarily for almost two months.

Three journalists—Rafael Marques, Alexandre Neto, and Coque Mukuta—were arrested on September 20 and severely beaten and threatened in police custody after they interviewed several just-released protesters on the street.

During those protests, youth groups demanded an official explanation on the whereabouts of Isaías Cassule and António Alves Kamulingue. Unknown men abducted Cassule and Kamulingue after they organized a protest of former presidential guards on May 27, 2012. In March 2013, police arrested Alberto Santos, who witnessed Cassule's abduction. Santos claimed that police tried to pressure him to incriminate opposition activists as responsible for the abductions. He was released on October 1 without charges. On November 9, an Angolan website published details of a leaked confidential report from the Ministry of the Interior that revealed that Kamulingue and Cassule were abducted, tortured, and killed by police and intelligence officials soon after their abduction.

In April, the authorities banned a teacher's union strike in Lubango, Huila province. Union leaders faced anonymous threats and intimidation. On April 30, police detained two union leaders and charged them with disobedience and defamation of the authorities. A court acquitted them for lack of evidence on May 2.

Arbitrary Detentions in the Enclave of Cabinda

An intermittent separatist insurgency persists in the oil-rich enclave of Cabinda despite a 2006 peace agreement. The government has used security as a pretext to crack down on peaceful dissent. Security forces continue to arbitrarily arrest supporters of the separatist guerilla movement Front for the Liberation of the Enclave of Cabinda (FLEC) and use torture in military custody to force detainees to confess or incriminate others. Such violations of due process rights, as well as harassment of journalists who document such cases and threats against defense lawyers, have undermined the credibility of trials for alleged national security crimes in Cabinda.

HUMAN RIGHTS WATCH

"Take That Filth Away"
Police Abuses Against Street Vendors in Angola

Between August 10 and September 12 2013, military and intelligence officials arrested, mistreated, in several cases tortured, and jailed at least 20 men in Cabinda, including an adviser to the deputy governor of Cabinda. They were charged with armed rebellion and remain in pretrial detention.

Nine men of Congolese origin and Angolan, Belgian and French nationalities, alleged to be former members of the defunct Armed Forces of Zaire (FAZ) were arrested on November 22, 2012, beaten and tortured by military and border guards while in incommunicado detention. In May, they were charged with armed rebellion against the government of the Democratic Republic of the Congo, illegal entry and stay in Angola. As of November 2012, the men remained in pretrial detention.

Since January 2013, Arão Tempo, a lawyer and local representative of the Angolan Bar, has received repeated death threats from intelligence officials warning him to stop defending the 20 men held in Cabinda and the 9 alleged FAZ members.

Police Brutality during Removals of Street Traders

In October 2012, the governor of Luanda ordered urgent measures to reduce street trade in the capital. Since then, the authorities have scaled up efforts to remove street vendors from the streets of Luanda.

During these operations, police and government inspectors have routinely mistreated street vendors, including pregnant women and women with children, by seizing their goods, extorting bribes, threatened them with imprisonment, and in some cases arresting them. The authorities have also intimidated, harassed, and arbitrarily arrested journalists, activists, and witnesses who seek to document the brutality of the operations.

Forced Evictions

The majority of Angola's urban population lives in informal settlements without legal protection. Angola's laws neither adequately protect people from forced eviction nor enshrine the right to adequate housing. In 2013, the government continued to carry out mass forced evictions in areas that it claimed were reserved for public use. The operations occurred without adequate prior notice and security forces used excessive force.

In the first days of February, security forces forcibly evicted an estimated 5,000 residents from an informal settlement in the peripheral Cacuaco municipality in Luanda. Following the evictions, security forces arbitrarily arrested dozens of residents, at least 40 of whom were charged with illegal land occupation and disobedience, and were convicted and given prison sentences.

On October 7, International Habitat Day, the authorities prevented a protest against forced evictions in Luanda organized by SOS Habitat, a nongovernmental organization.

Key International Actors

Angola is the second largest economy in the Southern African Development Community (SADC), and an increasingly influential power both in the sub-region and the continent due to its economic and military clout. Angola's oil wealth and soaring economic growth continue to attract business interests from all over the world, and few of its partners prioritize the governance and human rights concerns in their cooperation agenda.

Angola's periodic report to the UN Human Rights Committee, the treaty monitoring body for the International Covenant on Civil and Political Rights, was considered in 2013. The Committee urged the government to end impunity and investigate killings, torture, ill-treatment, and enforced disappearances by the security forces, among other recommendations.

In early April, the UN High Commissioner for Human Rights, Navi Pillay, visited Angola at the invitation of the government. During her visit, Pillay raised a wide array of human rights concerns, including restrictions on freedom of expression and of the media, the excessive use of force to repress protests, mistreatment and sexual violence against irregular migrants, forced evictions, and violations of economic and social rights. Pillay's visit was a rare spotlight on Angola's human rights record, which is mostly ignored by Angola's regional and international partners in favor of strengthening trade links.

Burundi

The Burundian government committed to strengthening human rights protections and made progress in certain areas, such as initiatives to address gender-based violence. A five-day national debate on the justice sector produced a set of recommendations on judicial reforms. However, the justice system remained weak and under-resourced and suffered from political interference and allegations of corruption.

Impunity for human rights abuses, particularly by state agents and youth of the ruling party, was a dominant concern. Most cases of extrajudicial killings and other acts of political violence between 2010 and 2012 remained unresolved. Prosecutions were initiated against a small number of alleged perpetrators, but proceedings were slow or seriously flawed, and several police officers accused of involvement in killings and ill-treatment were released.

Most leading opposition figures who had fled the country after boycotting the 2010 elections returned to Burundi, encouraged by the government, in advance of the 2015 general elections. However, opposition party members continued to face obstruction and harassment.

Journalists and civil society activists also encountered intimidation by the government, which accused them of siding with the opposition. In June, President Pierre Nkurunziza promulgated a new press law severely curtailing media freedoms.

Impunity for Political Killings and Other Abuses

Few of the perpetrators of the scores of political killings in 2010-2012 were brought to justice, due to a lack of political will and weak judicial system. In many cases, victims' families were too afraid to seek redress.

In a small number of cases, judicial authorities arrested, charged, and prosecuted police officers, following investigations by a commission of inquiry into extrajudicial killings and torture set up in 2012 by the prosecutor general. The High Court in Gitega tried Michel Nurweze, known as Rwembe ("razor blade" in Kirundi), a deputy police commissioner in Gitega province, for his alleged involvement in the November 2011 murder of Léandre Bukuru, a member of the

Movement for Solidarity and Democracy (MSD) opposition party. Nurweze was also tried for attempted murder and torture in two other cases. His trial could have set an important precedent in ending impunity, but at least two prosecution witnesses would not testify in court because of the absence of adequate protection.

On August 12, the court acquitted Nurweze of the murder and torture charges, changed the offense of attempted murder to grievous bodily harm, and sentenced him to three months' imprisonment. He was released, as he had already served a year in prison. The prosecution appealed. Appeal hearings opened in October but were postponed to January 2014.

Appeal hearings in the trial of those accused of involvement in an attack in Gatumba in September 2011, which killed 39 people, concluded in November. Proceedings were complicated by the escape from detention of one of the principal defendants, Innocent Ngendakuriyo. The trial in 2012 had been seriously flawed, with several defendants convicted despite claiming they had been tortured.

Political Parties

Most opposition party leaders who had fled the country after boycotting the 2010 elections returned to Burundi, including Alexis Sinduhije, president of the MSD, and Agathon Rwasa, former rebel leader and head of the National Liberation Forces (FNL). Following their return, members of opposition parties, including the FNL and the MSD, were harassed and intimidated, despite government promises that political parties could operate freely. Government officials and police disrupted or obstructed party meetings and arrested a number of FNL and MSD members.

Members of the *imbonerakure*—the youth league of the ruling National Council for the Defense of Democracy-Forces for the Defense of Democracy (CNDD-FDD)—committed acts of violence, including killings, beatings, rape, threats, and extortion against their perceived opponents and other Burundians. Despite a public outcry and promises by government and party officials to punish such actions, abuses continued throughout the year. Some opposition party members threatened to retaliate in kind through their own youth groups. A clash between *imbonerakure* and MSD youth in Gihanga, Bubanza province, on October 6 caused injuries on both sides.

Killings, Ill-Treatment, and Arbitrary Arrests of Religious Worshippers

Police opened fire on a large crowd of religious worshippers near Businde, Kayanza province, on March 12, killing nine people. The police then lined up the worshippers and beat them. The victims included men, women, and children. The worshippers, part of an informal spiritual movement that makes a monthly pilgrimage to Businde, consider themselves Roman Catholics, but have been rejected by the Catholic Church hierarchy in Burundi and have repeatedly clashed with local clergy, police, and governmental officials since 2012. The police, instructed by the government to prevent the worshippers from gathering at Businde, beat them severely on several previous occasions in late 2012 and January 2013. Some victims sustained broken bones and other serious injuries.

Hundreds of these worshippers were arbitrarily arrested in late 2012 and 2013. Most were accused of "rebellion" for disregarding the government decision to prohibit prayers at Businde. Many were released without charge but some were rearrested. In some cases, a condition for their release was that they would agree not to return to Businde, in violation of their right to religious freedom. More than 200 people arrested in March and April were tried summarily on the day of their arrest, without a defense lawyer, and received sentences of up to five years' imprisonment. On appeal, their sentences were reduced to a fine and all but two of them were released. Thirty-three others arrested in late 2012 remained in pretrial detention.

The prosecutor of the appeal court at Ngozi ordered the arrest on March 16 of Bosco Havyarimana, the police commander accused of ordering the shootings and supervising the beatings, and two other police officers, Syldie Nsengiyumva and Innocent Nizigiyimana. On May 29, all three were provisionally released, pending further investigations. At time of writing, they had not been brought to trial.

Harassment of Civil Society Activists and Journalists

Burundi has a vibrant independent civil society and media, but government officials have attempted to silence their criticisms and accused them of siding with
the political opposition. Government and judicial officials harassed, intimidated, and questioned several journalists about their reporting and threatened
them with legal action.

On April 27, a policeman threatened Patrick Niyonkuru, a journalist with Radio
Publique Africaine (RPA), as he attempted to investigate alleged extortion of
bicycle-taxi drivers by the police. The policeman then shot Niyonkuru, injuring
him in the arm. The policeman was arrested, tried summarily, and sentenced to
15 years in prison on the day of the attack.

On April 25, armed men broke into the house of Willy Abagenzinikindi of Radio
Television Renaissance, forced him to the ground, hit him with a machete, and
demanded that he hand over audio cassettes he had recorded as part of his
investigations.

Hassan Ruvakuki, journalist with Radio France Internationale and Bonesha FM,
who had been sentenced to life imprisonment in 2012 for alleged participation
in terrorist acts after interviewing a rebel group, was released in March after
spending 15 months in prison. His sentence had been reduced to three years on
appeal. Following much international attention on the case, he was released
early on medical grounds, then granted conditional release in October. On
February 19, police fired teargas to disperse journalists marching in support of
Ruvakuki in the capital Bujumbura.

The National Communication Council suspended the online readers' forum of
Burundi's main independent newspaper *Iwacu* for 30 days on May 31, claiming
that unspecified readers' comments had violated legal provisions on "endangering national unity, public order and security, incitement to ethnic hatred, justifi-
cation of crimes, and insults to the head of state."

In June, the government adopted a new restrictive press law, despite strong
national and international expressions of concern. The law undermines the protection of sources and limits the subjects on which journalists can report,
potentially criminalizing reporting and analysis on subjects such as inflation,

public order and security, and political killings. While eliminating prison sentences provided under the old law, it imposes new, heavy fines.

A draft law on public demonstrations and meetings, adopted by parliament but not yet promulgated, and another on nongovernmental organizations, awaiting parliamentary debate, also raised concerns about possible restrictions of freedom of association and assembly. Amendments by the National Assembly to the law on public demonstrations and meetings took into account many recommendations by Burundian civil society organizations, but the draft retained the right of an administrative official appointed to attend public meetings to suspend or dissolve them to maintain public order.

Transitional Justice

At time of writing, parliament had not yet adopted a draft law establishing a Truth and Reconciliation Commission to cover crimes committed since 1962, despite assurances by President Nkurunziza that the commission would be established by the end of 2012. The draft law does not provide for the establishment of a special tribunal to prosecute those accused of the most serious offenses.

Returnees

Around 35,000 Burundian refugees, many of whom had been living in Tanzania for several decades, returned to Burundi between October and December 2012 following an ultimatum by the Tanzanian government. Overall the returns took place peacefully, but there were tensions around property and land ownership, and controversy over some decisions of the National Commission for Land and Other Property, responsible for resolving such disputes.

Key International Actors

Burundi's Universal Periodic Review, which took place in January 2013, contained important recommendations on the protection of civil and political as well as social, economic, and cultural rights. While welcoming progress in some areas, many governments raised concerns in the Human Rights Council about extrajudicial killings, impunity for human rights abuses, and restrictions on press freedom, among other issues. The Burundian government rejected all the recommendations to fight impunity for extrajudicial killings, as well as those on the prevention of discrimination on the basis of sexual orientation and gender identity and the decriminalization of consensual same-sex conduct.

The United Nations Office in Burundi, BNUB, encouraged dialogue between political parties and organized a meeting between political actors in March. Participants agreed to create an environment conducive to free, fair, transparent, and peaceful elections in 2015, the right of all parties to carry out their activities unhindered, and a commitment not to use violence.

Central African Republic

A rebel coalition known as the Seleka took control of Bangui, the capital of the Central African Republic (CAR), on March 24, 2013, forcing out the former president, François Bozizé. A transitional government was established, and Michel Djotodia was formally named interim president in April. New elections were scheduled for early 2015.

Rebels belonging to the Seleka, which means "alliance" in Sango, the national language, engaged in widespread human rights abuses, particularly killing civilians indiscriminately. These killings, both in Bangui and outside the capital, were often followed by widespread looting and pillaging, leaving sections of an already-poor population homeless and destitute.

Djotodia denied that Seleka fighters committed abuses, initially blaming the violence on Bozizé loyalists, "false Seleka," or bandits. On September 13, he dissolved the Seleka as a group. However, members of the Seleka continue to kill with impunity and the central government does not appear to be in total control of the Seleka.

Armed groups originally created by Bozizé to fight banditry, the *anti-balaka* ("anti-machete"), clashed with the Seleka in late 2013. Violence and insecurity took on an alarming sectarian dimension, as the anti-balaka, who are predominantly Christian and include some soldiers who served under Bozizé in the Central African Armed Forces (FACA), attacked Muslim civilians around Bossangoa, the capital of Ouham province, in response to Seleka abuses, mostly against Christian civilians.

The dire security situation hampered the delivery of humanitarian aid and Seleka fighters intimidated and harassed journalists and civil society activists.

An African Union (AU)-led peacekeeping force, the International Support Mission in Central Africa (AFISM-CAR) has requested financial, logistical, and technical support from the international community, but as of October 31 had only 2,589 of the 3,500 personnel requested.

Seleka Abuses

The Seleka was created in late 2012 out of three main rebel factions, primarily from CAR's impoverished north. The group called for more political inclusiveness and an end to the marginalization of the predominantly Muslim northern region. The Seleka includes fighters from Chad and Sudan, and it has recruited child soldiers.

The group launched an offensive in December 2012 and swiftly moved toward the capital, capturing towns along the way. A peace agreement was reached with the government in January, but was soon ignored by both parties, as the rebels advanced on Bangui, forcing former President Bozizé to flee. Along the way towards the capital, they destroyed numerous rural villages, looted homes, and raped women and girls.

After taking power, the Seleka killed scores of civilians who were trying to flee attacks. In some villages, every single structure was at least partially burned. The destruction was often accompanied by pillaging, leaving civilian populations utterly destitute.

Many villagers, forced to abandon their homes, are living in extremely difficult conditions in the bush. Lacking humanitarian support, numerous people have died of illness, injuries, or exposure to the elements. International humanitarian agencies have been able to provide limited support to only a few affected areas. Governmental and nongovernmental health services were systematically targeted, and destroyed or closed.

In Bangui, the Seleka looted entire neighborhoods as they took control of the city. Areas such as Damala, Boy-Rabe, Kasai, and Walingba saw wanton attacks and scores of civilians killed. Boy-Rabe, in particular, has been routinely ransacked by the Seleka. Government officials claimed that these were disarmament operations.

Fighting escalated in September around Bossangoa in the north. Hundreds of people have been killed and numerous communities have been burned to the ground. The anti-balaka groups have singled out Muslim communities for attack, as they are perceived to be allied with the Seleka.

Almost all of the abuses have been carried out with complete impunity. A small number of alleged Seleka perpetrators have been arrested and some prosecutions initiated against them, but the judicial system remains severely hampered and trials, at time of writing, had yet to commence. The functioning of the government, especially in the rural areas, has been seriously disrupted and limited by the coup, with many administrative buildings destroyed.

Refugees and Internally Displaced Persons

The situation for displaced people is bordering on catastrophic because of their limited access to humanitarian assistance. In September 2013, the United Nations reported that about 170,000 people fled intense fighting in the north around Bossangoa. Most were left to fend for themselves in the bush, but about 36,000 found refuge in the compound of a Catholic church and at a local school in Bossangoa. The number of internally displaced persons stands at about 400,000. Almost 65,000 CAR refugees were in the Democratic Republic of the Congo (DRC) and other neighboring countries.

Commission of Inquiry

On May 22, a presidential decree established a national commission of inquiry to investigate human rights violations committed since 2002 and to identify the persons most responsible for these crimes. The commission, comprising judges, human rights defenders, and police officers, is also tasked with identifying individual victims and assessing levels of damage for eventual compensation.

The commission was initially incapable of doing its work due to a lack of funding, but in September it received technical assistance and vehicles from the government to conduct investigations. Some civil society actors have questioned the ability of a national commission to achieve results and have called for the establishment of an international commission of inquiry.

The International Criminal Court

CAR first accepted the jurisdiction of the International Criminal Court (ICC) in 2001, when it became a state party to the Rome Statute. On December 22, 2004, the government went one step further and referred the situation in the country to the ICC prosecutor, after a Bangui court of appeals ruled that domestic courts were unable to prosecute grave international crimes effectively. In

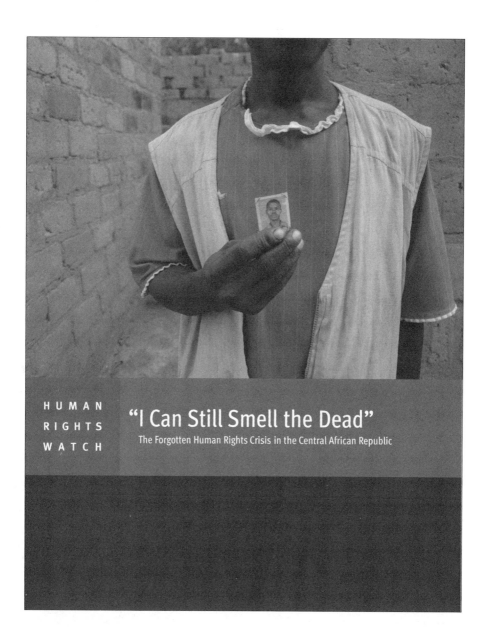

HUMAN
RIGHTS
WATCH

"I Can Still Smell the Dead"

The Forgotten Human Rights Crisis in the Central African Republic

2007, the ICC opened an investigation into crimes committed during the 2002-2003 civil war. The investigation has so far led to only one case, that of Jean-Pierre Bemba Gombo, a Congolese national and former vice-president of the DRC. Bemba and his Movement for Liberation of Congo forces were invited to CAR in 2002 by then-President Ange-Félix Patassé to support resistance of a coup attempt by Bozizé. Bemba is currently on trial at the ICC for war crimes and crimes against humanity.

ICC Prosecutor Fatou Bensouda continues to monitor developments in the country and has indicated that she may exercise jurisdiction over more recent crimes. She issued public statements on April 22 and August 7, warning those responsible for recent abuses that their crimes may fall under the ICC's jurisdiction and that her office would investigate and prosecute those most responsible for committing serious crimes "if necessary."

Peacekeeping Forces

In March, while trying to protect the Bozizé government, 13 soldiers of the South African Defence Force were killed outside of Bangui by Seleka forces. The soldiers were there under a bilateral arrangement between Bozizé and President Jacob Zuma of South Africa.

Also unable to stop the Seleka were the Multinational Forces for Central Africa (FOMAC), regional peacekeepers deployed in CAR through an agreement signed in late 2007 with the Economic Community of Central African States (ECCAS) under the Mission for the Consolidation of Peace in Central African Republic (MICOPAX). In April, ECCAS decided to deploy an additional 2,000 troops to support MICOPAX.

In August, MICOPAX was transitioned into the AU-led AFISM-CAR. Most of the requested 3,500 troops will be made up of contingents that were already serving in MICOPAX. The mandate of AFISM-CAR includes civilian protection and the creation of conditions for the provision of humanitarian assistance. As of October 31, 2013, AFISM-CAR had roughly 2,589 of the 3,500 requested peacekeepers on the ground.

French troops, meanwhile, maintain control over the international airport in Bangui.

Key International Actors

The international response to the Seleka takeover was initially regional. In December 2012, the Economic Community of Central African States (ECCAS) called on the Seleka to halt its advance on Bangui. In January, a power-sharing agreement brokered by ECCAS was signed between the Seleka and the Bozizé government, but was ignored by both sides. When the Seleka took Bangui in March, the ECCAS turned its focus to supporting and augmenting the FOMAC presence.

Ivan Simonovic, the assistant secretary-general for human rights at the United Nations, visited CAR from July 29 to August 2. In an August 14 report to the UN Security Council (Security Council), he stated that the current conflict "was marked by an unprecedented level of violence, looting and destruction" and that the Seleka were committing the most "serious violations of international human rights and international humanitarian law."

In October, the Security Council unanimously adopted a resolution strongly condemning the widespread human rights and humanitarian law violations, notably by "Seleka elements," strengthening the UN's mandate to monitor and report on human rights abuses on the ground, and demanding safe and unhindered access for humanitarian aid.

John Ging, the UN's operations director for the Office for the Coordination of Humanitarian Affairs, said in November after a visit to CAR that he was "very concerned that the seeds of a genocide are being sown."

In mid-November the secretary-general presented the Security Council with options for international support to the African peacekeeping force and the potential creation of a UN peacekeeping force. The Security Council was expected to pass an additional resolution toward the end of the year.

Côte d'Ivoire

During 2013, the government of President Alassane Ouattara made progress in creating the legislative framework for greater respect for human rights and in ensuring better discipline within the security forces. Inadequate headway was made in strengthening the judiciary's independence, ensuring accountability for crimes committed during the 2010-2011 post-election crisis, and addressing root causes of the country's decade of violence—notably impunity, corruption, land conflict, and the proliferation of small arms.

Security force abuses decreased from 2012, in part due to government efforts. However, members of the security forces continued to engage in numerous human rights violations and acts of criminality, including arbitrary arrests, cruel and inhuman treatment of detainees, and extortion at checkpoints.

One-sided justice for the post-election crisis undermined reconciliation and, together with ongoing weaknesses within the judiciary, hindered progress in establishing the rule of law. While Ivorian authorities have investigated and charged numerous supporters of former President Laurent Gbagbo for their role in the post-election violence, there has been a near complete absence of accountability for serious crimes committed by President Ouattara's forces. The government made some efforts to improve access to justice for other crimes, including by opening a new tribunal in western Côte d'Ivoire, but corruption and the judiciary's lack of independence remain a general concern.

The country's security situation improved, though land conflict simmered in western Côte d'Ivoire with ineffective government response, contributing to several cross-border attacks from Liberia and small-scale inter-communal violence. As disarmament proceeded slowly, the country remained awash in guns, often in the hands of disgruntled former combatants.

Some of Côte d'Ivoire's partners, notably the United Nations and the United States, showed more willingness to criticize the lack of accountability for past crimes, while others, particularly France, remained largely silent. The International Criminal Court continued investigations, though many Ivorians criticized the lack of progress in the investigation of crimes by pro-Ouattara forces.

HUMAN
RIGHTS
WATCH

TURNING RHETORIC
INTO REALITY
Accountability for Serious International Crimes in Côte d'Ivoire

National Justice for Post-Election Violence

The Ouattara government has failed to deliver on its promise to render fair and impartial justice for crimes committed during the 2010-2011 post-election crisis. This crisis was the culmination of a decade of politico-ethnic conflict in which security forces, rebel forces, and allied militia groups regularly committed serious crimes with complete impunity.

On the Gbagbo side, Ivorian authorities have charged more than 150 civilian and military leaders, including at least 55 with serious violent crimes. However, they have failed to charge a single member of the pro-Ouattara Republican Forces for the serious crimes they committed during the crisis. Ongoing investigations also appear one-sided. A national commission of inquiry reported in August 2012 that both sides had committed hundreds of summary executions, yet the UN reported that, as of July 2013, only three of the 207 investigations subsequently opened relate to perpetrators from pro-Ouattara forces.

Military trials against several key military leaders under Gbagbo were set to start in late November. At this writing, civilian courts had yet to begin trials for post-election crimes, meaning that most pro-Gbagbo defendants have languished in pre-trial detention for two and a half years, violating their right to a trial within a reasonable time. Ivorian authorities did provisionally release 14 pro-Gbagbo defendants in early August.

International Criminal Court

On September 30, the International Criminal Court (ICC) unsealed an arrest warrant against, Charles Blé Goudé, the youth minister under Gbagbo, for four counts of crimes against humanity, following the unsealing in 2012 of arrest warrants against Laurent and Simone Gbagbo. Many Ivorians grew disenchanted with the lack of progress in the investigation of crimes by pro-Ouattara forces, although the Office of the Prosecutor stressed that its investigations would ultimately target both sides.

On February 15, Côte d'Ivoire ratified the Rome Statute, taking a positive step in the fight against impunity. In October, 18 months after the ICC issued an arrest warrant against Simone Gbagbo, the Ivorian government filed an admissibility challenge contesting her transfer on the grounds that national proceedings are ongoing for substantially the same crimes. The government has yet to respond to the warrant against Blé Goudé, raising further concerns about its intent to cooperate fully with the ICC.

In June, the ICC's Pre-Trial Chamber asked the prosecutor to consider providing additional evidence in the case against Laurent Gbagbo, as it decides whether or not to confirm charges for four counts of crimes against humanity.

Security Force Abuses

The government and military prioritized human rights training for the armed forces, perhaps contributing to fewer abuses. However, members of the security forces continued to carry out arbitrary arrests and detentions; cruel and inhuman treatment of detainees; and frequent acts of extortion and theft at road checkpoints. The government took occasional action to reduce checkpoint extortion, including arresting some soldiers involved, though the problem remained widespread.

Authorities made little progress towards accountability for serious security force abuses committed since Ouattara took office, including the July 2012 attack on the Nahibly internally displaced persons camp, which left at least 12 dead; and the widespread arbitrary detention, cruel and inhuman treatment, and torture by soldiers that occurred in August and September 2012 following several attacks on military installations.

There have been no prosecutions for these crimes, although authorities have started investigations into the Nahibly case. The military prosecutor did investigate and prosecute some soldiers in other, less politically sensitive cases, including for murder and theft. While these prosecutions were significant, they also suggest that the failure to prosecute in more sensitive cases stems from lack of political will.

Land Rights

During the post-election crisis, violence displaced hundreds of thousands of people, either as refugees or internally within Côte d'Ivoire. Many people have returned to find their land illegally taken over through illegal sales or, in some

HUMAN
RIGHTS
WATCH

"That Land Is My Family's Wealth"
Addressing Land Dispossession after Côte d'Ivoire's Post-Election Conflict

cases, hostile occupations—violating their property rights and rights as returning refugees.

In August, the government passed reforms to land tenure and nationality laws, rightly recognizing their link to recent politico-military violence. However, it failed to adequately support local administrative and judicial mechanisms involved in resolving land conflicts, leaving many people unable to access their land more than two years after the crisis. Several attacks in March 2013 on Ivorian villages near the Liberian border were related to land dispossession, showing the potential for future violence if the government does not ensure the fair resolution of land disputes.

Disarmament and Security Sector Reform

The Ivorian government made slow progress in security sector reform and in disarming tens of thousands of former combatants who fought during the crisis. According to the UN, the government had by June 2013 disarmed and demobilized around 6,000 former combatants. Some armed former combatants engaged in violent criminality, while others staged demonstrations in several towns protesting the slow progress of reintegration programs.

There was improvement in 2013 in returning basic security functions from the military to the police and gendarmerie, but the military maintained a presence at road checkpoints and in leading the response to internal security threats. Although less visibly present than in 2011 and 2012, many youth who fought with pro-Ouattara forces during the crisis continued to perform security duties under military commanders. Several military commanders implicated in serious human rights abuses remain in key positions.

Sexual Violence

Sexual violence remained a major problem. The UN reported at least 100 cases of sexual violence in the first half of 2013, including many against children. Although not required by law, Ivorian authorities often refuse to undertake investigations unless the victim presents a medical certificate, for which she must pay. Accountability for sexual violence is further undermined by the dysfunctional state of the *cour d'assises*, the Ivorian courts mandated to try such cases. Authorities often have to downgrade rape to indecent assault, which can be prosecuted in other courts but carries significantly less penalties.

With assistance from the UN, the Ivorian government is finalizing a national strategy to combat sexual violence. The government and military have also prioritized reducing sexual violence by the security forces. While these represent important steps forward, deficiencies among law enforcement and the judicial system continued to hinder investigations and prosecutions of most sexual violence cases. In addition, victims' access to health and psychosocial services remains limited, particularly outside Abidjan.

Corruption

The UN Group of Experts, appointed by the Security Council to monitor the sanctions regime in Côte d'Ivoire, reported in April that former rebel warlords—now commanders in the Ivorian military—are plundering millions of dollars from the Ivorian economy through smuggling and a parallel tax system on cocoa, timber, and other export goods. Such corrupt practices could potentially undermine efforts to improve access to health and education, among other rights.

In November, 14 former cocoa sector officials, originally charged in 2008, were convicted for embezzling hundreds of millions of dollars between 2002 and 2008. Authorities have yet to credibly investigate the role of high-level political officials also believed to have been implicated and to have used the embezzled funds, in part, to purchase arms.

Key International Actors

Many of Côte d'Ivoire's international partners, including France, remained largely silent on the lack of accountability for past crimes, failing to learn from Côte d'Ivoire's own history the dangerous costs of impunity.

The European Union, France, and the United States supported justice and security sector reform, along with the UN mission in Côte d'Ivoire (UNOCI), which also monitored human rights abuses and helped implement human rights training for the security forces.

The UN Human Rights Council's (HRC) independent expert on human rights in Côte d'Ivoire published reports in January and June, highlighting, among other things, concerns about the one-sided nature of justice for post-election crimes and its impact on reconciliation.

Democratic Republic of Congo

Armed conflict continued in eastern Democratic Republic of Congo, with Congolese security forces and non-state armed groups responsible for serious abuses against civilians. The Rwandan-backed M23 armed group committed widespread war crimes, including summary executions, rapes, and forced recruitment of children. As the military focused attention on defeating the M23, many other armed groups also attacked civilians.

In the capital, Kinshasa, and elsewhere, government authorities have sought to silence dissent with threats, violence, and arbitrary arrests against human rights activists, journalists, and opposition political party leaders and supporters who were critical of government officials or participated in anti-government demonstrations.

In March, M23 leader and former Congolese military commander Bosco Ntaganda surrendered to the United States embassy in Rwanda. He is awaiting trial at the International Criminal Court (ICC) on charges of war crimes and crimes against humanity committed in northeastern Congo in 2002 and 2003. One of the region's most brutal warlords, Ntaganda commanded forces that terrorized civilians for the past decade.

Abuses by the Security Forces

When government soldiers fled the M23's advance on the eastern city of Goma in late November 2012, they went on a rampage and raped at least 76 women and girls in and around the town of Minova, South Kivu. In Kitchanga, North Kivu, soldiers from the 812th Regiment, allied with a Tutsi militia they had armed, clashed with a primarily ethnic Hunde armed group in late February through early March. At least 25 civilians died in the fighting. Many of the civilians killed were Hunde who appear to have been targeted by soldiers because of their ethnicity. Security forces also deliberately killed civilians during operations against Mai Mai fighters in Katanga province.

Military and intelligence officials detained many former M23 fighters and alleged collaborators for several weeks without bringing them before a court, often incommunicado and in harsh conditions.

War Crimes by M23 Rebels

During their occupation of Goma and nearby areas in late November 2012, M23 fighters summarily executed at least 24 people, raped at least 36 women and girls, looted hundreds of homes, offices, and vehicles, and forcibly recruited soldiers and medical officers, police, and civilians into their ranks. The M23 withdrew from Goma on December 1 when the government agreed to start peace talks in Kampala, Uganda.

Following infighting between two M23 factions and Ntaganda's surrender in March, abuses by the M23 continued. Between March and July, M23 fighters summarily executed at least 44 people and raped at least 61 women and girls. In August, after intense fighting resumed between the M23 and the Congolese army supported by MONUSCO, the UN peacekeeping mission in Congo, the M23 shelled populated neighborhoods in and around Goma, killing at least 7 civilians and wounding more than 40.

Since its inception, the M23 had received significant military support from Rwanda, including the deployment of Rwandan troops to Congo to fight alongside it; weapons, ammunition, and other supplies; training for new M23 recruits; and the forcible recruitment of men and boys in Rwanda, who were then sent across the border to fight for the M23.

Following public denunciations and aid suspensions to Rwanda by Western allies, when fighting resumed in late October, the M23 did not receive the military support from Rwanda on which it had previously relied. The rebels were quickly defeated by the Congolese army and UN forces. On November 5, the M23 announced an end to its armed rebellion. Many of its remaining leaders and fighters fled to Uganda and Rwanda.

Attacks on Civilians by Other Armed Groups

Numerous other armed groups have carried out horrific attacks on civilians in eastern Congo, including in North and South Kivu, Katanga, and Orientale provinces. Fighters from the Nduma Defense of Congo militia group, led by Ntabo Ntaberi Sheka, killed, raped, and mutilated scores of civilians between May and September in Masisi and Walikale territories, North Kivu. Sheka is sought on a Congolese arrest warrant for crimes against humanity.

Other armed groups have also carried out ethnically based attacks on civilians in North and South Kivu. They include the Raia Mutomboki, the Nyatura, the Mai Mai Kifuafua, and the Democratic Forces for the Liberation of Rwanda (FDLR), a largely Rwandan Hutu armed group, some of whose members participated in the Rwandan genocide in 1994. Some groups have targeted human rights activists who spoke out against their abuses. In September, FDLR fighters abducted a human rights activist in Miriki, North Kivu, detained him in an underground cell for eight days, and accused him of providing information about FDLR abuses to UN peacekeepers.

In Beni territory, North Kivu, the Allied Democratic Forces (ADF), a rebel group led by Ugandan fighters, as well as other militia groups active in the area, kidnapped several hundred Congolese civilians. In Orientale province, fighting between the Patriotic Resistance Force in Ituri (FRPI) and other militia groups and the Congolese army forced more than 80,000 people to abandon their homes.

In Katanga, Mai Mai fighters forcibly recruited hundreds of children into their ranks and killed, raped, and mutilated civilians. Some of these Mai Mai fighters are led by Gédéon Kyungu Mutanga, a warlord who was convicted by a military court in 2009 for crimes against humanity but escaped from prison in September 2011. On August 7, militia fighters in Pweto, Katanga, summarily executed a human rights activist who had denounced abuses by the group.

The Lord's Resistance Army (LRA), a Ugandan rebel group with a long record of atrocities, continued to attack civilians in northern Congo and eastern Central African Republic. At time of writing, the LRA's three senior leaders sought on arrest warrants from the International Criminal Court (ICC)—Joseph Kony, Odhok Odhiambo, and Dominic Ongwen—remained at large.

Few efforts have been made to curb abuses by these armed groups or to investigate, arrest, and prosecute those responsible. Elements of the Congolese army have in some cases collaborated with and provided support to armed groups responsible for serious abuses, including the FDLR and Nyatura.

Freedom of Expression and Peaceful Assembly

Government and security forces have used violence, intimidation, threats, arbitrary arrests, and judicial proceedings based on trumped-up charges to silence dissent and prevent political leaders and activists from freely expressing their peaceful opinions or demonstrating.

Eugène Diomi Ndongala, a former member of parliament and minister, has been detained since April. Diomi is the president of the Christian Democrats (*Démocratie chrétienne*) opposition party and a founding member of the Popular Presidential Majority (*Majorité présidentielle populaire*)—a political alliance supporting opposition leader Etienne Tshisekedi.

Another member of parliament, Muhindo Nzangi, was sentenced to three years in prison in August. Only two days after he made remarks on a radio program in Goma that were viewed as critical of President Joseph Kabila's policy in eastern Congo, Nzangi was tried and convicted for endangering internal state security. On August 20, police forcibly disrupted a peaceful sit-in by Nzangi's supporters outside the North Kivu governor's office in Goma. They beat several protesters, arrested five, and threatened to charge them with rebellion.

Security forces also threatened, beat, or detained journalists and human rights activists. On March 10, police and Republican Guard soldiers beat or threatened four journalists for covering Tshisekedi's return to Kinshasa from South Africa. In July, a human rights activist was accused of being a spy; soldiers beat him after he conducted a research mission to document M23 abuses.

Justice and Accountability

The vast majority of human rights abuses committed in Congo have gone unpunished. However, there have been some positive developments. On March 18, Bosco Ntaganda turned himself in to the US embassy in Kigali, Rwanda, and was flown to The Hague, where he faces charges of war crimes and crimes against humanity at the ICC. The Congolese government issued arrest warrants for several M23 leaders, and government officials have stated clearly that they will neither provide an amnesty nor integrate into the army those allegedly responsible for war crimes.

In November, the trial began in North Kivu's military operational court in Goma for 39 soldiers and officers allegedly involved in the mass rape and pillaging in and around Minova a year earlier.

In December 2012, the ICC acquitted and released Mathieu Ngudjolo Chui, who had been charged with crimes against humanity and war crimes allegedly committed in northeastern Congo in 2003. The trial of Ngudjolo's co-accused, Germain Katanga, continues. Sylvestre Mudacumura, the FDLR's military commander sought on an arrest warrant from the ICC for war crimes, remained at large at the time of writing.

Key International Actors

In February, 11 African countries signed the Peace, Security and Cooperation Framework for the Democratic Republic of Congo and the Region in Addis Ababa, under the auspices of the UN secretary-general. The signatories agreed not to tolerate or provide support of any kind to armed groups; neither to harbor nor provide protection of any kind to anyone accused of war crimes or crimes against humanity, or anyone who is listed under the UN sanctions regime; and to cooperate with regional justice initiatives. The former president of Ireland, Mary Robinson, was appointed UN special envoy for the Great Lakes region to support implementation of the agreement.

In March, the UN Security Council authorized the deployment of an Intervention Brigade. This 3,000-member force within MONUSCO, made up of African troops, is mandated to carry out offensive operations to neutralize armed groups operating in eastern Congo.

Equatorial Guinea

Corruption, poverty, and repression continue to plague Equatorial Guinea under President Teodoro Obiang Nguema Mbasogo, who has been in power since 1979. Vast oil revenues fund lavish lifestyles for the small elite surrounding the president, while a large proportion of the population continues to live in poverty. Mismanagement of public funds and credible allegations of high-level corruption persist, as do other serious abuses, including arbitrary detention, secret detention, and unfair trials.

The period surrounding legislative elections in May 2013 was marked by the denial of fundamental freedoms. The government blocked planned protests by political opponents and arrested the organizers. The ruling party gained an overwhelming victory in the election, but the poll lacked credibility because of biased electoral processes and restrictive conditions for international observers.

The new government that formed in September maintained a system that lacks effective checks on the powers of President Obiang. Obiang appointed his eldest son and possible successor, "Teodorin," to one of 15 senate seats he personally selects, under 2011 constitutional changes. Obiang retained Teodorin as second vice president, an appointed post not contemplated in the constitution.

Obiang and his government strongly defended Teodorin against allegations of corruption and money laundering, which are the focus of foreign law enforcement investigations in France and the United States. Although several legal decisions went in Teodorin's favor in August, notably a California judge's dismissal of part of a case against him, followed by Interpol's unexpected withdrawal of an international arrest warrant against him in a separate case filed in France, intensive investigations in both countries continue and a Europe-wide warrant issued at France's request remains in effect.

Economic and Social Rights

Equatorial Guinea is the third largest oil producer in sub-Saharan Africa and has a population of approximately 700,000 people. According to the United Nation's 2013 Human Development Report, the country has a per-capita gross domestic

product of US$32,026, which is the highest wealth ranking of any African coun-
try and one of the highest in the world, yet it ranks 136 out of 187 countries in
the Human Development Index. As a result, Equatorial Guinea has by far the
largest gap of all countries between its per-capita wealth and its human development score.

Despite the country's abundant natural resource wealth and government's obligations to advance the economic and social rights of its citizens, it has directed
little of this wealth to meet their needs. Figures released by the International
Monetary Fund in early 2013 showcase the government's spending priorities:
while half of Equatorial Guinea's capital spending in 2011 was used to build
infrastructure and another 22 percent was spent on public administration,
health and education together accounted for only 3 percent of capital spending.

About half of the population lacks clean water or basic sanitation facilities,
according to official 2012 statistics. A large portion of the population also lacks
access to quality health care, decent schools, or reliable electricity. The government does not publish basic information on budgets and spending, and citizens
and journalists lack the freedom to monitor the use of the country's natural
resource wealth.

Freedom of Expression and Association

Equatorial Guinea is notorious for its poor record on press freedom. Local journalists are unable to criticize the government or address issues the authorities
disapprove of without risk of censorship or reprisal. Only a few private media
outlets exist in the country, and they are generally owned by persons close to
President Obiang; self-censorship is common. Foreign news is available to the
small minority with access to satellite broadcasts and the Internet; others have
access only to limited foreign radio programming.

Freedom of association and assembly are severely curtailed in Equatorial
Guinea, greatly limiting the effectiveness of civil society groups. The government
imposes restrictive conditions on the registration and operation of nongovernmental groups. The country has no legally registered independent human rights
groups. The few local activists who seek to address human rights related issues
face intimidation, harassment, and reprisals.

Political Parties and Opposition

Only two political parties offered candidates independently in the May legislative elections. The other 10 officially recognized political parties aligned with the ruling party, which benefited from a virtual monopoly on power, funding, and access to national media. The May vote, like prior elections in the country, were marked by serious human rights violations and a denial of fundamental freedoms, including arbitrary arrests and restrictions on freedom of assembly. The National Election Commission is controlled by the ruling party and is headed by the interior minister, a prominent member of the governing party.

Requests by political activists and opposition political parties to hold peaceful demonstrations were denied. Protests planned for May and June were blocked and the organizers of the May event were arrested. At least 10 activists were arrested in May, following calls for a peaceful demonstration on May 15 to call for government reforms and to protest a government decision denying registration to a new political party, Partido Democrático de la Justicia Social (Democratic Party for Social Justice). Clara "Lola" Nsegue Eyí and Natalia Angue Edjodjomo, the party's co-founders and coordinators of the demonstration, were arrested on May 13 in Malabo and transferred to the city of Mongomo. They were both released after three weeks, but Nsegue was subsequently rearrested in Malabo and flown to Mongomo, an inland city, more than 200 miles away, where she remained in custody without charge from late June until her release in October.

Jerónimo Ndong, secretary general of the opposition party Unión Popular (People's Union), was arrested on May 13 and held for several days, also in connection with the planned protest. He went into hiding after his release, but turned himself in when the authorities arrested his wife and brother to force him to emerge from hiding. Ndong was then rearrested and held for another seven days.

A number of people were arrested on their way to the planned May 15 protest and later released, including Salvador Bibang Ela, a leader of the Convergencia Social Democrática Popular (CPDS, People's Social Democratic Convergence) opposition party. The protest was not held, due to these arrests and the heavy presence of security forces in the streets.

In June, security forces surrounded the CPDS headquarters in Malabo and several party leaders were briefly arrested in a successful effort to block a planned demonstration against alleged election fraud. The party's earlier request for a permit for the protest was denied.

On September 22, Weja Chicampo, coordinador of the Movimiento para la Autodeterminación de la Isla de Bioko (MAIB, Movement for the Self-Determination of Bioko Island), was deported to Spain from the Malabo airport as he returned from a visit to there. Chicampo had previously lived in exile in Spain, following repeated arrests and prison terms in Equatorial Guinea, but had moved back to Equatorial Guinea. He remained in Spain at time of writing.

Torture, Arbitrary Detention, and Unfair Trials

Due process rights are routinely flouted in Equatorial Guinea and prisoner mistreatment remains common. Many detainees are held indefinitely without knowing the charges against them. Some are held in secret detention. Lawyers and others who have visited prisons and jails indicate that serious abuses continue, including beatings in detention that amount to torture.

President Obiang exercises inordinate control over the judiciary, which lacks independence. The president is designated as the country's "chief magistrate." Among other powers, he chairs the body that oversees judges and appoints the body's remaining members.

Judicial processes are used to intimidate or punish those perceived as disloyal to those in power. In July, Roberto Berardi, a business associate of Teodorín, was convicted of theft of company property and given a two-and-a-half year sentence, following a brief trial at which Berardi's family said no evidence was presented. Beradi had been in government custody in Bata since January. According to his family, Berardi's arrest came after he asked Teodorin about a suspicious bank transfer to a US account. They also allege that he was held in secret detention for several weeks and subjected to torture.

Eleuterio Esono, an Equatoguinean citizen who returned to the country from exile in Sweden in early 2013, was held without charge in a Malabo jail from March 12 until the end of April. He was arrested without warrant in connection with an alleged conspiracy against the state.

Agustín Esono Nsogo, a teacher arrested in October 2012 for an alleged plot to destabilize the country, remained in custody without charge or trial.

Key International Actors

The US is Equatorial Guinea's main trading partner and source of investment in the oil sector. The US government openly criticized the May legislative elections in Equatorial Guinea, citing "serious concerns" about arbitrary detentions, limits on free speech and assembly, and the opposition's severely restricted ability to access the media and the Internet-based social networks.

Spain, the former colonial power, also applied some pressure on Equatorial Guinea to improve its human rights record by publicly criticizing the May vote.

In a speech during the G20 summit and subsequently, United Kingdom Prime Minister David Cameron prominently used Equatorial Guinea as an example of the so-called resource curse: a corrupt, poorly governed country with great wealth that does not benefit the majority of its people.

President Obiang continued to seek international attention as a statesman, hosting a summit with African and Latin American leaders in March and accepting from North Korea in July the International Kim Jong-il Prize "for his commitment to justice, development, peace and harmony."

Eritrea

Eritrea is among the most closed countries in the world; human rights conditions remain dismal. Indefinite military service, torture, arbitrary detention, and severe restrictions on freedoms of expression, association, and religion provoke thousands of Eritreans to flee the country each month. Among those fleeing in 2013 were the minister of information—whose 85-year-old father, brother, and 15-year-old daughter were immediately arrested—and the deputy head of economic affairs of the People's Front for Democracy and Justice (PFDJ), Eritrea's sole political party that controls most major domestic commercial enterprises.

In October, more than 300 Eritrean refugees drowned when a boat bringing them to Europe capsized near Lampedusa, Italy. According to the United Nations High Commissioner for Refugees (UNHCR), over 305,000 Eritreans (more than 5 percent of the population) have fled during the past decade.

Eritrea has no constitution, functioning legislature, independent judiciary, elections, independent press, or nongovernmental organizations; it does not hold elections. All power is concentrated in the hands of President Isaias Afewerki, in office since 1991.

In a rare sign of domestic dissent, on January 21, 2013, a group of soldiers with tanks, led by a brigadier general and three colonels, briefly occupied the Ministry of Information ("Forto") and forced the director of government television to read a statement demanding the release of political prisoners and implementation of the 1997 constitution. The transmission was cut after a few sentences and the protestors surrendered when other military units failed to deliver expected support. According to credible reports, 60 or more high-level alleged collaborators were arrested, several of whom are now dead, some by suicide. Among them is said to be Abdella Jaber, PFDJ's chief administrator.

Despite repeated requests, Eritrea denied the United Nation special rapporteur on Eritrea, Sheila Keetharuth, a visa. In a 2013 report based on refugee interviews, she concluded that "basic tenets of the rule of law are not respected." Following her report, the Council "strongly condemn[ed]" Eritrea's "continued widespread and systematic violations of human rights and fundamental freedoms."

Indefinite Conscription and Forced Labor

Eritrea conscripts all men and unmarried women into "national service." Although Eritrean law limits national service to 18 months, most conscripts serve for much of their working lives. Conscripts are routinely used as forced labor on essentially civilian jobs. In 2013, Human Rights Watch reported that conscripts were used by a state-owned construction company, Segen Construction Co., engaged by Canadian mining firm Nevsun Resources, to build infrastructure at its Bisha gold mine. Former conscripts described working long hours for minimal food rations, primitive lodging, and wages too low to sustain themselves, much less their families. They were not allowed to leave the work site.

Children as young as 15 are inducted and sent for military training, according to recent interviews by refugee agencies. They and other recruits are regularly subject to violence and ill-treatment for raising questions or for other perceived infractions. Beatings, torture, and prolonged incarcerations are common. Women are subject to sexual violence from military commanders, including rape. No mechanisms for redress exist.

Since mid-2012, all men in their 50s, 60s, and 70s are compelled to perform militia duty: carrying military weapons; reporting for training; and going on periodic patrols.

Arbitrary Arrest, Prolonged Detention, and Inhumane Conditions

Thousands of ordinary citizens are arrested and incarcerated without charge, trial, or opportunity to appeal, and without access to family, lawyers, or independent prison monitoring organizations. While some are freed without explanation and warned not to speak about their detention, most prisoners remain in jail indefinitely. Until the "Forto" incident in January 2013, the most prominent prisoners were 21 government officials and journalists arrested in September 2001 and still held incommunicado 12 years later. None have been formally charged, much less tried; former guards who have left Eritrea report that half of them have died.

Former detainees describe brutal detention conditions. Death in captivity is not unusual. Many prisoners disappear, their whereabouts and health unknown to their families. Former prisoners describe being confined in vastly overcrowded underground cells or shipping containers, with no space to lie down, little or no light, oppressive heat or cold, and vermin. Medical treatment is poor or non-existent. Food consists of a piece or two of bread a day, occasional servings of lentils or beans, a cup of tea, and insufficient water. Beatings and torture in detention are common; wardens are able to impose any physical punishment they devise. A former interrogator told Human Rights Watch he ordered beatings of prisoners until they confessed to whatever they were accused of; they were then beaten to implicate others.

Eritreans who were forcibly repatriated to Eritrea from Middle Eastern countries and then fled again told Human Rights Watch in 2012 they had been incarcerated in crammed cells and beaten shortly after their return. They displayed scars from beatings and electric shocks. One escapee reported that several prisoners in his group of returnees died from their beatings.

Freedom of Religion

Since 2002, the government has jailed and physically abused citizens for practicing religions other than the four government-controlled or recognized religions—Sunni Islam, Ethiopian Orthodox, Catholicism, and Lutheranism. Most arrests occur in private houses but many also occur during private Quran or Bible study at colleges or at national service training centers.

Some prisoners are offered release on condition that they sign statements renouncing their faith. Three deaths during captivity were reported by foreign-based religious monitoring groups in 2013, but given the difficulties of obtaining information, the number may be higher.

The octogenarian Orthodox patriarch, whom the government deposed in 2007, remains under strict house arrest.

Reprisals against Family Members

Family members of some draft evaders or national service deserters have been punished by fines of Nakfa 50,000 (US$3,333) and by detention, in a country with, according to the World Bank, per capita income in 2012 of $560.

Families are also punished when relatives living abroad fail to pay a 2 percent tax on foreign income, retroactive to 1992, or to contribute "national defense" fees. Punishments include revocation of resident families' business licenses, confiscation of houses and other property, and refusal to issue passports to allow reunification of children and spouses with overseas parents or spouses.

Freedom of Expression and Association

The government maintains a complete monopoly on domestic sources of information since it closed all local press outlets in 2001 and arrested their staff. Telephone and Internet communications are monitored. Eritrea expelled the last accredited foreign correspondent in 2008. Although foreign language transmissions are accessible, the government jammed Al Jazeera in early 2013 and has long jammed overseas transmissions from Eritrea diaspora stations. At least six government journalists arrested in 2009 and 2011 remain in solitary confinement without trial.

No independent civil society organizations are permitted. Labor unions remain a government monopoly.

Key International Actors

Eritrea's government has few allies. Relations with Ethiopia remain hostile following the 1998-2000 border war and Ethiopia's failure to implement an international boundary commission's ruling awarding disputed territory to Eritrea.

Eritrea has been under United Nations sanctions since 2009 because of its support for armed Islamic insurgents in Somalia and its refusal to release Djibouti prisoners of war captured during a 2008 invasion of Djibouti's border territory.

A UN monitoring group reported in July 2013 that although Eritrea had made a tactical decision to court the Somali government, it fostered regional destabilization by "maintain[ing]close links to a network of warlords and other spoilers

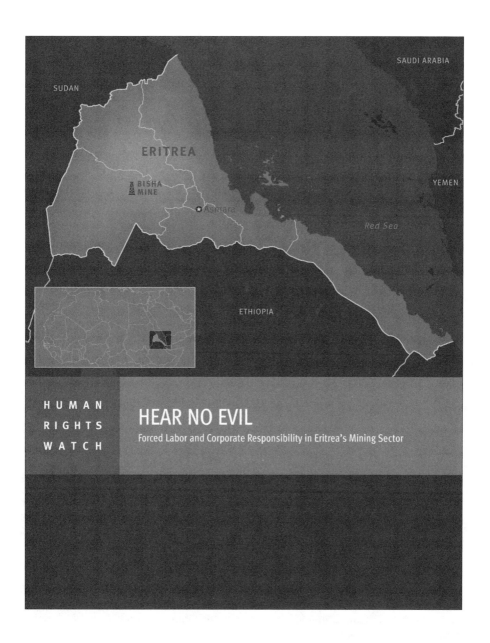

HUMAN
RIGHTS
WATCH

HEAR NO EVIL
Forced Labor and Corporate Responsibility in Eritrea's Mining Sector

in Somalia," including at least two Al-Shabaab leaders. Eritrea refuses to acknowledge that it holds Djibouti prisoners of war although three escaped in late 2011. Following the report, the UN Security Council retained sanctions and renewed the monitoring group's mandate for a year.

Eritrea's relationship with Qatar, which had been mediating Eritrea-Djibouti border issues, frayed in 2013 and Qatar apparently stopped funding a large Red Sea resort. The Yemeni Foreign Ministry complained that Eritrea seized Yemeni fishing vessels in international waters and detained their crews. In October, Eritrea released 81 Yemeni fishermen held for 18 months without trial; Yemen claims another 519 remain jailed.

In June 2013, Canada expelled Eritrea's Toronto consul for continuing to solicit "national defense" fees (and the 2 percent tax) from Eritrean expatriates despite Canadian demands that he stop because the practice violated UN sanctions.

Eritrea has warmer relations with China. The Chinese government provided a 630 million Yuan ($10.3 million) loan in 2013 to construct canning, food cold-storage, and PCV pipe manufacturing plants. The projects will be run by SFECO, a Shanghai Construction Co subsidiary. SFECO bought a 60 percent share of the Zara gold exploration site near Asmara in 2013 and has contracts to repair and enlarge Asmara's power plant. Lengthy power shortages occurred in 2013.

In earlier years, Eritrea expelled all nongovernmental aid agencies. In 2013, the UN and Eritrea agreed on a four-year $188 million "cooperation framework." The UN will provide $50 million and attempt to raise the remaining $138 million from donor countries for capacity building, food security, environmental improvements, and social services. Providing assistance presents "acute coordination challenges," according to the UN Office for the Coordination of Humanitarian Affairs, because of "access restrictions on international staff" and the "absence of up-to-date information" from the government.

The Bisha mine, a major hard currency generator, was expected to earn less in 2013 as production shifted from gold to copper and copper prices fell. Eritrea issues no budget; government finances are opaque and secret. President Afewerki nevertheless complained in 2013 that "international organization" statistics (ostensibly referring to the World Bank and International Monetary Fund) "are based on speculation and aimed at serving vested political interests" and "should be dismissed."

Ethiopia

Hopes that Ethiopia's new leadership would pursue human rights reforms following Prime Minister Meles Zenawi's death in August 2012 have been shattered; there was no tangible change of policy in 2013. Instead, the Ethiopian authorities continue to severely restrict the rights to freedom of expression, association, and peaceful assembly, using repressive laws to constrain civil society and independent media, and target individuals with politically motivated prosecutions.

Muslim protests against perceived government interference in their religious affairs were met by security forces with arbitrary arrests and detentions, beatings, and other mistreatment throughout the year. The trial of 29 protest leaders who were arrested in July 2012 has been closed to the public, media, and family members since January. Others convicted under the country's deeply flawed antiterrorism law—including opposition leaders and four journalists—remain in prison.

Ethiopia's ambitious development schemes, funded from domestic revenue sources and foreign assistance, sometimes displace indigenous communities without appropriate consultation or any compensation. Security forces have also used violence, threats, and intimidation to force some groups to relocate, such as in the Lower Omo Valley where indigenous people continue to be displaced from their traditional lands, which are earmarked for state-run irrigated sugar plantations.

Freedom of Peaceful Assembly

Since early 2012, members of Ethiopia's Muslim community—which constitutes at least 30 percent of the country's population—have organized regular public protests. Demonstrations were triggered by perceived government interference in the Supreme Council of Islamic Affairs and the Awalia mosque in Addis Ababa.

The government has clamped down heavily on the protests, arbitrarily detaining and beating protesters, including 29 prominent activists and leaders who were arrested in July 2012 and charged in October 2012 under the Anti-Terrorism

Proclamation. In January, the High Court closed those hearings to the public, including media, diplomats, and family members. Some defendants have alleged mistreatment in detention and the trials raise a number of due process concerns, including lack of access to legal counsel for some defendants for almost two months, and erratic access to relatives.

The government has also undermined the defendants' presumption of innocence by broadcasting inflammatory material and accusations against them on state television. In February, the state-run Ethiopian Television (ETV) broadcast a program called "Jihadawi Harakat" ("Jihad War") that included footage of at least five of the defendants filmed in pretrial detention. The program equated the Muslim protest movement with Islamist extremist groups, casting the protest leaders as terrorists.

Despite the arrests, protests continued throughout 2013. In early August, protests were organized in the capital, Addis Ababa, as well as in other cities to commemorate Eid al Fitr, the end of Ramadan. Witnesses described a heavy police presence in Addis Ababa, and credible sources said that police used excessive force to disperse the demonstrators and detained hundreds, at least temporarily.

The Semayawi Party ("Blue Party"), a newcomer to Ethiopia's political scene, held a peaceful protest in June—the first large-scale protest organized by a political opposition party in eight years. A planned protest in August was cancelled when the Blue Party offices were raided by security forces, resulting in the arrest of dozens of people and the confiscation of equipment. The Blue Party had earlier been denied a permit by government to hold the protest.

Arbitrary Detention and Ill-Treatment

Arbitrary detention and ill-treatment in detention continues to be a major problem. Students, members of opposition groups, journalists, peaceful protesters, and others seeking to express their rights to freedom of assembly, expression, or association are frequently detained arbitrarily.

Ill-treatment is often reported by people detained for political reasons, particularly in Addis Ababa's Federal Police Crime Investigation Center, known as Maekelawi, where most individuals are held during pre-charge or pretrial detention. Abuse and coercion that in some cases amount to torture and other ill-treatment are used to extract information, confessions, and statements from detainees.

Individuals are often denied access to legal counsel, particularly during pre-charge detention. Mistreated detainees have little recourse in the courts and there is no regular access to prisons and detention centers by independent investigators. Although the government-affiliated Ethiopian Human Rights Commission has visited some detainees and detention centers, there is no regular monitoring by any independent human rights or other organizations.

In July, a delegation from the European Parliament was denied access to Kaliti prison in Addis Ababa by Ethiopian authorities, despite having received prior authorization.

Freedom of Expression and Association

Since 2009, when the Anti-Terrorism Proclamation and the Charities and Societies Proclamation (CSO Law) were passed, freedoms of expression and association have been severely restricted in Ethiopia. The CSO law is one of the most draconian laws regulating nongovernmental activity in the world. It bars work on human rights, good governance, conflict resolution, and advocacy on the rights of women, children, and people with disabilities if organizations receive more than 10 percent of their funds from foreign sources.

Ethiopia's most reputable human rights groups have either dramatically scaled down their operations or removed human rights from their mandates. Several of the country's most prominent human rights activists have fled the country due to threats.

Ethiopian media remains under a tight government stranglehold, and many journalists practice self-censorship. Webpages and blogs critical of the government are regularly blocked, and foreign radio and TV stations are routinely jammed. Journalists working for independent domestic newspapers continue to face regular harassment and threats.

The Anti-Terrorism Proclamation has been used to target political opponents, stifle dissent, and silence journalists. In May, the Supreme Court upheld the 18-year sentence of journalist and blogger Eskinder Nega Fenta, who was convicted in July 2012 for conspiracy to commit terrorist acts and participation in a terrorist organization. Eskinder received the PEN Freedom to Write award in 2012. Reeyot Alemu Gobebo, a journalist for *Feteh,* was convicted on three counts under the terrorism law for her writings. Her sentence was reduced from 14 to 5 years on appeal, but her appeal of the remaining five-year sentence was dismissed in January. Reeyot was awarded the prestigious 2013 UNESCO/Guillermo Cano World Press Freedom Prize.

Journalists covering the Muslim protests were threatened and arbitrarily detained. Solomon Kebede, chief editor of the now-defunct *Yemuslimoch Guday* ("Muslim Affairs"), was arrested in January and charged under the Anti-Terrorism Proclamation. Yusuf Getachew, his predecessor, was charged under the same law in 2012. Several other journalists fled Ethiopia in 2013, making it one of the top three countries in the world in terms of the number of journalists in exile.

Forced Displacement Associated with Development Programs

Both the government of Ethiopia and the donor community have failed to adequately investigate allegations of abuses associated with Ethiopia's "villagization program." Under this program, 1.5 million rural people are being relocated, ostensibly to improve their access to basic services. However, some of the relocations in the first year of the program in Gambella region were accompanied by violence, including beatings and arbitrary arrests, and insufficient consultation and compensation.

On July 12, the World Bank's board of executive directors approved the recommendation of the Inspection Panel, the institution's independent accountability mechanism, to investigate a complaint from ethnic Anuak refugees alleging that the bank violated its own safeguards in Gambella. The investigation was ongoing at time of writing.

Ethiopia is proceeding with development of a sugar plantation in the Lower Omo Valley, clearing 245,000 hectares of land that is home to 200,000 indigenous peoples. Displaced from their ancestral lands, these agro-pastoralists are being moved to permanent villages under the villagization program.

Key International Actors

Ethiopia enjoys warm relations with foreign donors and most of its regional neighbors. Ethiopia has forged strong ties based on its role as the seat of the African Union (AU), its contribution to United Nations peacekeeping, security partnerships with Western nations, and its progress on some of the Millennium Development Goals (MDGs). These strong relationships have contributed to the international community's silence on Ethiopia's dismal human rights record.

The year 2013 saw Ethiopia continue to play a mediation role between Sudan and South Sudan, while its troops maintained an uneasy calm in the disputed Abyei region. Ethiopia continues to deploy its troops inside Somalia, but outside the AU mission.

Ethiopia also continues to receive significant amounts of donor assistance— almost US\$4 billion in 2013. As partners in Ethiopia's development, donor nations remain muted in their criticism of Ethiopia's appalling human rights record and are taking little meaningful action to investigate allegations of abuses associated with development programs.

Relations with Egypt worsened in 2013 due to Egyptian concerns that Ethiopia's Grand Renaissance Dam will divert valuable water from the Nile River. An estimated 85 percent of the Nile's waters originate in the Ethiopian highlands and Egypt is completely dependent on the Nile for all its water needs. At 6,000 megawatts of electricity, the dam will be Africa's largest hydroelectric project. Construction started in 2012 and the dam is scheduled to be completed in 2018.

In addition to Western donors, China, India, and Brazil are increasingly financing a variety of large-scale development initiatives. Foreign private investment into Ethiopia is increasing with agro-business, hydroelectric, mining, and oil exploration all gaining prominence in 2013. Agro-business investment is coming mainly from India, the Gulf, and the Ethiopian diaspora, attracted to very low land prices and labor costs. As seen in several of Ethiopia's other large-scale development projects, there is a serious risk of forced displacement of people from their land when some of these programs are implemented.

Guinea

Uncertainty over the organization of long-delayed parliamentary elections, envisioned to consolidate Guinea's full transition from authoritarian to democratic rule, dominated the political and human rights landscape and led to a worrying increase in violence in 2013. Months of violent protests involving militants from the opposition, the ruling party, and the security services left dozens dead and over 400 wounded.

Parliamentary elections, not held since 2002, were to have taken place six months after the largely free and fair 2010 election of Alpha Condé as president. However, they were repeatedly delayed by opposition demands to address technical concerns involving the electoral list and the right of the diaspora to participate, among other issues. The delay exacerbated ethnic tensions, deepened a concentration of power in the executive branch, and generated considerable frustration within Guinean civil society and the country's international partners.

The vote finally took place on September 28 but, according to Guinean and international observers, it was marred by organizational problems and irregularities including ballot stuffing by supporters of the ruling party, voter intimidation, and minors casting votes.

Endemic corruption, the chronically neglected judiciary, and the slow pace of security sector reform undermined respect for the rule of law. Rising ethnic tensions ignited political violence and led to communal clashes in the N'Zérékoré region in July, which left at least 98 dead and 160 wounded.

Excessive use of force by security forces in response to political demonstrations declined, but they were nevertheless implicated in numerous incidents of excessive use of lethal force and unprofessional conduct as they responded to the violent clashes between militants of opposing political parties. Attacks against freedom of the press increased in 2013.

Guinea made some progress in ensuring accountability for past atrocities, including the 2009 massacre of unarmed demonstrators by security forces, and indictment of a few powerful political and military figures for the 2010 torture of members of the political opposition. There was little progress in attempts to establish a reconciliation commission and an independent human rights body.

International actors—notably the United Nations Office of West Africa (UNOWA), European Union, France, the United States, and the *Organisation internationale de la francophonie* (OIF)—took proactive steps to resolve disputes over the organization of parliamentary elections, but rarely spoke out on the need for justice for past and recent crimes by state actors.

Accountability for the September 28, 2009 Massacre and Other Crimes

More than four years on, the domestic investigation into members of the security forces implicated in the September 2009 massacre of some 150 people and the rape of over 100 women during the military regime of Moussa Dadis Camara has yet to conclude. In 2010, the then-government committed to bringing the perpetrators to justice, and a Guinean prosecutor appointed a panel of three judges to investigate the crimes.

The panel has made important strides, having interviewed more than 300 victims and charged at least eight suspects including several high-level members of the security forces. However, progress continues to be stymied by insufficient government backing and support, including the government's failure to place high-level suspects on leave from their government posts pending investigation and to satisfactorily resolve the judges' outstanding request to question the former Guinean president, who is currently living in Burkina Faso. Some suspects have been in pretrial detention longer than the two years Guinean law permits.

Judiciary and Detention Conditions

Decades of neglect of the judiciary has led to striking deficiencies in the sector, allowing perpetrators of abuses to enjoy impunity for crimes. The allocation for the judiciary has for several years stood at around 0.5 percent of the national budget. As a result, there continue to be severe shortages of judicial personnel and insufficient infrastructure and resources, which, when coupled with unprofessional conduct, including corrupt practices, failing to show up in court, and poor record-keeping, contributed to widespread detention-related abuses.

The indictment in 2013 of Conakry's powerful governor and two high-level soldiers for alleged torture committed during the run-up to the 2010 elections, as well as the arrest and indictment of two suspects for the 2012 assassination of Guinea's treasury director, Aissatou Boiro, demonstrated progress in addressing impunity. However, the judiciary failed to make progress in ensuring justice for the 2012 killing of six men by members of the security forces in the village of Zoghota in southeastern Guinea.

Prison and detention centers in Guinea are severely overcrowded, and inmates and detainees lack adequate nutrition, sanitation, and medical care. The largest detention facility—designed for 300 detainees—accommodates some 1,100. An estimated 75 percent of prisoners in Conakry are held in prolonged pretrial detention. The failure of the *Cour d'assises*—which hears matters involving the most serious crimes—to meet regularly contributes to the problem. The government failed to establish the Superior Council of Judges, which is tasked with discipline, selection, and promotion of judges. International and Guinean legal aid groups helped ensure representation for the indigent.

Truth-Telling Mechanism and Independent Human Rights Institution

During 2013, the "Reflection Commission," created by presidential decree in June 2011 to promote reconciliation, made no visible progress in fulfilling its mandate. The interim co-presidents appeared to limit its mandate to promoting reconciliation largely through prayer, while local human rights groups pushed for a commission that could meaningfully address impunity.

Progress in setting up the independent human rights institution, as mandated by Guinea's 2010 constitution, was undermined by delays in holding legislative elections; the constitution stipulates that the institution can only be established through a law voted on by the national assembly.

While the Ministry for Human Rights and Civil Liberties, newly created in 2012, lacked resources, the minister actively advocated for strengthening the judiciary, an end to impunity for abuses, and respect for freedom of the press.

Conduct of the Security Forces

The government and military hierarchy made some progress in ensuring that their subordinates responded proportionately to civil unrest and to ensure the army remained in their barracks during protests. However, members of the police and gendarmerie were implicated in numerous incidents of excessive use of lethal force and unprofessional conduct as they responded to often-violent protests and clashes between militants of opposing political parties, and arbitrarily detained and beat others. Several security force members were killed during the violent demonstrations.

On at least three occasions, members of the security forces attacked or failed to protect members of the opposition or their family members from violence meted out by ruling party militants. On several occasions, members of the security forces engaged in theft, extortion, and other crimes directed at people living in neighborhoods that largely supported the opposition. The police and gendarmes also failed to equally protect people during violent street demonstrations, including by standing by while protestors supporting the ruling party attacked and at times robbed opposition supporters.

After 12 people were killed by the security forces in May, most by gunshot, President Condé tasked the justice minister with opening an inquiry into the violence and prosecuting those responsible.

Freedom of Media

Censorship measures were imposed in late 2012 by state media regulators against three popular current affairs talk shows, stemming from commentary critical of government officials. One debate program on the private Planète FM station was suspended on December 13 for five weeks, and the program's host was banned for a week, based on a defamation complaint. Another station, Espace FM, was formally warned for its coverage of deadly unrest in the southern town of Guéckédou. Several journalists and news outlets covering political unrest in the capital, Conakry, were attacked, detained, or threatened during political unrest in 2013.

In mid-August, soldiers stormed Bate FM in Kankan, shutting it down for airing President Condé being booed at a rally. At least three journalists were briefly detained. The station was later attacked and looted and one journalist was assaulted in the process. The attackers were allegedly supporters of the president.

Key International Actors

Guinea's key international partners, notably the United Nations, European Union, Economic Community of West African States (ECOWAS), France, and the United States, remained largely focused on ensuring progress in the long-delayed parliamentary elections. However, they remained largely silent on the need for those responsible for the September 2009 violence. While they made frequent calls to end the violent exchanges between supporters of the opposition and ruling party, they largely failed to condemn abuses by the security forces or demand that they be held accountable for their crimes.

Despite having a full mission in Guinea, the Office of the United Nations High Commissioner for Human Rights (OHCHR) failed to consistently denounce abuses by the security forces. OHCHR, together with the EU, and the UN Development Programme (UNDP) took the lead in strengthening Guinea's judicial system. However, much of the EU's development support was conditioned on the conduct of transparent legislative elections. In a resolution adopted in June, the Human Rights Council called on Guinea to further support the work of the Panel of Judges, protect survivors, and compensate families of victims of the 28 September massacre.

The UN Peace Building Commission (PBC) continued to fund programs supporting security sector reform and reconciliation. In May, the International Monetary Fund unlocked US$27 million in credits for Guinea, and in June Guinea benefitted from €74 million of debt relief from France.

The International Criminal Court (ICC), which in October 2009 confirmed that the situation in Guinea was under preliminary examination, visited the country in January and June to assess progress made in national investigations.

Kenya

Kenya's closely contested presidential election in March resulted in the election of President Uhuru Kenyatta and Deputy President William Ruto, after the Supreme Court rejected an opposition challenge. Both Kenyatta and Ruto face crimes against humanity charges at the International Criminal Court (ICC) for their alleged roles in post-election violence in 2007-2008.

Fears that the 2013 election would spark a repeat of the widespread violence of 2007-2008 did not materialize, but the run-up to the elections was marred by pockets of ethnic and political violence, and police used excessive force to disperse protests in Kisumu.

The slow pace of police reform, the lack of accountability for security force abuses—including extrajudicial killings, torture, and other human rights violations by the police— and the government's failure to hold accountable perpetrators of the 2007–2008 post-election violence remain key concerns.

The September 21 attack on Nairobi's Westgate mall killed at least 67 people and highlighted the security threat posed by the militant Islamist Somali group Al-Shabaab both within Somalia and in Kenya, which hosts an estimated 500,000 Somali refugees. The Somali refugee community has frequently been subjected to discrimination and reprisals in the wake of attacks in Kenya, including a brutal police operation from November 2012 to January 2013 in Nairobi's Eastleigh neighborhood. The community did not immediately report reprisals following the attack on Westgate mall, but there were reports of arbitrary arrests and extortion by the police in the Eastleigh area of Nairobi in October and November.

Lack of Accountability and the ICC

President Kenyatta, his deputy Ruto, and former radio journalist Joshua arap Sang are facing charges of crimes against humanity at the International Criminal Court (ICC) for their alleged roles in the 2007-2008 post-election violence. Ruto and Sang's trial began in September, while Kenyatta's trial is now expected to start in February 2014.

Kenya pledged to continue cooperating with the ICC, but since the election, the new government has actively campaigned at the United Nations and the African Union (AU) to have the cases dropped, deferred, or referred to a local justice mechanism. In September, the National Assembly and the Senate approved a motion calling on the Kenyan government to withdraw from the Rome Statute, the treaty establishing the ICC, which Kenya signed in 2005. The government has taken no steps to act on that motion, and any prospective withdrawal from the Rome Statute would not affect the ongoing cases at the ICC.

The ICC intervened in 2010 and summoned six people alleged to bear the greatest responsibility after parliament defeated a bill that would have established a domestic tribunal to try those responsible for the violence in 2007-2008. In 2012, a committee appointed by the director of public prosecutions said there was insufficient evidence in the 5,000 files it had reviewed, to proceed with criminal prosecutions.

In 2012, the chief justice announced plans to set up an International Crimes Division to deal with post-election violence and other related cases in the future, but the Judicial Service Commission is still assessing the modalities of setting up the division.

The ICC cases in Kenya have been marred by withdrawals of prosecution witnesses, allegedly because of bribery and intimidation; the defendants have also alleged evidence tampering or intimidation of witnesses. The ICC prosecutor described the level of witness tampering in the Kenyan cases as "unprecedented."

Extrajudicial Killings, Torture, and Other Abuses by Security Forces

Over the past five years police have been responsible for hundreds of extrajudicial killings but the perpetrators have not been prosecuted due to weak internal accountability mechanism and nascent civilian oversight.

A survey by the Kenya National Commission on Human Rights found that police had unlawfully killed 120 people between May and August 2013 under circumstances that could have been avoided, and that police did not report the killings

killings to the civilian oversight authority, the Independent Police Oversight Authority (IPOA), for investigation as required under the law.

Police have also been implicated in the torture, disappearance, and unlawful killing of alleged terrorism suspects and individuals of Somali origin, and Somali refugees in Mombasa, Nairobi, North Eastern region, and other parts of Kenya.

In August 2012, a Muslim cleric, Sheikh Aboud Rogo, whom Kenyan authorities said they were investigating over links with terror networks in Somalia, was shot dead by unknown people. Kenya police have denied allegations that they were responsible for Aboud Rogo's death. In September 2013, a Multi-Agency Task Force appointed by the director of public prosecutions in 2012 to investigate Aboud Rogo's killing said in its report that it did not get adequate evidence to identify the killers and recommended a public inquest. No police officer has been held accountable for any of the crimes.

Reforms and Implementation of the 2010 Constitution

The 2010 constitution provides the framework for institutional reforms to improve governance, accountability, and protection of human rights. Although reforms to the judiciary, the electoral system, and parliament have proceeded as outlined in the constitution, police reforms—including measures to improve accountability for police abuses—have lagged.

Key civilian oversight bodies, such as the National Police Service Commission and Independent Police Oversight Authority (IPOA), have been established, but important measures such as restructuring of the police service and vetting of officers—a process to remove those implicated in human rights violations from the police force—have been delayed for over a year due largely to resistance from senior officers.

Efforts to restructure the Ethics and Anti-Corruption Commission (EACC) dragged in the face of allegations that the commission's chair, Mumo Matemu, was implicated in suspected corruption at his previous post at the Kenya Revenue Authority. The restructuring is essential for investigations and important accountability measures against those suspected of corruption to proceed.

Treatment of Refugees

Following a series of grenade attacks in Nairobi's Eastleigh neighborhood in November 2012, police responded with widespread abuses, including torture, rape, and beatings of at least 1,000 people, mainly Somali refugees, as well as significant extortion and looting during subsequent police operation in Eastleigh. While several police units were involved, the paramilitary General Service Unit (GSU) was responsible for many of the worst abuses.

Police responded with similar abuses against residents of the surrounding villages following a grenade attack in Mandera in September 2012 and a gun attack in Garissa in October 2012.

The Kenyan government also increased its hostile rhetoric against Somali refugees in 2013, calling for the refugee camps to be closed and for Somalis to return to Somalia, despite the ongoing conflict and insecurity in Somalia.

Civil Society and Human Rights Defenders

Civil society has come under increased pressure for advocating for justice for the 2007-2008 post-election violence. During their election campaigns, Kenyatta and Ruto accused civil society of manufacturing evidence against them and coaching witnesses in the ICC cases; of receiving foreign funds and furthering foreign interests; and of preventing the ICC cases from being tried in Kenya or Tanzania.

In August 2013, Kenyan security officers in Moyale killed Hassan Guyo, a 40-year-old human rights defender who had travelled from Wajir to Moyale to document human rights abuses by security agents against villagers. The villagers were protesting the sacking of a local chief.

In September, two prominent civil society activists—Maina Kiai, the former head of the Kenyan National Commission for Human Rights and a UN special rapporteur on the rights to freedom of peaceful assembly and of association, and Gladwell Otieno, the director of AFRICOG—were threatened by supporters of the president and his deputy for their role in the ICC cases. A group of youths threatened to burn down Kiai's rural home while unknown people send messages to Otieno, threatening to kill members of her family if she did not stop opposing the idea of ICC partly sitting in either Kenya or Tanzania.

HUMAN
RIGHTS
WATCH

HIGH STAKES
Political Violence and the 2013 Elections in Kenya

New laws were introduced that, if enacted, would impose draconian restrictions on the media and on nonprofit organizations, including by restricting the amount of funds that organizations can receive from foreign sources. One such law, the Public Benefits Organizations (PBO) Act, which was passed in January 2013, but yet to come into force, prohibits political campaigning by nongovernmental organizations and introduces stricter accounting standards.

Key International Actors

The United States and European nations continued to call for accountability for 2007-2008 post-election violence and urged Kenya to cooperate with the ICC following the coming to power of the Jubilee Alliance. US President Barack Obama excluded Kenya from his second tour of Africa in June, but relations appeared to warm following the Westgate attack in September, given the increased attention to Kenya's counterterrorism concerns and role in the region.

The new administration moved to strengthen relations with Russia and China, with visits by President Kenyatta to both countries in August 2013. China approved a development loan of US$5 billion in August 2013 and announced the strengthening of trade ties with Kenya.

Kenya's engagement with the UN Security Council and the AU have focused on its bid to have the ICC cases terminated, deferred, or referred to a domestic mechanism. Kenya is strengthening relations with the AU member states and members of the East African community in the lead up to the next AU Heads of State Summit in January 2014.

East and Horn of Africa allies—Tanzania, Uganda, Rwanda, and Ethiopia—continue to be important players with regard to Kenya's anti ICC campaign and, together with Burundi, have all called for the Kenyan ICC cases to be dropped or referred to a domestic mechanism. The ICC's appeals chamber approved an application by five African countries to be enjoined in the Kenyan cases as friends of the court, in order to provide their views as to whether the deputy president should be excused from appearing in person at trial, an issue currently pending before the chamber.

Liberia

Longstanding deficiencies within the judicial system and security sector, as well as insufficient efforts to address official corruption, continue to undermine development and human rights in Liberia.

Ten years after the signing of a peace accord that ended over a decade of armed conflict, Liberians and the country's key international partners increased pressure on President Ellen Johnson Sirleaf's government to expedite reforms.

While President Sirleaf dismissed a number of high-ranking government officials accused of corruption, her government, as in past years, failed to pursue investigations into the alleged crimes, thereby undermining accountability efforts.

Police Conduct

Widespread police indiscipline and corruption continue to compromise equal and impartial justice and the establishment of the rule of law. Liberian police officers routinely demand bribes and participate in extortion schemes. Members of two armed units—the Emergency Response Unit and the Police Support Unit—regularly engage in armed robbery and other criminal acts during patrols.

Police officers operate with serious logistics shortages, including a lack of vehicles, fuel, uniforms, and basic tools to carry out their duties.

The police made some effort to address the abuse, notably through the Professional Standards Division (PSD), which receives and processes public and internal complaints against officers. From January to June, the PSD received 299 cases, investigated 96, and acted upon 80. Despite this progress, many Liberians are still unaware of the unit and its work.

Access to Justice

Persistent weaknesses in the judiciary undermined access to justice and due process. Prolonged pretrial detention is prevalent; fair and speedy trials are rare. The judiciary is able to conclude only a small number of cases every year. Poor management of the judiciary and corrupt practices by judges, jurors, ministry administrators, and others also severely undermine the dispensation of justice.

An estimated 80 percent of detainees are subjected to extended pretrial deten-tion as a result of the understaffing of the courts, inadequate funding for the judiciary, and lack of coordination between the police and the courts. But greater attention by both the government and donors led to some improve-ments in this sector. Liberian officials, with external support, created a regional hub system, which is intended to decentralize the security and justice sectors by placing armed police officers, immigration units, and judges in five regional centers outside of Monrovia. The first hub opened in Gbarnga, the capital city of Bong County, in 2013.

Sexual Violence

Sexual violence against women and girls is rampant. Hundreds of cases were reported to and documented by the Ministry of Gender and Development. The number of successful sexual violence prosecutions remains low due to poor evi-dence gathering, the reluctance of witnesses to testify, and deficiencies in the judicial sector. In large part because of these problems, the establishment in 2008 of Criminal Court 'E,' a special court designed to fast-track cases of sexual violence, has resulted in few prosecutions.

Truth and Reconciliation Commission and Accountability

The government made some progress in implementing the recommendations the Truth and Reconciliation Commission has made since 2009. In June, the government released a plan for promoting national peacebuilding and reconcili-ation, and in October launched the National Palava Hut Program, envisioned to foster reconciliation through community and grassroots dialogue. The plan advocates for reparations, but ignores the commission's call for prosecutions of those responsible for war crimes committed during Liberia's two armed con-flicts, for which there has still been no accountability.

Sexual Orientation and Gender Identity

Numerous members of the lesbian, gay, bisexual, and transgender (LGBT) community were, in 2013, subjected to verbal assaults, harassment, and stigmatization. Although Liberian law already criminalizes same-sex conduct for both men and women, the country's legislature has been considering even more repressive legislation. In February 2012, Liberia, like some other African countries, sought to pass new laws that would further punish LGBT people. At time of writing, there were two new bills pending before the legislature that, if passed, would increase penalties for same-sex conduct and explicitly criminalize same-sex marriage.

In July 2012, Liberia's upper legislative house, the Senate, passed the Amendment to the Domestic Relations Law of Liberia bill, commonly known as the "Anti-Same-Sex Marriage" bill. The proposed legislation criminalizes same-sex marriage with punishment of up to five years in prison.

At time of writing, another bill that seeks to criminalize same-sex practices was before the Judiciary Committee of the House of Representatives.

Freedom of Expression

There has been some improvement in the protection of freedom of expression, as evidenced by the creation of a number of independent media establishments and the passage of a Freedom of Information Act into law.

Despite these gains, Liberia's outdated and draconian defamation laws continue to pose a serious risk to freedom of expression. The August 2013 arrest and imprisonment for several weeks of editor Rodney Sieh, and the temporary closure of his prominent investigative paper, *FrontPage Africa,* raised concerns about the freedom of media to publish articles critical of government. Chris Toe, a former government minister, won the libel case he brought against Sieh and *FrontPage Africa.* The court ordered the defendants to pay Toe a judgment of US$1.5 million. Under Liberian civil procedure law, a defendant can be imprisoned for inability to pay a libel judgment. Sieh potentially faces a long prison sentence.

There are few protections in Liberian law to ensure that defamation judgments are not excessive. Furthermore, Liberia's appeals process—including the use of

HUMAN
RIGHTS
WATCH

"It's Nature, Not a Crime"
Discriminatory Laws and LGBT people in Liberia

disproportionate appeals bonds—effectively denies media centers and journalists the right to appeal a defamation ruling.

Human Rights and Anti-Corruption Institutions

The Liberia Anti-Corruption Commission (LACC), which is empowered to investigate and prosecute on its own initiative, has secured only two convictions since it was established in 2008. The second conviction occurred in 2013 against former Liberia National Police Inspector General Beatrice Munah-Sieh. The conviction was appealed on the basis of jury errors. At time of writing, the case was pending before the Supreme Court. In June, the Senate rejected a bill submitted by President Sirleaf to give the LACC more freedom to prosecute corruption cases. Currently, the LACC must submit its cases to the Ministry of Justice and wait three months for the ministry to decide whether it will pursue its own case.

The General Auditing Commission (GAC), Liberia's independent auditing agency, has completed and issued dozens of reports in the last five years with details of mismanagement and corruption. The Ministry of Justice has investigated or pursued very few of these reports, but it announced in September 2013 it was reviewing past GAC reports for possible prosecution of government malfeasance. That same month, the Senate began to hold public hearings on past GAC audits.

The Independent National Commission on Human Rights, established in 2010 and empowered to investigate and consider human rights complaints, remains ineffective and weak. While there was some progress—the commission dispatched its first field monitors to Nimba, Bong, and Lofa—the commission has yet to take meaningful steps toward fulfilling its mandate.

Key International Actors

Liberia's international partners, including the United Nations Mission in Liberia (UNMIL), the United States, and the European Union were more outspoken in 2013 than in past years about the need to address corruption and weaknesses in the security and justice sectors.

The UN Security Council extended the mandate of UNMIL until September 30, 2014. UNMIL began its plan to decrease the number of peacekeepers by half—

from over 8,000 to 3,750— between 2013 and 2015. In recognition of the lack of readiness of the Liberia National Police to fully take over security, the UN secretary-general decided to increase the number of UN police officers. The UN Peacebuilding Support Office contributed $13 million to strengthen the rule of law, notably by supporting the regional hub system.

Mali

An unexpected push south by Islamist armed groups in January 2013 provoked a French-led military offensive that quickly dislodged the groups and largely ended their abusive occupation of the north. During and after the offensive, Malian soldiers committed numerous abuses, particularly against civilians and rebel suspects in their custody.

Fears about the threat posed by Islamist armed groups linked to Al-Qaeda led to considerable diplomatic efforts to resolve the crisis and stabilize Mali. The French took the lead on military matters, the European Union on training and security sector reform, and the United Nations, through the establishment of a peacekeeping force, on rule of law and political stability. While most of these actors criticized abuses by the Islamist groups, they were reluctant to publicly criticize those by the Malian army.

Largely free, fair, and transparent presidential elections in August helped stabilize the political situation. However, security was undermined by persistent communal tensions, uncertainty about the status of Tuareg rebels; ongoing attacks by Islamist groups, including suicide bombings; divisions within the military; and rising criminality.

Malian authorities made little effort to investigate and hold accountable members of the security forces implicated in abuses. However, in January, the prosecutor of the International Criminal Court (ICC) opened an investigation into crimes allegedly committed in the three northern regions of the country. The Ouagadougou Accord signed in June by the Malian government and two Tuareg groups was ambiguous about whether those responsible for serious crimes would be prosecuted.

The rule of law in the north was undermined by the slow return of members of the judiciary and police to the north. Inadequate budgetary allocations for the criminal justice system in general limited due process throughout the country. Graft and corruption, endemic at all levels of government, further impeded Malians' access to basic health care and education.

Abuses by State Security Forces

Malian soldiers, in their campaign to retake the north, committed numerous abuses, including summary executions, enforced disappearances, and torture. The abuses, which targeted suspected Islamist rebels and alleged collaborators, included at least 26 extrajudicial executions, 11 enforced disappearances, and over 50 cases of torture or ill-treatment.

Detainees were severely beaten, kicked, and strangled; burned with cigarettes and lighters; injected or forced to swallow an unidentified caustic substance; exposed to simulated drowning akin to "waterboarding"; and subjected to death threats and mock executions.

The mistreatment ceased after the detainees were turned over to gendarmes, whom they sometimes bribed to secure their release. The presence of gendarmes, French soldiers, and West African troops served as a deterrent to the most serious abuses.

In August, the leader of the 2012 coup, Capt. Amadou Sanogo, was promoted to the rank of lieutenant general, despite being directly implicated in torture and enforced disappearances in 2012 and October 2013, when forces loyal to Sanogo allegedly killed four and disappeared at least seven of his loyalists who had mutinied. However, in August the interim president repealed a 2012 decree appointing Sanogo as head of the committee to carry out reforms in the army.

Abuses by Armed Islamist Groups and Tuareg Rebels

Before being driven out of northern Mali, combatants with the Islamist groups—Ansar Dine, the Movement for Unity and Jihad in West Africa (MUJAO), and Al-Qaeda in the Islamic Maghreb (AQIM)—committed serious abuses against prisoners and local residents. Enforcing their interpretation of Sharia, the groups beat, flogged, and arbitrarily arrested those who smoked cigarettes, consumed alcoholic beverages, or failed to adhere to the groups' dress code. In January, Islamist armed groups in Konna executed at least seven Malian soldiers.

AQIM continues to hold as hostages at least eight persons, including two Frenchmen, a Dutchman, a Swede, a South African, and at least three Algerians. AQIM claimed to have executed a Frenchman, Phillippe Verdon, on March 10 in retaliation for France's military intervention in northern Mali.

On June 1 and 2, forces of the Tuareg National Movement for the Liberation of Azawad (MNLA), which still controls parts of the Kidal region, arbitrarily detained about 100 people, most of them darker-skinned men from non-Tuareg ethnic groups. The MNLA robbed, threatened, and, in numerous cases, severely beat the men. On November 2, two French journalists were abducted in the MNLA stronghold of Kidal and later executed by armed men allegedly linked to AQIM. In September, the MNLA released some 30 prisoners being held by Islamist groups in Kidal.

Accountability

War crimes and other serious abuses were committed by all sides during Mali's recent armed conflict. These abuses include the summary execution of up to 153 Malian soldiers in Aguelhok; widespread looting and pillage, and sexual violence by the MNLA; the recruitment and use of child combatants, executions, floggings, amputations, and destruction of religious and cultural shrines by armed Islamist groups; and the summary execution, torture and enforced disappearance by soldiers from the Malian army. Many health facilities in the north were specifically targeted and looted.

In July 2012, the government of Mali, a state party to the ICC, referred "the situation in Mali since January 2012" to the ICC prosecutor for investigation. On January 16, 2013, the ICC prosecutor formally opened an investigation into grave crimes allegedly committed in the northern three regions of Mali. At time of writing, no arrest warrants had been issued.

The Malian government and military high command gave mixed signals regarding abuses by Malian soldiers, at times flatly denying violations and at others promising to hold alleged perpetrators to account. While Malian authorities investigated a few incidents, including the enforced disappearance of five men in Timbuktu in February and the September 2012 killing by soldiers of 16 Islamic preachers in Diabaly, numerous others have not been investigated, and no soldiers implicated in recent abuses have been put on trial. There was progress in justice for the enforced disappearance in May 2012 of at least 21 soldiers by forces loyal to Sanogo. In October, the judge investigating the case charged and detained three security force members and summoned for questioning 17 others, including Sanogo, for their alleged role in the crimes.

Truth Telling and Reconciliation Mechanism

In March, the interim government established the Commission for Dialogue and Reconciliation, but its efficacy was undermined by an unclear mandate and the hasty appointment of commissioners by the interim government, which failed to consult sufficiently with a wide variety of stakeholders. Because its mandate and powers appear limited to promoting reconciliation, some Malians have pushed for a commission that could address impunity for abuses and recommend individuals for prosecution.

The Judiciary

Neglect and mismanagement within the Malian judiciary led to striking deficiencies and hindered efforts to address impunity for the perpetrators of all classes of crimes. Coupled with unprofessional conduct and corrupt practices, personnel and logistical shortfalls within the justice sector contributed to violations of the right to due process.

Because of the courts' inability to adequately process cases, hundreds of prisoners are held in extended pretrial detention in overcrowded jails and detention centers. Very few of the estimated 250 men who were detained in relation with the offensive to retake the north had legal representation, and several died in custody as a result of inadequate medical care and poor detention conditions. The interim justice minister did, however, replace many corrupt prosecutors and made some progress in improving detention conditions.

Recruitment of Children and Child Labor

During their occupation of the north from April 2012 through February 2013, Islamist armed groups recruited, trained, and used several hundred children in their forces. Scores of children, some as young as 12, took part in battle, and many were killed while fighting or by aerial bombardments. A number of schools were destroyed by French bombings because Islamist groups were using them as command centers.

Child labor in agriculture, domestic service, mining, and other sectors was common, and often included dangerous work that Malian law prohibits for anyone under the age of 18. Child laborers in artisanal gold mining were exposed to health risks from accidents and exposure to toxic mercury. More than two years after its adoption, the government's action plan on child labor remained largely unimplemented.

Key International Actors

Mali's partners, notably France, the European Union, the United States, and the United Nations, issued numerous statements denouncing the offensive and abuses by Islamist groups, but were reluctant to publicly condemn abuses committed by the Malian army.

The establishment of a 6200-strong African-led International Support Mission to Mali (AFISMA), authorized by UN Security Council Resolution 2085 in December 2012, was envisioned to re-establish government control over northern Mali in 2013. This mission was overtaken by events after Islamist rebels attacked the government-controlled town of Konna in January. The attack prompted a six-month military operation by up to 4,500 French soldiers, who were assisted by African forces to re-establish government control of the north.

In recognition of the complex political and security challenges, the UN Security Council in April adopted Resolution 2100, establishing the 11,200-strong Integrated United Nations Mission for the Stabilization of Mali (MINUSMA). In July, most AFISMA troops were re-assigned as UN peacekeepers.

Meanwhile, the African Union and ECOWAS took the lead in supporting negotiations between armed Tuaregs and the Malian government, and in January the AU Peace and Security Council (PSC) mandated the deployment of some 50 human rights observers to Mali. In February, the EU Foreign Affairs Council launched the EU Training Mission in Mali (EUTM), mandated to train four battalions of Malian soldiers and help reform the Malian army. In May, a donors' conference organized by the EU and France resulted in pledges of US$4.2 billion for development efforts in Mali.

In February, the Office of the UN High Commissioner for Human Rights sent a second fact-finding mission to Mali and surrounding countries. In March, the UN Human Rights Council adopted a mandate for an independent expert

Nigeria

Horrific abuses in the north by the militant Islamist group Boko Haram and the Nigerian security forces' heavy-handed response to this violence dominated Nigeria's human rights landscape in 2013. In May, President Goodluck Jonathan imposed a state of emergency, which was extended for another three months in November in the three states where Boko Haram is most active. The emergency failed to curb atrocities and to sufficiently protect civilians. The prosecutor of the International Criminal Court said that there was reason to believe Boko Haram had committed crimes against humanity.

More than 400 people died in 2013 from violent inter-communal conflict in Nigeria's Middle Belt states, and scores were rendered homeless from the clashes. Security forces throughout the country engaged in human rights abuses. There were few investigations or prosecutions of these crimes.

The judiciary remained nominally free from interference and pressures from other branches of government, but corruption did impede pursuit of justice. Poverty and corruption continued to afflict the oil-rich Niger Delta, while the weakness of anti-corruption institutions in government inhibited the realization of social and economic rights and the fair and transparent functioning of the public and private sectors.

Boko Haram Violence

The four-year insurgency by Boko Haram, which seeks to impose a harsh form of Sharia, or Islamic law, in northern Nigeria and end government corruption, has killed more than 5,000 people. Although the Nigerian government set up a committee to develop an amnesty framework for Boko Haram, the group continued to target government security agents, churches, and mosques.

Since 2012, Boko Haram has burned more than 300 schools in the north and deprived more than 10,000 children of an education. In a particularly gory attack in July, suspected armed Islamists killed 42 pupils and teachers and burned down a government-owned boarding school in Mamudo village, Yobe state.

The Nigerian government's support for the formation of armed self-defense groups, mostly young men to assist in the apprehension of Islamist insurgents,

HUMAN
RIGHTS
WATCH

"Leave Everything to God"
Accountability for Inter-Communal Violence
in Plateau and Kaduna States, Nigeria

brought a new and alarming dimension to its anti-Boko Haram efforts. These young men themselves became targets of Boko Haram attacks. In one August incident in Borno state, Boko Haram killed 24 members of the "Civilian Joint Task Force," as the group is called. Thirty other members were declared missing.

Inter-Communal and Political Violence

Episodes of inter-communal violence in the Middle Belt states of Plateau, Taraba, Benue, and Nasarawa left more than 400 people dead and scores of houses destroyed. Federal and state authorities failed to hold accountable the perpetrators of these crimes and break the cycle of violence. In response, ethnic and religious groups in this region resorted to forming their own militias to deliver justice and security. State and local government policies fed discontent by discriminating against "non-indigenes"—people who cannot prove that they are descendants of the original inhabitants of an area.

Conduct of Security Forces

Government security forces were implicated in various human rights violations with regard to the Boko Haram insurgency. The large number of troops deployed to enforce the state of emergency engaged in the indiscriminate arrest, detention, torture, and extra-judicial killing of those suspected to be supporters or members of the Islamist group. Security forces razed and burned homes and properties in communities thought to harbor Boko Haram fighters. In Baga, a town in Borno state, Nigerian troops destroyed more than 2,000 buildings and allegedly killed scores of people, apparently in retaliation for the killing of a soldier by Boko Haram. The authorities have yet to bring anyone to justice for these crimes.

The Nigerian police have also been involved in frequent human rights violations, including extrajudicial killings, torture, arbitrary arrests, and extortion-related abuses. Despite the dismantling of many "road blocks" by the inspector general of police, corruption in the police force remains a serious problem. The police routinely solicit bribes from victims to investigate crimes and from suspects to drop investigations. Senior police officials embezzle or mismanage police funds, often demanding monetary "returns" that their subordinates extort from the public.

Government Corruption

The Economic and Financial Crimes Commission (EFCC) made little progress combating corruption in the public sector. In a major setback in ending impunity for corruption among political officeholders, President Goodluck Jonathan in March 2013 "pardoned" Diepreye Alamieyeseigha, a former governor of Bayelsa State, and the only governor to have served prison time in Nigeria for corruption.

Corruption cases against several dozen senior politicians, as well as oil marketers for their alleged role in a fraudulent fuel subsidy scheme, had still not been completed at time of writing. Executive interference with the EFCC, a weak and overburdened judiciary, and the agency's own missteps, including failing to appeal tenuous rulings or prosecute senior politicians credibly implicated in corruption, have continued to undermine its efficacy.

The country's other prominent anti-corruption agency, the Independent Corrupt Practices and Other Related Offences Commission (ICPC), established in 2000 to tackle corruption in the public sector, failed to file charges or achieve any major convictions in 2013.

Violence and Poverty in the Oil-Producing Niger Delta

The federal government's 2009 amnesty program—which saw some 26,000 militants, youth, and gang members surrender weapons in exchange for amnesty and monthly cash stipends—have reduced attacks on oil facilities in the Niger Delta. The government has doled out these financial incentives—some US$400 million annually—from the additional oil revenue accruing to government following the amnesty, but has still not addressed the region's underlying causes of violence and discontent, such as poverty, public sector corruption, environmental degradation from oil spills, and impunity for politically sponsored violence. In June, the government announced 2015 as the terminal date for the program and acknowledged that its inability to secure jobs for the trained ex-militants or implement an orderly exit strategy may portend more danger for the region.

Health and Human Rights

Widespread lead poisoning from artisanal gold mining in Zamfara State has killed at least 400 children since 2010. The release of funds in February by the federal government to clean up the environment allowed lead treatment programs to be expanded to reach an additional 1,500 children.

In February, nine female polio vaccinators were shot dead by suspected Islamic militants in Kano, and security for vaccinators remains fragile in the north. Attacks on health workers threaten the realization of the right to health.

Sexual Orientation and Gender Identity

Nigeria's criminal and penal codes punish consensual homosexual conduct with up to 14 years in prison. Sharia penal codes in many northern states criminalize consensual homosexual conduct with caning, imprisonment, or death by stoning.

In May 2013, Nigeria's House of Representatives passed the Same Sex Marriage (Prohibition) Bill, earlier passed by the Senate in November 2012, and at time of writing the bill was awaiting the president's approval. Same-sex marriages or civil unions, which could lead to imprisonment of up to 14 years, are so broadly defined in the bill that they include virtually any form of same-sex cohabitation. In addition, the bill seeks to impose prison sentences on lesbian, gay, bisexual, transgender, and intersex (LGBTI) people.

Human rights groups vocally opposed the bill because it would formalize discrimination against LGBTI people and have wide-ranging effects on the constitutionally guaranteed rights to dignity, personal liberty, freedom of speech, association and assembly, and freedoms of thought, conscience, and religion.

In July, Nigeria's Foreign Ministry announced that the country would not accredit diplomats with same-sex spouses, confirming that, if the law comes into effect, the country would extend to non-citizens its legal ban on LGBTI relationships.

Freedom of Expression and Media

Civil society and the independent media openly criticize the government and its policies, allowing for robust public debate. Yet journalists are still subject to arrest and intimidation when reporting on issues implicating Nigeria's political and economic elite. In August, the federal government arrested and charged the political editor and political reporter of Leadership newspaper, Tony Amokeodo and Chibuzor Ukaibe, respectively, for reporting on a story based on documents allegedly issued by the president. In September, Tukur Mamu, the publisher of *Desert Herald*, was arrested and detained allegedly for publishing a book criticizing the Minister of the Federal Capital Territory.

In January, Ikechukwu Udendu, the editor of *Anambra News*, a monthly newspaper in southeastern Anambra state, was gunned down in Onitsha. In September, the mutilated body of Aisha Usman, a reporter with the news magazine Mahangar Arewa in Zaria, was found on a highway in Kaduna state. The causes of these deaths remained unknown at time of writing.

Key International Actors

Nigeria's roles as a regional power, Africa's leading oil exporter, and a major contributor of troops to United Nations peacekeeping missions have made foreign governments reluctant to exert meaningful pressure on the country over its disappointing human rights record.

The British government in July designated Boko Haram as a foreign terrorist organization, aimed at preventing it from operating in the UK and blocking British-based support for the group. The UK continues to provide substantial foreign aid to Nigeria, including security sector assistance. It has not, however, openly demanded accountability for government officials or security force members implicated in corruption or serious human rights abuses.

The US government in November designated Boko Haram and its affiliate, Ansaru, as foreign terrorist organizations. The United States in 2013 restricted a Nigerian army battalion operating in Mali as part of an African force from receiving non-lethal equipment under a foreign aid law, which bars the US from providing training or equipment to foreign troops or units that commit gross human rights violations.

United Nations High Commissioner for Human Rights Navi Pillay consistently warned that Boko Haram's attacks might constitute crimes against humanity. The International Criminal Court continued its "preliminary examination" of the situation in Nigeria, with a focus on assessing the gravity of crimes committed and the extent to which national authorities are investigating and prosecuting them.

Rwanda

Rwanda adopted a number of new laws, including media laws and a revised law on genocide ideology. The country continued to make impressive progress in the delivery of public services, such as health care, but freedom of expression and association remain tightly controlled. The government obstructed opposition parties and independent civil society organizations, and threatened its critics. Parliamentary elections resulted in an overwhelming majority for the ruling party, with no meaningful challenge. The leadership of one of the last remaining independent human rights organizations was taken over by pro-government elements.

Despite mounting international concern, Rwanda provided significant military support to the M23, an armed group responsible for serious abuses against civilians in eastern Democratic Republic of Congo. In November, the M23 was defeated by the Congolese army and UN peacekeepers, after Rwanda appeared to withdraw its support for the M23 during military operations.

Political Parties

The ruling Rwandan Patriotic Front (RPF) won parliamentary elections in September with more than 76 percent of the vote. The only other parties that presented candidates were those broadly supporting the RPF.

The opposition Democratic Green Party of Rwanda, which had been trying to register as a party for almost four years, was finally granted registration by the government in August, on the day before the deadline for parties to submit their lists of election candidates. As a result, it decided not to take part in the polls.

Two opposition party leaders arrested in 2010—Victoire Ingabire of the FDU-Inkingi and Bernard Ntaganda of the PS-Imberakuri—remained in prison, serving sentences of respectively eight and four years, Ntaganda for endangering national security and divisionism, and Ingabire for conspiracy to undermine the government and genocide denial. Appeal hearings for Ingabire, who was sentenced in 2012, concluded at the High Court in Kigali on July 31. The judgment is expected in December.

Sylvain Sibomana, secretary general of the FDU-Inkingi, and Dominique Shyirambere, another party member, were arrested on March 25, after a confrontation with police outside the courtroom where Ingabire's trial was taking place. They were charged with contempt of public officials, illegal demonstration, and inciting insurrection or public disorder. Police and judicial officials questioned them about the possession of T-shirts bearing the slogan "democracy and justice" and badges calling for Ingabire's release. On November 22, Sibomana was found guilty of the first two charges and sentenced to two years in prison; Shyirambere was sentenced to five months.

Sibomana also faced charges in a second case linked to the prosecution of eight other FDU-Inkingi members in Karongi, arrested in September 2012 on charges of inciting insurrection or public disorder after allegedly holding illegal meetings. On July 11, seven of the original defendants were each sentenced to two years in prison. Sibomana's case has since been joined to that of the eighth, Anselme Mutuyimana. At time of writing, the verdict in Sibomana and Mutuyimana's trial had not yet been handed down.

Civil Society Organizations

Government officials were openly hostile toward independent nongovernmental organizations (NGOs) working on human rights. The pro-government media echoed these views with public attacks on international human rights organizations and other perceived critics.

In August, the last effective independent Rwandan human rights organization, the Rwandan League for the Promotion and Defense of Human Rights (LIPRODHOR), was taken over by members believed to be sympathetic to the government. On July 21, these members ousted the organization's leaders and voted in a new board, violating the organization's internal statutes and Rwandan legislation governing NGOs.

Three days later, the Rwanda Governance Board—the state body with oversight of national NGOs—recognized the new board. LIPRODHOR, through its ousted president, has taken the case to court. The case was pending at time of writing. During the forced handover between the old and new boards, police threatened LIPRODHOR staff with imprisonment if they did not cooperate with the new board.

Freedom of Media

New media laws adopted in February appeared to increase the scope for independent journalism, for example by enshrining journalists' rights to freedom of opinion and expression and by introducing media self-regulation. Some radio stations broadcast call-in programs in which listeners posed critical questions to political leaders. However, most print and broadcast media continued to be heavily dominated by pro-government views. Most journalists were unable or unwilling to engage in investigative reporting on sensitive issues and rarely criticized government policies, as a result of intimidation, threats, and prosecutions in previous years.

Saidati Mukakibibi, journalist with *Umurabyo* newspaper, arrested in 2010, was released on June 25 after serving a three-year sentence, reduced from seven years on appeal in 2012. The newspaper's editor, Agnès Uwimana, whose sentence had been reduced from seventeen to four years, remained in prison.

On March 25, the High Court in Kigali upheld the conviction of Stanley Gatera, editor of *Umusingi* newspaper, who was found guilty of discrimination and sectarianism in 2012. He was released on July 26 after serving a one-year prison sentence.

Justice for Genocide

The trial of Léon Mugesera, a former government official extradited from Canada to Rwanda in 2012 and accused of planning and incitement to genocide, took place in the High Court in Kigali. It was ongoing at time of writing.

In July, the International Criminal Tribunal for Rwanda (ICTR) transferred genocide suspect Bernard Munyagishari to face trial in Rwanda. After preliminary hearings, the trial of Jean Bosco Uwinkindi, the first such case to be transferred by the ICTR to Rwanda in 2012, was postponed and had not begun in substance at time of writing.

Criminal trials of Rwandan genocide suspects on the basis of universal jurisdiction took place in the national courts of Norway, Sweden, and the Netherlands, leading to convictions and prison sentences.

A United States court convicted a Rwandan of immigration fraud for concealing her role in the genocide, stripped her of US citizenship and sentenced her to 10 years' imprisonment. A genocide suspect in Norway was extradited to Rwanda while two others in Sweden and Denmark lost their appeals against extradition. Extradition cases were pending in several other countries, including the UK, Netherlands, and France.

Genocide Ideology Law

A revised version of the 2008 law on genocide ideology was promulgated in October. It contains several improvements to the 2008 law, including a more precise definition of the offense and the requirement to demonstrate intent behind the crime, thereby reducing the scope for abusive prosecutions. However, several articles retain language that could be used to criminalize free speech. The new law reduces the maximum prison sentence from 25 to 9 years.

Unlawful Detention, Torture, and Ill-Treatment

In a trial of 20 people that began in 2012 and concluded in September 2013, a court in Gasabo, Kigali, failed to investigate claims by defendants that they had been held in illegal detention centers and tortured. Several defendants, accused of stealing televisions and other goods, said they had been held unlawfully, in two unofficial detention centers known as Chez Kabuga and Chez Gacinya. They stated in court that the police had tortured them to force them to confess or incriminate others. The judge dismissed their allegations of torture, saying the detainees had no evidence. The court acquitted 7 defendants and sentenced the remaining 13 to prison terms of between 3 and 10 years.

Dozens of defendants charged with endangering state security in several group trials in Musanze claimed they had been detained unlawfully in military camps or other unrecognized detention centers. Some said they had been tortured. Many defendants spent lengthy periods in pretrial detention—in some cases, more than two years—before they were tried in 2013. Some were tried and convicted without a defense lawyer.

Refugees from Rwanda

Some Rwandan refugees and asylum-seekers faced security threats in their country of asylum, particularly in Uganda. Joel Mutabazi, a former presidential bodyguard in Rwanda with refugee status in Uganda, was abducted on August 20 by armed men from a safe-house in a suburb of the capital Kampala where he had been staying since escaping an attempt on his life in Uganda in July 2012. He was released the same day, thanks to an intervention by the Ugandan police. On October 25, he went missing from another location where he was living under 24-hour Ugandan police protection. His whereabouts were unknown for six days. On October 31, the Rwandan police confirmed he was detained in Rwanda but refused to disclose where he was held. On November 13, he appeared before a military court in Kigali with 14 co-accused, charged with terrorism and other offenses. The Ugandan government claimed that a Ugandan police officer had erroneously handed Mutabazi to the Rwandan police, without following correct legal procedures.

Another Rwandan, Pascal Manirakiza, who had fled to Uganda after escaping from the M23 in eastern Congo, was reported missing in August. He was found alive but unconscious, with serious injuries, near Kampala.

Rwanda's Involvement in the DRC

Rwanda provided military support to the M23, a Congolese armed group responsible for killings of civilians, rape, and recruitment of child soldiers in eastern Congo. This support included supplies of weapons and ammunition; the recruitment in Rwanda of young men and boys, some under 16, to fight with the M23 in Congo; training of M23 recruits by Rwandan military officers; and the deployment of Rwandan troops in Congo to assist the M23. As in 2012, the Rwandan government denied providing any support to the M23. In November, the M23 was defeated by the Congolese army and UN peacekeepers after Rwanda appeared to stop supporting the group during military operations.

Around 700 M23 fighters fled to Rwanda in March after infighting in the M23, and additional fighters fled in November when the M23 was defeated. They included several individuals implicated in serious abuses in eastern Congo, including four named on UN and US sanctions lists. Rwanda has yet to take steps to investigate alleged abuses by M23 fighters who fled to Rwanda.

M23 leader Bosco Ntaganda, who had long been backed by Rwanda until the M23 split into two factions in early 2013, surrendered to the US embassy in Kigali in March and was transferred to the International Criminal Court (see chapter on Democratic Republic of Congo).

Key International Actors

Several governments and other international actors expressed renewed concern for Rwandan military support to the M23. Some donors who had suspended or delayed parts of their assistance to Rwanda in 2012 in response to its support for the M23 resumed aid but channeled it to different sectors.

The United Kingdom decided not to resume general budget support and redirected its assistance to education and poverty alleviation programs instead. In October, the US government suspended military assistance to Rwanda under the Child Soldiers Protection Act, because of Rwanda's support to the M23, which uses child soldiers.

Somalia

Civilians continue to suffer serious human rights abuses as the new Somali government struggled to extend its control beyond the capital, Mogadishu, and to some key towns in south-central Somalia in 2013. Parties to Somalia's long-running armed conflict were responsible for serious violations of international law; abuses include indiscriminate attacks, sexual violence, and arbitrary arrests and detention.

The Islamist armed group Al-Shabaab maintains control of much of southern Somalia, and the group increased attacks on high-profile civilian locales in Mogadishu, including the courthouse, a popular restaurant, and the United Nations compound, killing scores of civilians. Those fighting against Al-Shabaab—a combination of Somali government armed forces, the African Union Mission in Somalia (AMISOM), Ethiopian government troops, and allied militias—have also committed abuses.

The new government's human rights record has been mixed. Despite public pledges to tackle rights violations, implementation has been poor. The government and its security forces undermined these commitments, for example, in February, by arresting a woman who alleged rape by government forces and also a journalist who interviewed her. They were convicted of tarnishing state institutions but eventually acquitted after significant international criticism.

The government gave priority to justice and security sector reform, essential to improving human rights, but insecurity in Mogadishu and other government-controlled areas remains a serious challenge. The unresolved implementation of the proposed federalism plan led to open conflict and abuses, notably in the contested port town of Kismayo, where fighting broke out in June between rival militia.

Abuses in Government-Controlled Areas

Civilians were killed and wounded by crossfire, including during infighting between government soldiers over control of roadblocks.

In June, fighting between rival clan militias in Kismayo and apparently indiscriminate attacks on civilian buildings caused dozens of civilian casualties. On June

8, three children were killed when a shell struck their house and a local health clinic was damaged.

In government-controlled areas, targeted killings including of traditional elders, civilian officials, and journalists increased. The perpetrators are frequently unknown, although Al-Shabaab is often believed to be responsible. On April 26, Deputy State Attorney Ahmad Shaykh Nur Maalin was killed in Mogadishu.

In addition, the government's military court sentenced at least six people—two civilians allegedly linked to Al-Shabaab and four soldiers—to death and executed them in Mogadishu and Beletweyne between July and August following trials that raise serious due process concerns.

In the run-up to council elections in the semi-autonomous region of Puntland, which were subsequently postponed, one journalist and two human rights defenders were killed. There were also executions by Puntland's military court.

Abuses by Al-Shabaab

Access to, and information about, Al-Shabaab areas is severely restricted, but credible reports indicate that Al-Shabaab has committed targeted killings, beheadings, and executions, particularly of individuals it accused of spying. Al-Shabaab continues to forcibly recruit adults and children, administer arbitrary justice, and restrict basic rights.

Al-Shabaab supporters carried out attacks with improvised explosive devices and grenades and suicide bombings that targeted civilians, particularly in Mogadishu. On April 14, Al-Shabaab attacked Mogadishu's main court complex leaving at least 30 civilians dead, including three lawyers and a judge. A June attack on the UN compound in Mogadishu killed at least 14 people. On September 7, at least 15 people were killed in an attack on Village restaurant, popular among journalists and politicians, for the second time in under a year.

In its most high-profile attack outside Somalia, Al-Shabaab claimed responsibility for a major attack on the Westgate shopping mall, an upscale shopping center in Nairobi, Kenya, on September 20 that killed 67 people (see Kenya chapter).

Sexual Violence

Women and girls face alarming levels of sexual violence throughout the country. Internally displaced women and girls are particularly vulnerable to rape by armed men including government soldiers and militia members. In January, a displaced woman, who alleged that she was raped by government soldiers, and a journalist who interviewed her were prosecuted in a deeply flawed and politicized judicial process. Security forces have also threatened individuals who have reported rape, and service providers.

Reports of sexual exploitation and abuse by AMISOM increased. In a March 2013 resolution, the UN Security Council called on AMISOM to take measures to prevent sexual abuse and exploitation and address allegations of abuse. In August, a woman alleged that she was abducted by soldiers and then transferred to AMISOM soldiers who raped her. A joint Somali and AMISOM high-level task force was established to investigate, during which AMISOM publicly denied the allegations. The alleged victim and witnesses were intimidated by government intelligence agents during the investigation.

Recruitment of Children and Other Abuses

All Somali parties to the conflict continue to commit serious abuses against children, including recruitment into armed forces and arbitrary detentions. Al-Shabaab in particular has targeted children for recruitment and forced marriage, and attacked schools.

Government authorities committed to implementing a July 2012 action plan against child recruitment but discussions about implementation were ongoing at time of writing.

Displaced Persons and Access to Humanitarian Assistance

According to the UN, at least 870,000 people, many of them displaced persons, are still in need of emergency humanitarian assistance. Tens of thousands of displaced people remain in dire conditions in Mogadishu and are subjected to rape, forced evictions, and clan-based discrimination at the hands of government forces, allied militia, and private individuals including camp managers

HUMAN
RIGHTS
WATCH

NO PLACE FOR CHILDREN
Child Recruitment, Forced Marriage, and Attacks on Schools in Somalia

known as "gatekeepers." Gatekeepers and militias controlling the camps have also diverted and stolen food aid intended for internally displaced persons.

In January, the government announced plans to relocate the capital's displaced population to new camps in the Daynile district, where Al-Shabaab retains a significant presence, prompting concerns that the new camps would lack basic security and protection, as well as services. Meanwhile, forced evictions of the displaced continue including from camps planned for relocation.

Humanitarian agencies face challenges accessing populations in need due to ongoing attacks and restrictions imposed by parties to the conflict. On April 14, a car bomb exploded on the airport road in Mogadishu hitting cars carrying Turkish aid workers. On August 14, Médecins Sans Frontières (MSF) ended its 22-year operation in Somalia, citing continuing attacks by armed groups and civilian leaders on health workers. Before its departure, MSF had treated about 50,000 people per month and the World Health Organization estimates that 1.5 million people may now lack access to health care.

Attacks on Media

Somalia remains one of the most dangerous countries in the world to be a journalist. Five journalists and media workers were killed in 2013, four of them in Mogadishu. On April 21, Mohamed Ibrahim Raage, a journalist working for the governmental Radio Mogadishu and Somali National Television who had recently returned to Mogadishu from exile in Uganda, was killed outside his home. A number of other journalists were also attacked, including in the town of Kismayo.

Impunity for these killings prevails. One individual was sentenced to death in March for the September 2012 killing of journalist Hassan Yusuf Absuge, and then executed in August after a trial that did not meet international due process standards.

The Puntland authorities temporarily closed media outlets and banned rebroadcasting of certain international programs. In April, the Ministry of Information banned Radio Daljir, One Nation, and Codka Nabada (Voice of Peace).

In June, a Somaliland court suspended the popular daily *Hubaal* upon request of the attorney general. The ban was lifted in August after a presidential pardon.

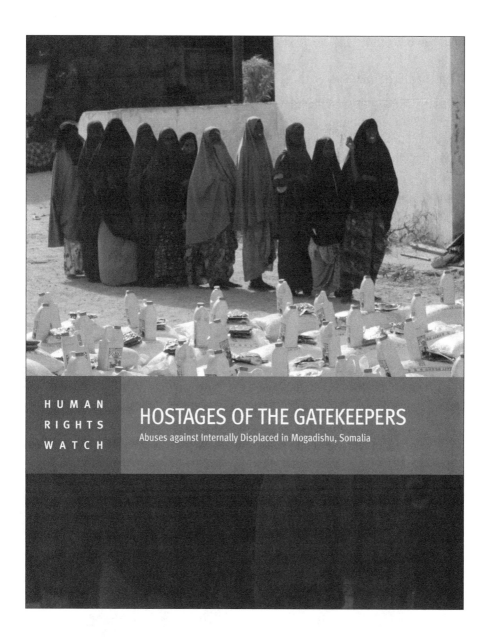

The newspaper's leadership has been intimidated and harassed, and the editor and managing director were convicted on criminal defamation charges in July.

Key International Actors

In a series of high-profile pledging conferences hosted by the United Kingdom and the European Union in May and September, international donors pledged significant funds to the new government's reform agenda. The plans included human rights components but no rights monitoring framework.

In November, the UN Security Council authorized the African Union to increase the number of AMISOM forces from 17,731 to 22,126 and approved the provision of non-lethal support to the Somali forces. Following the September attack on Kenya's Westgate mall, the United States claimed responsibility for at least one operation against Al-Shabaab inside Somalia.

In addition to their large military presence in Somalia, Kenya, and Ethiopia trained and provided military support to government-affiliated militia. Both focused on the status of border areas such as Lower Juba and Gedo, where they have been particularly involved in tense negotiations over the creation of the Jubaland region. Ahmed Mohamed Islam, known as "Madobe," a Kenyan ally, was chosen as the head of the interim administration.

The UN established a new country presence, the United Nations Assistance Mission in Somalia (UNSOM), which includes a human rights monitoring and reporting mandate.

Host countries of Somali refugees, particularly Kenya, seized on the apparent improvement of security in Mogadishu and the takeover of certain towns by AMISOM and government forces as grounds for potentially returning Somalis to their country. Furthermore, some EU member countries returned failed Somali asylum seekers to Mogadishu, contending that apparent improvements in Mogadishu meant they no longer needed protection on human rights grounds. The ongoing internal armed conflict in south-central Somalia means EU countries should carefully examine, on a case-by-case basis, whether returning a person to Mogadishu would pose a serious threat to that person.

In September, the European Court of Human Rights declared inadmissible a claim by a rejected Somali asylum seeker, paving the way for his return by Sweden to Somalia. The court failed to give sufficient weight to the ongoing displaced person crisis in Mogadishu and the volatile security situation, both of which could place anyone returned to the capital in serious jeopardy.

South Africa

South Africa continues to struggle with the legacy of apartheid and the challenges relating to addressing increasing demands from its citizens for the realization of economic and social rights as well as respect for fundamental civil and political freedoms. Although the government has been relatively successful in the provision of social services, financial mismanagement, and corruption—especially at the local government level—have seriously undermined progress in effective and efficient delivery of social and economic services.

Growing disaffection with local government, increasing poverty levels, and unemployment contributed to a resurgence of threats of violence against, and attacks on, property belonging to refugees, asylum-seekers, and migrants in the Eastern Cape and Gauteng provinces.

Xenophobic Attacks

In May and June, xenophobic attacks on the businesses and homes of refugees, asylum-seekers and migrants displaced hundreds of people in Gauteng. More than 60 foreign-owned shops were forced to close following violent looting and destruction by community members in the Orange Farm and Diepsloot areas of Gauteng. In June and September, similar attacks against Somali nationals in KwaZakhele and New Brighton in Port Elizabeth, in the Eastern Cape Province, left several shops looted and burnt. Due to the level of xenophobic violence, police had to relocate some of the foreign nationals to temporary shelters.

At time of writing no one had been arrested and charged with xenophobic violence. Instead, police arrested 21 people in Gauteng and charged them with public violence and arrested about 100 others in connection with the violence in Port Elizabeth. Official statements by members of both local and central governments have denied that violence against foreign nationals has been motivated by xenophobia or other forms of intolerance. Such statements have undermined the development of an effective, long-term strategy by the police to prevent xenophobic crimes by dealing with its root causes. On the other hand, some intervention strategies planned by local authorities in the affected areas, such as awareness campaigns and peace dialogues, sought to address xenophobia.

Inquiry into Killing of Marikana Miners

The investigation into the deaths of 44 people including the police killing of 34 miners between August 11 and 16, has been obstructed by delays of the work of the Farlam Commission of Inquiry, created to investigate the killings. The commission was asked by the government to conclude its investigation in four months, but its work slowed due to loss of vital documents (including video evidence), the deaths of witnesses, and an ongoing legal battle over state funding for lawyers representing the families of the miners killed, injured, and arrested.

The commission, which adjourned in May, resumed in July, but lawyers representing the injured and arrested miners requested another postponement, as they called on the government to cover the miners' legal fees. The presidency and minister of justice opposed the application for funding and the lawyers took their case to the North Gauteng High Court. In July, the High Court rejected the application for state funding, with Judge Raulinga ruling that the right to state funding was not absolute for the Marikana miners. Delays in submission of video evidence led to another extension of the inquiry to October 30. On October 31, President Jacob Zuma extended the term of the Farlam Commission to April 30, 2014.

Serious concerns remain about the ongoing conduct and capacity of the South African Police Services (SAPS), both in terms of the use of force in general, as well as the ability to deal with riots in a rights-respecting manner.

Sexual Orientation and Gender Identity

South Africa played an important but inconsistent role in advancing the human rights of LGBT people internationally. On the domestic front, South Africa faced challenges in responding to widespread violence (including rape and murder) against lesbians and transgender men in the country.

In 2011, South Africa was instrumental in introducing a precedent-setting resolution at the United Nations Human Rights Council on combating violence and discrimination against individuals on the basis of sexual orientation and gender identity, but has not played a decisive leadership role on this issue at the UN since then.

In May 2011, the Department of Justice and Constitutional Development established a National Task Team to address gender and sexual orientation-based violence against lesbian, gay, bisexual, transgender and intersex (LGBTI) persons. The Task Team, with representatives from government departments, independent bodies, and civil society, was tasked with developing, implementing, and monitoring a joint intervention strategy to address gender- and sexual orientation-based violence against LGBTI persons, especially in the courts and the criminal justice sector.

The Task Team became dormant and ineffectual, but has been moved to the Constitutional Development Branch of the Department of Justice and Constitutional Development and reinvigorated with new leadership, additional resources, the adoption of clear terms of reference, and the development of a national coordinated strategy to combat hate crime and ensure that bias crimes against LGBTI people are monitored and fast-tracked through the criminal justice system. If effective, this will go a long way to demonstrate the government's commitment to fight sexual and gender-based violence by conducting genuine and timely investigations and prosecutions of perpetrators of such violence.

Freedom of Expression

The controversial Protection of State Information Bill (the Secrecy Bill) remains a major concern in light of its restrictions on freedom of expression, freedom of information, press freedom, and democratic accountability. The bill, introduced in March 2010, has been criticized as inconsistent with South Africa's constitution and international human rights obligations. In April 2013, the bill was amended, and a slightly modified new version was adopted by the National Assembly. However, major concerns remain about the bill, as well as the lack of protection for whistleblowers and journalists exposing information as a matter of public interest. Under the new version of the bill, journalists or whistleblowers can potentially be arrested for reporting information deemed classified by the government that exposes corruption, mismanagement, or malfeasance—even in the face of a compelling public interest.

On September 10, President Zuma said he would not sign the Secrecy Bill, which he returned to parliament for redrafting. Zuma cited concerns with section 42 that relates to failure to report possession of classified information, and section

45 that relates to proper classification of information, stating that these lacked coherence and clarity and were therefore unconstitutional. Civil society groups welcomed the development but urged the government to address other draconian aspects of the bill including sections that provide harsh sentences and penalties for possession of information deemed by the government as classified.

Local civil society groups called on the government to amend the bill to ensure that it conformed to international standards on freedom of expression, including by providing a public interest defense. On November 12, parliament adopted a revised version of the bill but failed to address civil society concerns on its other draconian aspects. The bill was returned to the president for assent. At time of writing, he had not signed the bill.

Women's Rights

The controversial Traditional Court's Bill that was withdrawn from parliament in 2012 went through a new consultation process during the first half of 2013. Following public hearings on the draft bill, the government sent the report of the consultation to South Africa's nine provinces to determine whether they supported the bill. The bill has been criticized for giving traditional leaders the authority to enforce controversial versions of customary law that infringe upon women's rights such as the practice of *ukutwala* (forced marriage), as well as discriminatory social and economic practices, such as denial of access to land, and inheritance.

Disability Rights

Despite progressive legislation on disabilities and ratification of the Convention on the Rights of Persons with Disabilities, children with disabilities, especially those living in institutions in rural areas, have limited access to mainstream education and are particularly vulnerable to physical and sexual abuse. Disability advocates have raised serious concerns about the quality of institutional care provided to children with disabilities and the lack of government oversight.

Rights of Asylum Seekers

In defiance of court orders, the Department of Home Affairs refused to reopen three of its seven Refugee Reception Offices, closed in 2011. The closures, which were part of the department's plan to move asylum-processing to the country's borders, have limited asylum seekers' access not only to the asylum procedure, but also to work permits, adequate shelter, and assistance while their refugee claims are pending. On June 20, the Eastern Cape High Court once again ordered the government to reopen the Port Elizabeth Refugee Reception Centre and ensure that it was fully functional by October 1. At time of writing, the reception center had not been reopened.

South Africa's Foreign Policy

South Africa since the end of apartheid has been an important and influential voice in debates over international responses to human rights issues in Africa and globally. It has twice been elected non-permanent member of the United Nations Security Council; it is a member of the trilateral forum, IBSA, composed of India, Brazil, and South Africa; and the BRICS grouping of emerging economies of Brazil, Russia, India, China, and South Africa. Its role in the African Union (AU) and as a mediator and contributor to peacekeeping forces on the continent has also grown rapidly. In November, South Africa was elected to the UN Human Rights Council.

The post-apartheid South African government has successfully created domestic standards based on the ideals of fairness, justice, and human rights that have to a greater extent shaped the country's approach to its foreign policy. South African foreign policy has consistently reflected a desire to fully integrate the country into the global system. At the same time, its foreign policy remains sensitive to the country's apartheid history, leading to the country's desire to be seen as an internationally responsible actor, a bridge between developed and developing countries, and a representative of Africa's interests in global affairs.

South Africa's history has also led it to view foreign policy through the lens of its own history of achieving locally informed, negotiated solutions to political situations and conflicts where the achievement of peace and justice were sought as mutually reinforcing imperatives.

These different competing strands of foreign policy have often manifested in an inconsistent and sometimes contradictory application of South Africa's foreign policy ideals, and a failure to consistently align foreign policy with the human rights principles articulated in the country's constitution.

In the past year, South Africa took positions on political crises in various countries that have at times been at odds with its human rights principles. In August, South Africa, which played a key role in mediating the political crisis in Zimbabwe, endorsed Zimbabwe's flawed July elections which led to President Robert Mugabe winning a seventh term.

In Syria, South Africa's expressions of concern at the political situation and escalation of violence, including the use of chemical weapons by the Syrian government, have been tempered by reluctance to condemn abuses committed by President Bashar al-Assad against his own citizens. Instead, South Africa has repeatedly emphasized the importance of all parties involved in the Syrian conflict engaging in an inclusive national dialogue to reach a negotiated settlement. Conversely, South Africa has strongly condemned the July military takeover of power in Egypt and ongoing abuses by the military. South Africa has also strongly supported the AU's decision to suspend Egypt from the regional body for an "unconstitutional change of government."

South Africa has consistently worked to bring about peace and stability and an end to abuses in the Democratic Republic of Congo, with the deployment of South African forces to the intervention brigade under the auspices of the United Nations Organization Stabilization Mission in the Democratic Republic of the Congo (MONUSCO) in the eastern DRC. South Africa has also played key roles in peace and reconstruction initiatives and the restoration of rights in South Sudan and Somalia.

South Sudan

South Sudan's second year as an independent nation was marked by political and economic uncertainty, violence in the eastern state of Jonglei, and ongoing repression of civil and political rights.

South Sudan and Sudan signed a series of agreements to resolve various outstanding issues in September 2012, but the relations between the two governments remain tense. Southern oil began flowing again through Sudan in April after a 2012 shutdown by South Sudan, but in June Khartoum threatened to stop transportation, accusing Juba of supporting rebels in its territory.

In July, President Salva Kiir dismissed his entire cabinet and appointed a new vice president and 21 new ministers, downsizing the cabinet from 28 ministries. In Jonglei state, an abusive government anti-insurgency operation against a rebel group in the area worsened brutal ethnic violence in 2013.

The government has not adequately responded to unlawful killings, arrests and detentions, and other human rights violations by its security forces. Lack of capacity and inadequate training of police, prosecutors, and judges give rise to numerous human rights violations in the administration of justice.

Legislative Developments

The South Sudan Legislative Assembly (SSLA) passed three media bills in July, including a Right of Access to Information bill, more than six years after the bills were drafted. President Kiir had yet to sign the bills into law at time of writing. Journalists hope the legislation will reduce unlawful arrests and harassment of media workers, including by officers from the National Security Service (NSS) who continue to operate without legal authority.

Kiir's cabinet endorsed the ratification of seven core international human rights instruments in early 2013, including the International Covenant on Civil and Political Rights. The SSLA ratified the African Charter on Human and Peoples' Rights and the AU Convention Governing Specific Aspects of Refugee Problems in Africa, the UN Convention Against Torture and Other Cruel, Inhuman or Degrading Treatment or Punishment and the Convention on the Rights of the Child in late 2013, but others were still pending approval at time of writing.

South Sudan's first elections since independence are due in 2015, but preparations have lagged. The mandate of the National Constitution Review Commission, tasked with conducting broad consultation ahead of drafting a new constitution by January 9, 2013, was extended to December 31, 2014. At time of writing, President Kiir had not sworn in members of the political parties' council, delaying registration and re-registration of all political parties, required under the 2012 Political Parties Act. Parties cannot conduct any political work or other activities until registered.

Weaknesses in the justice system give rise to human rights violations, including prolonged periods of pretrial detention, lack of defense counsel, and poor detention conditions. Although South Sudan voted in favor of the UN General Assembly moratorium on the use of the death penalty in December 2012, at least four people were reported to have been executed in November.

South Sudan's laws on marriage, separation, divorce, and related matters requires urgent reform, as almost half of South Sudanese girls between 15 and 19 are married, some as young as 12. South Sudan has no legislation that clearly sets 18 as the minimum age of marriage. Lack of a national plan of action that sets out comprehensive strategies to address child marriage has undermined efforts to curb the practice. Marital rape is also still not recognized as a criminal offense.

Anti-Insurgency Abuses and Ethnic Conflict in Jonglei State

Conflict between South Sudan's army and a rebel group largely drawing support from the Murle ethnic group continued in 2013. Inter-ethnic conflict has intensified in recent years in Jonglei, with thousands killed.

An abusive 2012 government disarmament campaign helped reignite an earlier Murle insurgency. During its counterinsurgency the Sudan People's Liberation Army (SPLA) committed serious violations of international human rights and humanitarian law, especially in Murle areas. Soldiers unlawfully targeted and killed Murle civilians and caused thousands to flee their homes out of fear of attack. Soldiers also looted or destroyed homes, schools, churches, and the compounds of aid agencies, deepening Murle perceptions of persecution. At least three health facilities in Murle areas were looted and almost completely destroyed by government soldiers and rebels.

The government is conducting the anti-insurgency operation amid intense inter-ethnic fighting between Lou Nuer, Murle, and Dinka groups, often provoked by cattle raids and other attacks. The government has repeatedly failed to protect communities from these clashes or arrest or prosecute those responsible.

In revenge for Murle attacks on Lou Nuer in 2012 and in February 2013 in which at least 85 people were killed, thousands of armed Lou Nuer attacked Murle areas in July, killing over 300 Murle according to local government officials. The army did not attempt to protect Murle civilians, many of whom had fled towns to the bush because of army abuses. Credible allegations that the Lou Nuer were given ammunition by South Sudan's army have not been fully investigated. An investigation committee established by the government in 2012 to research human rights abuses and causes of violence in Jonglei state has still not received funds to begin its work.

Abuses by Security Forces

Soldiers detained, beat, and attacked civilians and civilian property in various locations across the country during 2013.

Citing worsening criminality including armed robbery and inter-clan attacks, the president in January replaced the elected governor of Lakes state with military strongman Matur Chuot Dhuol. Dhuol sidestepped the courts, police, and the prisons service and ordered the army to arrest and detain suspects. Soldiers rounded up dozens of men in February and March 2013, often detaining others from the same village if they could not find the suspects, and held them in military facilities in extremely harsh conditions for weeks or months and subjected many to severe beatings.

In Eastern Equatoria, soldiers reportedly killed six civilians when soldiers attacked Orema village on April 15, 2013, apparently in revenge for the killing of security forces by armed civilians during an earlier cattle raiding incident.

Soldiers continue to occupy schools, and 26 schools were occupied at some point in 2013, mostly in Jonglei and Eastern Equatoria states. On August 14, the army announced a zero tolerance policy of child recruitment or the occupation of schools.

HUMAN
RIGHTS
WATCH

"This Old Man Can Feed Us,
You Will Marry Him"
Child and Forced Marriage in South Sudan

Freedom of Expression and Association

Authorities have not fully investigated the killings of eight peaceful protesters in Wau in December 2012 by security forces or dozens of unlawful arrests of others, many from the Fertit ethnic group, who openly opposed the decision of the governor of Western Bahr el Ghazal state's to move a county headquarters. The courts conducted trials of individuals accused of ethnically-motivated crimes and perceived government opponents on a variety of charges. None of the cases brought before the court related to the protester shootings.

In January, three NSS officers arrested a journalist at gunpoint in Juba, slapped him in the face, and held him overnight in an NSS detention center. A radio journalist and two public commentators fled South Sudan after receiving threats in early 2013, including from government officials. In May, the editor and managing editor of the *Juba Monitor* were arrested, detained, and subsequently released for allegedly defaming the deputy minister of the interior. A government investigation into the killing on December 5, 2012, of a well-known commentator and journalist, Isaiah Abraham, by unidentified gunmen outside his home in Juba has stalled.

Two lawyers from South Sudan's Law Society received death threats after launching a legal challenge against a presidential decree that forbade Pagan Amum, former secretary general of South Sudan's leading Sudan People's Liberation Movement (SPLM) political party, from speaking to media.

Political Instability

Power plays within the ruling SPLM continued with Vice President Riek Machar announcing on July 4 that he will contest South Sudan's presidency in 2015. In mid-April, President Kiir, by presidential decree, withdrew executive powers delegated to Machar and replaced him with Archbishop Daniel Deng as head of the national reconciliation process.

In a sweeping move on July 23, President Kiir fired Machar and all national ministers and undersecretaries by presidential decree. He then appointed James Wani Igga as vice president and appointed a new, smaller cabinet of ministers. Kiir also sacked Pagan Amum on the same day for insubordination, including using public media to discredit the party.

HUMAN
RIGHTS
WATCH

"They Are Killing Us"
Abuses Against Civilians in South Sudan's Pibor County

Kiir removed governors of Unity and Lakes states in 2013, appointing new governors without holding fresh elections, as required under South Sudan's transitional constitution, triggering complaints of presidential heavy-handedness by some members of civil society.

Meanwhile, South Sudan's relations with Sudan remained tense. Both countries accused the other of supporting rebel groups in their territory. South Sudan halted oil production in February 2012 after a row between the two countries over oil transportation fees through Sudan's territory. A September 2012 agreement paved the way for the resolution of outstanding issues including oil flows, but implementation has been troubled with both sides threatening to cut oil flow and disagreements over the status of Abyei.

Key International Actors

The United Nations Mission in South Sudan (UNMISS) has a mandate to use force to protect civilians under imminent threat of serious harm, but its failure to intervene against a clear pattern of unlawful killings and other serious violations by South Sudan's army in Murle areas of Pibor state has undermined public confidence in the peacekeepers.

In addition, the mission failed to publicly report on violations by security forces in Jonglei and other locations where serious abuses occurred in 2012 such as in Wau and Rumbek, reinforcing a perception that the mission values its relationship with the government over holding authorities to account for violations.

South Sudan's army shot down an UNMISS helicopter in December 2012 in Jonglei, and peacekeepers have been attacked there several times by unknown attackers. On April 9, unknown gunmen killed five peacekeepers and seven civilian staff in Pibor county.

The mandate for the UN Interim Security Force for Abyei (UNISFA) peacekeeping force was renewed on May 29, increasing its authorized force number from 4,200 to 5,326 troops.

The United States, United Kingdom, and other western supporters of South Sudan's government were critical of the government's human rights record and especially violations in Jonglei state. The African Union continued to play a mediation role between Sudan and South Sudan.

Sudan

Fighting between Sudanese forces and rebel groups continued in Sudan's war-torn peripheries and was marked by serious violations of international humanitarian and human rights law.

In Darfur, authorities failed to protect people from intensified inter-communal clashes, particularly between Arab pastoral groups. Sudanese forces also attacked communities presumed to support rebel groups. In Southern Kordofan and Blue Nile, Sudan's indiscriminate bombing and ongoing clashes with rebels, and the obstruction of humanitarian assistance to rebel-held areas since the outbreak of conflict in June 2011, have displaced tens of thousands within those states and elsewhere in Sudan and forced more than 225,000 to flee to refugee camps in South Sudan and Ethiopia.

Sudanese security forces continued to arrest and detain activists, opposition party members, and people suspected of links to rebel groups. Authorities also censored the media and restricted space for civil society, stepping up at the end of 2012 the harassment of groups that receive foreign funding.

In September, protests, some of them violent, swept the country in response to hikes in the price of fuel and other basic commodities. Sudanese forces responded to the protests with live ammunition, and are implicated in the killing of more than 175 protesters. Security officials detained hundreds of protesters and opposition members and activists, many for weeks without charge, and stifled media coverage of the protests.

Conflict and Abuses in Darfur

More than 500,000 people were displaced by conflict in 2013, a number far exceeding previous years. The vast majority of Darfur's displaced population, estimated around 2.5 million people, remain in camps in Darfur and Chad.

Communal violence, especially between Arab pastoralist groups, significantly increased in 2013. Sudanese government forces were unwilling or unable to protect civilians and in some cases participated in the fighting. In April, Ali Kosheib, a known militia leader who is wanted by the International Criminal Court (ICC) for alleged crimes in Darfur, participated in large-scale attacks on ethnic Salamat villages in Central Darfur, before being seriously wounded in May.

Government forces and allied militia carried out large-scale attacks, including aerial bombing, on locations believed by the government to be controlled by rebel groups. In February, government forces attacked Golo and Guldo in eastern Jebel Mara, killing an unknown number of civilians and forcing tens of thousands to flee to safer areas. In early April, government forces bombed and attacked the towns of Labado and Muhajariya and several other villages in South Darfur, and reportedly burned and looted homes and killed dozens of civilians and displaced tens of thousands.

Sudan continued to deny peacekeepers from the African Union-United Nations Mission in Darfur (UNAMID) access to much of Darfur. Insecurity also undermined UNAMID's work. Armed attackers in Darfur killed 12 peacekeepers and injured many more between July and October alone.

Authorities have not prosecuted the vast majority of serious crimes committed in violation of international humanitarian and human rights law during the Darfur conflict. Although some pro-government media outlets reported that the government's special prosecutor investigated numerous cases, few if any Sudanese government forces or militia have been prosecuted, and Sudan has failed to implement justice reforms recommended in a 2009 report by the AU High-Level Panel on Darfur, the lead mediation body.

Sudan has not cooperated with the ICC; arrest warrants or summonses for six men, including President Omar al-Bashir, on charges of genocide, crimes against humanity and war crimes remain outstanding. A case involving alleged war crimes committed by one rebel leader proceeded at the ICC, while proceedings against a second rebel leader were terminated following his death.

Conflict and Abuses in Southern Kordofan and Blue Nile

In Southern Kordofan and Blue Nile, Sudanese government forces continued to fight with the Sudan Revolutionary Front (SRF), a rebel coalition formed by the Sudan People's Liberation Army-North (SPLA-North) and Darfur rebel groups in 2011. In April, fighting spread to North Kordofan, displacing tens of thousands.

The conflict remains marked by serious violations of international human rights and humanitarian law, including indiscriminate bombing that has killed and maimed scores of people; destroyed schools, clinics, and other civilian buildings; and instilled fear in the population.

More than a million people have been forced to flee from their homes; at least 230,000 live in refugee camps in South Sudan or Ethiopia. Sudan obstructed humanitarian access to tens of thousands displaced in areas controlled by the SPLA-North.

Sudanese government forces have also carried out mass detentions and prosecutions in the two states. From November 2012 until May 2013, authorities detained 32 ethnic Nuba women from Southern Kordofan without charge because of their suspected affiliation with the Sudan People's Liberation Movement-North (SPLM-North), the opposition party Sudan banned in 2011. Authorities have also brought charges against dozens of men from Blue Nile state in an anti-terrorism court on the basis of their presumed links to the rebel movement.

Restrictions on Freedom of Assembly, Association

In September, government security forces shot tear gas, rubber bullets, and live ammunition at protesters during sometimes violent mass protests, using excessive force. Sudanese human rights groups reported that more than 175 people, most of them teenagers or in their early twenties, were killed by shooting during the protests.

Security forces also shot and killed at least seven people including two children in Nyala, South Darfur, during September protests over the killing by militia of a prominent businessman. Government forces have also violently dispersed student protests on several other occasions across the country during the year. In May, security forces shot at students at El Fashir University, North Darfur, injuring eight.

Sudanese authorities targeted and harassed, intimidated, and closed some civil society organizations, in particular several that had received foreign funding. In December 2012, security officials shut down three civil society groups and one literary forum, and summoned leaders of other groups for questioning.

Authorities have obstructed groups from legally registering and refused permission for or cancelled public activities in towns across Sudan.

In early 2013, authorities also shut down Nuba and Christian groups, arresting staff and confiscating property. Church leaders were questioned about sources of funding, and the government deported or otherwise forced to leave Sudan more than 170 foreign church members.

Politically Motivated Arrest and Detention

After a cut in fuel subsidies sparked mass demonstrations in September, National Intelligence and Security Service (NISS) officials detained hundreds of protestors and opposition party members and activists, arresting many from their homes. NISS detained hundreds without charge, many of them for several weeks.

In January, security officials detained six leading members of Sudan's political opposition parties, apparently for attending a meeting of opposition groups that signed an opposition agreement known as the New Dawn Charter, and held them without access to lawyers or appropriate medical care for at least 10 weeks before their release without charge.

Despite a pledge in April by President al-Bashir to release all political prisoners, scores remained in detention without charges, many from conflict-affected parts of the country. In July, authorities arrested more than 24 people, including ethnic Nuba and Darfuri student activists, for their perceived links to rebel groups.

Restrictions on Press Freedom

Despite a pledge in May to halt prepublication censorship of newspapers, whereby security officials remove articles before a newspaper goes to print, authorities have continuously censored media. They have suspended publication of some papers, confiscated printed editions, suspended individual journalists, blocked websites, and harassed and threatened journalists with prosecution for criticizing the government

In September, authorities tightened restrictions on media to prevent coverage of the protests. Security officials instructed newspaper editors not to publish articles related to the protests, confiscated editions of three newspapers, sum-

moned several journalists for questioning, jammed the reception of international TV stations, and blocked the Internet for one day. Most newspapers and the
TV stations have resumed, but remain under tight scrutiny.

Stalled Law Reform

Sudan has yet to pass a new permanent constitution, despite the end of the
transition period in the 2005 Comprehensive Peace Agreement, during which it
had adopted an Interim National Constitution, and the secession of South
Sudan.

The National Security Act of 2010 and many other laws contravene basic human
rights norms. Authorities continued to apply Shari'a law sanctions that violate
international prohibitions on cruel, inhuman, or degrading punishment. On
February 14, Sudan implemented a penalty of cross-amputation, the amputation
of the right hand and the left foot. Women and girls continue to be subjected to
flogging and other humiliating punishments under discriminatory public order
laws.

In July, parliament passed amendments to the Sudan Armed Forces Act of 2007
that subject civilians to the jurisdiction of military courts for a range of broadly
defined offences such as undermining the constitutional system, leaking classified information, and the publication of "false news."

Key International Actors

Sudan's relations with South Sudan remained tense in 2013, with both countries accusing the other of support to rebel movements. Implementation of a
September 2012 agreement signed by Sudan and South Sudan was slow. The
agreement addresses a range of outstanding issues, including oil production,
debt, the status of the nationals of one country resident in the other, border
security, and resolution of border disputes. The status of the contested area of
Abyei remains unresolved.

The United Nations, African Union, and key nations involved in Sudan continued
to press for implementation of the September 2012 agreement but made little
progress addressing Sudan's internal armed conflicts or human rights record.

In September, the AU extended the mandate of its High-Level Implementation Panel to December 2014. The UN extended the mandates of the peacekeeping missions in Darfur and Abyei, while the UN Human Rights Committee extended the mandate of the independent expert on Sudan.

Efforts by advocacy groups in relation to the ICC arrest warrant for President al-Bashir's appeared to again restrict his international travel. He cut short a July trip to Nigeria and cancelled September plans to attend the UN General Assembly.

In October, the European Parliament adopted a strong resolution on the human rights situation in Sudan urging the Sudanese Government "to cease all forms of repression against those who exercise their right to freedom of expression, both online and offline, and to protect journalists."

Uganda

After 27 years in office, President Yoweri Museveni's government increasingly suppresses freedom of assembly, expression, and association while escalating threats to civil society. Two media houses faced temporary closure in 2013 for publishing articles suggesting that Museveni is grooming his son to take over the presidency. Debate around presidential succession, accountability of public resources, governance, and other politically sensitive topics is increasingly constrained. Activists who provide public information about government expenditure and corruption are obstructed from demonstrating and sometimes face criminal charges such as inciting violence, while opposition politicians are regularly prevented from holding public rallies.

Freedom of Assembly and Expression

After two years of sporadic debate, Parliament passed the Public Order Management bill in August 2013 and the president assented shortly after, further restricting space for dissent and public critiques of governance. The controversial bill was considerably amended just before passage, but it remains vague, making it open to abusive application. The law still grants police wide discretionary powers to permit or disallow public meetings.

Throughout the year opposition politicians faced arrest, detention, and criminal charges for holding public assemblies in Uganda. In July, seven opposition politicians were charged in a Kampala court for belonging to and managing an "unlawful society," Activists for Change (A4C), a political pressure group the government had banned in 2012 on spurious grounds. Earlier, in February, 15 people, including the mayor of Kampala and then-opposition leader Kizza Besigye, were charged with organizing an unlawful assembly. Both cases were pending at time of writing.

The government continues to be hostile to independent media publishing politically sensitive articles. On May 7, the *Daily Monitor* newspaper detailed an alleged conspiracy to frame or eliminate high-ranking members of the government who do not support the plan for Museveni's son to take over when his father steps down. On May 20, more than 50 uniformed police sealed off the *Daily Monitor*'s premises after it published a letter allegedly written by Uganda's coordinator of intelligence service, Gen. David Sejjusa. Two radio stations located in the same compound were also forced off air by the Uganda Communications Commission. The same day, police closed the *Red Pepper*, another newspaper, on similar grounds. Three days later, the court withdrew the search warrant but police defied the orders and increased their presence. Two journalists and eight civil society members protesting the closures were arrested, beaten, and detained by police. They were charged with inciting violence before being released. The newspapers and radio stations were opened 10 days later when the minister of internal affairs ordered the police to vacate the premises. The charges were still pending at time of writing.

Corruption

Corruption in Uganda remains pervasive at both low and high levels of public administration. Bribery, nepotism, and misuse of official positions and resources are widespread in spite of continuous assurances from the president that corruption will be eradicated. Major corruption scandals have surfaced repeatedly in the last few years, though no high-ranking officials have served prison sentences for corruption-related offences. Scandals have rocked the health services, particularly regarding the misuse of funds intended for the provision of immunizations and essential medicines to fight HIV, tuberculosis, and malaria.

The embezzlement in 2012 of US$12.7 million in donor funds from the Office of the Prime Minister, which was designated for the rehabilitation of the war-ravaged areas of northern Uganda, led donors to withdraw their budget support in February. Donors, who fund about 25 percent of Uganda's budget, demanded repayment when the auditor general discovered the misappropriation of the funds. The principal accountant in the Prime Minister's Office was convicted of abuse of office and forgery, but other officials implicated in the scandal were never charged.

Police have silenced and obstructed activists working to raise corruption issues and educate citizens about public sector accountability. Members of 50 civil society groups have come together in solidarity and wear black every Monday to raise awareness of corruption issues. Known as the Black Monday Movement, the campaign publishes and distributes monthly newsletters that highlight the

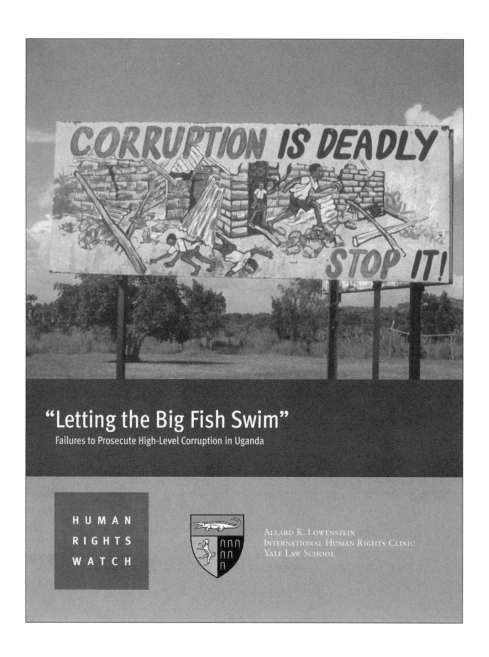

impact of corruption on various sectors, such as education and health, and protests the impunity that government officials enjoy.

In the first 10 months of 2013, police arrested and charged at least 28 individuals handing out Black Monday materials. Nineteen were charged with inciting violence; five with possession of prohibited publications; and three with spreading harmful propaganda. Most of the 28 were stopped from distributing Black Monday materials and were detained for between three and ten hours by police before being released without charge.

Illegal Arrest and Detention

The Ugandan government continues to grapple with the Allied Democratic Forces (ADF) rebels based in the Democratic Republic of Congo (DRC), a group composed predominantly of Ugandan Muslims of the Salaf sect. In 2013, Human Rights Watch documented over two dozen cases of illegal arrest and detention of Salaf Muslims. Those arrested were detained for between one week and four months, often moved to various detention locations, then released without charge or brought before a court. Family members often could not identify where their relatives had been detained, and police often denied knowledge of the arrests.

Accountability for Past Abuses

In 2009 and 2011, police and military police killed at least 49 people, but police have not conducted serious or meaningful investigations into these killings. Relatives continue to search for justice through civil cases against the government. The Uganda Human Rights Commission ordered compensation for two families for the deaths of their children at the hands of security forces, but the money was never paid. In December 2011, police disbanded its Rapid Response Unit but there have been no investigations into the killings or torture by officers in the unit. Similarly, no inquiries have been made by the Ugandan army into cases of people who were tortured or died in the custody of the Joint Anti-Terrorism Task Force (JATT).

The Lord's Resistance Army

The Ugandan rebel group the Lord's Resistance Army (LRA) was active across the Central African Republic, southern Sudan, and northern Democratic Republic of Congo (DRC), with allegations of killings and abductions, though on a much lesser scale than previous years.

Warrants issued in 2005 by the International Criminal Court (ICC) for LRA leaders remain outstanding. Former LRA fighter Thomas Kwoyelo, charged with willful killing, taking hostages, and extensive destruction of property, has been imprisoned in Uganda since March 2009 but his trial has not begun. The Supreme Court has not yet heard the state's 2012 appeal of the High Court ruling ordering Kwoyelo to be granted amnesty and released.

In May, Uganda's parliament reinstated legislation for another two years granting amnesty to members of armed groups who surrender, though those wanted on ICC warrants were explicitly not eligible. Sections of the Amnesty Act had been allowed to lapse in May 2012, and through the new extension of the powers of the Amnesty Commission, those who were not eligible during the interim period now will now in theory qualify for amnesty.

Bills Violating Human Rights Law

The Anti-Homosexuality Bill, which proposes the death penalty for some consensual same-sex activities, and the HIV/AIDS Prevention and Control Act, which criminalizes intentional or attempted transmission of HIV, are before parliamentary committees and could still be tabled for debate and vote at any time. Both have been pending since 2009.

Key International Actors

Following the October 2012 US$12.7 million corruption scandal in the Office of the Prime Minister, the governments of Denmark, Ireland, Norway, Sweden, and the United Kingdom suspended budget support. Donors reported that the government needed to take action to restore confidence before financial support would resume. The World Bank suspended the ninth Poverty Reduction Support Credit in December 2012 but eventually released it in June 2013. While the bank will not proceed with the tenth, it indicated it is open to using budget support in exceptional cases to support governance or sectoral reforms. Since then, most have turned to project support and reduced or stopped direct budget support. For international development assistance to address corruption, Uganda's donors should significantly increase the focus on accountability at the highest levels of government, and ensure that any reengagement is based on substantive changes to Uganda's anti-corruption structures. External donors should also actively and vocally support civil society working to document and raise awareness of corruption, by both financially supporting their work and publicly denouncing arrests and harassment of activists.

International bilateral donors continue to press the government to respect lesbian, gay, bisexual, transgender, and intersex (LGBTI) rights including pushing police leadership to meet with LGBTI activists and improve communication and response to threats to members of the LGBTI community.

In contrast, there continues to be minimal criticism of security force conduct, such as the killings during protests in 2009 and 2011 and past and current torture cases. The army continues to receive logistical support and training from the US for counterterrorism, its leading role in the African Union Mission in Somalia (AMISOM), and counter-LRA operations in the Central African Republic (CAR).

Zimbabwe

National elections in July ended a five-year power-sharing coalition, retained Robert Mugabe as president, and gave his Zimbabwe African Union–Patriotic Front (ZANU-PF) over two-thirds parliamentary majority. Although the election was peaceful, the electoral process had major flaws, including highly partisan statements by the leadership of the security forces, restrictions on and intimidation of journalists and civil society activists, and a skewed voter registration process.

The opposition party, Movement for Democratic Change (MDC), and key international actors including the United Kingdom, the United States, the European Union, and Australia criticized the electoral process, differing with the Southern African Development Community (SADC) and the African Union (AU), which endorsed the elections. The discord among key actors diminished international pressure to address the disputed election and help resolve Zimbabwe's pressing human rights and governance issues, which ZANU-PF has been unwilling to seriously address.

National Elections

A generally peaceful environment characterized the build-up to the holding of presidential, parliamentary, and local government elections on July 31. However, the elections were marred by widespread irregularities raised by local monitors, including reports of voter intimidation by Zimbabwe's security forces, traditional leaders coercing villagers to vote for ZANU-PF, a high number of "ghost" or duplicate voters present on the voters' roll, and credible reports that large numbers of people were unfairly turned away from polling stations. The Zimbabwe Electoral Commission (ZEC) failed to make available the voters' roll to political parties in advance of elections as required by law.

State-owned media openly aligned with, and campaigned for ZANU-PF, while vilifying the MDC. State media also failed to offer equal and impartial coverage to all political parties participating in the elections. These irregularities call into question the credibility and fairness of the election. The build-up to the elections was also marked by the failure of the former coalition government, made up of ZANU-PF and the two MDC factions, to implement needed human rights reforms.

The MDC presidential candidate, Morgan Tsvangirai, challenged in court the validity of the election in which Robert Mugabe won the presidential vote with his ZANU-PF party winning over two thirds of the parliamentary vote. When the court refused to compel ZEC to provide material that could be used to electoral malpractices and irregularities, Tsvangirai withdrew his court petition paving the way for Mugabe to be sworn as president on August 22.

The New Constitution

The enactment of a new constitution has not resulted in improving the human rights environment, largely due to ZANU-PF's failure to implement the rights provisions in the new constitution. The government has neither taken steps to enact new laws to operationalize the constitution, nor has it amended existing laws as necessary to bring them in line with the new constitution's provisions. The government also needs to fully and impartially enforce domestic laws by holding accountable all those responsible for human rights abuses and politically motivated violence.

Under the new constitution, political parties are able to propagate their views and canvass for support, free of harassment and intimidation. It enshrines respect for the rule of law, and commits the government to fully implement and realize the rights to freedom of association, assembly, expression, and information.

While the establishment of an independent and credible human rights commission is set out in the new constitution, there are significant concerns with the commission. The law establishing the commission states that it can only investigate alleged human rights abuses since February 2009. This prevents the commission from investigating previous serious crimes, including election-related violence in 2002, 2005, and 2008; the massacre of an estimated 20,000 people in the Matebeleland and Midlands provinces in the 1980s; and the government-led mass demolitions of homes and evictions of 2005. At time of writing, the human rights commission had no substantive chairperson, lacked sufficient resources, and had no support staff.

HUMAN RIGHTS WATCH

RACE AGAINST TIME

The Need for Legal and Institutional Reforms
Ahead of Zimbabwe's Elections

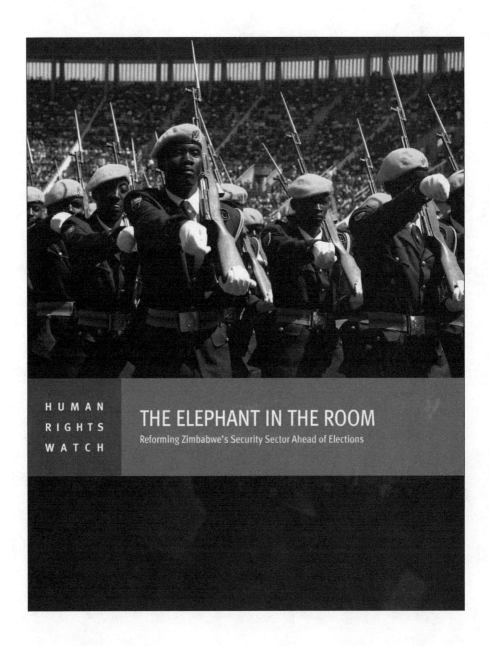

HUMAN
RIGHTS
WATCH

THE ELEPHANT IN THE ROOM
Reforming Zimbabwe's Security Sector Ahead of Elections

Conduct of Security Forces

The security forces have a long history of partisanship on behalf of President Mugabe and the ruling ZANU-PF party. The partisanship of the security forces' leadership has translated into abuses by these forces against MDC members and supporters, and civil society organizations.

Although the new constitution obligates the security forces to be politically neutral and impartial, this constitutional requirement has been disregarded. Beyond the open endorsement of ZANU-PF, in advance of the 2013 elections, security forces intimidated, beat, and committed other abuses against Zimbabweans perceived to be supporting the MDC or critical of the government. Members of the security forces have committed these abuses with almost absolute impunity.

Freedom of Expression, Association, and Assembly

Both the power-sharing government prior to August 2013 and the new administration have failed to amend repressive laws, such as the Access to Information and Protection of Privacy Act (AIPPA), the Public Order and Security Act (POSA), and the Criminal Law Codification and Reform Act, which severely curtail basic rights through vague defamation clauses and draconian penalties. Failure to amend or repeal these laws and to address the partisan conduct of the police severely limits the rights to freedom of association and assembly.

Sections of AIPPA and POSA that provide criminal penalties for defamation, or for undermining the authority of, or insulting the president, have routinely been used against journalists and human rights defenders. Police often misuse provisions of POSA to ban lawful public meetings and gatherings. Activists and journalists continue to be wrongly prosecuted and charged under these laws. For instance, on May 7, police arrested Dumisani Muleya, editor of the Zimbabwe *Independent*, and Owen Gagare, its chief reporter, following the publication of an article on the security forces. The two were detained for eight hours, then charged with "publishing or communicating false statements prejudicial to the State."

Sexual Orientation and Gender Identity

Attacks against lesbian, gay, bisexual, and transgender (LGBT) individuals and rights activists continue to emanate from the highest level of government. During his election campaign in July, President Mugabe (who has a long history of making homophobic statements) reiterated that LGBT citizens are "worse than dogs and pigs," and threatened to behead them. The new constitution does not explicitly recognize LGBT rights, and in his inauguration speech on August 22, Mugabe attacked same-sex marriage, which the new constitution prohibits, saying it was a "filthy, filthy, filthy disease."

These attacks on LGBT people, arbitrary arrests of LGBT activists by the police, and the harassment by state agents of the Gays and Lesbian of Zimbabwe (GALZ) nongovernmental organization in previous years, have driven many LGBT people underground.

Human Rights Defenders

A campaign of politically motivated abuses against civil society by the police began in December 2012 under the coalition government, and continues under the new administration. Police repeatedly arrested members of Women of Zimbabwe Arise as they peacefully protested human rights violations and the economic situation.

Other attacks included the arbitrary arrest on March 17 and eight-day detention of human rights lawyer Beatrice Mtetwa, on charges of obstructing justice despite a High Court order for her release. In the lead-up to the July elections, police charged a number of civil society leaders, including Jestina Mukoko, director of the Zimbabwe Peace Project, Okay Machisa, director of Zimbabwe Human Rights Association, and Abel Chikomo, director of Zimbabwe Human Rights NGO Forum, with alleged violations of various laws under what appeared to be politically motivated attempts to curtail the human rights work of civil society organizations. Chikomo was required to report to the Harare police station on numerous occasions throughout the year and was eventually summoned to stand trial on August 1. At time of writing, Chikomo and Mtetwa's trials were ongoing.

Key International Actors

Through its facilitation team, South Africa, appointed by SADC as mediator in Zimbabwe's political negotiations, strongly pushed for key reforms ahead of elections. However, South Africa eventually succumbed to pressure from Mugabe and ZANU-PF to stop raising concerns about electoral and human rights conditions ahead of the elections. ZANU-PF directed particularly venomous attacks at Ambassador Lindiwe Zulu, a vocal member of the Facilitation Team. Initially, South Africa did not comment on the elections, but eventually made an about-turn and congratulated Zimbabwe on holding "successful elections," while refraining from commenting on the credibility or fairness of the elections and the lack of the key reforms it had been pushing for.

SADC also failed to press Mugabe and ZANU-PF to implement key human rights and institutional reforms ahead of the elections, as its recommendations were repeatedly ignored by ZANU-PF. Subsequently, SADC and the AU endorsed the July elections, describing them as "free, peaceful, and generally credible," ignoring widespread electoral flaws that violated SADC's elections standards. Regional endorsement has emboldened the government of Zimbabwe to ignore pressing human rights and governance concerns.

The European Union welcomed the generally peaceful and orderly manner in which the elections were conducted but raised concerns about "alleged irregularities and reports of incomplete participation, as well as the identified weaknesses in the electoral process and a lack of transparency." Similarly the UK commended Zimbabwe on holding peaceful elections while expressing "grave concerns over the conduct of the election." The US said the Zimbabwe election was deeply flawed, while Australia called for a rerun of the election.

The ability of key international actors to apply pressure on Zimbabwe for a resolution of the election dispute, and for improvements in human rights and governance, was largely nullified by SADC and the AU's endorsement of the July elections. On Zimbabwe, the EU, the UK, and the US had previously deferred to SADC and the AU, whose response to the flawed July elections weakened international efforts to ensure restoration of the rule of law and respect for human rights.

THE RISK OF RETURNING HOME

Violence and Threats against Displaced People
Reclaiming Land in Colombia

WORLD REPORT

2014

AMERICAS

Argentina

In 2013, President Cristina Fernández de Kirchner secured passage of legislation that severely undermined judicial independence, although the Supreme Court subsequently struck down some of its key aspects. A vibrant but increasingly polarized debate exists in Argentina between the government and its critics. However, the Fernández administration has sanctioned individuals for publishing unofficial inflation statistics challenging official ones, and has failed to adopt rules regarding the distribution of public advertising funds. There is no national law regulating access to information.

Other ongoing human rights concerns include police abuse, poor prison conditions, torture, and failure to protect indigenous rights.

Argentina continues to make significant progress on LGBT rights and in prosecuting officials for abuses committed during the country's "Dirty War" (1976-1983), although trials have been subject to delays.

Judicial Independence

In April 2013, President Fernández put forward legislation to revise Argentina's justice system, which Congress swiftly approved. It included a bill to limit individuals' ability to request injunctions against government acts, and another that granted the ruling party an automatic majority in the Council of the Judiciary, which selects judges and decides whether to open proceedings for their removal, thereby granting the ruling party powers that undermined judicial independence. In June, the Supreme Court struck down critical aspects of the latter bill, including norms regarding the composition and selection of the Council of the Judiciary.

Fernández accused those who defended the role of the judiciary as a check on other branches of government of being a "check on the people."

Freedom of Expression

In 2009, Congress approved a law to regulate the broadcast media, which includes provisions to increase plurality in media. The federal authority in charge of implementing the law has yet to ensure a diverse range of perspectives in state-run media programming. Argentina's largest media conglomerate, the Clarin Group, had challenged the constitutionality of articles of the law requiring companies to sell off broadcast outlets that exceed the new limits of outlets that can be owned by a media company, and obtained an injunction that suspended their implementation during the trial. In October 2013, the Supreme Court upheld the constitutionality of the law, lifted the injunction, and ordered Clarin to comply with the law. The court also established clear parameters regarding how the law should be implemented to ensure the right of free expression is effectively protected.

Fernández accused the media in August 2013 of using "bullets of ink" to "overthrow elected governments." The president's general secretary called a journalist who aired several shows alleging government corruption of being a "media hit man."

High fines and criminal prosecutions undermine the right to freely publish information of public interest. In 2011, the Ministry of Commerce imposed a fine of 500,000 pesos on 11 economists and consulting firms for publishing unofficial inflation statistics challenging the accuracy of official ones. While the Supreme Court overturned some of the fines in October 2013, others remained pending at time of writing. Three of the fined economists were also being criminally investigated for allegedly "defrauding commerce and industry." In September, a judge charged the minister of commerce with "abuse of authority" for having imposed the fines.

The absence of transparent criteria for using government funds at the federal level and in some provinces to purchase media advertisements creates a risk of discrimination against media outlets that criticize government officials. In two rulings in 2007 and 2011, the Supreme Court found that while media companies have no right to receive public advertising, government officials may not apply discriminatory criteria when deciding where to place advertisements.

Argentina does not have a national law ensuring public access to information held by government bodies. An existing presidential decree on the matter only applies to the federal executive branch, and some provincial governments have adopted regulations for their jurisdictions.

Transnational Justice

At time of writing, no one had been convicted for the 1994 bombing of the Argentine Israelite Mutual Association (AMIA) in Buenos Aires that killed 85 people and injured over 300. Judicial corruption and political obstruction hindered criminal investigations and prosecutions from the investigation's outset. Iran, which is suspected of ordering the attack, has refused Argentina's requests for the extradition of former Iranian President Ali Akbar Hashemi-Rafsanjani and seven Iranian officials suspected of participating in the crime.

In January 2013, Argentina and Iran signed a memorandum of understanding (MoU) that creates an international commission of jurists with powers to review evidence against Iranians accused by Argentine judicial authorities of being responsible for the bombing, and to interrogate some of the suspects. Legislators from Fernandez's party ratified the agreement in February. In Iran, it was ratified by the Council of Ministers, but it is unclear from the agreement's vague terms whether it can be implemented without Iranian parliamentary approval, or if the Iranians' statements will be admissible as evidence in Argentine criminal proceedings. In September 2013, President Fernández de Kirchner called on Iran to ratify the agreement during her speech before the United Nations General Assembly. A legal challenge to the agreement filed in April by Jewish community leaders before Argentine courts remained pending at time of writing.

Confronting Past Abuses

Several cases of human rights violations committed during Argentina's military dictatorship (1976-1983) were reopened in 2003 after Congress annulled existing amnesty laws. The Supreme Court subsequently ruled that the amnesty laws were unconstitutional, and federal judges struck down pardons favoring former officials convicted of, or facing trial for, human rights violations.

By September 2013, out of 2,316 persons investigated by the courts for crimes against humanity, 416 had been convicted and 35 had been found not guilty, according to the Center of Legal and Social Studies (CELS). There are 11 ongoing oral trials involving multiple victims and suspects.

In December 2012, for example, a federal court convicted Jaime Smart, a minister of Buenos Aires province during the dictatorship, for the torture and subsequent death of one individual, and the illegal detention and abuse of 43 others. The first civilian government official convicted for these crimes, Smart was given life in prison. The tribunal also convicted 22 security officials for the same abuses, and requested the investigation of a prosecutor, members of the judiciary, and the Catholic Church for their alleged involvement.

Given the large number of victims, suspects, and cases, prosecutors and judges face challenges bringing those responsible to justice while respecting the due process rights of the accused. Other concerns include significant delays in trials; that three convicted military officers who escaped in July 2013 remain at large; and the unresolved fate of Jorge Julio López—a former torture victim who disappeared in September 2006, a day before he was due to attend the trial of one of his torturers.

In July 2013, President Fernández requested that Congress promote General César Milani, the head of the armed forces, to lieutenant general. After widespread criticism from human rights organizations and victims, who accused Milani of having participated in abuses during the dictatorship, the president asked Congress to postpone Milani's promotion until the end of the year.

Police Abuse

In April 2013, at least 100 officers from the Metropolitan Police Force of the city of Buenos Aires used excessive force to disperse doctors, nurses, union leaders, and lawmakers who were protesting the city government's plans to demolish a building at a hospital, according to the city Ombudsman Office. The police intervention resulted in injuries to dozens of civilians, including patients and journalists, according to media accounts. Seventeen police officers were also injured in the clash. At time of writing, the case was under investigation by a criminal judge.

Prison Conditions

Overcrowding, ill-treatment by prison guards, inadequate physical conditions, and inmate violence continue to be serious problems in prisons. According to the National Penitentiary Office (Procuración Penitenciaria de la Nación), an official body created by Congress, there were 86 deaths, including 41 violent ones, in federal prisons between January 2012 and mid-2013. The office also documented 429 cases of torture or ill-treatment in federal prisons in 2012, and 426 in the first seven months of 2013.

Indigenous Rights

Indigenous peoples in Argentina face obstacles in accessing justice, land, education, healthcare, and other basic services.

Existing laws require the government to perform a survey of land occupied by indigenous communities by November 2017, before which authorities cannot lawfully evict communities. In May 2013, the Supreme Court urged the government of Formosa province and the federal government to carry out the required survey for the Qom indigenous group. Before the survey was conducted, authorities opened criminal investigations against Félix Díaz, a Qom leader, for having "usurped" lands where community members live, and for participating in a 2010 protest in which a community member died and dozens more were injured due to excessive use of force by provincial security forces, according to CELS.

Women's Rights

Argentina adopted a new law in March 2013 extending key protections to domestic workers, the majority of whom are women and girls, including limits to work hours, a weekly rest period, overtime pay, sick leave, and maternity protections.

Abortion is illegal in Argentina, with limited exceptions, and women and girls face numerous obstacles to reproductive health products and services, such as contraception, voluntary sterilization procedures, and abortion after rape (one of the few circumstances when abortion is permitted). These barriers mean that women and girls may face unwanted or unhealthy pregnancies.

In a landmark ruling in March 2012, the Supreme Court determined that prior judicial authorization was unnecessary for abortion after rape and urged provincial governments to ensure access to legal abortions. As of March 2013, only 5 out of Argentina's 23 provinces had adopted protocols that met the court's requirements, according to the Association for Civil Rights (ADC).

Sexual Orientation and Gender Identity

In 2010, Argentina became the first Latin American country to legalize same-sex marriage. The Civil Marriage Law allows same-sex couples to enter into civil marriages and provides for equal rights and the legal protections of marriage afforded to opposite-sex couples including, among others, adoption rights and pension benefits.

In 2012, the Gender Identity Law established the right of individuals over the age of 18 to choose their gender identity, undergo gender reassignment, and revise official documents without any prior judicial or medical approval. The surgical and hormonal reassignment procedures are covered as part of public and private health insurance.

Key International Actors

In April 2013, the UN rapporteur on the independence of lawyers and judges stated that the changes to the justice system proposed by the Fernández administration "seriously compromise[d] the principles of separation of powers and independence of the judiciary, which are fundamental elements of any democracy." The Fernández government reacted by accusing the rapporteur of "lack of impartiality, restraint, and balance."

As a returning member of the Human Rights Council, Argentina voted in favour of a number of key resolutions addressing the human rights violations in countries such as Sri Lanka, Iran, and Syria. Argentina could do more to speak out and hold governments accountable for enforced disappearances given their priority focus on this issue at the UN.

In March 2013, the Organization of American States General Assembly adopted a resolution ending a process, begun in 2010, to strengthen the Inter-American human rights system. Several countries, however, used the process to attempt to undermine the independence of the Inter-American Commission on Human Rights and its special rapporteurship on freedom of expression. At the end of the March meeting, Argentina proposed language to adopt the final resolution by consensus, effectively opening the door to reinitiating a debate in which amendments to the system could undermine the commission's independence.

In May 2013, the Inter-American Court of Human Rights ruled that Argentina had violated the rights to liberty and freedom from cruel and inhuman treatment of five children who were sentenced to life in prison. The court ordered Argentina to modify laws to eliminate life imprisonment of children and to review cases in which others were serving similar sentences.

Bolivia

Long-standing problems in Bolivia's criminal justice system, such as extensive and arbitrary use of pre-trial detention and long delays in trials, undermine defendant's rights and contribute to serious overcrowding in prisons. Impunity persists for serious human rights abuses committed during the country's authoritarian rule from 1964 to 1982.

The administration of President Evo Morales continued to launch verbal attacks on the press, accusing critical journalists of politically motivated lies.

After several high-profile killings of women sparked public protests, the government passed a comprehensive law in March 2013 to combat gender-based violence.

Accountability for Past Abuses

Bolivia has made little progress investigating and prosecuting human rights violations committed under authoritarian governments between 1964 and 1982. A contributing factor has been the unwillingness of the armed forces to provide information that might clarify the fate or whereabouts of people killed or disappeared during this period.

Plans to create a truth commission announced by the Morales administration in 2008 have not materialized. Bolivia has failed to fulfill commitments to compensate victims of political violence during that period. A 2004 law budgeted US$3.6 million in government funds for this purpose, which would only cover about 20 percent of the proposed costs. The remaining funds were to be obtained from private donors, but were never raised.

In April 2012, Congress passed a law announcing one-off payments equivalent to roughly 20 percent of the compensation amounts approved in 2004. As of December 2012, 1,418 of the 1,714 approved beneficiaries had received one of these reduced payments, according to the government. Many additional potential beneficiaries said they were rejected due to overly stringent documentary evidence required by the government commission appointed to review claims.

Long delays in the trials of opposition leaders and government officials have obstructed justice for victims of violent clashes in 2008 between supporters and opponents of President Morales. Repeated changes of jurisdiction and prosecutorial inefficiency have also undermined the right of the accused to due process and a prompt trial. As of August 2013, a La Paz court was still hearing evidence in a case involving Leopoldo Fernández, former prefect of Pando department, and five local officials, charged in 2008 for their roles in a September 2008 massacre in which 13 people were killed. The judge repeatedly suspended proceedings when defendants failed to appear.

Despite international concern, the government has not reopened an investigation into the April 2009 killing of two Hungarians (one of Bolivian birth) and an Irishman, whom the government alleged were mercenaries involved in a separatist plot. Police shot them dead after storming their hotel rooms in Santa Cruz. Reports by an Irish government pathologist and an independent forensic consultant suggested that at least two of the victims may have been extrajudicially executed.

Military Jurisdiction

In a landmark December 2012 decision, the Constitutional Court ruled that a civilian court should have jurisdiction in the case of a conscript who died in 2011 following a combat training exercise—allegedly after instructors beat him on the head and chest. The court urged lawmakers to reform Bolivia's military justice code to bring it in line with international human rights standards, which affirm that all human rights violations should be handled in civilian jurisdiction.

Due Process Violations

The broad discretion that judges enjoy in ordering pretrial detention and lack of access to public defenders have greatly undermined due process rights for those accused of a crime, particularly among Bolivia's poor. According to a report published by the United Nations High Commissioner for Human Rights (UNHCR), as of September 2012, 84 percent of prisoners in Bolivia were awaiting trial. Bolivian law allows up to three years in pretrial detention, a limit often contravened in practice.

High-profile defendants have also suffered due process violations and judicial harassment. In October 2013, José María Bakovic, a 74-year-old former director of the National Road Service (SNC), died from a heart attack after prosecutors—

ignoring warnings from doctors that a journey to the high altitudes of La Paz could endanger his life—ordered him to attend a hearing there. Bakovic, who worked aggressively to eradicate corruption within the SNC while he was its director, himself became the target of a corruption investigation after President Morales took office in 2006. Before his death, he said that he had defended himself in 72 cases filed in different parts of Bolivia, and was eventually sentenced in August 2013 to three years in prison for economic damage to the state.

Prison Conditions

Extended pretrial detention and trial delays have led to increased overcrowding in Bolivia's prisons. As of September 2013, the government reported there were 14,770 inmates in prisons with a capacity of under 5,000. Eighty percent of those prisoners, President Morales said at the time, were being held due to "delays of the justice system."

Prison conditions are poor: most are dilapidated; food and medical attention are inadequate; and internal control is often left to prisoners. At least 35 inmates were killed and more than 50 injured in a fire resulting from a clash in August 2013 between rival gangs in Palmasola prison. The dead included an 18-month-old who was spending the night in the prison with his father, who reportedly died while trying to shield him from the flames.

In September, President Morales signed a decree that allowed the pardoning of prisoners serving sentences of up to eight years for lesser sentences, while those in pretrial detention for crimes with penalties of four years or less could be released and have their charges dropped under a government amnesty. While the government estimated this would affect roughly 2,000 prisoners, the Bolivian Catholic Church estimated that only approximately 600 prisoners in pretrial detention would be eligible for release, due to stringent eligibility requirements.

Gender-Based Violence and Reproductive Rights

Women and girls in Bolivia are at high risk for gender-based violence. According to police statistics reported in the press, in 2012 there were over 140 gender-based killings of women, and thousands of complaints filed for acts of gender-based violence. Public protests following several high-profile murders of women in early 2013, including the fatal stabbing in February of journalist Hanalí Huaycho by her husband—a former police officer—led the government to pass a comprehensive law in March to combat gender-based violence. Prior to her killing, Huaycho had repeatedly reported abuses by her ex-husband to authorities.

The new law adds "femicide" to the criminal code (with a mandatory 30-year sentence), establishes a task force to combat domestic violence, and mandates the construction of women's shelters, among other reforms.

In Bolivia, victims of sexual violence must receive judicial authorization before they may access legal abortion services. Failure to do so may result in prosecution: an indigenous woman served eight months in prison in 2012 after being convicted for obtaining an abortion without judicial authorization after she became pregnant from rape.

Freedom of Expression

While public debate is robust, on occasions President Morales or his ministers have aggressively criticized the press, accusing journalists of lies and politically motivated distortions. In August 2013, the minister of the presidency accused the La Paz newspaper, *Página Siete*, of being "indecorous, malicious, deceitful and mendacious," and of having links with Chilean right-wing politicians. The minister's comments followed an Independence Day speech the same month in which President Morales accused unnamed newspapers and television outlets of having a pro-Chilean stance (Bolivia has a long-standing maritime dispute with Chile). In August 2012, the government filed a criminal lawsuit against *Página Siete* and two other outlets for "inciting racism," by publishing a headline it alleged distorted a presidential speech about food shortages. As of September 2013, the case remained open.

As of October 2013, the National Assembly was debating a bill presented by the government on transparency and access to public information. The National Press Association criticized several of the grounds for confidentiality envisaged in the bill, which grants a wide range of government authorities broad powers determine exceptions to access.

Key International Actors

Bolivia supported a campaign by Ecuador to undermine the independence of the Inter-American Commission on Human Rights and limit the funding and effectiveness of its special rapporteurship on freedom of expression. While they were unable to win support for this effort at the March 2013 meeting of the Organization of American States General Assembly, both governments, as well as other members of the Bolivarian Alliance for the Americas (ALBA), made clear their intent to press for these changes in the future.

In June 2013, the Committee against Torture (CAT) urged Bolivia to adopt legislation establishing torture as a crime in its own right as defined in the Convention Against Torture and expressed concern at delays in investigations into allegations of torture.

In October 2013, in a draft version of its concluding observations on Bolivia's third periodic report, the UN Human Rights Committee urged Bolivia to implement alternatives to preventive detention and to strictly limit its duration, and to eliminate the requirement of prior judicial authorization for therapeutic abortion and abortion in cases of rape and incest, among other recommendations.

In April 2013, the UN Committee on Migrant Workers expressed concern at persistent discrimination against migrant workers and refugees in Bolivia and the absence of any record of compensation paid to migrant workers whose rights had been violated.

Also in April, Bolivia became the second International Labour Organization member state in Latin America to ratify the Domestic Workers Convention, which provides critical protections for millions of domestic workers—mostly women and girls—who perform essential household work in other persons' homes.

Brazil

Brazil is among the most influential democracies in regional and global affairs, and in recent years has emerged as an increasingly important voice in debates over international responses to human rights problems. At home, the country continues to confront serious human rights challenges, including unlawful police killings, the use of torture, prison overcrowding, and ongoing impunity for abuses committed during the country's military rule (1964-1985).

Faced with high levels of violent crime, some Brazilian police units engage in abusive practices with impunity. In recent years, the São Paulo and Rio de Janeiro state governments have implemented measures aimed at improving police performance and curbing abuses, yet police misreporting and other forms of cover-up persist.

Beginning in June, hundreds of thousands of protesters participated in nation-wide demonstrations against inadequate public services and the high cost of staging the World Cup and Olympics in 2014 and 2016 respectively, as well as government corruption and other grievances. In multiple incidents, police used teargas, pepper-spray, and rubber bullets disproportionately against the demonstrators. In October, Rio de Janeiro police arrested more than 200 people following a protest during which banks, stores, and buildings were destroyed. The federal minister of justice and public security officials in Rio and São Paulo states announced in November that they would work together more closely to prevent and punish violence by protesters and police alike.

In August, President Dilma Rousseff signed a law creating a National Mechanism to Prevent and Combat Torture that will consist of 11 experts and have authority to conduct unannounced visits to civilian and military establishments where individuals are deprived of their liberty.

Public Security and Police Conduct

Widespread violence perpetrated by criminal gangs and abusive police plague many Brazilian cities. According to the Brazilian Forum on Public Security, a non-governmental organization (NGO) that gathers official data from state and federal bodies, 1,890 people died during police operations in Brazil in 2012, averaging 5 people per day. In Rio de Janeiro and São Paulo states alone, police were responsible for 362 killings in the state of Rio de Janeiro, and 165 killings in the state of São Paulo in the first six months of 2013. Police routinely report these deaths as the result of shoot-outs with criminals. While some police killings result from legitimate use of force, others do not, a fact documented by Human Rights Watch and other groups and recognized by Brazilian criminal justice officials.

In an effort to prevent cover-ups of unlawful police killings, the São Paulo state government issued a resolution in January 2013 prohibiting police from removing victims' corpses from the scenes of the shootings. Police killings in the state subsequently fell by approximately 34 percent in the first six months of 2013, according to government figures. Yet significant obstacles to accountability for unlawful killings in São Paulo persist, including the failure of police to preserve crucial evidence, and the lack of sufficient staff and resources provided to prosecutors responsible for investigating these cases.

In the state of Rio de Janeiro, 11,749 police officers and other public servants received financial compensation in April 2013 for meeting reduction targets for crimes and acts of violence, including police homicides. As of September, 34 Pacifying Police Units (UPP) had also been established in low-income communities with the goal of providing a more effective police presence. The UPP program came under sharp scrutiny when a resident of the Rocinha community, Amarildo Dias de Souza, disappeared on July 14 after being arrested by UPP police, who later claimed to have released him. On August 2, the national minister of human rights called on the Rio government to ensure an adequate investigation into Souza's disappearance. Twenty-five police officers were subject to criminal charges for torture in October in connection with Souza's disappearance. Seventeen of these officers were also accused of unlawfully concealing Souza's body.

Prison Conditions, Torture, and Ill-Treatment of Detainees

Many Brazilian prisons and jails are severely overcrowded and plagued by violence. The country's incarceration rate increased almost 30 percent over the last five years, according to the Ministry of Justice's Integrated System of Penitentiary Information (InfoPen). The adult prison population now exceeds half a million people—43 percent more than the prisons were built for. An additional 20,000 children are currently serving prison sentences. Delays within the justice system contribute to the overcrowding. Nearly 200,000 inmates are in pretrial detention. In Piauí state, 66 percent of detainees are in pretrial detention, the highest rate in the country.

Overcrowding and poor sanitation facilitate the spread of disease, and prisoners' access to medical care remains inadequate. Torture is a chronic problem in police stations and detention centers. The United Nations Subcommittee on the Prevention of Torture and other Cruel, Inhuman or Degrading Treatment reported that it received "repeated and consistent" accounts from inmates of beatings and other allegations of ill-treatment during police custody. In July 2013, law enforcement officers in Paraná state allegedly beat, suffocated, and applied electric shocks to four men to force them to confess to the rape and murder of a 14-year-old girl. In August 2013, security camera footage from the Vila Maria prison complex in São Paulo state was leaked to the press showing prison guards beating six children. The prison unit director and three other employees allegedly involved in the incident were removed from their posts.

Law enforcement agents who commit abuses against inmates and detainees are rarely brought to justice. In a notable exception, in August 2013, 48 police officers were convicted of homicide for their participation in the 1992 killing of 111 detainees in the Carandiru prison in São Paulo state.

President Rousseff signed a law in August 2013 establishing the National Mechanism to Prevent and Combat Torture. The body will consist of 11 experts with power to conduct unannounced visits to civilian and military establishments where people are deprived of their liberty, open investigations into possible cases of torture, and make recommendations to public and private institutions. It was not operational at time of writing.

Freedom of Expression

Dozens of journalists who covered the nationwide demonstrations in June were injured or detained by state police. For example, during a protest in São Paulo on June 13, a reporter and a photographer were hit in the eyes with rubber bullets and seriously injured. Following this incident, the São Paulo military police internal affairs unit opened an investigation into the police's use of force against the journalists and federal authorities called on state governments to ensure their police forces provided "special protection" for members of the media.

Six journalists were killed in Brazil between January and November 2013. Two of the victims worked for the *Vale do Aço* newspaper in Minas Gerais state, where investigators concluded in August that police officers were involved in their killings. The officers implicated were subsequently detained and charged with aggravated homicide.

By November 2013, 16 out of 27 states had passed legislation to implement the federal access to information law that went into force in 2012. The law establishes that the public should have unfettered access to information regarding violations of fundamental rights.

Reproductive Rights and Gender-Based Violence

Brazil's criminal code prohibits abortion except in cases of rape or when necessary to save a woman's life. In 2012, the Supreme Court expanded the exceptions to include cases of anencephaly, in which the fetus has a fatal congenital brain disorder. Women and girls who obtain an abortion outside of these exceptions may face sentences of up to three years in jail, while people who perform abortions face up to four years imprisonment.

In August 2013, President Rousseff signed into law a bill that requires public hospitals to provide comprehensive care for victims of sexual violence, including "pregnancy prophylaxis" for rape victims and information on the right to access abortion in cases where it is legal. Rousseff concurrently sent a draft law to Congress clarifying that "pregnancy prophylaxis" consists of emergency contraception.

Sexual Orientation and Gender Identity

The national Human Rights Ombudsman's Office received more than 3,000 complaints of violence against lesbian, gay, bisexual, and transgender (LGBT) persons in 2012, 166 percent more than in 2011, when the Ombudsman's Office began to track these complaints through a hotline service.

In March 2013, the newly elected president of the Commission for Human Rights and Minorities of the federal Chamber of Deputies, Pastor Marcos Feliciano, proposed a legislative bill that would partially suspend a resolution by the Federal Psychology Council prohibiting psychologists from treating homosexuality as a disorder. The bill was withdrawn from voting in July following extensive public criticism.

In May 2013, the National Council of Justice (CNJ) issued a resolution establishing that notaries who refuse to perform same-sex civil marriages or convert stable same-sex unions into marriages shall be referred to the judiciary's internal affairs unit for disciplinary action. The Supreme Court recognized equal rights for same-sex couples in 2011.

Labor Rights

Federal government efforts to eradicate forced labor have resulted in more than 44,000 workers being freed from slave-like conditions since 1995, according to official data. However, the Pastoral Land Commission, a Catholic NGO, received complaints involving approximately 3,000 workers allegedly subject to forced labor in 2012. Criminal accountability for offending employers remains relatively rare.

In June 2013, the Constitution and Justice Commission in the Senate approved a constitutional amendment that would permit the government to confiscate properties where forced labor is used without providing compensation to the owners. Final approval will require a full Senate vote.

Brazil adopted a constitutional amendment in March 2013 that entitles the country's estimated 6.5 million domestic workers to overtime pay, unemployment insurance, pension, a maximum 8-hour workday, and 44-hour work week.

Rural Violence

Rural activists and indigenous leaders involved in conflicts over land continue to face threats and violence. According to the Pastoral Land Commission, 36 people involved in land conflicts were killed and 77 were victims of attempted murder throughout the country in 2012. Nearly 2,500 rural activists have received death threats over the past decade.

In May 2013, several members of the Terena indigenous group were wounded and one was fatally shot during a court-ordered eviction in the state of Mato Grosso do Sul. The National Indian Foundation (FUNAI) had designated the ranch as ancestral Terena land in 2010, but a state court ruled in 2012 that it belonged to a rancher. According to the Indigenous Missionary Council of the Catholic Church, 37 members of indigenous tribes were killed in Mato Grosso do Sul in 2012, the highest number of all Brazilian states.

Confronting Military-Era Abuses

In May 2012, a national truth commission began investigating the systematic human rights violations that occurred during military rule, from 1964 to 1985, which included extrajudicial killings, forced disappearances, torture, arbitrary detention, and the curtailment of free expression.

The perpetrators of these crimes have been shielded from justice by a 1979 amnesty law. In April 2010, the Brazilian Supreme Court reaffirmed lower courts' interpretation that the amnesty barred most prosecutions of state agents for these cases. However, six months later, the Inter-American Court of Human Rights ruled that this interpretation violated Brazil's obligations under international law, and that the amnesty should not be an obstacle to prosecuting serious human rights violations committed under military rule.

In April 2013, São Paulo prosecutors filed criminal charges against a retired army colonel and police investigator for concealing the body of a medical student killed during military rule. A federal judge determined in August that he will take this case to trial. In contrast, in June, a judge in Rio de Janeiro refused to try state agents for their alleged involvement in the forced disappearance of a journalist in 1970.

Key International Actors

In March 2013, the UN Working Group on Arbitrary Detention expressed concern regarding prolonged periods of pretrial detention and the lack of adequate public legal assistance for detainees. In June, the UN special rapporteur on adequate housing called on local authorities to "refrain from forced evictions" as

Brazil prepares to host the 2014 World Cup and 2016 Olympic Games and to comply with international guidelines when evictions are justified.

During a visit to Brazil in July, Pope Francis condemned unlawful police killings during a prayer with homeless children in Rio de Janeiro and urged state authorities and civil society to use dialogue as an alternative to "selfish indifference and violent protest."

Brazil's Foreign Policy

As a returning member to the Human Rights Council, Brazil maintained a positive voting record, supporting the adoption of resolutions on a number of critical human rights situations, including Iran and Sri Lanka. In June, for example, Brazil voted in favor of two resolutions addressing the deteriorating humanitarian situation in Syria and also approved the submission of the final report of the Independent Commission of Inquiry on Syria to the UN General Assembly. However, the Brazilian delegation significantly lowered its profile in the council proceedings and negotiations compared to its prominent engagement during its previous membership.

At the UN General Assembly, Brazil abstained from a resolution in May condemning violence in Syria and recognizing the opposition Syrian National Coalition as "an effective representative interlocutor for a political transition." It also abstained in November from a resolution at the UN General Assembly Third Committee expressing concern regarding ongoing human rights violations in Iran such as torture and public executions. However, that same month Brazil supported a resolution calling on all parties in Syria to immediately end all violations and abuses of international human rights and humanitarian law.

In 2011, the Rousseff administration recalled its ambassador to the Organization of American States after the Inter-American Commission on Human Rights issued precautionary measures for Brazil due to an alleged failure to consult with indigenous groups prior to beginning the construction of the Belo Monte hydroelectric dam. Brazil has yet to restore the ambassador.

Following press reports in September that the United States and the United Kingdom carry out massive surveillance of Brazilian citizens, companies and political leaders, President Rousseff cancelled a state visit to the United States planned for October and announced in a speech to the UN General Assembly that Brazil would seek to play a leading role in the development of a global Internet governance mechanism to protect the right to privacy.

Previously, Brazil had expressed concern to UK authorities that a Brazilian citizen was detained for questioning at Heathrow Airport in London apparently in connection with US surveillance information leaked to the press by his partner. In November, Brazil and Germany proposed a UN General Assembly resolution calling on countries to take measures to end violations of the right to privacy and ensure effective oversight of state surveillance of communications and collection of personal data.

Chile

The administration of President Sebastián Piñera has taken several important steps to strengthen human rights. Since September 2010, it has ended the jurisdiction of military courts over civilians, reformed some of the most objectionable parts of counterterrorism legislation, and promulgated a law to provide redress for LGBT individuals who suffer discrimination.

However, current laws continue to allow military courts to exercise jurisdiction over alleged human rights abuses committed by the Carabineros (police responsible for public order and crime prevention), and vague counterterrorism legislation remains subject to arbitrary enforcement. Police sometimes use excessive force when responding to public protests.

While courts continue to prosecute individuals for abuses committed during the Augusto Pinochet dictatorship (1973-1990), the Supreme Court has used its discretionary powers in many cases to reduce sentences against human rights violators, resulting in sentences that are incommensurate with the gravity of the crimes. Abortion continues to be prohibited in all circumstances, even when the mother's life is at risk.

Police Abuses

Occupations and street protests by students calling for education reform frequently end in violent clashes between demonstrators and police. Public protests are not regulated by law, but rather by a 1983 decree dating from the Pinochet dictatorship that gives wide discretion to local government officials to deny permission for protests, as well as broad powers to the police to disperse unauthorized gatherings.

Carabineros regularly use anti-riot equipment such as water cannons and tear-gas to break up unauthorized marches. And when violence occurs at authorized marches, the police response is sometimes indiscriminate or disproportionate. The National Institute for Human Rights (INDH—Chile's human rights ombudsman) noted that while Carabineros had made efforts in 2012 to improve police practices in response to authorized protests, they continued to use excessive force "regardless of the behavior" of demonstrators. Of particular concern in

2013 was Carabineros' lack of caution in firing paintball rifles at protesters, which they justified as a means of identifying law-breakers. Five people were hit in the eye by paintballs fired by police during a student demonstration in April 2013, one of whom lost an eye.

The executive branch proposed legislation in 2012 and 2013 to criminalize violent conduct in public protests. Some of the measures proposed, such as those outlawing the use of hoods or garments protecting the face against tear gas, would have increased the risk of arbitrary arrest and criminal prosecution of people exercising a legitimate right to protest, but the Senate rejected the proposed legislation in October 2013.

According to the INDH, courts have granted seven petitions since January 2012 asking them to protect individuals' constitutional rights following alleged abusive actions by police in Mapuche indigenous communities. The courts found that police had been responsible for arbitrary arrest, ill-treatment, and excessive use of force.

Military Jurisdiction

Legislation approved by Congress in September 2010 finally ended the jurisdiction of military courts over civilians, a reform urged by the Inter-American Court of Human Rights in its 2005 ruling in the Palamara Iribarne case. However, the reform left untouched the jurisdiction of military courts over abuses committed by Carabineros against civilians, and at time of writing the government had yet to present legislation to ensure that Carabineros accused of human rights violations are tried by civilian courts.

Military courts, which are composed of military officers on active service, lack the independence and due process guarantees of ordinary criminal proceedings. Investigations are secret, criminal proceedings conducted mainly in writing, and lawyers representing victims of police abuse have limited opportunities to cross-examine witnesses.

However, verdicts by military courts can be appealed to the Supreme Court. In August 2012, the Corte Marcial (military appeals court) revoked the conviction of a police officer responsible for the death of a Mapuche who had been participating in a land occupation, basing its verdict solely on the testimony of the accused—who claimed to have fired in self-defense—and ignoring evidence that showed that the victim had not fired a weapon. On appeal, in August 2013 the Supreme Court rejected the officer's self-defense argument and gave the officer a commuted sentence of three years for homicide due to unnecessary force (sentences of three years or less can be served without imprisonment).

Counterterrorism Law

In September 2010, following a hunger strike by indigenous Mapuche prisoners held on terrorism charges, the Piñera administration reformed the counterterrorism law. Positive reforms allowed for the defense to cross-examine anonymous witnesses and barred the law's application to children.

However, the law's overly broad definition of terrorism continues to allow for the prosecution on terrorism charges of those allegedly responsible for unrelated criminal acts such as arson and the destruction of private property, although judges may later reject terrorism charges as unfounded. In addition, a provision in the law allowing prosecution witnesses' identity to be kept anonymous makes it difficult for defense attorneys to obtain information relevant to witnesses' credibility. Although the Piñera administration has invoked the terrorism law against Mapuches engaged in land protests more selectively than its predecessors, the risk of arbitrary terrorism prosecutions remains without clear and appropriate legal criteria for its application.

Prison Conditions

In March 2013, the Ministry of Justice instituted a new data collection system to measure and monitor overcrowding, a chronic problem in Chile's prisons, among other poor conditions. In July 2013, there were 47,515 prisoners in a prison system with a capacity to hold just 38,088.

Confronting Past Abuses

In an interview prior to the 40th anniversary of the September 1973 military coup, President Piñera acknowledged civilian complicity in abuses under the Pinochet dictatorship, stating that "there are many who were passive accomplices [of human rights violations], who knew and did nothing, or did not want to know." The chief justice publicly acknowledged that the Supreme Court failed during the dictatorship to act against human rights violations and to protect victims. He announced in September that the appellate judges in Santiago who are responsible for trying perpetrators of abuses committed during the dictatorship would be ordered to dedicate themselves exclusively to these cases.

The chief justice stated in March 2013 that 1,104 cases of human rights violations were under adjudication by the courts. According to the human rights program of the Ministry of the Interior, a party to 837 of these cases, as of September 2013 courts had convicted 355 perpetrators, 262 of whom had received a final sentence. Sixteen of those convicted had held the rank of general in the armed forces or police and 39 had been colonels before retirement. Sixty-six were serving sentences in prison. Nevertheless, as of July 2013, only 33 cases of torture, a systematic practice under Pinochet, were under adjudication, according to the Human Rights Observatory of Diego Portales University, which monitors the progress of trials for dictatorship-era abuses.

In many cases, the Supreme Court has used its discretionary powers to issue lenient sentences against officials who committed serious human rights abuses by arguing that significant time has elapsed since the criminal act. In other cases, the court commuted the sentences of others previously convicted for such crimes. These practices raise concerns about Chile's fulfillment of its obligation to hold accountable perpetrators of crimes against humanity by imposing appropriate punishments or sanctions.

In September 2013 President Piñera ordered the closure of the Cordillera military prison, one of two built under previous administrations to house military officers convicted of human rights violations. Its 10 prisoners, who were enjoying privileges unavailable to ordinary prisoners, were transferred to Punta Peuco, the other prison for military personnel convicted for human rights abuses.

Reproductive Rights

Chile is one of only four countries in Latin America (the other three being El Salvador, Honduras, and Nicaragua) with an absolute prohibition on abortion, even in the event of medical necessity or rape.

In April 2012, the Senate rejected three bills to legalize abortion in cases in which the mother's life was at risk or the fetus was unviable. In July 2013, the widely publicized case of "Belén," an 11-year-old who became pregnant after being raped by her stepfather, brought renewed calls for legislation to allow abortion for rape victims. Belén stated publicly that she wanted to have the baby. However, due to the absolute prohibition of abortion, authorities cannot provide accurate, complete, and unbiased information about reproductive and sexual health to women and girls pregnant from rape, including youth-sensitive and confidential counseling to children. As of November 2013, two new bills to legalize abortion—one for medical reasons, and the other for medical reasons and rape—presented in May and July respectively, were still under consideration in committee in the Chamber of Deputies and the Senate.

Sexual Orientation and Gender Identity

In May 2013, five senators tabled Chile's first bill to achieve legal recognition of the gender identity of transgender people. The bill would allow individuals to change their name and legal gender on birth certificates and identity cards so that official documents match their gender identity. Discrimination based on gender identity was banned under an anti-discrimination law that entered force in 2012, providing avenues of redress for victims. At time of writing, the Senate was still discussing the bill.

Key International Actors

Following a visit to Chile in July 2013, the UN special rapporteur on the promotion and protection of human rights and fundamental freedoms while combating terrorism stated that the counterterrorism law had been "applied disproportionately against Mapuche defendants," and recommended that its use in connection with Mapuche land protests should cease. In September, the Committee on the Elimination of Racial Discrimination expressed concern about the "lack of objective legal criteria" for the application of the counterterrorism law in Mapuche cases, which could violate the principles of legality, equality, and freedom from discrimination.

In a landmark August 2013 decision, the Inter-American Court of Human Rights found Chile violated the right to a hearing within a reasonable time of torture victim Leopoldo García Lucero, who was detained five days after the September 1973 military coup. It was the first ruling of the court on the case of a survivor of human rights abuse during the Pinochet dictatorship.

While Chile played a positive role at the Human Rights Council by voting in favor of key human rights resolutions such as those on Sri Lanka, Iran, and Syria, the country could take its positive engagement further by speaking out more often on other human rights situations that warrant UN attention.

Colombia

Colombia's internal armed conflict continued to result in serious abuses by irregular armed groups in 2013, including guerrillas and successor groups to paramilitaries. More than 5 million Colombians have been internally displaced, and upward of 150,000 continue to flee their homes each year, generating the world's second largest population of internally displaced persons (IDPs). Human rights defenders, trade unionists, journalists, indigenous and Afro-Colombian leaders, and IDP leaders face death threats and other abuses. The administration of President Juan Manuel Santos has consistently condemned threats and attacks against rights defenders, but perpetrators are rarely brought to justice.

The Santos administration has adopted several measures that undermine accountability for human rights violations. The government promoted constitutional changes concerning transitional justice and the military justice system that threaten to ensure impunity for egregious abuses by guerrillas, paramilitaries, and the military. In proceedings before the Inter-American Court of Human Rights, the government denied the military's participation in atrocities for which military members had already been convicted in national courts.

The Colombian government and Revolutionary Armed Forces of Colombia (FARC) guerrillas have been engaged in peace talks in Cuba since 2012. Colombia's internal armed conflict has taken approximately 220,000 lives since 1958, 81.5 percent of whom were civilians, according to a report published in 2013 by the government-created National Center for Historical Memory.

Guerrilla Abuses

The FARC and the National Liberation Army (ELN) continue to commit serious abuses against civilians, including killings, threats, forced displacement, and recruiting and using child soldiers. In September 2013, the government's human rights Ombudsman's Office expressed alarm over the forced recruitment of children from indigenous Paeces communities in Cauca department, allegedly by the FARC.

The FARC and ELN continue to use antipersonnel landmines. The government reported that landmines and unexploded munitions killed 13 civilians and injured 107 between January and August 2013.

Top FARC and ELN commanders have been convicted in absentia to lengthy prison sentences for a range of serious crimes, including murders, abductions, and child recruitment.

Paramilitaries and Their Successors

Between 2003 and 2006, right-wing paramilitary organizations underwent a deeply flawed government demobilization process in which many members remained active and reorganized into new groups. Successor groups to paramilitaries, largely led by members of demobilized paramilitary organizations, commit widespread abuses against civilians, including killings, disappearances, sexual violence, and forced displacement. According to the 2012 annual report of the International Committee of the Red Cross (ICRC), these groups caused at least as many deaths, threats, incidents of displacement, and disappearances as the armed conflict between the FARC and government forces.

Despite notable gains in capturing their leaders, Colombian authorities have failed to significantly curb the power of paramilitary successor groups: in May 2013, the police reported that the groups had 3,866 members operating in 167 municipalities, as compared to the police's July 2009 estimate of 4,037 members in 173 municipalities. One source of the groups' ongoing power is the toleration and collusion of local security force members.

Implementation of the Justice and Peace Law, which offers dramatically reduced sentences to demobilized paramilitaries who confess their atrocities, has been very slow. As of July 2013, eight years after the law was approved, special Justice and Peace unit prosecutors had obtained convictions against only 18 individuals. In 2013, the unit adopted a new investigative method that has accelerated its progress bringing charges against paramilitaries.

Since the "parapolitics" scandal erupted in 2006, more than 55 current and former members of Congress have been convicted for conspiring with paramilitaries. In August 2013, the Supreme Court ordered the arrest of Luis Alfredo

Ramos, Senate president from 2002-2003, governor of Antioquia from 2008-2011, and a presidential hopeful for the 2014 elections.

The Inspector General's Office, which conducts disciplinary investigations of public officials, has made significantly less progress in sanctioning members of Congress for collaborating with paramilitaries. The office has cleared several former Congressmen who had previously been found guilty of such collaboration in criminal proceedings.

Former President Álvaro Uribe (2002-2010) and his inner circle faced an increasing number of allegations of paramilitary ties. In 2013, prosecutors reopened a preliminary investigation into alleged links between Uribe and paramilitaries. Uribe denies the allegations. Prosecutors also questioned Uribe's brother, Santiago Uribe, in relation to Santiago's alleged role in creating a paramilitary group and a killing in Antioquia department in the 1990s.

In October 2013, prosecutors formally identified Uribe's security chief while president, retired police Gen. Mauricio Santoyo, as a suspect in an investigation into the forced "disappearances" of two human rights activists in 2000. In 2012, Santoyo pled guilty in United States federal court for collaborating with paramilitaries between 2001 and 2008.

Abuses by Public Security Forces

During the Uribe administration, the Colombian army executed an alarming number of civilians, particularly between 2004 and 2008. In many cases—commonly referred to as "false positives"—army personnel killed civilians and reported them as combatants killed in action, apparently in response to pressure from superiors to boost body counts. There has been a dramatic reduction in cases of alleged unlawful killings attributed to security forces since 2009; nevertheless, some isolated cases were reported in 2012 and 2013.

The government does not keep statistics for cases of "false positives" as a separate category of crimes distinct from other types of unlawful killings. However, as of June 2013, the Human Rights Unit of the Attorney General's Office had been assigned investigations into 2,278 cases of alleged unlawful killings by state agents involving nearly 4,000 victims, and had obtained convictions for 189 cases. The convictions covered 605 army members, of whom 91 were (mostly junior) officers. More than 40 army colonels and lieutenant colonels were under investigation, but just four had been convicted at time of writing.

In 2012 and 2013, in cases before the Inter-American Court of Human Rights, the government denied the military's participation in human rights violations for which military members had already been convicted in national courts. The government claimed the FARC killed 17 civilians in Santo Domingo, Arauca in 1998, despite multiple judicial rulings in Colombia establishing the air force's responsibility for the massacre. The court rejected Colombia's arguments and held the state responsible. Similarly, in proceedings before the court concerning the 1985 Palace of Justice siege, the government did not accept that the army participated in enforced "disappearances" for which an army general had already been convicted.

Reforms Promoting Impunity

In July 2012, the government enacted the Legal Framework for Peace constitutional amendment, which paves the way for widespread impunity for atrocities by guerrillas, paramilitaries, and the military if a peace agreement is reached with the FARC. The amendment empowers Congress to limit the scope of prosecutions of atrocities to individuals found "most responsible," and provide statutory immunity to others who planned, executed, and covered up the same crimes but are not deemed "most responsible," a category the amendment did not define.

Furthermore, it gives Congress the authority to exempt from criminal investigation entire cases of atrocities—such as rapes or enforced "disappearances"—if they did not form part of a systematic attack. Lastly, the amendment enables Congress to fully suspend prison sentences for all guerrillas, paramilitaries, and military personnel convicted of heinous abuses, including those found "most responsible" for Colombia's worst crimes.

Colombia's Constitutional Court reviewed the Legal Framework for Peace and declared it constitutional in August 2013. However, the court corrected a major flaw in the amendment by prohibiting full suspension of penalties for those "most responsible" for atrocities, according to a press release summarizing the court's ruling, which was not public at time of writing.

In December 2012, the Santos administration enacted a constitutional change to the military justice system that created a serious risk that "false positive" investigations would be transferred from civilian prosecutors to military courts, which have long failed to hold perpetrators accountable.

In June 2013, as a result of the amendment, the case of an army colonel facing trial for two alleged false positive killings was transferred to the military justice system. In addition to opening the door to the transfer of false positive cases, the amendment's implementing law, which Congress approved in June 2013, also authorized security forces to use lethal force in a dangerously broad range of situations. In October 2013, the Constitutional Court struck down the change to the military justice system on procedural grounds; however, President Santos announced the government would resubmit a new draft of the exact same amendment to Congress in 2014.

Internal Displacement and Land Restitution

More than 5 million Colombians have been internally displaced since 1985, according to newly revised government figures. The government registered more than 150,000 newly displaced people in 2012, while CODHES, a respected Colombian nongovernmental organization (NGO), reports nearly 260,000 Colombians were displaced that year. Displacement levels are particularly high along the Pacific Coast, such as in the predominantly Afro-Colombian city of Buenaventura, where paramilitary successor groups caused the forced displacement of more than 2,500 people during the first week of November 2012.

The Colombian government has made limited progress implementing its land restitution program under the Victims Law, which was enacted in 2011 to restore millions of hectares of stolen and abandoned land to displaced people. The Agricultural Ministry estimated that by the end of 2014 there would be judicial rulings in nearly 80,000 land restitution cases under the Victims Law; however, as of September 2013, the government had obtained rulings ordering restitution for 666 of the more than 45,000 land claims it had received. By September 2013—more than two years since the Victims Law was enacted—the government reported just three families had returned to live on their land due to rulings under law.

IDPs face threats and violence for attempting to reclaim their land. Between January 2012 and September 2013, more than 700 displaced land claimants and their leaders seeking land restitution through the Victims Law reported to authorities that they had received threats. Prosecutors have not charged a single suspect in any of their investigations into such threats. As of August 2013, the Attorney General's Office reported that it was investigating 43 cases of killings of "leaders, claimants, or participants in land restitution matters" committed since 2008.

Gender-Based Violence

Gender-based violence (GBV) is widespread in Colombia. Lack of training and poor implementation of protocols create obstacles for women and girls seeking post-violence care, with the result that victims may face delays in accessing essential medical services. Perpetrators of GBV crimes are rarely brought to justice.

Violence against Human Rights Defenders, Journalists, and Trade Unionists

Rights advocates and journalists continue to be targeted for threats and attacks. On May 1, unidentified gunmen opened fire against Ricardo Calderón, a leading investigative journalist who had just exposed in *Semana* magazine how army members convicted of atrocities were enjoying extravagant privileges at the Tolemaida military detention center. Calderón escaped the attack without injuries.

The National Labor School (ENS), Colombia's leading NGO monitoring labor rights, continues to report killings of trade unionists, though the annual number of cases remains on the decline. Threats against trade unionists are common.

The Interior Ministry runs a protection program that covers thousands of at-risk members of vulnerable groups, including human rights defenders, trade unionists, and land restitution claimants.

Key International Actors

The United States remains the most influential foreign actor in Colombia. In 2013, it provided approximately US$473 million in aid, 59 percent of which went to the military and police. A portion of US military aid is subject to human rights conditions, which the US Department of State has not enforced. In September 2013, the State Department certified that Colombia was meeting human rights benchmarks, even though its military justice system reform directly contradicted the condition requiring that civilian authorities investigate and try all alleged human rights violations.

The UN Office of the High Commissioner for Human Rights (OHCHR) is active in Colombia. In April, the government announced it would renew the OHCHR country office mandate through 2016, but three months later, following a statement by the office calling for an investigation into the police's possible excessive use of force, President Santos said he had not decided if he would extend the mandate. The government ultimately extended the mandate through October 2014.

The ICRC is also active in Colombia, where its work includes providing assistance to IDPs. The office of the prosecutor of the International Criminal Court (ICC) continued to monitor local investigations into crimes that may fall within the ICC's jurisdiction. In July 2013, the ICC's chief prosecutor sent a letter to the Constitutional Court stating that full suspension of penalties for those most responsible for crimes against humanity and war crimes could trigger an investigation by the international body.

Cuba

In 2010 and 2011, Cuba's government released dozens of political prisoners on condition they accept exile in exchange for freedom. Since then, it has relied less on long-term prison sentences to punish dissent and has relaxed draconian travel restrictions that divided families and prevented its critics from leaving and returning to the island.

Nevertheless, the Cuban government continues to repress individuals and groups who criticize the government or call for basic human rights. Officials employ a range of tactics to punish dissent and instill fear in the public, including beatings, public acts of shaming, termination of employment, and threats of long-term imprisonment. Short-term arbitrary arrests have increased dramatically in recent years and routinely prevent human rights defenders, independent journalists, and others from gathering or moving about freely.

Arbitrary Detentions and Short-Term Imprisonment

The government continues to rely on arbitrary detention to harass and intimidate individuals who exercise their fundamental rights. The Cuban Commission for Human Rights and National Reconciliation—an independent human rights group the government views as illegal—received over 3,600 reports of arbitrary detentions from January through September 2013, compared to approximately 2,100 in 2010.

The detentions are often used preemptively to prevent individuals from participating in events viewed as critical of the government, such as peaceful marches or meetings to discuss politics. Many dissidents are beaten and threatened when detained, even if they do not try to resist.

Security officers virtually never present arrest orders to justify detentions and threaten detainees with criminal sentences if they continue to participate in "counterrevolutionary" activities. In some cases, detainees receive official warnings, which prosecutors may later use in criminal trials to show a pattern of delinquent behavior. Dissidents said these warnings aim to discourage them from participating in activities seen as critical of the government.

Victims of such arrests may be held incommunicado for several hours to several days. Some are held at police stations, while others are driven to remote areas far from their homes where they are interrogated, threatened, and abandoned.

On August 25, 2013, more than 30 women from the Damas de Blanco (Ladies in White)—a group founded by the wives, mothers, and daughters of political prisoners and which the government considers illegal—were detained after attending Sunday mass at a church in Santiago, beaten, forced onto a bus, and left at various isolated locations on the city's outskirts. The same day, eight members of the group in Havana and seven more in Holguín were arbitrarily detained as they marched peacefully to attend mass.

Political Prisoners

Cubans who criticize the government may face criminal prosecution. They do not benefit from due process guarantees, such as the right to fair and public hearings by a competent and impartial tribunal. In practice, courts are "subordinated" to the executive and legislative branches, denying meaningful judicial independence. Political prisoners are routinely denied parole after completing the minimum required sentence as punishment for refusing to participate in ideological activities, such as "reeducation" classes.

The death of political prisoner Orlando Zapata Tamayo in 2010 after his 85-day hunger strike and the subsequent hunger strike by dissident Guillermo Fariñas pressured the government to release the remaining political prisoners from the "group of 75" (75 dissidents sentenced to long prison terms in a 2003 crackdown). Yet most were forced to choose between ongoing prison sentences and forced exile. The overwhelming majority accepted relocation to Spain in exchange for their freedom.

Dozens of political prisoners remain in Cuban prisons according to local human rights groups, which estimate that there are more political prisoners whose cases they cannot document because the government prevents independent national or international human rights groups from accessing its prisons.

Luis Enrique Labrador Diaz was one of four people detained in January 2011 for distributing leaflets in Havana with slogans such as "Down with the Castros" and was subsequently convicted in May 2011 for contempt and public disorder in a closed, summary trial. He was still in prison at time of writing.

Freedom of Expression

The government controls all media outlets in Cuba and tightly restricts access to outside information, severely limiting the right to freedom of expression. Only a tiny fraction of Cubans are able to read independent websites and blogs because of the high cost of and limited access to the Internet. A May 2013 government decree directed at expanding Internet access stipulates that it cannot be used for activities that undermine "public security, the integrity, the economy, independence, and national security" of Cuba—broad conditions that could be used to impede access to government critics.

A small number of independent journalists and bloggers manage to write articles for websites or blogs, or publish tweets. Yet those who publish information considered critical of the government are sometimes subject to smear campaigns, attacks, and arbitrary arrests, as are artists and academics who demand greater freedoms.

After jazz musician Roberto Carcasses called for direct elections and freedom of information in a nationally televised concert in Havana in September 2013, officials told him that his words benefitted "the enemy" and that he would be barred from performing in state-run venues. The government lifted the ban— widely reported in the international press—a week later. In May, the director of the government-run Casa de las Americas cultural institute, Roberto Zurbano, published an article in the *New York Times* highlighting persistent inequality and prejudice affecting Afro-Cubans. He was subsequently attacked in the government-controlled press and demoted to a lesser job at the institute.

Human Rights Defenders

The Cuban government refuses to recognize human rights monitoring as a legitimate activity and denies legal status to local human rights groups. Meanwhile, government authorities harass, assault, and imprison human rights defenders who attempt to document abuses.

Travel Restrictions and Family Separation

Reforms to travel regulations that went into effect in January 2013 eliminate the need for an exit visa to leave the island, which had previously been used to deny the right to travel to people critical of the government and their families. Nearly 183,000 people traveled abroad from January to September 2013, according to the government. These included human rights defenders, journalists, and bloggers who previously had been denied permission to leave the island despite repeated requests, such as blogger Yoani Sanchez.

Nonetheless, the reform establishes that the government may restrict the right to travel on the vague grounds of "defense and national security" or "other reasons of public interest," which could allow the authorities to deny people who express dissent the ability to leave Cuba. The government also continues to arbitrarily deny Cubans living abroad the right to visit the island. In August, the Cuban government denied Blanca Reyes, a Damas de Blanco member living in exile in Spain, permission to travel to Cuba to visit her ailing 93-year-old father, who died in October before she could visit him.

The government restricts the movement of citizens within Cuba through a 1997 law known as Decree 217. Designed to limit migration to Havana, the decree requires that Cubans obtain government permission before moving to the country's capital. It is often used to prevent dissidents traveling there to attend meetings and to harass dissidents from other parts of Cuba who live in the capital.

Prison Conditions

Prisons are overcrowded, unhygienic, and unhealthy, leading to extensive malnutrition and illness. More than 57,000 Cubans are in prisons or work camps, according to a May 2012 article in an official government newspaper. Prisoners who criticize the government or engage in hunger strikes and other forms of protest are subjected to extended solitary confinement, beatings, restrictions on family visits, and denial of medical care. Prisoners have no effective complaint mechanism to seek redress.

While the government allowed select members of the foreign press to conduct controlled visits to a handful of prisons in April, it continued to deny international human rights groups and independent Cuban organizations access to its prisons.

Key International Actors

The United States' economic embargo of Cuba, in place for more than half a century, continues to impose indiscriminate hardship on the Cuban people and has done nothing to improve the country's human rights. At the United Nations General Assembly in October, 188 of the 192 member countries voted for a resolution condemning the US embargo.

In 2009, President Barack Obama enacted reforms to eliminate restrictions on travel and remittances by Cuban Americans to Cuba put in place during the administration of President George W. Bush in 2004. In 2011, Obama used his executive powers to ease "people-to-people" travel restrictions, allowing religious, educational, and cultural groups from the US to travel to Cuba.

The European Union continues to retain its "Common Position" on Cuba, adopted in 1996, which conditions full economic cooperation with Cuba on the country's transition to a pluralist democracy and respect for human rights.

Former US Agency for International Development contractor Alan Gross remained in prison despite a UN Working Group on Arbitrary Detention report in November 2012 that called for his immediate release. Gross was detained in Cuba in December 2009 and later sentenced to 15 years in prison for distributing telecommunications equipment to religious groups. The working group said Gross's detention was arbitrary and that Cuba's government had failed to provide sufficient evidence of the charges against him.

In May, Cuba underwent its second Universal Periodic Review at the UN Human Rights Council. Several countries expressed concern with repression of human rights defenders, increased arbitrary detentions, and lack of freedom of expression. Cuba rejected many of these recommendations on the grounds that they were "politically biased and built on false premises, resulting from efforts to discredit Cuba on the part of those who, with their hegemonic ambitions, refuse to accept the diversity and the right to freedom of determination of the Cuban people."

In November, Cuba was re-elected to a seat on the UN Human Rights Council, defeating Uruguay for a regional position despite its poor human rights record and consistent efforts to undermine the council's work to respond to human rights violators.

Ecuador

After being re-elected to a third term in February 2013, President Rafael Correa promulgated a sweeping new Communications Law in June regulating broadcast and print media, which undercuts press freedom. The Correa government continues to subject members of the media to public recrimination. Prosecutors use overly broad counterterrorism and sabotage offences against government critics who engage in public protests.

Other ongoing problems include vaguely worded restrictions affecting civil society organizations, and asylum application procedures that do not provide rigorous safeguards that international standards require. Unable to obtain a legal abortion, rape victims may resort to illegal and unsafe abortions that endanger their life and health.

Freedom of Expression

The Communications Law that the National Assembly approved in June 2013 contains vague provisions that allow arbitrary prosecutions and censorship. The law's invocation of a constitutional right to information that is "verified, contrasted, precise, and contextualized," opens the door to censorship by giving the government or judges the power to decide if information is truthful.

A government regulatory body, the Superintendent of Information and Communication, may order media outlet directors to rectify and publicly apologize for information deemed to be untruthful, impose fines for repeated incidents, and pursue judicial action against them. Moreover, the law grants the government extremely broad regulating powers that could severely limit free speech by defining social communication through media as a "public service" that should be provided with "responsibility and quality" and "contribute to the good life of people."

In addition, journalists responsible for "media lynching"—defined as persistent critical reporting "with the purpose of undermining the prestige or credibility of a person or legal entity" may be obliged to issue a public apology, and may face criminal prosecution for other crimes.

In August, citing provisions of the law that define matters of public relevance and the right to a correction for disseminating inaccurate information, the communications minister ordered *El Universo* newspaper to publicly apologize for publishing tweets he alleged undermined the president's honor and reputation. The minister accused *El Universo* of "quoting out of context" and "frivolity" (*ligereza*), and of publishing information of no "public relevance." *El Universo* had published tweets by Correa explaining his decision to allow oil exploitation in the Yasuní national park, and tweets by individuals to Correa opposing his decision.

President Correa continues to use criminal defamation laws to target his critics. In September 2013, the National Court of Justice upheld the conviction of opposition legislator José Cléver Jiménez for slandering the president, sentenced him to 18 months in prison, and ordered him to publicly apologize to the president and pay him approximately US$140,000. Together with two union members whose conviction the court also upheld, Jiménez had asked the attorney general to investigate Correa's responsibility for violence that led to five deaths during a September 2010 police mutiny, accusing him of ordering an armed assault on a hospital where civilians were present.

The attorney general—who had been Correa's personal lawyer during part of his first term of office—found that there was insufficient evidence to open an investigation and, in May 2012, a judge dismissed the case. In August 2012, Correa filed a complaint before the National Court of Justice accusing Jiménez and the others of slander. A proposal to reform the Ecuadoran Criminal Code under debate in the National Assembly as of October 2013 would eliminate several defamation provisions from the current code, but retain the crime of slander.

The Correa government frequently requires private outlets to transmit official broadcasts to refute information or critical opinions, which authorities argue is necessary to fulfill the government's obligation to refute media falsehoods and distortions.

Judicial Independence

Corruption, inefficiency, and political influence have plagued Ecuador's judiciary for years. With a popular mandate following a 2011 referendum, the Correa administration initiated an ambitious judicial reform process that included appointing a new National Court of Justice and hundreds of lower level judges. In December 2012, government-invited observers from Argentina, Brazil, Chile, Guatemala, Mexico, and Spain, published a report finding anomalies in the judicial appointment process, including that of top justices. The observers urged the passage of a law to regulate disciplinary procedures, defining faults clearly in order to avoid the risk of judges being suspended or punished simply for exercising their duties.

Disproportionate Criminal Charges against Protesters

The Criminal Code contains sweeping provisions on sabotage and terrorism, which prosecutors have repeatedly applied inappropriately against participants in public protests and other gatherings. Acts classified as terrorism in Ecuador include vaguely defined crimes such as "crimes against the common security of people or human groups of whatever kind or against their property," by individuals or associations "armed or not." Such crimes carry a possible prison sentence of four to eight years. A new draft of the criminal code that was under congressional debate as of October 2013 would modify the existing definition of terrorism, but the new definition could still allow prosecutors to bring terrorism charges against participants in public protest.

In February 2013, a court sentenced ten people, known as the Luluncoto 10 (after the Quito neighborhood where they were detained), to one year in prison for attempted sabotage and terrorism. Arrested in March 2012 while holding a peaceful meeting to plan a public protest, most were held in pretrial detention for nine months. Their lawyers maintained the only evidence against them consisted of personal objects found in their homes, such as innocuous books, clothing, and music. As of October 2013, their appeal alleging mistrial was still pending.

Prosecutors have filed other serious charges against participants in public protests that are disproportionate to alleged acts. In February 2013, 12 students were charged for rebellion, a crime that carries a prison sentence of up to six years, for their alleged participation in violent incidents during a protest in Quito against the decision to change the name of their university. A judge later dismissed the charges after the prosecutor was unable to substantiate them. After Correa criticized the judge's decision in his weekly TV broadcast, another prosecutor reopened the case. In a second trial in July, the 12 were convicted and sentenced to 21 days in prison.

Accountability for Past Abuses

Efforts to hold to account those responsible for human rights violations committed by governments from 1984 to 2008 made significant progress in 2013. In 2010, a special prosecutorial unit was formed to investigate 118 cases involving 456 victims (including 68 victims of extrajudicial execution and 17 of enforced disappearance), which had been documented by a truth commission created by the Correa administration. In 2012, the number of cases under investigation rose to 138. In October 2013, two former government defense ministers and eight retired military and police officers were charged with enforced disappearance and torture in connection with the illegal arrest in 1985 and torture of three people linked to a guerilla group. As of October 2013, work by a human rights investigative unit attached to the Attorney General's Office had led to charges being filed against 36 government agents in three other cases from the period covered by the Truth Commission report.

Reproductive Rights

Women and girls in Ecuador have the right to seek abortions only when their health or life is at risk or when pregnancies result from the rape of an "idiot or demented" woman. In October, as part of the drafting of the new criminal code, the National Assembly was considering a change in terminology, substituting "mental disability" for "idiot or demented." The new language continues to imply that women and girls with disability would be "unfit" mothers, and to prevent all other victims of rape from accessing legal abortion. One in four women in Ecuador have been victims of sexual violence, according to government figures. Threat of criminal penalty drives some women and girls to have illegal and unsafe abortions, and impedes health care and post-rape services for victims of sexual violence. Fear of prosecution also hinders detection and prevention of sexual and gender-based violence.

Sexual Orientation and Gender Identity

Private drug and alcohol rehabilitation centers continue to operate to "cure" gay people of homosexuality, a practice Ecuador's health minister has said is illegal. Following the June 2013 escape by 22-year-old psychology student Zulema Constante from confinement in one such center, the minister of health announced a crackdown on clinics engaging in this practice. According to the minister, from March 2012 to July 2013 authorities closed 15 clinics for alleged human rights violations.

Human Rights Defenders and Civil Society Organizations

Correa's government has routinely sought to discredit human rights defenders by accusing them of seeking to destabilize the government. On at least two occasions in 2013, the communications ministry interrupted programming on the Ecuavisa channel to excoriate the nongovernmental press freedom group Fundamedios after the station transmitted interviews with its director.

The Correa administration has issued sweeping executive decrees that allow greater control over nongovernmental organizations (NGOs), some of which have been outspoken critics of the government. In June 2013, Correa issued a decree granting the government broad powers to intervene in NGO operations. The decree's vague language, which includes authority to dissolve Ecuadorian groups for "compromis[ing] public peace," provides scope for arbitrary application and poses a threat to a robust civil society.

Refugees

As of August 2013, Ecuador had nearly 55,000 registered refugees, the largest number of any Latin American country. Most are Colombians fleeing armed conflict. Presidential Decree 1182, which Correa issued in May 2012 to regulate asylum procedures, narrows the definition of who may be considered a refugee, and establishes an unfair procedure to determine which asylum claims should be deemed "manifestly unfounded." It also allows officials to reject an asylum application before a substantive review if well-founded reasons exist to believe the applicant had committed a crime, without providing for rigorous procedural safeguards that international standards require to ensure a full factual and legal assessment of the case. The decree also grants overly broad powers to revoke refugee status.

These provisions are counter to international standards in the Convention Relating to the Status of Refugees and its Protocol, the Cartagena Declaration on Refugees, and guidelines adopted by the United Nations High Commissioner for Refugees.

Key International Actors

In March 2013, the Organization of American States (OAS) rejected proposals led by Ecuador with the support of other members of the Bolivarian Alliance for the Americas (ALBA) to block outside funding for the Inter-American Commission on Human Rights, including the special rapporteur on freedom of expression. However, Ecuador, as well as other ALBA members, made clear its intent to continue pressing for these changes.

In a speech to the OAS General Assembly in June, Ecuador's foreign minister complained that the funds available to the special rapporteur on freedom of expression discriminated against OAS bodies dealing with other human rights issues, and that the rapporteur's 2012 report on Ecuador distorted information, used biased sources, and was politically motivated. The special rapporteur continues to play an important role in advocating for press freedom in Ecuador. In October at an ALBA meeting in Cochabamba, Bolivia, President Correa said he would "think seriously" about continuing to participate in the Inter-American system of human rights protection if the changes that Ecuador advocated were not implemented.

Guatemala

Former Guatemalan leader Efraín Ríos Montt was found guilty in May 2013 of genocide and crimes against humanity, the first time that any head of state has been convicted of genocide in a national court. The ruling was overturned on procedural grounds days later, however, and a new trial is scheduled for January 2015.

The Attorney General's Office has made progress on other prominent human rights cases, though impunity remains high. The mandate of the United Nations International Commission against Impunity in Guatemala (CICIG), which since 2007 has supported efforts to investigate and prosecute organized crime, was extended for two years in September. President Otto Pérez Molina has said that this will be the commission's final term.

President Pérez Molina has continued to expand the role of the Guatemalan military in public security operations, despite its poor human rights record.

Guatemala hosted the 43rd General Assembly of the Organization of American States in June 2013, where the main topic of discussion was drug policy reform. The Pérez Molina administration has taken a leading role in promoting alternative approaches to drug policy, arguing that regulating the trade, allowing limited legal consumption and production of narcotics, could reduce violence and abuses tied to organized crime.

Accountability for Past Atrocities

In a landmark ruling, former head of state Efraín Ríos Montt was found guilty in May of genocide and crimes against humanity, and sentenced to 80 years in prison. The retired general led a military regime from 1982 to 1983 that carried out hundreds of massacres of unarmed civilians. However, the verdict was overturned 10 days later, when the Constitutional Court ruled that all proceedings in the final three weeks of the trial had been invalid due to irregularities relating to an incident in March, when Ríos Montt was briefly without his own defense attorney. The case will likely have to be retried in full, with witnesses testifying once more before a different criminal court. Proceedings are scheduled to begin in January 2015. Representatives of the victims filed a petition before the Inter-

American Commission of Human Rights in November, accusing the Guatemalan state of failing to provide justice in the case.

Ríos Montt's defense has made repeated requests for the former leader to be protected from prosecution under amnesty legislation.

In April, while the genocide trial was ongoing, President Pérez Molina expressed his support for a public letter signed by a group of prominent politicians that called genocide charges against members of the army a "fabrication," and said that the charges endangered peace.

Ríos Montt has been charged in a separate case involving a 1982 massacre in the town of Dos Erres, in the Petén region, in which soldiers murdered more than 250 people, including children. Proceedings, which are ongoing, have been delayed by legal challenges from Ríos Montt's lawyers.

Five former members of army special forces have received lengthy prison sentences for their role in the Dos Erres massacre, while several high-level former members of the security forces have been convicted in recent years of human rights crimes committed in previous decades. They include former National Police Chief Héctor Bol de la Cruz, who received a 40-year sentence in September for ordering the disappearance of a student activist in 1984.

Public Security and the Criminal Justice System

Powerful criminal organizations engage in widespread acts of violence and extortion. The intimidation and corruption of justice system officials, as well as the absence of an effective witness protection program, contribute to high levels of impunity. Frustrated with the lack of criminal enforcement, some communities have resorted to vigilantism. According to the Human Rights Ombudsman, 23 people were killed in lynchings in 2012, and another six by February 2013.

Despite these challenges, prosecutors have made progress in cases of violent crime, as well as torture, extrajudicial killings, and corruption—due in large part to the work of Attorney General Claudia Paz y Paz, as well as the support of CICIG.

In August, Víctor Hugo Soto Diéguez, a former head of Criminal Investigation of the National Civil Police, was sentenced to 33 years in prison for forming part of a group that executed 10 prisoners from Pavón and El Infiernito prisons in 2005 and 2006, with the alleged participation of senior government officials.

In November 2012, the CICIG released a report accusing 18 judges of issuing "illegal judicial decisions" to protect criminal networks and corrupt officials. The prosecutor's office launched proceedings to strip 13 of the judges of their immunity, several of which have been rejected by the Supreme Court.

The Attorney General's Office arrested eight soldiers and a colonel accused of responsibility for the killing of six protesters in Totonicapán in October 2012. Their case has been delayed by legal challenges, and at time of writing the trial had not begun.

The progress made by the Public Prosecutor's office and CICIG in bringing charges against officials has been undercut by the dilatory practices of defendants' lawyers, including the abuse of *amparo* protection appeals leading to trial postponements of months or even years.

Use of Military in Public Security Operations

The government deployed more than 2,500 additional members of the military in public security roles in 2013, including three newly created army units with a total of 1,500 members.

The government declared a state of emergency in several municipalities in the south of the country in May following violent clashes involving anti-mining protesters, police, and the mine's private security guards. The measure, lifted before its 30 days were up, gave the military the power to carry out arrests without a warrant, and suspended freedom of assembly and other basic rights.

Child Labor and Exploitation

A 2013 report, produced by the government with support from the International Labour Organization, found that the proportion of children working below Guatemala's legal minimum working age of 14 had dropped more than one-third between 2000 and 2011. The number was some 300,000, equivalent to eleven percent of those aged 7 to 13. Twenty-one percent of these children carried out work the government considers dangerous.

The exploitation of children in sexual tourism, pornography, and organized crime is a widespread problem.

Gender-Based Violence

Violence against women and girls is a chronic problem in Guatemala and perpetrators rarely face trial. According to official figures quoted by Guatemala's Human Rights Ombudsman's Office, reported rapes and sexual assaults of women and girls increased by more than a third between 2008 and 2011, while in more than 9 of every 10 of these cases, those responsible were not punished.

Abortion is illegal, even in cases of rape, except where there is a threat to the life of the woman.

Palliative Care

Palliative care is very limited in Guatemala, even though more than 10,000 people die of cancer or HIV/AIDS each year, many in severe pain. Although the introduction of immediate release morphine in 2012 was a positive development, the country maintains some of the most restrictive regulations on opioid medications in the world, effectively denying access to essential pain medicines to thousands of patients each year.

Attacks on Human Rights Defenders, Trade Unionists, and Journalists

Attacks and threats against human rights defenders are common, significantly hampering human rights work throughout the country. Acts of violence and intimidation against trade unionists endangers freedom of assembly and association, and the right to organize and bargain collectively.

Journalists, especially those covering corruption and drug trafficking, also face threats and attacks. The UN special rapporteur on freedom of opinion and expression said in August that the level of aggression against the press had reached a level not seen in a decade. In August President Pérez Molina promised a thorough investigation into the attacks carried out in 2013, and said that the government would move forward with the creation of a UN-backed Program to Protect Journalists, promised since 2012.

Key International Actors

The CICIG, established in 2007, plays a key role in assisting the Guatemala's justice system in prosecuting violent crime, working with the Attorney General's Office, the police, and other government agencies to investigate, prosecute, and dismantle criminal organizations operating in Guatemala. The CICIG can participate in criminal proceedings as a complementary prosecutor, provide technical assistance, and promote legislative reforms. As of September 2013, it had initiated 320 investigations, which resulted in 88 convictions.

The CICIG's mandate was renewed in September 2013 for two additional years, but President Pérez Molina has stated that it will not be renewed again when it expires in 2015. Iván Velásquez Gómez, a prominent Colombian jurist, was appointed to lead the CICIG following the resignation of the previous head. Formerly an auxiliary magistrate on Colombia's Supreme Court, Velásquez played a leading role in investigating ties between politicians and paramilitary groups in that country.

The UN High Commissioner for Human Rights has maintained an office in Guatemala since 2005. The office monitors the human rights situation in the country and provides policy support to the government and civil society.

In January, the Guatemalan government published a resolution restricting the jurisdiction of the Inter-American Court of Human Rights to incidents that took place after 1987, but withdrew the resolution later that month amid criticism.

The Inter-American Commission on Human Rights' (IACHR) rapporteur on the rights of indigenous peoples carried out a working visit to Guatemala in August 2013, and expressed concern that licenses for mining and hydroelectric plants had been granted without properly consulting affected indigenous communities, as required by international law.

Two former Guatemalan officials allegedly involved in a plan to execute prisoners from Pavón and El Infiernito prisons in 2005 and 2006 are currently facing criminal prosecution in Switzerland, and Spain, while a third former official was acquitted in October by an Austrian court.

In October, Jorge Vinicio Sosa Orantes, a former Guatemalan soldier who allegedly participated in the Dos Erres massacre, was found guilty by a US court of lying about his role in the incident on his application for US citizenship, which he received in 2008.

The Pérez Molina government has asked the US to lift military aid restrictions established in 1990. Some military aid was restarted nearly a decade ago. In April, the US donated 42 armored vehicles to a new military-police task force operating close to the Mexican border.

Haiti

Election delays, natural disasters, and the persistence of a deadly cholera epidemic continue to hinder the Haitian government's efforts to meet the basic needs of its people and address long-standing human rights problems, such as violence against women and inhumane prison conditions.

Postponement of national and local elections originally scheduled for 2011 continued to foster political uncertainty and undermine the right to political participation. As of October, one-third of Senate seats remained vacant and the fate of another third was uncertain due to conflicting interpretations of a 2008 electoral law. At the local level, terms for elected posts in 129 of the country's 140 municipalities also expired in 2011. The administration of President Michel Martelly filled these posts with political appointees in 2012. With prompting by the United Nations and other international actors, Martelly convoked a special session of Parliament on November 22 to consider a draft electoral law for regulating the overdue elections. At time of writing, the session had not met.

A wave of anti-government protests beginning in October led to confrontations between protestors and Martelly supporters, which raised concerns about the resurgence of political violence in the country.

As of June 2013, 280,000 internally displaced persons (IDPs) were living in camps established in the aftermath of the 2010 earthquake, according to the UN. The International Organization for Migration estimated that of 71,000 displaced households, 57,000 have no prospect of IDP sites, while at least 21,000 could face eviction. Nearly 1,200 households were evicted between January and June, often with the involvement of the police or other government entities.

The three-year-old cholera epidemic continues to claim lives, with an estimated 8,500 people killed and 694,000 infected since October 2010. Damage caused by Hurricane Sandy in October 2012 and droughts affected harvests, contributing to high levels of food insecurity.

Deficiencies in the Criminal Justice System and Detention Conditions

Haiti's prison system remains severely overcrowded, in large part due to high numbers of arbitrary arrests and prolonged pretrial detentions. Public health efforts by the government and the UN Stabilization Mission in Haiti (MINUSTAH) reduced the rate of inmate deaths in the first half of the year, which had spiked in 2012.

The weak capacity of the Haitian National Police (HNP) contributes to overall insecurity in the country. While the government and MINUSTAH have made reforming the police a priority, there have been difficulties training sufficient numbers of entry-level cadets. Oversight and accountability within the HNP remain weak, and investigations made by the Inspectorate General of the police into human rights abuses by police made little progress.

Accountability for Past Abuses

Former President Jean-Claude Duvalier returned to Haiti in January 2011 after nearly 25 years in exile. He was charged with financial and human rights crimes allegedly committed during his 15-year tenure as president. From 1971 to 1986, Duvalier commanded a network of security forces that committed serious human rights violations, including arbitrary detentions, torture, disappearances, summary executions, and forced exile.

In 2012, the investigating judge in the case found, contrary to international standards, that the statute of limitations prevented prosecuting Duvalier for his human rights crimes. An appellate court heard testimony in a challenge to the ruling over several months beginning in February. Duvalier appeared in court on February 28 and answered questions posed by the court and victims' attorneys. At time of writing, the court had not issued its ruling.

Violence against Women

Gender-based violence is a widespread problem. Draft revisions to Haiti's criminal code, which at time of writing were awaiting approval of the Council of Ministers before introduction to Parliament, include acts of gender-based violence, such as rape and sexual assault, not currently in the code.

Women seeking accountability for sexual violence crimes encounter multiple obstacles, including reproach by members of the public or threats. In one high-profile case, a woman pressed charges against a former justice minister, claiming he had raped her in 2012. She subsequently reported receiving multiple death threats, which led her to withdraw her criminal complaint.

Violence Based on Sexual Orientation and Gender Identity

Public statements by religious leaders in June led to a spate of protests and violence targeting lesbian, gay, bisexual, transgender, and intersex (LGBTI) people. The Haitian nongovernmental organization SEROvie documented 47 cases violence targeting LGBTI persons between July 17 and 24, including attacks with knives, machetes, cement blocks, rocks, and sticks. At least three victims were hospitalized. On July 21, the Haitian government issued a statement condemning homophobic violence. Investigations into crimes against LGBTI persons rarely progress, however, and police and justice officials lack training on issues related to sexual orientation and gender identity.

Children's Domestic Labor

Use of child domestic workers—known as restavèks—continues. Restavèks, the majority of whom are girls, are sent from low-income households to live with wealthier families in the hope that they will be schooled and cared for in exchange for performing light chores. Though difficult to calculate, some estimates suggest that 225,00 children work as restavèks. These children are often unpaid, denied education, and physically or sexually abused. Haiti's labor code does not set a minimum age for work in domestic services, though the minimum age for work in industrial, agricultural and commercial enterprises is set at 15.

Human Rights Defenders

Human rights defenders face threats of violence. Patrick Florvilus, a pro bono lawyer, reported receiving death threats since representing two men injured (one later died) during a police intervention in an IDP camp in April. In August, the court in Port-au-Prince summoned Florvilus in connection with a criminal arson case against him, which he alleged is frivolous and meant to intimidate him.

The Inter-American Commission on Human Rights issued precautionary measures in October 2012 for human rights lawyer Mario Joseph and considered
measures for two other lawyers, André Michel and Newton Saint Juste. On
October 22, 2013, police detained Michel, who has filed corruption charges
against members of Martelly's family. The following morning his supporters
stormed the Port-au-Prince courthouse where he was due to appear, freed him,
and brought him to the offices of the powerful Port-au-Prince Bar Association.
The attempted arrest sparked a lawyers' strike preventing courts in the capital
from functioning.

In August, unknown gunmen shot into the home of Malya Villard Apollon, co-
director of the Commission of Women Victims for Victims (KOFAVIV). In
September and October, unknown assailants harassed and threatened activists
working at KOFAVIV, and poisoned Apollon's two dogs. In November, three
armed men attacked the offices of the LGBTI organization Kouraj, assaulted two
of its members, and stole computers and files containing confidential information about people in the group. The incident followed months of anonymous
threats instructing organization leaders to cease advocacy on behalf of LGBTI
persons.

Key International Actors

The UN mission, MINUSTAH, has been in Haiti since 2004 and has contributed
to efforts to improve public security, protect vulnerable groups, and strengthen
the country's democratic institutions.

In October 2010, allegations surfaced that a contingent of UN peacekeepers was
the source of the cholera epidemic. A 2011 UN independent investigation found
that the outbreak was caused by a South Asian strain of the cholera bacteria,
but stopped short of identifying peacekeepers as the source. However, in July
2013, scientists from the UN panel stated that evidence presented by numerous
scientific studies now supported the conclusion that MINUSTAH soldiers most
likely had introduced the strain.

The Ministry of Public Health and Population continues to document hundreds of cases of the illness weekly, resulting in dozens of deaths monthly: in August, it reported that cholera had killed 8,173 people and infected 664,282 since October 2010, with 258 deaths and 28,800 infections in the first half of 2013. The UN reports the number of humanitarian organizations participating in the cholera response, as well as medical stocks needed to treat projected cases, has fallen significantly since 2012.

In October 2013, UN High Commissioner for Human Rights Navi Pillay publicly stated that cholera victims should be provided compensation, although she did not specify who should be responsible for funding the reparation. Also in October, the Institute for Justice and Democracy in Haiti and the Bureau des Avocats Internationaux filed a class-action law suit against the UN in a US federal court in New York. The claim calls for the UN to pay US$2.2 billion for a cholera eradication program and an unspecified amount in damages for 679,000 individual victims. At time of writing, plaintiffs had not affected service of notice of the complaint on the UN; therefore the UN had not responded to the claim in court.

The Institute for Justice and Democracy in Haiti and the Bureau des Avocats Internationaux filed a claim directly with the UN in November 2011 on behalf of 5,000 cholera victims, alleging that MINUSTAH was the proximate cause of their illness. The claim sought the installation of a national water and sanitation system, financial compensation for individual victims, and a public apology from the UN. In February 2013, the UN informed the victims by letter that the claims were not "receivable," citing the Convention on the Privileges and Immunities of the UN.

According to UN figures, at least 81 allegations of sexual abuse or exploitation have been made against MINUSTAH personnel in the last six years, including 16 in 2013, as of mid-November.

The UN Security Council extended MINUSTAH's mandate through October 15, 2014.

Honduras

Honduras suffers from rampant crime and impunity for human rights abuses. The murder rate, which has risen consistently over the last decade, was the highest in the world in 2013. Perpetrators of killings and other violent crimes are rarely brought to justice. The institutions responsible for providing public security continue to prove largely ineffective and remain marred by corruption and abuse, while efforts to reform them have made little progress.

Journalists, peasant activists, and LGBTI individuals are particularly vulnerable to attacks, yet the government routinely fails to prosecute those responsible and provide protection for those at risk.

After it arbitrarily dismissed four Supreme Court judges in December 2012, Congress passed legislation empowering itself to remove justices and the attorney general, further undermining judicial and prosecutorial independence.

Police Abuses and Corruption

Impunity for serious police abuses is a chronic problem. Police killed 149 civilians from January 2011 to November 2012, including 18 individuals under age 19, according to a report by Honduras's National Autonomous University. Then-Commissioner of the Preventive Police Alex Villanueva affirmed the report's findings and said there were likely many more killings by police that were never reported. The government did not respond to calls by the university's rector to provide information on how many of those killings had been subject to investigations or resulted in criminal convictions.

Compelling evidence in a May 2013 investigation by the Associated Press suggested police involvement in at least five extrajudicial executions or disappearances of suspected gang members in Tegucigalpa. Authorities have provided conflicting reports of progress in efforts to weed out police corruption. Such efforts have been protracted and inefficient. In April 2013, the then-chief of Directorate for Investigation and Evaluation of the Police Career told Congress that, of 230 police evaluated for corruption, 33 failed. However, only seven of those who failed were suspended, and some were later reinstated.

Use of Military in Public Security Operations

In November 2011, Congress passed an emergency decree allowing military personnel to carry out public security duties, which has since been extended periodically. In August 2013, Congress passed a law authorizing the creation of a military police force with powers to seize control of violent neighborhoods and carry out arrests, among other duties, despite a history of abuse by the military against civilians.

Judicial and Prosecutorial Independence

In December 2012, the Supreme Court's Constitutional Chamber ruled that a law governing police oversight, which had support from a majority in Congress and the president, was unconstitutional. Shortly thereafter, Congress removed four of the chamber's five members for unsatisfactory "administrative conduct." Replacements were appointed in January 2013, and the Supreme Court rejected a legal challenge by the dismissed judges in February. The Council of the Judiciary, an independent body established by a 2001 constitutional reform to appoint and remove judges, could help protect against political interference in judicial processes, but at time of writing, its members had still not been named.

In April 2013, Congress suspended Attorney General Luis Rubi and his chief deputy, and appointed an intermediate commission to serve in their place, pending an investigation into the office's effectiveness and alleged corruption within it, a power granted to Congress by a 2002 constitutional reform. Rubi and his deputy resigned in June before the investigation was completed.

Lack of Accountability for Post-Coup Abuses

Following the June 2009 military coup, the de facto government suspended key civil liberties, including freedom of the press and assembly. In the ensuing days, security forces responded to generally peaceful demonstrations with excessive force and shut down opposition media outlets, which caused several deaths, scores of injuries, and thousands of arbitrary detentions. A truth commission established by President Porfirio Lobo published a report in July 2011 that documented 20 cases of excessive use of force and killings by security forces. Honduras made very little progress prosecuting the abuses in 2013.

Attacks on Journalists

Journalists in Honduras continue to suffer threats, attacks, and killings. Authorities consistently fail to investigate these crimes effectively. According to Honduras's National Human Rights Commission (CONADEH) 36 journalists were killed between 2003 and mid-2013, and 29 have been killed since President Lobo took office. In June 2013, TV news anchor Aníbal Barrow was abducted while driving in San Pedro Sula, and his dismembered remains found weeks later. While several suspects have been charged in his kidnapping and murder, none have been convicted.

Rural Violence

Over 90 people have been killed in recent years in land disputes in the Bajo Aguán Valley, most of them since 2009, according to a March 2013 report by CONADEH. Scores more have been victims of attacks and threats. The disputes often pit international agro-industrial firms against peasant organizations over the rightful ownership of lands transferred following a reform to the country's agrarian law. While most victims have been peasants, private security guards have also been killed and wounded. None of the investigations into the killings in the CONADEH report led to a conviction.

Violence against LGBTI Persons

Bias-motivated attacks on lesbian, gay, bisexual, transgender, and intersex (LGBTI) people are a serious problem in Honduras. According to local rights groups, more than 90 LGBTI people were killed between 2009 and 2012, and many more subjected to attacks and harassment. The alleged involvement of Honduran police in some of these violent abuses is of particular concern. In 2011 and 2012, the government established special prosecutors units to investigate these crimes, yet impunity remains the norm.

Prison Conditions

Inhumane conditions, including overcrowding, inadequate nutrition, and poor sanitation, are systemic in Honduran prisons. The country's jails, which can hold a maximum of approximately 8,200 inmates, were holding more than

12,600 in May 2013, according to CONADEH. Corruption among prison officials is widespread. An August 2013 report by the Inter-American Commission on Human Rights (IACHR) found that the government had failed to allocate sufficient resources to address these chronic problems, or to thoroughly investigate disasters such as the 2012 fire at Comayagua prison that killed 362 people.

Human Rights Defenders

Human rights defenders continue to be subject to violence and threats. In July, two international human rights observers who were accompanying activists under threat for opposing a mining project in Nueva Esperanza said they were abducted by armed men, threatened, and told they would be disappeared if they did not abandon the community.

While the administration submitted draft legislation to Congress in August 2013 to protect human rights defenders, journalists, and legal practitioners, Honduran human rights groups said the proposal fails to provide adequate safeguards. The law had not been passed at time of writing. Similarly, the government has not fulfilled its pledge to create a national protection mechanism for human rights defenders and journalists at risk, which in February 2013 it told the IACHR was "in the consultation phase."

Key International Actors

The United States allocated over US$50 million in security aid to Honduras from 2010 to 2012, and continues to provide assistance through the Central America Regional Security Initiative (CARSI). US legislation granting military and police aid to Honduras states that 20 percent of the funds will only be available if the US State Department reports that the Honduran government has met several human rights requirements.

In its 2012 report on those requirements, the US State Department released the conditioned funds, but stipulated that no aid be directed to the chief of Honduras's National Police, Juan Carlos Bonilla, or anyone under his direct supervision, due to an investigation into previous abuses. However, press reports suggest that US assistance continues to flow to police officers who report to Bonilla. In a November 2013 Associated Press interview, Bonilla said that he receives ongoing logistical support from the US Embassy for police operations. At time of writing, the US Congress was withholding approximately $10 million of 2012 funding pending investigations of serious abuses.

In January 2013, the United Nations special rapporteur on the independence of judges and lawyers called the dismissal of four Supreme Court justices on administrative grounds a violation of international norms and "a grave threat to democracy."

In February, the UN Working Group on the use of mercenaries stated the government had failed to properly regulate private security firms and expressed concern regarding their "alleged involvement … in widespread human rights violations including killings, disappearances, forced evictions, and sexual violence."

In April 2012, the ombudsman of the International Finance Corporation (IFC), the private-sector lending arm of World Bank group, initiated an investigation into a 2008 loan to Corporación Dinant, a Honduran palm oil and food company. The IFC report, which had not been released at time of writing, will examine whether the IFC adequately followed its own policies regarding security and human rights in relation to the loan, including whether it responded adequately to "intensifying social and political conflict" after issuing the loan.

Mexico

Upon taking office in December 2012, President Enrique Peña Nieto acknowledged that the "war on drugs" launched by predecessor Felipe Calderón had led to serious abuses by the security forces. In early 2013, the administration said that more than 26,000 people had been reported disappeared or missing since 2007—a problem it called a "humanitarian crisis"—and promulgated broad legislation aimed at ensuring victims' rights.

Yet the government has made little progress in prosecuting widespread killings, enforced disappearances, and torture committed by soldiers and police in the course of efforts to combat organized crime, including during Peña Nieto's tenure. Members of the military accused of human rights violations continue to be prosecuted within the biased military justice system, ensuring impunity. Some criminal suspects can be held for 80 days without charge under the *arraigo* provision.

Disappearances

Mexico's security forces have participated in widespread enforced disappearances since former President Calderón (2006-2012) launched a "war on drugs." Members of all security force branches continue to carry out disappearances during the Peña Nieto administration, in some cases collaborating directly with criminal groups. In June 2013, Mexico's National Human Rights Commission (CNDH) said it was investigating 2,443 disappearances in which it had found evidence of the involvement of state agents.

Prosecutors and police routinely fail to carry out basic investigative steps to search for missing people or to identify those responsible for disappearances, often blaming victims and telling their families to investigate. Families of the disappeared may lose access to basic social services that are tied to the victim's employment, such as child care.

In February 2013, the Peña Nieto administration acknowledged that more than 26,000 people had been reported disappeared or missing since December 2006. In May, the government created a unit in the Federal Prosecutor's Office to investigate enforced and other disappearances, but at time of writing it had

not demonstrated meaningful progress in criminal investigations or searches for the victims. Mexico still lacks a national database for disappeared people, and a national database of thousands of unidentified human remains, many of which were found in mass graves.

Military Abuses and Impunity

Mexico has relied heavily on the military to fight drug-related violence and organized crime, leading to widespread human rights violations. From December 2006 to mid-September 2013, the CNDH received 8,150 complaints of abuse by the army, and issued reports on 116 cases in which it found that army personnel had committed serious human rights violations.

The soldiers who commit these abuses are virtually never brought to justice, largely because such cases continue to be investigated and prosecuted in the military justice system, which lacks independence and transparency. The Military Prosecutor's Office opened over 5,600 investigations into alleged abuses by soldiers against civilians from January 2007 to mid-2013. However, as of October 2012, military judges had sentenced only 38 members of the military for human rights violations.

At time of writing, the Senate's Justice Commission was considering a proposed reform to the military justice code that would aim to ensure that abuses committed by members of the military against civilians were handled in the civil justice system.

Torture

Torture is widely practiced in Mexico to obtain forced confessions and extract information. It is most frequently applied in the period between when victims are arbitrarily detained and when they are handed to prosecutors, when they are often held incommunicado at military bases or other illegal detention sites. Common tactics include beatings, waterboarding, electric shocks, and sexual torture. Many judges continue to accept confessions obtained through torture, despite the constitutional prohibition of such evidence.

Justice officials rarely apply the Istanbul Protocol, a set of principles to assess a potential victim of torture or ill-treatment. The Federal Prosecutor's Office applied the protocol in 302 cases from 2003 to August 2012, and found signs of torture in 128. Yet during this period it only opened 39 investigations for torture, none of which led to convictions. Between January and September 2013, the National Human Rights Commission received more than 860 complaints of torture or cruel or inhuman treatment by federal officials.

Criminal Justice System

The criminal justice system routinely fails to provide justice to victims of violent crimes and human rights violations. Causes of this failure include corruption, inadequate training and resources, and the complicity of prosecutors and public defenders. In response to the demands of a broad-based movement, Mexico enacted a Victims Law in January 2013 intended to ensure justice, protection, and reparations for victims of crime. At time of writing, implementing regulations had not yet been passed. The failure of law enforcement has contributed to the emergence of new armed citizen self-defense groups in some parts of the country.

In 2008, Mexico passed a constitutional reform to transform its inquisitorial, written justice system to an adversarial, oral one. But implementation of the reform, which authorities have until 2016 to complete, has been sluggish. At time of writing, only 3 of Mexico's 32 states had fully implemented the reform, while 13 had partially transitioned to the new system.

The reform also introduced the provision of *arraigo*, which allows prosecutors, with judicial authorization to hold organized crime suspects for up to 80 days before they are charged with a crime. In April 2013, the House of Representatives passed reforms to reduce the maximum time that such individuals can be held without charge to 35 days, rather than eradicating the measure. The Senate still had not approved the reform at time of writing.

In September 2013, the Supreme Court ruled that rights guaranteed by international human rights treaties have equal weight to those guaranteed by the constitution. However, in cases where the constitution expressly limits a right, this limitation would prevail over international treaties—a restriction that cuts against the *pro homine* principle that requires states to interpret legal obligations in the way that best protects the human rights of the individual.

Prison Conditions

Prisons are overpopulated, unhygienic, and fail to provide basic security for most inmates. Prisoners who accuse guards or inmates of attacks or other abuses have no effective system to seek redress.

Approximately 65 percent of prisons are controlled by organized crime, and corruption and violence are rampant, according to the CNDH. Some 108 inmates had died in 2013, as of November.

Freedom of Expression

Journalists, particularly those who report on crime or criticize officials, face harassment and attacks. At least 85 journalists were killed between 2000 and August 2013, and 20 more were disappeared between 2005 and April 2013, according to the CNDH. Authorities routinely fail to adequately investigate crimes against journalists, often preemptively ruling out their profession as a motive.

Journalists are often driven to self-censorship by attacks carried out both by government officials and by criminal groups, while under-regulation of state advertising can also limit media freedom by giving the government disproportionate financial influence over media outlets.

Mexico created a special prosecutor's office for Crimes against Freedom of Expression in 2006, but to date it has obtained only one criminal sentence from the 378 investigations it has opened. Legislation enacted in May 2013 gave the Federal Prosecutor's Office power to take over any investigation into attacks on media.

Gender-Based Violence

Mexican laws do not adequately protect women and girls against domestic violence and sexual violence. Some provisions, including those that make the severity of punishments for some sexual offenses contingent on the "chastity" of the victim, contradict international standards. Women and girls who have suffered these types of human rights violations generally do not report them to authorities, while those who do generally face suspicion, apathy, and disrespect. In January 2013, Mexico amended its law on violence against women to expedite emergency protection measures for victims of gender-based violence.

Reproductive Rights

In August 2008, the Supreme Court affirmed the constitutionality of a Mexico City law that legalized abortion in the first 12 weeks of pregnancy. Since that time, 16 of Mexico's 32 federal entities have legislated to recognize the right to life from the moment of conception, limiting women's ability to exercise their right to health. In 2010, the Supreme Court ruled that all states must provide emergency contraception and access to abortion for rape victims. However, in practice many women and girls face serious barriers to accessing abortions after sexual violence, including inaccurate information and intimidation by officials.

Marriage Equality

In August 2010, the Supreme Court recognized the right of same-sex couples in Mexico City to adopt children and to marry, and ruled that all 31 Mexican states must recognize same-sex marriages that take place in Mexico City. Yet the ruling does not require that states recognize the right themselves, and many still deny same-sex couples the right to marry. In December 2012, the Mexican Supreme Court struck down a law in Oaxaca that defined marriage as being between a man and a woman.

Access to Palliative Care

Tens of thousands of patients face major and often insurmountable obstacles in accessing end-of-life care, even though Mexican law grants them a right to such care. Health insurance schemes do not yet adequately address the health needs of incurable patients; drug control regulations unnecessarily restrict access to morphine, an essential medication for severe pain; and training in palliative care for healthcare workers remains insufficient.

Migrants

Hundreds of thousands of undocumented migrants pass through Mexico each year and many are subjected to grave abuses en route—such as disappearances and sexual violence—at the hands of organized crime, migration authorities, and security forces. Authorities have not taken adequate steps to protect migrants, or to investigate and prosecute those who abuse them. Despite the approval in 2011 of a new migration law ostensibly aimed at protecting migrants' rights, police continue to detain and harass undocumented migrants.

The staff of migrant shelters face threats and harassment from criminal groups and officials, yet the government has failed to implement protective measures granted to these centers by national and international human rights bodies. At least three migrant centers were forced to close or saw staff forced to flee in 2013.

In September, the Federal Prosecutor's Office authorized the creation of a team, including international forensic experts, to identify more than 200 human remains thought to belong to migrants.

Labor Rights

The dominance of pro-management unions continues to obstruct legitimate labor-organizing activity. Independent unions are often blocked from entering negotiations with management, while workers who seek to form independent unions risk losing their jobs. A 2012 labor law failed to address the lack of transparency and democracy in the powerful pro-management unions, and failed to protect workers' right to form independent unions and carry out collective bargaining.

Human Rights Defenders

Human rights defenders and activists continue to suffer harassment and attacks, often in the context of opposition to infrastructure or resource extraction "mega-projects." In many cases, there is evidence—including witness testimony or traced cell phones—that state agents are involved in aggressions against human rights defenders. Of 89 aggressions against human rights defenders registered by the Office of the UN High Commissioner for Human

Rights between November 2010 and December 2012, none resulted in a conviction.

In June 2012, Mexico enacted a law to protect human rights defenders and journalists. At time of writing, the protection mechanism created by the law had not been effectively implemented, with protective measures slow to arrive, insufficient, or incomplete in some cases. The mechanism suffers from too few and inadequately trained staff, delays in accessing funds, coordination failures with state-level institutions, poor dissemination to those at risk, and a lack of public support from high level government officials.

Key International Actors

The United States has allocated over US$2 billion in aid to Mexico through the Merida Initiative, an aid package agreed upon in 2007 without a year cap, to help Mexico combat organized crime. Fifteen percent of select portions of the assistance can be disbursed only after the US secretary of state reports that the Mexican government is meeting human rights requirements.

However, the impact of these requirements has been undermined by the fact the US State Department has repeatedly reported to the US Congress that they are being met, despite overwhelming evidence to the contrary, often citing vague and incomplete progress towards meeting the requirements, leading Congress to release the funds.

The UN special rapporteur on extrajudicial, summary or arbitrary executions conducted a fact-finding mission to Mexico in April-May 2013, and stated that extrajudicial executions by security forces were widespread and often occurred without accountability.

In October 2013, Mexico underwent its second Universal Periodic Review in the United Nations Human Rights Council, where key recommendations included placing human rights violations by the military under civilian jurisdiction, and strengthening the protection mechanism for human rights defenders and journalists.

Peru

In recent years, public protests against large-scale mining projects, as well as other government policies and private sector initiatives, have led to numerous confrontations between police and protesters, and resulted in the shooting deaths of civilians by state security forces. While the number of deaths declined significantly during the first nine months of 2013, there has been little progress in investigating these cases or taking steps to ensure that police comply with international norms on the use of lethal force.

Despite the landmark convictions in 2009 and 2010 of former President Alberto Fujimori, his advisor Vladimiro Montesinos, several army generals, and members of a government death squad, progress on cases involving abuses committed under earlier administrations has been very limited.

Deaths in Protests

As of September 2013, 27 civilians had been killed during protests since President Ollanta Humala took office in July 2011. The number of these fatal shootings declined from 18 in the first eight months of 2012 to three in the same period of 2013. The National Office for Dialogue and Sustainability, a government body created in August 2012, has promoted dialogue to seek peaceful resolution of social conflicts that drive protests. However, there has been little progress determining the circumstances in which the deaths occurred and holding to account police or military personnel who used force unlawfully.

Confronting Past Abuses

Peru's Truth and Reconciliation Commission estimated that almost 70,000 people died or were subject to enforced disappearance during the country's armed conflict between 1980 and 2000. Many were victims of atrocities by the Shining Path and other insurgent groups; others were victims of human rights violations by state agents.

Former President Fujimori was sentenced in 2009 to 25 years in prison for killings and "disappearances" in 1991 and 1992. His intelligence advisor, Vladimiro Montesinos, three former army generals, and members of the Colina

Group, a government death squad, are also serving sentences ranging from 15 to 25 years for the assassination in 1991 of 15 people in the Lima district of Barrios Altos, and for six enforced disappearances. In June 2013, President Humala rejected a petition to grant Fujimori a presidential pardon requested by his family on grounds of ill-health. Media reports indicated that a commission on presidential pardons had determined that Fujimori was not suffering from a terminal or degenerative illness or grave psychological problems.

Judicial investigations into other cases have been subject to long delays and have resulted in few convictions. In a report issued in August 2013 to mark the tenth anniversary of the Truth and Reconciliation Commission's report, the human rights ombudsman found that, despite initial efforts, Peru had failed to implement a specialized judicial system with sufficient staff and resources to bring most cases to court. According to the ombudsman, as of April 2013, 113 of the 194 cases it monitors had been closed or were in the early stages of investigation, and only 32 had resulted in a sentence.

In June 2013, the Constitutional Court held that a 1986 massacre in El Frontón prison during the first administration of former President Alan García, in which at least 130 inmates were killed, was subject to a statute of limitations since it did not constitute a crime against humanity. The court's opinion disregarded a 2000 ruling of the Inter-American Court of Human Rights in the case of Durand and Ugarte, which ordered Peru to investigate these events and hold those responsible accountable. In September, the Ministry of Justice asked the Constitutional Court to correct the ruling on the grounds that a majority of the judges had rejected the petitioners' argument that the opening of trial proceedings in the El Frontón case was unconstitutional, and that the court had not been asked to rule on whether the crimes committed were crimes against humanity. As of October 2013, the court had not responded.

Military Jurisdiction

The jurisdiction of military courts to hear human rights cases involving members of the military remains an issue. Legislative Decree 1095 adopted in 2010 by the administration of President García permits military courts to try cases in which members of the military engaged in public security operations are accused of abuses against civilians. International human rights bodies have consistently rejected the use of military prosecutors and courts in cases involving human rights violations throughout the region. As of September 2013, the Constitutional Court had still to rule on the decree's constitutionality, which has been challenged by Peruvian human rights advocates.

Torture

Torture is a chronic problem. One third of the 144 victims whose cases have been monitored over the past decade by the nongovernmental organization Human Rights Commission (COMISEDH) died or suffered permanent physical disabilities as a result of torture, most allegedly committed by members of the police.

Freedom of Expression

In August 2012, in response to the growing public profile of a small group advocating amnesty for Shining Path prisoners, President Humala introduced a bill that would undermine freedom of expression by criminalizing the "denial" of crimes carried out by terrorist organizations. As subsequently amended by Congress, the bill would impose prison sentences of 6 to 12 years for "denying" such crimes or individuals' participation in them, if such participation was established in a final judicial ruling. To be criminalized, the expressions would need to have the "purpose of promoting the commission of terrorist crimes or publicly defending terrorism or to serve as a medium to indoctrinate terrorist objectives." If the denial is made through social media or information technologies, the sentence would increase up to 15 years. As of October 2013, the bill still awaited a final vote in Congress.

Journalists continue to face suspended prison sentences and fines for defamation. For example, in May 2013, a judge in Huaraz, Ancash, handed down a two-year suspended prison sentence against journalist Alcides Peñaranda, director of *Integración* magazine, for defaming the regional president of Ancash, César Alvarez, and ordered him to pay monetary damages. The accusation concerned an article in *Integración* discussing corruption in the regional government that quoted from an article published in a Lima magazine by César Hildebrandt, a well-known investigative journalist. Alvarez separately sued Hildebrandt and his colleague Melissa Pérez. A Lima judge acquitted them, citing a Supreme Court ruling that public personalities must assume a greater burden of proof in libel cases where a public interest is involved.

A bill that would replace such prison sentences for criminal defamation with community service and fines is still awaiting a vote in the legislature. Although Congress approved the bill in July 2011, former President García lodged objections, and an amended version was never approved.

Reproductive Rights

Women and girls in Peru have the right to seek abortions only in cases of risk to the health or life of the woman. However, the country lacks clear protocols that enable health providers to determine in which specific circumstances an abortion may be lawful. Multiple United Nations human rights monitoring bodies have all called on Peru to establish such protocols, as well as to legalize abortion in cases in which the pregnancy results from rape. At time of writing, the government had failed to comply with these recommendations.

Disability Rights

Under Peru's system of judicial interdiction, judges can determine that individuals with certain intellectual or mental disabilities are legally "incompetent" and assign them legal guardians, effectively suspending their basic civil rights, including the right to vote. International and regional human rights bodies have called on Peru to abolish judicial interdiction—or guardianship—because it is incompatible with Peru's obligations under the Convention on the Rights of Persons with Disabilities.

In December 2012, the General Law on People with Disabilities entered force, but as of October 2013 the executive had yet to adopt its implementing regulations. The law aims to bring existing national legislation into line with the convention, protecting the right of people with disabilities to act in their own interests, with appropriate support when necessary. However, a commission to revise the civil code, created by the General Law on People with Disabilities, had not been established as of October 2013. Peruvian law still permits involuntary detention for treatment of people with disabilities who are under guardianship.

Key International Actors

In March 2013, in its concluding observations on Peru's fifth periodic report, the UN Human Rights Committee recommended that Peru "effectively prevent and eradicate the excessive use of force by law enforcement officials and members of the security forces" and "intensify its efforts to eradicate torture." It also called on Peru to adopt legislation to prohibit discrimination on the basis of sexual orientation and gender identity, to allow abortion in cases of rape, and to "swiftly adopt a national protocol regulating the practice of therapeutic abortion."

In September 2013, the UN Subcommittee on Prevention of Torture and Other Cruel, Inhuman or Degrading Treatment or Punishment visited 26 prisons and police stations in different parts of Peru. Peru ratified the Optional Protocol to the Convention against Torture in 2006. The subcommittee's chairperson expressed hope that by the end of 2013, Peru would have instituted a national prevention mechanism against torture and ill-treatment, and given it sufficient funds to function effectively.

As a relatively new member of the UN Human Rights Council, Peru has played a positive role in voting for a number of resolutions that address human rights violations in countries like Sri Lanka, Belarus, and Iran. However, Peru took a step back backwards by deciding to no longer sponsor country-specific resolutions at the UN.

Venezuela

The April 2013 presidential election, held weeks after the death of President Hugo Chávez, resulted in a narrow victory for Chávez's hand-picked successor, Nicolás Maduro, according to Venezuelan electoral authorities. The Supreme Court and the National Electoral Council rejected appeals filed by the opposition candidate, Henrique Capriles Radonski, challenging the results. The controversy over the results touched off street demonstrations and counterdemonstrations, which led to at least nine deaths and dozens of injured, as well as excessive use of force and arbitrary detentions by security forces.

Under the leadership of President Chávez and now President Maduro, the accumulation of power in the executive branch and the erosion of human rights guarantees have enabled the government to intimidate, censor, and prosecute its critics. While many Venezuelans continue to criticize the government, the prospect of facing reprisals—in the form of arbitrary or abusive state action—has undercut the ability of judges to fairly adjudicate politically sensitive cases, and forced journalists and rights defenders to weigh the consequences of publicizing information and opinions that are critical of the government.

In September 2013, the Venezuelan government's decision to withdraw from the American Convention on Human Rights took effect, leaving Venezuelans without access to the Inter-American Court on Human Rights, an international tribunal that has protected their rights for decades in a wide array of cases.

Police abuse, prison conditions, and impunity for abuses by security forces remain serious problems.

Post-Election Violence

Security forces used excessive force and arbitrary detentions to disperse antigovernment demonstrations after the April elections, according to local groups. For example, the Forum for Life, a network of 18 Venezuelan human rights organizations, reported that security forces had arbitrarily detained at least 62 individuals and injured 38 others in demonstrations in the state of Lara on April 15 and 16. The detainees reported that they were severely beaten, threatened with sexual violence, and deprived of food for more than 24 hours.

According to official information, six "violent and aggressive" demonstrations took place after the elections, in which 35 people were injured; and 15 health centers, five headquarters of political parties, and one ombudsman's office were vandalized. Official sources reported that nine individuals were killed at the time, although the circumstances in which the deaths occurred remain unclear.

President Maduro and other high level officials have used the threat of criminal investigations as a political tool, attributing responsibility for all acts of violence during demonstrations to Capriles. The Attorney General's Office has investigated incidents involving victims who were government supporters, but has failed to conduct thorough investigations into credible allegations of post-electoral abuses by security forces.

Judicial Independence

Since then, President Chávez and his supporters in the National Assembly conducted a political takeover of the Supreme Court in 2004, the judiciary has largely ceased to function as an independent branch of government. Members of the Supreme Court have openly rejected the principle of separation of powers, publicly pledged their commitment to advancing the government's political agenda, and repeatedly ruled in favor of the government, validating the government's disregard for human rights.

Judge María Lourdes Afiuni remains under criminal prosecution as a result of a 2009 ruling against the government. In December 2009, Afiuni was detained on the day she authorized the conditional release of a government critic who had spent nearly three years in prison awaiting trial on corruption charges. Although Afiuni's ruling complied with a recommendation by international human rights monitors—and was consistent with Venezuelan law—a provisional judge who had publicly pledged his loyalty to Chávez ordered her to stand trial on charges of corruption, abuse of authority, and "favoring the evasion of justice." Afiuni spent more than a year in deplorable conditions in a women's prison, and over two years under house arrest. In June 2013, she was granted conditional liberty, but at time of writing remained bound by a court order forbidding her to make any public statements about her case.

Freedom of Media

Over the past decade, the government has expanded and abused its powers to regulate media. While sharp criticism of the government is still common in several newspapers and some radio stations, fear of government reprisals has made self-censorship a serious problem.

In 2010, the National Assembly amended the telecommunications law to grant the government power to suspend or revoke concessions to private outlets if it is "convenient for the interests of the nation." It also expanded the scope of a restrictive broadcasting statute to cover the Internet, allowing the arbitrary suspension of websites for the vaguely defined offense of "incitement." Previously, amendments to the criminal code had expanded the scope and severity of defamation laws that criminalize disrespect of high government officials.

The government has taken aggressive steps to reduce the availability of media outlets that engage in critical programming. Venezuela's oldest private television channel, RCTV, which was arbitrarily removed from public airwaves in 2007, was then driven off cable TV in 2010.

The government subsequently pursued administrative sanctions against Globovisión, which was for years the only major channel that remained critical of Chávez. The broadcasting authority opened nine administrative investigations against the channel. In one case, it imposed a fine of US$2.1 million for allegedly violating the broadcasting statute when Globovisión aired images of a prison riot in 2011. In April 2013, Globovisión was sold to government supporters because, according to its owner, it had become politically, economically, and legally unviable. Since then, it has significantly reduced its critical programming.

The government has also targeted other media outlets for arbitrary sanction and censorship. For example, in a case brought by the ombudsman, a specialized court to protect children fined *El Nacional* newspaper in August 2013 for publishing on its front page a photograph of a dozen naked corpses in the Bello Monte morgue in Caracas. The image accompanied an article about illegal arms and violence, which are major public concerns in Venezuela. Since the picture was printed in 2010, the court forbade the paper from publishing "images, information and publicity of any type containing blood, arms, and messages of terror, physical aggression, images with contents of war and messages about deaths that could alter the psychological well-being of boys, girls, and adolescents in Venezuela."

In November 2013, the broadcasting authority opened an administrative investigation against eight Internet providers for allowing web sites that published information on unofficial exchange rates, and threatened to revoke their licenses if they did not immediately block the sites. Days later, it asked Twitter to suspend accounts related to such websites.

Human Rights Defenders

The Venezuelan government has sought to marginalize the country's human rights defenders by repeatedly accusing them of seeking to undermine Venezuelan democracy with the support of the US government. For example, in July 2013, the minister of interior accused Rocío San Miguel, the director of the nongovernmental organization Citizen Control, of being a "CIA operator in Venezuela" who is conducting a "psychological campaign" against the government's security policies.

In 2010, the Supreme Court ruled that individuals or organizations that receive foreign funding could be prosecuted for "treason." In addition, the National Assembly enacted legislation blocking organizations that "defend political rights" or "monitor the performance of public bodies" from receiving international assistance.

In October 2013, the National Assembly created a "special commission" to investigate the sources of funding of "offices or organizations with political purposes and groups that act with the purpose of destabilizing and generating social commotion and coup d'etat[s] to undermine the constitutional order."

Abuses by Security Forces

Violent crime is rampant in Venezuela. In May 2013, President Maduro launched the "Secure Homeland Plan," deploying 3,000 military officials to participate in joint public security operations with police forces. Military officials lack the training to perform these tasks.

Killings by security forces are a chronic problem. According to the most recent official statistics, law enforcement agents allegedly killed 7,998 people between January 2000 and the first third of 2009. In July 2013, military officials opened fire at a car in the state of Falcon, killing the driver and one of her daughters, and injuring her two other children. After the case received widespread media coverage, prosecutors charged 10 military officials for their alleged responsibility in the killings. However, impunity remains the norm.

In April 2008, the government created the National Bolivarian Police (NBP) and enacted measures to promote non-abusive policing proposed by a commission comprised of government and NGO representatives. As of August 2013, there were 14,478 NBP officers working in eight states.

In June 2013, the National Assembly passed a new Law to Prevent and Sanction Torture and other Cruel or Inhuman Treatment, which penalizes the commission, collaboration, cover up, and obstruction of criminal investigations into these acts. The law, which has entered in force, imposes penalties of up to 25 years for these crimes.

Prison Conditions

Venezuelan prisons are among the most violent in Latin America. Weak security, deteriorating infrastructure, overcrowding, insufficient and poorly trained guards, and corruption allow armed gangs to effectively control prisons. Hundreds of violent prison deaths occur every year. For example, in January 2013, at least 56 prisoners and one member of the National Guard were killed during a clash between members of the National Guard and inmates in which security forces used lethal force during a weapons search in the Uribana prison in Lara state. Forty-six prisoners were hospitalized with serious injuries.

Labor Rights

Political discrimination against workers in state institutions remains a problem. In April 2013, Minister of Housing Ricardo Molina called on all ministry personnel who supported the opposition to resign, saying that he would fire anyone who criticized Maduro, Chávez, or the "revolution." The Human Rights Center of the Catholic University Andrés Bello received complaints involving hundreds of workers from public institutions —including the state oil company, the office in charge of customs and taxes, and state electrical companies— who were allegedly threatened with losing their positions for supporting Capriles, or for not openly supporting the government, after the April elections.

Labor legislation adopted in April 2012 includes provisions that limit the full freedom that unions should have to draft their statutes and elect their representatives. In practice, the National Electoral Council (CNE), a public authority, continues to play an excessive role in union elections, violating international standards that guarantee workers the right to elect their representatives in full freedom, according to conditions they determine.

Key International Actors

On September 10, 2013, the Venezuelan government's decision to denounce the American Convention on Human Rights entered into effect. Venezuelan citizens and residents are unable to request the Inter-American Court of Human Rights' intervention when local remedies are ineffective or unavailable for any abuses committed since that date.

As a member of the UN Human Rights Council, Venezuela has spoken out against UN action to respond to human rights violations in places such as North Korea. During the September 2013 session of the Human Rights Council, it was the only country to vote against a resolution condemning human rights violations committed against the Syrian people. For years, Venezuela's government has refused to authorize UN human rights experts to conduct fact-finding visits in the country.

In June 2013, Venezuela became the pro-tempore president of Mercosur, a year after joining the regional bloc. The Asunción Protocol on Commitment with the Promotion and Protection of Human Rights of Mercosur states that "full respect of democratic institutions and the respect of human rights" are essential for regional integration, and that state parties will "cooperate for the effective promotion and protection of human rights." By not addressing the absence of an independent judiciary in Venezuela, as well as the government's efforts to undermine human rights protections, the other Mercosur member states have failed to uphold these commitments.

Venezuela supported a campaign by Ecuador to undermine the independence of the Inter-American Commission on Human Rights, and limit the funding and effectiveness of its special rapporteurship on freedom of expression. While they were unable to win support for this effort at the March 2013 meeting Organization of American States General Assembly, both governments, as well as other members of the Bolivarian Alliance for the Americas (ALBA), made clear their intent to continue pressing for these changes in the future.

HUMAN
RIGHTS
WATCH

IN RELIGION'S NAME
Abuses against Religious Minorities in Indonesia

WORLD REPORT

2014

ASIA

Afghanistan

Preparations for the end-2014 withdrawal of international combat troops continued in 2013, with international troops largely departed, sequestered in bases, and focused on the logistics of shipping military equipment out of the country. The Afghan army and police stepped forward to lead the fight against the Taliban and other insurgents, with mixed results.

The ability of Afghan security forces to hold government-held territory, let alone retake insurgent-controlled areas, is unclear, and security concerns for much of the population remain high. The United Nations recorded a 23 percent rise in civilian casualties for the first six months of 2013 compared to 2012, most caused by insurgents, with the Taliban explicitly targeting civilians they see as supporting the government. The security concerns are reflected in the fact that almost half of the 7,000 polling centers planned for the 2014 presidential election face serious threats.

There was continued instability and declining respect for human rights in the country over the past year. This was reflected in attacks on women's rights, growing internal displacement and migration, and weakened efficacy of the Afghanistan Independent Human Rights Commission (AIHRC). Impunity for abuses was the norm for government security forces and other armed groups. These problems raised concerns about the fairness of the upcoming presidential election.

Women's Rights

With international interest in Afghanistan rapidly waning, opponents of women's rights seized the opportunity to begin rolling back the progress made since the end of Taliban rule. A May parliamentary debate on the groundbreaking Law on the Elimination of Violence Against Women (EVAW Law), passed by presidential decree in 2009, was halted after 15 minutes after numerous lawmakers argued for the law's repeal and spoke out against legal protections for women and girls. The law remains valid, but enforcement is weak. The EVAW debate heralded, and perhaps triggered, subsequent attacks and setbacks within the government during the year, including:

- A call by Abdul Rahman Hotak, a new AIHRC commissioner, to repeal the EVAW Law;

- A decision by parliament to reduce the 25 percent of seats set aside for women on Afghanistan's 34 provincial councils;

- A revision by the Ministry of Justice to the new criminal procedure code, adding a provision that bans family member testimony in criminal cases that makes it extremely difficult to prosecute domestic violence and child and forced marriage— and the law's subsequent passage by the lower house of parliament;

- The release from prison after just one year of the parents-in-law of Sahar Gul, the 13-year-old bride of their son whom they had starved and tortured for months. The in-laws had initially received a 10-year sentence.

A string of physical assaults in 2013 against high-profile women highlighted the danger to activists and women in public life. These included:

- July 5: Former parliamentarian Noor Zia Atmar revealed that she was living in a battered women's shelter due to attacks from her husband. She later confirmed that she was seeking asylum abroad.

- August 7: Unknown attackers shot Rooh Gul, a parliamentarian in the upper house, as she travelled by road through Ghazni province. She and her husband survived, but her eight-year-old daughter and driver were killed.

- September 4: A self-described Taliban breakaway group dragged Sushmita Banerjee, an Indian woman married to an Afghan health worker, from her house in Paktika province, shot her repeatedly, and dumped her body outside a religious school.

- September 16: Lieutenant Nigara, the highest ranking female police officer in Helmand province, was shot and killed on her way to work less than three months after the July 3 assassination of her predecessor, Lt. Islam Bibi.

Security Transition

Overall declining international interest in Afghanistan contributed to mounting fears among Afghans for the country's future.

Afghan security forces filled in many of the gaps left by departing international forces. Some 400 Afghan security force members were killed each month during the 2013 "fighting season," and attrition rates reached 50 percent in some units.

Preparations for the April 2014 presidential election were plagued with difficulties, with voter registration off to a slow start; delays in the adoption of necessary legislation; controversy over the membership of the Independent Election Commission and the Electoral Complaints Commission; low rates of female voter registration; and concerns about the ability of Afghan security forces to provide adequate security on election day.

Candidacy by individuals implicated in serious human rights abuses raised questions about the efficacy of vetting processes, and increased cynicism among potential voters.

Internally Displaced Persons and Refugees

Deteriorating security and growing fears for the future contributed to an increasing number of Afghans fleeing their homes for other parts of the country, other countries, or choosing not to return home from overseas. The United Nations High Commissioner for Refugees (UNHCR) documented an increase of over 106,000 in the number of internally displaced people from January through June 2013, bringing the total to over 583,000. The main causes of displacement were armed conflict and diminished security.

The number of Afghans seeking safety outside the country also grew, with some making dangerous journeys from Afghanistan through the mountains into Iran toward Europe or by boat to Australia. The number of refugees returning to Afghanistan from neighboring countries has fallen in recent years, according to the UNHCR.

Afghans arriving in other countries often faced increasing hostility, including draconian new policies in Australia diverting asylum seekers to third countries and governmental proposals in European countries, including the United Kingdom and Norway, to deport unaccompanied Afghan children back to Afghanistan.

Abusive Security Forces

In recent years, the government has largely denied documentation by the UN and the Afghanistan Independent Human Rights Commission that Afghan police and the intelligence service tortured detainees. However, on February 10, 2013, a government investigation that President Hamid Karzai ordered into allegations of ill-treatment acknowledged widespread torture. Karzai followed up on February 16 with a decree ordering anti-torture measures, including prosecuting officials responsible for torture.

In September, Karzai issued an order creating a new government committee to investigate prison conditions. However, at time of writing there was no indication that torture prosecutions had advanced, or that Karzai's actions had substantially reduced torture and other ill-treatment in detention.

Abuses by the Afghan Local Police (ALP)—a network of local defense forces established largely by the US military in cooperation with the Afghan government—continued to be a serious problem. Designed to operate in areas with limited Afghan police or army presence, the ALP has been plagued from its beginnings in 2010 by structural problems that include poor vetting of recruits, weak command and control structures, and lack of accountability mechanisms. These problems persist, as do allegations of ALP involvement in murder, rape, theft, extortion, and child recruitment.

Human Rights Defenders and Transitional Justice

Although praised globally as an effective human rights body, the AIHRC—the independent government agency—was largely in limbo from December 2011 until June 2013 due to multiple commissioner vacancies that President Karzai did not fill for a year-and-a-half.

However, after donors set a deadline for filling these positions as part of the follow-up to the 2012 Tokyo Conference, at which donors pledged US$16 billion in development aid in return for commitments by the Afghan government including support for human rights, Karzai in June 2013 filled all vacant seats, albeit without the consultation with civil society that the Paris Principles on national human rights commissions requires. Several of the five new appointees had little or no experience in human rights or had expressed overt hostility to the concept of universal human rights. Abdul Rahman Hotak, a former member of the Taliban government, after his appointment publicly criticized the EVAW Law. In June, the UN high commissioner for human rights took the unusual step of raising "serious concerns" about the appointments and called for the Afghan government "to reconsider the recent appointments and re-open the selection process."

One of the AIHRC's key achievements in recent years was the completion of an 800-page report that maps war crimes and crimes against humanity in Afghanistan since the communist era. Completed in December 2011, it will provide a foundation for future steps to prosecute those implicated in past abuses. However, at time of writing there was no planned release date for the report: President Karzai has blocked the release with the encouragement of international donors including the US and UK, which have argued that releasing the report could be destabilizing in the current tense security environment since it likely implicates a number of powerful figures.

Freedom of Expression and Association

The rights to freedom of expression and association of media and political parties, hailed as one of Afghanistan's clear human rights successes since 2001, came increasingly under threat in 2013.

Two credible Afghan media organizations, *Nai* and the Afghanistan Journalists' Safety Committee, compiled statistics demonstrating a rise in the risks faced by journalists during 2013 as compared to 2012. Both groups documented around 40 attacks on journalists in the first six months of 2013, compared to around 20 attacks in the same period in 2012. The attacks included threats, armed assaults, and kidnappings. Of particular concern was the growing number of cases where the attacks implicated government officials, including members of the Afghan security forces. There were also cases in which journalists who were attacked sought help from the security forces but were denied assistance or subjected to abuse by the security forces.

Key International Actors

International fatigue with Afghanistan among most countries that have contributed troops or significant amounts of aid post-2001—particularly the US,
which has had the largest military and aid involvement—negatively impacted
human rights in 2013 by reducing political pressure on the government to
respect human rights, especially those of women.

While many countries are pledging continued aid to Afghanistan, political
engagement is waning sharply and the US is scaling back most forms of assistance. A sense that involvement in Afghanistan is ending is palpable in discussions with diplomats, and cuts in international aid are already leading to the
closure of some schools and health clinics.

The end-2014 deadline for the withdrawal of international military troops will
further hasten disengagement. Disagreements between the Afghan and US governments, including over the opening of a Taliban office in Doha, Qatar, delayed
the pending Bilateral Security Agreement (BSA), expected to set out US support
for Afghanistan's security post-2014. Similar agreements with other key foreign
partners were on hold pending resolution of the BSA. These delays have
increased the sense of uncertainty and instability in Afghanistan.

In April 2013, President Karzai admitted that the CIA had been dropping off bags
of cash, totaling tens of millions of dollars, at his office for more than a decade.
The acknowledgement led the ranking member of the US Senate Foreign
Relations Committee to put a temporary hold on certain assistance programs
while he sought more information.

Afghanistan remained under preliminary analysis by the prosecutor of the
International Criminal Court, who since 2007 has been looking into allegations
of serious international crimes, including torture, recruitment of child soldiers,
attacks on humanitarian objects and the UN, and attacks on schools.

Australia

Australia has a strong record protecting civil and political rights, but has damaged its record and its potential to be a regional human rights leader by persistently undercutting refugee protections. In 2013, successive Australian governments continued to engage in scare-mongering politics at the expense of the rights of asylum seekers and refugees. The Labor government reintroduced offshore processing, and the Liberal Party-led coalition government elected in September continued and expanded these punitive resettlement policies, repeatedly trumpeting their refusal to consider resettling in Australia even a single additional asylum-seeker arriving by sea.

Australia also has been increasingly unwilling to publicly raise human rights abuses in countries with which it has strong trade or security ties, fearing that doing so would harm its relations with Asian governments. Such reluctance to speak out validates the stance of those who mistakenly view raising human rights as an act of diplomatic aggression rather than a normal part of principled diplomacy, making it all the more difficult to use foreign relations as a means of improving human rights protections globally.

Asylum Seekers and Refugees

Successive governments have prioritized domestic politics over Australia's international legal obligations to protect the rights of asylum seekers and refugees, many of who have escaped from appalling situations in places like Afghanistan and Sri Lanka. Too often, the government has attempted to demonize those trying to reach Australia by boat and has insisted that officials refer to all asylum seekers who do so as illegal maritime arrivals.

In October 2012, the Labor government introduced "enhanced screening" for Sri Lankan asylum seekers arriving by boat, whereby immigration officials conduct cursory interviews with asylum seekers, who often have no access to legal representation or right to appeal. An unfavorable finding means the asylum seeker is immediately deported back to his or her country of origin. This policy poses a serious risk of refoulement, returning genuine refugees to face persecution and threats to their life and liberty. At this writing, the government had returned at least 1,191 Sri Lankans under this procedure.

In July 2013, the United Nations Human Rights Committee found that Australia had breached the International Covenant on Civil and Political Rights and committed 143 human rights violations by indefinitely detaining 46 refugees on the basis of Australian Security Intelligence Organisation "adverse security assessments." The committee directed Australia to provide the refugees with an effective remedy, including release from detention, rehabilitation, and compensation. So far, the government has yet to act on the committee's recommendations.

Australia has continued the practice of mandatory detention for those arriving in Australia without a visa. As of September 30, 2013, 6,403 people were in secure immigration detention facilities (onshore and offshore), including 1,078 children; 106 people had been in detention for more than two years.

Another deterrent measure is the offshore processing of asylum seekers on Manus Island, Papua New Guinea, and Nauru. Offshore processing was first implemented in 2001 and subsequently abandoned in 2008, only to be reintroduced by the Labor government in August 2012. In July and August 2013, the Australian government concluded agreements with Papua New Guinea and Nauru through which all asylum seekers who arrive in Australia by boat after July 19, 2013, are to be transferred to offshore processing centers. The United Nations High Commissioner for Refugees (UNHCR) has repeatedly expressed concern regarding the mandatory and indefinite detention of asylum seekers in offshore centers, where conditions are harsh and unsatisfactory and individuals get little help making their claims.

The new agreements mean that those found to be refugees, despite the limitations of the offshore processing system, will never be eligible for resettlement in Australia and instead will be permanently resettled in Papua New Guinea, Nauru, or another country.

Upon taking office in September, Prime Minister Tony Abbott declared his intention to expand the offshore processing and regional resettlement arrangements and implement the government's new "Operation Sovereign Borders" policy. The policy empowers military commanders to turn around boats at sea "where safe to do so." The new government stopped referring asylum seekers to refugee casework organizations. Abbott also announced the reintroduction of temporary protection visas for the approximately 30,000 asylum seekers in

Australia awaiting assessment of their refugee claims, though in December this was blocked in the Senate.

Indigenous Rights

While some health and socioeconomic indicators are improving for indigenous Australians, they still on average live 10-12 years less than non-indigenous Australians, have an infant mortality rate almost two times higher, and continue to die at alarmingly high rates from treatable and preventable conditions such as diabetes and respiratory illness. Although they live in one of the world's wealthiest countries, many indigenous Australians do not have access to adequate health care, housing, food, or water.

In March 2013, Parliament passed legislation recognizing indigenous Australians as the first inhabitants of Australia, an important step toward constitutional recognition and toward addressing Australia's history of exclusion. As part of his election campaign, Prime Minister Abbott promised to propose a referendum on recognition within 12 months of taking office and to establish an indigenous advisory council. In September, he established the council to focus on "practical changes to improve the lives of Aboriginal people." It is not clear what role this council will play relative to the national representative indigenous body, the Congress of Australia's First Peoples.

Disability Rights

In July 2013, the government introduced the National Disability Insurance Scheme, allowing people with disabilities to receive support based on their needs and be actively involved in choosing the types of support they need. Disability rights have also been a focal point in Australia's international aid programs.

In 2013, the Australian Law Commission launched an inquiry into barriers to equal recognition before the law and legal capacity for individuals with disabilities. Current laws promote guardianship, which strips people with disabilities of their ability to make decisions about their lives instead of recognizing their legal capacity on an equal basis as others, as required by the Convention on the Rights of Persons with Disabilities (CRPD).

Alarmingly, Australian law allows women and girls with disabilities to be involuntarily sterilized if the family court or a guardianship tribunal determines that the procedure is in their best interests. A Senate committee review in 2013 merely recommended that the practice of involuntary sterilization be "regulated" rather than banned. In September 2013, the UN Committee on the Rights of Persons with Disabilities (CRPD Committee) urged the Australian government to take immediate steps to prohibit involuntary sterilization and provide assistance enabling people with disabilities to make decisions about their own lives (supported decision-making).

Shackles and restraints are often still used on people with mental disabilities in Australia, sometimes because of lack of beds in psychiatric wards in public hospitals. According to local disability advocates, women with mental disabilities experience a high rate of physical and sexual abuse, including in psychiatric facilities. The CRPD Committee recommended that the government develop more inclusive gender-based violence prevention programs and ensure access for women with disabilities to an effective, integrated redress mechanism.

Sexual Orientation and Gender Identity

Cohabiting same sex couples are accorded de facto status and civil unions are recognized in some states. Marriage, however, remains restricted to heterosexual relationships under the federal Marriage Act.

The Australian Capital Territory became the first state or territory in Australia to recognize same-sex marriage with the passage of the Marriage Equality Act in October 2013. The Federal Government later signaled its intention to challenge the new law in the High Court.

Long overdue amendments to the Sex Discrimination Act in August 2013 made discrimination on the basis of sexual orientation, gender identity, intersex status, and relationship status unlawful in Australia. However, exemptions for religious organizations mean that, for instance, religious schools can continue to refuse to admit or expel LGBTI students.

Freedom of Media

In September 2013, the High Court rejected an appeal by three award-winning journalists working for the *Age* newspaper who refused to comply with an order to disclose their confidential sources in a defamation case for articles written in 2009. The journalists face charges of contempt of court, which could lead to fines and imprisonment if they refuse to reveal their sources.

Since the publication of these articles, shield laws protecting journalistic sources have been introduced in six of the nine legal jurisdictions in Australia. In these jurisdictions, there is now a presumption that journalists do not have to reveal their sources. The presumption can be overridden where the benefit of disclosure would outweigh the harm. Whether these new shield laws will offer adequate protection remains to be seen. No such protections exist in Queensland, South Australia, and the Northern Territory.

Australia's Foreign Policy

Australia held a two-year rotating seat on the UN Security Council starting in 2013. It used its presidency of the Security Council in September to push for a resolution restricting the trade in and distribution of small arms and light weapons and a presidential statement on humanitarian access in Syria. The government continued its leadership role in international disarmament by presiding over the successful final Arms Trade Treaty negotiations in New York.

Despite calls for a boycott over lack of war crimes accountability in Sri Lanka, Australia sent a high-level delegation to the Commonwealth Heads of Government Meeting (CHOGM) in Colombo in November 2013. Prime Minister Abbott and Foreign Minister Julie Bishop repeatedly sidestepped or downplayed the importance of accountability and respect for human rights. Most egregiously, Abbott, addressing allegations of torture by Sri Lankan security forces, defended the Sri Lankan government, saying "We accept that sometimes, in difficult circumstances, difficult things happen."

This rationalization of torture, which was endemic during the war years and continues to be a serious problem in Sri Lanka today, seems to have been motivated in part by the goal of enlisting Sri Lanka's support in preventing asylum seekers from leaving Sri Lanka for Australia, and, on the same visit, Abbott announced a gift of two patrol boats to the Sri Lankan navy to combat people smuggling. The Australian government was seemingly oblivious to the role Sri Lankan government abuses play in prompting outflows of ethnic Tamil asylum seekers.

Abbott continued his predecessors' foreign policy focus on the Asia-Pacific region, declaring he would be an "Asia-first" prime minister. He also continued the practice of turning a blind eye to human rights abuses in neighboring countries. Abbott made Indonesia his first foreign visit as head of state in September in order to seek cooperation on combatting "people smuggling," with no mention of the rights of those seeking asylum. Australian aid remained focused on Asia and the Pacific, with Indonesia and Papua New Guinea the top two aid recipients. In September, the government said it would slash Australia's aid budget by US$4.2 billion over the next three years, reducing foreign aid spending from 0.37 percent to 0.32 percent of gross national income.

Bangladesh

Bangladesh tumbled backwards on human rights in 2013. The government led by Prime Minister Sheikh Hasina, which has long claimed to be liberal and democratic, engaged in a harsh crackdown on members of civil society and the media. In August, it jailed prominent human rights defender Adilur Rahman Khan on politically motivated charges. "Atheist" bloggers were arrested, as was a newspaper editor. The government increasingly accused those who criticized its actions or policies, ranging from the World Bank to Grameen Bank founder and Nobel laureate Muhammad Yunus, of being involved in plots against it.

On many occasions the government employed violent and illegal measures against protesters, including against followers of the Hefazat-e-Islami movement and those demonstrating against deeply flawed war crimes trials which ended in death sentences against many accused.

Dire conditions for workers in the garment and other industries remained largely unreformed in spite of promises of improvements following the tragic collapse of the Rana Plaza garment factory in April and the deaths of over 1,100 workers. The government finally dropped frivolous charges against several labor rights leaders. The courts also ordered all charges to be dropped against Limon Hossain, a young man wrongfully shot and maimed by security forces in a botched operation in 2011.

Elections scheduled for January 2014 led to increased tensions. Although the Awami League campaigned for a caretaker system while in opposition to guard against fraud and manipulation, once in power it abolished the system, leading to opposition party threats to boycott the elections and increasing the chances of violent confrontations between security forces and protesters.

Crackdown on Civil Society, Media, and Opposition

In February, Bangladesh was gripped by large-scale protests, political unrest, and violence after the International Crimes Tribunal (ICT) sentenced a leader of the Jamaat-e-Islaami party, Abdul Qader Mollah, to life in prison instead of death. Hundreds of thousands of people throughout Bangladesh took to the streets in peaceful protests to demand that Mollah be hanged. The situation took a more violent turn after the ICT, on February 28, sentenced another Jamaat leader, Delwar Hossain Sayedee, to death for war crimes. Following this verdict, Jamaat supporters took to the streets. Jamaat supporters were responsible for a number of deaths, but the security forces killed many more with often indiscriminate attacks on protesters and bystanders.

At the same time, the government began a crackdown on critics. Several bloggers who criticized the government for appearing to appease Islamic extremism were arrested.

In April, the law minister announced that the government would increase its control over social media, blogs, and online news websites. On February 16, the Bangladesh Telecommunication Regulatory Commission shut down the *Sonar Bangla* blog, known to be operated by Jamaat activists, for spreading "hate speech and causing communal tension." In a further attack on free speech, on April 11 the police arrested Mahmdur Rahman, the editor of an opposition news outlet, *Amar Desh*. Rahman was subsequently charged with sedition and unlawful publication of a hacked conversation between the ICT judges and an external consultant initially published by the *Economist* magazine. On April 14, police raided the offices of another opposition newspaper, *Daily Sangram*, and its editor was subsequently charged for printing *Amar Desh*.

In August, Adilur Rahman Khan of Odhikar, a leading human rights group, was arrested under the Information and Communication Technology Act for allegedly false reporting about killings by government security forces when they dispersed the May 5-6 demonstration by Hefazat, a fundamentalist group demanding greater adherence to Islamic principles. Police raided Odhikar's offices on the night of August 11, seizing computers which may contain sensitive information on victims and witnesses. Khan was denied bail several times and kept in prison for two months before being granted bail in October on appeal.

In October, parliament passed a bill amending the Information and Communication Technology Act to increase the length of sentences, according the police greater powers to arrest, and making certain offenses non-bailable.

War Crimes Trial

At time of writing, the ICT, set up to prosecute war crimes during the country's independence war in 1971, had handed down eight convictions, five of which resulted in death sentences. While human rights organizations have long called for fair trials of those responsible, the trials fell short of international human rights standards. In December 2012, the *Economist* published damning evidence of collusion between judges, prosecutors, and the government showing that judges were instructing the prosecution on the conduct of the trials, the questioning of witnesses, and written submissions. The revelations led to the resignation of the ICT's chief judge, but defense motions for retrials were rejected.

Although the ICT had the authority to order measures for victim and witness protection, it summarily dismissed credible claims of witness insecurity. In the Delwar Hossain Sayedee case, judges dismissed credible evidence that an important defense witness was abducted from the courthouse gates and did not order an independent investigation into the allegation. Contradictory statements by key prosecution witnesses were not taken into account in several cases, and judges severely limited the number of defense witnesses. The Appellate Division of the Supreme Court reversed the life sentence given to Abdur Qader Mollah and imposed the death penalty after the government pushed through retrospective amendments to the ICT Act, in clear violation of Bangladesh's obligations under article 15 of the International Covenant on Civil and Political Rights (ICCPR). The amendment allowed the prosecution to appeal against the life sentence handed down by the trial judges, which the ICT Act had not previously allowed.

Human Rights Watch and the *Economist*, journalists and television show guests were issued orders by the ICT to show cause for contempt for critical remarks and reporting on the tribunal.

Unlawful Violence Against Protesters

Bangladeshi security forces frequently used excessive force in responding to street protests, killing at least 150 protesters and injuring at least 2,000 between February and October 2013. While large numbers of protesters were

arrested, Bangladeshi authorities made no meaningful efforts to hold members of the security forces accountable. At least 90 protesters were killed by security force gunfire during the clashes among the Shahbagh movement, Jamaat-e-Islaami supporters, and security forces in March and April.

In response to the May 5-6 Hefazat protests, the police, the paramilitary Rapid Action Battalion (RAB), and the Border Guards Bangladesh (BGB) fired indiscriminately into crowds and brutally and unlawfully beat protesters, leading to approximately 50 deaths. At least a dozen members of the security forces and police officers were also killed, as well as three members of the ruling Awami League party.

Labor Rights and Conditions of Workers

Bangladesh has long had notoriously poor workplace safety, with inadequate inspections and regulations. This issue was spotlighted in April, when the Rana Plaza building, which housed five garment factories, collapsed. The building had been evacuated the day before due to cracks in the structure, but the workers had then been ordered back to work. More than 1,100 workers died.

Under domestic and international pressure, on July 15, 2013, the Bangladeshi parliament enacted changes to the Labour Act. The amendments, which did away with the requirement that unions provide the names of leaders to employers at the time of registration and allow workers to seek external expert assistance in bargaining, failed to lift a number of other restrictions on freedom of association. The law also provided exemptions to export processing zones where most garments are made. Even after Rana Plaza, Bangladeshi law remains out of compliance with core International Labour Organization standards, including Convention No. 87 on freedom of association and Convention No. 98 on the right to organize and bargain collectively.

The government also undertook to have more regular inspections of factories in 2013, but inspections which were due to start in September remained stalled by administrative delays.

In a welcome move, the authorities dropped charges against the leaders of the Bangladesh Centre for Worker Solidarity, who had been hampered and harassed in their work for years by frivolous criminal charges.

Tannery workers in the Hazaribagh neighborhood of Dhaka, one of the world's most polluted urban sites, continue to face highly toxic working conditions. Some 150 leather tanneries operate in the area, producing leather primarily for export and discharging 21 thousand cubic meters of untreated effluent into the nearby Buriganga River each day. The government's planned relocation of the tanneries to a dedicated industrial zone, delayed numerous times since 2005, was again put off in mid-2013.

The Department of the Environment fined two tanneries for their failure to treat waste in 2013, the first time environmental laws have been enforced against Hazaribagh tanneries. Enforcement of environmental and labor laws is otherwise lacking, with negative consequences for the health and well-being of tannery workers and local residents.

Women's Rights

Leading human rights groups in the country had discussions with doctors to revise medico-legal protocols for the treatment and examination of rape victims to exclude degrading practices like the two-finger test to draw conclusions about a woman's "habituation to sex." Such groups are challenging the practice as a violation of the fundamental rights to life and health with dignity in the High Court Division of the Bangladesh Supreme Court.

Key International Actors

India, Bangladesh's most influential international interlocutor, remained largely silent on the human rights situation. Bangladesh and India continued to hold talks on issues linked to their shared border including illegal trade and the use of excessive force by Indian border guards leading to deaths and injuries to Bangladeshi and Indian nationals.

Bangladesh's donors were more vocal, pressing the government to end its crackdown on critics. Donors were swift in denouncing the arrest of Adilur Rahman Khan, with members of the international community observing court proceedings. However, donors were largely silent on the lack of fair trials at the ICT.

Following the Rana Plaza collapse, over 70 European companies signed an international accord designed to better protect Bangladeshi workers by requiring regular inspections of factories and making the results public. However, American buyers refused to join this accord and signed a separate agreement which has been criticized for not allowing workers to freely form unions.

The government publicly agreed to allow international monitors to observe the January 2014 elections. The international community, in particular the US, have been vocal in calling for the various parties to come to an agreement well beforehand in order to avoid contentious and potentially violent protests and a non-credible election result.

Burma

Burma's uneven reform process continued in 2013 with notable improvements in some sectors, but serious problems continuing throughout the country. Basic freedoms of assembly and association improved but laws were enforced inconsistently and in several instances peaceful demonstrators still faced arrest. Media freedoms continued to flourish in 2013, but at time of writing the government was seeking new laws that could roll back important recent gains.

Burma released more than 200 political prisoners in amnesties in 2013, including 56 in October and 69 in November. Despite this progress, it still had an estimated 60 political detainees at time of writing. New arrests of peaceful political activists continue to be reported.

The national parliament has proven to be a more robust venue for debate and legislative reform than many observers predicted, with surprisingly open discussion of issues such as land grabbing by the military, constitutional reform that would reduce military representation, and rule of law initiatives.

Violence against Muslims

Communal violence against Muslim communities in central Burma spread during 2013, with a series of apparently coordinated attacks against Muslim communities and property. In late March, Burmese Buddhist mobs attacked Muslim communities in the central Burmese town of Meiktila. At least 44 people were killed and 1,400 mostly Muslim-owned businesses and houses were destroyed. Burmese police forces failed to intervene during much of the violence and in most cases did not act to protect Muslim lives or property; in some instances they actively participated in the anti-Muslim violence. More than 12,000 people were displaced by the violence, and many remained in government-protected displacement camps in the town at time of writing.

Similar outbreaks of violence were reported during the year in Pegu and Okkan north of Rangoon, and in Lashio in Shan State. In October, attacks against Kaman Muslims in southern Arakan State around the town of Thandwe killed at least six people and destroyed nearly 100 houses. The attacks coincided with a

HUMAN
RIGHTS
WATCH

"All You Can Do is Pray"
Crimes Against Humanity and Ethnic Cleansing
of Rohingya Muslims in Burma's Arakan State

visit to the region by President Thein Sein. Authorities arrested senior Arakanese political party members accused of instigating the violence.

Legal proceedings against perpetrators of violence were initially asymmetrical, with more Muslims tried and sentenced in more cases than Burman Buddhist instigators. However, in June, 25 Buddhists involved in violence in Meiktila were sentenced for murder and arson, in July, 6 suspects were arrested in connection with the killing of Muslim pilgrims in 2012 that sparked violence in Arakan State, and in September two men were sentenced to five years in prison for arson and violence in Okkan. At time of writing, no members of the security forces were known to have been disciplined or prosecuted for involvement in violence.

In some cases, anti-Muslim violence and hate speech is being spread by nation- alist Buddhist monks such as U Wirathu, active proponent of the so-called 969 movement that has urged Buddhists to boycott Muslim businesses and refrain from marrying Muslims and converting to Islam. U Wirathu has even drafted leg- islation that would ban such marriages and conversions. Key political leaders such as Aung San Suu Kyi did not publicly denounce this movement in 2013, although in an important speech in April, President Thein Sein warned that the rise in communal violence had the potential to derail the fragile reform process.

During a country visit in August, the UN special rapporteur on human rights in Burma, Tomas Ojea Quintana, was attacked in his car by Burman Buddhist mobs in Meiktila; security forces in the vicinity failed to intervene. Compounding their failure to adequately ensure Quintana's safety, senior government officials accused him of exaggerating the incident. Many in the Burmese-language media also lambasted Quintana, a disturbing reflection of rising Burman nationalism and backlash against international pressure to end human rights abuses.

The condition of the displaced Rohingya Muslim minority in northern Arakan State remained precarious in 2013, even with a considerable international humanitarian response. At time of writing, an estimated 180,000 people, mostly Muslims, remained in over 40 IDP camps throughout Arakan State, many living in deplorable conditions. While more international assistance reached them in 2013 than in 2012, serious concerns remain over restrictions on movement, lack of livelihoods, inadequate basic services, and continued threats from hostile Arakanese. In Buthidaung and Maungdaw townships, local ordinances reportedly prohibited Rohingya women from having more than two children; when the policy became publicly known and met with international outrage, national officials backtracked and claimed no such policy was in effect.

A government commission of inquiry report on the anti-Rohingya violence of June and October 2012 in Arakan State failed to investigate cases or assign responsibility for the violence, and made no recommendation for prosecution of security forces involved in the violence. Human Rights Watch had found that the attacks on Rohingya had amounted to a campaign of "ethnic cleansing" and crimes against humanity. On several occasions in 2013, Rohingya IDPs were abused for staging protests; in one incident in June, police shot and killed three women protesters at an IDP camp.

The government continues to refuse to amend Burma's draconian 1982 Citizenship Law that effectively denies citizenship to Rohingya, despite many families having lived in Burma for generations. In July, the president ordered the disbanding of the notoriously abusive and corrupt Na Sa Ka paramilitary border security force, although doubts remain as to whether all personnel have been withdrawn from Arakan State or reassigned to other agencies.

Laws on Basic Freedoms

Burma's legislative reform process remains opaque and consultation with key community groups uneven. Many longstanding repressive laws have not been repealed or amended and some are still used to target activists. Several important laws related to land rights and farmers rights were enacted in 2013, but concerns remain that they will be insufficient to protect against mass land grabs by the Burmese military and companies.

The Law on Peaceful Assembly and Peaceful Processions was applied haphazardly in 2013, with the authorities permitting some demonstrations and denying permission for others. An increasing number of public protests over land issues were reported during the year, some of which turned violent with clashes between communities and police. Long-time activist Naw Ohn Lah was sentenced in August to two years in prison for leading a demonstration against the Letpadaung mine project in Monywa; 11 Arakanese protesters were sentenced in September to three months in prison for demonstrating against a Chinese pipeline project, although all were eventually pardoned in the November

H U M A N
R I G H T S
W A T C H

REFORMING
TELECOMMUNICATIONS IN BURMA
Human Rights and Responsible Investment in Mobile and the Internet

amnesty. The government permitted a major gathering on August 8 to commemorate the 25th anniversary of the 1988 democratic uprising.

A draft Association Law proposed in July contained numerous provisions that would have severely restricted the establishment and activities of Burmese and international NGOs. Following coordinated pressure from Burmese civil society, including consultations with the parliament and government and public letters by over 500 Burmese groups, a much improved draft was released in August, albeit still with the potential to restrict the right to freedom of association.

The media in Burma continued to flourish in 2013, even as the government pressed forward with proposed new laws such as the draft Printers and Publishers Act that, if passed, would significantly curtail media freedom. The nascent Burmese Press Council drafted its own version of the law, but the government rejected it. In June, the government banned the sale of an issue of *Time* magazine with a cover story on the nationalist monk U Wirathu.

A draft telecommunications law proposed in 2013 contained numerous provisions that could imperil basic rights. Passage was pending at time of writing.

The governmental National Human Rights Commission continues to receive numerous reports of alleged human rights violations but it has not adequately investigated the reports. At time of writing, it had received approximately 4,000 cases since it was established in 2011. Chairman Win Mra said in early 2013 that the commission would not investigate any alleged Burmese army abuses in Kachin State. A draft law to provide a stronger legislative basis for the commission's independence is pending.

Ethnic Conflict and Displacement

Although the government has concluded ceasefire agreements with about 15 non-state armed groups in Burma, serious human rights violations continued in ethnic areas in 2013.

The government reached a shaky preliminary ceasefire agreement with the Kachin Independence Army in March after nearly two years of fighting and displacement of over 80,000 Kachin civilians. However, reports of Burmese army abuses against civilians persist. Humanitarian access to IDPs has been uneven and insufficient, with some local Burmese army commanders denying access that national-level authorities previously granted. No major returns of displaced civilians had been reported at time of writing.

Conflict spread to parts of northern Shan State involving Kachin, Shan, and Palaung rebels, with reports of civilian displacement and attacks against civilians by both government and opposition forces.

At time of writing, an estimated 400,000 internally displaced persons remained in eastern Burma, and another 130,000 refugees live in nine camps along the Thailand-Burma border. Thailand, Burma, and the UN refugee agency have agreed that conditions for the refugees' return in safety and dignity are not yet present.

Key International Actors

Most sanctions on Burma were lifted in 2013, including all relevant provisions of the EU Common Position except its arms embargo. The United States suspended many of its sanctions, but maintained bans on the importation of jade and rubies as well as targeted financial sanctions on certain individuals implicated in past human rights abuses. New human rights reporting requirements for US investments in Burma took effect in May.

Burma continued its re-engagement with the international community by expanding programs with the World Bank and Asian Development Bank, and negotiating marked increases in humanitarian and development assistance from the US, EU, UK, Australia, and Japan. Foreign investment increased, mainly in the extractive and resource sectors.

President Thein Sein made visits to the United States, Europe, and Australia in 2013, pledging to continue the reform process. However, despite his public pledges in November 2012 that the government would permit the establishment of an office of the UN High Commissioner for Human Rights in Burma, the initiative was repeatedly blocked by the Burmese government.

Burma continued desultory cooperation with the UN on a child soldier action plan signed in 2012. Progress on demobilizing child soldiers and ending forced recruitment was slowed by government denials of access to military sites and to government-controlled border militias.

The US announced tentative re-establishment of defense links with the Burmese military, inviting Burmese officers in February to observe the Thailand-based multilateral Cobra Gold exercises, and in July sending US military experts to begin basic instruction in human rights norms. The chief of the UK defense forces visited Burma in June and the governments later announced that Britain would invite 30 Burmese military officers to attend a major defense conference in the UK. The year also saw UK and Australian announcements that they would station defense attachés in Burma for the first time since 1988, and the initiation of a European Union police reform program in the country.

The US government included Burma in its list of four countries banned from receiving certain forms of US military assistance in 2014 under the Child Soldiers Prevention Act. Affected programs include International Military Education and Training (IMET), which helps train foreign militaries, and Foreign Military Financing (FMF), which funds the sale of US military material and services.

In June, the UN Human Rights Council urged the Burmese government to take immediate steps to stop violence and human rights violations committed in the name of religion. It called on the government to take all necessary measures to ensure accountability for such abuses and expedite the establishment of a UN human rights office in Burma.

Cambodia

Cambodia became engulfed in a human rights crisis after national assembly elections on July 28, 2013. Final results announced by the National Election Committee (NEC), a body controlled by the ruling Cambodian People's Party (CPP), returned the CPP, in power since 1979, to a majority in the National Assembly. The assembly then chose Hun Sen as prime minister, a post he has held since 1985. Large-scale demonstrations ensued amidst credible allegations that electoral irregularities and CPP control over election bodies affected the final outcome. Security forces repeatedly used excessive force to suppress post-election protests and social unrest, resulting in two deaths and many injuries.

Although Cambodia's rapidly growing social media sector remains largely unrestricted, almost all state and private television stations and almost all print media, domestic radio stations, and news websites are controlled by or are loyal to the CPP. While many labor unions exist, strikes are often violently broken up by the security forces.

National Elections

Cambodian King Norodom Sihamoni amnestied the leader of the opposition Cambodia National Rescue Party (CNRP), Sam Rainsy, on July 14, 2013, making it possible for Rainsy to return to Cambodia without facing imprisonment for previous convictions on trumped-up charges. However, his right to vote and run in the July 28 elections was not restored.

The CPP controls the media, security forces, and all election management bodies, including the NEC and its provincial and local affiliates, and the Constitutional Council. Voter registration in 2013 was marred by CPP-orchestrated fraud and other irregularities. The NEC announced that the CCP won 68 seats and the CNRP won 55 seats in the election, a much closer result than the CPP expected, but it rejected CNRP demands for an independent investigation into the irregularities.

In the run-up to elections, commanders of the army, gendarmerie, and police openly campaigned for the CPP and Hun Sen. After the ballot, they proclaimed their support for the contested CPP victory. Hun Sen then ordered a massive deployment of troops and police in Phnom Penh and elsewhere in an attempt to prevent demonstrations. A security force lockdown of the capital, Phnom Penh, on September 15 was accompanied by excessive force against social unrest following the demonstrations, killing one person and injuring approximately two dozen others.

On September 20 and 22, security force operations broke up small peaceful protest vigils in Phnom Penh, on the second occasion deliberately attacking human rights monitors and journalists along with protesters, injuring at least 20 people. On November 12, 2013, security forces again employed excessive force, this time while obstructing a march by striking workers, shooting and killing one person and wounding nine others.

Attacks on Civil Society and Imprisonment of Human Rights Defenders

In the months before the July 28 elections, security forces violently broke up peaceful gatherings by civil society groups, especially those protesting alleged land-grabbing. Excessive force resulted in serious injuries to protesters. After the elections, government-backed religious authorities threatened and in some cases assaulted Buddhist monks in order to prevent them from joining opposition demonstrations.

At time of writing, at least five human rights defenders were serving prison terms and three others sentenced *in absentia* were facing prison if apprehended. All were tried on politically motivated charges, mostly in connection with defending land tenure rights. They included Bun Roatha, a key figure opposed to land grabbing in Kratie province, who was sentenced in absentia to 30 years in prison. Yorm Bopha, sentenced to prison on trumped up charges for leading a protest against illegal evictions in Phnom Penh, was temporarily released on November 22, 2013, when the Supreme Court referred her case to a lower court for further review.

Impunity

Forces under Hun Sen and the CPP have committed frequent and large-scale abuses, including extrajudicial killings and torture, with impunity. Instances in

HUMAN
RIGHTS
WATCH

"They Treat Us Like Animals"

Mistreatment of Drug Users and "Undesirables" in Cambodia's Drug Detention Centers

2013 included the case of the CPP governor of Bavet municipality, Chhouk Bandit: although convicted of "unintentional injury" on June 25, 2013, in connection with his shooting of three women workers during a strike near the town in February 2012, he was not detained for trial and was allowed to abscond despite his guilty verdict. Disregarding considerable evidence implicating government authorities, no one was convicted in a 2013 trial for the brutal murder of journalist Hang Serei Udom in September 2012 after he published reports alleging official involvement in illegal logging. No serious investigations were carried out into the killing and injury of protesters and bystanders during post-election protests and unrest in September and November 2013.

Those responsible for the 2004 killing of labor leader Chea Vichea remain at large. After the killing, the government arrested and then instructed the courts to convict Born Samnang and Sok Sam Oeun. The two were released in 2009 after the prosecution admitted that there was no evidence against them, but a court later re-imprisoned them in 2012, sentencing them to 20 years in prison. Under intense international pressure on the government, the Supreme Court acquitted and released both men on September 25, 2013. The court, however, refused their demand for compensation.

Land Rights

A government moratorium remained in place on the granting of Economic Land Concessions (ELCs) for industrial-scale corporate agriculture on state lands. Such ELCs have adversely affected hundreds of thousands of people. Economically and politically powerful actors, however, continue to grab land to which impoverished residents and cultivators have legitimate tenure claims, provoking sometimes violent confrontations.

A program organized and run by Hun Sen in his own name to bestow land titles on some people living within the peripheries of ELCs and other state lands ended just before the elections with claims the program had benefited up to 360,000 needy households. While many indeed benefitted, in many places wealthy and powerful interests diverted the program to increase their land-holdings. Hun Sen suspended the program in the run-up to the election. However, in November 2013, the government announced it would resume the program shortly.

Arbitrary Detention

The authorities routinely detain alleged drug users, homeless people, "street" children, sex workers, and perceived people with disabilities in "correction centers" around the country holding at least 2,000 people each year without due process, where the mainstays of ostensible "treatment" are exhausting physical exercises and military-like drills. Guards and other staff whip detainees with rubber water hoses, beat them with bamboo sticks or palm fronds, shock them with electric batons, sexually abuse them, and punish them with physical exercises intended to cause intense physical pain. Detainees from some centers are forced to work on construction sites, including in at least one instance to help build a hotel.

Khmer Rouge Tribunal

The United Nations-assisted Extraordinary Chambers in the Courts of Cambodia (ECCC) continues to suffer the long-term effects of government obstruction of and non-cooperation with efforts to bring leaders of the Khmer Rouge to justice for genocide, crimes against humanity, and war crimes committed during their rule from 1975 to 1979. The ECCC has fully tried and convicted only one person since it was established in 2006, the head of the infamous Tuol Sleng torture center. It is currently trying just two alleged Khmer Rouge senior leaders, Nuon Chea and Khieu Samphan, both elderly and in ill-health, and only for a few of the crimes for which the ECCC originally indicted them in 2010. Another ECCC indictee, Leng Sary, died on March 14, 2013.

Government non-cooperation slowed UN investigations into five other suspects begun in 2006, one of whom died in 2013. Popular interest and support for the ECCC has greatly waned.

Key International Actors

The Cambodian government remained heavily dependent on foreign assistance. Japan was the major aid donor, while China was the largest direct foreign investor. Vietnam continued to maintain close connections at national and local levels with government and security force agencies.

The United States provided some non-lethal military aid plus military training, but was the most forthright foreign government in raising human rights concerns. Meeting in September, the United Nations Human Rights Council extended for two years the mandate for a special rapporteur on the human rights situation in Cambodia.

China

Rapid socio-economic change in China has been accompanied by relaxation of some restrictions on basic rights, but the government remains an authoritarian one-party state. It places arbitrary curbs on expression, association, assembly, and religion; prohibits independent labor unions and human rights organizations; and maintains Party control over all judicial institutions.

The government censors the press, the Internet, print publications, and academic research, and justifies human rights abuses as necessary to preserve "social stability." It carries out involuntary population relocation and rehousing on a massive scale, and enforces highly repressive policies in ethnic minority areas in Tibet, Xinjiang, and Inner Mongolia. Though primary school enrollment and basic literacy rates are high, China's education system discriminates against children and young people with disabilities. The government obstructs domestic and international scrutiny of its human rights record, insisting it is an attempt to destabilize the country.

At the same time, citizens are increasingly prepared to challenge authorities over volatile livelihood issues, such as land seizures, forced evictions, environmental degradation, miscarriages of justice, abuse of power by corrupt cadres, discrimination, and economic inequality. Official and scholarly statistics, based on law enforcement reports, suggest there are 300-500 protests each day, with anywhere from ten to tens of thousands of participants. Despite the risks, Internet users and reform-oriented media are aggressively pushing censorship boundaries by advocating for the rule of law and transparency, exposing official wrongdoing, and calling for political reforms.

Civil society groups and advocates continue to slowly expand their work despite their precarious status, and an informal but resilient network of activists monitors and documents human rights cases as a loose national "weiquan" (rights defense) movement. These activists endure police monitoring, detention, arrest, enforced disappearance, and torture.

The Xi Jinping administration formally assumed power in March, and proposed several reforms to longstanding policies, including abolishing one form of arbitrary detention, known as re-education through labor (RTL), and changes to the household registration system. It staged high-profile corruption investigations, mostly targeting political rivals. But it also struck a conservative tone, opposing constitutional rule, press freedom, and "western-style" rule of law, and issuing harsher restrictions on dissent, including through two legal documents making it easier to bring criminal charges against activists and Internet critics.

Bo Xilai, once a rising political star, was sentenced to life imprisonment in September after a show trial that captured public attention but fell short of fair trial standards and failed to address widespread abuses of power committed during his tenure in Chongqing.

Human Rights Defenders

China's human rights activists often face imprisonment, detention, torture, commitment to psychiatric facilities, house arrest, and intimidation.

One of the most severe crackdowns on these individuals in recent years occurred in 2013, with more than 50 activists put under criminal detention between February and October. Human rights defenders are detained for ill-defined crimes ranging from "creating disturbances" to "inciting subversion" for organizing and participating in public, collective actions. In July, authorities detained Xu Zhiyong, who is considered an intellectual leader of the New Citizens Movement, a loose network of civil rights activists whose efforts include a nationwide campaign that calls on public officials to disclose their assets.

In September, Beijing-based activist Cao Shunli was detained after she was barred from boarding a flight to Geneva ahead of the United Nations Human Rights Council (HRC) review of China on October 22. Cao is known for pressing the Chinese government to include independent civil society input into the drafting of China's report to the HRC under a mechanism called Universal Periodic Review (UPR). Another activist, Peng Lanlan, was released in August after she spent one year in prison for "obstructing official business" for her role in the campaign.

Nobel Peace Prize winner Liu Xiaobo continues his 11-year jail term in northern Liaoning province. His wife Liu Xia continues to be subjected to unlawful house arrest. In August, Liu Xiaobo's brother-in-law, Liu Hui, was given an 11-year sen-

HUMAN
RIGHTS
WATCH

"SWEPT AWAY"

Abuses Against Sex Workers in China

tence on fraud charges; it is widely believed the heavy sentence is part of broader effort to punish Liu Xiaobo's family.

Legal Reforms

While the government rejects judicial independence and prohibits independent bar associations, progressive lawyers and legal scholars continue to be a force for change, contributing to increasing popular legal awareness and activism.

The Chinese Communist Party maintains authority over all judicial institutions and coordinates the judiciary's work through its political and legal committees. The Public Security Bureau, or police, remains the most powerful actor in the criminal justice system. Use of torture to extract confessions is prevalent, and miscarriages of justice are frequent due to weak courts and tight limits on the rights of the defense.

In November, the government announced its intention to abolish re-education through labor (RTL), a form of arbitrary detention in which the police can detain people for up to four years without trial. There were about 160,000 people in about 350 camps at the beginning of the year, but numbers dwindled rapidly as the police stopped sending people to RTL. The official press, however, reported that some of these facilities were being converted to drug rehabilitation centers, another form of administrative detention. At time of writing it was unclear whether the government would fully abolish administrative detention as a way to deal with minor offenders, or whether it would instead establish a replacement system that continued to allow detention without trial.

China continues to lead the world in executions. The exact number remains a state secret, but experts estimate it has decreased progressively from about 10,000 per year a decade ago to less than 4,000 in recent years.

Freedom of Expression

Freedom of expression deteriorated in 2013, especially after the government launched a concerted effort to rein in micro-blogging. The government and the Party maintain multiple layers of control over all media and publications.

Internet censors shape online debate and maintain the "Great Firewall," which blocks outside content from reaching Internet users in China. Despite these restrictions, the Internet, especially microblog services known as "weibo" and other social media tools, are popular as a relatively free space in which China's 538 million users can connect and air grievances. However, those who breach sensitive taboos are often swiftly identified and their speech deleted or disallowed; some are detained or jailed.

In January, *Southern Weekly*, a Guangzhou-based newspaper known for its boundary-pushing investigative journalism, was enveloped in a censorship row after the paper's editors found that their New Year's special editorial was rewritten on the censors' orders and published without their consent. The original editorial had called for political reform and respect for constitutionally guaranteed rights, but the published version instead praised the Chinese Communist Party. The paper's staff publicly criticized the provincial top censor, called for his resignation and went on a strike; the paper resumed printing a week later.

In May, the General Office of the Chinese Communist Party's Central Committee issued a gag order to universities directing them to avoid discussions of "seven taboos," which included "universal values" and the Party's past wrongs, according to media reports.

Since August, authorities have waged a campaign against "online rumors." The campaign has targeted influential online opinion leaders and ordinary netizens. The authorities have detained hundreds of Internet users for days, closed down over 100 "illegal" news websites run by citizen journalists, and detained well-known liberal online commentator Charles Xue.

Also in August, the government official in charge of Internet affairs warned Internet users against breaching "seven bottom lines," including China's "socialist system," the country's "national interests," and "public order." In September, the Supreme People's Court and the Supreme People's Procuratorate (state prosecutor) issued a new judicial interpretation applying four existing criminal provisions to Internet expression, providing a more explicit legal basis for charging Internet users.

Freedom of Religion

Although the constitution guarantees freedom of religion, the government restricts religious practices to officially approved mosques, churches, temples, and monasteries organized by five officially recognized religious organizations. It audits the activities, employee details, and financial records of religious bodies, and retains control over religious personnel appointments, publications, and seminary applications.

Unregistered spiritual groups such as Protestant "house churches" are deemed unlawful and subjected to raids and closures; members are harassed and leaders are detained and sometimes jailed.

The government classifies Falun Gong, a meditation-focused spiritual group banned since July 1999, as an "an evil cult" and arrests, harasses, and intimidates its members. After releasing a new documentary about a labor camp in which Falun Gong practitioners were detained and tortured, filmmaker and photographer Du Bin was detained in May. He was released after five weeks in detention.

In April, a court in Henan province sentenced seven house church leaders to between three and seven years in prison on charges of "using a cult to undermine law enforcement;" evidence suggested they had only attended meetings and publicized church activities.

Health and Disability Rights

The government has developed numerous laws, regulations, and action plans designed to decrease serious environmental pollution and related threats to public health, but the policies are often not implemented.

In February, a lawyer's request under the Open Government Information Act to reveal soil contamination data was rejected; according to the authorities, such data was a "state secret." Also in February, after years of denial and inaction, the Ministry of Environmental Protection finally acknowledged the existence of "cancer villages," those with abnormally high cancer rates. Victims had long pressed for justice and compensation and domestic media had written extensively on the issue.

Despite a review in 2012 under the Convention on the Rights of Persons with Disabilities (CRPD), protections of the rights of persons with disabilities remain inadequate. These individuals face serious discrimination in employment and education, and some government policies institutionalize discrimination.

HUMAN
RIGHTS
WATCH

"As Long as They
Let Us Stay in Class"

Barriers to Education for Persons with Disabilities in China

In February, the State Council's Legislative Affairs Office announced amendments to the 1994 Regulations of Education of Persons with Disabilities in China. While welcome, the amendments do not ensure that students with disabilities can enroll in mainstream schools or mandate appropriate classroom modifications ("accommodations") enabling them to participate fully in such schools.

In May, China's first Mental Health Law came into effect. It filled an important legal void but does not close loopholes that allow government authorities and families to detain people in psychiatric hospitals against their will. In July, after the law came into effect, Gu Xianghong was detained for five weeks in a Beijing psychiatric hospital for petitioning the authorities about her grievances.

Women's Rights

Women's reproductive rights and access to reproductive health remain severely curtailed under China's population planning regulations. While the government announced in November that Chinese couples will now be allowed two children if either parent was a single child, the measure does not change the foundations of China's government-enforced family planning policy, which includes the use of legal and other coercive measures—such as administrative sanctions, fines, and coercive measures, including forced abortion—to control reproductive choices.

The government's punitive crackdowns on sex work often lead to serious abuses, including physical and sexual violence, increased risk of disease, and constrained access to justice for the country's estimated 4 to 10 million sex workers, most of whom are women. Sex workers have also documented abuses by public health agencies, such as coercive HIV testing, privacy infringements, and mistreatment by health officials.

In January, the Supreme People's Court upheld a death sentence against Li Yan, a woman convicted of murdering her physically abusive husband. Domestic violence is not treated as a mitigating factor in court cases.

In May, Ye Haiyan, China's most prominent sex worker rights activist, was detained by police for several days after being assaulted at her home in Guangxi province over her exposure of abusive conditions in local brothels.

Although the government acknowledges that domestic violence, employment discrimination, and gender bias are widespread, it limits the activities of independent women's rights groups working on these issues by making it difficult for them to register, monitoring their activities, interrogating their staff, and prohibiting some activities.

Migrant and Labor Rights

The official All-China Federation of Trade Unions (ACFTU) continued to be the only legal representative of workers; independent labor unions are forbidden.

Despite this limitation, workers have become increasingly vocal and active in striving for better working conditions across the country, including by staging protests and strikes. In September, Shenzhen dock workers went on strike to demand better pay and working conditions. Ten days later, the workers accepted a government-brokered deal that met some of their demands.

In May, the official All-China Women's Federation issued a new report revealing that the number of migrant children, including those living with their parents in urban areas and those "left behind" in rural areas, had reached 100 million by 2010. Migrant workers continue to be denied urban residence permits, which are required to gain access to social services such as education. Many such workers leave their children at home when they migrate so that the children can go to school, rendering some vulnerable to abuse.

Although China has numerous workplace safety regulations, enforcement is lax, especially at the local level. For example, in June, a fire at a poultry farm killed 121 workers in Jilin province. Subsequent investigations revealed that the local fire department had just days before the fire issued the poultry farm a safety certificate even though it failed to meet a number of standards.

Sexual Orientation and Gender Identity

The Chinese government classified homosexuality as a mental illness until 2001. To date there is still no law protecting people from discrimination on the basis of sexual orientation or gender identity, which remains common especially in the workplace.

Same-sex partnership and marriage are not recognized under Chinese law. In February, a lesbian couple attempted to register at the marriage registry in Beijing but their application was rejected.

On May 17, the International Day against Homophobia, Changsha city authorities detained Xiang Xiaohan, an organizer of a local gay pride parade, and held him for 12 days for organizing an "illegal march." In China, demonstrations require prior permission, which is rarely granted.

Tibet

The Chinese government systematically suppresses political, cultural, religious and socio-economic rights in Tibet in the name of combating what it sees as separatist sentiment. This includes nonviolent advocacy for Tibetan independence, the Dalai Lama's return, and opposition to government policy. At time of writing, 123 Tibetans had self-immolated in protest against Chinese policies since the first recorded case in February 2009.

Arbitrary arrest and imprisonment remains common, and torture and ill-treatment in detention is endemic. Fair trials are precluded by a politicized judiciary overtly tasked with suppressing separatism.

Police systematically suppress any unauthorized gathering. On July 6, police opened fire in Nyitso, Dawu prefecture (Ch. Daofu), on a crowd that had gathered in the countryside to celebrate the Dalai Lama's birthday. Two people died on the spot, and several others were injured. The government censored news of the event.

In an apparent effort to prevent a repetition of the popular protests of 2008, the government in 2013 maintained many of the measures it introduced during its brutal crackdown on the protest movement—a massive security presence composed largely of armed police forces, sharp restrictions on the movements of Tibetans within the Tibetan plateau, increased controls on monasteries, and a ban on foreign journalists in the Tibetan Autonomous Region (TAR) unless part of a government-organized tour. The government also took significant steps to implement a plan to station 20,000 new officials and Party cadres in the TAR, including in every village, to monitor the political views of all residents.

建美好家园 过幸福生活

中共石渠县委 石渠县人民政府宣

"They Say We Should Be Grateful"

Mass Rehousing and Relocation Programs in Tibetan Areas of China

The government is also subjecting millions of Tibetans to a mass rehousing and relocation policy that radically changes their way of life and livelihoods, in some cases impoverishing them or making them dependent on state subsidies, about which they have no say. Since 2006, over two million Tibetans, both farmers and herders, have been involuntarily "rehoused"—through government-ordered renovation or construction of new houses—in the TAR; hundreds of thousands of nomadic herders in the eastern part of the Tibetan plateau have been relocated or settled in "New Socialist Villages."

Xinjiang

Pervasive ethnic discrimination, severe religious repression, and increasing cultural suppression justified by the government in the name of the "fight against separatism, religious extremism, and terrorism" continue to fuel rising tensions in the Xinjiang Uyghur Autonomous Region.

In 2013, over one hundred people—Uyghurs, Han, and other ethnicities—were killed in various incidents across the region, the highest death toll since the July 2009 Urumqi protests. In some cases, heavy casualties appear to have been the result of military-style assaults on groups preparing violent attacks, as in Bachu prefecture on April 23, and in Turfan prefecture on June 26. But in other cases security forces appear to have used lethal force against crowds of unarmed protesters.

On June 28, in Hetian prefecture, police tried to prevent protesters from marching toward Hetian municipality to protest the arbitrary closure of a mosque and the arrest of its imam, ultimately shooting into the crowd and injuring dozens of protesters. On August 8, in Aksu prefecture, police forces prevented villagers from reaching a nearby mosque to celebrate a religious festival, eventually using live ammunition and injuring numerous villagers. After each reported incident the government ritualistically blames "separatist, religious extremist, and terrorist forces," and obstructs independent investigations.

Arbitrary arrest, torture, and "disappearance" of those deemed separatists are endemic and instill palpable fear in the population. In July, Ilham Tohti, a Uyghur professor at Beijing's Nationalities University published an open letter to the government asking for an investigation into 34 disappearance cases he documented. Tohti was placed under house arrest several times and prevented from traveling abroad.

The government continues to raze traditional Uyghur neighborhoods and rehouse families in planned settlements as part of a comprehensive development policy launched in 2010. The government says the policy is designed to urbanize and develop Xinjiang.

Hong Kong

Despite the fact that Hong Kong continues to enjoy an independent judiciary, a free press, and a vocal civil society, freedoms of the press and assembly have been increasingly under threat since Hong Kong returned to Chinese sovereignty in 1997. Prospects that election of the territory's chief executive starting in 2017 would be genuinely competitive dimmed after Beijing indicated that only candidates who did not "oppose the central government" would be able to run.

Hong Kong has witnessed slow erosion of the rule of law in recent years, exemplified by increasingly strict police controls on assemblies and processions, and arbitrary Immigration Department bans on individuals critical of Beijing, such as members of the Falun Gong and exiled dissidents from the 1989 democracy spring.

Key International Actors

Most governments that have bilateral human rights dialogues with the Chinese government, including the United States, European Union, and Australia, held at least one round of those dialogues in 2013; most acknowledge they are of limited utility for promoting meaningful change inside China.

Several of these governments publicly expressed concern about individual cases, such as those of Xu Zhiyong or Liu Hui, or about trends such as restrictions on anti-corruption activists. Ambassadors from the US and Australia, as well as the EU's special representative for human tights, were allowed to visit the TAR or other Tibetan areas.

None of these governments commented on the denial of Chinese people's political rights to choose their leaders during the 2012-2013 leadership transition, and few successfully integrated human rights concerns into meetings with senior Chinese officials.

China participated in a review of its compliance with the Convention on the Rights of Persons with Disabilities by the international treaty body charged with monitoring implementation of the convention and a review of its overall human rights record at the UN Human Rights Council, but it failed to provide basic information or provided deeply misleading information on torture, arbitrary detention, and restrictions on freedom of expression. There are eight outstanding requests to visit China by UN special rapporteurs, and UN agencies operating inside China remain tightly restricted, their activities closely monitored by the authorities.

China's Foreign Policy

Despite China's continued rise as a global power and its 2013 leadership transition, including the appointment of a new foreign minister, long-established foreign policy views and practices remained relatively unchanged.

China has become more engaged with various United Nations mechanisms but has not significantly improved its compliance with international human rights standards or pushed for improved human rights protections in other countries. In a notable exception, shortly after it was elected to the UN Human Rights Council in November, China publicly urged Sri Lanka "to make efforts to protect and promote human rights."

Even in the face of the rapidly growing death toll in Syria and evidence in August 2013 that the Syrian government used chemical weapons against civilians, Beijing has continued to object to any significant Security Council measures to increase pressure on the Assad regime and abusive rebel groups. It has opposed referral of the situation to the International Criminal Court (ICC) and an arms embargo against forces that commit widespread human rights or laws of war violations. China has also slowed down Security Council-driven efforts to deliver desperately needed humanitarian assistance across the border to rebel controlled areas in northern Syria.

In a minor change of tactics, if not of longer-term strategy, Chinese authorities have become modestly more vocal in their public and private criticisms of North

Korea, particularly following actions by Pyongyang that increased tensions between members of the six-party talks aimed at addressing security concerns posed by North Korea's nuclear weapons program.

Both private and state-owned Chinese firms continue to be a leading source of foreign direct investment, particularly in developing countries, but in some cases have been unwilling or unable to comply with international labor standards.

India

India took positive steps in 2013 by strengthening laws protecting women and children, and, in several important cases, prosecuting state security force personnel for extrajudicial killings. The impact of these developments will depend in large part on effective follow-up by central government authorities. The year also saw increased restrictions on Internet freedom; continued marginalization of Dalits, tribal groups, religious minorities, sexual and gender minorities, and people with disabilities; instances of remained marginalized and often without redress; and persistent impunity for abuses linked to insurgencies, particularly in Maoist areas, Jammu and Kashmir, Manipur, and Assam.

Widespread protests over the gang-rape and death of a female student in New Delhi in December 2012 yet again drew international and domestic attention to the need for institutional reforms to ensure human rights protections in India. The government responded by enacting long-overdue reforms to India's criminal laws to better address gender-based violence. But new reports of violence against women and girls exposed the wide gap between laws on the books and their implementation.

The fact that the government responded to public outrage confirms India's claims of a vibrant civil society. An independent judiciary and free media also acted as checks on abusive practices. However, reluctance to hold public officials to account for abuses or dereliction of duty continued to foster a culture of corruption and impunity.

Investigations into Extrajudicial Killings

In December 2012, the National Human Rights Commission told the Supreme Court it had received 1,671 complaints of extrajudicial killings in the last five years. Following his 2012 visit to India, the UN special rapporteur on extrajudicial, summary or arbitrary executions, Christof Heyns, stressed the need to end impunity and bring perpetrators promptly to justice.

The courage and persistence of human rights activists and victims' families resulted in a number of court interventions and investigations into deaths at the

the hands of security forces. In many cases the authorities had falsely claimed that the deaths occurred during armed exchanges or in self-defense.

In July 2013, the Supreme Court set up an independent panel led by a retired judge after groups from Manipur state filed a public interest petition seeking an investigation into 1,528 alleged extrajudicial executions between 1979 and 2012. The panel looked into six emblematic cases of alleged unlawful killings and found all violated the law. It also observed that security forces were wrongly being shielded by the Armed Forced Special Powers Act (AFSPA), which forbids the prosecution of soldiers without approval of the central government. Because officials rarely grant approvals, troops often enjoy effective immunity from prosecution.

In January 2012, the Supreme Court ordered an independent panel led by a retired judge to look into 22 alleged extrajudicial killings by police in Gujarat state between 2002 and 2006. On Supreme Court orders, court martial proceedings began in September 2012 against army officers accused by the Central Bureau of Investigation in the extrajudicial executions of five villagers from Pathribal in Jammu and Kashmir in 2000. The Armed Forces Special Powers Act shielded the officers from prosecution in a civilian court.

In July 2013, the Central Bureau of Investigation filed charges against policemen responsible for the 2004 killing of Ishrat Jahan, a young student, and three others in a faked armed encounter. In September, D.G. Vanzara, a senior official arrested along with 31 others from the Gujarat police for their alleged role in extrajudicial killings, wrote a letter claiming the killings took place while they were implementing Gujarat government policy.

Repeal of the AFSPA remained a core demand in northeast states and Jammu and Kashmir, where it is in operation. However, despite calls from judicial inquiries and national and international human rights bodies, the government failed to abide by its promise to repeal the abusive law because of strong opposition from the army.

Communal Violence

According to government estimates, 451 incidents of communal violence were recorded in the first eight months of 2013, compared to 410 incidents in all of

2012. Among these were clashes between Hindu and Muslim communities in August in Kishtwar town in Jammu and Kashmir, which killed three people and injured many others. In Bihar, an August altercation at a roadside eatery led to Hindu-Muslim clashes killing two people and injuring nearly a dozen. Over 50 people died in Hindu-Muslim violence in Muzaffarnagar in western Uttar Pradesh state in September. There is a risk of more violence in the run-up to the 2014 elections as political interest groups exploit tensions between the two communities.

Maoist Insurgency

Violence linked to an armed campaign in central and eastern India by the Communist Party of India (Maoist), known as Naxalites, led to the death of 384 people, including 147 civilians, in 2013. In May, Maoists attacked a convoy in Chhattisgarh, killing at least 20 people, including senior Congress Party politicians.

Tribal villagers and civil society activists, caught between the Maoists and the police, remained at risk of arbitrary arrest and torture by government forces, and of extortion and killings by Maoists.

Contrary to court orders, government security forces continued to occupy school buildings as bases for operations in Maoist-affected areas, endangering students and teachers, and depriving some of India's most marginalized children of access to education. Maoists continue to target schools in bombing attacks.

In 2013, members of a Dalit cultural group, charged in 2011 under India's draconian counterterrorism law, remained subject to prosecution for their alleged support of Maoist militants. Courts have repeatedly ruled that ideological sympathy alone does not justify criminal charges.

Freedom of Expression

Repeated abuse of section 66A of the Information Technology Act by police and other state authorities to stifle Internet freedom led the central government to issue an advisory in January 2013 making it mandatory for police to seek clearance from high-ranking officials before making arrests under the law. While this was an improvement, the provisions are still subject to abuse and used to criminalize free speech.

In April 2013, India started rolling out a Central Monitoring System to monitor all phone and Internet communications raised further concerns of abuse since current legal frameworks may not provide adequate oversight or safeguards for the right to privacy. According to recent transparency reports from Google and Facebook, India is second only to the United States in seeking private information about users from these companies.

On occasion, state governments gave in to the demands of interest groups to censor material such as books, talks, and film screenings.

Restrictions on Civil Society

India continued to use the Foreign Contribution Regulation Act (FCRA) to stifle dissent by restricting access to foreign funding for domestic nongovernmental organizations (NGOs) that have been critical of the government. The government targeted groups protesting against nuclear plants and big infrastructure projects. Among groups that lost permission to receive foreign funds was Indian Social Action Forum, a network of more than 700 NGOs across India.

Protection of Children's Rights

Many children in India remained at risk of abuse and deprived of education. Despite efforts to forbid any employment of children under 14, millions remained in the work force, including the worst forms of labor. By some estimates nearly half of India's children under the age of five are malnourished. Thousands of children remain missing, many of them trafficked within and outside the country.

The 2009 Right of Children to Free and Compulsory Education Act led to increased enrollment. However, children from vulnerable communities, particularly Dalits and tribal groups, faced various forms of discrimination, with many dropping out and eventually becoming child workers.

Despite enacting a strong law in 2012, the government failed to embark upon systemic reforms that are needed to ensure the protection of children from sexual abuse.

Women's Rights

After the uproar over the gang-rape and death of a student in New Delhi in December 2012, the government instituted a three-member committee to propose legal reforms to better address gender-based violence. Based on the commission's findings, parliament adopted amendments introducing new and expanded definitions of rape and sexual assault, criminalizing acid attacks, providing for a right to medical treatment, and instituting new procedures to protect the rights of women with disabilities who experience sexual assault.

Despite these important reforms, key gaps remain. For example, Indian law still does not provide adequate legal remedies for "honor killings," or victim and witness protection. Parliament disregarded opposition by rights groups and in April 2013 expanded the scope of death penalty in rape cases.

In June, a local court ordered the reopening of the investigation into alleged mass rapes in the villages of Kunan and Poshpora in Jammu and Kashmir's Kupwara district in 1991. Residents of the villages allege that soldiers raped women during a cordon and search operation.

Hundreds of rapes were reported across the country in 2013. Protests renewed in August after the gang rape of a journalist in Mumbai, accompanied by new calls for greater safety measures for women in public spaces.

In April, India adopted the Sexual Harassment of Women at Workplace (Prevention, Prohibition, and Redressal) Act 2013, which includes domestic workers employed in homes, and sets out complaint mechanisms and the obligations of employers to provide a safe working environment.

Palliative Care

After a series of positive steps in 2012 to address the suffering of hundreds of thousands of persons with incurable diseases from pain and other symptoms, progress on palliative care in India slowed considerably in 2013. The government has so far not allocated a budget to implement India's progressive national palliative care strategy and parliament failed to consider critical amendments to the Narcotic Drugs and Psychotropic Substances Act that would dramatically improve the availability of strong pain medications. More than 7 million people in India require palliative care every year.

HUMAN
RIGHTS
WATCH

BREAKING THE SILENCE
Child Sexual Abuse in India

Rights of Persons with Disabilities

Even as India engages in a reform process to implement national disability and mental health laws, activists remain concerned that these laws are not in line with the Convention on the Rights of Persons with Disabilities, which India ratified in 2007.

Instances of violence against women and girls with mental or intellectual disabilities including voluntary confinement, physical and sexual abuse, inhumane or degrading treatment, and excessive electroshock therapy remained particularly high in state-run and private residential care facilities, which lack adequate oversight. Within the family and community, women and girls with disabilities also experience violence, including involuntary sterilization.

Death Penalty

India ended its eight-year unofficial moratorium on capital punishment in November 2012 with the hanging of Mohammad Ajmal Kasab, a Pakistani convicted of multiple murders in the high-profile November 2008 attacks on luxury hotels and the main railway station in Mumbai. In February 2013, the government executed Mohammad Afzal Guru, convicted for a December 2001 attack on the Indian parliament. Since taking office in July 2012, President Pranab Mukherjee has rejected 11 clemency pleas, confirming the death penalty for 17 people.

Indian law permits the death penalty only in the "rarest of rare" cases, but in November 2012 the Supreme Court ruled that this standard had not been applied uniformly over the years and death penalty standards needed "a fresh look."

Key International Actors

Sexual violence against women in India drew international condemnation in 2013. After the notorious December 2012 New Delhi gang rape and murder, UN Secretary-General Ban Ki-moon called on India to take "further steps and reforms to deter such crimes and bring perpetrators to justice." Attacks on foreign tourists led some countries such as the United States and the United Kingdom to issue travel advisories telling women travelers to exercise caution.

Despite the enormity of India's human rights problems, countries that normally raise human rights issues in their foreign relations continued their low-profile approach to the world's largest democracy.

India's Foreign Policy

India did not live up to expectations in promoting respect for democracy and human rights in its foreign policy. Although the country aspires to a growing role in world affairs and a permanent seat on the UN Security Council, it did little to address some of most pressing problems confronting the world in 2013, such as the crises in Syria and Egypt.

At the UN Human Rights Council, India has rarely supported human rights resolutions on specific countries. While it usually opts for a policy of "non-interference in the internal affairs" of other countries, India notably supported HRC resolutions in 2012 and 2013 calling for accountability for alleged war crimes in Sri Lanka. It has also backed restoration of an elected government in Nepal.

In bilateral engagements, India called on the Burmese government to promote religious tolerance and harmony after attacks on Rohingya Muslims in Arakan State and on Muslim communities in central Burma in several incidents during 2013.

India engaged in promoting stability and human rights in Afghanistan, pledging nearly US$2 billion for the country's rehabilitation and reconstruction efforts, supporting education of girls, providing some police training, and granting asylum to a number of activists fleeing Taliban threats.

Indonesia

Human rights showed little improvement in 2013, President Susilo Bambang Yudhoyono's last full year in office.

Although the president made public appeals for greater religious freedom and tolerance, national authorities continued to respond weakly to growing violence and discrimination against religious minorities. Other areas of concern include new onerous restrictions on the activities of nongovernmental organizations (NGOs), the proliferation of local decrees that violate women's rights, and mistreatment of the increasing number of refugees and migrants, including unaccompanied migrant children, reaching Indonesia.

Forestry sector reforms made some headway in 2013, but timber concessions on lands with pre-existing community claims continue to generate rural conflict and abuse. Corruption and mismanagement deprive government coffers of billions of dollars in forest revenues, and threaten Indonesia's ability to deliver on its "green growth" promises.

Conditions in Papua, still virtually off-limits to foreign journalists, remain volatile, with security forces enjoying virtual impunity for abuses, including excessive and at times lethal use of force against peaceful proponents of independence. Meanwhile, the armed Free Papua Movement, though small and poorly organized, continues to carry out attacks against government forces.

Local elections in Indonesia in recent years have resulted in the emergence of young politicians, including Jakarta's governor Joko Widodo, who have pledged to break with traditional patronage-style politics by tackling corruption, poverty, and crumbling infrastructure. National parliamentary and presidential elections scheduled for 2014 will give an indication of whether these politicians reflect a national trend.

Freedom of Expression

The Alliance of Independent Journalists documented 23 cases of violence against journalists in the first six months of 2013. They included a March 2 attack on Normila Sari Wahyuni of Paser TV while she was covering a land dispute in Rantau Panjang village in East Kalimantan. The assailants repeatedly kicked her stomach, prompting a miscarriage. Police later arrested a village chief and village secretary as suspects in the assault. On March 27, supporters of Gorontalo mayor, Adnan Dhambea, burned down the office of the local TV station, TVRI Gorontalo, following Dhambea's defeat in local elections. Two TVRI journalists were assaulted during the arson attack.

On July 2, Indonesia's parliament enacted a new law on NGOs that infringes on rights to freedom of association, expression, and religion. The law imposes a variety of vague obligations and prohibitions on NGO activities, severely limits foreign funding of NGOs, and forbids NGOs from espousing atheism, communism, Marxist-Leninism, beliefs deemed contrary to Pancasila, the state philosophy.

In a positive step, the government in August signaled a possible end to the informal national taboo on public discussion of the army-led massacres of between 500,000 and over a million communist party members and alleged sympathizers in 1965-66 by allowing the release of the award-winning documentary on the massacre, *The Act of Killing*, as a free Internet download.

Military Reform and Impunity

A military court in September sentenced 12 members of the Special Forces Command (Komando Pasukan Khusus, Kopassus) to prison terms of between several months and 11 years for their role in the well-orchestrated murder of four detainees in a prison in Yogyakarta. The guilty verdicts marked an important departure from the usual impunity enjoyed by soldiers implicated in serious crimes, but the sentences imposed on the three most culpable soldiers failed to match the gravity of their crimes.

Women's Rights

A gender equality bill first submitted to parliament in 2009 remained stalled in 2013 due to opposition from Islamist politicians.

Meanwhile, discriminatory regulations continued to proliferate. An August update by Indonesia's official Commission on Violence against Women reported that national and local governments had passed 60 new discriminatory regulations in 2013. Indonesia has a total of 342 discriminatory regulations, including

79 local bylaws requiring women to wear the *hijab*. As of July, the Ministry of Home Affairs had signaled its intention to revoke only eight of them.

These regulations include one banning women from straddling motorcycles—only riding side-saddle is permitted—in Lhokseumawe, Aceh. In neighboring Bireuen, a local regulation prohibits women from dancing. In Gorontalo, Sulawesi Island, the government transferred its entire female support staff to other offices in July, replacing them with men as part of an initiative to discourage "extramarital affairs."

In August, an education office in Prabumulih, southern Sumatra, cancelled plans to have high school girls undergo mandatory "virginity tests" to tackle "premarital sex and prostitution." Despite a public outcry, plans are afoot to introduce similar tests in Pamekasan, East Java.

Freedom of Religion

President Yudhoyono has repeatedly called Indonesia "a moderate Muslim democracy." On May 31, Yudhoyono said his government "would not tolerate any act of senseless violence committed by any group in the name of the religion" and on August 16 said he was "very concerned" about rising religious intolerance and related violence.

Despite the rhetoric, the Yudhoyono administration has failed to enforce Supreme Court decisions against local officials who have long blocked building permits for the Christian churches in Bogor and Bekasi. It also maintains dozens of regulations, including ministerial decrees on building houses of worship and a decree against religious practice by the Ahmadiyah community, which discriminate against religious minorities and foster intolerance.

According to the Jakarta-based Setara Institute that monitors religious freedom, there were 264 attacks on religious minorities in 2012 and 243 cases in the first 10 months of 2013. The perpetrators were almost all Sunni militants; the targets include Christians, Ahmadiyah, Shia, and Sufis.

On March 21, Bekasi authorities bowed to the demands of the local Islamic People's Forum and demolished a church built by the Batak Protestant Christian Church. The church had fulfilled local requirements, but had been denied a denied a building permit for five years running due to pressure from groups opposed to all church construction in the area.

On June 20, a mob of more than 800 Sunni militants pressured local authorities to evict hundreds of displaced Shia villagers from a stadium in Sampang, Madura, where they had been living since August 2012 after more than 1,000 Sunni villagers attacked their homes, killing one resident. The displaced Shia villagers were then forcibly driven to an apartment building that the government had prepared in Sidoarjo, Java, three hours away.

On September 11, a long-simmering dispute between two Muslim communities in Puger in East Java's Jember regency boiled over into violence when a group of 30 machete-wielding militants vandalized the local Darus Sholihin Islamic boarding school. More than 100 policemen at the scene failed to intervene. An hour later, one of those militants, Eko Mardi Santoso, 45, was found dead on the village pier with machete wounds to his face and torso after an apparent revenge attack.

Papua/West Papua

Tensions heightened in Papua in 2013 following a February 21 attack on Indonesian military forces by suspected Free Papua Movement rebels that killed eight soldiers.

As of August, according to the "Papuans Behind Bars" website, 55 Papuans were imprisoned for peaceful advocacy of independence. Indonesia denies holding any political prisoners.

On April 30, police fired upon a group of Papuans who had gathered in Aimas district, near Sorong, for a prayer gathering to protest the 1963 handover of Papua to Indonesia from Dutch colonial rule. One account said police opened fire when protesters approached police vehicles that had arrived at the scene. Two men were killed on the spot; a third victim died six days later from gunshot wounds. Police detained at least 22 individuals and charged 7 of them with treason. The other 15 were subsequently released.

In May the *Sydney Morning Herald* reported that thousands of Papuan children, mostly Christians, had been induced to leave Papua to attend Islamic schools in Java for religious "re-education" over the last decade. The program has resulted in large numbers of Papuan children fleeing the schools and living destitute in major cities.

Human rights abuses in Papua were in the spotlight during the Asia Pacific Economic Cooperation summit in Bali on October 6 after three Papuan activists scaled a wall and entered the Australian consulate. Markus Jerewon, Yuvensius Goo, and Rofinus Yanggam demanded that Indonesia lift travel restrictions on international visitors and release political prisoners.

Land Rights

In May, the Constitutional Court declared unconstitutional a provision of the 1999 Forestry Law that includes customary territories within state forests. The landmark decision rebuked the Ministry of Forestry for allocating community lands as concessions to logging and plantation companies.

Forestry sector corruption and mismanagement continued to bleed Indonesian government coffers, the annual losses reaching US$2 billion, more than the entire national health budget. Forest mismanagement fuels often violent land disputes and taints Indonesia's self-proclaimed image as a leader in sustainable "green growth."

Refugees and Asylum Seekers

Indonesia is a transit point to Australia for refugees and asylum seekers fleeing persecution, violence, and poverty in countries including Somalia, Afghanistan, Pakistan, and Burma. As of March 2013, there were almost 10,000 refugees and asylum seekers in Indonesia, all living in legal limbo because Indonesia lacks an asylum law. This number includes an unprecedented number of unaccompanied migrant children; more than 1,000 such children arrived in Indonesia in 2012 alone.

While Indonesia delegates the responsibility for refugees and asylum seekers to the office of United Nations High Commissioner for Refugees (UNHCR), it often refuses to release even UNHCR-recognized refugees from detention centers, where conditions are poor and mistreatment common. Those who are released face constant threat of re-arrest and further detention.

HUMAN
RIGHTS
WATCH

THE DARK SIDE OF GREEN GROWTH

Human Rights Impacts of Weak Governance in Indonesia's Forestry Sector

HUMAN
RIGHTS
WATCH

BARELY SURVIVING
Detention, Abuse, and Neglect of Migrant Children in Indonesia

Key International Actors

On May 8, Germany approved the sale to Indonesia of 164 tanks, including 104 Leopard 2 battle tanks. On August 25, US Defense Secretary Chuck Hagel disclosed a $500 million deal to sell eight Apache attack helicopters to Indonesia, which he said was aimed at strengthening military ties as part of the US "pivot" towards the Asia-Pacific.

On September 30, new Australian Prime Minister Tony Abbott made Jakarta his first foreign visit, seeking better trade relationships and cooperation over migration and people smuggling. Abbott failed to raise human rights concerns in discussions in Jakarta and, several days later, when three Papuan activists entered the Australian consulate during the APEC summit in Bali, he took the opportunity to denounce Papuans who "grandstand" against Indonesia and then dangerously conflated an attempt to spotlight human rights violations with Papuan separatism.

Indonesia signed a timber trade agreement with EU on September 30, requiring that timber exported to the EU be certified as legally produced, an important step in combatting illegal logging. The agreement, however, does not require any assessment of whether the timber is produced in violation of community land rights or rights to compensation, an important source of conflict and human rights abuse.

A visit by the UN special rapporteur on freedom of expression, Frank La Rue, scheduled for January 2013 was postponed over Jakarta's objection to his plan to visit Papua; no new date had been set at this writing.

Malaysia

Malaysia's general election on May 5, 2013, resulted in historic losses for the ruling Barisan Nasional (BN) coalition. Although the BN won 133 seats out of 222, it lost the popular vote to the opposition Pakatan Rakyat (PKR) coalition amid widespread allegations of election irregularities. In an attempt to explain away the election results, Prime Minister Najib Tun Razak blamed a "Chinese tsunami" favoring the opposition, and raised concerns about ethnic and religious fractures in multi-ethnic Malaysia.

The election was followed by a significant deterioration in human rights and the apparent abrupt end to Prime Minister Najib's oft-touted reform agenda. Relevant developments in the second half of 2013 included passage of new and revised laws again permitting administrative detention without trial, new arrests of opposition activists for organizing peaceful protests, and repression of political speech.

Administrative Detention

Following the May election, the government launched a major campaign against an apparent rise in crime that some officials attributed to the June 2012 expiration of the Emergency (Public Order and Crime Prevention) Ordinance 1969. The home minister recommended that the ordinance be reintroduced and then helped push through amendments to the Prevention of Crime Act 1959 that reauthorize administrative detention without trial. The amendments empower a five-person government-appointed panel to impose up to two years' preventive detention on certain criminal suspects, decisions that are not subject to judicial review except on procedural grounds. Up to five years of restricted residence in remote locations could follow, renewable for another five years as decided by the home minister.

The government also has proposed electronic monitoring for felons who have served out their sentences in violation of their basic rights.

Freedom of Assembly and Association

To protest alleged malfeasance during May 5 parliamentary elections, the opposition PKR coalition organized "Black 505" rallies throughout Malaysia. The government responded by arresting persons deemed to be rally organizers for failing to notify the police 10 days in advance as required by the Peaceful Assembly Act (PAA). To date, police have arrested at least 43 persons on such charges. The PAA also requires that organizers negotiate with the police on conditions for holding assemblies. At the so-called People's Uprising Rally in Kuala Lumpur on January 12, 2013, the police set 27 conditions and followed up by investigating rule violations that were either trivial or protected under international law, such as carrying placards with "inappropriate slogans."

In Sabah, police ordered organizers of the February 22 "Idle No More Long March" for indigenous rights and fair elections to apply for a permit, claiming that it was not an "ordinary" march as defined under the PAA.

The government restricts the right to freedom of association by requiring that organizations of seven or more members register with the Registrar of Societies in order to legally function. The registrar, appointed by the Ministry of Home Affairs, has broad authority to deny registration and has continually delayed or denied registration to groups critical of the government and to opposition political parties. During 2013, an application by the three opposition parties to register as a coalition remained mired in bureaucratic requirements, and the registrar forced a re-run of the opposition Democratic Action Party's Central Executive Committee elections on a technicality. The home affairs minister has "absolute discretion" to declare a society unlawful.

Freedom of Expression

Despite pledges by Prime Minister Najib to revoke the Sedition Act, the government uses sedition charges to silence and punish those who question government policies. Police charged five prominent opposition activists with sedition for their May 13 remarks at the Kuala Lumpur and Selangor Chinese Assembly Hall about election fraud and popular dissatisfaction with the government. One of the five, student activist Adam Adil Abd Halim, was detained for five days and is suspended from the university until his trial is over. In April, the government charged opposition member of parliament Tian Chua with sedition for alleging that the United Malays National Organisation (UMNO), the lead party in the government coalition, was linked to the armed incursion at Lahad Duta in Sabah in 2013.

Malaysian authorities maintain control over television and radio, printed newspapers, magazines and books, and films and video. The Printing Presses and Publication Act (PPPA) requires print publications to obtain a government license that the home minister may revoke at any time. The Malaysian Communications and Multimedia Act (MCMA) provides broad authority to act against service providers that "provide content which is indecent ... or offensive in character with intent to annoy, abuse, threaten or harass any person."

In January 2013, the government banned screening of the Tamil language movie *Vishwaroopam*. In September, the police charged Lena Hendry, an NGO staff member, with violating the Film Censorship Act by screening *No Fire Zone, The Killing Fields of Sri Lanka*. The case was still pending at time of writing.

In May 2012, the Home Ministry banned the book *Allah, Liberty & Love* by female Canadian author Irshad Manji. In September 2013, the High Court overturned the ban on the Malay translation, but the Attorney General's Chambers planned an appeal. The publisher's application for judicial review of his arrest and prosecution under the Sharia Criminal Offenses (Selangor) Enactment 1995 was pending at time of writing, as was his effort to have the Federal Court declare the law unconstitutional. The publisher also faces charges in the Petaling Sharia Court. Although the High Court ruled in favor of Berjaya Books (Borders Malaysia) that had stocked the book, criminal prosecution in the Sharia court of a store salesperson for being in possession of the book was still pending at time of writing. The English language version of the book is still banned.

Police Abuses and Impunity

The Malaysia police force has been frequently faulted for use of excessive or lethal force during apprehension of suspected criminals, and the torture of detainees. During 2013, at least 12 persons died in suspicious circumstances in police custody. In a particularly egregious case in May, truck driver N. Dhamendran died in custody at Kuala Lumpur police headquarters—a postmortem examination found 52 injuries resulting from "sustained multiple blunt force trauma." In an exceptional development, five police officers have been charged with murder. In other death-in-custody cases, police have flatly denied any abuse, blamed illness for the deaths, resisted family-requested second post-mortems, or relied on frequently inconclusive judicial inquests.

The government has rejected establishment of an Independent Police Complaints and Misconduct Commission (IPCMC), an external oversight body recommended in 2005 by a Royal Commission, which would have power to receive and investigate complaints and to sanction those found guilty of misconduct. The existing Enforcement Agencies Integrity Commission (EAIC) does not have power to sanction misconduct.

Political Prosecution of Opposition Leader Anwar Ibrahim

The Malaysia government continued its politically motivated prosecution of opposition leader Anwar Ibrahim for sodomy, appealing his January 2012 acquittal to the Court of Appeal. If convicted, Anwar faces up to 20 years in prison and caning, and the loss of his seat in parliament.

Human Rights Defenders

Suara Rakyat Malaysia (SUARAM), a leading Malaysian human rights organization, faced hostile government investigations throughout the year. The Malaysian government investigated SUARAM under three different laws between July 2012 and February 2013, under pressure from ministers who publicly attacked SUARAM for receiving foreign funds. In August 2013, police questioned a member of the SUARAM secretariat about a fund-raising dinner SUARAM had held in support of its work on the Scorpene submarine corruption case.

Police also harassed Samad Said, Malaysia's 81-year-old poet laureate and co-chair of Bersih 2.0, the civil society coalition working for clean and fair elections. Police detained him in September for reciting a poem in the presence of pre-independence flags. A government civil suit against Bersih 2.0 steering committee members, including Samad Said and co-chair Ambiga Sreenevasan, was pending at time of writing.

Refugees, Asylum Seekers, and Trafficking Victims

Malaysian immigration law does not recognize refugees and asylum seekers. The government is not a party to the 1951 Refugee Convention and lacks domestic refugee law and asylum procedures. It takes no responsibility for migrant children's education. There is no evidence that an announced plan to allow refugees to work legally had been implemented at time of writing.

The Anti-Trafficking in Persons and Anti-Smuggling of Migrants Act conflates trafficking and people smuggling, and fails to provide meaningful protection to victims of either crime. The government confines trafficking victims in sub-standard government shelters without access to services until adjudication of their legal case is complete.

Detention and Drug Policy

The Dangerous Drugs (Special Preventive Measures) Act authorizes administrative detention without trial. The National Anti-Drug Agency maintains over 20 *puspens* (drug detention centers) where users are held for a minimum of two years. Drug traffickers face mandatory death sentences, but the number of people executed is not publicly available.

Sexual Orientation and Gender Identity

Discrimination against lesbian, gay, bisexual, and transgender (LGBT) persons remains a persistent problem that is reinforced by government policy. In 2012, Prime Minister Najib declared that LGBT activities do not "have a place in the country." In April 2013, Deputy Prime Minister Muhyiddin Yassin accused LGBT rights activists of "poisoning" the minds of Muslims with "deviant practices." The Malaysian government led efforts to ensure that LGBT rights were excluded from the ASEAN Human Rights Declaration adopted in November 2012.

Police regularly arrest transgender persons, especially Muslims who are considered to be violating Sharia law provisions against cross-dressing, ridicule and humiliate them, and jail them in lock-ups where they are subject to physical and sexual abuse by police staff and male inmates.

The Malaysian government took no steps to repeal Penal Code article 377B, which criminalizes consensual "carnal intercourse against the order of nature" between persons who have reached the age of consent, or to replace article 377C on non-consensual sexual acts with a modern, gender-neutral rape law.

Key International Actors

Prime Minister Najib has announced Malaysia's intention to seek a non-permanent seat on the United Nations Security Council for the 2015-2016 term. Malaysia is a member of the UN Human Rights Council but has not signed or ratified most core human rights treaties.

The US plays an important role in Malaysia, strengthening mutual security ties and promoting negotiations on the free trade Trans-Pacific Partnership Agreement (TPPA), but says little publicly about Malaysia's human rights record. President Barack Obama was scheduled to visit Malaysia in October but cancelled the trip due to a US budget impasse and partial government shutdown. It would have been the first visit by a sitting US president since 1966. In prepared remarks delivered at the time of the scheduled visit, Obama praised Malaysia as a global model for "diversity, tolerance, and progress," but said nothing publicly about continuing human rights problems in the country.

Malaysia, which is a member of the Organization of Islamic Cooperation and has been positioning itself as a leading moderate Muslim state, also continues to cultivate its ties with Middle Eastern states.

At the regional level, Malaysia has blocked efforts to reach a comprehensive agreement to protect the rights of all migrant workers in ASEAN. Relations with the Philippines were strained in 2013 when an armed group from the Philippines calling itself the "Royal Security Forces of the Sultanate of Sulu and North Borneo" tried to claim a portion of the eastern Malaysian province of Sabah. The Philippines did not support the group but sought to negotiate their return. Malaysian forces ultimately routed the militants.

Malaysia continues to deepen its ties with China, exemplified in 2013 by an October state visit to Malaysia by new Chinese President Xi Jinping. The two countries agreed to improve bilateral ties and to triple the volume of bilateral trade by 2017.

Nepal

Elections held in November to elect the second Constituent Assembly were considered free and fair by international observers. The United Communist Party of
Nepal (Maoist) suffered a significant loss in seats from 2008, while the more
centrist Congress and United Marxist Leninist parties gained significantly. But
the year saw little human rights progress and new setbacks to efforts to end
impunity for abuses committed by both government and Maoist forces during
the country's 1996-2006 civil war. A decline of more than 5 million in the number of registered voters since the last Constituent Assembly elections in 2008
raised concerns that millions of Nepalis were being disenfranchised.

A new Truth and Reconciliation Commission established to address the war
years is deeply flawed and, unless reformed, unlikely to answer repeated calls
for accountability and justice from victims, rights groups, and the international
community. At least 13,000 people were killed and over 1,300 subjected to
enforced disappearance during the decade-long conflict. Political leaders have
shown little interest in justice, with Maoist leaders even threatening an elderly
couple that went on hunger strike to demand an investigation into their son's
2004 murder. An interim relief program providing financial compensation and
other benefits to individuals whose family members were killed or disappeared
during the conflict did not extend to victims of torture and sexual assault.

Nepal has made significant progress in protecting the rights of lesbian, gay,
bisexual, transgender, and intersex (LGBTI) individuals in the last decade, but
2013 saw troubling instances of private actor violence and seemingly arbitrary
arrest of LGBTI activists. Women, migrant workers, people with disabilities, and
members of disadvantaged communities such as Dalits continue to be marginalized and suffer discrimination.

Accountability for Past Abuses

Instead of taking steps to ensure the prosecution of those responsible for the
worst crimes committed during the country's civil war, the cabinet pushed an
ordinance that could lead to amnesty for perpetrators. Nepal's Truth,
Reconciliation and Disappearance Ordinance, signed into law by the president
in March 2013, calls for a high-level commission to investigate serious conflict-

related violations. The law does not define which crimes are eligible for amnesty and which are excluded, giving commissioners potentially wide discretion to make determinations. As a result, some perpetrators of torture, war crimes, and crimes against humanity could win amnesties in contravention of international law.

The high-level commission has yet to be formed, and in April the Supreme Court suspended the ordinance pending further review.

In September, after mounting national and international pressure, the police finally announced an arrest for the 2004 abduction and murder of Krishna Adhikari. In August 2013, Adhikari's parents had begun a hunger strike demanding information about their son's murder, allegedly at the hands of Maoist forces. Threats by the Maoist leadership did not deter the fasting couple.

Women's Rights

In December 2012, a female migrant worker returning from Saudi Arabia was raped by an airport police constable in Kathmandu, sparking widespread protests. On December 27, protesters gathered near the prime minister's residence beginning "Occupy Baluwatar," a movement named after the neighborhood. Due in part to intense public pressure, the police constable responsible for the rapes was sentenced in April to five-and-a-half years in prison.

Women's rights groups demanded fast-track courts to deal with cases of gender-based violence, and a review of the 35-day limitation period on filing police complaints, which restricts the ability of victims to seek redress. A government review committee submitted a report in April on laws and policies related to violence against women, but the government had not acted on its recommendations at time of writing.

The government also has not yet investigated credible allegations of sexual violence during the 1996-2006 conflict, and has not included sexual assault victims in its interim relief compensation program.

Migrants' Rights

As part of the Occupy Baluwatar movement, women's groups called for a review of Nepal's migration policies, which currently lack adequate protections. Rights groups demanded that the government revoke an August 2012 decree banning women under age 30 from traveling to Gulf countries for work. The ban was imposed to protect Nepali domestic workers from physical or sexual abuse, but rights groups fear that it will push women to migrate through informal channels and increase the risk of abuse.

Disability Rights

Although the government has ratified the Convention on the Rights of Persons with Disabilities (CRPD) and is committed to inclusive education—whereby children with and without disabilities attend school together in their communities—it continues to maintain a system of separate schools for children who are deaf, blind, or have physical and intellectual disabilities, and to put children with disabilities in segregated classes in mainstream schools. The government has taken steps to increase school scholarships for children with disabilities, and has created a team tasked with developing a new national inclusive education policy.

However, disability rights activists say they have been excluded from the political process, and that recently enacted constitutional amendments have not addressed their concerns.

Sexual Orientation and Gender Identity

The government has advanced transgender and intersex rights in the last decade by recognizing a third category on official documents. Nevertheless, the government failed to prevent an escalation in threats and violent attacks on LGBTI rights activists in 2013. In early February, four transgender women were arrested under the Public Offense Act, a vaguely worded law that can result in up to 25 days in detention and a fine amounting to more than US$300.

Authorities did little to investigate threatening phone calls and harassment of members of the Blue Diamond Society, the national LGBTI umbrella organization. It instead launched an investigation into the organization for alleged corruption, despite the fact it had passed third party audits and inspections. The group's 2012-2013 license renewal process was delayed and its bank accounts frozen, temporarily halting its health and human rights work.

Statelessness

Nepal failed to reform its citizenship laws in 2013, leaving an estimated 2.1 million people effectively stateless, unable to secure drivers' licenses, passports, bank accounts, or voting rights. The flawed citizenship law makes it particularly difficult for women to secure legal proof of citizenship, especially when male family members refuse to assist them or are unavailable to do so, and it denies citizenship to children of non-Nepali fathers.

Tibetan Refugees

Nepal imposes strict restrictions on Tibetan refugees, forbidding protests and gatherings. Two Tibetan monks in Nepal self-immolated in 2013 to protest China's rule over Tibet.

In April, Pushpa Kamal Dahal, also known as Prachanda, former prime minister and chairman of the Unified Communist Party of Nepal (Maoist), assured China's President Xi Jinping that Nepal will repress any "anti-China" activities by Tibetan refugees.

Key International Actors

The international community, including India, the United Kingdom, United States, and European Union pressed the government to announce and conduct free and fair elections and end the political deadlock that has paralyzed governance in Nepal.

China increased financial assistance to Nepal, but demanded that the government curb protests by Tibetans and other "anti-China" activities.

In a positive move, in January 2013 the UK arrested a Nepali army colonel suspected of torture during the civil war.

UN High Commissioner for Human Rights Navi Pillay called for an independent and impartial investigation into serious violations of international law during the country's 10-year conflict, and expressed concern that the Truth, Reconciliation and Disappearance Ordinance could allow perpetrators of serious crimes to obtain amnesties. "Such amnesties would not only violate core principles under international law but would also weaken the foundation for a genuine and lasting peace in Nepal," Pillay said.

North Korea

There has been no discernible improvement in human rights in the Democratic People's Republic of Korea (DPRK or North Korea) since Kim Jong-Un assumed power after his father's death in 2011. The government continues to impose totalitarian rule. In response to the systematic denial of basic freedoms in the country, the United Nations Human Rights Council unanimously established a commission of inquiry in April 2013 to investigate whether such abuses amount to crimes against humanity and who should be held accountable.

Although North Korea has ratified four key international human rights treaties and technically possesses a constitution with some rights protections, in reality the government represses all forms of freedom of expression and opinion and does not allow any organized political opposition, independent media, free trade unions, civil society organizations, or religious freedom. Those who attempt to assert rights, fail to demonstrate sufficient reverence for the party and its leadership, or otherwise act in ways deemed contrary to state interests face arbitrary arrest, detention, lack of due process, and torture and ill-treatment. The government also practices collective punishment for supposed anti-state offenses, effectively enslaving hundreds of thousands of citizens, including children, in prison camps and other detention facilities with deplorable conditions and forced labor.

Torture and Inhumane Treatment

North Korean refugees living in exile—some of whom fled after Kim Jong-Un took power—told Human Rights Watch that people arrested in North Korea are routinely tortured by officials seeking confessions, bribes, and obedience. Common forms of torture include sleep deprivation, beatings with iron rods or sticks, kicking and slapping, and enforced sitting or standing for hours. Guards also sexually abuse female detainees.

Executions

North Korea's criminal code stipulates that the death penalty can be applied for vaguely defined offenses such as "crimes against the state" and "crimes against the people." A December 2007 amendment to the penal code extended the death penalty to additional crimes, including non-violent offenses such as fraud and smuggling, as long as authorities determine the crime is "extremely serious."

Political Prisoner Camps

North Korean refugees also confirm that persons accused of political offenses are usually sent to brutal forced labor camps, known as *kwan-li-so*, operated by North Korea's National Security Agency.

The government practices collective punishment, sending to forced labor camps not only the offender but also their parents, spouse, children, and even grand-children. These camps are notorious for horrific living conditions and abuse, including induced starvation, little or no medical care, lack of proper housing and clothes, continuous mistreatment and torture by guards, and executions. Forced labor at the *kwan-li-so* often involves difficult physical labor such as min-ing, logging, and agricultural work, all done with rudimentary tools in often dan-gerous and harsh conditions. Death rates in these camps are reportedly extremely high.

North Korea has never acknowledged that these *kwan-li-so* camps exist, but United States and South Korean officials now estimate that between 80,000 and 120,000 people may be imprisoned in them, including in camp No. 14 in Kaechun, No. 15 in Yodok, No. 16 in Hwasung, and No. 25 in Chungjin. During the year, new satellite imagery indicated camp No. 22 in Hoeryung has been closed; it is unclear what happened to the estimated 30,000 prisoners previ-ously held at the camp.

Freedom of Information and Movement

The government uses fear—generated mainly by threats of detention, forced labor, and public executions—to prevent dissent, and imposes harsh restric-tions on freedom of information and travel.

All media and publications are state controlled, and unauthorized access to non-state radio or TV broadcasts is punished. North Koreans are punished if found with mobile media such as DVDs or computer 'flash drives' containing unauthorized TV programs, such as South Korean drama and entertainment shows. Unauthorized use of Chinese mobile phones to communicate with people outside North Korea is also harshly punished.

Refugees and Asylum Seekers

North Korea criminalizes leaving the country without state permission. Upon Kim Jong-Un's ascension to power, the government issued a shoot-on-sight order to border guards to stop illegal crossing at the northern border into China. Since then, the government has increased rotations of North Korean border guards and cracked down on guards who turn a blind eye when people cross.

People seeking to flee North Korea have also faced greater difficulties making the arduous journey from the North Korea border through China to Laos, and then into Thailand from where most are sent to South Korea. In a sign of the increased risks, the DPRK in May 2013 persuaded Laos to return nine young defectors arrested in Vientiane, at least five of whom were children, to an unknown fate in North Korea.

China continues to categorically label all North Koreans in China "illegal" economic migrants and routinely repatriates them, despite its obligation to offer protection to refugees under the Refugee Convention of 1951 and its 1967 protocol, to which it is a state party. The certainty of harsh punishment upon repatriation has led many in the international community to argue that North Koreans fleeing into China should all be considered refugees *sur place*. Beijing regularly denies the office of UN High Commissioner for Refugees (UNHCR) access to North Koreans in China.

Former North Korean security officials who have defected told Human Rights Watch that North Koreans handed back by China face interrogation, torture, and referral to political prisoner or forced labor camps. The severity of punishments depend on North Korean authorities' assessments of what the returnee did while in China.

Those suspected of simple trading schemes involving non-controversial goods are usually sent to work in forced labor brigades (known as *ro-dong-dan-ryeon-dae*, literally labor training centers) or *jip-kyul-so* (collection centers), criminal penitentiaries where forced labor is required. Harsh and dangerous working conditions purportedly result in significant numbers of people being injured or killed.

Those whom authorities suspect of religious or political activities abroad, especially having any sort of contact with South Koreans, are often given lengthier terms in horrendous detention facilities known as *kyo-hwa-so* (correctional, reeducation centers) where forced labor is combined with chronic food and medicine shortages, harsh working conditions, and regular mistreatment by guards.

North Korean women fleeing their country are frequently trafficked into forced *de facto* marriages with Chinese men. Even if they have lived there for years, these women are not entitled to legal residence and face possible arrest and repatriation. Many children of such unrecognized marriages lack legal identity or access to elementary education.

Labor Rights

North Korea is one of the few nations in the world that still refuses to join the International Labour Organization (ILO). Forced labor is essentially the norm in the country, and workers are systematically denied freedom of association and the right to organize and collectively bargain. The government firmly controls the only authorized trade union organization, the General Federation of Trade Unions of Korea.

In April, the North Korea government unilaterally shut down the Kaesong Industrial Complex (KIC), close to the border between North and South Korea, where 123 South Korean companies employ over 50,000 North Korean workers. The KIC reopened in September after intensive negotiations to set up a joint North Korea-South Korea committee to oversee the complex. However, there was no change to the law governing working conditions, which fall far short of international standards.

Key International Actors

North Korea's record of cooperation with UN human rights mechanisms is arguably among the worst in the world. It ignores all resolutions on the human rights situation in North Korea adopted by the UN Human Rights Council (HRC) and the UN General Assembly, and has never responded to requests for visits from the UN special rapporteur on human rights in the DPRK.

The April HRC resolution establishing a UN Commission of Inquiry (COI) on human rights in the DPRK constituted an important and warranted increase in UN scrutiny of the government's rights record. The COI is due to report to the HRC in March 2014 on nine distinct areas of abuse "including the violation of the right to food, the violations associated with prison camps, torture and inhuman treatment, arbitrary detention, discrimination, violations of freedom of expression, violations of the right to life, violations of freedom of movement, and enforced disappearances, including in the form of abductions of nationals of other States, with a view to ensuring full accountability, in particular where these violations may amount to crimes against humanity."

In an oral update given to the HRC on September 16, Michael Kirby, chair of the COI, stated that "testimony heard thus far points to widespread and serious violations in all areas that the Human Rights Council asked the Commission to investigate" and to "large-scale patterns that may constitute systematic and gross human rights violations."

The COI has visited South Korea, Japan, Thailand, the United States, and United Kingdom, but to date North Korea has refused to cooperate. China has also declined to let the three COI commissioners visit the country to conduct investigations.

Two weeks before conservative Park Geun-hye was sworn-in as new president of South Korea in February, North Korea conducted its third nuclear test in seven years, earning widespread international condemnation, including from its closest ally, China.

North Korean threats, canceling of family reunification visits, and the five-month long shuttering of the Kaesong Industrial Complex, further contributed to a chill in North-South relations. Six-party talks on denuclearizing the Korean peninsula—involving North and South Korea, China, Japan, Russia, and the US—remained moribund during the year.

Japan continues to demand the return of 17 Japanese citizens that North Korea abducted in the 1970s and 1980s. Some Japanese civil society groups insist the number of abductees is much higher. South Korea's government expanded its attention and efforts to press for the return of hundreds of its abducted citizens.

Pakistan

Pakistan had another violent year in 2013. Nawaz Sharif's Pakistan Muslim League won parliamentary elections in May and Sharif became prime minister in June. The elections were marred by a bombing and targeted killing campaign by the Taliban and their affiliates to sabotage the elections. The new government replaced the Pakistan People's Party-led government, in office since 2008. The constitutional transfer of power from one civilian government to another was the first in Pakistan's history.

While the military did not hinder the electoral process, it remained unaccountable for human rights violations and exercised disproportionate political influence, especially on matters of national security and counter-terrorism. The deep-rooted security crisis in the country was underscored by the inability or unwillingness of military and civilian institutions to end attacks on the population by militant groups. Islamist militant groups continued to target and kill hundreds of Shia Muslims—particularly from the Hazara community—with impunity. In September, the Christian community experienced the deadliest attack on its members in Pakistan's history when 81 were killed in a bombing on a church in Peshawar.

There has been a breakdown of law enforcement in the face of politically motivated attacks particularly throughout the province of Balochistan and targeted killings in Karachi. The police and other security forces have been responsible for numerous abuses, including, torture and other ill-treatment of criminal suspects, extrajudicial killings, and unresolved enforced disappearances of terrorism suspects.

The country also faces acute economic problems, exemplified in 2013 by growing electricity shortages and rising food and fuel prices, which hit the country's poor disproportionately.

At least 22 polio vaccination workers were killed, and 14 wounded in 2012 and 2013 in attacks for which the Taliban claimed responsibility.

Elections

During the election campaign, at least 130 people were killed and over 500 were injured by the Taliban and its affiliates, who declared elections "un-Islamic" and warned voters to stay away from ruling coalition political rallies. The European Union Election Observer Mission noted that "violence by non-state actors unbalanced the playing field and distorted the election process considerably in affected areas," but the political parties in the outgoing government accepted the results. In September, President Asif Ali Zardari retired upon completion of his term after overseeing an orderly democratic transition.

Sectarian Attacks

Sunni militant groups such as the ostensibly banned Lashkar-e Jhangvi (LEJ), an Al-Qaeda affiliate, operate with virtual impunity across Pakistan, as law enforcement officials either turn a blind eye or appear helpless to prevent attacks.

In 2013, over 400 members of the Shia Muslim population were killed in targeted attacks that took place across Pakistan. In Balochistan province, at least 200 Shias, mostly from the Hazara community, were killed in and around the provincial capital, Quetta. In January, a suicide bomb killed 96 Hazaras and injured at least 150. In February, at least 84 were killed and over 160 injured when a bomb exploded in a vegetable market in Quetta's Hazara town. The LEJ claimed responsibility for both attacks. In March, at least 47 Shias were killed and 135 injured in the port city of Karachi when a Shia-majority neighborhood was targeted in a bomb attack. Some 50 apartments and 10 shops were destroyed. Throughout the year, dozens of other Shia across Pakistan were targeted and killed.

Religious Minorities

Abuses are rife under the country's abusive blasphemy law, which is used against religious minorities, often to settle personal disputes. Dozens of people were charged with the offense in 2013. At least 16 people remained on death row for blasphemy, while another 20 were serving life sentences at time of writing. Aasia Bibi, a Christian from Punjab province, who in 2010 became the first woman in the country's history to be sentenced to death for blasphemy, languished in prison. Rimsha Masih, a 14-year-old Christian girl accused of blasphemy and subsequently released in 2012, was granted asylum in Canada in June. In March, several thousand Christians were forced to flee their homes in Lahore after allegations of blasphemy against a local resident, Sawan Masih. A mob of thousands then looted and burned some 150 homes and two churches as police looked on. Sawan Masih remained in jail at time of writing.

In September, a suicide bombing during Sunday Mass at a church in Peshawar killed 81 worshippers and wounded more than 130, the deadliest attack in Pakistan's history on the beleaguered Christian minority.

Members of the Ahmadiyya religious community continue to be a major target of blasphemy prosecutions and are subjected to longstanding anti-Ahmadi laws across Pakistan. In 2013, they faced increasing social discrimination as militant groups accused them of illegally "posing as Muslims," barred them from using their mosques in Lahore, vandalized their graves across Punjab province, and freely engaged in hate speech, inciting violence against them as authorities looked the other way or facilitated extremists.

Women and Girls

Violence against women and girls—including rape, "honor" killings, acid attacks, domestic violence, and forced marriage—remains a serious problem in Pakistan.

There have been several thousand "honor" killings in Pakistan in the past decade, with hundreds reported in 2013. Provisions of the Islamic Qisas and Diyat law that allow the next of kin to "forgive" the murderer in exchange for monetary compensation remain in force and continue to be used by offenders to escape punishment.

Despite high levels of domestic violence, parliament failed in 2013 to enact laws to prevent it and protect women who experience it. Efforts to raise the minimum age of marriage to 18 remained stalled.

Judicial Activism and Independence

Pakistan's judiciary remains an independent but controversial actor. Despite the adoption of a National Judicial Policy in 2009, access to justice remains poor, as case backlogs mount throughout the country. The courts are rife with corruption.

Judges often use *suo motu* proceedings—the court acting on its own motion—to help people gain access to justice. In other cases, the judiciary has used such proceedings to interfere with legislative or executive powers, part of a long-standing power struggle between Chief Justice Iftikhar Chaudhry, the government, and the army.

The Supreme Court was active in raising enforced disappearances and government abuses in Balochistan in 2013, yet did not hold any high-level military officials accountable, demonstrating the limits of judicial independence in a state in which the military is the most powerful actor.

Judges also continued to muzzle media and other criticism of the judiciary through threats of contempt of court proceedings. The judiciary's conduct came under severe criticism during the election campaign when judges tried to disqualify political candidates in violation of Pakistan's international human rights commitments, using vague and discriminatory laws requiring candidates to be pious Muslims, and although repealed in 2009, to be university graduates. Chief Justice Chaudhry, who took a leading role in acting against those critical of the judiciary, retired from office in December.

Balochistan

The human rights crisis in the mineral-rich province continues unabated. As in previous years, 2013 saw enforced disappearances and killings of suspected Baloch militants and opposition activists by the military, intelligence agencies, and the paramilitary Frontier Corps. Baloch nationalists and other militant groups stepped up attacks on non-Baloch civilians.

The government of Nawaz Sharif attempted to achieve reconciliation in the province after the election of Baloch nationalist leader Malik Baloch as chief minister. However, the military continued to resist government reconciliation efforts and attempts to locate ethnic Baloch who had been subject to "disappearances." Successive Pakistani governments have appeared powerless to rein in abuses by the military and both sectarian and nationalist militant groups. As a result, many members of the Hazara community and non-Baloch ethnic minorities under attack by militants fled the province or country, while Baloch nationalists have continued to allege serious abuses by the military.

Counterterrorism Abuses

Security forces routinely violate basic rights in the course of counterterrorism operations, with suspects frequently detained without charge or convicted without a fair trial. Thousands of suspected members of Al-Qaeda, the Taliban, and other armed groups—who were rounded up in a nationwide crackdown in 2009 in the Swat Valley and the Tribal Areas—remained in illegal military detention at time of writing; few had been prosecuted or produced before the courts.

The army continues to deny lawyers, relatives, independent monitors, and humanitarian agency staff access to persons detained during military operations. In July, Attorney General Munir Malik admitted that more than 500 "disappeared" persons were in security agency custody.

Aerial drone strikes by the US on suspected members of Al-Qaeda and the Taliban continued in northern Pakistan in 2013, though less frequently than in 2012. An estimated 25 strikes had been launched through late November. Hakimullah Mehsud, leader of the Pakistani Taliban, was killed in such a strike in November. As in previous years, many of the strikes were accompanied by claims of large numbers of civilian casualties; a 2013 Amnesty International report documented unlawful civilian casualties in several strikes, but lack of access to the conflict areas largely prevented independent inquiries into their scope, scale, and legality under international law.

Freedom of Expression

At least six journalists were killed in Pakistan in 2013 while reporting stories or as a result of deliberate attacks. Three journalists, Mirza Iqbal Husain, Saif ur Rehman, and Imran Shaikh, were killed in a suicide bombing targeting the Hazara community in Quetta on January 10. In April, Aslam Durrani, news editor of the Urdu-language *Daily Pakistan*, was killed in a suicide bomb attack during an election rally. In August, the mutilated body of Abdul Razzaq Baloch, a journalist working for the Urdu-language Baluch nationalist newspaper *Daily Tawar,* was found in Karachi. Razzaq had disappeared in March. In November, Salik Ali Jafri, a producer with *Geo TV*, a television channel, was killed in a bomb attack in Karachi that targeted Shia Muslims.

A climate of fear impedes media coverage of both state security forces and militant groups. Journalists rarely report on human rights abuses by the military in counterterrorism operations, and the Taliban and other armed groups regularly threaten media outlets over their coverage. YouTube, banned by the government since September 2012 for hosting "blasphemous content," remained blocked in 2013.

In May, the longtime *New York Times* Islamabad bureau chief, Declan Walsh, was expelled from the country at the behest of the military because of his coverage of Balochistan and militant groups. Pakistani and international journalists protested his expulsion. The authorities had not allowed Walsh permission to return at time of writing.

Key International Actors

The US remains the largest donor of development and military assistance to Pakistan, but relations remained unsteady through 2013 despite a meeting between US President Barack Obama and Prime Minister Nawaz Sharif in October. Reasons include increasing public anger in Pakistan over US drone strikes and US allegations of Pakistani support for the Haqqani network, a militant group that US officials accuse of attacking US troops in Afghanistan. Pakistan raised concerns about US drone strikes at the United Nations General Assembly in September.

Despite a 2012 law authorizing creation of a national human rights commission, Pakistan failed to constitute the commission in 2013. In March, during its quadrennial "Universal Periodic Review" appearance before the UN Human Rights Council, Pakistan accepted recommendations that it take measures against religious hatred, prevent violence against religious minorities, and hold to account those responsible for such violence. The government, however, had taken no action to implement these commitments at time of writing. Despite the serious problem of enforced disappearances in the country, Pakistan has not ratified the

International Convention for the Protection of All Persons from Enforced Disappearance.

Historically tense relations between Pakistan and nuclear rival India remained poor in 2013 despite a meeting between the prime ministers of the two countries in September. Pakistan and China continued to deepen their already extensive economic and political ties.

Papua New Guinea

Human rights conditions in Papua New Guinea (PNG) remain poor. PNG's significant oil, gas, and gold reserves have continued to fuel strong economic growth, but improving living standards remains a challenge with consistently poor governance and endemic corruption. PNG's corruption taskforce made strides in investigating cases and initiating court action, but more concerted efforts are needed given the scope of the problem.

Violence against women in PNG is rampant. A series of gruesome crimes involving mob torture and murder of accused sorcerers was reported in 2013. Police violence is also common; authorities have publicly condemned specific instances of police violence, but impunity for perpetrators remains the norm.

Torture and Other Police Abuse

Physical and sexual abuse of detainees—including children—by police and paramilitary police units is widespread. Two years after the UN special rapporteur on torture issued a report on PNG, the government has failed to adequately respond to his recommendations addressing police abuse and impunity.

In May, police beat and slashed the ankles of 74 men following a street brawl in Port Moresby, the capital. Two police officers were charged with unlawful wounding and five others investigated for the attack. A judge called for the prosecution of other police implicated in the incident.

Other reported incidents of police violence during the year included beatings, robberies, attempted murder, and the fatal shooting of a child. Although the official response to police violence improved in 2013, there had been no reported convictions of perpetrators in 2013 at time of writing.

Some of PNG's notorious paramilitary police units (Mobile Squads) have been deployed to Manus Island to assist with security issues at an Australian-funded detention center for asylum seekers. In July, members of the squad beat a local man to death on the island. Five members of the squad were charged with murder.

Violence against Women and Girls

In February, PNG Health Minister Michael Malabag reported that up to 68 percent of women in PNG have suffered violence; up to a third have been raped. In September, PNG's parliament unanimously passed the Family Protection Bill 2013, which criminalizes domestic violence.

Accusations of sorcery are pervasive across the country and are routinely invoked to justify violence. Most victims are women. In February, a mob in Western Highlands Province accused a 20-year-old woman of being a witch and burned her to death. Two people were charged in the incident. Local media have reported that at least eight other women were victims of such attacks between February and this writing in late 2013; police reportedly were investigating the attacks.

The UN special rapporteur on violence against women, Rashida Manjoo, visited PNG in 2012 and released her report in March 2013. The report calls for the repeal of the 1971 Sorcery Act, which allows accusation of sorcery as a defense to murder. In April, a UN human rights official renewed calls for a repeal of the Sorcery Act and demanded an end to the extrajudicial killing of accused sorcerers. The PNG government repealed the Sorcery Act in May.

Disability Rights

Children with disabilities in PNG face abuse, discrimination, exclusion, lack of accessibility, and a wide range of barriers to education.

Death Penalty

In a step backwards, in May the parliament expanded the scope of crimes eligible for the death penalty. Sorcery-related killings, aggravated rape, and armed robbery are now predicate crimes. The amendment signals PNG's intention to resume executions after nearly 60 years (no executions have taken place since 1954). There are currently 10 prisoners on death row.

Corruption

Corruption remains a chronic problem in PNG. In September, the trials of 31 people charged in corruption cases began following investigations by PNG's anti-corruption task force. Also in September, task force Chairman Sam Koim estimated that 40 percent of the national budget is misappropriated each year. In November, the government introduced a bill to create an independent anti-corruption commission, a step that has been discussed for many years.

Extractive Industries

Extractive industries are an important engine of PNG's economic growth, but have given rise to serious human rights problems and environmental harm.

In 2011, Human Rights Watch documented gang rape and other violent abuses by private security personnel at PNG's Porgera gold mine, operated by Canadian mining giant Barrick Gold. Along with other steps, Barrick has responded by rolling out an ambitious remediation program to compensate victims of sexual violence. That program has been dogged by controversy, but could be an important global precedent if it succeeds.

The country's $US19 billion Liquefied Natural Gas (LNG) project, led by ExxonMobil, is reportedly on track to begin production in 2014. LNG revenues could have a transformative impact on the national economy but, without additional safeguards, could also exacerbate corruption. Violent clashes related to compensation claims marred construction for the project.

Key International Actors

Australia is the country's most important international partner and provided $469 million dollars in development assistance in 2012-2013.

In July, Australia announced a new agreement with PNG whereby Australia will transfer to PNG some of the asylum seekers arriving irregularly by boat in Australian waters. Under the agreement, PNG will undertake refugee status determinations and individuals determined to be refugees will be settled permanently in PNG or wait to be settled in a third country with no option to settle in Australia. PNG has agreed to withdraw its seven reservations to the 1951

Refugee Convention—including refugee rights to wage-earning employment, public education, and freedom of movement—but how and when this will take place remains unclear. At time of writing, 780 asylum seekers were detained in the Australian-funded processing center on PNG's Manus Island.

In July, the UN High Commissioner for Refugees (UNHCR) raised concerns about PNG's lack of capacity and expertise to determine refugee status, its mandatory and arbitrary detention of asylum seekers in substandard facilities, and likely resettlement difficulties facing non-Melanesians. The fate of LGBT asylum seekers is particularly precarious because the PNG criminal code outlaws sex "against the order of nature," which has been interpreted to apply to consensual homosexual acts.

The Australian government pledged to send 50 unarmed police officers to PNG by the end of 2013 to act in advisory roles and help combat the surge in reported violence in the country. This is a short-term engagement aimed at building the capacity of PNG's police force.

Philippines

As Philippine President Benigno Aquino III enters the second half of his six-year term in office, there are growing doubts about his administration's willingness to deliver on many of its human rights commitments.

On January 18, 2013, Aquino signed a landmark law, Republic Act No. 10361, designed to protect the rights of the country's estimated 1.9 million domestic workers. The Philippines also ratified the International Labor Organization's Domestic Workers Convention No. 189, which would help protect the rights of the 1.5 million Filipino domestic workers abroad.

The Aquino administration, however, has not made significant progress on its pledge to expedite the investigation and prosecution extrajudicial killings, torture, and enforced disappearances, among other serious violations of human rights. The number of extrajudicial killings has dropped significantly since Aquino took office, but politically motivated killings are still frequently reported and the murder of petty criminals by "death squads" in urban areas continues unabated. Only two cases of extrajudicial killings have resulted in convictions in the past three years, and even in those cases, the individuals believed most responsible for the killings have not faced justice. The government took some steps to set up an inter-agency committee in 2013 to help investigate and prosecute high-profile extrajudicial killings, but it was not yet operational at time of writing.

Harassment of and violence against leftist political activists and environmentalists continues.

Insurgency and Ethnic Conflicts

In September, serious fighting erupted in the southern city of Zamboanga between a faction of the Moro National Liberation Front (MNLF), and the Philippine military and police. A reported 161 civilians, MNLF fighters, and government soldiers and police were killed in three weeks of fighting in Zamboanga and neighboring Basilan. Nearly 120,000 people were displaced by the fighting and remained homeless at time of writing. Many of those relocated to evacuation centers are at risk due to overcrowding and poor sanitation.

The Islamist armed group Abu Sayyaf remains active and engages mainly in kidnappings, including the abduction of two people in September.

The communist New People's Army (NPA) conducted attacks against government forces in various parts of the country. The latest proposal for peace talks with the government collapsed in February 2013.

Attacks on Journalists and Criminal Defamation

The Philippines remains one of the most dangerous places in the world to be a journalist. In 2013, seven journalists were killed, according to the Center for Media Freedom and Responsibility, a Manila media advocacy group. Vergel Bico, the 41-year-old editor of Kalahi, a weekly newspaper in Calapan City in the central Philippines, had been writing on the drug trade, among other issues. Motorcycle-riding assailants fatally shot him in the head on September 4. Nanding Solijon, a broadcaster at radio station DXLS, was shot seven times by two motor-riding assailants as he was crossing a street in Iligan City in Mindanao on August 29. On August 1, gunmen entered the home of photojournalist Mario Sy in General Santos City in Mindanao and shot him twice, killing him. According to local monitors, 18 journalists have been killed since Aquino became president.

Three journalists were convicted of criminal libel in 2013. The most recent, in September, was Stella Estremera, editor-in-chief of *Sun Star Davao* who, together with the paper's former publisher, Antonio Ajero, was convicted for a 2003 story identifying people a police report said were suspects in the illegal drug trade in Digos City. The previous month, a columnist for the Cebu City daily the *Freeman* was convicted of libel for a 2007 column that criticized the governor of Cebu province at the time, Gwendolyn Garcia. The defendants faced prison. Free expression groups urged the Philippine government to decriminalize libel. Several journalists have been imprisoned over the years for criminal defamation.

Extrajudicial Killings and Enforced Disappearances

While there has been a notable decline in extrajudicial killings under the Aquino administration, they remain a serious problem and rarely result in a prosecution.

Killings by "death squads" in urban centers including Metro Manila, Davao City, and Zamboanga City remain a serious problem. The victims are frequently petty criminals, drug dealers and street children. By all accounts these killings largely go uninvestigated and there are no reports of death squad members being prosecuted.

In November 2012, the government announced that it would create a judicial "superbody," composed of various government and law enforcement agencies, to give priority to the investigation and prosecution of extrajudicial killings. However, the agency was not yet operational at this writing.

Abuses by Paramilitary Forces

Paramilitary forces controlled by the Philippine government and military committed serious human rights abuses in 2013. Alleged militia members working with the military murdered Benjie Planos, a tribal leader in Agusan del Sur province, on September 13.

President Aquino has not fulfilled his 2010 campaign promise to revoke Executive Order 546, which local officials cite to justify providing arms to their "private armies."

The trial in the Maguindanao Massacre case, in which 58 people linked to a local politician and journalists were summarily executed by members of the Ampatuan political clan in Maguindanao province, continued in 2013. However, families of victims were increasingly impatient at the slow pace of the trial. Four years after the killings, the court is still hearing the bail petitions of several of the suspects. In August, five more suspects were arraigned, including the operator of the backhoe that was used to bury the victims. Of 197 identified suspects, 107 have been arrested, all but 6 of whom have been indicted.

Children and Armed Conflict

A faction of the MNLF took children hostage and used them as human shields during the fighting in Zamboanga City. Several children were killed and wounded. A 15-year-old boy brought by his family to attend a "peace rally" was taken by MNLF rebels when fighting broke out and was forced to help the rebels feed their hostages. Two other children were arrested on suspicion that they were MNLF rebels.

The Philippines government violated domestic and international law by detaining children with non-family member adults for several days in extremely cramped conditions.

Women's Rights

The Supreme Court suspended implementation of the country's landmark Reproductive Health Law following a legal petition from individuals and lay Catholic groups opposing the law. Hearings on the law were ongoing at time of writing. Women's rights advocates point out that the petition delayed government funding for family planning services and reproductive rights education.

Key International Actors

The Philippines' verbal conflict with China heightened in 2013, with increasingly heated rhetoric from both sides over disputed territory in the South China Sea. As a result of China's alleged incursions into territory claimed by the Philippines, the Aquino government turned for help to the United States, which promised to help finance modernization of the Philippines' antiquated naval defense system. Several US senators sought to restrict military assistance to the Philippine army because of continuing rights violations and lack of accountability.

Singapore

Despite controlling an overwhelming majority in Parliament, the Singapore government continues to impose wide-ranging restrictions on core civil and political rights.

On January 26, 2013, the opposition Workers Party raised its number of parliamentarians to an all-time high of eight when it defeated the ruling People's Action Party in a by-election. Increasingly open debate in online blogs and news portals is now echoed by more open parliamentary debate, but the government still punishes speech and peaceful actions that it deems a threat to public order, especially on matters of ethnicity and religion.

Freedom of Expression, Peaceful Assembly, and Association

The rights to freedom of expression, peaceful assembly, and association are limited in Singapore in the name of security, public order, morality, and racial and religious harmony. The restrictions are interpreted broadly.

In June, the government added restrictions on Internet news websites by requiring submission of a S$50,000 (US$39,430) bond and annual licensing for any website averaging at least one Singapore-related news article a week, and receiving a monthly average of 50,000 unique visits from Singapore-based users. Sites determined by the Media Development Authority (MDA) to meet the criteria must, on notification, remove "prohibited content" or face forfeiture of their bond. Any content in the article, or associated readers' comments, which the MDA decides violates broadly defined conceptions of public interest, public security, or national harmony can trigger a take-down order that requires sites to remove the content within 24 hours. Although the MDA said bloggers would not be affected, it added that "if [blogs] take on the nature of news sites, we will take a closer look and evaluate them accordingly."

Printed materials continue to be regulated by the Newspaper and Printing Presses Act, which requires all newspapers to renew their registration annually and limits circulation of foreign newspapers which the government determines "engage in the domestic politics of Singapore." The two corporations that dominate media regularly take a pro-government stance. Media Corp, owned by a government investment company, dominates broadcasting. Singapore Press Holdings Limited (SPH) dominates print media, and although a private company, the government controls appointment of its shareholders.

Singapore uses criminal defamation and contempt of court charges to rein in criticism of the government and the ruling People's Action Party. In July, Leslie Chew, a cartoonist posting his work on "Demon-cratic Singapore," his Facebook page, was charged with "scandalizing the judiciary" for four cartoons that authorities said implied the Singapore judiciary was not impartial or independent. In exchange for dropping the charges, Chew apologized, took down the cartoons and accompanying reader comments, and agreed not to "put up any post or comic strip ... that amounts to contempt of court."

Under the Public Order Act 2009, Singapore requires a permit for any cause-related assembly in any public place or to which members of the general public are invited, or any procession of two or more persons. Grounds for denial of the permit are broad and left largely to the discretion of police. They include the likelihood that the assembly would cause disorder or a "public nuisance," lead to property damage, obstruct roads, "plac[e] the safety of any person in jeopardy," or cause enmity between different groups in Singapore. Demonstrations and rallies are restricted to the city-state's Speakers' Corner, require advance notice, can only be organized by Singapore citizens, and can only be attended by citizens and permanent residents.

Associations with more than 10 members must seek approval to exist, and the Registrar of Societies has broad authority to deny registration if he determines that the group could be "prejudicial to public peace, welfare or good order."

Yale-NUS College, a joint initiative of Yale University and the National University of Singapore, opened its doors to its first classes in August 2013. College President Pericles Lewis has said that students can express their views but will not be allowed to organize political protests on campus or form partisan political societies, thereby undermining human rights principles that are a crucial part of a liberal arts education.

Criminal Justice System

Singapore authorities continue to use the Internal Security Act (ISA) and Criminal Law (Temporary Provisions), which permit arrest and detention of suspects for virtually unlimited periods of time without charge or judicial review. In September 2013, Asyrani Hussaini was ordered to serve two years in detention for attempting to take part in an armed insurgency in southern Thailand. In September, Mustafa Kamal Mohammad, a member of the Moro Islamic Liberation Front in the Philippines, was placed on a two-year Restriction Order.

Singapore made welcome legal reforms in 2012, granting judges some discretion in setting punishments for certain crimes. Three people on death row for murder, Fabian Adiu Edwin, Gopinathan Nair Remadevi Bijukumar, and Kho Jabing had their death sentences commuted to life imprisonment accompanied by caning, though prosecutors said they intended to appeal Kho Jabing's commutation.

In drug cases, judges now have discretion to bypass the mandatory death penalty and sentence low-level offenders to life in prison and caning in cases in which prosecutors attest that the offenders have been cooperative.

In April, convicted drug trafficker Abdul Haleem bin Abdul Karim had his death sentence commuted, and in November, following years of campaigning by anti-death penalty activists in Singapore and the region and prominent international attention given to his case, Yong Vui Kong had his death sentence commuted.

Corporal punishment is common in Singapore. Judicial caning, an inherently cruel punishment, is a mandatory additional punishment for medically fit males aged 16 to 50 who have been sentenced to prison for a range of crimes, including drug trafficking, rape, and immigration offenses. Sentencing officials may also, at their discretion, order caning in cases involving some 30 other violent and non-violent crimes.

Sexual Orientation and Gender Identity

In February, a constitutional challenge to section 377A of the penal code failed, leaving intact a statute criminalizing sexual acts between consenting adult men. The High Court dismissed the case because repeal of the law would further a societal norm that the judge claimed has yet to "gain currency." The plaintiffs argued the law is discriminatory and violates Singapore's constitutional equal protection guarantee. The plaintiffs appealed to the Court of Appeal, which in October decided to hear the case with another challenge to article 377A also pending at the court. A decision is expected by mid-2014. In a third case, a plaintiff has sued to seek a declaration that the constitution "prohibits discrimination against gay men on account of their sexual orientation in the course of employment."

Prime Minster Lee Hsien Loong has spoken dismissively of the challenges to article 377A: "Why is that law on the books? Because it's always been there and I just think we leave it. I think that's the way Singapore will be for a long time."

Singapore's Media Development Authority issued a regulation effective on June 1 that banned major news websites available in Singapore from "advocating homosexuality or lesbianism."

In August, in what was widely seen an affirmation of lesbian, gay, bisexual, and transgender (LGBT) rights, over 20,000 participants joined the fifth annual Pink Dot pride festival. The festival continued to attract prominent corporate sponsors, including Google, Barclays, and J.P. Morgan.

Migrant Workers and Labor Exploitation

Foreign workers in Singapore, both men and women, are subject to labor abuses and exploitation through debts owed to recruitment agents, non-payment of wages, restrictions on movement, confiscation of passports, and, in some cases, physical and sexual abuse. Foreign domestic workers are still excluded from the Employment Act and key labor protections, such as limits on daily work hours. Although the government is still not in compliance with minimum standards for trafficking elimination, it has made some improvements in prevention and protection, but prosecutorial efforts have been weak. Singapore has not yet ratified the ILO Domestic Workers Convention or the UN Protocol to Prevent, Suppress and Punish Trafficking in Persons.

A government-mandated standard contract for migrant workers does not address work-related discrimination issues such as lower wages, longer work hours, and poorer living conditions. Labor laws discriminate against foreign workers by prohibiting them from organizing and registering a union or serving as union leaders without explicit government permission.

On November 26, 2012, 171 Chinese nationals working as bus drivers for the public transport company SMRT, whose majority shareholder is the government-owned Temasek investment company, refused to report to work. They demanded that SMRT management end discrimination against migrants in pay and selection of bus routes, and improve company-provided unhygienic living quarters. The government prosecuted four work-stoppage leaders for conducting an illegal strike, sentencing them to prison for a number of weeks before deporting them. Two of the four alleged that police beat them in custody. Another 29 drivers who participated in the strike were not charged but were deported.

Human Rights Defenders

In January 2013, Prime Minister Lee demanded that activist Alex Au take down a blog post and readers' comments and apologize or face legal action. It was the third time in 11 months that Alex Au had faced such demands. In July 2012, the Attorney General's Chambers had sent a similar demand, as did Law Minister Shanmugam in February 2012. Prosecutors issued a warning to Lynn Lee, a freelance journalist filming interviews with striking bus drivers.

Nizam Ismail resigned as a member of the Board of Directors of the Association of Muslim Professionals (AMP) and as board chairman of the Centre for Research on Malay and Islamic Affairs under pressure from two government ministers who expressed concerns to AMP about his political activities and threatened to cut government funding for AMP.

Key International Actors

Singapore serves as a major trade and commercial hub for the region. It has concluded 18 bilateral and regional free trade agreements with 24 trading partners, including Australia, China, India, Japan, South Korea, New Zealand, the United States, and the European Union.

The US and Singapore maintain strong trade and military ties, with security cooperation continuing to grow under President Barack Obama. In April 2013, a US Navy littoral combat ship docked in Singapore, an illustration of the country's importance in the US "pivot" to the region. At the same time, Singapore continues to maintain a close and warm relationship with China, and remains a central player in the regional Association of Southeast Asian Nations (ASEAN) bloc.

Sri Lanka

The Sri Lankan government of President Mahinda Rajapaksa made little progress in 2013 in addressing accountability for serious human rights abuses committed during the country's nearly three-decades-long civil war, which ended in 2009. In March, the United Nations Human Rights Council (HRC) adopted a second resolution in as many years that called on Sri Lanka to implement the recommendations made by its own Lessons Learnt and Reconciliation Commission (LLRC) and provide accountability for alleged war crimes committed by both sides in the civil war. The government claimed it was implementing the LLRC recommendations, but its claims were difficult to verify and accountability efforts lacked credibility.

The year saw an escalation in attacks by militant Buddhist groups against Hindus and Muslims.

The independence of the judiciary came under question after the Rajapaksa government orchestrated the impeachment of Chief Justice Shirani Bandaranayake in December 2012 after she had ruled against the government in a major case.

Elections for three provincial councils were conducted in September. Independent observers reported dozens of incidents of intimidation, violence, and improper military interference. The Tamil National Alliance (TNA) won a large majority in the Northern Provincial Council, an ethnic Tamil-majority area that was the site of much of the fighting during the civil war.

By September, the government was detaining 230 of the estimated 12,000 members and supporters of the defeated Liberation Tigers of Tamil Eelam (LTTE) held at the end of the civil war for "rehabilitation."

Accountability

Sri Lanka's failure over several years to address war crimes allegations prompted the HRC in March to issue a resolution calling on Sri Lanka to independently and credibly investigate violations of international humanitarian and human rights law. The resolution also called on UN High Commissioner for Human Rights Navi Pillay to give an oral update on the human rights situation in Sri

Lanka during the HRC's September session, and to present a written report at the March 2014 session.

Following the HRC resolution, the government issued several updates regarding its implementation of LLRC recommendations, including investigations into a few war crimes allegations. Many of its claims were difficult to verify due to lack of government transparency, and, even if accurate, in important respects fell far short of the steps called for in the resolution.

Special army courts of inquiry established in 2012 wholly exonerated the army of any laws of war violations despite significant evidence to the contrary. While the government arrested 12 members of the police Special Task Force as part of its investigation into the murder of five Tamil youths in Trincomalee in January 2006, it failed to arrest senior police officials implicated. In response to LLRC concerns about enforced disappearances, the government established the latest in a long line of special commission with a limited mandate and no clarity as to whether the government would publicize its findings.

High Commissioner Pillay travelled to Sri Lanka in August. Her September oral report to the HRC was a scathing critique of the government's failures on postwar accountability. Pillay said she found no evidence of government efforts "to independently or credibly investigate the allegations" of war crimes and reported that the government had failed to implement many of the LLRC recommendations. Pillay said that the separation of the police from the Ministry of Defence, a key LLRC recommendation, remained incomplete as the police were placed under the command of a former army officer.

Torture and Rape

Torture and other ill-treatment of persons in custody by the security forces has been a widespread problem both during and since the armed conflict. Human Rights Watch published new evidence in February that rape and sexual violence has been a key element of broader torture of suspected LTTE members and supporters even since the war's end. The torture is used to obtain "confessions" of LTTE involvement, and to instill terror in the broader Tamil population to discourage involvement with the LTTE.

The government rejected these findings and claimed they were fabrications by individuals seeking to embellish their overseas asylum claims. Human Rights Watch is unaware of any government investigations into the reported sexual abuse.

Several European countries have since suspended deportations of Tamils with connections to the LTTE, finding them to be at risk of torture on return. UNHCR revised its guidelines on assessing asylum claims in December 2012, and recommended that persons with certain links to the LTTE be regarded as being at risk on return.

Arbitrary Detention and Enforced Disappearances

Sri Lanka's Prevention of Terrorism Act gives police broad powers over suspects in custody and is the law most commonly invoked by officials to justify prolonged detention without trial of security suspects. It is still in regular use. The government asserts it has made available comprehensive lists of the names of those detained under the law as well as their places of detention, but family members in 2013 reported difficulty accessing the information. Pillay said during her trip in August that she had "never seen this level of uncontrollable grief" when visiting with families of the forcibly disappeared in northern Sri Lanka.

Civil Society Organizations and Media Freedom

Civil society organizations and media continue to face arbitrary restrictions and intimidation. In June, the government proposed a dangerously ambiguous media code that would have prohibited 13 types of substantive speech, including content that "offends against expectations of the public, morality of the country, or tends to lower the standards of public taste and morality." Also prohibited would have been any content that "contains material against the integrity of the Executive, Judiciary, and Legislative"—which could have been interpreted as barring criticism of the government. The proposed code was withdrawn in the face of a storm of negative media coverage.

The government continues to block public access to certain news websites critical of the government. Several cases of journalists killed or "disappeared" in recent years remained unsolved.

HUMAN
RIGHTS
WATCH

"We Will Teach You a Lesson"
Sexual Violence against Tamils by Sri Lankan Security Forces

Activists and organizations, particularly those working in the north and east, report ongoing harassment and intimidation. Pillay reported that people who she met with in the north and east were visited by security forces within hours of her visit. Instead of investigating these reports, the government denied Pillay's allegations and demanded the names of her sources. Repression by the government is not limited to the north and east: in August, the army opened fire on protesters in Weliweriya demanding clean drinking water, killing three.

In July, a senior Sri Lankan diplomat launched a public attack on Callum Macrae, producer of "No Fire Zone," a documentary film about alleged war crimes at the end of the civil war, tweeting suggestions that Macrae was a terrorist receiving "blood money" from the LTTE. The government did not censure the diplomat for his remarks, and a Channel 4 crew including Macrae was subjected to continual harassment during the Commonwealth summit in November.

A disturbing trend was the rise in violence against religious minorities, led largely by the militant Buddhist group Bodhu Bala Sena (BBS). The government did little to investigate or prevent these attacks. During an ongoing campaign by the BBS targeting Sri Lanka's Muslim population, the secretary to the Ministry of Defence, the president's brother, was the group's guest at a public event. In her September oral report to the HRC, High Commissioner Pillay expressed alarm at the rise in hate speech against religious minorities, and called for more forceful government intervention to prevent violence.

Military Abuses in the North and East

The government contends to have considerably decreased its military presence in the north and east, but credible accounts indicate that military personnel still frequently intervene in civilian life. The Defence Ministry and army websites both regularly post articles about the role of the military in civilian affairs that appear intended to exert control over the local population and development. Independent observers of provincial council elections in September expressed concern about military campaign activities in favor of the ruling party there, and the resulting heightened sense of insecurity and tension among the Tamil population ahead of the elections.

Women and girls in the north and east remained especially vulnerable to sexual harassment and violence that the army neither prevented and may have contributed to. Women's rights groups working in Tamil areas reported particular difficulty documenting abuses because of an oppressive military presence.

Key International Actors

At the March HRC session, the government unsuccessfully tried to block the council from adopting a resolution focusing on accountability for serious wartime abuses. The resolution, backed by the United States and India among others, sets the stage for calling for an independent investigation at the 2014 HRC session if Sri Lanka does not take meaningful steps to implement the resolution.

Canadian Prime Minister Stephen Harper, as well as the prime minister of Mauritius, did not attend the Commonwealth Heads of Government Meeting (CHOGM) in November in Colombo because of human rights concerns. The prime minister of India also did not attend the summit, citing domestic concerns. The human rights situation in Sri Lanka and lack of accountability for wartime atrocities became the focus of media coverage. United Kingdom Prime Minister David Cameron attended the summit, and spent much time touring war-ravaged parts of the north and talking to local activists. He publicly said the UK would back an international investigation into war crimes if the Sri Lankan government did not undertake an independent investigation, a position supported by the US and Canada.

China kept up its high-profile engagement and investment in Sri Lanka and vocally opposed the HRC resolution. After pressing for Sri Lanka to hold meaningful provincial council elections, India continued to call for the full implementation of the 13th amendment to the constitution, which calls for devolution of powers to the provinces.

Thailand

The government of Prime Minister Yingluck Shinawatra made little progress in 2013 in resolving ongoing, serious human rights problems, and continued to protect the military from accountability for the political violence in 2010.

More than 100,000 opposition supporters took to the streets in November and December in response to the ruling Pheu Thai Party's attempt to pass a blanket amnesty for all individuals responsible for political violence and corruption from 2004 to 2011. This led to a series of clashes that had left at least four dead and over 200 wounded at time of writing.

Despite pro-rights rhetoric, the government achieved very limited success addressing other serious human rights concerns, including abuses in southern border provinces, free speech restrictions, and violations of refugee and migrant rights.

Accountability for Political Violence

At least 90 people died and more than 2,000 were injured in the 2010 political violence, with most casualties resulting from unnecessary and excessive use of lethal force by soldiers. Elements of the United Front for Democracy against Dictatorship (UDD), popularly known as the "Red Shirts," were also responsible for deadly armed attacks on soldiers, police, and civilians.

Court inquests found that 15 of the victims in the 2010 violence were shot dead by soldiers acting under orders from the Center for the Resolution of the Emergency Situation (CRES), established by then-Prime Minister Abhisit Vejjajiva and chaired by then-Deputy Prime Minister Suthep Thaugsuban. While Abhisit and Suthep have been charged with premeditated murder based on command responsibility, no military personnel have been charged in the killings.

The status of government investigations into alleged crimes by the UDD-linked "Black Shirt" militants remains unclear. Despite clear photographic and other evidence, the UDD leadership and its supporters, including those holding positions in the government and the parliament, continue to assert that the UDD had no armed elements at the time of the 2010 events.

The government commendably has provided reparations to all those harmed by the 2010 violence. Some victims and their families, however, have expressed concern that financial compensation is serving as a substitute for bringing perpetrators of violence to justice.

On November 1, 2013, the House of Representatives passed an amnesty bill proposed by the Pheu Thai Party that promised a full amnesty for protesters from all political sides charged with or convicted of actions against the state from 2004 to 2011, for authorities who ordered crackdowns on protesters, for soldiers who carried out the crackdowns, and for individuals convicted of corruption after the 2006 coup. Even though the Senate rejected this bill on November 11, anti-amnesty protests in Bangkok and other provinces escalated. More than 100,000 people took to the streets in what protest leaders publicly called an attempt to topple the Yingluck government and eliminate the political network of former Prime Minister Thaksin Shinawatra.

Clashes on November 30 between pro and anti-government groups at Ramkhamhaeng University and Rajamangala Stadium in Bangkok left at least 4 dead and 60 wounded. Protesters from the People's Democratic Reform Committee (PDRC) and other anti-government groups clashed with police when they tried to storm the Government House and the Bangkok Metropolitan Police headquarters on December 1 and 3, leading to more than 200 injuries—mostly side-effects from exposure to teargas.

Freedom of Expression

Criticizing the monarchy is a criminal offense in Thailand. The number of arrests and convictions for *lese majeste* (insulting the monarchy) offenses has significantly declined since Prime Minister Yingluck entered office in 2011, but authorities continue to use the *lese majeste* law (in article 112 of the penal code), as well as the Computer Crimes Act, to suppress free speech and prosecute critics of the monarchy. Persons charged with *lese majeste* offenses are routinely denied bail and remain in prison for many months awaiting trial. In most cases, convictions result in harsh sentences.

On January 23, the Bangkok Criminal Court sentenced Somyot Prueksakasemsuk—a magazine editor and prominent pro-democracy activist—to 11 years in prison for publishing two articles in his *Voice of Taksin* magazine that made negative references to the monarchy. Authorities denied bail to Somyot eight times during the course of his 20-month pretrial detention. The United Nations Working Group on Arbitrary Detention determined in August 2012 that the pretrial detention of Somyot violated international human rights law. Somyot has appealed his conviction.

On September 13, the Bangkok Criminal Court acquitted Yuthaphum Madnok of *lese majeste* charges filed against him by his own brother. Authorities had detained Yuthaphum without bail since September 2012 because the court determined that his alleged insults to the monarchy posed a threat to national security. The case, in which the *lese majeste* law became a weapon in a family feud, shows how easily the law can be misused. Often the police, courts, and prosecutors are afraid they will be accused of disloyalty to the monarch if they fail to prosecute allegations of *lese majeste*.

The ruling Pheu Thai Party, the government's allies in the UDD, the military leadership, the opposition Democrat Party, and anti-government groups have all explicitly and publicly argued that those accused of committing *lese majeste* offenses should not be included in any amnesty proposal. In 2013, the palace pardoned three individuals convicted of the offense.

On November 25, anti-government PDRC protesters assaulted Nick Nostitz, a German freelance journalist, after a former Democrat Party member of parliament, Chumpol Junsai, asserted from a protest stage that Nostitz was affiliated with the UDD. Nostitz's photograph subsequently was disseminated widely on anti-government social media sites, raising concerns for his safety.

Led by politicians from the Democrat Party, thousands of PDRC supporters marched to the headquarters of TV channels 3, 5, 7, 9, 11 and Thai PBS on December 1 to pressure them to broadcast Suthep's speech and not to transmit government-provided information on the political confrontations.

Violence and Abuses in Southern Border Provinces

On February 28, the government agreed to hold talks with Hassan Taib from the separatist Barisan Revolusi Nasional (BRN) movement, seeking an end to the armed conflict that has claimed more than 5,000 lives in Thailand's southern border provinces since January 2004. The two sides agreed to cease hostilities during the holy month of Ramadan from July 10 to August 18.

The Fatoni Fighters (also known as Pejuang Kemerdekaan Fatoni), insurgents in the loose BRN network, continued to target civilians in bomb attacks, roadside ambushes, drive-by shootings, and assassinations. The attacks by the ethnic Malay Muslim insurgents appear aimed at intimidating and ultimately driving out the ethnic Thai Buddhist population in Narathiwat, Yala, and Pattani provinces, keeping the Muslim population under their control, and discrediting government authorities for being unable to protect citizens. Thai security forces have also been responsible for killings and other abuses against ethnic Malay Muslims.

The government provided financial compensation to hundreds of Muslim victims of abuses committed by the security forces. However, security personnel still operate with impunity, and not a single security officer has been held accountable for involvement in extrajudicial killings, torture, enforced disappearances, and other abuses in the region.

Insurgents also launched bomb attacks against government-run schools and attacked Buddhist teachers whom they accuse of representing the ideology of the Thai Buddhist state. Since January 2004, 164 teachers have been killed in southern Thailand.

Insurgents have recruited children from private Islamic schools to participate in armed hostilities and to perform secondary tasks such as distributing separatist leaflets; some have used private Islamic schools as areas to assemble improvised explosive devices.

Enforced Disappearances

The government signed the International Convention for the Protection of All Persons from Enforced Disappearance in January 2012, but has taken no steps to obtain parliamentary ratification of the treaty. The penal code does not recognize enforced disappearance as a criminal offense. Authorities have continually failed to give priority to solving any of the 63 known cases of enforced disappearance.

Human Rights Defenders

On February 25, a gunman killed Prajob Nao-opas, a well-known environmental activist leading a campaign to expose the dumping of toxic waste in Chachoengsao province. Since 2001 more than 20 environmentalists and human rights defenders have been killed. Investigations into the killings have frequently suffered from inconsistent and shoddy police work, and been plagued by political interference in law enforcement efforts and, in several cases, by the Justice Ministry's failure to provide witnesses adequate protection.

In a chilling development for human rights research, on February 14, the Natural Fruit Company Ltd. filed criminal defamation charges against labor activist Andy Hall for allegations made in an investigative report about serious labor rights violations at its factory.

In the southern border provinces, the security agencies have profiled ethnic Malay Muslim human rights defenders, paralegals, and student activists as "insurgent sympathizers" and subjected them to surveillance and arbitrary arrest and detention.

Refugees, Asylum Seekers, and Migrant Workers

The government has given public assurances that the 140,000 Burmese refugees living in camps on the Thai-Burmese border will not be forced to return home against their will. Some 40 percent of camp residents remain unregistered, however, and Thailand restricts their freedom of movement and bars all refugees from working.

Thailand is not a party to the 1951 Refugee Convention and has no law that recognizes refugee status. Asylum seekers and refugees who are arrested often face long periods of detention until they are accepted for resettlement or agree to be repatriated at their own expense.

Authorities regularly intercept and push back boats carrying ethnic Rohingya from Burma. The government considers all Rohingya arriving on Thailand's coast to be illegal migrants. Between January and October, more than 2,000 Rohingya were detained. Rohingya men are restricted to poor and extremely cramped conditions in small cells, and at least eight of them have died from illness while in immigration detention. Starting in July, Rohingya men—fearful of being sent back to persecution in Burma or detained indefinitely in Thailand—staged protests at immigration detention facilities in many provinces. Human traffickers have gained access to government shelters and tried to lure out Rohingya women and children.

Thailand's labor laws provide little protection to migrant workers. A migrant worker registry and "nationality verification" scheme provides legal documentation for workers, but does little to counter the impunity with which employers violate such workers' rights. Domestic workers remain excluded from key protections such as a minimum wage, limits to working hours, and maternity leave. Migrant workers remain extremely vulnerable to exploitation, with female migrants enduring sexual violence and labor trafficking, and male migrants facing extreme labor exploitation, including being trafficked onto fishing boats.

Anti-Narcotics Policy

The government still denies any official involvement in the more than 2,800 extrajudicial killings that accompanied then-Prime Minister Thaksin's 2003 "war on drugs." Criminal investigations of extrajudicial killings related to police anti-drug operations have progressed very slowly.

The government continues to send drug users to "rehabilitation" centers, mostly run by the military and the Interior Ministry, where "treatment" consists mainly of military-style physical exercise. Routinely detained in prison prior to compulsory rehabilitation, detainees get little or no medical assistance for drug withdrawal symptoms.

Key International Actors

In November and December, the United Nations secretary-general—together with officials from the European Union, United States, United Kingdom, and Australia—raised concerns about the ongoing political confrontations, urging all sides to reject violence, respect human rights, and resolve their differences peacefully.

Thailand in 2013 launched a bid for a non-permanent seat on the UN Security Council for 2017-2018, and for election to the UN Human Rights Council (HRC) for 2015-2017. Thailand is one of the few countries in the Southeast Asia region that has extended a standing invitation for HRC special procedures. On September 9, 2013, Prime Minister Yingluck became the first Thai leader to speak at the HRC. However, her speech did not substantively address Thailand's outstanding human rights problems.

Vietnam

The human rights situation in Vietnam deteriorated significantly in 2013, worsening a trend evident for several years. The year was marked by a severe and intensifying crackdown on critics, including long prison terms for many peaceful activists whose "crime" was calling for political change.

The Communist Party of Vietnam (CPV) continued its one-party rule, in place since 1975. While it maintained its monopoly on state power, it faced growing public discontent with lack of basic freedoms. Denial of rights and endemic official corruption are widely seen as stifling Vietnam's political and economic progress. Political infighting and economic policy disagreements within the CPV about how to handle the crisis of legitimacy and economic stagnation created an opening for members of the public to offer their opinions, particularly through social media.

The year saw a significant expansion of critical commentary in digital and other media. Critics questioned official policies, exposed official corruption, protested land-grabs, defended religious freedom, and called for democratic alternatives to one-party rule. One remarkable effort was "Petition 72," originally signed by 72 intellectuals but later signed by some 15,000 people, calling for constitutional changes to allow multi-party elections. Another was "Statement 258," calling for reform of article 258 of the penal code ("abusing democratic freedoms"), a provision often used to punish freedom of speech.

The government took some positive steps. On November 7, 2013, Vietnam signed the UN Convention Against Torture. On September 24, 2013, it issued a decree ending administrative sanctions for same-sex wedding ceremonies, although government sponsored amendments to the Marriage and Family Law did not grant legal recognition to same-sex marriage. The government also began phasing out detention and forced rehabilitation of sex workers in 2013.

Political Prisoners and the Criminal Justice System

Vietnam had an estimated 150-200 political prisoners at time of writing, including lowland Vietnamese and upland ethnic minority prisoners, some of whom were detained at least in part in connection with their religious activities. The total included at least 63 political prisoners convicted by politically controlled courts in 2013, an increase over the roughly 40 sentenced in 2012, which in turn exceeded the numbers sentenced in 2011 and 2010.

Vietnamese courts lack the independence and impartiality required by international law. Where the party or government has an interest in the outcome of a case, they—not the facts and the law—dictate the outcome. Trials are often marred by procedural and other irregularities that go along with achieving a politically pre-determined outcome.

The penal code provisions used most often against proponents of peaceful political change are articles 79, 87, 88, 89, 91, and 258, though other laws, such as tax laws, are also used. For example, prominent human rights lawyer and blogger Le Quoc Quan was arrested on December 27, 2012, shortly after he criticized the Communist Party's political monopoly, but his arrest was justified by trumped up charges of tax evasion. Following domestic and international calls for him to be released, his trial was delayed but on October 2, 2013, he was sentenced to 30 months' imprisonment.

Freedom of Expression, Opinion, and Information

Government repression targets many independent writers, bloggers, and rights activists. They face police intimidation, harassment, arbitrary arrest, prolonged detention without access to legal counsel or family visits, court convictions, and often severe prison sentences. Enhancing already extensive government powers to punish and otherwise deter digital freedom, Prime Minister Nguyen Tan Dung on September 1, 2013, put into force Decree 72, which contains provisions legalizing content-filtering and censorship, and outlawing vaguely defined "prohibited acts." It also forbids individuals from synthesizing news on their blogs or personal websites.

The 2013 persecution of bloggers was highlighted by the arrests of Truong Duy Nhat and Pham Viet Dao for allegedly violating article 258. They face up to seven years in prison if convicted.

Freedom of Assembly, Association, and Movement

Vietnam bans all political parties, labor unions, and human rights organizations independent of the government or CPV. The authorities require official approval for public gatherings and refuse to grant permission for meetings, marches, or protests they deem politically or otherwise unacceptable. If such events go ahead, organizers and participants are sometimes punished. In 2013, such measures were applied to individuals who questioned government domestic and foreign policies and to individuals who demonstrated against alleged land-grabs.

In May 2013, authorities in three Vietnamese cities intervened with violence, temporary arrests, and concerted harassment to prevent and break up peaceful "human rights picnics" at which activists planned to disseminate and discuss the Universal Declaration of Human Rights and other human rights standards.

The government also repeatedly prevented critics from making trips outside Vietnam, citing "national security reasons." Prominent intellectuals Huynh Ngoc Chenh and Nguyen Hoang Duc were prohibited from going abroad in May and July 2013.

Freedom of Religion

In January 2013, the prime minister put Decree 92 into effect, further extending controls on religious groups. In its enforcement actions, the government monitors, harasses, and sometimes violently cracks down on religious groups that operate outside of official, government-registered and government-controlled religious institutions. Targets in 2013 included unrecognized branches of the Cao Dai church, the Hoa Hao Buddhist church, independent Protestant and Catholic house churches in the central highlands and elsewhere, Khmer Krom Buddhist temples, and the Unified Buddhist Church of Vietnam.

The January 2013 conviction and imprisonment of 14 mostly Catholic activists by the People's Court of Nghe An province initiated the year's upsurge of government attacks on critics. The vehicle this time was article 79 of the penal code, prohibiting activities aimed at "overthrowing the government," even though the 14 activists were exercising fundamental human rights, such as participating in volunteer church activities and peaceful political protests.

Abuses in Detention and Prison

Official media and other sources continue to report many cases of police abuse, torture, or even killing of detainees. In May 2013, Nguyen Van Duc died in the custody of Vinh Long province police due to "brain bleeding with cracks on his skull, crushed right brain, blood-clotted left brain, two broken ribs, and broken sternum." Human Rights Watch is unaware of any investigation into his death.

Many political prisoners suffer from poor health but do not receive adequate medical attention. Several, such as Cu Huy Ha Vu, Nguyen Van Hai (Dieu Cay), and Ho Thi Bich Khuong, went on hunger strikes in 2013 to protest denial of their internationally recognized prisoner's rights, such as adequate medical care.

Constitutional Amendment

On November 28, 2013, the National Assembly adopted an amended constitution, the provisions of which disappointed those hoping for significant reforms to the political and economic system. Government-proposed amendments that were approved include rhetorical commitments to human rights, but they leave serious loopholes in place. The amended constitution falls far short of ensuring effective promotion and protection of many fundamental rights.

Arbitrary Detention

People dependent on drugs, including children, continued to be held in government detention centers where they are forced to perform menial work in the name of "labor therapy." Their detention is not subject to judicial oversight. Violations of the rules—including the work requirement—are punished by beatings and confinement to disciplinary rooms, where detainees told us they were deprived of food and water.

Key International Actors

Vietnam's most important foreign relations are with China and the United States, but linkages with Japan, the European Union, the Association of Southeast Asian Nations, and Australia are also significant.

Vietnam's relationship with China was complicated in 2013 by maritime territorial disputes, though perhaps more important for both was the shared commitment by each country's communist parties to maintain their rule.

The United States continued to pursue improved military and economic relations with Vietnam, although an American ban on the sale of lethal military equipment remained in place in 2013. The US made some efforts to press Vietnam to improve its human rights record, but the issue was not prominent in meetings between President Barack Obama and President Truong Tan San in July. The EU made only tepid efforts on promoting respect for rights, while Japan remained silent and failed to use its status as Vietnam's largest bilateral donor to publicly press for reforms.

The EU and Vietnam continued negotiations on a Free Trade Agreement and a third round of their annual human rights dialogue took place in September 2013. In April 2013, the European Parliament adopted a resolution condemning continuing human rights violations in Vietnam and called on the EU to raise concerns with Vietnamese authorities. While high level EU officials, such as EU High Representative Catherine Ashton were silent, the EU delegation to Vietnam issued public statements expressing concern over the crackdown on dissidents, the resumption of execution as a criminal penalty, and the cyber restrictions of Decree 72.

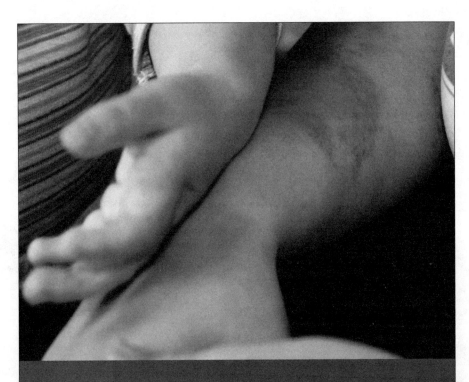

UNLESS BLOOD FLOWS
Lack of Protection from Domestic Violence in Hungary

WORLD REPORT

2014

EUROPE
AND CENTRAL ASIA

Armenia

President Serzh Sargsyan was re-elected in February and the ruling Republican Party dominated Yerevan municipal elections in May. Although generally well-administered, reports of voter harassment, vote-buying, misuse of administrative resources to favor incumbents, and police unresponsiveness to citizens' complaints marred both elections.

Ill-treatment in police custody persists. The government has yet to offer conscientious objectors a genuine civilian alternative to military service. The authorities did not adequately investigate a troubling number of noncombat deaths in the military. They also failed to investigate violent attacks against peaceful protesters by unidentified assailants.

Broadcast media lacks pluralism and there were several instances of violence and harassment against journalists and media workers during the year. Violence and discrimination based on sexual orientation and gender identity by both state and non-state actors are serious problems. Bureaucratic restrictions prevent people with terminal illnesses from accessing strong pain medications.

Presidential and Municipal Elections

International observers, led by the Organization for Security and Co-operation in Europe (OSCE), concluded that the February presidential election "was generally well-administered" but noted "some serious violations" of OSCE and Council of Europe standards, such as pressure on voters. The OSCE also noted other breaches, including public administration bias in favor of incumbents, misuse of administrative resources, and interference by the incumbent's proxies. Local observers reported the presence of unauthorized persons in polling stations, numerous attempts to pressure observers and journalists by political parties and election commission members, and widespread ballot stuffing for the incumbent candidate.

Yerevan Mayor Taron Markaryan, a Republican Party member, won re-election in the May 5 city council elections. Local groups observed instances of vote buying, multiple voting, and bullying of election observers by pro-government activists.

Freedom of Assembly and Attacks Against Activists

In August, police used force to disperse a crowd of local residents and civic activists in central Yerevan, demanding to halt construction of a high-rise apartment building in the city center. Police briefly detained some 26 protesters and beat at least one as he was transported to a police station; he required brief hospitalization. In October, the Armenian ombudsman's office found that the police had used disproportionate force but no disciplinary action had been taken at time of writing.

September saw a spate of attacks against peaceful protesters in Yerevan, apparently intended to discourage participation in two peaceful protests. On September 5, about six unidentified assailants attacked Haykak Arshamyan and Suren Saghatelyan, well-known civil society activists, as they returned from a peaceful demonstration in front of the Republican Party headquarters where they were protesting President Sargsyan's announcement that Armenia would join the Russia-led customs union. Saghatelyan suffered a broken nose, requiring surgery and hospitalization, and Arshamyan was treated for multiple bruises. On September 4, about 10 unidentified assailants attacked activist Arman Alexanyan after he left a sit-in at the municipal building to protest a temporary price increase in municipal transport fares. He was hospitalized briefly for bruises and head trauma. On August 25, about six unidentified assailants attacked two activists, Babken Der Grigoryan and Mihran Margaryan, shortly after they left the municipal building protest. Investigations were pending at time of writing.

The Women's Resource Center, a nongovernmental rights organization, has faced an increasing number of threats by nationalist groups, including Facebook comments by users who threatened to blow it up and slit the throats of its activists. While these threats have been reported to the police, authorities had yet to investigate at time of writing.

In November, authorities arrested Shant Harutyunyan, an opposition leader, and 13 activists, after they clashed with riot police following an attempted march to the presidential administration building. The government claims that the group intended to forcibly occupy the building. At time of writing, all those detained remained in pretrial custody, facing criminal charges of violence against the authorities. Harutyunyan claimed that police officials physically abused him in custody, but authorities have not initiated an investigation into the allegations. In late November, a Yerevan court ordered Harutyunyan be sent to a psychiatric institution for a forced examination.

Torture and Ill-Treatment in Custody

According to local human rights defenders, torture and ill-treatment in police custody persist, and the definition of torture in Armenian law does not meet international standards, as it does not include crimes committed by public officials. Authorities often refuse to investigate allegations of ill-treatment or pressure victims to retract complaints. Police use torture to coerce confessions and incriminating statements from suspects and witnesses.

For example, Artur Karapetyan, detained in October 2012 on charges of illegal drug distribution, complained of police abuse in custody. According to his lawyer, Karapetyan showed him wounds on his feet that he said were from a beating. Although Karapetyan was released in December and the charges against him dropped in April 2013, police failed to conduct an effective investigation into his ill-treatment allegations.

In November 2012, Mger Andreasyan testified in a local court that Yerevan police officers severely beat him after his arrest on robbery charges. Andreasyan stated that, unable to bear sustained beatings, he attempted suicide by using his head to break a window in the investigator's office and trying to jump out, but police prevented him. Although a Yerevan court dropped escape charges against Andreasyan in March, there was no investigation into his ill-treatment allegations.

Army Abuses

As of October 31, the Helsinki Citizens' Assembly Vanadzor office had reported 29 noncombat army deaths, including 7 suicides. Local human rights groups have documented the Defense Ministry's failure to investigate adequately and expose the circumstances of noncombat deaths and to account for evidence of violence in cases where the death is ruled a suicide.

In June, parliament amended the law on alternative military service to remove military supervision from alternative labor service and reduce it from 42 to 36 months. Local activists voiced concerns about the amendments, including the Defense Ministry's continued role in application decisions, vague eligibility requirements, and length of service, which would still be longer than regular military service. By mid-November, 33 Jehovah's Witnesses who had been convicted for refusing alternative service were released but were still required to perform alternative service.

Freedom of Expression

Armenia has diverse print and online media, but broadcast media lacks pluralism; for example, only 1 of Armenia's 13 television stations carries live political talk shows. International election observers noted the media's "selective approach" in covering post-presidential election developments, notably limiting views critical of the conduct of the election.

The Committee to Protect Freedom of Expression, a local media monitoring group, reported six instances of physical violence against journalists during the first half of 2013. In one case, several young men forcibly prevented Artak Hambardzumyan, from Journalists for Human Rights, from documenting alleged ballot box stuffing in Artashat during the presidential election. As of June, the committee had documented 34 instances of pressure on media outlets and journalists.

Palliative Care

Armenia's complicated and time-consuming prescription and procurement procedures for opioid medications obstruct the delivery of adequate palliative care, condemning most terminally ill patients to unnecessary suffering. Although morphine is a safe, effective, and inexpensive way to improve the lives of terminally ill people, Armenia's current consumption levels of morphine and alternative strong opioid medicines are insufficient to provide care to all terminally ill cancer patients, leaving many without adequate pain relief during the last stages of their illness.

Sexual Orientation and Gender Identity

Local lesbian, gay, bisexual, and transgender (LGBT) rights activists have expressed concern for the alarming level of homophobia in Armenia. According to PINK Armenia, a local rights group, transgender women who engage in sex work are frequently assaulted and receive no police protection when they report abuse. PINK Armenia also reported that the LGBT population continues to experience employment discrimination, obstacles to health care, and physical and psychological abuse in the army, in public, and in families.

According to an August Amnesty International report, government officials frequently condone violent attacks against LGBT people, characterizing the violence as an expression of "traditional values." In July, the Armenian police made a proposal to amend the code of administrative offenses to establish a fine of up to US$4,000 for promoting "nontraditional sexual relationships." The proposal was subsequently withdrawn.

Also in July, a Yerevan court convicted two people for damage to property stemming from a bomb attack in May 2012 against DIY, a bar frequented by LGBT and women's rights activists. Graffiti identified LGBT people as targets of the attack. One attacker was sentenced to 19 months in prison and the other received a two-year suspended sentence. They were both amnestied in October. Local human rights groups expressed frustration that the sentence was too lenient. Armenia does not have hate speech legislation.

Key International Actors

Armenia's international partners noted that the February presidential election was conducted smoothly, but in addition to the OSCE, the European Union, the Council of Europe, and others also highlighted violations of OSCE election standards, including misuse of administrative resources, lack of impartiality of public administration, and cases of pressure on voters.

In September 2013, the EU delegation in Yerevan expressed deep concern about attacks on members of civil society and cases of intimidation targeting human rights defenders.

In its March European Neighborhood Policy progress report, the EU commended Armenia for its "serious effort to address issues related to human rights and fundamental freedoms" but also highlighted a rise in homophobia and insufficient media independence in the country.

In its April annual human rights report, the United States State Department highlighted a number of human rights concerns in Armenia, including arbitrary or unlawful deprivation of life; torture and other cruel, inhuman, or degrading treatment or punishment; and denial of freedom of speech and peaceful assembly.

In September, Armenia signed the United Nations Convention on the Protection of the Rights of All Migrant Workers and Members of Their Families, affording them equitable, humane, and lawful conditions.

Azerbaijan

The Azerbaijani government's poor record on freedom of expression, assembly, and association dramatically deteriorated during the year. The authorities arrested dozens of political activists on bogus charges, imprisoned critical journalists, broke up several peaceful public demonstrations, and adopted legislation that further restricted fundamental freedoms. This crackdown was the backdrop for the October 2013 presidential election, in which incumbent President Ilham Aliyev was re-elected for a third term with 84.5 percent of the vote.

The government continued its urban renewal campaign in the capital Baku, forcibly evicting hundreds of families without adequate compensation. Torture and ill-treatment persists with impunity.

Azerbaijan's international partners failed to fully realize the potential of their relationships with the government to press for rights improvements.

Elections

International observers from the Organization for Security and Co-operation in Europe (OSCE) criticized the presidential election for failing to meet international standards. It assessed counting in 58 percent of polling stations observed as bad or very bad. It also said arrests and intimidation of opposition political activists, a restrictive media environment, and violations of the freedoms of assembly and association marred the pre-election campaign. International observers from the Council of Europe Parliamentary Assembly and the European Parliament were less critical.

Politically Motivated Prosecutions

In 2013, the authorities used a range of spurious charges—including narcotics and weapons possession, hooliganism, incitement, and even treason—to imprison political activists critical of the government. These activists included several high-ranking opposition political party members such as Ilgar Mammadov, chair of the opposition group REAL, arrested on February 4 and charged with inciting violence; Tofig Yagublu, Musavat party deputy chair, also arrested in February on similar charges; Yadigar Sadigov, an advisor to Musavat,

HUMAN
RIGHTS
WATCH

TIGHTENING THE SCREWS
Azerbaijan's Crackdown on Civil Society and Dissent

arrested in June on hooliganism charges for allegedly beating up a Nagorno-Karabakh war veteran; and Ilkin Rustemzade, a Free Youth activist, arrested in May on hooliganism charges for alleged involvement in filming a comedy video but later charged with inciting violence.

Seven members of the youth opposition movement NIDA were arrested in March and April on drugs and other charges related to an alleged plan to instigate violence at a peaceful protest. At time of writing their trials were ongoing.

In November, courts sentenced Rashad Ramazanov, a well-known blogger and government critic, and Taleh Bagirov, a religious scholar and activist who sharply criticized the government, to seven and nine years, respectively, on bogus drug possession charges.

Dashgin Malikov, a Popular Front Party activist, was arrested in March shortly after he criticized the government on social media and sentenced in July to two-and-a-half years' imprisonment on drug charges.

In two separate incidents in March and May, security personnel detained, blind-folded, handcuffed, and mistreated Ibrahim Ibrahimli, a leader of an opposition alliance, and Rahim Gaziyev, a former defense minister who had publicly criticized President Aliyev. Both were released after several hours.

Freedom of Media

In May 2013, the parliament amended a law expanding the definition of slander and insult to specifically include content published on the Internet.

At least five journalists were arrested or convicted in 2013 on spurious charges in apparent retaliation for critical and investigative journalism. In March, Avaz Zeynalli, editor-in-chief of the opposition newspaper *Khural*, was sentenced to nine years' imprisonment upon conviction for dubious extortion and tax evasion charges. In April, Araz Guliyev, editor-in-chief of the news site *Xeber44.com*, was convicted on charges of possessing illegal weapons and organizing public order disturbances and sentenced to eight years' imprisonment.

In November, Sardar Alibeyli, editor of the pro-opposition newspaper *Nota Bene* and the *PS Nota* news portal, was convicted on spurious hooliganism charges and sentenced to four years in prison.

In September, a court sentenced Hilal Mamadov, editor-in-chief of the *Tolishi Sado* newspaper, arrested in 2012, to five years' imprisonment for illegal drugs possession, treason, and other charges. Also in September, police arrested Parviz Hashimli, editor of the news website *Moderator* and a reporter for the opposition daily *Bizim Yol*. At time of writing, he was awaiting trial on charges of smuggling and illegal weapons possession.

In March, the executive director and editor-in-chief of Khayal TV, a local station, was convicted on several charges, including participating in social unrest, and sentenced to three years' probation and released.

A smear campaign begun in 2012 against Khadija Ismayilova, a Radio Liberty journalist, continued throughout 2013 in apparent retaliation for her investigations into the business holdings of the president's family and close associates. Pro-government newspapers and sites published articles and videos personally attacking the journalist and her family. Yafez Hasanov, another Radio Liberty journalist, was the target of blackmail and threats by security services after he refused to stop investigating a 2012 suspicious death in custody.

In February, a government smear campaign targeted Akram Aylisli, a well-known writer, after he published a novel containing critical analysis of Azerbaijan's modern history and treatment of Armenians. President Aliyev stripped Aylisli of his government stipend and honorary title of "Peoples' Writer"; his wife and son were also fired from their jobs.

In November, major opposition daily *Azadlig* temporarily ceased publishing due to financial constraints after mounting defamation claims brought by officials, frozen bank accounts, and government-imposed restrictions on distribution.

Freedom of Assembly

The authorities broke up several peaceful protests, at times violently, and arrested protesters. In November 2012 and May 2013, parliament amended laws increasing by more than hundredfold the fines for involvement in unauthorized protests and increasing from 15 to 60 days the maximum jail sentence for minor public order offenses often used to incarcerate protesters.

On January 26, police rounded up more than 60 people at an unsanctioned, peaceful rally in central Baku, using excessive force during the arrests. Courts sentenced 5 people to up to 15 days of administrative detention and fined 20 people up to 2,500 manat (US$3,200) for resisting police and participating in an unsanctioned protest.

On March 10, police used water cannons and teargas to disperse another peaceful gathering in central Baku. Police arrested dozens and courts convicted over twenty on misdemeanor charges, sentencing five to up to seven days' detention and fining others up to 600 manat (US$760).

Freedom of Association

In February 2013, parliament adopted legislative amendments making it impossible for unregistered groups to legally receive grants and donations, a measure that will jeopardize groups that the government refuses to register, often because they engage in work that is controversial or critical of the authorities. Other amendments increased by five-fold fines for nongovernmental organizations that receive funding from a donor without first concluding a grant agreement and registering it with the Ministry of Justice.

The government continues to refuse to register the Human Rights Club, an advocacy group that first filed its registration papers in 2011.

Torture and Ill-Treatment

Torture and ill-treatment continue with impunity. In the first nine months of 2013, the Azerbaijan Committee Against Torture, an independent prison monitoring group, received 96 complaints alleging ill-treatment in custody.

The authorities did not effectively investigate credible allegations of beatings, threats, and other abuses in custody made by several arrested political activists. In March 2013, NIDA activist Mahammad Azizov told his lawyer that after he retracted a confession made under duress, Ministry of National Security officials punched him and beat him with clubs. As a result he could not walk for four days and lost hearing in his left ear.

In May, Rashad Ramazanov told his lawyer that he was beaten in a police car on the day of his arrest and during the first three days of questioning.

Forced Evictions and Illegal Demolitions

In 2013, the authorities continued urban renewal in Baku, involving expropria-tion of many properties—primarily apartments and homes in middle class neighborhoods. Some homeowners continued to face forced eviction in the lead-up to May 2013 opening of central Baku's Winter Garden, a complex with parks and shops. Hundreds more have been forcibly evicted in previous years to make way for parks, roads, a shopping center, and luxury residential buildings. Most evictees have not received fair compensation based on market values of their properties.

Human Rights Defenders

In February 2013, a court convicted Bakhtiyar Mammadov, a human rights lawyer, on apparently politically motivated charges of large-scale extortion and sentenced him to eight years in prison. Mammadov represented several resi-dents who were forcibly evicted from their homes in Baku in 2012.

In May, police briefly detained, slapped, and threatened human rights lawyer Aslan Ismayilov after he publicly claimed that Rashad Ramazanov had been beaten in custody. In September a court stripped Ismayilov of his bar member-ship.

Key International Actors

The European Union, United States, and other international and regional actors and institutions expressed concern about the deterioration in Azerbaijan's human rights record but did not impose any consequences for it.

In its January 2013 resolution, the Parliamentary Assembly of the Council of Europe (PACE) expressed concern about "the alleged use of fabricated charges against activists and journalists" and called on Azerbaijan to, among other things, release prisoners "whose detention gives rise to justified doubts and legitimate concerns." The PACE voted down a parallel resolution dedicated exclusively to the issue of political prisoners in Azerbaijan.

In his July 2013 report, Nils Muižnieks, the Council of Europe's commissioner for human rights, expressed serious concern about "the apparent intensification of

... unjustified or selective criminal prosecution of journalists and others who express critical opinions." Other criticism included restrictions on freedom of expression, assembly, association, and property rights.

In February 2013, EU High Representative Catherine Ashton and Commissioner Štefan Füle jointly urged the authorities to "ensure speedy, fair, transparent, and independent investigation of the charges" against Ilgar Mammadov and Tofig Yagublu. In June, they expressed disappointment regarding legislation expanding the definition of criminal libel.

In its March European Neighborhood Policy progress report, the EU noted that Azerbaijan "addressed only a few of the key recommendations" contained in last year's report and highlighted serious, ongoing human rights violations related to freedom of expression, association, and assembly.

In April, Azerbaijan underwent the second cycle of the Universal Periodic Review at the United Nations Human Rights Council. The government announced an open invitation to UN human rights experts and accepted all critical recommendations regarding, inter alia, freedom of expression, assembly, and association but continued to deny allegations of rights violations.

OSCE Special Representative on Freedom of the Media Dunja Mijatovic criticized the Azerbaijani authorities' failure to respect freedom of expression, including the expansion of criminal libel laws and Avaz Zeynalli's nine-year prison sentence. In July, Azerbaijan successfully pushed to downgrade the OSCE's presence in Baku from a full-fledged mission to a project coordinator. At time of writing, the OSCE's new mandate was not made public.

In its annual human rights report published in April, the US Department of State flagged a concern about restrictions on freedom of expression and assembly and politically motivated imprisonment. The US embassy issued several statements of concern on related issues during 2013.

Belarus

The human rights situation in Belarus saw little improvement in 2013. The state suppresses virtually all forms of dissent and uses restrictive legislation and abusive practices to impede freedoms of association and assembly. Journalists are routinely harassed and subjected to arbitrary arrests and detention. Eight political prisoners remain jailed. Those who have been released continue to face restrictions, ranging from travel limitations to inclusion in law enforcement agencies' 'watch lists'. Civil society groups cannot function freely. Belarusian courts sentenced two more people to death during 2013.

Media Freedom, Attacks on Journalists

Most media are state-controlled, and authorities harass the few independent journalists and outlets that remain. In 2013, police arrested 25 journalists as they covered public protests. Courts sentenced at least four to short-term detention following convictions on misdemeanor charges. The authorities frequently prohibit reporting on public marches and open court hearings.

In March, the authorities once again denied registration to *Belsat*, the Poland-based satellite television channel known for its critical reporting on Belarus. Law enforcement officials warned Belarusian journalists reporting for *Belsat* that they would face misdemeanor charges if they continue working for an unregistered foreign media outlet.

In May, the prosecutor's office issued a warning to Radio Liberty journalist Aleh Hruzdzilovich following him publishing a book about the 2011 explosion in the Minsk metro. The warning noted Hruzdzilovich's doubt regarding the official investigation's results, which led to two people being charged with committing a terrorist attack, sentenced to death, and executed in 2012. The Prosecutor's Office warned Hruzdzilovich he could be stripped of his journalistic accreditation if he continued to spread "false information."

In April, a court designated as "extremist" the 2012 Belarus Press Photo Contest photo album, following a complaint filed by a regional department of the state security service (KGB), and ordered that its entire print-run be destroyed. The album's images included news and art-related topics, and included photos depicting police violence against protesters. The KGB complaint claimed that the album contained "intentionally distorted" facts about Belarus and undermined the country's "national honor and dignity." In November 2012, Belarusian customs officials at the Lithuanian-Belarusian border confiscated the album's entire print-run.

In two positive developments, the authorities in June allowed a visit to Belarus by the Organization for Security and Co-operation in Europe's (OSCE) Representative on Freedom of the Media, and in May 2013 registered *Arche-Pachatak*, an independent monthly that had been denied registration four times in previous years. In March, *Arche-Pachatak*'s bank account was reactivated, after being frozen in October 2012 due to a criminal investigation into its finances, which revealed no violations.

In June, the KGB dropped criminal charges against blogger Anton Surapin, who had been charged in 2012 with complicity in illegal border crossing after posting in his blog photographs of a cross-border freedom of speech protest.

In March, the authorities dropped a criminal investigation against Andrey Pochobut, the *Belsat* journalist accused of libel by President Aliaxander Lukashenka. In July, a court lifted all restrictions imposed on *Novaya Gazeta* journalist Iryna Khalip in connection with the two-year suspended sentence she received in 2011 for "rioting"; the court confirmed the restrictions did not require renewal. Khalip's sentence appears to have been retaliation for her critical reporting on the December 2010 protests in Minsk.

Freedom of Association

Belarusian legislation provides for a wide range of grounds to deny registration to nongovernmental organizations (NGOs) and establishes a maximum two-year prison sentence for involvement in an unregistered group. The authorities rigorously enforce this legislation and burdensome NGO reporting requirements, and also conduct sudden NGO inspections. These actions force civil society groups to function on the margins of the law. Unregistered groups are not able to rent office space officially and are frequently raided by the state security services.

In 2013, the authorities issued warnings to at least three activists for involvement in unregistered groups. In June, the authorities pressed unfounded criminal charges against Aliaksei Shchadrou, a devout Catholic, for allegedly establishing an unregistered religious organization by opening a shelter with a prayer room for homeless people in his house. Police raided Shchadrou's house twice, in February and April. During the February raid, the police confiscated his religious books. In September, the criminal case against Shchadrou was dropped.

In July, parliament adopted amendments to laws regulating political parties and public associations, but failed to loosen draconian regulations for NGOs. Parliament refused to hold hearings on a proposal by 25 Belarusian NGOs to improve legislation governing NGOs, including by simplifying the registration procedure.

Freedom of Assembly

Authorities showed little tolerance in 2013 for peaceful gatherings: most were prohibited and some marred by excessive police force.

Throughout 2013, dozens of peaceful protesters were convicted on misdemeanor charges and sentenced, some repeatedly, to short-term detention. In April, police held four environmental activists in "preventative" custody to stop them from attending a march in Minsk to commemorate the 1986 Chernobyl nuclear disaster. Police severely beat a protester at the march, which was peaceful, and detained four journalists who covered it.

In August, police detained two members of the Viasna Human Rights Center while handing out postcards in support of the group's imprisoned leader Ales Bialiatski. A court fined each 3 million Belarusian rubles (approximately US$350) for violating regulations on organizing public events.

Harassment of Civil Society Groups

In October 2012, the Economic Court of Minsk ruled to dissolve *Platforma*, a prison monitoring group, for alleged tax violations. In November, the appeals court upheld the ruling in absentia, ignoring the group's request for its representatives to be present for the hearing.

In March, Taxation Ministry officials attempted to seize the property of the Belarusian Helsinki Committee (BHC), the oldest human rights organization in Belarus, for the group's alleged failure to pay taxes on foreign grants it received in 2002 and 2003. In previous years, the authorities attempted to dissolve the BHC for alleged tax violations and issued warnings against the group for violating NGO legislation, apparently in retaliation for its human rights work.

In February, following the second, unsuccessful attempt by Gay Belarus—the lesbian, gay, bisexual, and transgender rights group—to register, the authorities launched an anti-LGBT campaign. Police raided gay clubs in various Belarusian cities, and law enforcement authorities questioned at least 60 group members.

Imprisonment of Critics and Opposition Members

At time of writing, 11 political prisoners remain behind bars, including Ales Bialiatski, the head of Viasna Human Rights Center, who has been in jail since 2011 on politically motivated charges of tax evasion. They have limited access to lawyers and face arbitrary reprimands (administrative punishment) and ill-treatment.

Among those arrested in 2013 was Andrei Haidukou, a political opposition activist and leader of the unregistered Union of Young Intellectuals. In July, a court convicted him on charges of attempted cooperation with foreign intelligence services, which may be linked to him seeking a grant from the United States government to support his work. The court sentenced him to one-and-a-half years' imprisonment.

Former political prisoners who have been pardoned or released early remain on police "watch lists," which give police grounds to frequently question them. None have had their civil and political rights fully restored: they are prohibited from running for or occupying public office and must obey restrictions that limit their ability to engage in activism, including a curfew; bans on involvement in demonstrations; and a requirement to inform the authorities about any changes to their places of residence—all misdemeanor offenses. Committing three misdemeanor offences in one year may result in another criminal sentence.

Death Penalty

Belarus remains the only country in Europe and Central Asia that uses capital punishment. In 2013, Belarusian courts sentenced three people to death. In

October, the Supreme Court of Belarus annulled one of these, regarding a murder case, and ruled that the case be re-investigated.

Those condemned to death in Belarus are refused the opportunity to bid farewell to their relatives, families are not informed of the date of execution in advance, and the burial place is not disclosed.

At time of writing, no one had been executed during 2013.

Key International Actors

Throughout the year, Belarus continued to demonstrate little interest in changing its international pariah status. In the lead up to the November 2013 Eastern Partnership Summit, the European Union demonstrated willingness to engage in dialogue with the Belarusian government by suspending a visa ban against the foreign minister, enabling him to travel to Brussels in July for the first high-level visit of a Belarusian official to EU headquarters since the 2010 government crackdown.

A European Parliament recommendation to EU institutions on EU policy towards Belarus, adopted in September, suggested to use the important opportunity presented by the November summit to gradually improve EU-Belarus relations. Progress on visa facilitation and readmission agreements, however, remained stalled over Belarus' failure to release political prisoners and make steps towards improving the human rights situation. Stefan Fule, European commissioner for enlargement and neighborhood policy, noted in September that use of death penalty, political prisoners, and harassment of civil activists meant that Belarus "had little progress to report."

In his first and highly critical report on Belarus published in May, United Nations Special Rapporteur on Belarus Miklos Haraszti called human rights restrictions in the country "systemic and systematic." In June, the UN Human Rights Council voted to extend the special rapporteur's mandate, which Belarusian authorities refused to recognize, denying Haraszti a visa.

In June, the OSCE representative on freedom of the media urged Belarusian authorities to address the problems of the country's restrictive media legislation.

Bosnia and Herzegovina

Political deadlock in Bosnia and Herzegovina (BiH) continued to impede necessary human rights reform in 2013. The government failed to meet a European
Union deadline to end discriminatory restrictions on Jews and Roma running for
political office. Roma remain the most vulnerable group in the country, subject
to widespread discrimination. The number of returns of refugees and internally
displaced persons (IDPs) decreased due to concerns about conditions in pre-
war communities.

Ethnic and Religious Discrimination

The authorities failed to implement a 2009 European Court of Human Rights
(ECtHR) ruling requiring BiH to amend its constitution to eliminate ethnic discrimination, including in the national tri-partite presidency and House of
Peoples, both currently restricted to the three main ethnic groups (Bosniaks,
Serbs, and Croats). An October agreement between political leaders of BiH
failed to specify how the ruling will be implemented. The EU announced that it
will not accept the results of general elections in 2014 unless the constitution is
amended.

In October, BiH conducted its first census since 1991, after delays due to concerns over the questionnaire and technical unpreparedness voiced by the
International Monitoring Operation (IMO) established by the EU and the Council
of Europe (CoE). The census went ahead amid criticism by civil society groups
including regarding improper storage of completed questionnaires. In an
October report, the IMO concluded that despite some problems the census was
conducted in accordance with international standards.

Roma, the most vulnerable minority group, continue to face widespread discrimination, high unemployment, low levels of school enrollment, political representation, and standards of living. Many Roma are not on the national public registry, impeding their access to public services, including health care. The practice of placing Roma children in Mostar, a city in the federation, in special
schools instead of mainstream schools continued. Many Roma, particularly
refugees and IDPs, including from Kosovo, continue to live in informal
settlements.

Refugees and Internally Displaced Persons

Implementation of a 2010 strategy to support the return of refugees and IDPs to their pre-war homes remained slow. Although a housing project to promote return to pre-war communities was launched in April, the number of returns declined, with only 104 refugees and 96 IDPs returning to their areas of origin in the first half of 2013, according to the United Nations High Commissioner for Refugees (UNHCR). As of October 2013, there were still 103,353 registered IDPs. Impediments to returns remain lack of economic opportunity, political instability, and reluctance to return to areas where other ethnic groups constitute the majority.

Additionally, excessive compensation awards to temporary occupants negatively affected displaced people wanting to return to pre-war homes. In several cases, returnees lost their property in compulsory auctions to satisfy compensation claims, prompting repeated criticism from the Office of the High Representative (OHR).

War Crimes Accountability

In February the new chief state prosecutor publicly committed to expedite some 600 pending war crime investigations and prepare for an increased caseload once the mandate of the International Criminal Tribunal for the former Yugoslavia (ICTY) expires at the end of 2014. Implementation of the national war crimes strategy is hindered by insufficient capacity and funding, particularly at the local level. In March the Organization for Security and Co-operation in Europe (OSCE) launched a judicial capacity program that includes district and cantonal courts. By November 2013 the War Crimes Chamber of the State Court of BiH had reached verdicts in 25 cases, raising the number of completed cases to 199.

The State Prosecutor's Office signed a cooperation agreement on the prosecution of war crimes, crimes against humanity, and genocide with its counterparts in Serbia and Croatia.

In February, the ICTY Appeals Chamber acquitted Momcilo Perisic, wartime chief of the General Staff of the Yugoslav Army, who had been convicted to 27 years in prison for aiding and abetting crimes against humanity and violations of the laws or customs of war. The Appeals Chamber found that the criterion of specific direction was not proven beyond reasonable doubt.

The ICTY trial of Bosnian Serb wartime General Radko Mladic, charged with genocide, war crimes, and crimes against humanity—including the murder of 7,000 men and boys from Srebrenica in July 1995—continued, subject to repeated interruptions due to Mladic's ill-health.

In the case of Bosnian Serb wartime president Radovan Karadzic, on trial at the ICTY for many of the same crimes as Mladic, a charge of genocide in seven Bosnian municipalities was reinstated in July by the Appeals Chamber of the ICTY, after being dropped in 2012 on the grounds of insufficient evidence. On September 3 Karadzic sought to have the decision overturned.

Also in July, the ECtHR ruled that the application of the 2003 criminal code in two war crimes cases at the BiH State Court violated the right to protection from retroactive criminal law under article 7 of the ECHR. In response, in October and November the State Court ordered the retrial of 12 convicted war criminals, including six involved in the Srebrenica massacre, and their release from custody pending retrial.

National Security and Human Rights

BiH continued to subject foreign nationals to indefinite detention on national security grounds. BiH failed to implement a 2012 ECtHR ruling halting the deportation to Syria of Imad Al Husin, a naturalized Bosnian in indefinite detention since 2008 on suspicion of terrorism, and ordering BiH to charge him, find a safe third country to resettle him, or release him. He remains in indefinite detention. Zeyad Khalad Al Gertani, another foreign national security suspect from Iraq, also remains in detention without trial at time of writing.

In November, after a retrial, Mevlid Jasarevic was convicted of an act of terrorism for firing on the United States embassy in Sarajevo in 2011, injuring one policeman, and sentenced to 15 years in prison. The appeals court annulled the previous verdict of 18 years in prison due to violations of the right to defense and fair trial.

Civil Society and Media

Numerous threats and acts of intimidation by political and religious authorities impeded investigative journalism. The national journalists' association recorded 44 violations of freedom of expression in as of November, including 3 physical assaults.

In April, the OSCE representative on freedom of the media voiced concern over threats against journalists Predrag Lucic on online forums and Nebojsa Vukanovic by a religious leader and the overall hostile atmosphere for journalists.

A broad civil society association, the Coalition for Combating Against Hate Speech and Hate Crime, formed in January. The coalition pushed to amend the federation's criminal code to include gender identity and sexual orientation as grounds for hate crimes. The House of Peoples rejected the amendment in September.

Sarajevo Open Centre—a lesbian, gay, bisexual, and transgender (LGBT) rights organization—facilitated an EU-supported training for police officers in September. The center documented 16 hate crimes and 18 cases of hate speech against LGBT people in 2013.

Political Gridlock

Repeated threats of secession by the authorities of Republika Srpska prompted criticism by the OHR for undermining state integrity.

Political quarrels hindered the adoption of new legislation on Single Reference Numbers, an identification number usually issued at birth that allows access to state services and documents, drawing criticism from the EU, the OSCE, and the OHR. The constitutional court rejected the previous law in February due to discrepancies of names of some municipalities. New legislation was adopted in November.

Mass protests outside the BiH parliament erupted in June when an infant requiring urgent medical treatment abroad could not travel without an ID number. Temporary measures have been enacted to issue numbers, but a permanent solution is still needed.

Protest continued throughout July, expressing generalized dissatisfaction with political gridlock and stalled progress. On several occasions police arbitrarily detained peaceful protestors for interrogation.

Key International Actors

Continued political stalemate and failure to implement the 2009 ECtHR ruling drew repeated criticism from EU, US, and CoE officials. EU foreign ministers in July strongly criticized lack of implementation and other impediments for the country's move toward the EU and urged the government to bring the country's constitution into compliance with the European Convention on Human Rights. After the third high-level meeting between the authorities of BiH and the EU in October, Commissioner for Enlargement Stefan Füle voiced regret about the lack of agreement and political will on the part of the authorities to solve the issue.

US Deputy Assistant Secretary for European and Eurasian Affairs Philip Reeker said in a May speech that constitutional reform is possible and had been within reach in March, although it was thwarted at the last minute.

A September resolution by the CoE Parliamentary Assembly threatened sanctions unless BiH implements the ruling and complies with other outstanding obligations as a CoE member by the October 2014 presidential elections.

In June, the UN Human Rights Committee found several violations of the International Covenant on Civil and Political Rights in the case of five individuals who were tortured and then forcibly disappeared in 1992, marking the first time BiH has been held accountable for forced disappearances during the war.

On July 23, BiH ratified the Istanbul Convention of the CoE on preventing and combating violence against women and domestic violence.

In September, the Dutch Supreme Court found the Netherlands responsible for the death of three Bosnian Muslims during Srebrenica because Dutch peacekeepers had sent the men away from the UN compound. The decision was the first to hold a government liable for events occurring under a UN mandate, highlighting that principles of accountability also apply to peacekeeping missions.

In a September report, the CoE Committee for the Prevention of Torture and Inhuman or Degrading Treatment or Punishment confirmed allegations of ill-treatment in police custody, particularly in Banja Luka, and recommended an independent assessment, training of the police, and other safeguards.

The EU delegation strongly condemned attacks on journalists in BiH after a September arson attack on the investigative weekly *Slobodna Bosna*.

In October, the US embassy, OHR, and EU mission in BiH criticized proposed legislative amendments in the Republika Srpska National Assembly that could undermine the editorial independence of the entity's broadcast media.

The European Commission's annual progress report, published in October, highlighted among the main outstanding issues the need for constitutional changes and to combat discrimination, including against Roma and LGBT people.

In his November report to the UN Security Council, High Representative for Bosnia and Herzegovina Valentin Inzko raised concerns over political instability and challenges to the rule of law.

European Union

Amid economic crisis and much contested austerity measures in many member states, discrimination, racism, and homophobia remained serious problems in European Union member states. Roma, migrants, and asylum seekers are particularly marginalized.

The Council of the European Union acknowledged for the first time that more is needed to ensure human rights violations within EU borders are adequately addressed, with an ongoing policy debate focused on improving responses to rule of law crises. Meanwhile, abusive practices around the EU continued without adequate action by EU institutions and member states.

EU Migration and Asylum Policy

The EU took final steps toward the creation of a Common European Asylum System with the adoption by the European Parliament (EP) in June of an asylum package, including recast versions of the Dublin regulation, the Asylum Procedures Directive, and the Reception Conditions Directive. While the package contains certain improvements, it provides broad grounds for detention of asylum seekers, does not obligate member states to provide free legal assistance at first instance, and fails to exempt especially vulnerable asylum seekers, including torture survivors and unaccompanied children, from accelerated procedures.

The Dublin III regulation, in force as of July, leaves intact the general rule that the first EU country of entry is responsible for asylum claims while improving safeguards, including the right to information, a personal interview, and an appeal against a transfer decision. States must now assess the risk of inhuman or degrading treatment before transfer to another EU country. The European Union Court of Justice (CJEU) ruled in June that member states must examine asylum claims by unaccompanied children present in their territory even if they have previously applied elsewhere.

In November, the CJEU ruled that sexual orientation is grounds for seeking asylum in the EU if the applicant comes from a country where laws criminalizing same-sex activity are enforced, and that no one should be expected to conceal his or her sexual orientation.

EU member states adopted widely divergent approaches to Syrian asylum seekers. For example Sweden said it would grant permanent residence to Syrians to whom it previously granted temporary protection, whereas Greece tried to return them to Turkey. Germany and Austria pledged to resettle 5,000 and 500 Syrian refugees respectively, but few other EU countries made more than token resettlement offers.

In June, the European Commission (EC) and the EU high representative for foreign affairs jointly called for a comprehensive approach to the Syrian crisis, focusing on humanitarian assistance for refugees in neighboring countries, while acknowledging the need for greater convergence in member states' approach.

Boat migration to Europe increased, with over 35,000 migrants and asylum seekers arriving by the end of October. An estimated 500 people had died at sea by mid-October, including over 360 in a single boat tragedy in October. In July, the European Court of Human Rights (ECtHR) blocked Malta's proposed summary return to Libya of a group of Somalis.

At time of writing, negotiations continued on proposed new regulations for the EU Border Agency (Frontex). The EC Proposal would clarify Frontex's role in search and rescue operations at sea, as well as matters relating to disembarkation, but would also allow for returns to third countries of those intercepted on the high seas following a cursory assessment of protection needs and the situation in the country of return. The then- European ombudsman concluded his inquiry into Frontex in April with recommendations to Frontex to clarify the legal framework for its operations as well as the agency's responsibilities for rights violations.

In September, the EP called for strategic guidelines to better protect unaccompanied migrant children beyond the EC's Action Plan, and Council of Europe (CoE) Commissioner for Human Rights Nils Muižnieks reminded states of the primacy of the best interests of the child in implementation of migration policies.

UN Special Rapporteur on Migrants Rights François Crépeau criticized the EU's securitized approach to migration, with its focus on strengthening external borders, detention, and removals. In his April report, Crépeau recommended increased safeguards, including ensuring alternatives to detention and human rights provisions in migration cooperation agreements with non-EU countries, and called on the EC to initiate infringement procedures against EU countries for violating migrants' rights.

Discrimination and Intolerance

Xenophobic sentiment and violence sparked concern among EU institutions and the CoE. In March, an EP resolution called for adequate recording, investigation, and prosecution of hate crimes, as well as assistance, protection, and compensation for victims. In June, the council of the EU called for more efforts to counter extreme forms of intolerance, such as racism, anti-Semitism, xenophobia, and homophobia. In May, CoE Commissioner Muižnieks called for systematic, continuous training for police, prosecutors, and judges, and effective measures to address bias within law enforcement agencies.

Repeated racial slurs against a black minister in Italy prompted seventeen EU ministers to sign a declaration in September condemning intolerance and extremism.

Politicians in the UK and the authorities in Catalonia, Spain, proposed banning the full-face Muslim veil, and voters in Ticino, Switzerland (not an EU country) approved a ban in a September referendum. In November, the ECtHR heard the case of a woman against the French ban on concealment of one's face in public on the grounds it allegedly violates her rights to private and family life and to freedom of religion and expression.

A Fundamental Rights Agency (FRA) survey published in May found that 47 percent of LGBT respondents reported experiencing discrimination or harassment in the previous twelve months, while 25 percent said they had been attacked or threatened with violence in the previous five years. A FRA survey reported in November that 21 percent of Jewish respondents had experienced anti-Semitic insults or harassment in the 12 months preceding the survey, while 2 percent reported a physical attack during the same period.

Roma experience discrimination and destitution across the EU. In June, the EC made recommendations to guide member states in effectively implementing their Roma integration strategies. In September, France's interior minister stated that most Roma have no wish to integrate, while news emerged that Swedish police kept unlawful Roma registries. In October, allegations that proved unfounded of blonde-haired, blue-eyed children being abducted by Roma families in Greece and Ireland prompted CoE Commissioner Muižnieks to warn against irresponsible reporting.

In February, Portugal became the first EU country to ratify the CoE Convention on preventing and combating violence against women and domestic violence, followed by Italy in September.

In November, the ECtHR found that the exclusion of same-sex couples from civil unions in Greece violated anti-discrimination norms and the right to private and family life.

Counterterrorism

In its first ruling on European complicity in CIA renditions, in December 2012 the ECtHR found Macedonia had violated the torture prohibition and German citizen Khaled el-Masri's rights to liberty and security, an effective remedy, and private and family life by illegally detaining him in 2003 and transferring him to US custody, and for the failure of Macedonian authorities to effectively investigate his allegations of ill-treatment.

The similar cases of Guantánamo detainees Abu Zubaydah, against Poland and Lithuania, and Abd al-Rahim al-Nashiri, against Poland and Romania, were pending before the ECtHR at time of writing. CoE Commissioner Muižnieks and the European Parliament in September and October respectively reiterated calls for accountability for European complicity and for US cooperation in investigations.

In September, the EP opened an inquiry into the impact of the US National Security Agency's surveillance program on EU citizens' privacy. The EP is expected to adopt conclusions and recommendations on the matter in January 2014.

EU Foreign Policy

Although there were some positive initiatives undertaken during the course of 2013, such as the establishment of the European Endowment for Democracy and two new sets of European Union (EU) guidelines on LGBTI rights and freedom of religion and belief, EU members states and institutions lacked the vitality and united efforts on human rights that existed in the run up to the adoption by EU foreign ministers of the EU Strategic Framework on Human Rights and Democracy in June 2012.

The EU's 28 member states and institutions have yet to utilize their combined leverage and unite behind a common message and approach to strategic partners such as Russia and China on human rights, despite calls from the European Parliament to do so. While the EU high representative did express some concerns in statements, a principled and collective EU response that would enable the EU's human rights concerns to be placed firmly at the highest levels of policy dialogues and public discussions with Russia and China was still missing.

The EU as a whole remained the largest humanitarian donor for the Syrian crisis. However, despite the EU's stated commitment to both the International Criminal Court (ICC) and to justice for serious crimes, the EU high representative failed to ensure strong collective EU voice and strategy that would advance the chances of bringing the crimes in Syria before the ICC. Twenty-seven EU member states—all but Sweden—joined a Swiss-led initiative calling on the United Nations Security Council to refer the situation in Syria to the ICC.

In reaction to the occupation of Northern Mali by Islamist armed groups, France took the lead in responding to the request for military assistance issued by the president of Mali by launching Operation Serval in January. Later in January, the EU established a mission to train and advise the Malian security forces, including a specific component on human rights and international humanitarian law.

The year 2013 marked a new era for EU-Burma relations. In April, the EU lifted all targeted sanctions on Burmese army and government individuals and entities, except its export ban on arms. A Comprehensive Framework for the EU's policy and support to Burma was subsequently endorsed by EU foreign ministers in July. Also in July, the European Parliament adopted a resolution condemning the "grave violations of human rights and the violence perpetrated against Rohingya Muslims in Burma/Myanmar." The EC allocated €14.5 million to Burma in humanitarian assistance in addition to € 5.5 million it allocated in December 2012. The priority for the humanitarian aid remained Rakhine and Kachin states and the eastern border areas. The EU continued to sponsor critical Burma resolutions in the UN's Human Rights Council and General Assembly.

In June, human rights appeared to have been left on the margins of the EU-Gulf Cooperation Council Ministerial meeting that took place in Bahrain. The EU high representative and EU member states failed to use their collective weight to actively and publically press for the immediate and unconditional release of imprisoned Bahraini activists, three of whom are dual nationals of Bahrain and EU member state, despite repeated calls from the EP and civil society to do so.

During the course of 2013, the EU appeared to lack any policy to secure improvements in countries with systematic rights repression such as Ethiopia, Uzbekistan, Turkmenistan, UAE, and Saudi Arabia.

The EU deployed different, sometimes inconsistent approaches to human rights concerns in Central Asia, the Caucasus, and non-EU states in Eastern Europe. In 2013, the EU suspended a long-standing visa ban against the Belarusian foreign minister, imposed in 2011, enabling him to travel to Brussels in July for the first high-level visit of a Belarusian official since 2010. At the same time, throughout the year the EU reiterated the need for Belarus to meet EU human rights benchmarks, including immediate release of political prisoners, as a condition for reopening dialogue.

Human Rights Concerns in Select EU Member States

Croatia

Croatia joined the EU in July amid continuing human rights concerns. The EC called in March for improving the efficiency of the judiciary, domestic war crimes prosecution, and protection of minorities.

Domestic and international war crimes prosecution continued. In January, a local court ordered the state to compensate the children of Serb victims for the attack on Varivode during "Operation Storm" in 1995.

Voluntary returns to Croatia increased, with 358 returns in the first five months compared to 132 in all of 2012. Reintegration of members of the Serb minority remains problematic, with continued discrimination and hostility in some regions of the country and obstacles in relation to the right to housing. In

November, the Vukovar city council halted the implementation of bilingualism after protests against Cyrillic street signs.

Roma, particularly stateless Roma, face difficulties accessing basic state services, including health care, social assistance, and education.

Few applied for asylum in Croatia—928 people by mid-October—with Syrians forming the third largest national group, yet reception centers are overcrowded, and there were reports of some asylum seekers being placed in closed detention facilities. Protection for unaccompanied children remains problematic, with poorly trained guardians usually far from centers where children are placed, often in unsuitable accommodation.

Voting rights for people with mental or intellectual disabilities were restored in December 2012. Proposals to lift full legal guardianship from thousands of people would still allow courts to vastly restrict legal capacity. Implementation of a 2011 deinstitutionalization plan for those with mental or intellectual disabilities progressed slowly, with two projects targeting around 400 individuals launched in May, while almost 9,000 remain institutionalized.

Following a December 2012 Supreme Court ruling, Turkish journalist Vicdan Özerdem was released immediately from detention and returned to Germany where she has political asylum. Özerdem was detained in mid-2012 for extradition to Turkey where she is wanted on terrorism charges, sparking widespread international criticism.

France

The European Roma Rights Centre and the Human Rights League reported that over 13,400 Roma were evicted from informal settlements between January and September, compared to 9,400 in all of 2012. In August, France's National Consultative Council for Human Rights called the mass distribution of removal orders to Roma "administrative harassment" and urged the government to halt evictions from slums and squats without offering adequate alternative housing and to respect EU free movement rules.

In October, the ECtHR ruled that France breached the right to private and family life of a group of French Travelers by ordering their eviction from land they had occupied for many years.

At its Universal Periodic Review in June, France accepted recommendations to end ethnic profiling, and announced amendments to the police and gendarmerie code of ethics. No further action was taken to stop discriminatory identity checks. In October, a Paris court ruled against plaintiffs alleging ethnic profiling, arguing anti-discrimination norms did not apply.

In May, the UN Committee on Enforced Disappearances expressed concern that the lack of a suspensive appeal in the fast-track asylum procedure creates a risk of return to enforced disappearance, and too frequent use of police custody in France.

Riots erupted in the Paris suburb of Trappes in July after police stopped a woman wearing a full-face veil. A 14-year-old lost an eye by what appeared to be a flashball fired by police. Rights groups reported a rise in attacks against Muslims, particularly women.

In April, the Defender of Rights raised concerns about an estimated 3,000 unaccompanied migrant children in the overseas French department of Mayotte, hundreds of whom are left to fend for themselves.

In July, the parliament abrogated the criminal offense of insulting the president of the republic following a March ECtHR ruling that it violated freedom of expression.

Parliament legalized same-sex marriage in April. SOS Homophobie, a non-profit association aimed at countering homophobic discrimination and violence, recorded testimonies of 3,200 homophobic incidents as of November, compared to 2,000 in all of 2012. In May, the government pledged to begin publishing statistics on homophobic violence in 2014.

In August, a new law introduced a crime of "reduction to slavery" into the penal code, also criminalizing forced labor, reduction to servitude and exploitation of people reduced to slavery.

In two separate cases, the ECtHR ruled in September and November that France's return of a failed Tamil asylum-seeker to Sri Lanka and of a Congolese national to the Democratic Republic of Congo would breach the torture prohibition.

Amid reports of mass data interception by US and British intelligence agencies, Prime Minister Ayrault denied allegations in a July *Le Monde* article that French intelligence services were systematically collecting data on communications in France. At time of writing, parliament was examining a bill to increase moderately oversight of intelligence agencies.

Germany

Asylum seekers and refugees launched protests and hunger strikes against conditions in reception centers and restrictions on freedom of movement and access to the labor market throughout 2013.

The trial of an alleged member of a neo-Nazi cell accused of murdering nine immigrants and a policewoman, and four alleged accomplices, began in May. A federal commission of inquiry made recommendations in August towards improving German police practices, including increased attention to hate crimes, more diversity among the police, and a greater emphasis on human rights in police training. Parliament rejected bills to enhance penalties for racially-motivated crimes as well as a bill to introduce hate crimes as a specific category.

In April, Baden-Württemberg issued a decree requiring individual risk assessments before returning Roma, Ashkali, and Egyptians to Kosovo, but deported 127 people in April and 90 to Serbia and Macedonia in July. At least three German states continued to forcibly return Roma, Ashkali, and Egyptians to Kosovo without adequate risk assessments and despite concerns about discrimination and inadequate integration measures upon return.

The German Institute for Human Rights reported in June that ethnic profiling is a common police practice, particularly in transportation hubs for immigration control purposes, and recommended legal and policy reforms.

The government denied allegations that German intelligence and police services profited from US mass surveillance technology and collaborated with US intelligence agencies despite leaked information suggesting the contrary.

In September, Germany ratified the ILO Domestic Workers Convention. In December 2012, the parliament adopted a bill clarifying that parents have the right to have their sons circumcised for religious reasons in accordance with certain medical standards.

Greece

Political uncertainty marked Greece's third year of economic crisis. In May, the UN independent expert on foreign debt and human rights warned that bailout conditions undermine human rights. The sudden closure of the national public broadcaster in June raised media freedom concerns, and resulted in a government reshuffle.

Despite the creation in January of anti-racism police units and some arrests, attacks on migrants and asylum seekers continued, with an NGO network recording 104 incidents by the end of August. Anti-LGBT attacks appeared to increase. The Greek ombudsman warned in September that racist violence and impunity for the perpetrators undermine social cohesion and rule of law. In November, the government tabled a bill to sanction hate speech and incitement to violence, failing to address problems in existing legislation and practice with respect to racist violence. Two people were convicted of racially aggravated crimes in November, the first known time the 2008 statute has been applied.

The fatal stabbing of an anti-fascist activist in Athens in September by an alleged member of Golden Dawn sparked a crackdown on the party and the arrest of the party leader and five parliamentarians on charges of managing a criminal organization. An internal police investigation found in October that 10 Greek police officers were linked to Golden Dawn.

In November, two Golden Dawn members were murdered outside a party's branch in Athens, and a third man was seriously injured. At time of writing, no arrests had been made.

In April, three Greek foremen were arrested after shooting at 100 to 200 Bangladeshi strawberry pickers demanding unpaid wages. The 35 injured were granted humanitarian visas while the foremen and the farm's owner were in pretrial detention at time of writing.

In July, the Joint United Nations Programme on HIV/AIDS expressed concern after the government reintroduced a health regulation used in the past to justify detention and forced HIV testing of alleged sex workers. A separate law allowing

439

police to detain foreigners based on overly broad public health grounds was still in force.

In October, the ECtHR held that the failure by the Greek Supreme Court to condemn a private company's dismissal of an employee, because he was HIV-positive, amounted to a violation of his right to protection from discrimination taken together with his right to a private life.

Increased security along the land border with Turkey rerouted flows of irregular migrants and asylum seekers, including Syrians, to Aegean Sea islands. Sea crossings were marked by at least ten deaths. UNHCR expressed concern over allegations of pushbacks to Turkey, including of people fleeing Syria.

The UN Working Group on Arbitrary Detention, the UN special rapporteur Crépeau, and CoE Commissioner Muižnieks criticized abusive stops and arbitrary detention during an ongoing police operation Xenios Zeus against irregular migrants, and noted substandard conditions of migrants and asylum seekers in often systematic and prolonged detention. The ECtHR condemned Greece over inhuman and degrading treatment in immigration detention in three separate cases. Detainees rioted at the Amgydaleza facility in August.

The new asylum service began processing applications in Athens in June, but access to asylum in the rest of the country, and in detention, remains difficult. Data published in 2013 show Greece had the lowest protection rate at first instance in the EU (0.9 percent in 2012).

In May, the ECtHR ruled for the third time since 2008 that school segregation of Roma pupils in Greece amounted to discrimination. CoE Commissioner Muižnieks expressed concern over persistent reports of ill-treatment of Roma by law enforcement agencies. In the first nine months of 2013, Greek police conducted 1,131 operations in Roma camps throughout the country, raising concerns about ethnic profiling.

In March, the UN Committee on the Elimination of Discrimination against Women (CEDAW) expressed concern over Greece's response to violence against women noting the lack of statistical data, and urged authorities to ensure that victims have access to immediate means of redress and protection, and that perpetrators are prosecuted and punished.

Hungary

Legal changes introduced by the government continued to threaten the rule of law and weaken human rights protections. Constitutional amendments in March further undermined judicial independence, stripped the Constitutional Court of significant powers, and introduced several legal provisions previously ruled unconstitutional.

Despite piecemeal changes to the media laws in March, the main media regulator, the Media Council, continues to lack political independence. Potential fines for journalists remain excessive, and requirements for content regulation are still unclear. In March, independent news station Klubradio was able to renew license after four favorable court rulings.

In response to international criticism, including a detailed opinion by the CoE Venice Commission and a damning EP report highlighting concerns about, inter alia, the independence of the judiciary, the legal status of churches, and political advertising, the government made cosmetic changes to the constitution in September that did not put an end to discrimination of religious groups and only partially addressed limitations on political advertising in private media.

Roma continue to face discrimination and harassment. The mayor of northern city Ozd shut off public water supplies to Roma settlements, affecting some 500 families. The ECtHR ruled in January that Hungary discriminated against two Roma pupils by enrolling them in special education and in July upheld a Hungarian court's ban of the Hungarian Guard, an anti-Roma and anti-Semitic group. In August, a Budapest court convicted four men of killing six Roma, including one child, in racist attacks in 2008 and 2009.

Anti-Semitism remains a problem. Police are investigating the April assault on the president of the Raoul Wallenberg Association after a soccer game where supporters chanted the Nazi slogan *sieg heil*.

In March, the UN CEDAW Committee urged Hungarian authorities to strengthen legal protections for domestic violence victims and increase space in shelters. A domestic violence offense introduced in July created stiffer penalties and widens public prosecution but excludes non-cohabiting partners without common children and is only triggered by repeated abuse. In September, the UN Committee on the Rights of People with Disabilities told Hungary to repeal a constitutional provision restricting voting rights for persons under legal guardianship and reinstate six such applicants to electoral lists.

In July, the government reinstated detention for asylum seekers on overly broad grounds. In October, the UN Working Group on Arbitrary Detention urged Hungary to take effective measures to prevent arbitrary detention of asylum seekers and irregular migrants. By the end of August, 15,069 people, including 588 Syrians, had applied for asylum, a significant increase from 1,195 applications during the same period last year.

In September, parliament adopted a law enabling local governments to criminalize homelessness, punishable by fines, community service, and even prison.

Italy

Over 35,000 people reached Italy by sea by October, a significant increase over the previous year; over one-fourth were Syrians. Reports emerged of Italy instructing commercial vessels to return rescued migrants to ports in Libya if closest, raising concerns about refoulement.

After several extensions, the North Africa emergency plan for receiving migrants that was initiated in 2011 during the Libyan conflict ended officially on March 31, and emergency shelters closed. Rejected asylum seekers were given the chance to reapply or receive a one-year permits to stay and 500 euros; many traveled elsewhere in Europe. In September the government announced an increase from 3,000 to 16,000 spaces in specialized reception centers for asylum seekers and refugees. In July, UNHCR, which welcomed the move, emphasized the need for a comprehensive reform of the reception system to improve vastly insufficient support measures for refugees.

In April, UN special rapporteur Crépeau criticized Italy's immigration detention system, including substandard conditions and inadequate access to justice. Detainees protested in several centers, including over the death of a Moroccan man in the Crotone center in August. Crépeau reiterated concerns about automatic summary returns to Greece, and inadequate safeguards in "quick return" agreements with Tunisia and Egypt. Crépeau and UNHCR called on Italy to introduce an effective age determination procedure to ensure that children enjoy appropriate protections.

HUMAN RIGHTS WATCH

TURNED AWAY

Summary Returns of Unaccompanied Migrant Children and Adult Asylum Seekers from Italy to Greece

Three UN experts expressed concern over the illegal deportation of the wife and daughter of Mukhtar Ablyazov, a critic of the Kazakhstan government, from Rome in May, saying it appeared to be "extraordinary rendition." Acknowledging improper involvement of Kazakh authorities, the government rescinded the deportation order in July, though mother and daughter remain in Kazakhstan under travel restrictions.

A European Committee for the Prevention of Torture (CPT) report in November criticized overcrowding in prisons and ill-treatment, particularly of foreigners, by police and Carabinieri.

The lower house of parliament approved a bill in September to extend hate crime protections to lesbians, gays, bisexuals, and transgender people (LGBT). LGBT organizations criticized an amendment to the bill, which must pass the Senate, exempting a range of organizations from criminal liability for hate speech.

In February, an appeals court sentenced three US citizens, including a former Rome CIA station chief, for their role in the 2003 abduction of an Egyptian cleric in Milan, overturning a lower court's finding of diplomatic immunity. Separately, the court found guilty five Italian intelligence officers whose involvement had been cloaked in state secrecy.

In January, Italy became the first EU country to ratify the ILO Convention on Decent Work for Domestic Workers. In October parliament converted into law an August government decree creating new measures against domestic violence and stalking including stiffer penalties in certain cases, and humanitarian visas for undocumented victims. UN expert Joy Ngozi Ezeilo called on the government in September to ensure a national approach to all forms of trafficking, including for labor as well as sexual exploitation.

The Netherlands

Concerns about immigration and asylum policy persist. In June, the UN Committee against Torture (CAT) expressed concerns about immigration detention beyond the legal 18-month limit of unaccompanied children asylum seekers and of families with children pending age determination, and conditions and treatment in detention. The committee recommended effective use of alternatives to detention. Detainees in Rotterdam and at Schiphol airport went on hunger strikes in May to protest their poor treatment.

At time of writing, parliament is examining a bill to make irregular stay a crime punishable by fines up to € 3,900 and prison up to six months for repeat offenders. The Ministry of Security and Justice set a police target of 4,000 arrests of irregular migrants during the year.

As of June, unaccompanied asylum-seeking children are processed under an accelerated procedure; those over the age of 16 whose asylum requests have been rejected may be returned immediately unless adequate care in their home country is unavailable or the child is unable to provide for him or herself. The Dutch children's rights ombudsman expressed concern that the procedure does not adequately take into account the best interests of the child.

The government acknowledged in April that almost 300 people were misclassified as "removable" despite pending asylum appeals, including a Russian who committed suicide in January while in detention pending deportation. In September, the government announced plans to reduce detention of asylum seekers.

In September, the government granted permanent residence to 620 children (and 690 family members) who had been living in the Netherlands for at least five years and had applied for asylum, less than half of those who applied for the program.

The Netherlands decided it could return failed Somali asylum seekers in late 2012, though court appeals halted deportations throughout 2013. In September, shortly after the ECtHR ruled (in a case involving Sweden) that improved security in the Somali capital allowed for returns, the government began returns. In November, a Somali man was injured in a blast in Mogadishu three days after his deportation from the Netherlands.

At time of writing, the Senate was examining a bill, already passed by the lower house in February, to eliminate the sex reassignment surgery requirement for transgender people wanting new identification documents.

Poland

The five-year investigation into secret CIA detention in Poland continued amid lack of transparency. In November, the UN Committee Against Torture urged Poland to complete the investigation within reasonable time. News emerged early in the year that charges, never officially confirmed, against Poland's former intelligence chief would be dropped. In October, the prosecutor general granted victim status in the case to a Yemeni national detained at Guantánamo Bay.

In January, an appeals court acquitted the editor of the *Antykomor.pl* website of charges of defaming the president. His conviction by a lower court in September 2012 prompted the Organization for Security and Co-operation in Europe to call for repeal of criminal defamation in Poland.

In February, the ECtHR found Poland in violation of the prohibition of inhuman and degrading treatment for detaining a paraplegic in a prison unsuitable for persons with disabilities.

At time of writing, Parliament was examining a bill to protect against discrimination on grounds of sexual orientation and gender identity, and broaden the legal definition of harassment.

The Senate was examining a bill to create a high-security facility for convicts who are deemed to pose a threat to the life, health or sexual freedom of others or to children. While safeguards are written into the bill, concerns remain that the measure could lead to indefinite detention of individuals who have already served out their sentences.

Romania

The European Commission concluded in January that the 2012 constitutional crisis had been averted following implementation of its recommendations, but pointed to continuing problems with the rule of law and judicial independence and stability, due in part to intimidation and harassment of judges.

Discrimination and forced evictions of Roma, on short notice and without alternative accommodation, persist. In August, authorities demolished 15 homes in the Craica Roma settlement in Baia Mare. At this writing, the remaining 15 families in the settlement face eviction. In September, local authorities in Eforie Sud evicted 100 Roma, including 60 children. Also in September, the secretary of state for minorities said that he would not send his child to a school with many Roma students, fueling negative stereotypes and rationalizing segregation in education.

Spain

UN special rapporteur on contemporary forms of racism, Mutuma Ruteere, raised concerns in January about the worsening of the situation of migrants including unemployment, restrictions on access to health care and de facto segregation of migrant neighborhoods, as well as anti-Roma sentiment. In October, CoE Commissioner Muižnieks raised concerns about the impact of budget cuts on vulnerable groups including children and persons with disabilities, and impunity for law enforcement officials for ill-treatment and torture.

Rejecting a bill promoted by civil society calling for mortgage debt cancellation, parliament adopted limited reforms to address the housing crisis in May. The law improves judicial review of mortgage contracts, following a March European Union Court of Justice ruling that existing law violated EU consumer protection rules, slightly broadens the moratorium on evictions, and includes measures to alleviate mortgage debt.

The national ombudsperson called on the police in May to introduce stop forms recording ethnicity, race and/or nationality and the reason for the identity check. In June the central government representative in Lleida, Catalonia, stated that police applied ethnic criteria when conducting immigration-related stops.

In October, a judge in Argentina exercised universal jurisdiction and requested extradition of two former Franco regime officials for torture. In November, the UN Committee on Enforced Disappearances urged Spain to investigate all enforced disappearances regardless of when they were committed, and concluded that incommunicado detention breaches the prohibition of secret detention under the UN Convention on Enforced Disappearance.

In February, Spain's Supreme Court annulled the Lleida, Catalonia, city ordinance banning full-face veils, saying it violated freedom of religion. The regional government announced its intention in July to prohibit face coverings in public on security grounds, while news emerged in August that Catalonia police were collecting data on women wearing the full-face veil.

The CPT expressed concerns in April about allegations of ill-treatment of incommunicado terrorism-suspects and of people in police custody, and prison conditions. The committee also criticized the "prison-like" atmosphere in immigration detention centers.

In October, the ECtHR upheld its 2012 ruling that retroactive lengthening of prison sentences, limiting eligibility for parole for people convicted of terrorism offenses, violated fair trial standards. By mid-November, 31 prisoners—24 of them ETA members—had been released in compliance with the ruling.

The Interior Ministry reported in September that almost 3,000 migrants attempted to enter the Spanish enclave of Melilla since January, almost double the number in the same period in 2012. Over three-quarters were prevented from entering, amid allegations that Spanish law enforcement officials summarily returned migrants to abuse at the hands of Moroccan police.

United Kingdom

Senior ministers regularly attacked the Human Rights Act and the ECtHR, and Home Secretary Teresa May stated that if re-elected in 2015 the Conservative party would scrap the Act and possibly withdraw from the European Convention on Human Rights.

Accountability for counterterrorism and overseas abuse suffered setbacks. An April law extended secret hearings on national security grounds in civil courts. The government did not establish a new inquiry into UK involvement in rendition and torture overseas, nor had it published any part of the aborted Gibson inquiry's interim report.

The UN Committee Against Torture (CAT) urged the UK in May to establish a comprehensive inquiry into allegations of torture and other ill-treatment during the UK's military intervention in Iraq between 2003 and 2009. The same month, the High Court said there had been no adequate inquiry into the deaths of Iraqis in British custody except in one case, and in a second ruling in October ordered public inquiries into alleged killings of Iraqis by British forces. A public judge-led inquiry investigating the alleged torture and execution of up to 20 Iraqis by

British soldiers in Iraq in 2004 began in March. In November, a military court convicted a UK marine of murdering an injured Afghan prisoner in September 2011 in Afghanistan.

Jordanian cleric Abu Qatada was deported in July to face terrorism charges in Jordan on the basis of a treaty guaranteeing the right to a fair trial, but concerns remained about the use of torture evidence.

Same-sex marriage became legal in July.

In November, the trial began of two men for the brutal murder in May of British soldier Lee Rigby in London. Attacks against Muslims and Islamic centers, including arson attacks, rose in the months following Rigby's murder. In London, the Metropolitan police recorded a 51 percent rise in anti-Muslim crime in the 12 months leading up to October 2013, compared to the previous year.

In July, the CEDAW Committee urged the UK to mitigate the impact of cuts to services to women, particularly women with disabilities and older women. In September, the UN special rapporteur on the right to housing, Raquel Rolnik, criticized the impact of austerity measures, noting also testimonies of discrimination in housing against Roma and Traveller communities, migrants, and asylum seekers.

Rights groups reported worsening abuse of migrant domestic workers since their right to change employers was removed in 2012.

In September, UN special rapporteurs on freedom of expression and on human rights and counterterrorism requested further information on the August detention of David Miranda, the partner of a *Guardian* newspaper journalist who wrote articles about US surveillance programs, for nine hours at Heathrow airport, the maximum time allowed under UK anti-terrorism law. The High Court heard Miranda's challenge to the legality of his detention in November. In October Prime Minister David Cameron specifically mentioned the *Guardian* when he warned that the government could take unspecified action against newspapers if they did not show "social responsibility" in reporting on mass surveillance.

In May, the UN CAT called for a "comprehensive framework for transitional justice" in Northern Ireland. An inter-party group in the Northern Ireland executive was expected to deliver recommendations on controversial issues by the end of the year.

In February, the High Court suspended returns of Tamils to Sri Lanka pending a review of an immigration tribunal's country guidance on Sri Lanka. The new guidance in July acknowledged torture, bribery, and availability of mental health treatment in Sri Lanka as relevant factors, but narrowed the group of people whose asylum claims are likely to succeed.

Georgia

The October 2013 presidential election completed a peaceful transition of power in Georgia after difficult cohabitation between Prime Minister Bidzina Ivanishvili and his political rival President Mikheil Saakashvili. Investigations into torture and ill-treatment in custody were slow and lacked transparency. Investigations into past abuses raised some concerns regarding selective justice and politically motivated prosecutions. Police did not adequately respond to several violent incidents against religious minorities and lesbian, gay, bisexual, and transgender (LGBT) people.

Georgia deepened its political and economic ties with the European Union through the Eastern Partnership process, which was closely tied to progress in governance and human rights.

Presidential Election

International observers, led by the Organization for Security and Co-operation in Europe, positively assessed the October 27 presidential election, highlighting respect for fundamental freedoms of expression, movement, and assembly. However, observers also noted allegations of political pressure, "including on United Nations Movement (UNM) representatives at local self-government institutions."

In July 2013 violent mobs attacked UNM campaign events in Zugdidi and Batumi. Police detained over a dozen assailants; courts convicted them on administrative charges, fined them, and released them.

Torture and Ill-Treatment, Prison Conditions

In June 2013, courts convicted 14 former prison officials implicated in beatings and torture in prison revealed in videos released in 2012. Six received prison terms ranging from three to six years; eight plea-bargained, receiving sentences ranging from six months to five years. However, the prosecutor general fully released from criminal responsibility Vladimer Bedukadze, who provided information about the torture in which he was also involved. Many local and international observers criticized the move.

In July, a court acquitted five former police officers who faced multiple charges, including ill-treatment and rape of a detainee, leading to an exchange of accusations between the Prosecutor's Office and the judiciary. The former claimed that it provided forensic examinations, victim and witness statements, and other evidence at trial, while the latter asserted that some evidence was contradictory and the prosecution failed to substantiate the charges.

In July, Mamuka Mikautadze, 36, was found hanged a day after police interrogated and then released him regarding drug possession. According to his wife, Mikautadze complained that police had beaten and forced him to sign false testimony incriminating his friend. Local rights groups alleged that police were slow to respond to Mikautadze's family's allegations. The investigation was ongoing at time of writing.

In January, parliament adopted a broad prison amnesty, leading to the release of over 8,000 inmates. This alleviated severe overcrowding, a chronic problem in Georgian prisons.

Investigations into Past Abuses

In response to over 20,000 complaints about alleged past abuses, the authorities charged 35 former officials from a variety of ministries with, inter alia, abuse of office, embezzlement, and false arrest; 14 of them were in custody at time of writing. The authorities did not explain the criteria they used to determine which cases of past abuses to investigate, and while investigating past abuses prosecutors questioned over 6,000 persons, mostly UNM party activists. Both factors caused the opposition to allege its activists were subject to politically motivated pressure.

Among those arrested was Vano Merabishvili, the UNM's secretary general and former interior minister, who faces charges including embezzlement and abuse of office for obstructing a high-profile murder investigation. Merabishvili's prosecution, ahead of the presidential election, raised concern among some observers that it was politically motivated.

On June 27, financial police briefly detained 23 Tbilisi municipal officials, including many UNM members. The authorities claimed they were interrogated as witnesses, but handcuffed the officials and provided neither prior notification to appear nor a court order required to forcefully bring witnesses before investigation. Four of the officials, including a deputy mayor, were later arrested in connection with an ongoing embezzlement investigation.

Right to Privacy

In September 2013, officials destroyed over 181 hours of secret video recordings of individuals' private lives, mostly of a sexual nature, obtained in recent years through illegal government surveillance. Opposition politicians, journalists, and civil society activists had been particular targets.

In May, a deputy interior minister leaked one of the videos involving a journalist who had been fiercely critical of senior officials. The deputy minister was dismissed and is awaiting trial on charges of illegal use or distribution of private information.

Other illegal, secret recordings have not been destroyed. In July, parliament adopted an amnesty bill exempting from criminal responsibility those who had been involved in illegal surveillance, and those who were in possession of such recordings but voluntarily handed them over by November 20.

The Interior Ministry maintains surveillance equipment on the premises of telecommunication operators, giving it automatic access to all communications without judicial oversight.

Freedom of Religion

Since November 2012, Orthodox Christian communities in several villages prevented, at times violently, Muslims from holding religious services in houses converted into mosques. Although the prime minister made several public statements condemning the violence, little action was taken to hold the offenders accountable.

In August 2013, local authorities in western Georgia forcefully removed a minaret from a mosque, leading to a clash between local Muslim residents and police. Officials claimed they wanted to inspect the minaret because it allegedly lacked the proper import license. Several days later, the authorities returned the minaret but did not reinstall it due to protests by the local Christian community.

In April three drunk military police officers verbally assaulted residents in a village in Adjara region—which has a significant Muslim population—arbitrarily stopping cars and searching people, calling them "Tatars" and demanding they show crosses around their necks. The Defense Ministry sacked the officers, and police arrested at least two of them.

Sexual Orientation and Gender Identity

On May 17, 2013, a peaceful gathering to mark International Day Against Homophobia was violently disrupted by thousands of counter-demonstrators, including some Orthodox clergy. The day before, the patriarch of the Georgian Orthodox Church publicly urged the authorities not to allow the gathering, calling it an "an insult" to Georgian traditions.

Police had to evacuate the LGBT activists to safety, but they failed to contain the mob, which attacked a van carrying the activists, throwing stones and other objects; one journalist was hit on the head and briefly hospitalized. Authorities charged two Orthodox priests and three other men with obstructing freedom of assembly and petty hooliganism. The Tbilisi City Court ordered that charges be dropped against one priest. At time of writing, the trials against the others were ongoing.

Identoba, a local LGBT rights group, reported 34 incidents of violence and intimidation against LGBT people during and after the May 17 incident. The group noted that many victims do not report homophobic violence due to fear of retribution and police failure to investigate adequately.

Freedom of Assembly

On February 8, hundreds of protesters gathered in front of the Tbilisi National Library, where President Mikheil Saakashvili planned to hold his annual State of the Nation address. The protesters verbally insulted and physically attacked several UNM members and the Tbilisi mayor. The public defender criticized police for failing to proactively ensure the safety of the UNM members, despite the fact that they had accurate information on the protesters' numbers, demands, and mood. A court convicted two protesters of petty hooliganism and released them after imposing a fine.

Freedom of Media

Georgia has a diverse print and broadcast media. In spring 2013 parliament approved a package of amendments to media laws, supported by a coalition of media organizations. The amendments envisage a more democratic composition of the board of Georgia Public Broadcaster (GPB), greater financial transparency of television companies, and a requirement that cable networks and satellite content providers broadcast all television stations that carry news. Previously, they were required to do so only for 60 days before elections.

Eka Kvesitadze and Davit Paichadze, the hosts of two GPB policy talk shows, alleged that the GPB's decision not to renew their contracts in September 2013 was politically motivated. Although the station director's written order attributed the non-renewal to the start of the new television season, he told one of the journalists it was because he "did not like their tone."

Key International Actors

The European Union closely engaged with the new Georgian government to monitor the rights record and urge much-needed reforms. It created and funded an expert position to advise the government on legal and constitutional and human rights, and appointed to the post former Council of Europe Commissioner for Human Rights Thomas Hammarberg.

In September—after regular visits to Georgia and extensive consultations with officials, the political opposition, and civil society—Hammarberg published a report with recommendations to the government to address religious intolerance, independence of the judiciary, prison conditions, ill-treatment and torture, illegal surveillance, minority rights, and other human rights issues.

In its March European Neighborhood Policy (ENP) progress report, the EU noted that Georgia "acted on most …. [of the ENP's] key recommendations," but also highlighted the need to ensure the independence of the judiciary, avoid selective justice, and increase accountability and democratic oversight of law enforcement agencies.

In its annual human rights report in April, the United States Department of State flagged concerns about shortfalls in the rule of law and lack of judicial independence, as well as restrictions on freedom of association and assembly.

The International Criminal Court prosecutor continued to monitor local investigations into crimes committed during the 2008 Georgia-Russian conflict over South Ossetia, while noting in a November 2012 report that these investigations had yet to yield any results.

Kazakhstan

Kazakhstan's poor human rights record continued to deteriorate in 2013, with authorities cracking down on free speech and dissent through misuse of overly broad laws. Authorities maintain strict controls on freedom of assembly and religion. Despite flawed trials, courts upheld the prison sentences of people convicted in the aftermath of violent clashes in December 2011 between police and people in the western oil town of Zhanaozen. Torture remains common in places of detention, even as authorities in July adopted a law on a National Preventive Mechanism on torture.

The government continues work on overhauling its criminal legislation, but based on a September draft of the criminal code, some amendments, if adopted, would further restrict freedom of speech, assembly, religion, and association.

Arrest and Detention of Government Critics

On December 7, 2012, civil society activist Vadim Kuramshin was sentenced to 12 years' imprisonment on extortion charges, despite a trial marred by procedural violations and concerns his detention was retribution for public criticism of the government.

On May 28, 2013, Kazakhstan's Supreme Court upheld labor activist Rosa Tuletaeva's conviction and five-year prison sentence (reduced from seven years by an earlier appeal) for organizing mass riots in connection with the Zhanaozen violence. Prosecutorial authorities have declined to investigate Tuletaeva's allegations of torture in detention.

On August 5, Kazakhstan's Supreme Court declined to review political opposition leader Vladimir Kozlov's seven-and-a-half-year prison sentence, despite procedural violations and the broad, vague charges, such as inciting social discord, used to convict him. As recently as mid-November, Kozlov's wife reported that Kozlov had not been receiving adequate and timely medical care in prison.

On August 9, Zinaida Mukhortova, a lawyer who in 2009 had alleged a member of parliament from the ruling party interfered in a civil case in which she was involved, was detained and forcibly admitted to a psychiatric hospital, violating her rights to liberty and security. She was initially denied access to her lawyer. Mukhortova was released from psychiatric detention on November 1. Her case against forcible detention was ongoing at time of writing.

On July 31, government critic Mukhtar Ablyazov was detained in France. His extradition is sought by Ukraine, Russia, and Kazakhstan on multiple charges, including embezzlement. Rights groups expressed serious concern that, if returned, he would be at serious risk of ill-treatment and denied a fair trial. His wife and child were illegally deported to Kazakhstan from Italy in May. United Nations experts said that the move resembled an "extraordinary rendition."

Freedom of Expression

Starting in late 2012, there was a marked escalation in the government's crackdown on independent and opposition media. In December 2012, in rushed trials, courts banned the newspapers *Vzglyad, Golos Respubliki*, and their affiliated sites, and prohibited K+ and Stan.TV from broadcasting. In 2013, several newspapers including *Pravda Kazakhstana* and *Tribuna,* were suspended for three months on technical grounds. In January, the *Zhezkazgan* youth newspaper was ordered to close.

Despite widespread criticism of the government's misuse of the overbroad and vague criminal offense of "inciting social, national, clan, racial, or religious discord," authorities opened new cases. Authorities also proposed broadening the scope of the criminal offense and increasing penalties on those found guilty of it. One such case was against journalist Aleksandr Kharlamov in March 2013. In mid-April, Kharlamov was forced to undergo a month of forced psychiatric observation. He was later released and put under house arrest. His case was ongoing at time of writing.

Some websites are blocked in Kazakhstan and libel remains a criminal offense. Media watchdog AdilSoz reported that between January and August 2013, there were 10 attacks on journalists, including on Igor Larra in August. In July, 4 men were sentenced to between 11 and 15 years in prison for attacking independent journalist Lukpan Akhmedyarov in April 2012.

Legal Reforms

Work on new criminal, criminal procedural, and penal codes continues amid serious concerns that proposed amendments would further restrict fundamental freedoms. In September, Dunja Mijatovic, the Organization for Security and Co-operation in Europe's media freedom representative, noted the proposed draft legislation "still contains and even strengthens sanctions that could limit free expression and freedom of the media," and in particular highlighted the "disproportionate sanctions" of suspending newspapers for minor administrative offenses.

Torture

In 2013, several police officers were convicted for torture and in July, authorities adopted a law on a National Preventative Mechanism against torture. Despite this, the Anti-Torture Coalition, a civil society alliance, reported receiving 201 complaints of torture and ill-treatment in the first half of 2013 alone. Perpetrators of torture often go unpunished. To date, there has been no effective investigation into serious and credible allegations of torture by detainees in the aftermath of the December 2011 Zhanaozen violence.

On November 18, a Kostanai court ordered local police to pay Aleksandr Gerasimov 2 million Tenge (US$13,000) in compensation following a May 2012 United Nations Committee Against Torture (CAT) decision finding Kazakhstan responsible for torturing Gerasimov in 2007. The committee had urged Kazakhstan to conduct an impartial investigation and provide full and adequate reparation.

Counterterrorism

In January 2013, amendments to counterterrorism laws were adopted in response to stated government concerns about increasing radicalization and armed attacks by alleged extremists. In October, President Nursultan Nazarbayev approved a five-year State Program to Counter Religious Extremism and Terrorism aimed at ensuring security and preventing terrorist attacks.

461

Forum18, an international religious freedom group, criticized the plan for its "all-embracing controls" on religious activities.

Vladislav Chelakh, a 19-year-old border guard accused of murdering 14 border guards and one ranger at a Kazakhstan-China border post in December 2011, was sentenced to life in prison in December 2012 despite an investigation and trial marred by irregularities. His sentence was twice upheld on appeal during 2013.

Freedom of Religion

Since the adoption in 2011 of a restrictive law on religion, religious groups have been subjected to raids, fines, and confiscation of literature. Between January and mid-November, authorities fined 119 individuals and sentenced 2 to short-term administrative detention for violating the religion law, according to Forum18. In February, a Kazakh court banned the minority Islamic group Jamaat Tablighi as "extremist."

In May, Protestant pastor Bakhytzhan Kashkumbayev was arrested on a dubious charge of "intentional infliction of grievous bodily harm" of a congregation member. In July, he was subjected to a month of forced psychiatric observation. In October, authorities brought an additional charge of propagandizing extremism against him. His case was ongoing at this writing.

Freedom of Assembly

Authorities maintain restrictive rules on freedom of assembly, and throughout the year detained and fined activists and others for organizing and/or participating in peaceful unsanctioned protests. For example, in mid-May, a court in Astana sentenced two civil society activists to between seven and fifteen days in detention and fined nearly two dozen others for violating the law on public assemblies.

Labor Rights and Child Labor in Agriculture

Legislation governing the organization, financing, and collective bargaining rights of trade unions remains restrictive and violates Kazakhstan's obligations under international law. Proposed provisions in the new draft criminal code would further restrict workers' right to strike—already subject to a broad prohibition in certain sectors of the economy—and continue to criminalize funding of trade unions by sources outside Kazakhstan. Work on a draft law on trade unions was ongoing at time of writing.

In response to concerns about debt bondage, forced labor, hazardous child labor, and other violations against migrant tobacco workers, Philip Morris International and Philip Morris Kazakhstan continued to implement policies aimed at decreasing such risks. In August 2012, the Ministry of Education and Science issued an order permitting children of migrant workers employed in accordance with migration laws to attend schools in Kazakhstan.

Returns to Risk of Torture

Kazakhstan continues to extradite individuals to Uzbekistan despite the risk of torture there. On March 13, authorities extradited Khairullo Tursunov to Uzbekistan, ignoring a February 28 UN Committee Against Torture communication to stall his extradition until it could fully review his complaint.

Key International Actors

There was criticism of Kazakhstan's rights record in 2013, notably by the European Parliament (EP), but overall concern was toned down as Kazakhstan's partners prioritized trade and energy interests. In a statement issued following her November 2012 visit to Kazakhstan, the EU High Representative for Foreign Affairs and Security Policy Catherine Ashton did not mention any human rights concerns, and asserted that her discussions "focused on economic and trade issues."

In June, European Commission President Jose Manuel Barroso did not raise publicly any specific human rights concerns during his first trip to Kazakhstan to discuss the European Union-Kazakhstan Enhanced Partnership and Cooperation Agreement (PCA). Enhanced PCA negotiations, which had stalled for over a year, resumed in October.

On April 11, United States Ambassador to the OSCE Ian Kelly voiced concern that Kazakhstan's 2011 religion law "falls short of upholding Kazakhstan's international obligations and commitments regarding freedom of religion." However, a July US-Kazakhstan annual Strategic Partnership Commission meeting focused on trade and investment without explicit concern about rights abuses in Kazakhstan.

On April 18, the EP adopted a resolution that flagged serious concerns about Kazakhstan's rights record, in particular about the closure of *Alga!* opposition party and media outlets and the imprisonment of activists on "vague criminal charges which could be considered to be politically motivated," including Vladimir Kozlov. The resolution stressed the importance of workers' rights and called for review of religion legislation. It also called for the EU to closely monitor developments in Kazakhstan.

British Prime Minister David Cameron visited Kazakhstan in late June, during which UK businesses concluded trade and other deals worth an estimated £700 million (US$1.1 million). Cameron said he and President Nursultan Nazarbayev discussed human rights issues "at some length." President Nazarbayev rejected concerns, saying "nobody has the right to instruct us how to live and build our country."

Kyrgyzstan

Shortcomings in law enforcement and the judiciary contribute to the persistence of grave abuses in connection to the ethnic violence in southern Kyrgyzstan in June 2010. Ethnic Uzbeks and other minorities remain especially vulnerable. Courtroom attacks on lawyers and defendants, particularly in cases related to the June 2010 events, occur with impunity.

Human rights defender Azimjon Askarov remains wrongfully imprisoned. In 2013, authorities proposed legislative initiatives to tighten restrictions on non-governmental groups. Violence and discrimination against women and lesbian, gay, bisexual, and transgender (LGBT) persons remain concerns. Some religious groups have faced harassment by the authorities. "Insult" and "insult of a public official" remain criminal offenses.

Government officials and civil society representatives formed a national center for the prevention of torture in 2013. In practice, ill-treatment and torture remain pervasive in places of detention, and impunity for torture is the norm.

Access to Justice

Three years on, justice for crimes committed during the ethnic violence in southern Kyrgyzstan in June 2010 remains elusive. The flawed justice process has produced long prison sentences for mostly ethnic Uzbeks after convictions marred by torture-tainted confessions and other due process violations. Authorities have not reviewed convictions where defendants alleged torture or other glaring violations of fair trial standards. At least nine ethnic Uzbeks continue to languish in pretrial detention, some for a third year. New convictions in August 2013 of three ethnic Uzbeks in Osh, and pending extradition orders of at least six others in Russia again point to judicial bias against ethnic Uzbeks.

The authorities failed to tackle the acute problem of courtroom violence by audiences in trials across Kyrgyzstan, including at the trial of three opposition members of parliament in June, perpetuating an environment that undermines defendants' fair trial rights. Lawyers were harassed or beaten in court in 2013, including for defending ethnic Uzbek clients in June 2010 cases. Mahamad Bizurukov, an ethnic Uzbek defendant, and his lawyers have been subjected to repeated threats, harassment, and physical attacks for two years, most recently in September 2013, with no accountability for perpetrators.

Torture

Despite the adoption of a national torture prevention mechanism in 2012, and the organization of a related National Center for the Prevention of Torture in 2013, authorities often refuse to investigate allegations of torture and perpetrators go unpunished. On rare occasions when charges are filed against police, investigations, and court proceedings are unduly protracted.

A telling example is the criminal case against four police officers following the August 2011 death of an ethnic Uzbek detained on charges related to the June 2010 ethnic violence. Usmonjon Kholmirzaev died several days after his release without charge, apparently from injuries he sustained from beatings in custody. The prosecution has been subjected to repeated delays over the last two years and no one has yet been held accountable for his death.

In July 2013, Nurkamil Ismailov was found dead in a temporary detention facility in southern Kyrgyzstan after police detained him for disorderly conduct. Authorities alleged he committed suicide by hanging himself with his t-shirt. The Jalalabad-based human rights group *Spravedlivost* intervened after which authorities opened a criminal investigation on charges of negligence. In September, Ismailov's relative and the police settled out of court for an undisclosed sum, with no admission of liability.

Freedom of Expression

In April 2013, internet providers in Kyrgyzstan lifted a 14-month ban on the independent online Central Asian news agency *Ferghana.ru*, after Kyrgyzstan's state media agency wrote a letter stating its previous notice urging providers to block *Ferghana.ru* was only a recommendation, not compulsory.

In June, OSCE representative on freedom of the media, Dunja Mijatovic, noted Kyrgyzstan's "progress in promoting media freedom and freedom of expression." Mijatovic urged authorities to bring to justice individuals responsible for the 2007 death of journalist Alisher Saipov, whose killers have not been identified.

Although Osh-based *Yntymak* Radio began broadcasting in Russian, Kyrgyz, and Uzbek languages in March 2012, concerns persist regarding restrictions on Uzbek-language media in southern Kyrgyzstan. In March 2013, the UN Committee on the Elimination of Racial Discrimination (CERD) noted "that the use of minority languages in media has decreased in particular in the Osh region." In July, an Osh court banned the Uzbek-language news site *Harakat.net* for allegedly inciting racial hatred.

Sexual Orientation and Gender-Based Violence

The authorities' approach to long-standing problems of gender-based violence, including domestic violence and bride abduction, remains ineffective. In February 2013, the Kyrgyz legislature adopted an amendment to increase the maximum jail sentence for bride-kidnapping from three to seven years (10 years if the girl is younger than 17).

In 2013, Labrys and Kyrgyz Indigo, LGBT rights groups, documented at least four new cases of police extortion and harassment of at least seven LGBT people. Gay and bisexual men are at particular risk of extortion, beating, and sexual violence. They rarely report abuses to the authorities due to fear of disclosure and retaliation, and abuses largely go unpunished. In March, unidentified assailants attacked two Labrys staff in Bishkek at a disco; one suffered a concussion. Police initially refused to register their complaint, which alleged the attack was a hate crime, and had yet to investigate at time of writing.

Civil Society

On November 17, 2012, agents of the State Committee on National Security (GKNB) temporarily detained an international staff member of the International Crisis Group (ICG), an international NGO working on peace and security issues, and without explanation, illegally searched and interrogated him, and confiscated his computer. He was later expelled from Kyrgyzstan. The GKNB later summoned five people for questioning apparently in connection with the ICG's work.

In 2013, the government sought to tighten control over civil society, proposing three legislative amendments that would impose burdensome reporting obligations and restrictions on civil society groups. Activists successfully lobbied to remove discriminatory provisions from two proposals. The third would require groups accepting foreign funding to register and identify themselves publicly as "foreign agents." At time of writing, it had not been reviewed by parliament.

In May, human rights lawyer Ulugbek Azimov, an ethnic Uzbek, and two members of his family were viciously assaulted after a traffic incident in Bishkek. Police found and prosecuted one of the attackers, but others remain at large. Azimov's colleagues believe the attack may have been ethnically-motivated.

Azimjon Askarov, a human rights defender who worked to document police treatment of detainees, continues to serve a life sentence, despite a prosecution marred by serious violations of fair trial standards. Askarov was found guilty of "organizing mass disorders," "inciting ethnic hatred," and taking part in killing a police officer on June 13, 2010. Despite repeated complaints filed by Askarov's lawyer, including in 2013, prosecutorial authorities have refused to investigate Askarov's credible allegations of torture in custody. Askarov's November 2012 complaint to the United Nations Human Rights Committee is under review.

Refugees

In recent years, Kyrgyzstan's efforts to host refugees and asylum seekers have been undermined by the government's failure to implement fully its obligations to protect the rights of asylum seekers and refugees from Uzbekistan. After a long court battle, in May 2013, a Bishkek court overturned the Prosecutor General's Office's extradition order for Khabibullo Sulaimanov, a former Imam from Uzbekistan, after he was granted refugee status by the United Nations High Commissioner for Refugees. In February, Shukhrat Musin, a refugee from Uzbekistan who fled religious persecution, was reported missing in Bishkek. In October, he was located in a pretrial detention center in Andijan, Uzbekistan.

Freedom of Religion

In December 2012, President Atambaev signed amendments to Kyrgyzstan's religion laws authorizing greater control over religious literature deemed "extremist." Forum18, an international religious freedom watchdog, reported harassment of smaller religious communities in 2013, including of Jehovah's Witnesses and Ahmadi Muslims.

Key International Actors

Kyrgyzstan's partners raised human rights concerns throughout the year, but did not consistently seize opportunities to urge concrete improvements.

Statements issued by European Union leaders on the occasion of Kyrgyz president's September 2013 visit to Brussels noted challenges in upholding the rule of law and the rights of minorities, but stopped short of urging any concrete improvements. The ministerial-level cooperation council meeting with Kyrgyzstan, held in November, urged "further steps to address human rights concerns," stressing "inter-ethnic reconciliation" and the "significant role" played by civil society.

In December 2012, German Chancellor Angela Merkel specifically noted concern about Azimjon Askarov's imprisonment and the rights of ethnic minorities. During a Kyrgyzstan visit in May, UN Assistant Secretary General for Human Rights Ivan Simonovic raised Askarov's case, violence against women, and the need to address discrimination on grounds of ethnicity, religion, and gender.

Following her mission to Kyrgyzstan in April 2013, UN special rapporteur on the sale of children, child prostitution, and child pornography, Najat Maalla M'jid, highlighted the country's insufficient protection of children from violence, exploitation, and abuse, and urged law enforcement agencies to do more to investigate, prosecute, and punish perpetrators.

In its March 2013 concluding observations, the Committee on the Elimination of Racial Discrimination (CERD) voiced serious concerns about the treatment of ethnic minorities in Kyrgyzstan, including due process violations in court proceedings following the June 2010 violence, allegations of torture, restrictions on Uzbek-language media, and violence against ethnic minority women. The committee also noted a few positive developments, including the adoption of a policy on inter-ethnic relations.

During its review of Kyrgyzstan in November, the UN Committee Against Torture noted that "[fundamental safeguards] were not upheld in practice" and expressed "serious concern about prison conditions."

Russia

Russian authorities continued the crackdown on civil society and government critics that began in 2012. Enforcement of the "foreign agents" law led to an unprecedented, nationwide inspection campaign of hundreds of nongovernmental organizations (NGOs). Dozens of groups are fighting the prosecutors in courts, refusing to register as "foreign agents." Parliament adopted laws restricting LGBT rights and freedom of expression and infringing on the right to privacy. Abuses in the North Caucasus continue.

Civil Society

A 2012 law requires NGOs receiving foreign funding and conducting broadly defined "political activity" to register as "foreign agents," effectively demonizing them as foreign spies. Authorities define as "political" such work as urging reforms, raising awareness, and assisting victims of abuse.

From March to May 2013, authorities subjected hundreds of NGOs to invasive inspections to intimidate groups and pressure them to register as "foreign agents."

At time of writing, the authorities filed administrative lawsuits against at least nine inspected organizations and five administrative cases against leaders of these groups for refusing to register. Two groups were forced to close as a result; at least another three chose to wind up operations to avoid further repressive legal actions. The Prosecutor's Office ordered dozens of other groups to register or warned they might need to do so. Many organizations also faced sanctions for alleged violations of fire safety, tax and labor regulations, and sanitary norms.

Sexual Orientation and Gender Identity

In June 2013, parliament unanimously adopted a law banning promotion among children of "propaganda of nontraditional sexual relationships," meaning lesbian, gay, bisexual, or transgender (LGBT) relationships. Violators risk stiff fines, and in the case of foreigners, up to 15 days' detention and deportation.

Beginning in 2006, similar laws outlawing "propaganda of homosexuality" among children were passed in 11 Russian regions.

Also in June, parliament passed a law banning adoption of Russian children by foreign same-sex couples and by unmarried individuals from countries where marriage for same-sex couples is legal. In September, several deputies introduced a bill that would make a parent's homosexuality legal grounds for denial of parental rights. It was withdrawn later for revision.

Homophobic rhetoric, including by officials, and rising homophobic violence accompanied debate about these laws. Three homophobic murders were reported in various regions of Russia in May 2013.

Vigilante groups, consisting of radical nationalists, and Neo-Nazis, lure men or boys to meetings, accuse them of being gay, humiliate and beat them, and post videos of the proceedings on social media. For example, in September 2013 a video showed the rape of an Uzbek migrant in Russia who was threatened with a gun and forced to say he was gay. A few investigations were launched, but have not yet resulted in effective prosecution.

Freedom of Expression

In June 2013, President Vladimir Putin signed a law imposing a maximum three-year prison sentence for publicly "insult[ing] the feelings of religious believers." The law provides no clear definition of acts or speech considered "insulting." The law is yet to be enforced.

At time of writing, parliament was debating a bill to ban criticism challenging the fairness of Nuremberg Trial judgments or actions of anti-Hitler coalitions, with a maximum three-year prison sentence. Doing so in the media or while holding a public office carries a harsher criminal penalty of up to five years in prison.

Arrests and Harassment of Human Rights Defenders, Government Opponents, and Other Critics

The authorities continue to prosecute people who participated in a large demonstration at Moscow's Bolotnaya Square on the eve of Putin's May 2012 inauguration, based on disproportionate "mass rioting" charges and alleged acts of violence against police. At time of writing, two people were sentenced to two-and-a-half and four-and-a-half years respectively in prison, and one was sentenced to indefinite compulsory psychiatric treatment. A further 24 were charged, of whom 14 were held in pretrial detention, some ten of them for more than a year. Twelve of the twenty-four were on trial.

In July, a court sentenced anti-corruption blogger and opposition leader Alexei Navalny to five years in prison on politically tainted embezzlement charges and released him pending appeal. On October 16, an appeals court suspended the sentence.

Two members of the punk group Pussy Riot, convicted on August 17, 2012, for a 40-second stunt in Moscow's largest cathedral, were repeatedly denied parole and continued to serve their two-year prison sentences. In September one of them, Nadezhda Tolokonnikova, went on a hunger strike protesting alleged inhuman work conditions, sleep deprivation, and threats by prison staff. She renewed her hunger strike in October to emphasize the threats against her. Russian authorities held Tolokonnikova incommunicado for over 26 days during her transfer to a prison facility in Kransoyarsk.

In July, a court in Nizhny Novgorod rejected a petition by the Prosecutor's Office to ban the book *International Tribunal for Chechnya* as "extremist." The book calls for the creation of an international tribunal to investigate alleged war crimes and crimes against humanity committed during two wars in Chechnya. In October, an appeals court upheld this decision.

In September, Russian authorites arrested 30 activists with the environmental organization Greenpeace for staging a protest in the Pechora Sea. Investigative authorities charged them with piracy, then reclassified the charge to hooliganism. At time of writing, 29 of the 30 had been granted bail and released.

In November, Mikhail Savva, an NGO leader on trial in Krasnador for allegedly mismanaging a government grant, stated in court that authorities were planning to press treason charges against him in an effort to intimidate him. Savva said the authorities referenced the fact that he had received foreign grants for years and met with US embassy officials, among other things.

North Caucasus

The Islamist insurgency in the North Caucasus republics continued in 2013, particularly in Dagestan. According to *Caucasian Knot*, an independent online media portal, in the first nine months of 2013, 375 people were killed in the North Caucasus region, including 68 civilians, and 343 people were wounded, including 112 civilians. Approximately 64 percent of the killings and 71 percent of the injuries reported by *Caucasian Knot* occurred in Dagestan.

According to the Memorial Human Rights Center, one of Russia's most prominent independent rights groups, from January to June 2013, eight people suffered abduction-style detentions by government agencies in Dagestan, with five still unaccounted for at time of writing. Ramazan Abdulatipov, Dagestan's new leader, abandoned the "soft power" counterinsurgency policies of his predecessor, including a commission for return of insurgents to peaceful life and promoting dialogue with Salafi Muslims. In 2013, persecution by law enforcement officials of Salafis increased. Unprosecuted abuses, including torture, abductions, and attacks against suspected insurgents and their families served to alienate Salafi communities. To combat "extremists," the authorities condoned the rise of people's militias, which have driven some Salafis to flee their homes.

In July, unidentified assailants shot dead Akhmednabi Akhmednabiev, an independent journalist and critic of abuses by law enforcement and security agencies. The official investigation, ongoing at time of writing, acknowledged that he was killed because of his journalism. Prior to the murder, Akhmednabiev reported to the authorities death threats he received, but they did not take adequate steps to investigate. Akhmednabiev is the second journalist covering counterinsurgency issues murdered in less than two years in Dagestan. The 2011 killing of Khadzhimurad Kamalov remains unresolved.

Five people suffered abduction-style detentions in Ingushetia between January and March 2013, and two of them "disappeared," according to Memorial. In August, the head of Ingushetia's Security Council, Akhmet Kotiev, was killed in an alleged insurgent attack.

According to Memorial, one person "disappeared" after abduction by security forces in Chechnya in the first six months of 2013. Law enforcement and security agencies under the de facto control of Chechnya's leader, Ramzan Kadyrov, continued collective punishment against relatives and suspected supporters of alleged insurgents. Victims increasingly refuse to speak about violations due to fear of official retribution. Abuses remain unpunished and largely under-reported.

In September, Russia's Prosecutor General's Office berated the Chechen minister of international affairs for lack of cooperation in investigating cases of disappearances dating to 1990-2000.

Women are forced to wear headscarves in public buildings, and according to local women's rights activists, "honor" killings are on the rise in Chechnya.

Cooperation with the European Court of Human Rights

At time of writing, the European Court of Human Rights (ECtHR) had issued over 200 judgments holding Russia responsible for grave human rights violations in Chechnya. At least three pertain to violations that law enforcement officials perpetrated under Kadyrov's de facto control.

While Russia continues to pay the required monetary compensation to victims, it fails to meaningfully implement the core of the judgments by not conducting effective investigations, and failing to hold perpetrators accountable In October, when the ECtHR ruled on the case of *Abdulkhanov and Others v. Russia*, for the first time in a case concerning the armed conflict in Chechnya, the Russian government acknowledged that there had been a violation of the right to life.

In June 2013, the ECtHR ruled that Russia violated the European Convention on Human Rights during the trial and sentencing, on tax evasion and fraud charges, of former Yukos oil company owner Mikhail Khodorkovsky in 2005 and awarded US$13,500 damages to the jailed businessman.

Abuses Linked to Preparations for the 2014 Olympic Games

Authorities continued to intimidate and harass organizations, individuals, and journalists who criticized the local government in the Black Sea city of Sochi, including for its preparations for the 2014 Winter Olympic Games.

Some migrant workers involved in building Olympic venues and other infrastructure continued to report that employers failed to provide contracts or promised

HUMAN
RIGHTS
WATCH

RACE TO THE BOTTOM

Exploitation of Migrant Workers Ahead of Russia's
2014 Winter Olympic Games in Sochi

**HUMAN
RIGHTS
WATCH**

BARRIERS EVERYWHERE
Lack of Accessibility for People with Disabilities in Russia

wages. Police detained on false charges at least one worker who tried to complain about exploitation. Local authorities failed to effectively investigate workers' complaints and, in September, initiated large-scale raids to detain and deport irregular migrants ahead of the games in 2014.

The authorities are resettling more than 2,000 families to obtain land for Olympic venues and infrastructure. Not all of those evicted have received fair compensation. The authorities refuse to compensate or resettle other families whose properties have been severely damaged or altered by Olympic construction.

Palliative Care

Restrictive government policies and limited availability of pain treatment persists and severely hinders the delivery of palliative care. Each year, tens of thousands of dying cancer patients are denied their right to adequate pain relief. In May 2013, a doctor in Krasnoyarsk and another woman were found guilty and fined on charges of illegal trafficking of controlled substances, after they helped a man in the final stages of cancer and in debilitating pain obtain opioid pain medicines. In September, an appeals court sent the case for retrial. The court hearing the retrial excluded a lead defense lawyer from the case.

A May 2013 government decree somewhat eased patients' access to narcotic pain medications. However, implementation is problematic.

Disability Rights

The government has taken several high-profile steps to demonstrate its commitment to ensuring an accessible environment for its approximately 13 million citizens with disabilities, including implementing its multibillion-ruble Accessible Environment Program and its decision to host the Sochi 2014 Winter Paralympics.

However, for many people living with disabilities in Russia, taking part in the basic activities of daily life can be extremely difficult or even impossible due to a range of barriers they encounter. These include the lack of ramps and elevators, leading to isolation in their homes; employers' unwillingness to hire people with disabilities; and inadequate visual, auditory, and sensory accommoda-

tions in buses, trains, and train stations. Most people with disabilities interviewed by Human Rights Watch who submitted written complaints to local government about inaccessible facilities or services reported that the response was
not timely or effective.

Hundreds of thousands of adults and children with disabilities considered to
need constant care currently live in closed institutions, including many who
would like to and could hold jobs and live independently, with certain social
supports.

Migrant's Rights

In July 2013, Moscow police launched a discriminatory campaign against irregular migrants, detaining people based on their non-Slavic appearance with the
stated aim of identifying alleged violations of migration and employment regulations. Several thousand were allegedly taken into custody. Some were released
and others were expelled. Several hundred were put in a makeshift tent camp
and held in inhumane conditions. The campaign to detain and deport irregular
migrants spread to other regions of Russia with high concentration of labor
migrants, including Sochi.

Key International Actors

International actors raised a range of concerns about developments in Russia,
condemning the anti-LGBT "propaganda" law, the "foreign agents" law and the
burdensome inspections of NGOs that followed its adoption, and the flawed
conduct of high-profile trials against political opponents.

In May 2013, the United Nations special rapporteurs for freedom of association,
human rights defenders, and freedom of expression voiced serious concerns
about the "obstructive, intimidating, and stigmatizing effects" of waves of
inspections of Russian NGOs in connection with the "foreign agents" law.

During its Universal Periodic Review at the Human Rights Council, Russia rejected key recommendations related to freedom of association, LGBT rights, and
abuses of migrant workers in Sochi. The Council of Europe's secretary general
and its commissioner for human rights urged Russia to reevaluate the NGO law,
as did Parliamentary Assembly of the Council of Europe rapporteurs.

HUMAN
RIGHTS
WATCH

LAWS OF ATTRITION

Crackdown on Russia's Civil Society after Putin's Return to the Presidency

European Union High Representative for Foreign Affairs and Security Policy Catherine Ashton spoke out against several "deeply troubling" trends in Russia, including the crackdown on civil society and political activists, impunity for past human rights violations, and discriminatory legislation against LGBT persons. At the conclusion of the June 2013 EU-Russia summit, European Council President Herman van Rompuy acknowledged that human rights remain an "important, although difficult, element of our relations."

EU governments also publicly criticized the human rights situation in Russia. Germany and France condemned the "foreign agents" law, particularly after German and French organizations operating in Moscow were inspected. Officials of many foreign governments and intergovernmental organizations also voiced strong concerns about the anti-LGBT "propaganda" law.

Although the International Olympic Committee (IOC) publicly affirmed its commitment to nondiscrimination regarding LGBT people, it has refused to ask Russia to repeal the "propaganda" law. Former IOC President Jacques Rogge went no further than to ask Russia for "assurances" that there will be no discrimination in Sochi. Current IOC head Thomas Bach declined to condemn the law and stated that the IOC "cannot claim to rise above sovereign states."

Relations between the US and Russia were particularly strained in 2013. In December 2012, the US Congress adopted legislation introducing a visa ban and asset freeze against Russian government officials involved in the death of whistleblower tax lawyer Sergei Magnitsky and the torture or killing of other whistleblowers. The initial list included 18 names, 16 of which were directly connected to the Magnitsky case. In response, the Duma adopted a law banning US adoptions of Russian orphans. In January 2013, the US withdrew from the civil society component of the US-Russian Bilateral Presidential Commission due to disagreements over the "foreign agents" law.

US President Barack Obama canceled a planned September summit with Putin, citing lack of progress on the bilateral agenda, including on human rights abuses. A meeting between US and Russian foreign and defense ministers went ahead, but did not address human rights. Obama later noted that he was personally "offended" by Russia's "antigay and lesbian legislation."

Russia's Foreign Policy

Russia's foreign policy impeded accountability for humanitarian law violations and, for much of the year, humanitarian assistance for all in Syria. In its drive to ensure no "regime change," no military intervention, and no singling out of the Syrian government for abuses, Russia, a close ally and supporter of the Syrian government, also failed to take actions to end war crimes and crimes against humanity, hold their perpetrators accountable, and ensure access to humanitarian assistance for people in all parts of Syria, including rebel-held areas.

Until the chemical weapons attacks of August 21, Russia and China continued to block meaningful action by the UN Security Council regarding Syria. Following the attack, Russia supported a council resolution requiring the Syrian government to eliminate its chemical weapons program. Russia also allowed the passage of a statement by the council's president calling for immediate, safe, and unhindered humanitarian access throughout Syria. Russia continued to obstruct efforts by some council members to refer the situation in Syria to the International Criminal Court, which would then have the mandate to examine serious crimes committed by all parties to the conflict.

In 2013, Russia continued proposals to weaken the autonomy of UN treaty bodies. These included the "supervision" by member states, allowing states under review to negotiate questions the particular committee would ask.

Despite the explicit mandate of the UN Human Rights Council to respond to situations of human rights violations, Russia continued to play a negative role by questioning the council's engagement in specific countries where engagement was needed, including Sri Lanka, Belarus, and Syria, branding the council's response politicized.

Serbia

Despite a historic agreement in April by the European Council to start European Union membership talks in January 2014 with Serbia, human rights concerns persist. The situation of ethnic minorities remains precarious, especially for Roma. Journalists continue to be targets of threats despite attempts to bring perpetrators to justice. The asylum system is weak and overburdened. The signing of a cooperation protocol between Serbian and Bosnian prosecutors offers potential to improve the slow progress in war crimes prosecutions.

Accountability for War Crimes

War crimes prosecutions progressed slowly in 2013. The Belgrade War Crimes Chamber reached convictions in six cases and acquitted two people in one case. The Office of the War Crimes Prosecutor indicted three people for crimes against civilians. Fourteen prosecutions were pending at time of writing.

In February, the chamber sentenced seven members of the "Sima's Chetniks" paramilitary unit to a total of 72 years' imprisonment for killing 28 Roma civilians, raping and torturing three Roma women, and destroying the mosque in Skocic in Bosnia and Herzegovina.

In July, the chamber sentenced Petar Ciric, of the Vukovar Territorial Defense corps of the Yugoslav National Army, to 20 years imprisonment for participating in the torture and murder by firing squad of 200 Croatian prisoners of war in November 1991.

Also in July, the chamber ordered the Serbian government to compensate three Kosovo Albanians for torture and inhuman treatment following their unlawful detention in May 1999 when Serbian forces occupied the Kosovar village of Novo Cikatovo.

In February, Serbia signed a war crimes protocol with Bosnia facilitating the mutual transfer of information and evidence of war crimes. In July, this resulted in an agreement to cooperate on investigations against 30 suspected war criminals believed to live in Serbia.

In April, Serbian President Tomislav Nikolic offered an apology on Bosnian TV in the name of the Serbian people for war crimes committed by Serb forces in

Bosnia during the 1992-1995 war. The apology stopped short of calling the massacre in Srebrenica a genocide.

In late May, the International Criminal Tribunal for the Former Yugoslavia (ICTY) acquitted former Serbian security officials Jovica Stanisic and Franko Simatovic of criminal responsibility for the removal of Bosniaks and Croats from parts of Bosnia and Croatia between 1991 and 1995.

In November, the war crimes prosecutor charged two former officers in the Yugoslav army with the killing of 27 people in the Kosovo village Trjnje in 1999. Also in November, in a pending case against 11 former members of the Yugoslav armed forces, the war crimes prosecutor added the indictment of former army commander Toplica Miladinovic for ordering the attacks on four Kosovo villages where at least 45 people were killed in 1999.

Freedom of Media

In April, the editor-in-chief of *Juzne Vesti*, a Serbian investigative journalism platform, received threats over the phone from the director of the Nis Heating Plant, Milutin Ilic, and two others saying "watch what you publish" due to reporting on operations at the plant. The three men were charged in September with threatening the safety of a person performing tasks of public importance.

In June, *Koreni* and *Intermagazin* web-portals published an article calling Nedim Sejdinovic, a well-known journalist and human rights activist from the Vojvodina region in northern Serbia, an "Islamic thinker" and "Vojvodina separatist," and suggesting that he should not feel safe in his hometown.

A long-awaited government commission was established in January to investigate the murders of three prominent journalists in Serbia more than a decade ago. The seven-member commission is tasked with analyzing all prior investigations, ascertaining why they failed, and creating the basis for future investigations.

Treatment of Minorities

Attacks and harassment against the Roma minority continued, but authorities brought some alleged perpetrators to justice. In March, a 17-year-old Roma boy died as a result of injuries sustained during a beating by several assailants. A

14-year-old boy was charged with manslaughter in connection with the attack. In August, a group of hooligans attacked a Roma settlement in Resnik, threatening residents and shouting racist slurs. At time of writing police had made four arrests.

Forced evictions and discrimination against Roma in education remain concerns. Authorities demolished approximately 40 homes in an informal Roma settlement in Belgrade in April, providing no alternative accommodation. Also in Belgrade, 50 Roma families faced imminent threat of eviction from their social housing at time of writing. Roma children continue to be disproportionally enrolled in schools for children with developmental disabilities. According to the European Roma Rights Centre, in the 2012-2013 school year, 22.8 percent of all students enrolled in special needs education were Roma.

Tensions between members of the Hungarian minority and Serb majority in the Vojvodina region in northeast Serbia continued. Groups of Serbs attacked Hungarians in separate incidents in January and February, in Temerin and Subotica, respectively, allegedly because of they were ethnic Hungarians. Police were investigating both cases at time of writing.

Sexual Orientation and Gender Identity

Despite landmark court decisions and a strengthened legal framework for the protection of lesbian, gay, bisexual, and transgender (LGBT) rights, members of the LGBT community continue to face intolerance and harassment. A local human rights group reported at least 30 threats per month on social media against members of the LGBT community involved in organizing the 2013 Pride Parade. In September, Serbia's National Security Council banned the Pride Parade for the third consecutive year again citing security concerns. The Constitutional Court in May held that the ban on the 2011 Pride Parade violated the right to freedom of assembly and awarded damages to the Pride Parade Belgrade association. The Appellate Court in Novi Sad, northern Serbia, set a legal precedent in January when it fined a man for discriminating against a colleague on grounds of sexual orientation by calling him a derogatory term.

The criminal code was amended in December 2012 to prohibit hate speech on grounds of sexual orientation and gender identity, and to include hate motivation, including against LGBT people, as an aggravated circumstance in sentencing. The government adopted a national strategy for prevention and protection against discrimination in June.

Asylum Seekers and Displaced Persons

In the first eight months of 2013, Serbia registered 2,232 asylum seekers, up from 1,454 during the same period in 2012. Syrians comprised the largest national group (432 people).

Concerns remain with the capacity of Serbia's two reception centers, which can only accommodate 280 people and are operating at near maximum capacity. According to the UN High Commissioner for Refugees (UNHCR), national asylum authorities are considering locations for a third reception center at this writing. For the first time since it assumed responsibility for the asylum procedure in 2008, the Asylum Office granted subsidiary protection to two applicants in 2013; to date it has never granted refugee status.

No movement occurred in finding a lasting solution for refugees and internally displaced persons (IDPs) from the Balkan wars. According to data from the Serbian Commissariat for Refugees and Migrations, as of September there were 54,000 refugees in Serbia, most from Croatia, and 210,000 IDPs, a majority of whom are from Kosovo. According to UNHCR estimates, 90,000 IDPs are in a situation of need, primarily with respect to housing.

In December 2012, the Serbian parliament criminalized the act of helping Serbian citizens to leave to seek asylum abroad. EU and individual member states, including Germany, Sweden, and Belgium, had pressured Serbian authorities to address the flow of so-called "fake" asylum seekers to the EU, most of whom appear to be Roma. There were no reported cases of people prevented from leaving Serbia in 2013.

Key International Actors

The European Court of Human Rights in a March decision ordered Serbia to investigate hundreds of cases of missing children following suspected deaths in hospital wards between 1970-1990 and to provide adequate compensation to parents.

In July, UN Secretary-General Ban Ki-moon urged Serbia to intensify efforts to determine the fate of over 1,700 people who disappeared during the 1990s war. The same month, the UN Committee on the Elimination of Discrimination against Women expressed concerns about the increasing number of women murdered or abused by their spouses and ex-spouses and urged the government to ensure effective investigations, prosecutions, and punishment of perpetrators.

In October, while acknowledging some improvements in the areas of media freedom and judicial reforms, the European Commission's annual progress report on Serbia urged authorities to strengthen the independence of key public institutions, including the judiciary, and stressed the need for further reforms. It also called on authorities to enhance the protection of journalists, human rights defenders, and the LGBT population from threats and attacks.

Kosovo

Human rights protection remains weak in Kosovo. Despite reforms, the justice system continues to have a large backlog. Ethnic minority communities, Roma, Ashkali, and Egyptians in particular, continue to suffer discrimination. Journalists and human rights defenders were subjected to threats and attacks during 2013.

Tensions sometimes flared up in the divided north, despite improved political relations with Serbia, demonstrated by an April agreement establishing a special police commander and appeal court for the Serbian minority; an August agreement to establish permanent border crossings between Kosovo and Serbia in 2014; and the September dissolution of Serb parallel structures in northern Kosovo. In September, unknown assailants killed an EU Rule of Law Mission (EULEX) police officer in an attack against two EULEX police vehicles. Police were investigating at time of writing.

Impunity, Accountability, Access to Justice

Justice system reform enacted in January restructured the courts in an attempt to address the years-long case backlog. A new criminal code also entered into force in January, without three contested provisions deemed to restrict media freedom.

In the first nine months, EULEX judges handed down five war crimes judgments, reaching acquittals in all but one case. The September acquittal of Fatmir Limaj and nine others in a case concerning the 1998 mass murder of Serb and Albanian civilians in Klecka by Kosovo Liberation Army (KLA) forces illustrates weaknesses in Kosovo's witness protection program and challenges to prosecute crimes committed during and after the war. Testimony from a key witness, found dead in a park in Germany in December 2012, in what police called a suicide, was first ruled inadmissible and then, in the retrial, contradictory and unreliable.

In June, three men were sentenced to six, four, and three years respectively for beating and torturing Kosovo Albanian civilians illegally detained in the KLA Llapashtica detention center between 1998 and 1999. In October, the EULEX special prosecutor charged 15 people with war crimes against civilians and prisoners in 1998 at a KLA detention center in Likovac.

Hundreds of cases are pending before the Kosovo Special Prosecution Office, the War Crimes Investigative Unit of the Kosovo Police, and EULEX. At time of writing, 13 arrest warrants were outstanding concerning Serbs who are believed to reside outside Kosovo. EULEX continues to investigate 94 war crimes cases from the 1998-1999 Kosovo war, including massacres in Meja, Dubrava, and Krusha thought to involve more than 1,000 victims.

At the end of August, the Human Rights Review Panel (HRRP), an independent body set up in 2009 to review allegations of human rights violations by EULEX staff, handed down 15 decisions, finding violations in 5 cases. In the case concerning attacks by Kosovo Police and ethnic Albanians against Serbs during the 2012 Vidovdan Serbian religious holiday, the HRRP found that EULEX had failed to allocate adequate resources to provide protection or to conduct an effective investigation into allegations of human rights abuse.

Freedom of Media

Journalists continue to face a hostile environment. In May, a gas bomb was thrown into the house of the editor-in-chief of Radio Television of Kosovo, the public service broadcaster, causing damage but no injuries. Kosovo authorities condemned the attack and police were investigating. At time of writing, no arrests had been made.

In June, a mixed panel of Kosovo and EULEX judges acquitted former Mayor of Skenderaj Sami Lushtaku; the former owner of *Infopress*, Rexhep Hoti; its former editor-in-chief, Avni Azemi; and two other journalists of threats against Jeta Xharra, the director of *BIRN*, a regional news group. The court held that the 12 news items where *Infopress* referred to Xharra as "a Serbian spy," and "embassy slut," in response to a BIRN TV program dealing with alleged mismanagement in Skenderaj where Lushtaku was mayor at the time, did not pose a threat to Xharra.

Treatment of Minorities

Roma, Ashkali, and Egyptian communities, numbering approximately 40,000 people, are the most vulnerable and marginalized groups in Kosovo and continue to face difficulties obtaining personal documents, impeding their access to health care, social assistance, and education.

In July, the Ministry of Social Welfare changed the eligibility criteria for social assistance in a way that effectively prevents many Roma, Ashkali, and Egyptian families from accessing social benefits. The 2010 Strategy for Integration of Roma, Ashkali, and Egyptians continues to exist on paper only, with the government failing to allocate necessary funds to implement the strategy.

Movement occurred with respect to the 2010 Strategy on Reintegration of Repatriated Persons, including Roma, Ashkali and Egyptians, as central funds were transferred from the Ministry of Internal Affairs to the Municipal Offices for Communities and Return, responsible for identifying and supporting Roma, Ashkali, and Egyptian returnees. The impact of the fund transfer was too early to tell at time of writing.

Tensions between the Serb minority and Albanian majority flared in the second half of 2013, particularly in northern Kosovo, with a fatal shooting of an EULEX officer in September and threats against a Serb politician and his family in Mitrovica in the lead-up to local elections in November. Police were investigating both incidents at this writing. In defiance of a Constitutional Court ruling, the Kosovo Assembly passed in September an amnesty for certain crimes committed up until June 20, 2013, in "resistance" to Kosovo law enforcement authorities, including destroying property, assisting offenders after they committed crimes, and falsifying documents. Supporters of the amnesty law argue it is intended to facilitate the integration of Kosovo's Serb minority.

Between January and August, Kosovo Police Services reported only 10 inter-ethnic incidents, without specifying whether such incidents involved physical injuries or property damage. International observers remained concerned that many inter-ethnic incidents are unreported, unregistered, and misclassified.

In January, approximately sixty graves in four orthodox graveyards were vandalized in Serb minority areas in Kilokot, Obilic, Prizren, and Kosovo Polje. Police arrested five people in January, including four under 18. Prime Minister Hashim Thaci condemned the vandalism and allocated 97, 000 EUR (US$ 131,000) to repair the graves. In February, two Serbian children were injured when an unknown assailant threw a hand grenade at a house in a suspected act of ethnic violence. The police were investigating at time of writing.

Human Rights Defenders

In March, at least two assailants severely beat prominent human rights defender Nazlie Bala outside her apartment. Anonymous death threats preceded the attack, citing her public support of a proposed amendment to an existing law that would provide compensation and rehabilitation to survivors of war crimes of sexual violence. A letter under her door read: "Do not protect the shame. Otherwise we will kill you." Police were investigating at this writing.

A mob of about twenty men with clubs destroyed equipment and beat one employee during the launch of magazine Kosovo 2.0's "sexuality" issue in December 2012. The issue included several articles related to lesbian, gay, bisexual, and transgender (LGBT) issues. In September, the EULEX mission and the Kosovo state prosecutor charged three people for inflicting bodily harm and inciting hatred.

Sexual Orientation and Gender Identity

LGBT people face social stigma and a culture of silence. *Qesh*, the only public LGBT organization in Kosovo, reported receiving several threats via social media related to an LGBT event in May hosted in cooperation with the government ministry for good governance. The organization reported one of these threats and police were investigating at time of writing.

Asylum Seekers and Displaced Persons

During the first eight months of the year, the Office of the United Nations High Commissioner for Refugees (UNHCR) registered 483 voluntary returns, including people from outside Kosovo and internally displaced persons, compared to 589 during the same period in 2012.

Deportations to Kosovo from Western Europe continued, with limited assistance provided upon return. Between January and August, the UNHCR registered 2,149 forced returns to Kosovo, including 378 Roma, 143 Ashkali, and 6 Egyptians. Most minorities were returned from Sweden (243) followed by Germany (150).

The lead-contaminated Osterode camp outside Mitrovica closed in December 2012 and the remaining five Roma, Ashkali, and Egyptian families were resettled to an apartment building in north Mitrovica.

Key International Actors

In a resolution adopted in January, the Parliamentary Assembly of the Council of Europe called on Kosovo authorities to fight corruption, make judicial reforms, address war crimes, protect and promote the rights of Roma, Ashkali, and Egyptians, ensure independence of media and adequate protection for journalists, and strengthen the fight against human trafficking. It also urged the European Union to focus its policy dialogue with Kosovo on strengthening the rule of law.

EU High Representative for Foreign Affairs Catherine Ashton welcomed Kosovo's April agreement with Serbia aiming to normalize relations and advance European integration, but failed to stress the importance of strengthening human rights protection.

In an October progress report, a stabilization agreement between the EU and Kosovo, the European Commission (EC) raised serious concerns about the rule of law and protection of minorities. The EC urged Kosovar authorities to address corruption, organized crime, and attacks on the judiciary by strengthening legislation and its implementation and ensure security and protection measures for judges, prosecutors, witnesses, and plaintiffs. It also urged authorities to take further measures to reduce the backlog of court cases by enforcing court rulings. The report called on authorities to investigate and prosecute attacks motivated by ethnicity or religion and for prompt implementation of the national strategy and action plan for the Roma, Ashkali, and Egyptian communities.

During a June visit, UN High Commissioner for Human Rights Navi Pillay expressed serious concerns about rule of law, including the independence of the judiciary and case backlogs, as well as discrimination against Roma, Ashkali, and Egyptians, Serbs, Gorani, and other minorities and called for vigorous implementation of laws and tougher responses to hate speech and ethnic intolerance.

In July, UN Secretary General Ban Ki-moon called on Kosovo and Serbia to cooperate to resolve the issue of missing persons in Kosovo. To date, more than 1,700 people remain missing as a result of the war with Serbia.

Tajikistan

President Emomali Rahmon was re-elected to a fourth term in office in November in an election that lacked meaningful political competition. Oinihol Bobonazarova, the only genuine independent candidate, was forced to exit the race prematurely in October after the authorities interfered with her campaign and intimidated her relatives and supporters. During the lead-up to the election, authorities widened a crackdown on freedom of expression, imprisoned opposition leaders, shut down a leading nongovernmental organization (NGO), and stepped up efforts to extradite political opponents from abroad.

The government also persisted with enforcing a repressive law on religion, restricting media freedoms, and pressuring civil society groups. There were widespread complaints by NGOs of the authorities' use of torture to obtain confessions.

In positive developments, Tajikistan passed a long-awaited law on domestic violence and committed to accede to the Second Optional Protocol to the International Covenant on Civil and Political Rights on the elimination of the death penalty.

Government Opponents and Other Critics

Authorities cracked down on government critics and the political opposition ahead of November's presidential election.

In February, former Prime Minister and one-time presidential candidate Abdumalik Abdullanjanov, a refugee in the United States since 1994, was detained in Kiev on an Interpol warrant. Tajikistan sought his extradition on charges ranging from embezzlement to involvement in a plot to assassinate President Rahmon. Abdullanjanov was released following an intervention by United Nations High Commissioner for Refugees.

In March, Salimboy Shamsiddinov, head of the Uzbek society of the Khatlon region, was reported missing after leaving his home in Qurghonteppa. The authorities declared that there was no sign that Shamsiddinov was beaten or kidnapped. In July, officials claimed that a body resembling Shamsiddinov's was found in a river in neighboring Uzbekistan, but Shamsiddinov's family stated they did not recognize the body from the picture they were shown.

In April, unknown assailants attacked Mahmadali Hayit, deputy head of the Islamic Revival Party of Tajikistan (IRPT), outside his home in Dushanbe. The attack happened days before the IRPT's planned 40-year anniversary convention. Hayit told Human Rights Watch that he had been under surveillance before the attack, and that unknown individuals in plain clothes were regularly coming to his home to inquire about his whereabouts.

In May, businessman and former Minister of Industry Zaid Saidov was detained at the Dushanbe airport on returning from a trip abroad. In April, Saidov had announced the creation of an opposition political party, New Tajikistan. Fellow New Tajikistan members believe that Saidov, currently on trial in a security services detention center on corruption, embezzlement, polygamy, and rape charges, was targeted for his opposition activity.

Also in May, Sherik Karamkhudoev, an IRPT leader from the autonomous province of Gorno-Badakhshan, was sentenced to 14 years' imprisonment for "participating in mass disorders" in a closed trial. Karamkhudoev was reported missing in April 2012 after government troops launched a military operation in his home region. He resurfaced two weeks later in security services custody in Dushanbe. His lawyers and family publicly stated that he was tortured in pretrial detention.

In September, authorities in Dubai pardoned Umarali Kuvvatov, head of the opposition movement Group of 24, following 10 months of detention on a Tajik extradition request. Kuvvatov, who was detained in Dubai's airport in December 2012, stated that he feared assassination were he to be returned to Tajikistan and is now in hiding outside Tajikistan. A former businessman with close ties to the Rahmon family, Kuvvatov believes he is being pursued because of his opposition activities and his knowledge of high-level corruption.

Criminal Justice and Torture

Despite reforms in 2012 to make the criminal code's definition of torture comply with international standards, torture remained an enduring problem in 2013. Torture is often used to coerce confessions and the right to counsel is routinely denied in pretrial custody. In January, UN Special Rapporteur on Torture Juan Mendez stated in his report on his May 2012 visit to Tajikistan that with regard to torture, "numerous loopholes and inconsistencies" persist in criminal procedure and law enforcement practices. In July 2013, the Coalition against Torture, a group of Tajik NGOs, reported that despite some reforms, claims of torture by detainees have increased since the beginning of 2012.

In January, a Sughd region appellate court upheld a lower court's decision to shut down a leading human rights organization on charges that appeared politically motivated. The group, the Association of Young Lawyers "Amparo," had investigated torture and advocated for the rights of army conscripts. The Justice Ministry filed a motion to liquidate Amparo in June 2012, only weeks after an Amparo representative spoke publicly about the need to monitor severe torture and hazing in Tajikistan's army.

While impunity for torture was still the norm, authorities took a few positive steps to hold perpetrators accountable. In May, an appellate court upheld a ruling requiring the Interior Ministry to compensate the widow of Safarali Sangov approximately US$10,000 for damages relating to Sangov's death in police custody in March 2011, which human rights groups deemed to be the result of torture.

In May, a prison official was convicted of negligence in connection with the death of Hamza Ikromzoda, who had died as a result of torture in a Dushanbe prison in September 2012. Investigations against three others accused of involvement are still pending. Relatives reported that Hamza's body bore traces of torture, including burns from a heated iron.

Freedom of Media

Tajikistan further restricted media freedoms in 2013. Authorities periodically blocked access to independent websites and filed defamation suits against, or otherwise intimidated, critical journalists. While the 2012 decriminalization of libel was a step forward, Tajik law retains criminal sanctions for insulting the president or any government representative, creating a chilling effect on the freedom of speech.

In January, according to Internet service providers, the state telecommunications agency ordered the blocking of several websites, including Facebook and *Radio Ozodi*, the *Radio Free Europe* Tajik service. State Telecommunications Chief Beg Zukhorov stated that the sites were blocked at "the request of the public" and accused social media users of insulting "respectable people."

Throughout the year there were also reports that access to YouTube had been blocked, including for several days in May after a video appeared on the site showing President Rahmon singing and dancing at his son's wedding.

In February, authorities denied journalistic accreditation to veteran journalist and former *Radio Ozodi* correspondent Abdukayumov Kayumzoda, known for his journalistic independence.

Also in February a Dushanbe court ordered the independent weekly *Imruz News* to pay approximately $10,500 in civil libel damages and publicly apologize to the son of a high-ranking government official after the paper published a story questioning his early release from prison where he had been serving a nine-and-a-half-year sentence for drug trafficking.

On April 25 IPRT's website became unavailable to Tajik users for several weeks. In response to an inquiry regarding the blocking of the site, Telecommunications Chief Zukhurov denied government involvement. But a spokesperson for the Internet provider told an IRPT representative, "You represent a political party; therefore, we can only say that the problem isn't with us."

Freedom of Religion

Tajik authorities maintained tight restrictions on religious freedoms, including on religious education and worship. Authorities suppress unregistered Muslim education throughout the country, bring administrative charges against religious instructors, and have closed many unregistered mosques.

The government has increased the powers of the State Committee for Religious Affairs to enforce the country's restrictive religion law and impose large administrative fines without due process. Authorities also maintained tight controls on those seeking to receive religious education abroad.

Rights groups, religious communities, and international bodies continued to criticize the 2011 highly controversial Parental Responsibility Law, which stipulates that parents must prevent their children from participating in religious activity, except for state-sanctioned religious education, until they turn 18.

Under the pretext of combating extremism, Tajikistan continues to ban several peaceful minority Muslim groups. Some Christian minority denominations, such as Jehovah's Witnesses, are similarly banned.

Sexual Orientation and Gender Identity

Although Tajikistan decriminalized same-sex sexual activity in 1998, lesbian, gay, bisexual, and transgender (LGBT) people are subject to wide-ranging discrimination and homophobia. In 2013, Tajik NGOs documented several cases of police violence against LGBT people. LGBT people are especially vulnerable to extortion, fearing that their sexual orientation could be revealed to their family or employers.

The Rights of Women and Children

In March, President Rahmon signed a law on the prevention of domestic violence. The law allows law enforcement officers, not solely victims, to initiate criminal charges. For years, civil society groups had been pushing the government to adopt such a law because of their concerns of the seriousness of the problem of domestic violence in Tajikistan.

Key International Actors

In November, following the re-election of President Rahmon by an overwhelming majority, the Organization for Security and Co-operation in Europe election observer mission issued a statement finding that while the election had taken place peacefully, restrictive registration requirements resulted in a lack of genuine choice. The report also found that extensive positive state media coverage of President Rahmon provided him with a "significant advantage," with widespread reports on election day of "group voting, and indications of ballot box stuffing."

In a May visit, UN Assistant Secretary General for Human Rights Ivan Simonovic welcomed the country's preparations to abolish the death penalty and expressed concern over the widespread problem of violence against women.

While welcoming the Tajik government's willingness to cooperate with UN human rights mechanisms and to bring national legislation in line with international standards, Simonovic specifically called on the Tajik authorities to empower women by increasing their representation among the ranks of police officers and prosecutors.

During her November 2012 visit to Dushanbe, EU High Representative Catherine Ashton raised public concern with President Rahmon about the government forcing the closure of Amparo, the anti-torture NGO.

The United States embassy issued a statement in April regarding the beating of opposition leader Mahmadali Hayit, urging the authorities to conduct a thorough and impartial investigation. Also in April, for the second year in a row, the US Commission on International Religious Freedom designated Tajikistan a "country of particular concern" based on the government's "systematic, ongoing, and egregious violations of religious freedoms."

Turkey

In office for three terms since 2002, and enjoying a strong parliamentary majority, the ruling Justice and Development Party (AKP) has demonstrated a growing intolerance of political opposition, public protest, and critical media.

In May, police violently dispersed campaigners staging a peaceful sit-in protest against a plan to build on Istanbul's Taksim Gezi Park, triggering weeks of anti-government protests in cities throughout Turkey in late May and June. In repeatedly and harshly clamping down on protests, the government failed to uphold human rights.

On September 30, the government announced what it called a "democratization package" of reforms that demonstrated that the government is more focused on addressing the undemocratic legacy it inherited than abuses that have proliferated under its watch. Positive steps included ending the headscarf ban for women in the civil service; signaling that the 10 percent election threshold that has kept minority parties out of parliament will be lowered; and easing the restriction on mother-tongue education by permitting it in private schools. Cross-party efforts to reach a consensus on a new constitution stalled over contested elements such as the definition of citizenship and minority rights provisions.

The government made important initial steps in a peace process with the country's Kurdish minority. At the start of 2013, the government announced talks with imprisoned Kurdistan Workers' Party (PKK) leader Abdullah Öcalan to end the decades-long armed conflict with the PKK. Bolder steps to address the rights deficit for Turkey's Kurds could address the root causes of the conflict and help further human rights for all ethnic and religious minority groups in Turkey. Significantly, the government and the PKK maintained a ceasefire through 2013 and there were no deaths reported on either side.

The Syrian conflict continued to be strongly felt in Turkey's border towns, and, as of November, Turkey was hosting 500,000 Syrian refugees, including 200,000 living in camps, according to Turkish government estimates. Turkish authorities periodically prevented tens of thousands of Syrian asylum seekers from crossing into Turkey, forcing them to live in internally displaced persons camps and Syrian villages in the border areas, including in areas hit by Syrian aerial attacks. A February car bombing killed 18 at the Cilvegözü, Hatay border crossing with Syria, and a May bomb attack in the Hatay town of Reyhanlı killed 52 civilians. The Turkish authorities suspect Syrian government involvement in both attacks. Five suspects have been indicted for the former bombing and 33 suspects for the Reyhanlı bombing.

Freedom of Expression, Association, and Assembly

The government's response to the Taksim Gezi Park protests in Istanbul and anti-government protests in other cities demonstrated its intolerance of the right to peaceful assembly and free expression. The authorities charged hundreds of individuals involved in the protests—mostly in Istanbul, Ankara, and Izmir—with participating in unauthorized demonstrations, resisting the police, and damaging public property. Several dozen people face additional terrorism charges in connection with the protests. Around 50 protesters remained in pretrial detention at time of writing. A criminal investigation into the organizers of Taksim Solidarity, a platform of 128 nongovernmental organizations supporting the Gezi Park campaign and sit-in was ongoing.

The mute or biased coverage of the Taksim Gezi protests in much of Turkey's media highlighted the reluctance of many media companies to report news impartially when it conflicts with government interests. In the course of the year, scores of media workers, among them highly respected mainstream journalists and commentators writing critically of the government in different media, were fired from their jobs.

Turkey continued to prosecute journalists in 2013, and several dozen remain in jail. The trial continued of 44 mainly Kurdish journalists and media workers (20 in detention since December 2011, at time of writing) for alleged links to the Union of Kurdistan Communities (KCK), a body connected with the PKK.

The government continued efforts to amend some laws that are used to limit free speech. In April, parliament passed a reform bill—known as "the fourth reform package" following three others since March 2011—amending various laws in response to violations identified by the European Court of Human Rights (ECtHR) in many judgments against Turkey. Positive changes included lifting limits on severe restrictions on publishing or reporting statements by illegal organizations (article 6/2, Anti-Terror Law) and narrowing the scope of the crime of "making terrorist propaganda" (article 7/2, Anti-Terror Law; article 220/8, Turkish Penal Code).

Reforms undertaken in 2013 did not remedy the situation of the thousands of prosecutions of individuals on charges of "membership of an armed organization" (article 314, Turkish Penal Code) for activities amounting to nonviolent political association. Demonstrating the government's widespread misuse of terrorism laws to prosecute and incarcerate individuals, hundreds of Kurdish political activists, elected mayors, parliamentarians, officials of the Peace and Democracy Party, students, and lawyers have been in prison for long periods, in some cases for over four-and-a-half years, during their trials for association with the KCK. The human rights defender Muharrem Erbey has spent four years in prison on these charges.

There was a spate of trials in 2013 against public figures for insulting the religious sentiments of a part of the population, similar to the prosecutions of individuals for "insulting Turkishness" common in the recent past. Pianist Fazil Say received a 10-month suspended prison sentence for sending tweets that poked fun at believers and Islam. An Istanbul court in April, and again during a retrial in September, determined the tweets had "insulted the religious sentiments of a part of the population" (under article 216/3 of the Turkish Penal Code). The case was at appeal at time of writing. Lawyer Canan Arın stood trial under the same charge, plus the charge of insulting the president, for her December 2011 comments at an Antalya Bar Association seminar on women's rights mentioning the practice of early marriage in Islam and a reference to the fact that President Abdullah Gül's bride had been a child. In May, the trial was suspended on condition that Arın does not commit a similar offense for the next three years.

Police Ill-treatment and Excessive Use of Force

The Taksim Gezi Park protests saw police repeatedly disperse protesters, most of whom were entirely peaceful, with water cannons, rubber bullets, and teargas, resorting to excessive use of force and beatings of detainees. Police also unlawfully shot teargas canisters directly at protesters, leading to scores of protesters receiving serious head injuries as a direct result. The Turkish Medical Association reported that 11 people lost an eye in this way. Fourteen-year-old Berkin Elvan was hit by a teargas canister in June and remained in a critical condition in a coma at time of writing. Six demonstrators and one police officer died in the course of demonstrations between May and September. Ali İsmail Korkmaz, a protester in Eskişehir, died of his head injuries in July after being beaten during a June 2 demonstration. The trial of four police and four civilians for his murder was scheduled to begin in February 2014. A police officer stood trial in September for the fatal shooting of Ethem Sarısülük, a protester in Ankara.

A report of the Interior Ministry's inspectorate quoted in the press in September found that police in Istanbul and Izmir had used excessive force. The Security Directorate's inspectorate announced in September that 164 police officers, 32 of them senior officers, faced administrative investigation. There was no information about the progress of criminal investigations into the police for excessive use of force at time of writing. Investigation and prosecution of demonstrators proceeded at a much faster pace.

Combatting Impunity

Great obstacles remain in securing justice for victims of abuses by police, military, and state officials. The lifting of the statute of limitations for the prosecution of torture was a positive element in the April reform bill, though prosecution of unlawful killings by state perpetrators is still subject to a 20-year time limit, raising concerns about impunity for abuses committed in the early 1990s.

In June 2013, the Diyarbakır prosecutor's office said it lacked jurisdiction in the case of an attack by the Turkish Air Force in December 2011 that killed 34 Kurdish villagers close to the Iraqi Kurdistan border near Uludere. The prosecutor referred the case to the military prosecutor, but the lack of an effective investigation to date supports concerns about an official cover-up.

The retrial of a group of young men for the January 2007 murder of journalist Hrant Dink began in September following the Court of Cassation decision to quash the first verdict on procedural grounds. To date there has been inadequate investigation of evidence of state collusion in Dink's murder.

The trial of anti-AKP coup plotters (the Ergenekon gang) ended in August with 259 defendants receiving a range of long sentences and 21 acquitted. The case was under appeal. While the Ergenekon case represented a milestone in civilian control over the military, it illustrates the serious concerns regarding the proliferation in recent years, and the fairness, of "mass trials" in which multiple defendants are alleged to have been part of terrorist groups. In the Ergenekon case, there are concerns too there was no investigation of the human rights abuses in which a core group of the military suspects were implicated.

In September, the trial began of 103 retired members of the top military (5 in detention at time of writing) charged with removing the government of former Prime Minister Necmettin Erbakan in 1997.

Key International Actors

The European Union, leading EU member states, and the United States expressed strong support for a peace process to end the conflict with the PKK and solve the Kurdish issue. They also raised to varying degrees concerns over the Turkish government's handling of the Taksim Gezi Park protests, including police use of excessive force in dispersing nonviolent demonstrations. The European Commission also expressed concern over the handling of the Taksim Gezi Park protests in its annual progress report released in October. In November, the EU revived EU accession negotiations with Turkey, opening a new chapter on regional policy.

Among ECtHR rulings against Turkey in 2013, a July decision (Abdullah Yaşa and Others v. Turkey) found that improper firing of teargas by Turkish police directly at protestors, injuring a 13-year-old, had violated human rights standards, and called for stronger safeguards to minimize the risk of death and injury resulting from its use.

Following a visit in November 2012, the UN special rapporteur on extrajudicial, summary or arbitrary executions concluded "the most important and urgent challenge is the lack of accountability in cases of killings, both those perpetrated recently and those from the 1990s."

In July, the UN Working Group on Arbitrary Detention issued an opinion stating the detention of 250 military personnel on trial for coup-plotting (the so-called Sledgehammer trial) was arbitrary and violated the International Covenant on Civil and Political Rights.

Turkmenistan

Turkmenistan remains one of the world's most repressive countries. The country is virtually closed to independent scrutiny, media and religious freedoms are subject to draconian restrictions, and human rights defenders and other activists face the constant threat of government reprisal. The government continues to use imprisonment as a tool for political retaliation. The release of several political prisoners and the adoption of some new laws that some have hailed as "reform," have barely dented this stark reality.

Cult of Personality, No Pluralism

President Gurbanguly Berdymukhamedov, his relatives, and associates enjoy unlimited power and total control over all aspects of public life in Turkmenistan. Berdymukhamedov's cult of personality continued to grow in 2013. His portraits permeate the country.

After Berdymukhamedov led a mass bicycle ride in August, civil servants and students were pressured to purchase bicycles at high prices. The government often forces people, sometimes by the thousands, to gather for hours for events attended by Berdymukhamedov. They are not permitted to leave, even to use the toilet.

In a June 2013 by-election, Ovezmammed Mammedov, chairman of the Party of Industrialists and Entrepreneurs, became the first parliamentary deputy who is not a member of the ruling party. Founded by a close associate of Berdymukhamedov, with the government's active involvement, Mammedov's party presents no alternatives to government policies.

Civil Society

Repressive government policies make it extremely difficult for independent non-governmental organizations (NGOs) to operate. Civil society activists and journalists, including those living in exile and their families in Turkmenistan, face a constant threat of government reprisal. NGOs are legally banned from carrying out any work unless they are registered, yet no independent NGO has obtained registration in the past five years.

A January 2013 presidential decree required all foreign grants to be registered with the government. Funding proposals require at least five layers of government approval, including a government assessment that assistance in the proposed area is desirable. Funding for "political" activities is prohibited.

Freedom of Media and Information

In December 2012, parliament adopted a law banning censorship and affirming citizens' right to freedom of expression and information. In practice, however, there is a total absence of media freedom in Turkmenistan. The state controls all print and electronic media, with the exception of one newspaper founded by an individual close to Berdymukhamedov.

Lack of access to Turkmenistan makes foreign media coverage very difficult. In May 2013, police arrested Rovshen Yazmuhamedov, a local correspondent for *Radio Free Europe/Radio Liberty* who reported on social issues and whom authorities questioned after his articles generated online reader responses. After two weeks of international pressure, the authorities released Yazmuhamedov. The reason for his detention remains unknown.

An example of conspicuous state interference with freedom of information occurred in April 2013, when Berdymukhamedov fell off his horse during a hippodrome race. Security forces forced spectators to delete from their cameras any image of the fall.

Internet access remains limited and heavily state-controlled. The country's only Internet service provider is state-operated, and social media and many websites are blocked, including those of foreign news organizations.

Monthly Internet connectivity costs roughly US$100, making it inaccessible for many. Internet cafes require visitors to present their passports. The government is known to monitor electronic and telephone communications.

Freedom of Movement

Turkmenistan's government continues to restrict the right of its citizens to travel freely outside the country by means of an informal and arbitrary system of travel bans commonly imposed on civil society activists and relatives of exiled dissidents. While a handful of persons previously banned from foreign travel were permitted to travel abroad in 2013, others were not, including family members of political prisoners.

Students studying abroad frequently face obstacles leaving Turkmenistan when returning to their studies. In September 2013, border officials prohibited, without explanation, several Turkmen students from leaving the country to return to Tajikistan to resume studies. Tajikistan's Ministry of Education confirmed that no Turkmen students studying at Tajik universities have returned.

In June, the migration service announced it would issue new biometric passports to Turkmen citizens who also have had Russian passports since June 2003. However, according to the Turkmenistan Initiative for Human Rights, a Vienna-based group, these individuals report continued problems obtaining the new passports. The new passports are required for all travel abroad for all Turkmen citizens, with very few exceptions.

Freedom of Religion

No congregations of unregistered religious groups or communities are allowed, and religious communities have been unable to register for years. A new administrative offenses code, adopted in August 2013, establishes new fines for involvement in unregistered religious activity, although the amount of the fines will be known only when the code enters into force in 2014.

According to Forum 18, an independent international religious freedom group, in September 2013, police in Mary province summoned for questioning Ilmurad Nurliev, a Protestant pastor who was released from prison in 2012 after serving 18 months on bogus swindling charges. They questioned, harassed, and threatened him and others who signed an unsuccessful 2007 petition to register Nurliev's congregation.

Forum 18 reported that in March, police in Lebap province raided the homes of several Protestant believers and confiscated their Bibles. Courts sentenced two of them to fines of twice the average monthly wage for possession of banned religious literature.

Forum 18 also reported that in January, police raided the home of a Jehovah's Witness who had filed a complaint to the United Nations Human Rights Committee, detained and beat six visitors, and threatened one with rape. All were released, and a court fined three of the six for violating laws on religious literature.

Political Prisoners, Enforced Disappearances, and Torture

In February 2013, civil society activists Annakurban Amanklychev and Sapardurdy Khajiev were released from prison after fully serving nearly seven-year sentences on bogus weapons charges. Before their arrest, they had been affiliated with the Turkmenistan Helsinki Foundation, an exiled human rights group. Both suffer numerous health problems related to their incarceration.

Also in February, the authorities released two popular singers, Murad Ovezov and Maksat Kakabaev, sentenced on bogus charges in 2011 to five and seven years' imprisonment respectively.

In July, authorities released Geldymyrat Nurmuhammedov, a former minister of culture and tourism, who had openly criticized the government and was forced to undergo nine months of forced drug rehabilitation treatment, despite having no history of drug abuse.

However, many others continue to languish in Turkmen prisons on what appear to be politically motivated charges. The actual number of those jailed on political grounds is impossible to determine because the justice system lacks transparency, trials are closed in political cases, and the overall level of repression precludes independent monitoring of these cases.

Political dissident Gulgeldy Annaniazov, arrested in 2008, remains imprisoned on charges that are not known even to his family. He is serving an 11-year sentence.

A decade after their arrest and show trials, several dozen persons convicted in relation to the November 2002 alleged assassination attempt on former President Saparmurat Niyazov remain victims of enforced disappearances. Some of those disappeared include former Foreign Minister Boris Shikhmuradov and Turkmenistan's Former Ambassador to the Organization for Security and Co-operation in Europe (OSCE) Batyr Berdiev. Their fate is unknown, even to their families. Human Rights Watch is aware of longstanding unconfirmed reports that several defendants in the case have died in detention.

Torture remains a grave problem, particularly in high-security facilities. The International Committee for the Red Cross does not have full access to Turkmen prisons. The government has persistently denied access to the country for independent human rights monitors, including international NGOs and 10 United Nations special procedures.

Sexual Orientation and Gender Identity

Consensual sex between men is criminalized with a maximum prison sentence of two years. Turkmenistan rejected recommendations made during the April 2013 United Nations Universal Periodic Review to decriminalize consensual sex between adults of the same sex.

Key International Actors

After having had no active projects on Turkmenistan since 1997, the World Bank in July approved an interim strategy to provide analytical and technical services to Turkmenistan.

The upgrading of relations between the European Union and Turkmenistan, in the form of a Partnership and Cooperation Agreement (PCA), remained stalled. The European Parliament continued to postpone its necessary approval of the PCA, in part over human rights concerns. But there was no apparent effort on the part of the EU institutions to press for human rights reforms in exchange for the finalization of the agreement.

In November 2012, during her first trip to Central Asia, EU High Representative Catherine Ashton met with Foreign Minister Rashid Meredov to discuss energy and other issues. Ashton's public statement noted that human rights concerns were also discussed, although she did not articulate them publicly. The annual EU-Turkmenistan human rights dialogue bore no concrete results.

In April, Turkmenistan was reviewed under the UN Universal Periodic Review. While Turkmenistan accepted most of the recommendations made by UN member states during the review, it rejected eighteen among the most pressing ones, five of which related to demands to release political prisoners or make known the whereabouts of prisoners who have disappeared in the country's prison system.

In May, Assistant Secretary General for Human Rights Ivan Simonovic met with high-level officials in Turkmenistan, and emphasized the need for access to the country for UN special procedures.

Ukraine

In 2013, Ukraine derailed its long-standing ambition of deeper political and economic integration with the European Union by suspending signature of the EU-Ukraine Association Agreement, including a Deep and Comprehensive Free Trade Area that it had initialed in March 2012. The government's unexpected decision to suspend signing the agreement sparked large and mostly peaceful protests in Kiev and other major cities. The protests grew after the authorities used excessive force to disperse protesters, injuring dozens, and arrested several activists for allegedly "rioting."

Parliament considered homophobic bills aimed at criminalizing the "promotion" of homosexuality among children and failed to revise the labor code to include lesbian, gay, bisexual, and transgender (LGBT) people as a protected category. Although activists participated in an LGBT equality march in May, attacks on LGBT groups and individuals remain a serious concern. There were many more attacks on journalists than in 2012. President Viktor Yanukovich pardoned several politicians imprisoned on politically motivated charges, yet former Prime Minister Yulia Tymoshenko and several others remain in prison. Ukraine's asylum system remains flawed. The government took important steps to improve access to palliative care, but has yet to implement new regulations or expand access to opiate substitution treatment for drug users.

Rule of Law

October 2013 marked two years since former Prime Minister Yulia Tymoshenko's conviction on charges of abuse of office. In April, the European Court of Human Rights determined Tymoshenko's pre-trial detention had been arbitrary, because she was not allowed a review of her detention or to seek compensation for unlawful detention. The European Court dismissed Tymoshenko's complaints concerning conditions of pre-trial detention and found no violation concerning alleged ill-treatment during her transfer from prison to a hospital in April 2012. The European Court will rule separately on the legality of Tymoshenko's criminal conviction and sentence.

In a September report on its 2012 visit to Ukraine, the Council of Europe's Committee for the Prevention of Torture confirmed Tymoshenko's allegations of use of excessive force during her April 2012 hospital transfer.

In November, police briefly detained Tymoshenko's lawyer Serhiy Vlasenko on domestic violence charges. Vlasenko was later released on bail. Ten days later, parliament failed to pass a bill that would allow Tymoshenko to receive medical treatment in Germany, which she has requested out of concerns for her safety in Ukrainian medical institutions.

In April, President Yanukovych pardoned several former officials from Tymoshenko's government, including former Minister of Internal Affairs Yuri Lutsenko, imprisoned in 2010 on charges of embezzlement and abuse of office. Lutsenko is barred from running for public office for at least four years, until his conviction is expunged.

In March, Ukraine issued an extradition request for Viktor Romanyuk, a candidate for the Batkovchina opposition party in the October 2012 parliamentary elections, on allegations of attempting to steal state property in 2008. Italian authorities arrested Romanyuk in March, but refused to extradite him, after a court found no grounds to support a criminal prosecution. Romanyuk led in his district when results in several districts were annulled at the request of a candidate for the pro-government Party of Regions. The case against Romanyuk appears aimed at preventing him from returning to campaign in repeat elections yet to be scheduled.

Migration and Asylum

Ukraine's asylum system remains deeply flawed. Despite 2011 changes to the refugee law, asylum seekers often encounter barriers in accessing asylum procedures, face prolonged periods of administrative detention, and have difficulty challenging their detention or appealing expulsion decisions by the courts. Ukraine's refugee recognition rates continue to decline. Because of flaws in the asylum system, there is no effective protection against refoulement, although there were no known new cases in 2013.

In February, Kyiv airport officials detained former Prime Minister of Tajikistan Abdoumalik Abdoulladjanov, as he arrived from the United States, where he has refugee status, in response to a politically motivated extradition request by Tajikistan, in violation of domestic law. Following an outcry from human rights groups and international organizations, authorities denied the extradition request and released Abdoulladjanov in April.

Ukrainian authorities failed to properly investigate the refoulement of a Russian political activist, Leonid Razvozzhayev, who went missing in October 2012 while in the process of applying for asylum in Ukraine and reappeared several days later in custody in Russia. The activist alleged mistreatment by the Russian authorities upon his forcible return to Russia, including being held in incommunicado detention and forced to sign a confession under duress.

Health

The government took important steps to improve care for tens of thousands of patients suffering from severe pain, by approving local production of oral morphine and adopting new drug control regulations that significantly simplify prescription of strong pain medications. As of September 2013, however, the Ministry of Health had not operationalized the new norms, limiting patients' access to essential medications. The expansion of treatment for dependence on opium-based drugs slowed considerably. Just 7,500 patients were receiving opiate substitution treatment in 2013, far short of the 20,000 approved in the National HIV/AIDS Program. Opiate substitution treatment remains unavailable in prisons, which hold many injecting drug users.

Sexual Orientation and Gender Identity

Two homophobic bills pending in parliament propose heavy fines or a prison sentence of up to six years for the production, publication, or distribution of materials aimed at the "promotion" of homosexuality among children. In February, the Cabinet of Ministers proposed amendments to the Labor Code introducing sexual orientation as protected grounds against discrimination, but parliament twice postponed consideration of the amendments. The EU requires Ukraine to adopt comprehensive anti-discrimination legislation for completion of the EU-Ukraine visa liberalization process.

Neo-Nazi and nationalist groups led a campaign through social networks and organized rallies in different regions threatening violence against LGBT people and calling for cancellation of the May Pride Equality March. After a Kyiv court banned all public events in the city center for the day of the march, it was held on the outskirts of Kyiv with a heavy police presence protecting march participants from counter-protestors. Police investigations into online threats against LGBT activists had no results.

Several LGBT activists were attacked. In May, members of the ultra-right Svoboda political party threw sour cream at LGBT activist Olena Shevchenko outside a club in Kyiv. Shevchenko filed a complaint with police but has received no response. Also in May, unidentified assailants attacked an LGBT activist in Mykolayiv, in southern Ukraine, punching, kicking and shouting homophobic slurs at him. The police opened an investigation into the attack, which is ongoing.

The law requires transgender people to undergo forced sterilization and a mandatory 45-day psychiatric institution stay as part of legal gender recognition procedures.

During its March UN Human Rights Council Universal Periodic Review Ukraine rejected recommendations to adopt anti-discrimination legislation and drop homophobic bills.

Civil Society and Media

Thirty-five journalists were attacked in the first six months of 2013, more than twice as many as during the same period in 2012. Two journalists covering a May opposition rally in Kyiv suffered multiple injuries after a group of nationalist youth severely beat them. Police reportedly stood by without intervening. In September, a court handed suspended sentences to three of the attackers for hooliganism and obstructing journalists' work.

In July, unknown attackers assaulted journalist Sergei Ostapenko outside his apartment in Lugansk, resulting in multiple bruises. Also in July, two men beat Oleg Bogdanov, a journalist from an online outlet, "Road Control," near his home in Donetsk, breaking his nose and jaw. Both journalists had reported on police corruption. Criminal investigations into both cases are ongoing, but have produced no results.

In January, following a closed trial, a Kyiv court sentenced Oleksy Pukach, former chief of the Interior Ministry's Criminal Investigations Directorate, to life in prison for the premeditated murder in 2000 of outspoken journalist Georgi Gongadze. In 2005, a court sentenced three former policemen for carrying out the murder. Despite Pukach's testimony implicating several senior government officials, including former Ukrainian President Leonid Kuchma, with giving the order to murder Gongadze, no one else has been charged.

In July, a district court ordered that 70-year-old Raisa Radchenko from Zaporizhzhya, who publicized corruption and police abuse, be placed in a psychiatric facility, alleging that her behavior "posed a threat to society." Doctors diagnosed Radchenko, who had no history of mental illness, with a personality disorder and paranoia and forcibly gave her strong sedatives. Officials denied Radchenko access to her lawyer in police custody and in the psychiatric facility. Radchenko was released after two weeks, following an outcry by human rights groups and the Ukrainian human rights ombudsperson.

Key International Actors

Throughout the year, the EU consistently urged Ukraine's authorities to fulfill the human rights criteria the EU had set out in order to enable signature of the EU-Ukraine Association Agreement at the November 2013 Eastern Partnership summit. These included tangible progress on: ending politically motivated prosecutions; fair and transparent elections; and judiciary reform. In a sudden move, one week before the summit, the Ukrainian government announced its decision to halt the association agreement with the EU, citing among other reasons the need to "restore trade volumes" with Russia.

Earlier in the year, Russia exerted pressure on Ukraine, stating that the EU Association Agreement, including the Deep and Comprehensive Free Trade Area, would harm relations with Moscow and preclude Ukraine's participation in a regional Russia-led Customs Union. In August, Russia imposed stricter customs controls on goods from Ukraine and threatened to cut the gas supply and permanently tighten customs procedures should Ukraine sign the agreement with the EU. In September, EU Commissioner for Enlargement and European

Neighbourhood Policy Štefan Füle called Russian pressure unacceptable. EU High Representative Catherine Ashton called the Ukrainian government's decision not to sign the Association Agreement with the EU "a disappointment not just for the EU but also for the people of Ukraine."

In April, Ashton and Füle welcomed President Yanukovich's pardon of several officials imprisoned on politically motivated charges and urged the authorities to continue addressing cases of selective justice.

In July, the Representative on Freedom of the Media from the Organization for Security and Co-operation in Europe condemned attacks on journalists in Ukraine and called on the authorities to ensure journalists' safety.

In a July report, the Office of the United Nations High Commissioner for Refugees (UNHCR) said Ukraine's asylum system still requires fundamental improvements, including better protection against refoulement.

Uzbekistan

Uzbekistan's human rights record remained abysmal across a wide spectrum of violations. The country is virtually closed to independent scrutiny. Freedom of expression is severely limited. Authorities continue to crack down on rights activists, harass activists living in exile, and persecute those who practice their religion outside strict state controls. Forced labor of adults and children continues.

Torture remains systematic in the criminal justice system. The International Committee of the Red Cross took the unusual step in April of announcing publicly its decision to end prison visits in Uzbekistan. It cited its inability to follow standard procedures for visits, including being able to access all detainees of concern and speaking with detainees in private.

Despite continuing grave abuses, the United States and the European Union advanced closer relations with Uzbekistan, seeking cooperation in the war in Afghanistan.

Human Rights Defenders and Journalists

Human rights defenders face the threat of government reprisal, including imprisonment and torture. Authorities block international rights groups and media from operating in Uzbekistan.

Uzbekistan has imprisoned more than a dozen human rights defenders on wrongful charges and has brought charges against others because of their work. Those currently serving prison sentences include: Solijon Abdurakhmanov, Azam Formonov, Mehrinisso Hamdamova, Zulhumor Hamdamova, Isroiljon Holdarov, Nosim Isakov, Gaibullo Jalilov, Turaboi Juraboev, Abdurasul Khudoinazarov, Ganihon Mamatkhanov, Chuyan Mamatkulov, Zafarjon Rahimov, Yuldash Rasulov, Bobomurod Razzakov, Dilmurod Saidov, Nematjon Siddikov, and Akzam Turgunov.

Other peaceful opposition figures remain imprisoned on politically motivated charges following unfair trials, including: Muhammad Bekjanov, Batyrbek Eshkuziev, Ruhiddin Fahruddinov, Hayrullo Hamidov, Bahrom Ibragimov, Murod Juraev, Davron Kabilov, Matluba Karimova, Samandar Kukanov, Gayrat

Mehliboev, Erkin Musaev, Yusuf Ruzimuradov, Rustam Usmanov, Ravshanbek Vafoev, and Akram Yuldashev. Many detained activists are in serious ill-health and have been tortured in prison.

On January 17 Khorezm-based activist Valerii Nazarov appeared outside his home heavily drugged and unable to speak. He went missing on December 7, 2012, the day before he was to take part in an opposition rally marking the 20th anniversary of Uzbekistan's Constitution. Before going missing, Nazarov's house was surrounded by security services. Friends believe he was held in a mental hospital.

On February 5, 25 men broke into the home of Fergana-based rights activist Nematjon Siddikov, beating him and his three sons. Days earlier Siddikov had alleged the involvement of officials in a smuggling ring along the Uzbek-Kyrgyz border. Although in the vicinity, police failed to protect Siddikov during the attack but intervened later to arrest him on charges of defamation and assault. In May, Siddikov and one of his sons were sentenced to six years' imprisonment.

In June, authorities deported Kyrgyz rights defender Tolekan Ismailova when she arrived at the Tashkent airport. Also in June, Ergashbai Rahimov, an activist who had advocated for the release of imprisoned journalist Solijon Abdurakhamanov, was detained for over a month in Karakalpakstan on defamation charges.

On July 8, a court in Karshi fined rights defenders Elena Urlaeva, Malohat Eshonkulova, and others a total of US$15,500 for staging a peaceful protest over the incommunicado detention of Hasan Choriev, father of the leader of Birdamlik, an opposition movement. Several women attacked Urlaeva and others moments before they began their protest outside the local office of the prosecutor general. Officials in the building did not stop the beating but later arrested the activists.

In August, 60-year-old Bobomurad Razzakov, the Bukhara region representative of the rights group Ezgulik ("Compassion"), was convicted of involvement in human trafficking and sentenced to four years' imprisonment.

On August 23, a court in Jizzakh sentenced 75-year-old activist Turaboi Juraboev to five years in prison. Arrested in May, Juraboev was found guilty of extortion despite the fact that three of the plaintiffs withdrew their complaints. Juraboev is known for his anti-corruption work.

In July, a Tashkent court sentenced in absentia France-based activist Nadejda Atayeva, her father, and her brother to six, seven, and nine years' imprisonment, respectively, on trumped-up charges of embezzlement. Prosecutors never informed Atayeva about the trial, which was held in secret.

In September, authorities arrested Sergei Naumov, a journalist known for his independent reporting on politically sensitive issues such as ethnic discrimination, under circumstances that appeared orchestrated to keep him from carrying out his work. Naumov was held in incommunicado detention for 12 days after a hearing marred by procedural violations and without access to independent counsel.

The Andijan Massacre

Eight years on, authorities continue to refuse an independent investigation into the 2005 government massacre of hundreds of people in Andijan. They had gathered to protest in connection with the prosecution of local businessmen on terrorism charges. Authorities persecute anyone suspected of having witnessed the atrocities or who attempts to speak publicly about them.

On May 13, authorities arrested activists Elena Urlaeva and Adelaida Kim as they attempted to lay a wreath of flowers at a public monument in Tashkent to commemorate the massacre's eighth anniversary.

Criminal Justice and Torture

Torture plagues Uzbekistan's places of detention, where it is often used to coerce confessions and occurs with impunity. Methods include beating with batons and plastic bottles, hanging by the wrists and ankles, rape, and sexual humiliation.

There is no evidence that the introduction of habeas corpus in 2008 has reduced torture in pretrial custody or ensured due process for detainees. Authorities routinely violate the right to counsel. Defense lawyers that take on politically sensitive cases have been disbarred since the passage of a law in 2009 dissolving the independent bar association.

The government regularly denies the existence of torture and has failed to implement meaningful recommendations made by the United Nations special rapporteur in 2003 or similar ones by international bodies in the past decade.

Authorities refuse to investigate torture allegations and Human Rights Watch continues to receive credible reports of torture, including suspicious deaths in custody. In March a Tashkent court sentenced 16-year-old Grigorii Grigoriev, son of rights activist Larisa Grigorieva, on trumped-up charges of theft. The judge ignored Grigoriev's testimony that he required hospitalization after police beat him into a confession.

In June, police in Urgench hit Sardorbek Nurmetov, a Protestant Christian, five times with a book on the head and chest, kicked him in the legs, and refused him medical attention. Police ignored Nurmetov's formal complaint and initiated charges for illegally storing religious materials in his home.

Forced Sterilization

Human Rights Watch received credible reports that some women who have given birth to two or more children have been targeted for involuntary sterilization, especially in rural regions. In some areas, doctors are pressured to perform sterilizations. Lack of access to information and safe medical facilities resulted in many unsafe surgical sterilizations sometimes performed without consent of the women.

Freedom of Religion

Authorities continued their campaign of arbitrary detention and torture of Muslims who practice their faith outside state controls. In April, the Initiative Group of Independent Human Rights Defenders estimated there were 12,000 persons currently imprisoned on vague and overbroad charges related to "religious extremism," with over 200 convicted this year alone.

Followers of the late Turkish Muslim theologian Said Nursi were imprisoned for religious extremism. Authorities also imprison and fine Christians who conduct peaceful religious activities for administrative offenses, such as illegal religious teaching.

517

Authorities often extend sentences of prisoners convicted of "religious" offenses for alleged violations of prison regulations. Such extensions occur without due process and add years to a prisoner's sentence. They appear aimed at keeping religious prisoners incarcerated indefinitely.

Sexual Orientation and Gender Identity

Consensual sexual relations between men are criminalized with a maximum prison sentence of three years. According to a local nongovernmental organization, police sometimes use blackmail and extortion against gay men due to their sexual orientation.

Forced Labor

State-sponsored forced labor of children and adults in the cotton sector continues on a massive scale. Authorities forcibly mobilize over a million adults and schoolchildren, mainly ages 15-17 but some as young as 9, to pick cotton for up to two months each autumn. Living in the fields for weeks at a time, workers live in filthy conditions without access to safe drinking water. They contract illnesses, miss work or school, and pick cotton daily in line with quotas for which they receive little to no pay.

In response to international pressure, authorities reduced the numbers of young children picking cotton but compensated by shifting the burden to older children and adults. The forced labor of adults disrupts the availability of essential services, as authorities draw heavily on public sector workers—doctors, nurses, teachers, and other civil servants—to fulfill quotas.

After years of refusing the International Labour Organization access to monitor the harvest, Tashkent agreed to a limited monitoring mission in 2013. However, it insisted that the mission's mandate be limited to child labor and that monitoring teams include Uzbek officials, raising serious concerns about the mission's ability to credibly investigate abuses and to ensure the safety of those being interviewed.

Key International Actors

Uzbekistan faced virtually no consequences for its continuing refusal to cooperate with international institutions on human rights. For the past 11 years, it has denied access to all 11 UN special monitors who have requested invitations and has failed to comply with recommendations that various expert bodies have made. At its Universal Periodic Review in April, Uzbek officials categorically declared that "there are no political prisoners in Uzbekistan" and that "the issue [of Andijan] is closed" and rejected most recommendations on key human rights issues, stating that they "do not correspond to... reality."

The European Union's position on human rights in Uzbekistan remained weak, with no public expressions of concern about the government's deteriorating record and no policy consequences for Tashkent's failure to meet the EU's reform expectations articulated by EU foreign ministers in 2010. In November 2012, EU High Representative Catherine Ashton visited Tashkent but did not publicly voice concern with its worsening human rights situation.

The US government continued to avoid attaching any serious policy consequences for Uzbekistan's failure to improve its rights record. The Obama administration views Uzbekistan as a critical part of the Northern Distribution Network through which it has sent non-lethal supplies to Afghanistan since 2009.

Since 2004, the US Congress has restricted assistance to Tashkent based on its rights record and imposed further limits following the Andijan massacre. However, beginning in 2012 the Obama administration exercised authority Congress granted it to waive rights-related sanctions and restarted military aid to Tashkent.

The State Department's human trafficking report placed Uzbekistan in the lowest category—Tier 3—based on Tashkent's systematic use of forced labor, but the Obama administration waived the sanctions provided for under this status citing national security grounds.

HUMAN
RIGHTS
WATCH

"Between a Drone and Al-Qaeda"

The Civilian Cost of US Targeted Killings in Yemen

WORLD REPORT

2014

MIDDLE EAST
AND NORTH AFRICA

Algeria

Despite the lifting of the state of emergency in April 2011 and the adoption of new laws on association, media, and political parties, Algeria has made little progress on the protection of human rights. Authorities continued to restrict freedom of assembly and association, prohibiting meetings and protests. They clamped down on union rights, frequently resorting to arrests and prosecutions of union leaders and activists.

Security forces and armed groups continued to enjoy impunity for atrocities they committed during the civil war of the 1990s. Armed militants committed a significant number of attacks against government officials, members of security forces, and civilians, culminating in the attack against the gas facility of In Amenas. After lifting the state of emergency back in 2011, authorities adopted new legislation authorizing the long-established practice of holding alleged terrorists in assigned secret residences for up to nine months.

Freedom of Assembly

Algerian authorities continue to restrict freedom of assembly, relying on pre-emptive techniques, including blocking access to sites of planned demonstrations and arresting organizers in advance to prevent public protests from even beginning. During peaceful demonstrations in the south of the country organized by associations of the unemployed, police arrested protesters. Courts later sentenced several of them to fines or suspended prison terms. Police arrested Taher Belabès, a coordinator for the National Committee for the Defense of the Rights of the Unemployed, in the southern town of Ouargla on January 2, after police dispersed peaceful protesters demanding jobs and the sacking of local officials for failing to tackle unemployment. Prosecutors charged Belabès with "obstructing the flow of traffic" and "inciting a gathering" and sentenced him on February 3 to one month in prison and a fine of 50,000 Algerian dinars (US$614).

Freedom of Association

On February 20, 2013, police arrested and expelled 10 non-Algerian members of associations of unemployed workers in other Maghreb countries who had traveled to Algiers to attend the first Maghreb Forum for the Fight Against Unemployment and Temporary Work (*Forum maghrébin pour la lutte contre le chômage et le travail précaire*) that was to take place on February 20 and 21 at the labor union center in the Bab Ezzouar neighborhood. Officials held them at the Bab Ezzouar police station, then took them to the airport, from where they expelled five Tunisians and three Mauritanians that same day, and two Moroccans the following day.

Freedom of Speech

The state operates all television and radio stations, and on key issues, such as security and foreign and economic policy, they broadcast the official line and allow no dissident commentary or critical reporting.

The January 2012 Law on Information eliminated prison sentences but raised fines for journalists who commit speech offenses. The offenses include defaming or showing contempt for the president, state institutions, and courts. The law has also broadened restrictions on journalists by requiring them to respect vaguely worded concepts, such as national unity and identity, public order, and national economic interests.

Other speech offenses still pervade the penal code, which provides for up to three years in prison for tracts, bulletins, or flyers that "may harm the national interest" and up to one year for defaming or insulting the president of the republic, parliament, the army, or state institutions. Prosecutors haul journalists and independent publishers into court for defaming or insulting public officials, and first instance courts sometimes sentence them to prison and heavy fines, only to have appeals courts overturn or convert to suspended sentences the penalties imposed by the lower courts.

On May 19, the public prosecutor in Algiers charged Hisham Abboud, director and owner of the private newspaper *Jaridati* and its French edition *Mon Journal*, of compromising state security by publishing a story about President Abdelaziz Bouteflika's health. The Telecommunications Ministry had banned the two newspapers from publishing a front page report on the deteriorating health of the president, based on French medical sources and sources close to Bouteflika.

Judicial Harassment

In 2013, authorities charged several human rights activists and union leaders with crimes related to the peaceful exercise of their right to assemble or their voicing of support for strikes and demonstrations. A court on May 6 sentenced Abdelkader Kherba, a member of the National Committee to Defend the Rights of the Unemployed (*Comité national pour la défense des droits des chômeurs-CNDDC) to* two months in prison, and fined him 20,000 dinars (US$250) after he distributed leaflets about national unemployment.

Rights of Unions

Algerian authorities in 2013 have increasingly clamped down on workers' efforts to form independent unions and organize and participate in peaceful protests and strikes. Authorities have blocked union demonstrations, arbitrarily arrested trade unionists, and prosecuted some on criminal charges, when the real motive behind their prosecution appears to have been punishment for union activities.

Algerian authorities engage in administrative maneuvers to withhold legal status from independent unions. The law on legalizing new unions requires these groups only to notify the authorities that they exist, not to seek their permission to form. But authorities sometimes refuse to issue a receipt proving they have been notified.

The Union of Higher Education Teachers in Solidarity (*Syndicat des Enseignants du Supérieur Solidaires*), for example, filed its papers on January 19, 2012. It received no receipt at the time and has yet to receive any response from the government, which means it cannot legally operate.

Accountability for Past Crimes

The 2006 Law on Peace and National Reconciliation provides a legal framework for impunity for perpetrators of atrocities during the civil war. The law also makes it a crime to denigrate state institutions or security forces for the way they conducted themselves during the political strife, potentially penalizing people who allege that the forces perpetrated human rights violations. Associations of the disappeared, which continue to call for truth and justice, face harassment.

Terrorism and Counterterrorism

On January 16, 2013, militants linked to Al-Qaeda and affiliated with a brigade led by a man named Mokhtar Belmokhtar took more than 800 people hostage at the Tigantourine gas facility In Amenas, near the Algeria-Libya border. The Algerian Special Forces raided the site in an effort to free the hostages. At the end of the episode, at least 37 foreign hostages and 29 members of the armed group were killed.

Algeria strengthened its role as a regional player on counterterrorism, and continued to participate in the Global Counterterrorism Forum, a multilateral group that the US created to expand counterterrorism discussions beyond Western, industrialized countries.

Key International Actors

The European Union, which has an "association agreement" with Algeria, agreed to provide Algeria with €172 million (US$234 million) in aid between 2011 and 2013.

On July 2013, the government applied for candidature on the United Nations Human Rights Council for the period of 2014 to 2016. Yet despite pledges to UN High Commissioner for Human Rights Navi Pillay during her visit to Algeria in September 2012, the government is still denying access to the UN special rapporteur on torture and other cruel, inhuman or degrading treatment or punishment, the UN Working Groups on Enforced or Involuntary Disappearances and on Arbitrary Detention, and the special rapporteur on summary, arbitrary, or extrajudicial executions.

In its most recent Universal Periodic Review of Algeria in 2012, the UN Human Rights Council recommended the release of prisoners detained solely for exercising freedom of expression, the removal of barriers to free assembly and expression, and the ratification of several international treaties, including the Rome Statute of the International Criminal Court. However, to date the Algerian authorities have implemented none of these recommendations. On November 12, 2013, the General Assembly of the UN elected Algeria as a member to the Human Rights Council.

Bahrain

Bahrain's human rights record regressed further in key areas in 2013 and the government made little real progress regarding reforms it claimed to pursue.

Security forces continued to arrest scores of individuals arbitrarily in towns where anti-government protests regularly take place. Continuing reports of torture and ill-treatment in detention were consistent with the findings of the 2011 Bahrain Independent Commission of Inquiry (BICI). The government's failure to implement key recommendations of the BICI stand in contrast to its claims it is making progress on human rights. The judicial system, headed by ruling family members, has yet to hold any senior official responsible for serious human rights violations that have occurred since 2011, including torture-related deaths in detention.

High-profile critics of the government remain in jail on charges that relate solely to exercising their rights to freedom of expression and assembly. Authorities continue to arrest and prosecute dissidents, including human rights defenders, on security-related charges. The arrest of the deputy head of al-Wefaq, the largest opposition group, prompted all the other opposition groups participating in a deeply flawed national dialogue process to suspend their involvement. The process resumed in February after a one-year hiatus. Of the 27 participating groups, 18 are linked to the government and they had still had not agreed on an agenda at time of writing.

In August, the government passed a set of laws that further restrict the right to freedom of assembly and may further restrict the right to freedom of expression.

Arbitrary Detentions, Ill-Treatment, and Torture

Security forces continued to detain scores of individuals arbitrarily every month, according to local rights activists. In May, masked plainclothes police conducted targeted night-time raids in towns around Bahrain's motor racing circuit in advance of the Formula 1 Grand Prix. Arresting officers failed to produce arrest or search warrants. Authorities often deny holding detainees when family members seek to locate them and initial interrogations typically take place without the presence of a lawyer, in violation of Bahrain's constitution and code of criminal procedure. The Bahrain Centre for Human Rights documented approximately 200 cases in a six-week period between July and mid-August during which authorities falsely denied holding detained individuals for two to ten days.

Many detainees complained of ill-treatment in detention, sometimes rising to the level of torture. Four former detainees told Human Rights Watch that they were severely beaten, and in one case sexually assaulted, while in detention at the Interior Ministry's Criminal Investigations Directorate (CID) in 2013. Bahrain's constitution forbids the use of torture and use of evidence secured by torture, and Bahrain is a state party to the United Nations Convention Against Torture.

According to local rights groups, authorities detained scores of children for participating in anti-government protests in 2013 and regularly held them in detention facilities alongside adults. One 17-year-old boy detained at CID headquarters told Human Rights Watch that he was forced to stand in a corridor, handcuffed, and blindfolded for several hours as passing officers insulted him and one officer threatened they would rape him.

In April, authorities indefinitely postponed the planned visit of UN Special Rapporteur on Torture Juan Mendez.

Prosecution and Harassment of Government Critics

In January, Bahrain's Court of Cassation upheld lengthy convictions for 13 high-profile critics of the government. The evidence against them consisted of public statements advocating reforms to curtail the power of the ruling family, Al Khalifa, and confessions that the defendants alleged were coerced while they were in incommunicado detention.

In September, authorities arrested Khalil al-Marzooq, the assistant secretary-general of al-Wefaq, the main legal opposition group. Prosecutors ordered al-Marzooq to be held for 30 days to investigate charges that he had been "inciting and advocating terrorism." The charges relate to comments he made at a rally in which he publicly denounced violence. Shortly after his arrest, al-Wefaq and other participating opposition groups announced they were suspending their involvement in the national dialogue.

On September 29, a Bahrain court sentenced 50 persons, including several rights activists, alleged to be part of the February 14th Youth Coalition, to jail terms ranging from 5 to 15 years for security-related offenses, including "establishing a terrorist group for the purpose of disturbing public security, disabling constitution and law, preventing public institution and authorities from performing their duties, attacking public and personal rights, and harming national unity."

At time of writing Human Rights Watch was unable to determine if any of the convictions were for recognizable criminal acts warranting such serious sentences. Defense lawyers and detainees alleged that confessions were coerced.

One defendant, rights and opposition activist Naji Fateel, who received a 15-year sentence, claimed he was badly tortured in April during his first three days in detention. He alleged that authorities handcuffed and blindfolded him, beat him severely, subjected him to electric shocks, and suspended him from the ceiling. Political activist Reyhana al-Mousawi, who received a five-year sentence, alleged she was subjected to electro-shocks and forced to sign a confession.

Abdul Ghani Kanjar, the former spokesperson for the National Committee for Martyrs and Victims of Torture who fled Bahrain in 2012 and is now the overseas spokesperson for the Haq Movement for Liberty and Democracy, an unrecognized opposition group, received a 15-year sentence in absentia. Kanjar told Human Rights Watch he had no relation to the 14th February Coalition and was not familiar with the names of many of those convicted.

In August, staff at Copenhagen Airport, apparently acting on directions from Bahraini authorities, prevented the acting director of the Bahrain Center for Human Rights, Maryam al-Khawaja, from boarding a flight to Manama. Al-Khawaja, whose father and sister are in jail in Bahrain as a result of their protests against the government, had publicly announced her plans to fly to Bahrain to monitor anti-government protests planned for August 14.

The targeting of medical professionals continues to be a concern. In January, seven physicians and one nurse were dismissed from their positions at the Ministry of Health and convicted for providing medical care to protesters in 2011. The continuing presence of security forces around hospitals prevents neutral medical access, in violation of medical ethics and the right to health.

Accountability

Since 2011, Bahrain established an ombudsman's office in the Ministry of Interior and a Special Investigations Unit in the Public Prosecution Office, but neither of these offices took steps to hold senior officials accountable for serious human rights abuses or address what the BICI characterized as a "culture of impunity." Senior officials told Human Rights Watch that a platoon commander in the police and a battalion commander in the criminal investigations division had been found responsible for rights violations, but it is not clear what action, if any, was taken in these cases.

In May, a Bahrain appeals court reduced the seven-year sentence of a Bahrain police lieutenant convicted of the April 2011 murder of Hani Abd al-Aziz Jumaa to six months. The lieutenant is the highest ranking security official known to have been convicted for abuses.

Freedom of Assembly, Association, and Expression

In April, Bahrain's cabinet endorsed an amendment to article 214 of the penal code to increase from two to five years the maximum sentence for insulting the king. Lawyer Mahdi al-Basri was one of at least five individuals sentenced to prison in 2013 for allegedly insulting King Hamad bin Isa Al Khalifa on social media.

In early August, the parliament issued 22 recommendations to King Hamad in advance of planned anti-government protests on August 14. One recommendation led to the amendment of article 11 of the 1973 Law on Public Gatherings. All demonstrations, marches, rallies, or sit-ins must now have the prior written permission of the head of state security, who can stipulate the number of permitted protesters and the time and place of any protest.

Political parties remain prohibited, but in 2013, 20 licensed political societies operated in the country, including Islamist and secular, pro-government and opposition groups. In September, Justice Minister Shaikh Khalid bin Ali Al Khalifa announced an amendment to the 2005 Law for Political Societies to require that political groups secure advance government permission to meet with foreign diplomats in Bahrain and abroad and that a Foreign Ministry representative accompany them in such meetings.

Authorities continue to restrict freedom of association by arbitrarily rejecting registration applications for civil and political groups and intrusively supervising independent organizations. The provisions of a 2012 Draft Law on Civil Organizations and Institutions submitted to parliament in January 2013 for approval are much more restrictive than those in an earlier 2007 draft, and in some respects worse than the 1989 law still in effect. At time of writing the parliament had not acted on the draft.

Women's Rights

Law no.19 of 2009 on the Promulgation of the Law of Family Rulings regulates matters of personal status in Bahrain's Sunni courts, but it does not apply in the country's Shia courts, which means that the majority of Bahraini women are not covered by a codified personal status law. Domestic violence is not specifically addressed in the penal code and marital rape is not considered a crime.

Migrant Workers

Approximately 460,000 migrant workers, primarily from Asia, make up 77 percent of Bahrain's private workforce. Due to shortcomings in Bahrain's legal and regulatory framework and failure to enforce laws, they endure serious abuses such as unpaid wages, passport confiscation, unsafe housing, excessive work hours, physical abuse, and forced labor. Conditions for domestic workers are of particular concern. A regional Gulf Cooperation Council unified contract for domestic workers, expected to be approved in early 2014, falls short of the minimum standards outlined in the Domestic Workers Convention that the International Labour Organization adopted in 2011.

International Actors

Two European Parliament resolutions strongly criticized Bahrain's human rights record, as did a joint statement supported by 47 states in September 2013 at the United Nations Human Rights Council in Geneva. The United Kingdom and the United States, key allies of Bahrain, joined the HRC statement but generally failed to criticize publicly abusive steps taken by Bahrain in 2013. The European Union failed to use its collective weight in actively and publicly pressing for the immediate and unconditional release of imprisoned Bahraini activists, three of whom are dual nationals of Bahrain and EU member states. In August, media reported that Britain was in talks with Bahrain over the sale of 12 Typhoon jets.

Egypt

After mass protests on June 30 against the Muslim Brotherhood, General Abdel Fattah al-Sissi on July 3 deposed President Mohamed Morsy, who had come to power through democratic elections one year earlier, and appointed Constitutional Court judge Adly Mansour as interim president. Mansour issued a Constitutional Declaration setting out a roadmap, which included drafting a new constitution and elections. A constituent assembly of 50 appointed members completed a draft of the constitution in December. In the months following the ouster of President Morsy, police used excessive lethal force, killing over 1,300 persons at protests, and arrested over 3,500 Brotherhood supporters. Armed group escalated attacks in North Sinai killing scores of police and soldiers. A Sinai-based armed group, Ansar Bayt al-Maqdes, claimed responsibility for a Cairo assassination attempt in September on the interim government's minister of interior.

Prior to his removal, President Morsy's Muslim Brotherhood-dominated government had shown disregard for rights protections, with an increase in the prosecutions of journalists, police abuse, and sectarian violence. In December 2012, 33 percent of eligible voters (the lowest turnout for any poll since the 2011 uprising) approved Morsy's controversial new constitution by 64 percent in a referendum. The constitution further undermined key rights protections following Morsy's November 2012 Constitutional Declaration which immunized his decisions from judicial review. Legislation issued by the Shura Council, Egypt's interim legislative body following the June 2012 dissolution of the People's Assembly, included deeply restrictive draft public assembly and draft associations laws.

Extrajudicial Killings and Torture by Security Forces

In January, police in Port Said killed 46 people over three days after gunmen killed two policemen during a demonstration outside a prison. In response, President Morsy praised the police and declared a one-month state of emergency in the Canal cities of Port Said, Suez, and Ismailia. In January and February, police shot dead at least 22 other anti-Morsy protesters in Cairo, Mansoura, and Mahalla.

Clashes between pro- and anti-Brotherhood protesters in the week of Morsy's overthrow between June 30 and July 5 killed at least 54 people around the country. Security forces used excessive lethal force in dealing with pro-Brotherhood protests that involved some violence on the part of protesters. On the morning of July 8, the military broke up a Brotherhood sit-in outside the Republican Guard headquarters, killing 61 protesters who responded with stone-throwing and some gunfire, which killed two security officers.

On July 27, the police clashed with a pro-Brotherhood march, killing 95 protesters, many of them with single-shot wounds to the head and chest. On August 14, police forcibly broke up the two Muslim Brotherhood sit-ins at Rab'a al-Adawiya and al-Nahda in Cairo, killing up to 1,000 people, according to Prime Minister Hazem Beblawy. A small number of protesters in the Rab'a sit-in responded to the police with gunfire, killing seven policemen. Security officials failed to allow ambulances safe access to the sit-in to transfer severely wounded protesters to hospitals, failed to allow safe exit for patients, and shot dead one ambulance worker. Attacks on health workers and facilities threaten the realization of the right to health. Residents and officials had complained about the tens of thousands of Morsy supporters blocking the streets, and detaining and abusing suspected "infiltrators."

Impunity for Abuse by Security Forces

There was no effort to account for the crimes of the Mubarak era or those killed by the police and military during and after the January-February 2011 uprising. In January, Morsy received a report by a fact-finding committee he had set up on police and military abuses against protesters, but refused to make its findings or recommendations public. In July 2013, the interim government established a Ministry for Transitional Justice but it took no steps towards accountability. The government failed to set up a fact-finding committee to look into the mass killing of protesters, despite Interim President Adly Mansour's July 8 promise to do so.

In a rare case of police accountability, a court in March sentenced one officer to three years imprisonment for shooting protesters during the protests in Mohamed Mahmoud Street in Cairo in November 2011. Only 5 of the 38 trials of middle and low-ranking police officers accused of killing protesters in January

2011 resulted in prison sentences. Two of them were suspended, so that only two officers have served actual prison time. In January, the Court of Cassation overturned the conviction of former president Hosni Mubarak. His retrial opened in May and was ongoing at time of writing. In October, the trial opened of four police officers for the deaths of 37 detainees they were transporting to Abu Zaabal prison on August 18 on charges of "negligence and involuntary manslaughter."

Prosecutors failed to investigate security forces for the killing of the hundreds of protesters in July and August, yet were quick to refer protesters to trial on violence-related charges. In November, a minor offenses court sentenced 12 students to 17 years imprisonment for a protest on October 30.

Mass Arrests and Torture

In January and February, the police arrested over 800 protesters outside the presidential palace and elsewhere and illegally held hundreds, including at least 264 children, in Central Security Forces camps where they subjected dozens to torture, including sexual abuse. Between January and June, at least eight people died in custody as a result of torture by the police. In March, Morsy praised the police as the "heart of the revolution."

After the military deposed Morsy in July, military officials detained the former president along with 10 of his senior aides incommunicado at an unknown location for weeks. On November 4, the authorities eventually transferred Morsy to court for the opening of his trial. The judge then ordered his detention in a regular prison. Five of Morsy's aides remained detained incommunicado without legal basis at the time of writing.

In the weeks following the dispersal of the sit-ins on August 14, police arrested the majority of the high-level and much of the mid-level leadership of the Brotherhood. They also arrested thousands of demonstrators, including 1,400 detained in the immediate aftermath of the sit-in dispersals—150 of whom were children. Prosecutors ordered their pretrial detention pending interrogation on charges of inciting or participating in violence and have continued renewing their detention on the basis of requests from security agencies but little independent evidence.

Military Trials

Throughout the year military prosecutors continued to try civilians before military courts despite government claims, first by Morsy and subsequently by the post July 3 government that this was no longer occurring. The number of military trials of civilians increased following Morsy's overthrow. Although the military mostly refrained from bringing people before military courts in Cairo, even in cases where clashes with protesters involved the military, they tried at least 96 civilians before military courts in the other governorates. In September, a military court in Suez sentenced 51 Muslim Brotherhood members to imprisonment on charges of assaulting military officers. In October, a military court sentenced *Watan* journalist Hatem Abdel Nour to one year in prison for impersonating a military officer. In October and November, military trials sentenced two Sinai-based journalists, Ahmad Abu Draa' and Mohamed Sabry, to suspended prison sentences in relation to their work as journalists.

Freedom of Religion and Sectarian Violence

In the first half of the year under Morsy, prosecutors interrogated at least 14 people on charges of blasphemy, referring 11 of them to trials which resulted in prison sentences for opinions protected by freedom of expression. Incidents of sectarian violence continued and increased dramatically after his overthrow. In April, sectarian violence in the town of Khosus left five Christians and one Muslim dead. Two days later, the police failed to intervene to halt clashes that broke out after a funeral at the main Coptic cathedral in Cairo, and at times themselves shot at Christian protesters inside church grounds.

In June, a mob of hundreds of Islamists lynched four Shia Egyptians in the village of Abu Musallim just outside Cairo after weeks of anti-Shia hate speech by Islamist extremists. The Morsy administration condemned the lynching but failed to condemn the sectarianism that incited it or to uphold the right of Shia to religious freedom.

In the aftermath of Morsy's overthrow, there was an unprecedented increase in attacks on churches and property of Christians. Immediately following the August 14 dispersals of Muslim Brotherhood sit-ins in Cairo, mobs chanting Islamist slogans attacked at least 42 churches, burning or damaging 37, and leaving 4 people dead. The attacks came after weeks of anti-Christian discourse in speeches at the two Brotherhood sit-ins in Cairo. Security forces failed to intervene to halt the attacks but subsequently arrested dozens of suspects. Prosecutors ordered their pretrial detention.

Freedom of Expression

Under Morsy there was a sharp increase in prosecutions of journalists and political activists on charges of "insulting" officials or institutions and "spreading false information," using Mubarak-era penal code provisions. An investigative judge appointed by the justice minister questioned over 15 journalists and politicians on criminal charges of "insulting the judiciary" after they publicly criticized the judiciary's lack of independence. Courts ordered fines and suspended sentences in at least five defamation cases. In April, the president's office withdrew nine criminal complaints it had filed against journalists for "insulting the president" in response to public criticism.

On July 3, the military-installed authorities shut down the Muslim Brotherhood TV station along with two other Islamist stations. Over the following two months, security officers raided the Arabic and English offices of Al Jazeera and the offices of Turkish broadcaster TRT, and police arbitrarily arrested at least 40 journalists during mass arrests after clashes. At least seven remain detained, including Al Jazeera Arabic journalist Abdallah al-Shamy who was arrested during the dispersal of the Rab'a sit-in on August 14. In September, security forces raided and sealed the premises of *Freedom and Justice*, the Muslim Brotherhood newspaper. In October and November, police arrested dozens of protesters for peaceful activities such as the possession of flyers or balloons with anti-military slogans on them.

Freedom of Association and Labor Rights

The repressive Mubarak-era Law 84 on Associations remains in force, and security agencies blocked funding for human rights projects at registered NGOs, leading to a freeze on activities. From March to June, the Shura Council and the presidency drafted a deeply restrictive law on associations. In June, a Cairo criminal court sentenced 43 Egyptian and foreign nongovernmental organization workers to prison sentences, some of them suspended. Morsy's government failed to pass a new trade unions law and, by the end of the year, hundreds of independent trade unions remained without legal protection. With the change in government in July, a cabinet drafting committee completed a new draft law on associations, but the government did not formally propose the law.

The Rights of Women and Girls

Systematic sexual harassment of women and girls in public spaces continued without serious government attempts to halt or deter the practice. In January, Egyptian groups reported at least 19 cases of mob sexual assaults, including one woman who attackers raped with a bladed weapon and cut her genitals. In June and July, women's rights groups confirmed 186 sexual attacks on women in Cairo's Tahrir Square over one week. The government's response has typically been to downplay the extent of the problem or to seek to address it through legislative reform alone. There is no law criminalizing domestic violence specifically. Other forms of violence against women, including child marriage and female genital mutilation continued to take place in some areas, despite laws prohibiting them. Personal status laws in Egypt continue to discriminate against women in relation to marriage, divorce, child custody, and inheritance. Drafters of the 2013 constitution failed to include a provision ensuring equality between men and women in the constitution.

Refugee, Asylum-Seeker, and Migrant Rights

The population of refugees from Syria in Egypt grew to 300,000 by the end of the year. Over 125,000 Syrians have registered with the United Nations High Commissioner for Refugees (UNHCR); Egypt, however, has prevented UNHCR from registering Palestinians from Syria. Airport officials sent three Syrian men—two in January and one in October—back to Syria against their will in violation of the principle of non-refoulement.

After Morsy's overthrow, security officials implemented a visa requirement and security clearance for Syrians. As a result airport officials denied entry to at least 276 Syrians and returned them to Syria again in violation of the international prohibition against refoulement. In July, police and military police arrested at least 72 Syrian men and 9 boys at checkpoints on main Cairo roads in an arrest sweep following a media campaign accusing Syrians of supporting the

Muslim Brotherhood. Since August, Egypt has detained without legal basis over 1,500 refugees from Syria, including 250 children, and coerced over 1,200 to leave Egypt under threat of indefinite detention.

African migrants continued to report torture and rape at the hands of traffickers operating in Sinai, a problem the government failed to address or acknowledge. In May, prosecutors interrogated a Sudanese man on charges of human trafficking, torture, and rape in the Sinai but failed to refer anyone to trial. Egyptian prosecutors have investigated only one person on Sinai-related trafficking offenses but have made no effort to investigate collusion on the part of members of the security forces, including at the Suez Canal and along the route from the southern border.

Key International Actors

The United States and European Union member states occasionally raised human rights concerns publicly but did not strongly condemn rights abuses under Morsy, including in response to police violence in January and February. After the military deposed Morsy, and in light of pressure in the US Congress to suspend US military aid to Egypt, the US canceled scheduled joint military exercises and later, after the violent dispersal of the two sit-ins, suspended the delivery of F16 fighter jets.

In October, President Barack Obama suspended additional military and economic assistance, including US$260 million in cash aid, and withheld certain large-scale military systems, such as Apache helicopters. Despite this step, little was said about ongoing abuses and the lack of accountability.

In June, the European Court of Auditors said in a report that EU aid to Egypt achieved little progress in support of human rights and democracy. In August, the EU Foreign Affairs Council reminded member states of their obligation to suspend commercial weapons sales to Egypt in accordance with the EU's Common Position on arms exports, but failed to take any other measures. In September, member states at the Human Rights Council in Geneva failed to take collective action on Egypt, although some member states raised Egypt as a country of concern.

Iran

Millions of Iranians participated in presidential and local elections in June 2013. Executions, especially for drug-related offenses, continued at high rates. The judiciary released some political prisoners, but many civil society activists remained in prison on political charges.

Freedom of Assembly, Association, and Voting

During Iran's June 14 presidential and local elections, dozens of opposition party members were serving prison sentences and prevented from participating. Opposition figures Mir Hossein Mousavi, Zahra Rahnavard, and Mehdi Karroubi remained under house arrest or detention at time of writing.

On May 21, the Guardian Council, an unelected body of 12 religious jurists, disqualified all but eight of the more than 680 registered presidential candidates using vague criteria that enabled authorities to make sweeping and arbitrary exclusions. Nonetheless, turnout was high and voters overwhelmingly elected cleric and former diplomat Hassan Rouhani whose campaign promises included a "civil rights charter," improving the economy, and greater political engagement with the West.

Following Rouhani's inauguration, authorities in September released at least a dozen rights activists and political opposition figures, but scores of others jailed for their affiliation with banned opposition parties, labor unions, and student groups remain in prison. The judiciary continued to target independent and unregistered trade unions.

Iran's interim minister of science, responsible for management of the country's universities, announced in September that universities could reinstate professors and students suspended for their political activities from 2005 to 2012, but at time of writing dozens remained unable to continue their studies or teach.

In September, the Ministry of Culture ordered the reopening of the country's largest independent film guild, the House of Cinema, which authorities had shut down in January 2012.

Death Penalty

According to official sources, Iranian authorities executed at least 270 prisoners as of October 2013, though the real number is thought to be much higher. In 2012, Iran carried out more than 544 executions, second in number only to China, according to Amnesty International, which reported that at least 63 executions were carried out in public. Crimes punishable by death include murder, rape, trafficking and possessing drugs, armed robbery, espionage, sodomy, adultery, and apostasy. Most of those executed were convicted of drug-related offenses following flawed trials in revolutionary courts.

On October 2, a local news website reported that authorities executed a child offender on murder charges close to the southwestern town of Kazeroun. It is believed that dozens of child offenders (individuals under 18 when they allegedly committed the crime) are currently on death row in Iran's prisons. Iranian law allows capital punishment for persons who have reached puberty, defined as 9 for girls and 15 for boys.

In early 2013, Iran's judiciary implemented an amended penal code under which children convicted of "discretionary crimes" such as drug-related offenses would no longer be sentenced to death. A judge may still sentence to death juveniles convicted of crimes such as rape, sodomy, and murder if he determines that the child understood the nature and consequences of the crime, a vague standard susceptible to abuse. The amended law retains stoning as punishment for the crime of adultery.

Authorities executed at least 16 people in 2013 on the charge of *moharebeh* ("enmity against God") or "sowing corruption on earth" for their alleged ties to armed opposition groups, including eight Baluch prisoners executed in "retaliation" for the killings of more than a dozen border guards along the Iran-Pakistan border. Dozens of others are on death row for terrorism-related charges following politically-motivated prosecutions and unfair trials, including Iranian Arab men for their alleged links to groups involved in attacking security forces. At time of writing, at least 40 Kurdish prisoners, including Sunni rights activists branded as "terrorists" by the government, were awaiting execution on national security charges such as *moharebeh*.

Freedom of Expression and Information

At least 40 journalists and bloggers were in Iran's prisons at time of writing, according to Reporters Without Borders. On December 28, 2012, Supreme Leader Ayatollah Ali Khamenei publicly warned journalists and others against suggesting that Iran's elections would not be free.

In late January, authorities arrested more than a dozen journalists, apparently in connection with their coverage of the upcoming elections and alleged affiliations with foreign media but released most by late February. On October 28, authorities shut down the reformist daily, Bahar, five days after it published a controversial article thought to question a historical event in Shia Islam. They also severely cut back Internet speeds and blocked proxy servers and virtual private networks that Iranians used to circumvent government filtering of websites.

An investigation by judiciary officials into the November 6, 2012 death in custody of blogger Sattar Beheshti stalled. Authorities harassed Beheshti's family to cease criticism regarding the slow pace of the investigation. Iran's cyber police arrested Sattar Beheshti on October 30, 2012, apparently because of his blogging activities.

Since the June election, despite promises by the new minister of technology to remove restrictions on online and press freedoms, authorities continued to block websites and jam foreign satellite broadcasts.

Human Rights Defenders and Political Prisoners

In September and October, authorities released a few dozen rights activists and political prisoners such as journalist Isa Saharkhiz, but many of them had completed or were close to completing their prison terms. Authorities released Nasrin Sotoudeh on September 18 after she had served three years of a six-year prison sentence. It is not clear whether the judiciary has thrown out her sentence completely, including a 10-year ban on practicing law. At time of writing, dozens of other rights defenders, including prominent lawyers such as Mohammad Seifzadeh and Abdolfattah Soltani, remained in prison on politically motivated charges.

Iranian authorities regularly subject prisoners, especially those convicted on politically-motivated charges, to abuse and deprive them of necessary medical treatment. Security forces deprived Hossein Ronaghi, a rights activist and blogger, and opposition leaders Mousavi and Karroubi, from receiving the regular check-ups doctors had recommended for serious medical conditions.

On June 22, Afshin Osanlou's family learned of his death at Rajai Shahr Prison in the city of Karaj, 25 kilometers from Tehran. According to his brother, the death could have been avoided if prison officials had transferred Osanlou to a hospital after he suffered a heart attack in prison on June 20. Since 2009, officials have reported the suspicious deaths in custody of at least seven political prisoners whom rights activists believe died as a result of torture, ill-treatment, or medical neglect.

In September, Evin prison authorities denied that student activist Arash Sadeghi, whom security forces arrested in January 2012 and transferred to Evin prison, was being detained there, raising concerns among his family and activists. Authorities had held Sadeghi in solitary confinement in Evin prison and prevented his family from visiting him regularly. Sadeghi reportedly initiated a hunger strike in June after alleging that prison guards abused him. Officials released Sadeghi on bail on October 20.

Women's Rights

The Guardian Council disqualified all of the approximately 30 women who had registered as candidates for the presidential election.

Iranian women face discrimination in many areas including personal status matters related to marriage, divorce, inheritance, and child custody. A woman needs her male guardian's approval for marriage regardless of her age, and cannot generally pass on her nationality to her foreign-born spouse or their children. A woman may not obtain a passport or travel outside the country without the written permission of a male guardian. Child marriage, though not the norm, continues in Iran, where the law provides that girls can marry at the age of 13 and boys at the age of 15; and below such ages with the permission of a judge. In October, the Guardianship Council ratified the Law on Protection of Children and Adolescents with No Guardian (adoption) after they amended a provision, despite opposition, to allow adoptive parents to marry children in their care if a judge deems it to be in the latter's best interest.

Treatment of Minorities

The government denies freedom of religion to adherents of the Baha'i faith, Iran's largest non-Muslim religious minority, and discriminates against them. On July 31, an Iranian daily reprinted a *fatwa*, or religious edict, previously issued by Supreme Leader Ayatollah Khamenei, stating that Baha'is are part of a "deviant and misleading sect" and urging Iranians to "avoid" them. One hundred and fourteen Baha'is were in Iran's prisons as of September 2013, according to the Baha'i International Community.

On August 24, unknown assailants murdered Ataollah Rezvani, a member of the Baha'i community, in the southern port city of Bandar Abbas. According to the Baha'i International Community, individuals and government officials had threatened Rezvani numerous times because of his faith and activism. He is one of at least nine Baha'is who have been murdered or died under suspicious circumstances since 2005. The Baha'i International Community reported that in 2013, 52 Baha'is were physically assaulted by plainclothes government agents or unidentified attackers.

Authorities restrict political participation and employment of non-Shia Muslim minorities, including Sunnis, who account for about 10 percent of the population. They also prevent Sunnis from constructing mosques in major cities and conducting separate Eid prayers. Government targeting of Sufis, particularly members of the Nematollahi Gonabadi sect, continued unabated. In July, revolutionary courts in Tehran and Shiraz sentenced members of the Nematollahi Gonabadi sect to terms of one to 10.5 years for their peaceful activities.

The government restricted cultural as well as political activities among the country's Azeri, Kurdish, Arab, and Baluch minorities.

In September, Iran threatened to expel hundreds of thousands of Afghans without allowing them to have their asylum claims considered fairly and to challenge any order to deport them. At time of writing, authorities had not carried out plans to deport the Afghans, but the 2.5-3 million Afghan refugees and migrant workers living and working in Iran continue to face serious abuses.

HUMAN
RIGHTS
WATCH

UNWELCOME GUESTS
Iran's Violation of Afghan Refugee and Migrant Rights

Key International Actors

Activists inside Iran reported that unilateral financial and banking sanctions imposed against Iran by the United States and European Union had an adverse effect on access to specialized medicines and medical equipment.

On March 11, Ahmed Shaheed, the United Nations special rapporteur on the human rights situation in Iran, issued his second annual report to the UN Human Rights Council (HRC), which found an "apparent increase in the degree of seriousness of human rights violations" and expressed alarm at the "rate of executions in the country, especially for crimes that do not meet serious crimes standards." On March 22, the HRC renewed the mandate of the special rapporteur, established in 2011. On November 19, the UN General Assembly's Third Committee voted to support the resolution on the promotion of human rights in the Islamic Republic of Iran.

In October, UN Secretary-General Ban Ki-moon released his annual report on the situation of human rights in Iran, saying there was continued concern regarding the rights situation in the country. Later that month, Shaheed released his report, which said there was "no sign of improvement" on rights issues previously raised by UN monitoring mechanisms.

The government continued to block access to Shaheed and to experts with other UN rights bodies.

Iraq

Human rights conditions in Iraq continued to deteriorate in 2013. Security dramatically declined as sectarian tensions deepened. Al Qaeda in Iraq and other insurgent groups emboldened by the Syrian conflict and Iraq's political crisis carried out nearly daily attacks against civilians, making 2013 the bloodiest of the last five years. Suicide attacks, car bombs, and assassinations became more frequent and lethal, killing more than 3,000 people and injuring more than 7,000 between May and August alone.

The government responded to largely peaceful demonstrations with violence and to worsening security with draconian counterterrorism measures. Borders controlled by Iraq's central government remained closed to Syrians fleeing civil war, while as of November, nearly 206,600 Syrians fled to the Kurdistan Regional Government (KRG)-controlled area.

In December 2012, thousands of Iraqis took part in demonstrations in mostly Sunni areas, demanding reform of the Anti-Terrorism Law and the release of illegally held detainees. Prime Minister Nuri al-Maliki announced in January 2013 that he had created special committees to oversee reforms, including freeing prisoners and limiting courts' use of secret informant testimony. At time of writing, there was little indication that the government had implemented reforms. Security forces instead used violence against protesters, culminating in an attack on a demonstration in Hawija in April, which killed 51 protesters. Authorities failed to hold anyone accountable.

The government responded to increasing unrest with mass arrest campaigns in Sunni regions, targeting ordinary civilians and prominent activists and politicians under the 2005 Anti-Terrorism Law. Security forces and government supporters harassed journalists and media organizations critical of the authorities.

Detention, Torture, and Executions

Iraq's security forces abused detainees with impunity. Throughout the year, detainees reported prolonged detentions without a judicial hearing and torture during interrogation. In February, Deputy Prime Minister Hussein al-Shahristani told Human Rights Watch that security forces frequently carried out mass arrests without arrest warrants. Courts continued to rely on secret informant testimony and coerced confessions to issue arrest warrants and convictions.

On May 11, villagers south of Mosul found the bodies of four men and a 15-year-old boy, which bore multiple gunshot wounds. Witnesses had last seen them alive on May 3 in the custody of the federal police 3rd Division, but at time of writing, the government had not announced any investigation into the deaths.

Iraq executed at least 151 people as of November 22, up from 129 in 2012 and 68 in 2011. In mid-March, after Justice Minister Hassan al-Shimmari announced that the ministry was about to execute 150 people, United Nations High Commissioner for Human Rights Navi Pillay likened Iraq's justice system to "processing animals in a slaughterhouse." The Justice Ministry rarely provides information about the identities of those executed, the charges against them, or the evidence presented against them at trial.

Freedom of Assembly

Security forces responded to peaceful protests with threats, violence, and arrests. In April, army and police forces used lethal force on demonstrators who had been gathering largely peacefully for five months. In Fallujah and Mosul in February and March, respectively, security forces fired on demonstrators, killing at least seven people in both incidents.

On April 23 in Hawija, soldiers, federal police, and Special Weapons and Tactics (SWAT) forces fired on a crowd of about 1,000 demonstrators. A ministerial committee tasked with investigating the attack has so far failed to interview any witnesses or participants or hold any members of the security forces accountable. Security forces from the police, army, and SWAT responded to protests against corruption and lack of services in August in Baghdad and Nasiriya with force, arresting, and in some instances, beating protesters, then prosecuting them on specious charges of "failure to obey orders." The Interior Ministry invoked broad and restrictive regulations on protests to refuse permits for peaceful demonstrations, in contravention of Iraq's constitutional guarantee of free assembly.

Freedom of Expression

The Committee to Protect Journalists (CPJ) named Iraq the "worst nation" on its 2013 Impunity Index of unsolved journalist murders. There have been no convictions in more

than 90 murders of journalists since 2003, and the government shows no will to solve the murders.

On April 1, unknown assailants attacked the Baghdad offices of four independent daily newspapers, destroying equipment, setting fire to the buildings, and injuring several employees. Police announced an investigation into the attacks but released no results.

On April 28, the government Communications and Media Commission of Iraq (CMC) suspended the licenses of 10 satellite television stations and prevented them from broadcasting. These were all pro-Sunni opposition stations, leaving other channels, including all state-run channels, free to broadcast. A senior CMC official told Human Rights Watch that the CMC had no legal basis for the suspensions, but ordered them because the 10 stations were "promoting violence and sectarianism." The commission announced on its website that the suspensions were in response to the coverage of the Hawija attack.

Journalists reported that security forces blocked them from accessing antigovernment demonstrations, effectively restricting media coverage. A television correspondent told Human Rights Watch that men in military uniforms and vehicles who refused to identify themselves abducted him on December 28 in Ramadi when he tried to cover one of the ongoing demonstrations. They blindfolded and threatened to kill him before releasing him.

Between July and September, unknown gunmen assassinated at least five journalists in Mosul. Two worked for the Sharqeyya news channel, one for the Mosuleyya news channel, and two were spokesmen for Mosul's governor. The government has not announced the results of any investigations into the killings.

Rights of Women and Girls

Female prison inmates suffer from overcrowding and lack sufficient access to female-specific health care. Women are frequently detained with their young children, who are deprived of access to education and adequate health care as well as light, fresh air, food, and water. Dozens of women reported that security forces detained, beat, tortured, and in some instances, sexually abused them as a means of intimidating or punishing male family members suspected of terrorism.

On October 27, Iraq's Justice Ministry announced that it had sent a draft law on Jaafari (Shia) jurisprudence and personal status to the Cabinet for approval and referral to the Parliament for passage. The draft law stipulates that Jaafari jurisprudence in Islamic Sharia would govern Shia Iraqis in personal status issues such as marriage, divorce, inheritance, and adoption. Local rights groups expressed concern that the proposed legislation would feed sectarianism because, if adopted, different sects will be governed by different rules in matters of personal status laws. The proposed legislation contains numerous provisions that violate women's and children's rights. Particularly troublesome are articles that would lower the marrying age for females—18 for both men and women under Iraq's current Personal Status Law (1959)—to the age of 9 for females and 15 for males; prevent Muslim males from marrying non-Muslim females except on a temporary basis; broaden the permissible conditions for polygamy; give men the right to prevent their wives from leaving the house without permission; and restricts women's rights in matters of divorce and inheritance even more than the current Personal Status Law.

Many Iraqi women have lost their husbands as a result of armed conflict, generalized violence, and displacement. The resulting financial hardship has made them vulnerable to trafficking for sex trafficking and sexual exploitation. The parliament passed a counter-trafficking law in April 2012, but authorities have done little to enforce or prevent it. In February, a government official told Human Rights Watch that security officers and judges are not educated about the law and courts continue to prosecute trafficking victims under laws criminalizing prostitution.

The KRG passed the Family Violence Law in 2011, but officials have done little to implement the provisions criminalizing domestic violence and "honor" killings. Dozens of male family members have abused or killed female relatives since the law was passed. Local organizations report that the government has not created special courts to prosecute domestic violence cases, hired additional female security officers, or educated security officers about the law, as the law requires.

Refugees and Displacement

According to the United Nations High Commissioner for Refugees (UNHCR), over 206,600 Syrian refugees have fled to Iraq since 2011, a dramatic increase from the 30,000 Syrians who reportedly took refuge in Iraq in 2012.

Since August 2012, the Baghdad government-administered al-Qaim and al-Rabia border crossings have been closed to Syrian refugees. On August 15 2013, the KRG reopened the Peshkapor crossing, near Duhok, after having closed the crossing for over a month. Over 60,000 refugees fled into the KRG-controlled territory in the two months that followed.

Thousands of Iraqis remain displaced within their own country. They continue to reside in squatter settlements without access to basic necessities, such as clean water, electricity, and sanitation, and the government has no plan for their return. In July, hundreds of families fled the Moqdadeya area of Diyala province when Asa'ib Ahl al-Haq, a pro-government Shia militia, distributed leaflets to Sunni residents threatening them with death. Diyala residents said that security forces did nothing to protect them or to facilitate their return.

In September 2012, the UN Assistance Mission for Iraq (UNAMI) oversaw the transfer of about 3,200 members of the exiled Iranian opposition organization, Mojahedin-e Khalq (MEK), from Camp Ashraf, a former military base where the group had resided since 1986, to Camp Liberty, another former military base. On February 9 and June 15, unidentified armed men attacked Camp Liberty, killing 11 and injuring many more. The MEK reported that 52 of its members were shot and killed in an attack on September 1 at Camp Ashraf. The group said that Iraqi security officials carried out the attacks, but officials denied the allegations and blamed the deaths on infighting among camp residents.

In his outgoing address to the UN Security Council, former UNAMI envoy Martin Kobler voiced concern over residents' reports that the MEK leadership prevents group members from participating in the UNHCR resettlement process, denies them access to medical treatment, and threatens them for disagreeing with camp leaders or voicing a desire to leave.

Attacks on Civilians by Non-State Actors

Al Qaeda in Iraq issued statements claiming responsibility for lethal suicide, car bomb, and other attacks in Iraq including: a bombing at a football field on June 30 that killed 12 people, mostly boys under 16; a car bomb explosion on July 12 at a Shia funeral in Moqdadeya, west of Baghdad, that killed 10 people, including emergency services workers who died when a suicide bomber targeted them as they assisted the first set of casualties; and July 21 attacks on two Baghdad prisons that, according to the Justice Ministry, killed at least 68 members of the security forces and an unknown number of prisoners. Taken together, such attacks amount to an ongoing and systematic policy of killing civilians that may constitute crimes against humanity.

Shia militias carried out targeted assassinations and high-ranking officials reported that members of the Shia militia group Asai'b Ahl al-Haqq were increasingly formally integrated into the government, largely through posts in the security ministries. Residents of mixed Sunni-Shia neighborhoods in Baghdad and other areas in the country reported that Shia armed groups Asa'ib Ahl al-Haqq and Kita'ib Hezbollah threatened Sunni residents with death if they did not leave the areas.

Key International Actors

Ten years after the US-led invasion of Iraq, the US government has turned a blind eye to serial abuses. Accountability for abuses committed by coalition forces in Iraq remains almost nonexistent.

On his first visit to the US in two years, Prime Minister Maliki met with President Barack Obama on November 1 to request a range of security aid from the US, including heavy weapons, increased intelligence and other forms of counterterrorism support. On the occasion of the visit, several senators wrote to Obama expressing their concern over Maliki's "sectarian and authoritarian agenda" and stressed the need for Maliki to present a plan for reconciliation with Iraq's disenfranchised Sunni population.

Israel and Palestine

Israeli forces killed at least 15 Palestinian civilians in the West Bank, most in circumstances that suggest the killings were unlawful. Israeli authorities destroyed homes and other property under discriminatory practices, forcibly displacing hundreds of Palestinian residents in West Bank areas under Israeli control, as well as hundreds of Bedouin citizens of Israel.

In the West Bank, including East Jerusalem, Israeli authorities took inadequate action against Israeli settlers who attacked Palestinians and damaged their property in 361 incidents as of October 31, the United Nations reported. Israel imposed severe restrictions on Palestinians' right to freedom of movement, continued to build unlawful settlements in occupied territory, and arbitrarily detained Palestinians, including children and peaceful protesters.

Israel, along with Egypt, impeded the rebuilding of Gaza's devastated economy by blocking virtually all exports from Gaza.

Hamas authorities in Gaza executed three men in 2013 and sentenced 12 others to death after unfair trials. Security forces conducted arbitrary arrests and tortured detainees. The authorities permitted some local human rights organizations to operate, but suppressed political dissent, free association, and peaceful assembly.

In the West Bank, Palestinian Authority (PA) security services beat peaceful demonstrators, detained and harassed journalists, and arbitrarily detained hundreds. Credible allegations of torture committed by the PA's security services persisted.

In July, Israeli and Palestinian leaders agreed to resume final-status negotiations, facilitated by the United States.

Gaza Strip

Israel

Israel Defense Forces (IDF) conducted occasional aerial attacks and ground incursions in Gaza. As of September 30, Israeli forces had killed three civilians in Gaza, according to the UN. They continued to shoot at Palestinian civilians in the "no-go" zone just inside Gaza's northern and eastern borders and beyond six nautical miles from the shore, wounding farmers and fishermen.

Israel did not open any criminal investigations against members of its forces for wrongdoing during "Operation Pillar of Defense" in November 2012, during which aerial bombs and air-to-surface missiles killed scores of Palestinian civilians in attacks that apparently violated the laws of war. Hamas did not prosecute anyone for rocket launches by Palestinian armed groups unlawfully targeting Israeli population centers during the conflict that killed three Israeli civilians.

Palestinians from Gaza with complaints that Israeli forces had unlawfully killed their relatives were barred from traveling to Israeli courts to testify.

Blockade

Israel's punitive closure of the Gaza Strip, particularly the near-total blocking of exports, continued to have severe consequences for the civilian population. Egypt also blocked all regular movement of goods at the crossing it controls, and imposed increased restrictions on the movement of people after the military-backed government came to power in July. More than 70 percent of Gaza's 1.7 million people receive humanitarian assistance.

Israel allowed imports to Gaza that amounted to less than half of 2006 pre-closure levels. As of August 31, a monthly average of 78,810 tons of construction materials entered Gaza from Israel in 2013, as opposed to 174,212 tons per month before Israel imposed a closure following Hamas's takeover, according to Gisha, an Israeli rights group.

In July, Egypt's new military-backed government significantly tightened restrictions on the movement of Palestinians at the Rafah crossing between Gaza and Sinai, citing attacks by armed groups in the Sinai against Egyptian security forces. The number of Gaza residents passing through the crossing fell from a monthly average of 20,000 earlier in 2013 to 6,281 in July, according to Gisha. Egypt did not permit regular imports or exports of goods through Rafah and destroyed or closed many of the tunnels beneath the border that have been used for smuggling, leading to increased prices and unemployment, particularly in the construction sector. Imports of construction materials through the tunnels fell to 1,500 tons per day in July, from 7,500 tons previously. As of September, Gaza was unable to build some 250 new schools needed to adequately serve the population, according to Gisha.

"No-Go" Zones

As part of an Egyptian-brokered ceasefire agreement after hostilities in November 2012, Israel agreed to reduce the "no-go" zones it imposed inside Gaza to lands within 100 meters of the Israeli perimeter fence. Yet as of July 2013, Palestinian farmers reported that Israeli forces continued to shoot at them at distances of up to 800 meters. As of September 30, Israeli forces had killed at least one Palestinian civilian in the "no-go" zones, according to the United Nations.

Israel eased its restrictions on Palestinian fishermen, allowing them to sail up to six nautical miles from shore rather than three miles as previously. From March to May 2013, Israel again extended the fishing restriction to the prior limit in response to rockets launched by Palestinian armed groups. The UN reported that Israeli navy forces shot at Palestinian fishermen in 95 incidents during the first half of the year, double the number in the previous six months, wounding five fishermen. The closures prohibited access to 70 percent of Gaza's maritime area as recognized under international law.

Hamas and Palestinian Armed Groups

Palestinian armed groups launched 31 rockets into Israel as of November 19, causing no casualties, compared with 1,632 indiscriminate rocket attacks in 2012. The rockets launched by armed groups in Gaza cannot be accurately aimed at military objectives and amount to indiscriminate or deliberate attacks on civilians when directed at Israeli population centers.

On June 22, Hamas executed by hanging Emad Abu Ghalyon and Hossein al-Khatib, convicted in separate cases of "collaboration with the enemy." Courts in Gaza have repeatedly accepted coerced confessions as evidence of guilt in other capital cases. In October, Hamas executed by hanging Hani Abu Aliyan, who was a child at the time of one of his two capital offenses. Abu Aliyan's lawyer said that his client had confessed to that crime under torture.

Hamas took no apparent steps to arrest or prosecute gunmen who killed seven men for allegedly collaborating with Israel in 2012. At least six of the men had been sentenced to death but were appealing their sentences when the gunmen took them from detention centers and killed them. The faces of some of the gunmen were visible in photographs widely published in the media. Hamas's armed wing claimed responsibility for the killings.

The internal security agency and Hamas police tortured or ill-treated 180 people as of October 31, according to complaints received by the Independent Commission for Human Rights (ICHR), a Palestinian rights body.

Hamas security forces arbitrarily summoned and detained civil society activists, university professors, and members of the rival Fatah political faction.

On July 25, the prosecutor general ordered the closure of the Gaza offices of the regional broadcaster al-Arabiya and the Ma'an News Agency, a Palestinian outlet, for news stories suggesting that Hamas supported Egypt's Muslim Brotherhood. In November, Hamas allowed Ma'an to re-open and pledged to allow al-Arabiya to do so.

West Bank

Israel

The IDF fatally shot at least 15 Palestinian civilians including 3 children in the West Bank as of September 31, most in circumstances that suggest the killings were unlawful. In January, Israeli forces shot Samir `Awad, a 16-year-old student, in the back as he fled from soldiers who had hidden and surprised him as he approached the separation barrier near the secondary school in the village of Budrus. In August, Israeli forces used lethal force against residents of the

Qalandia refugee camp after clashes erupted during an arrest raid, killing three, including Roubin Zayed, 34, shot from close range while walking to work.

In August, the Israeli military closed its investigation into the death of Bassem Abu Rahmeh, who died after a high-velocity IDF tear-gas canister hit him in the chest in 2009. Video recordings of the incident showed Israeli forces firing from a short distance directly at Abu Rahmeh, who was not throwing stones or near any demonstrators. The military said it had "insufficient evidence" to prosecute any soldier for his death.

In April, Israeli forces arrested and detained a Palestinian volunteer paramedic for assisting an injured protester at the Damascus Gate in Jerusalem, Physicians for Human Rights-Israel reported. Similar cases have been reported during other protests, violating international human rights law.

Israeli authorities took inadequate action against Israeli settlers who injured Palestinians and destroyed or damaged Palestinian mosques, homes, schools, olive trees, cars, and other property. As of October 31, the UN reported 361 such attacks in 2013.

Settlement Building and Discriminatory Home Demolitions

Construction work began on 1,708 settlement housing units during the first half of 2013, an increase of 70 percent over the number begun during the same period in 2012, according to Peace Now and Israel's Central Bureau of Statistics. After US Secretary of State John Kerry announced the resumption of Israeli-Palestinian peace talks in July, Israel advanced plans for around 3,000 more units as of September.

As of November 18, Israeli authorities demolished 561 Palestinian homes and other buildings in the West Bank (including East Jerusalem), displacing 933 people. Israeli authorities demolished every structure in the Palestinian communities of Tel al-`Adassa, near Jerusalem, and Khillet Mak-hul, in the northern Jordan Valley, in August and September respectively.

Building permits are difficult or impossible for Palestinians to obtain in East Jerusalem or in the 60 percent of the West Bank under exclusive Israeli control (Area C), whereas a separate planning process readily grants settlers new construction permits. In October, following the suggestion of the High Court of

Justice, the military decided to negotiate with 1,300 Palestinian residents of eight villages in an area designated as a military training zone rather than demolish their homes.

Freedom of Movement

Israel maintained onerous restrictions on the movement of Palestinians in the West Bank, including checkpoints and the separation barrier. Settlement-related movement restrictions forced Palestinians to take time-consuming detours and restricted their access to agricultural land. In July, Israel opened a road to Hebron to Palestinians that had been closed for eight years.

Israel continued construction of the separation barrier around East Jerusalem. Some 85 percent of the barrier's route falls within the West Bank rather than along the Green Line, isolating 11,000 Palestinians on the Israeli side of the barrier who are not allowed to travel to Israel and must cross the barrier to access livelihoods and services in the West Bank. Palestinian farmers in 150 communities on the West Bank side of the barrier were separated from their lands on the Israeli side, the UN reported.

Arbitrary Detention and Detention of Children

Israeli military authorities detained Palestinians who advocated nonviolent protest against Israeli settlements and the route of the separation barrier.

Israeli security forces continued to arrest children suspected of criminal offenses, usually stone-throwing, in their homes at night, at gunpoint; question them without a family member or a lawyer present; and coerce them to sign confessions in Hebrew, which they did not understand. The Israeli military detained Palestinian children separately from adults during remand hearings and military court trials, but often detained children with adults immediately after arrest.

As of September 30, Israel held 135 Palestinian administrative detainees without charge or trial, based on secret evidence. Israeli prison authorities shackled hospitalized Palestinians to their hospital beds after they went on long-term hunger strikes to protest their administrative detention.

Palestinian Authority

Complaints of torture and ill-treatment by West Bank PA security services persisted. The ICHR reported 126 complaints as of October 31.

PA security services and men in civilian clothes identified as security employees violently dispersed peaceful protests and arbitrarily detained protesters and journalists. The PA continued to ban the distribution of two pro-Hamas weekly newspapers in the West Bank.

Palestinian courts did not find any West Bank security officers responsible for torture, arbitrary detention, or prior cases of unlawful deaths in custody. To our knowledge, the PA did not prosecute officers for beating demonstrators in Ramallah on August 28.

Attacks by Palestinian civilians injured 60 settlers in the West Bank as of September 30, the UN reported. On April 30, a Palestinian civilian killed Eviatar Borovsky, a security guard from Yitzhar settlement. In July, an Israeli military court convicted a Palestinian man for the attack.

Palestinian governing authorities in the West Bank, as well as in Gaza, delegated jurisdiction over personal status matters such as marriage and divorce to religious courts. In practice, women seeking marriage and divorce suffered discrimination. Courts required Muslim women to obtain a male relative's consent to marry and to obtain the husband's consent to divorce except in limited cases.

Israel

Bedouin citizens of Israel who live in "unrecognized" villages suffered discriminatory home demolitions on the basis that their homes were built illegally. Israeli authorities refused to prepare plans for the communities or approve construction permits, and rejected plans submitted by the communities themselves, but retroactively legalized Jewish-owned private farms and planned new Jewish communities in the same areas.

In September, according to the Israeli rights group Adalah, the Interior Ministry stated that it had demolished 212 Bedouin homes in 2013 and that Bedouin themselves, under threat of heavy fines, demolished an additional 187 homes. In June, the Israeli parliament gave initial approval to a proposed law that would bar Bedouin from contesting home demolition orders in court or appealing zoning plans that discriminate against Bedouin communities, raising the likelihood of increased numbers of home demolitions. Government officials estimated that the law, if implemented, would displace 30,000 Bedouin.

There are an estimated 200,000 migrant workers in Israel. In March, the Supreme Court ruled that Israel's Work Hours and Rest Law, which provides for overtime pay, does not apply to migrant workers, mostly from the Philippines, who work as live-in caregivers for ill or elderly Israelis. Many caregivers are indebted to recruiting agencies, beholden to a single employer for their livelihood, and unable to change jobs without their employer's consent. A 2012 bilateral agreement with Thailand significantly reduced recruitment fees for Thai agricultural workers and made it easier for them to change employers.

Government policies restrict migrant workers from forming families by deporting migrants who marry other migrants while in Israel, or who have children there.

Around 60,000 African migrants and asylum seekers have entered Israel irregularly from Egypt since 2005; Israel's almost-completed fence along its border with Egypt reduced new arrivals in 2013 to a few dozen. Israel continued to deny asylum seekers who entered the country irregularly the right to a fair asylum process and detained around 2,000 people, primarily Eritrean and Sudanese nationals. In June, the Ministry of Interior began to implement a "voluntary returns procedure" under which asylum seekers could "choose" to be deported, waiving their right to an asylum procedure, rather than remain in indefinite detention under the "anti-infiltration law." Earlier, in May, Israel stated it had "voluntarily" deported around 500 Sudanese from detention and another 1,500 who had not been detained, and it later deported smaller groups of Eritreans through an undisclosed third country. The Supreme Court overturned the anti-infiltration law in September for violating the right to liberty under Israel's Basic Law, and gave the government 90 days to review the cases of detainees.

Israel continued to delegate jurisdiction over marriage, divorce, and some other aspects of personal status to Jewish, Muslim, Christian, and Druze religious courts. In practice, women seeking divorces suffered discrimination, such as refusal of divorce by state-funded Jewish religious courts without the husband's consent in up to 3,400 cases per year, according to women's rights groups. The government did not publish figures of spouses denied divorce but women were reportedly the vast majority.

Key International Actors

The US allocated US$3.1 billion in military aid to Israel in 2013 and $427 million in assistance to Palestinian security forces and economic support to the PA. In July, Israeli and Palestinian leaders agreed to resume final-status negotiations, facilitated by the US.

In March 2013, the prosecutor of the International Criminal Court (ICC) stated that the "ball is now in the court of Palestine" to seek the court's jurisdiction, after the UN General Assembly voted to recognize Palestine as a non-member observer state in 2012. Israel and the US reportedly pressured Palestinian leaders not to join the ICC, and the Canadian foreign minister threatened unspecified "consequences."

The EU allocated €168 million (about $227 million) in direct financial support to the PA and €300 million ($406 million) in development and security sector support to the Palestinian territory for 2013.

Jordan

Jordan received and hosted hundreds of thousands of refugees fleeing the conflict in Syria in 2013, although the authorities prevented or restricted some from entry. In January, the political wing of the Muslim Brotherhood called for a boycott of the first parliamentary elections held under the amended election law, according to which some seats are elected using party lists. In March, King Abdullah II reappointed Abdullah Ensour as prime minister. Authorities stepped up attacks on independent media, censoring over 260 websites that refused to comply with new government registration requirements.

Freedom of Expression and Belief

Jordanian law criminalizes speech deemed critical of the king, government officials, and institutions, as well as Islam and speech considered defamatory of others. In 2013, the authorities failed to amend the penal code to bring it into compliance with constitutional free speech guarantees strengthened in 2011, and continued to prosecute individuals on charges such as "insulting an official body," using vaguely worded penal code articles that place impermissible restrictions on free expression.

In October 2012, Jordan's parliament approved amendments to the Press and Publications Law that require all independent news websites operating within the country to register with the Press and Publications Department, and empower the director of the press department to close down or censor unregistered sites. The amendments also make an electronic publication's owner, editor-in-chief, and director responsible, along with the author, for comments or posts that users place on its website. They also require the editor-in-chief of each news website to have been a member of the Jordan Press Association (JPA) for four years, although the JPA's bylaws limit its membership to employees of print publications.

On June 2, 2013, the director of the Press and Publications Department ordered the blocking of over 260 news websites. They had refused to register in protest against the new press law requirements and to preserve their independence. Some blocked news websites registered with the press department in November after losing a lawsuit to overturn the censorship order.

On September 17, police arrested Nidhal al-Fara`nah and Amjad Mu`ala, respectively publisher and editor of the Jafra News website, after it posted a third-party YouTube video that authorities deemed insulting to the brother of Qatar's ruler. Prosecutors charged both men with "disturbing relations with a foreign state" before the State Security Court, whose judges include serving military officers.

Following a visit in September, United Nations Special Rapporteur on Freedom of Religion or Belief Heiner Bielefeldt praised Jordan as "a safe haven and voice of religious moderation," but noted that unrecognized religious groups such as Baha'is, Druze, and Evangelical Christians face difficulties adjudicating personal status issues.

In March, prosecutors referred five university students from Al al-Bayt University in Mafraq to the State Security Court on charges of "inciting sectarian or racist strife" and "insulting a religious symbol," alleging that their style of dress and musical tastes indicated that they were "devil worshippers." The State Security Court exonerated them on the first charge, but at time of writing they remained on trial before an ordinary court in Mafraq on the second charge, which they deny.

Freedom of Association and Assembly

Since the amended Public Gatherings Law took effect in March 2011, Jordanians no longer require government permission to hold public meetings or demonstrations. However, prosecutors continued to charge protesters with participating in "unlawful gatherings" under article 165 of the penal code.

At time of writing, dozens of cases arising from protest-related incidents in 2011 and 2012 were in process before the State Security Court. In many cases, prosecutors had charged defendants with "subverting the system of governance or inciting opposition to it," using article 149 of the penal code.

On September 1, Prime Minister Ensour announced that the government planned to amend the State Security Court law to end trials of civilians before the court unless they faced terrorism, espionage, treason, money counterfeiting, or drug charges. This would bring the court into compliance with article 101 of the constitution, which allows military judges to try civilians only for these five groups of crimes; however, as the penal code classifies vaguely worded offenses such as "undermining the system of governance" as terrorism, the court will still be able to try civilians on such charges.

Refugees and Migrants

By November, over 550,000 persons from Syria had sought refuge in Jordan since 2011, according to the United Nations High Commissioner for Refugees (UNHCR). Of these, approximately 113,000 were then housed at the Zatari Refugee Camp in northern Jordan, down from over 200,000 in April, and 4,000 others were at the Emirates-Jordan camp in Zarqa Governorate. Another camp for Syrians was under construction near al-Azraq, east of Amman.

The authorities did not permit entry to all those fleeing Syria's conflict. In particular, they denied entry, in breach of international law, to Palestinian and Iraqi refugees residing in Syria, single males of fighting age, and people without documents. Human Rights Watch estimates that several thousand have been affected.

In late May, the daily number of Syrian refugee arrivals fell abruptly from over 1,500 to 300 or less. Refugees reported that Jordanian officials had closed the country's border or imposed a strict limit on refugee entry. Jordanian officials attributed the fall to intense fighting between Syrian government and opposition forces, impeding refugees' access to the border.

Hundreds of foreign migrants working in the duty-free Qualified Industrial Zones and in agriculture and domestic work complained about labor violations, including unpaid salaries, confiscation of passports, and forced labor. Government inspections and judicial redress remained lax.

Jordan hosted over 70,000 migrant domestic workers in 2013, mostly from the Philippines, Sri Lanka, and Indonesia. Nongovernmental organizations repeatedly referred domestic workers who had suffered multiple abuses to labor ministry investigators but they rarely classified any of them as victims of the crime of trafficking. Instead they treated each aspect of abuse such as non-payment of salaries separately, sometimes even detaining workers for "escaping" employers.

The Rights of Women and Girls

Jordan's personal status code remains discriminatory despite a 2010 amendment. Marriages between Muslim women and non-Muslims are not recognized. A woman separated from a Muslim husband forfeits her custodial rights after the child reaches seven years old.

Article 9 of Jordan's nationality law denies women married to foreign-born spouses the ability to pass on their nationality to their husbands and children.

Articles 98 and 340 of Jordan's penal code, which provide for reduced sentences for perpetrators of "honor crimes," remained in force. Honor crimes continued to take place in 2013. In one case, local media reported in April that a 25-year-old man in Zarqa Governorate murdered his 20-year-old sister, stabbing her 10 times in the chest, back, and throat, and dumped her body in the desert near their home. The man confessed to the police that he murdered his sister because she repeatedly left the house for long hours.

Torture, Arbitrary Detention, and Administrative Detention

Perpetrators of torture or other ill-treatment continued to enjoy near-total impunity. Credible allegations of torture or other ill-treatment are routinely ignored because it remains up to police, intelligence prosecutors, and judges to investigate, prosecute, and try fellow officers. At the Police Court, where many such cases are heard, two out of three sitting judges are serving police officers appointed by the police. To date, no police or intelligence officer has even been convicted of torture under article 208 of the penal code.

In late March 2013, a public prosecutor investigated the death-in-custody of Sultan al-Khatatba, whom authorities had arrested on a drug possession charge. The public prosecutor recommended that at least six police officers should face charges of torture under article 208, the first such recommendation known. Judicial authorities, however, transferred the case to the police court, which at time of writing had not released any public information on the progress of the case.

Local governors continued to use provisions of the Crime Prevention Law of 1954 to place individuals in administrative detention for up to one year in circumvention of the Criminal Procedure Law. The National Center for Human Rights reported that 12,410 persons were administratively detained, some for longer than one year, in 2012.

Key International Actors

The United States has a memorandum of understanding to provide Jordan with a minimum of US$360 million in economic assistance, and $300 million in foreign military financing annually. The US granted an additional $200 million in 2013 to help Jordan cope with the refugee crisis, and announced plans to increase aid by an additional $340 million in 2014. The US did not publically criticize human rights violations in Jordan in 2013 except in annual reports.

Jordan received a grant from Saudi Arabia of $200 million in February and finalized a deal for a $667 million grant in April as part of a $5 billion aid package pledged to Jordan by Gulf Cooperation Council (GCC) countries in December 2011.

In April, the US military deployed approximately 1,000 soldiers to northern Jordan, as well as scores of F-16 aircraft and patriot missiles, to mitigate the potential spillover effects of the Syrian civil war.

The United Kingdom deported Muslim cleric Abu Qatada to Jordan in July after the two countries signed a mutual legal assistance treaty to facilitate cooperation on criminal matters. The treaty guaranteed deportees from the UK would not face torture or other ill-treatment in Jordan, or face prosecutions based on torture-tainted confessions.

Kuwait

Recurring political disputes between the government and Parliament paralyzed political institutions and the passage of most new legislation. A constitutional court ruling in June 2013 dissolved the parliament formed in December 2012. However, the court upheld controversial amendments to the electoral law that had prompted the opposition's boycott of the polls in 2012 and sparked violent street protests. Elections in July 2013 led to the formation of a new parliament, including two women among its 50 members, one less than in 2012.

Kuwait continues to exclude thousands of stateless people, known as Bidun, from full citizenship, despite their longstanding roots in Kuwaiti territory.

The government has aggressively cracked down on free speech, often resorting to a law forbidding any offense to the ruler (emir).

A new effort to dramatically reduce the number of migrant workers in Kuwait has led to the implementation of regulations to allow for swift and unlawful deportation.

Treatment of Minorities

There are at least 105,702 stateless people in Kuwait, known as Bidun. After an initial registration period for citizenship ended in 1960, authorities shifted Bidun citizenship claims to a series of administrative committees that for decades have avoided resolving the claims. Authorities claim that many Bidun are "illegal residents" who deliberately destroyed evidence of another nationality in order to get the generous benefits that Kuwait provides its citizens.

In March 2011, the government granted Bidun certain benefits and services, such as free health care and education, as well as registration of births, marriages, and deaths. Some Bidun have complained there are still administrative hurdles to accessing these benefits.

In March 2013 the Parliament passed a law to naturalize 4,000 "foreigners" in 2013, touting this as a measure to address the citizenship of Bidun. Activists in the Bidun community have said this measure has not benefitted their community, but is being used to grant citizenship to children born to Kuwaiti mothers and foreign fathers. The government confirmed to Human Rights Watch that so far no Bidun had benefited from the law.

Some Bidun activists say that the real number of Bidun in Kuwait is closer to 240,000, reflecting the government's failure to update its statistics.

Members of the Bidun community frequently take to the streets to protest the government's failure to address their citizenship claims, despite government warnings that Bidun should not gather in public. Article 12 of the 1979 Public Gatherings Law bars non-Kuwaitis from participating in public gatherings.

Women's Rights

In January, Kuwait gave women the right to apply for posts as prosecutors, which until then were only open to male candidates. This will allow women to pursue careers as judges in the future. However women continue to face discrimination in many other aspects of their lives, and large legal gaps remain in protections for women. Kuwait has no laws prohibiting domestic violence, sexual harassment, or marital rape. In addition, Kuwaiti women married to non-Kuwaiti men cannot give their spouses or children Kuwaiti citizenship. Kuwaiti law does not let women marry a partner of their choice if their father will not grant permission.

In May, the Kuwaiti authorities announced that Saudi Arabian women would not be provided with drivers' licenses while in Kuwait without the permission of their male guardians; women are not allowed to drive in Saudi Arabia.

Freedom of Assembly

According to local activists and lawyers, government forces responded with excessive violence to multiple demonstrations by Bidun and Kuwaiti citizens. Human Rights Watch documented one case where special forces officers beat a demonstrator in April 2013 when detaining him, and heard allegations of many more cases.

Freedom of Expression

The year 2013 saw increased violations of free speech in Kuwait. The authorities brought cases against at least 29 people who expressed critical views of the government over Twitter, Facebook, blogs, other social media platforms, and at protests. Human Rights Watch knows of nine cases in 2012.

Most of these cases have been brought under article 25 of Kuwait's penal code of 1970, which prescribes a sentence of up to five years in prison for anyone who publicly "objects to the rights and authorities of the emir or faults him." The article gives no detail on what constitutes an offense. Kuwait would have to demonstrate incitement to violence or similar crimes for these cases to meet international standards on permissible restrictions of free speech. Human Rights Watch documented eight cases of political commentary that did not amount to incitement to violence, but that Kuwaiti courts in 2013 found violated article 25.

In July, during the Muslim fasting month of Ramadan, Kuwaiti ruler Emir Sabah al-Ahmad al-Jaber Al Sabah issued a pardon for all those been jailed under article 25. However, the authorities subsequently brought charges against at least one individual under that article, indicating that the pardon does not represent a change in government policy.

Migrant Workers

Migrant workers make up around 2 million of Kuwait's population of 2.9 million, including more than 600,000 domestic workers. In March 2013, the government announced that it intended to reduce the number of expatriate workers by 100,000 every year for the next 10 years, in order to bring the total down to one million. Kuwait has since adopted a number of mechanisms facilitating quick, non-judicial deportations in order to reach its goals.

In April, Kuwait implemented a policy of deporting migrants after they had committed their first major traffic violation. By September, according to local human rights organizations, the Ministry of Interior had deported 1,258 expatriates for traffic violations. In August, the health ministry announced that it would deport any expatriates with confirmed cases of infectious diseases, though Human

Rights Watch had not documented any such deportations at time of writing. These deportations occur without any judicial review.

Kuwait has also adopted indirect methods to push migrants to leave. In March, Kuwait adopted regulations requiring expatriates applying for a driving license to be 18 or over, pass a driving test, be a legal resident for at least two years, have a university degree, and earn at least KWD400 (US$1,400) per month.

Local media reported in August that authorities began evicting expatriate tenants from private homes owned by Kuwaiti citizens. According to local NGOs, residential buildings that are rented out to expatriates must be classified as "investment accommodations."

Death Penalty

On June 18, 2013, Kuwaiti authorities hanged two Egyptian men, one convicted of abduction and rape, and the other on murder charges. It was Kuwait's second round of executions in 2013, and the first time it had applied the death penalty since 2007.

Key International Actors

The United States, in its 2013 US State Department's annual Trafficking in Persons report, classified Kuwait as Tier 3—among the most problematic countries—for the seventh year in a row. The report cited Kuwait's failure to report any arrests, prosecutions, convictions, or sentences of traffickers for either forced labor or sex trafficking, and weak victim protection measures.

Lebanon

The security situation in Lebanon deteriorated in 2013 with violence spilling over from the armed conflict in Syria. Sectarian tensions led to deadly clashes in Tripoli and Saida amidst a climate of impunity for gunmen. Syrian refugees registering in Lebanon topped 816,000 in November, and with limited international support, the Lebanese government struggled to meet the refugees' needs. The prime minister resigned in early 2013, and at time of writing, a new government had not yet formed, leaving draft laws to stop torture, improve the treatment of migrant domestic workers, and protect women from domestic violence, stalled in Parliament for most of 2013.

Spillover Violence from Syria

Violence from neighboring Syria spilled over into Lebanon including through kidnappings, cross border shelling, and car bombings in Beirut and Tripoli.

Kidnappings of Lebanese in Syria by both Syrian government forces and armed opposition groups led to retaliatory kidnappings in Lebanon by victims' relatives. Lebanese authorities helped to facilitate the release of some kidnapped victims, but have not taken law enforcement measures either to prevent or prosecute kidnappings.

On April 14, a Syrian opposition group indiscriminately shelled Shia villages in northern Bekaa killing two civilians and wounding three. Syrian government forces also attacked targets in Lebanon with air and artillery strikes, wounding two individuals in a helicopter strike in Arsal, in the Bekaa, on June 12.

On July 9, a car bombing in the mostly Shia Beir al-Abed neighborhood in Beirut's suburbs left dozens wounded. On August 15, a previously unknown Syrian opposition group, the Aisha Brigades, claimed responsibility for a car bombing in Beirut's Shia suburbs that killed some 70 people and injured hundreds more. Eight days later, on August 23, two car bombs targeting two Sunni mosques in Tripoli, where sheikhs who support the Syrian opposition were giving sermons, left more than 40 dead and 400 wounded. No one claimed responsibility for these bombings.

On October 30, Ali Eid, the chief of the Arab Democratic Party and a former parliamentarian, was summoned by the Internal Security Forces' Information

Branch in connection to the car bombings in Tripoli. At time of writing, Eid was still refusing to respond to the summons.

Lebanese government forces were largely absent in the targeted neighborhoods until late September, when Internal Security Forces were first deployed to the Beirut suburbs.

Authorities planned similar measures for Tripoli, and in November, Internal Security Forces deployed in several neighborhoods there including Jabal Mohsen and Bab al-Tabbaneh as the security plan began to be implemented.

Clashes in Tripoli and Saida

Sustained violence between armed groups in Tripoli took a deadly toll, particularly in the mainly Alawite Jabal Mohsen and Sunni Bab al-Tabbaneh neighborhoods where the Syrian conflict exacerbates existing tensions. In May, major clashes erupted between the neighborhoods killing at least 28 and wounding over 200. In October, a week of fighting between the neighborhoods also resulted in at least 13 dead and 91 wounded. On October 28, the army deployed to the two neighborhoods and restored calm.

On November 12, amidst fears of renewed violence, the army also deployed to several neighborhoods in Tripoli and set up checkpoints following the assassination of Sheikh Saad Eddine Ghaya, a pro-Syrian government Sunni sheikh.

The Tripoli clashes have resulted in a sharp increase in sectarian attacks, including attacks against Alawite workers and the destruction of Alawite shops. On May 31, Sunni militants told Alawite workers at the Tripoli municipality not to come to work or face death. On November 2, a bus transporting Alawite workers stopping at the entrance of Bab al-Tabbaneh came under attack and nine workers were injured. On November 3, the army said that it had detained one man in relation to the incident.

The government failed to take steps that could protect residents, such as confiscating weapons, arresting and prosecuting fighters, and maintaining an active security presence.

Heavy clashes broke out in the southern city of Saida on June 23, after armed followers of Sheikh Ahmed al-Assir, a pro-Syrian opposition Imam, fired on an army checkpoint and the army counterattacked. Two days of clashes left 18 soldiers and 28 of al-Assir's supporters dead, according to media reports.

Torture, Ill-Treatment, and Prison Conditions

Following the June clashes in Saida, the Lebanese army detained individuals it suspected of supporting al-Assir. Many of whom reported being beaten and tortured. Seven individuals told Human Rights Watch that security officers kicked them and beat them with fists and, in some cases, sticks and cables. Nader Bayoumi died while in military custody, apparently as a result of beatings in custody. A military judge issued arrest warrants in July for four soldiers and one officer implicated in Bayoumi's death. Their trial was ongoing at time of writing.

Internal Security Forces (ISF) subjected suspected drug users, sex workers, and lesbian, gay, bisexual, and transgender people in their custody to ill-treatment and torture. The most common forms of alleged abuses were beatings with fists, kicks with boots, and assault with implements such as sticks, canes, and rulers.

Lebanon, with substantial assistance from donor countries, has taken a number of steps to expand and reform the ISF in the last five years, including by establishing a new code of conduct. However, these efforts remain inadequate and have failed to address ongoing abuses. Despite repeated government pledges to prevent torture and ill-treatment, accountability remains elusive. Lebanon has not yet established a national preventive mechanism to visit and monitor places of detention, as required under the Optional Protocol to the Convention against Torture (OPCAT), which it ratified in 2008.

Refugees

By September, over 816,000 Syrian refugees in Lebanon had approached UNHCR for registration. Registration does not grant Syrians legal status, but enables them in some cases to receive assistance. Syrians who enter at official border crossings are granted a six-month residency permit with one-time possibility of renewal, after which extension requires a $200 renewal fee. Absent legal status, refugees face the risk of detention for illegal presence in the country. Lebanon, the last of Syria's neighboring countries to maintain an open border policy, began arbitrarily barring Palestinians from Syria from entering the country in August.

Over 60,000 Palestinians from Syria have entered Lebanon since the conflict began, joining the estimated 300,000 Palestinian refugees already living in

HUMAN
RIGHTS
WATCH

"It's Part of the Job"
Ill-treatment and Torture of Vulnerable Groups
in Lebanese Police Stations

Lebanon in appalling social and economic conditions. The year 2013 saw no tangible improvement in Palestinian access to the labor market despite a 2010 labor law amendment that was supposed to ease such access. In 2013, a decision by the minister of labor exempted Palestinians from insurance and medical examination requirements typically required to get a work permit but its impact was limited as Lebanese laws and decrees still bar Palestinians from working in at least 25 professions requiring syndicate membership, including law, medicine, engineering, and from registering property.

Migrant Workers' Rights

Migrant domestic workers are excluded from the labor law and subject to restrictive immigration rules based on employer-specific sponsorship—the *kafala* system—which put workers at risk of exploitation and abuse. While outgoing Labor Minister Charbel Nahhas announced in January 2012 that he would look at abolishing the *kafala* system, in 2013 Labor Minister Salim Jreissati failed to do so or to put forward legislation that would protect the estimated 200,000 migrant domestic workers in the country. In July, a criminal court sentenced an employer to two months in prison, imposed a fine, and required her to pay damages and compensation to a migrant domestic worker whose wages she had not paid for years. Migrant domestic workers suing their employers for abuse continue, however, to face legal obstacles and risk imprisonment and deportation due to the restrictive visa system.

In June, the Association of Owners of Recruitment Agencies in Lebanon adopted a self-regulating code of conduct to protect the rights of migrant domestic workers, but the impact was limited in the absence of enforcement mechanisms.

Following the March 2012 suicide of Alem Dechasa-Desisa, an Ethiopian domestic worker, the trial of recruitment agency owner Ali Mahfouz, who is accused of contributing to her suicide, began in February 2013 but was postponed until February 2014.

Women's Rights

In July 2013, a parliamentary subcommittee approved a 2010 draft bill that seeks to protect women and children from domestic violence, criminalizing domestic abuse for the first time. At time of writing, parliament had yet to vote

575

on the bill. Discriminatory provisions that significantly harm and disadvantage women continue to exist in personal status laws, determined by an individual's religious affiliation. Women suffer from unequal access to divorce and, in the event of divorce, to child custody. Lebanese women, unlike Lebanese men, cannot pass on their nationality to foreign husbands and children, and continue to be subject to discriminatory inheritance law.

Legacy of Past Conflicts and Wars

In October 2012, Justice Minister Shakib Qortbawi put forward a draft decree to the cabinet to establish a national commission to investigate the fate of Lebanese and other nationals who "disappeared" during and after the 1975-1990 Lebanese civil war. The cabinet formed a ministerial committee to examine the draft, but at this writing, no action had been taken.

In September, a criminal case brought by Najat Hashisho against three members of the Lebanese Forces militia for "disappearing" her husband over 30 years ago was dismissed for lack of evidence. Hashisho and her attorney argued there was significant evidence against the accused and planned to appeal the decision.

In February 2012, the UN's Special Tribunal for Lebanon announced that the in-absentia trial of four indicted members of Hezbollah, for the killing of former Prime Minister Rafik Hariri in 2005, would go forward. The trial is tentatively scheduled to begin on January 13, 2014.

Key International Actors

Syria, Iran, and Saudi Arabia maintain a strong influence on Lebanese politics through local allies, and increasingly so as Lebanon becomes more involved in the conflict in Syria.

Many countries have given extensive, albeit insufficient, support to help Lebanon cope with the Syrian refugee crisis and to bolster security amidst spillover violence. In July, the UN Security Council issued a presidential statement calling for strong international support to Lebanon to help it meet its security challenges and to assist the government in responding to the refugee influx.

Libya

Libya's interim government faced multiple challenges in 2013. Myriad armed groups controlled security in many parts of the country, thousands of detainees remained in government and militia-controlled detention facilities without access to justice, and rampant ill-treatment and deaths in custody persisted. Forced displacement of tens of thousands of people from the town of Tawergha by militias from nearby Misrata had yet to be resolved.

Authorities failed to conclude any investigations into politically motivated assassinations, attacks on protesters in Benghazi and Tripoli, and attacks on journalists and foreign diplomatic missions, citing lack of resources and the precarious security situation.

Political Transition

The General National Congress (GNC), Libya's first elected parliament, has yet to fulfill its core mandate to organize elections for the Constituent Assembly (CA). On July 16, the GNC approved a law for electing the 60-member CA, which will draft Libya's constitution but at time of writing the law had not been issued, and the elections date had not been fixed.

The GNC suffered from political discord between its main political parties, in particular the Muslim Brotherhood-affiliated Justice and Construction Party (JCP) and the more liberal leaning National Forces Alliance (NFA); resignations by some Congress members; and removal of some congress members due to a sweeping lustration law that banned from office persons who had held any office in the Gaddafi era.

Security and Militias

The interim government failed to control deteriorating security in the country, especially in the capital, Tripoli, and in Benghazi, Libya's second largest city.

Myriad armed groups with varying agendas and allegiances, some affiliated with the government, controlled large swathes of the country and its resources—including Libya's oil terminals, its main income source—and operated with impunity. The government failed to demobilize militias or merge fighters who fought against Muammar Gaddafi's forces in the 2011 uprising into government forces with proper vetting procedures.

Authorities "contracted" militias, comprised of former revolutionary fighters, to help impose order, instead of prioritizing establishing a military and police force. These militias, including the Libya Shield Brigades and the Supreme Security Committee (SSC) that operated under the army chief of staff and Interior Ministry respectively, operated parallel to state security forces.

Attacks by unknown groups increased against foreign diplomatic missions in Tripoli and Benghazi, including the Tripoli embassies of France and the United Arab Emirates, and the Egyptian consulate in Benghazi.

Criminal investigation units under the police and Prosecutor's Office failed to arrest suspects or complete investigations into at least 30 seemingly politically-motivated assassinations. Authorities cited lack of capacity and the security situation as reasons for their inaction.

Tribal clashes among various armed groups, mostly vying for territorial control, increased in the Nafusa Mountains; Zawiya and Warshafana on the west coast; Sirte in center of the country; and in Kufra and Sebha in the south. Different militias clashed frequently in Tripoli.

There was an increase in violence in Tripoli in November when militias mainly from Misrata attacked overwhelmingly peaceful protesters. In ensuing clashes, 51 people died and more than 500 were injured. This prompted the government to implement law 27/2013 and law 53/2013 which called on all "illegitimate" armed formations to disband.

Violence escalated in the east, particularly in Benghazi and Derna, as armed groups with a religious agenda and other militias increased attacks on the government. In June, 31 protesters, some armed, were killed during clashes outside the Benghazi headquarters of the government-aligned Libya Shield Forces militia. The protesters were demonstrating against the militia's presence in city and its alleged abuses, such as arbitrary detentions.

The Cyrenaica Transitional Council, headed by Ahmed Zubair al-Senussi, and the Political Bureau of Cyrenaica, headed by Ibrahim Jadhran—two rival political groups with a military wing calling for an autonomous federalist form of government—competed for recognition in Libya's Eastern region. After months of occupying vital oil terminals in the East, Jadhran announced a parallel rival government on October 24, and created a "National Oil Company" to rival Libya's central national oil company.

Libya's south remained a closed military region throughout 2013. Lack of border control and tribal infighting destabilized the region and trafficking of humans, drugs, and weapons with neighboring Chad and Algeria surged.

Arbitrary Detention, Torture, and Deaths in Custody

Around 8,000 detainees held in relation to the 2011 armed conflict are still in detention facilities; around 3,000 of these are held in government custody, the rest by militias. Most have no access to lawyers or judicial reviews. Militias were responsible for continuing widespread abuses, and some deaths, in custody.

The judicial police, tasked with running detention facilities, remained weak and ill-equipped. There were at least two prison riots in Tripoli and Benghazi, including one at al-Roueimy prison in Tripoli in September when authorities wounded at least eight detainees with live fire. Armed groups attacked at least two convoys transferring detainees between their prison and a Tripoli court. Numerous prison breaks occurred in Sabha. In Benghazi, 1,200 detainees managed to escape after a riot in August.

Migrant workers from sub-Saharan Africa and South Asia continued to face harassment by militias, arbitrary arrests by militias and government forces, and forced labor by criminal gangs and militias.

Judicial System and Transitional Justice

The judicial system continued to face considerable challenges, including the slow pace of screening detainees and transferal to state custody. Prosecutors' inability to bring conflict-related cases to court and gaps in the judiciary's application of fair trial standards also plagued the system.

Militias subjected judges, prosecutors, lawyers, and witnesses to threats and violence, which authorities failed to challenge. At time of writing, the general prosecutor had not concluded an investigation into the killing of Muammar Gaddafi and his supporters in October 2011.

On September 19, Libyan authorities started the pre-trial stage of domestic proceedings against one of Gaddafi's sons, Saif al-Islam Gaddafi, his intelligence chief, Abdullah Sanussi, and 36 other senior Gaddafi-era officials. They faced charges of murder, torture, and indiscriminate killings committed during the 2011 uprising. The trials of these former officials were expected to start in December.

At time of writing, the GNC had yet to pass the draft transitional justice law, which calls for a commission to investigate abuses, refer perpetrators for prosecution, and compensate victims directly. It would cover abuses committed during the Gaddafi era and during the transitional phase following the 2011 conflict. A draft law that would provide some compensation for mainly female victims of physical and sexual violence had yet to pass.

Death Penalty

Military and civil courts imposed at least 28 death sentences, 12 of them passed in absentia, since Gaddafi's fall in October 2011. The Misrata Military Court sentenced two members of Gaddafi's military to death for violations committed during the 2011 conflict, including indiscriminate attacks against civilians and torture. A civil court in Misrata sentenced a former Gaddafi official and pro-Gaddafi fighter to death for unlawful killings during the 2011 uprising. Civil courts in Misrata, Benghazi, Zawiya, and Tripoli sentenced 12 civilians to death on charges related to the 2011 conflict and common crime charges, including murder. Lawyers and family of the accused alleged serious due process violations, including the inability to call defense witnesses. The Supreme Court had yet to approve the death sentences at time of writing.

International Justice and the International Criminal Court

Saif al-Islam Gaddafi and Abdullah Sanussi, who are wanted by the International Criminal Court (ICC) for crimes against humanity, remained in Libyan custody, without access to lawyers.

Libya filed a legal bid at the ICC to prosecute Gaddafi domestically in May 2012, and was told it could postpone surrendering him to the court until the ICC made its decision. In May 2013, the ICC judges rejected Libya's bid and reminded the

Libyan authorities of their obligation to surrender him. Libya has appealed the decision rejecting its bid.

On October 11, the ICC ruled Sanussi's case inadmissible thereby granting Libya the right to try him domestically. Sanussi's lawyers at the ICC appealed that decision. At time of writing, the ICC had yet to rule on the appeal.

Forced Displacement

Approximately 35,000 people from the town of Tawergha, in Libya's northeast, remained forcibly displaced at the end of 2013, with militias from nearby Misrata preventing them from returning to their homes. The militias accuse Tawerghans of supporting Gaddafi and committing serious crimes, including rapes and torture, against people in Misrata in 2011.

Militias mainly from Misrata continued to arbitrarily detain, torture, harass, and kill Tawerghans in custody. At time of writing, 1,300 people from Tawergha were detained, mainly in Misrata, or unaccounted for. The same militias also prevented residents of Tomina and Karareem, towns near Tawergha, from returning home.

Freedom of Speech and Expression

Attacks on journalists increased amid instability. In August, unknown assailants killed a journalist in Benghazi, two other journalists escaped separate assassination attempts. Throughout the year, militias threatened and beat scores of other media workers, mainly in Tripoli and Benghazi

Two politicians faced blasphemy charges and possible death sentences if found guilty for using posters during the GNC elections campaign in June 2012 that militia members claimed insulted Islam.

An editor of *al-Ummah* newspaper faced charges of insulting members of the judiciary after he published a list of allegedly corrupt judges and prosecutors. If found guilty, he could face up to 15 years in jail.

Freedom of Religion

Attacks on Sufi religious sites across the country continued in 2013, although fewer in number than in 2012. Authorities made no effort to protect the religious sites of minorities or arrest those responsible for attacks. In August, unknown persons desecrated Sufi graves in Tripoli and, in September, desecrated a Sufi gravesite in Mizdah, southern Libya. In September, a Sufi religious leader was assassinated by unknown gunmen in the Eastern city of Derna.

Women's Rights

In February, Libya's Supreme Court lifted restrictions on polygamy, enabling a man to marry up to four wives without the prior consent of his first wife. In April, the Ministry of Social Affairs suspended issuing marriage licenses for Libyan women marrying foreigners after a call by Grand Mufti al-Sadeq al-Ghariani to avoid spreading "other" religions in Libya. In the absence of a Personal Status Law, the law Concerning the Specific Provisions on Marriage and Divorce and their Consequences, Law No. 10 of 1984 is the only current legislation dealing with domestic violence, but enforcement remains weak.

Political Isolation

After months of controversy, the GNC in May passed the Political Isolation Law, barring Gaddafi-era officials from holding public office for 10 years. The law's sweeping provisions, vague procedures, and lack of judicial review, meant it violated human rights standards. Armed groups surrounded the Foreign Affairs, Justice, and Interior ministries, as well as the GNC, demanding that the GNC pass the law.

Key International Actors

The United States, European Union countries, and the United Nations played significant roles throughout the year. In May, the EU signed a border assistance agreement with Libya supporting border security efforts. The US, UK, Germany, France and Italy expanded cooperation, particularly in the security sector, although promised trainings of security forces for the most part did not materialize.

HUMAN
RIGHTS
WATCH

A REVOLUTION FOR ALL
Women's Rights in the New Libya

In March, the UN Security Council adopted resolution 2095, which extended the mandate of the United Nations Mission to Libya (UNSMIL) for one more year. The resolution modified the arms embargo to allow Libyan authorities access to non-lethal weapons and equipment in certain circumstances. Also in March 2013, the UN Human Rights Council (HRC) adopted a resolution that urged the government to implement reform, but failed to condemn ongoing and serious violations. The HRC asked the UN High Commissioner for Human Rights to report back in March 2014 on the situation on the ground.

On May 8, the US, UK, and France expressed concern for the armed protests and violence during the democratic transition. On September 10, the US, UK and Italy issued a statement supporting the Libyan government in its efforts to restore security and build its institutions and cautioning against disruption of Libyan oil exports due to protests by armed groups at Libya's main exporting oil terminals.

In response to ongoing insecurity, the US, UK, France, Italy, and Turkey announced plans to train more than 8,000 militia members for a General Purpose Force to be merged into Libya's army and police forces.

Morocco/Western Sahara

Morocco's 2011 constitution incorporated strong human rights provisions, but these reforms did not lead to improved practices, the passage of implementing legislation, or the revision of repressive laws. In 2013, Moroccans exercised their right to peaceful protest in the streets, but police continued to violently disperse them on occasion. Laws that criminalize acts deemed harmful to the king, the monarchy, Islam, or Morocco's claim over the disputed Western Sahara limited the rights to peaceful expression, assembly, and association. In February, a military court sentenced 25 civilian Sahrawis to prison terms, including nine to life imprisonment. The trial was just one of many unfair trials in recent years that have resulted in politically motivated convictions.

Freedom of Expression

Independent print and online media continue to investigate and criticize government officials and policies, but face prosecution and harassment when they cross certain lines. The press law prescribes prison terms for "maliciously" spreading "false information" likely to disturb the public order, or for speech that is ruled defamatory.

Moroccan state television provides some room for debate and investigative reporting but little for direct criticism of the government or dissent on key issues. Authorities allowed Al Jazeera to resume operations in Morocco, having ordered it to shut its bureau in 2010 on account of its coverage of the dispute over the status of Western Sahara. On September 17, authorities arrested Ali Anouzla, director of the independent news site Lakome.com, because of an article describing, and providing an indirect link to, a militant Islamist recruitment video attacking King Mohammed VI. Released on October 25, he faced trial at time of writing on charges under the 2003 counterterrorism law, including "intentionally aiding those who perpetrate acts of terrorism."

Abdessamad Haydour, a student, continued to serve a three -year prison term for insulting the king by calling him a "dog," "a murderer," and "a dictator" in a YouTube video. A court sentenced him in February 2012 under a penal code provision criminalizing "insults to the king."

Freedom of Assembly

Moroccans have continued to hold marches and rallies to demand political reform and protest government actions since popular protests swept the region in February 2011. The police mostly allow these protests, but on some occasions in 2013 they attacked and severely beat protesters. For example, on August 2, police violently dispersed a small protest in front of the Parliament in Rabat against a royal pardon that had been granted to a convicted pedophile. However, authorities tolerated subsequent street protests against the pardon, which authorities said had been granted in error.

In Western Sahara, security forces routinely repressed any public gathering deemed hostile to Morocco's contested rule over that territory. This included gatherings in the territory's main town, El-Ayoun, on March 23, April 29, and October 19. Authorities allowed an unprecedentedly large demonstration in favor of self-determination on May 4.

Freedom of Association

The 2011 constitution introduced protection for the first time for the right to create an association yet, in practice, officials continue to arbitrarily prevent or impede many associations from obtaining legal registration, undermining their freedom to operate. Groups affected include some that defend the rights of Sahrawis, Amazighs (Berbers), sub-Saharan migrants, and the unemployed. Others include charitable, cultural, and educational associations whose leaders includes members of al-Adl wal-Ihsan (Justice and Spirituality), a well-entrenched, nationwide movement that advocates for an Islamic state and questions the king's spiritual authority. The government, which does not recognize Justice and Spirituality as a legal association, tolerated many of its activities, but prevented others. In Western Sahara, authorities withheld legal recognition for all local human rights organizations whose leaders support independence for that territory, even associations that won administrative court rulings that they had wrongfully been denied recognition.

Terrorism and Counterterrorism

Hundreds of suspected Islamist extremists arrested in the aftermath of the Casablanca bombings of May 2003 remain in prison. Many were convicted in unfair trials after being held in secret detention and subjected to ill-treatment and, in some cases, torture. Police have arrested hundreds more suspected militants since further terrorist attacks in 2007 and 2011. Courts have convicted and imprisoned many of them on charges of belonging to a "terrorist network" or preparing to join Islamist militants fighting in Iraq or elsewhere.

Police Conduct, Torture, and the Criminal Justice System

Moroccan courts continue to impose the death penalty, but the authorities maintained a de facto moratorium under which they have carried out no executions since the early 1990s.

In his final report on his 2012 visit to Morocco, United Nations Special Rapporteur on Torture Juan Mendez concluded in February 2013, "In cases involving State security, such as terrorism, membership in Islamist movements, or supporters of independence for Western Sahara, there is a pattern of torture and ill-treatment by police officers during the arrest process and while in detention…. Many individuals have been coerced to confess and sentenced to prison on the basis of such a confession." The rapporteur's recommendations included amending the law to ensure that "access to lawyers of a suspect's own choosing is granted from the moment of apprehension" and shortening the length of pre-charge detention in police custody from the current maximum of 12 days allowed in terrorism related cases. Moroccan authorities responded in detail, noting steps they were taking, such as an engagement by "the Ministry of Justice and Liberties … to ensure the video recording of all statements made to the police during investigations and interrogations."

Courts failed to uphold the right of defendants to receive fair trials in political and security-related cases. In some cases, they failed to order medical examinations that might substantiate defendants' allegations of torture, refused to summon exculpatory witnesses, and convicted defendants based on apparently coerced confessions.

In February 2013, the Rabat Military Court sentenced 25 Sahrawi men to prison terms, imposing nine life sentences, after convicting them on charges arising from violence that occurred on November 8, 2010, when security forces dismantled the Gdeim Izik protest encampment in Western Sahara. Eleven members of the security forces died in the violence. The court failed to probe the allegations made by defendants, most of whom had spent 26 months in pretrial detention, that police officers had tortured or coerced them into signing false statements. Yet, the court relied on these contested statements as the main, if not sole, evidence to convict them.

Prison conditions were reportedly harsh, due in large part to severe overcrowding, a problem aggravated by investigating judges' frequent resort to the pretrial detention of suspects. The Justice Ministry stated that as of October 2012, 31,000 of the country's 70,000 prison inmates were pretrial.

On September 12, 2013, Justice Minister Moustapha Ramid—a well-known human rights lawyer who was appointed following the 2011 election victory of the Islamist-oriented Hizb al-Adalah wal-Tanmiya (Justice and Development) party—unveiled proposals on judicial reform that, if implemented, could enhance judicial independence. These proposals include diminishing executive control over prosecutors.

Migrants and Refugees

Migrants from sub-Saharan Africa continued to experience police abuse in 2013. On several occasions, police rounded up migrants, transported them to the Moroccan-Algerian border and dumped them there without formally verifying their status or informing them of their rights.

In September, the National Council of Human Rights (CNDH), a state-funded body that reports to the king, issued a report on the plight of migrant workers and recommended that the government take measures to protect their rights. These included the establishment of a "national legal and institutional framework of asylum." Currently, Morocco delegates asylum status determination to the UN High Commissioner for Refugees (UNHCR), and generally refrains from expelling migrants who have documents proving that they have applied for or received recognition from the UNHCR. King Mohammed VI publicly welcomed the CNDH's recommendations, and ordered a government task force to examine

HUMAN
RIGHTS
WATCH

"Just Sign Here"
Unfair Trials Based on Confessions to the Police in Morocco

the status of migrants whose asylum claim the UNHCR had already recognized with a view toward regularizing them.

Women's and Girls' Rights

The 2011 constitution guarantees equality for women, "while respecting the provisions of the Constitution, and the laws and permanent characteristics of the Kingdom." The Family Code contains discriminatory provisions for women with regard to inheritance and the right of husbands to unilaterally divorce their wives. Reforms to the code in 2004 improved women's rights in divorce and child custody and raised the age of marriage from 15 to 18.

Domestic Workers

Despite laws prohibiting the employment of children under the age of 15, thousands of children under that age—predominantly girls—are believed to work as domestic workers. According to the UN, nongovernmental organizations, and government sources, the number of child domestic workers has declined in recent years, but girls as young as 8 years old continue to work in private homes for up to 12 hours a day for as little as US$11 per month. In some cases, employers beat and verbally abused the girls, denied them an education, and refused them adequate food.

Morocco's labor law excludes domestic workers from its protections, including a minimum wage, limits to work hours, and a weekly rest day. In 2006, authorities presented a revised draft law to regulate domestic work and reinforce existing prohibitions on under-15 domestic workers, but at this writing the parliament has yet to adopt it.

Key International Actors

In 2008, the European Union awarded Morocco "advanced status," placing it a notch above other members of the European Neighbourhood Policy (ENP). Morocco is the largest beneficiary of EU aid in the Middle East and North Africa after the Occupied Palestinian Territories, with €580 million (US$757 million) earmarked for 2011 to 2013, plus an additional €35 million in 2013 under the

EU's SPRING program that aids countries judged to be undergoing democratic transitions.

On September 10, EU Ambassador to Morocco Rupert Joy praised the CNDH report on migrants in Morocco, which, he said, "recognizes violations to the rights of migrants that have concerned us for a long time, but also proposes concrete recommendations for migration policies that are more just and more effective." Joy pledged "considerable financial assistance" from the EU and its member states toward projects that are "inspired by" the CNDH's recommendations.

On a state visit, French President François Hollande refrained from any public human rights criticism. During an address to parliament and at a press conference on April 4, he insisted that France, Morocco's leading trading partner and source of public development aid and private investment, did not wish "to give lessons." However, the Foreign Ministry, in a rare remark that could be interpreted as criticism, reacted on April 29 to the police's repression of a demonstration in Western Sahara by "recall[ing] our attachment to the right to protest peacefully."

In 2013, the United States, a close ally to Morocco with which it maintains a formal human rights dialogue, gave the final portion of a five year $697 million grant from the Millennium Challenge Corporation to reduce poverty and stimulate economic growth. At the annual UN Security Council debate in April on renewing the mandate of the peacekeeping force for Western Sahara (MINURSO), the US initially proposed enlarging the mandate to include human rights monitoring but backed down in the face of Morocco's vehement opposition.

On November 22, King Mohammed VI was received by a US president in Washington for the first time since 2002. President Barack Obama praised Morocco's intentions and commitments to make various human rights improvements, but did not publicly criticize Morocco's human rights practices.

Morocco has facilitated the visits of several UN human rights mechanisms over the past two years, including the special rapporteur on trafficking in persons in June 2013. At time of writing the Working Group on Arbitrary Detention was scheduled to take place in December 2013.

591

Oman

Omani authorities in 2013 restricted the right to freedom of expression through the use of criminal defamation laws. Despite a royal pardon on March 21 of more than 35 activists convicted in 2012 on charges of "insulting the Sultan" and participating in unauthorized protests, officials continued to harass and detain pro-reform activists in 2013, creating little opportunity for citizens to impact the government and its policies.

Omani authorities restricted the right to freedom of assembly both in law and in practice, using force to break up peaceful demonstrations, and arresting individuals present at protests. In one case, officials arrested and detained a Shura Council member who attended the demonstration on charges of inciting violence and wrongful public assembly.

Although Oman's constitution bans discrimination based on gender, women and girls face discrimination in family law.

Pro-Reform Activists

The government continued to harass and detain Omani pro-reform activists in 2013. In March, Sultan Qabus pardoned activists convicted in 2012 on charges of "insulting the sultan" and "illegal gathering" after the courts had sentenced them to between 6 and 18 months in prison. At least 31 of the activists had gone on a hunger strike in February to protest the delay of the Omani Supreme Court in hearing their appeals.

In January, Omani authorities arrested human rights activist and blogger Saeed Jaddad, 43, and held him for eight days in solitary confinement on charges including calling for demonstrations and heaping discredit on state officials before releasing him on bail. Jaddad has called for political and social reforms in posts on Facebook and on his blog.

On July 3, Omani authorities arrested Jaddad again at a rural property he owns in the Dhofar region, claiming he was inhabiting the property illegally. Jaddad said he obtained the property through a property swap with the local municipality and had yet to receive proper documentation. When Jaddad refused to vacate

vacate the property, authorities arrested him on charges of "resisting the authorities" and held him in detention overnight.

On July 21, the public prosecution summoned Jaddad on a new charge of "undermining the status and prestige of the state." Authorities released him on bail but threatened that he may again be interrogated and brought to trial on these charges.

Freedom of Expression

Articles 29, 30, and 31 of Oman's Basic Law protect freedom of expression and the press, yet other legislation restricts these freedoms and in practice authorities did not respect these rights. Oman's Telecommunications Act of 2002 restricts online content. Article 26 penalizes "any person who sends, by means of telecommunications system, a message that violates public order or public morals."

On July 29, Omani authorities arrested pro-reform activist Sultan al-Saadi at a gas station as he was traveling with his family. Fourteen armed men from the Omani Intelligence Service detained al-Saadi, confiscated his laptop and other personal items, and took him to an undisclosed location. They released him on August 20 without charge. Al-Saadi claimed that security forces subjected him to ill-treatment in detention.

Authorities had previously arrested al-Saadi in 2011 on the basis of his participation in pro-reform demonstrations in the northern industrial town of Sohar, and in 2012 on charges of "insulting the Sultan" because of his pro-reform Facebook and Twitter advocacy. Sultan Qabus had included him in his pardon of activists in March 2013.

On September 13, Omani security forces arrested blogger Noah Saadi, who had criticized Omani authorities on his blog for arresting Dr. Talib al-Maa'mari, a Shura Council member who had participated in anti-pollution protests. At time of writing, authorities had prevented Saadi from contacting his family and denied him access to a lawyer. Authorities previously arrested Saadi for his participation in protests in Sohar in 2011, when thousands of Omanis took to the streets demanding jobs and an end to corruption.

Freedom of Assembly

Omani authorities require citizens to request government approval for all public gatherings, and regularly arrest citizens at unapproved gatherings.

In July, the sultan reportedly pardoned another group of 14 activists jailed in 2011 anti-government protests in Sohar. The Sohar prisoners were serving sentences of between 30 months and 5 years for their role in the protests. To Human Rights Watch's knowledge, authorities have not expunged the convictions of any of the pardoned activists.

On August 22, activists gathered in Liwa, a town north of Sohar near the port, to protest pollution from the industrial zone at the port, which they consider a public health risk. Police used tear gas to disperse demonstrators who had blocked the entrance to the port. On August 24, security forces arrested Dr. Talib al-Maa'mari, a member of Oman's Shura Council, who was present at the anti-pollution demonstration. Authorities did not permit al-Maa'mari to meet with a lawyer until September 10, 2013, almost 14 days after his arrest. On September 9, the public prosecution charged al-Maa'mari with inciting a crowd and wrongful assembly at a public place. According to the verdict, which Human Rights Watch reviewed, the court sentenced both al-Ma'mari to seven years in prison with a fine of 1,000 riyals (US$2,600), and al-Baloushi to four years with a fine of 500 riyals ($1,300) on charges of "illegal gathering" and "blocking traffic." At time of writing, this case was before an appeals court.

Women's Rights

Article 17 of Oman's Basic Law officially provides that all citizens are equal and bans discrimination on the basis of gender, however despite such constitutional guarantees, women continue to face discrimination in law and practice.

Women continue to be discriminated against in the Personal Status Law that governs family law in matters of divorce, inheritance, child custody, and legal guardianship, granting men privileged status in these matters.

In December 2012, Oman held its first municipal council elections with a total of over 1,400 candidates, including 46 women, competing for 192 seats. Four women were elected.

Key International Actors

Both the United States and the United Kingdom provide significant economic and military aid to the sultanate. Neither country publicly criticized Oman's human rights abuses in 2013, except in annual reports.

In late 2012, the Gulf Cooperation Council (GCC), of which Oman is a member, revised and re-signed its security cooperation agreement enabling each state party to take legal action against its own or other GCC citizens when they are judged to have interfered in the internal affairs of any GCC state.

Qatar

Unlike most other Gulf states, Qatar has not experienced serious domestic unrest. Yet the human rights climate remains problematic, particularly for the large and growing migrant worker population. Migrants continue to experience serious rights violations, including forced labor and arbitrary restrictions on the right to leave Qatar, which expose them to exploitation and abuse by employers. Qatar's poor record on freedom of expression declined further with the announcement of a draft cyber crime law.

Migrant Workers' Rights

Qatar is upgrading its infrastructure in preparation for the 2022 FIFA World Cup, but authorities have yet to implement reforms that are needed to afford foreign migrant workers adequate protection against serious rights abuses, including forced labor and trafficking.

According to official 2013 statistics, Qatar has a population of about 2million, of whom only 10 percent are Qatari nationals. The number of economically active foreign nationals increased by 122,000, almost 10 percent, in the 12 months from April 2012, and is expected to rise further in response to the demands of Qatar's burgeoning construction sector.

Qatar's Law 14 of 2004 regulating labor in the private sector limits workers' hours requires that they receive paid annual leave, sets requirements on health and safety, and requires on-time payment of wages each month. However, the authorities fail to enforce this and other laws intended to protect workers' rights.

Workers typically pay exorbitant recruitment fees and employers regularly take control of their passports when they arrive in Qatar. The *kafala* (sponsorship) system ties a migrant worker's legal residence to his or her employer, or sponsor. Migrant workers commonly complain that employers fail to pay their wages on time if at all, but are barred from changing jobs without their sponsoring employer's consent other than in exceptional cases and with express permission of the Interior Ministry. Adding to their vulnerability, they must obtain an exit visa from their sponsor in order to leave Qatar. Migrant workers are prohibited from unionizing or engaging in strikes, although they make up 99 percent of the private sector workforce.

Many migrant workers live in cramped, unsanitary conditions, especially those working without documentation.

Workers can become undocumented when employers report them as having absconded, or when they fail to pay to renew workers' annual ID cards. A lack of proper documentation leaves workers at risk of arrest and detention or deportation. It also leaves them at risk of further labor exploitation. Authorities rarely, if ever, bring criminal prosecutions against employers for violating Qatar's labor or anti-trafficking laws.

In May 2013, the Qatar Foundation, a quasi-governmental organization heavily engaged in property development, announced a code of conduct relating to workers' conditions that it requires contractors and sub-contractors on its projects to respect. Another quasi-governmental organization, the 2022 Supreme Committee, plans to follow suit for projects related to the World Cup. These codes, if properly enforced, would improve conditions for workers on certain projects and possibly bring them up to international minimum standards. However, they are no substitute for enforced state-led regulation and they will not alleviate conditions for most of Qatar's low-paid migrant workers, since these projects constitute only a fraction of those ongoing in Qatar.

Domestic migrant workers, almost all women, are especially vulnerable. In addition to the problems the general migrant worker population face, they are also subject to verbal, physical, and in some cases, sexual abuse. Some are not allowed to speak to strangers or are locked up in the homes where they work. Many do not receive a day off. They are not afforded any protection under Qatari labor law, which could provide them with days of rest and limit their working hours among other measures. A regional unified contract for domestic workers, expected to be approved in 2014, falls well short of the minimum standards outlined in the recently adopted International Labour Organization's Domestic Workers' Convention.

Freedom of Movement

A number of foreign professionals working as expatriates in Qatar complained they were unable to leave the country because their employers failed or refused to issue them exit visas.

Law No. 4 of 2009, which regulates the sponsorship, employment, and residence of expatriate workers, requires they obtain residence permits, and exit permits when they wish to leave the country. Under the *kafala* system, these permits are provided by "residence sponsors," who can effectively prevent those they sponsor from leaving Qatar.

The law does not require residence sponsors to justify their failure to provide an exit permit, instead placing the onus on the sponsored expatriate to find another Qatari national willing to act as an exit sponsor. Alternatively, the expatriate must publish a notice in two daily newspapers and then provide a certificate 15 days later showing that he or she faces no outstanding legal claims. The exit visa requirement cannot be justified as a means of preventing foreigners fleeing court cases in Qatar, as the Interior Ministry has separate powers to impose travel bans on non-citizens facing criminal charges or civil claims in Qatar's courts.

There are also concerns over the arbitrary manner in which Qatar imposes indefinite travel bans against individuals accused of criminal or civil offences by their employers.

The exit visa requirement and the authorities' use of arbitrary travel bans means that Qatari employers can prevent their foreign employees from leaving Qatar indefinitely, a power they may use unfairly to secure concessions from foreign employees with whom they are in dispute. Formerly highly-paid expatriates trapped in Qatar in 2013 included the French professional footballer, Zahir Belounis, and three former employees of the Al Jazeera Children's Channel.

Freedom of Expression

In February, an appeal court reduced to 15 years the life imprisonment sentence imposed on poet Mohammed Ibn al-Dheeb al-Ajami, a Qatari national, in November 2012, by a court in Doha. The court convicted him of incitement to overthrow the regime after he recited poems critical of Qatar's then-emir, Sheikh

Sheikh Hamad bin Khalifa al-Thani. In June 2013, the emir abdicated, handing power to his son, Sheikh Tamim bin Hamad al-Thani.

In May, Qatar's cabinet approved a draft cyber-crimes law, but it remained unclear when it would be enacted. The authorities did not consult the state-funded Doha Center for Media, whose role is to promote media freedom in Qatar, when preparing the draft law and they did not disclose its full contents.

According to state media, however, it "punishes anyone who infringes on the social principles or values or otherwise publishes news, photos, audio or visual recordings related to the sanctity of the private and familial life of persons, even if they were true; or infringes on others by libel or slander via the Internet or other information technology means." As yet, authorities have also not enacted a problematic draft media law of 2012 that would expose journalists in Qatar to prohibitive financial sanctions if they criticize any Gulf Cooperation Council states.

Provisions of Qatar's penal code are inconsistent with international free speech standards. Article 134, for example, prescribes a penalty of up to five years' imprisonment for anyone who is convicted of criticizing the emir or vice-emir.

Women's Rights

Provisions of Law No. 22 of 2006, Qatar's first codified law to address issues of family and personal status law, discriminate against women. Article 36 states that two men must witness marital contracts, which are concluded by male matrimonial guardians. Article 57 prevents husbands from hurting their wives physically or morally, but article 58 states that it is a wife's responsibility to look after the household and to obey her husband. Marital rape is not a crime.

Saudi Arabia

Saudi Arabia stepped up arrests, trials, and convictions of peaceful dissidents, and forcibly dispersed peaceful demonstrations by citizens in 2013. Authorities continued to violate the rights of 9 million Saudi women and girls and 9 million foreign workers. As in past years, authorities subjected thousands of people to unfair trials and arbitrary detention. In 2013, courts convicted seven human rights defenders and others for peaceful expression or assembly demanding political and human rights reforms.

Freedom of Expression, Association, and Belief

On March 9, the Criminal Court of Riyadh sentenced rights activists Dr. Mohammed al-Qahtani and Dr. Abdullah al-Hamid to 10 and 11 years in prison respectively and lengthy travel bans, after convicting them on charges that included "breaking allegiance with the ruler," and "setting up an unlicensed organization." The charges related solely to the men's peaceful human rights advocacy. The verdict also ordered the dissolution of their organization, the Saudi Civil and Political Rights Association (ACPRA). A court in Buraida convicted APCRA activist Abd al-Karim al-Khodr on similar charges in June and sentenced him to eight years in prison.

The Specialized Criminal Court in June sentenced human rights advocate Mikhlif al-Shammari to five years in prison and a 10-year travel ban based on his writings and exposure of human rights abuses. Human rights activists Waleed Abu al-Khair and Fadhel al-Manasef remained on trial at this writing on charges based solely on their peaceful exercise of the rights to free expression and association.

Saudi officials continue to refuse to register political or human rights groups, leaving members subject to prosecution for "setting up an unregistered organization." In August, an appeals court upheld the Social Affairs Ministry's denial of registration to the Eastern Province-based Adala Center for Human Rights. The ministry said it can only license charitable organizations, and that Adala's activities are not covered under the ministry's definition of a charity.

Saudi Arabia does not tolerate public worship by adherents of religions other than Islam and systematically discriminates against Muslim religious minorities, in particular Twelver Shia and Ismailis.

On February 8, officers from the Committee for the Promotion of Virtue and the Prevention of Vice, or religious police, raided a gathering of around 40 Ethiopian women in al-Khobar on the pretext that it was a Christian religious gathering. Authorities jailed them and deported them in groups, the last in July.

In July, a Jeddah court convicted liberal activist Raif Badawi and sentenced him to six years in prison and 600 lashes for "insulting Islam" by founding a liberal website, and for his comments during television interviews. In October, authorities released journalist Hamza Kashgari, who had been held since February 2012 without charge on blasphemy allegations related to his fictitious Twitter dialogue with the Prophet Muhammad.

Criminal Justice

Detainees, including children, commonly face systematic violations of due process and fair trial rights, including arbitrary arrest, and torture and ill-treatment in detention. Saudi judges routinely sentence defendants to hundreds of lashes.

Judges can order arrest and detention, including of children, at their discretion. Children can be tried for capital crimes and sentenced as adults if physical signs of puberty exist.

Authorities do not always inform suspects of the crime with which they are charged, nor of supporting evidence. Saudi Arabia has no penal code, so prosecutors and judges largely determine criminal offenses at their discretion. Authorities generally do not allow lawyers to assist suspects during interrogation and often impede them from examining witnesses and presenting evidence at trial. Previous court rulings do not bind judges, and there is little evidence that they seek consistency in sentencing for similar crimes.

Authorities continued to arrest and hold suspects for months and sometimes years without judicial review or prosecution. Security forces detained Jordanian activist Khaled al-Natour at King Khalid International Airport in Riyadh on January 6, 2013, as he attempted to enter Saudi Arabia on a business trip. Al-

Natour had appeared in videos of protests in Amman that criticized Saudi Arabia's armed intervention in Bahrain. Authorities held him incommunicado and without charge for three months until releasing him on April 7. The governmental Human Rights Commission told Human Rights Watch in July that over 2,500 terrorism suspects still languish in prisons without charge or trial for up to 10 years.

According to media reports, Saudi Arabia executed at least 64 persons between January and November 2013, mostly for murder, drug offenses, and armed robbery. The vast majority of executions were carried out via public beheading. On May 21, authorities in Jizan governorate executed five Yemenis for armed robbery and murder by "crucifixion"— a punishment of beheading followed by display of the decapitated body in public. At time of writing, prosecutors in the Specialized Criminal Court were pursuing a "crucifixion" sentence against prominent Shia cleric Nimr al-Nimr.

In April, authorities in the southern city of Abha executed seven Saudi men by firing squad for armed robberies in 2005; at least two were under 18 at the time of the alleged robberies. Saudi Arabia is one of just four countries worldwide that continues to execute child offenders.

Women's and Girls' Rights

Under the guardianship system, girls and women are forbidden from traveling, conducting official business, or undergoing certain medical procedures without permission from their male guardians. Likewise, under un-codified rules on personal status, women are not allowed to marry without the permission of their guardian; unlike men, they do not have unilateral right to divorce and often face discrimination in relation to custody of children.

On October 26, at least 50 Saudi women got behind the wheel throughout the kingdom in defiance of the ban on women driving. Police officials said that officers had pulled over at least 18 women driving in various areas of the country, though it is unclear whether any faced fines or other penalties. On October 27, police arrested Tariq al-Mubarak, a secondary school teacher and columnist for the London-based Arabic newspaper *Asharq al-Awsat*, who had expressed support for an end to the driving ban. Authorities released al-Mubarak on November 3.

The Ministry of Education announced in May that girls enrolled in private schools could take part in supervised sports if they wear "decent clothing," but failed to announce a promised national strategy to promote sports for girls in government-funded schools.

In January, King Abdullah appointed 30 women to the Shura Council and amended the council statute to guarantee representation of women. The Ministry of Justice granted the first lawyer-trainee license to a woman, Arwa al-Hujaili, in April.

Punishment for domestic violence remained lax, but in August the Council of Ministers issued a new law criminalizing domestic abuse for the first time. The law does not detail enforcement mechanisms to ensure prompt investigations of abuse allegations or prosecution of those who commit abuses and does not explicitly criminalize marital rape.

Migrant Workers' Rights

Over 9 million migrant workers fill manual, clerical, and service jobs, constituting more than half the workforce. Many suffer abuses and exploitation, sometimes amounting to conditions of forced labour or servitude.

The *kafala* (sponsorship) system ties migrant workers' residency permits to "sponsoring" employers, whose written consent is required for workers to change employers or exit the country. Some employers illegally confiscate passports, withhold wages, and force migrants to work against their will.

On November 4, following a seven month "grace period" for foreign workers to correct their status and documentation, authorities raided businesses and set up checkpoints across the country to apprehend workers without required documentation or not working for their legal sponsors. Interior Minister Mohammed bin Nayef announced in late November that authorities had expelled over 60,000 foreign workers in the crackdown's first three weeks.

Some 1.5 million migrant domestic workers remain excluded from the 2005 Labor Law, though in July the Council of Ministers passed a new regulation on domestic work. The law would offer domestic workers certain basic protections for the first time, such as requiring a nine-hour daily break, prompt salary payment at the end of each month, sick leave, and a one-month paid vacation every two years. The law would prohibit sponsors from employing workers outside the sponsor's home or assigning work harmful to a worker's health.

Domestic workers, most of them women, frequently endure a range of abuses including overwork, forced confinement, non-payment of wages, food deprivation, and psychological, physical, and sexual abuse. Workers who attempted to report employer abuses sometimes faced prosecution based on counterclaims of theft or "sorcery."

Authorities executed 24-year-old Sri Lankan domestic worker Rizanna Nafeek in January for the 2005 death of a 4-month-old child in her care, though Nafeek was only 17 at the time of her alleged crime and despite her claims that investigators obtained her confession under duress and she did not have access to a competent translator during interrogation.

Key International Actors

The United States, a key ally, did not publicly criticize Saudi human rights violations beyond Congressionally mandated annual reports, though State Department spokespeople expressed "concerns" over the convictions of al-Hamid, al-Qahtani, and Badawi.

In August, the US Department of Defense approved the sale of 1,300 cluster bombs to Saudi Arabia for more than US$640 million. Neither country is party to the Convention on Cluster Munitions.

In March 2013, UN High Commissioner for Human Rights Navi Pillay "strongly condemned" the executions of the seven Saudi men from Abha, including two who were children at the time of the crimes for which they were convicted.

Syria

Syria's armed conflict escalated even further in 2013 as the government intensified its attacks and began using increasingly deadly and indiscriminate weapons, culminating in a chemical weapons attack on the Damascus countryside on August 21. Government forces and pro-government militias also continued to torture detainees and commit executions.

Armed opposition forces, including a growing number of pro-opposition foreign fighters, have also carried out serious abuses including indiscriminate attacks on civilians, executions, kidnapping, and torture. According to United Nations Secretary-General Ban Ki-moon, as of July 2013 more than 100,000 people had been killed in the conflict. The spread and intensification of fighting have led to a dire humanitarian crisis with millions internally displaced or seeking refuge in neighboring countries.

Attacks on Civilians, Unlawful Use of Weapons

On August 21, hundreds of civilians, including many children, were killed in a chemical weapons attack on areas near Damascus. A UN investigation determined that the nerve agent sarin was used. While the Syrian government denies responsibility, available evidence strongly suggests that government forces were responsible for the attack. In response to US and French threats of strikes in response to the attack, Syria acceded to the Chemical Weapons Convention and agreed to eliminate its chemical weapons in the first half of 2014.

Syrian armed forces have also continued to use cluster bombs—weapons banned by the 2008 Convention on Cluster Munitions, which Syria has not signed. Human Rights Watch has identified 152 locations where government forces used at least 204 cluster munitions, in 9 of the country's 14 governorates. The actual number of cluster munitions used by Syrian government forces is probably higher.

The Syrian air force has dropped incendiary weapons in populated areas in dozens of instances, including on a school playground in al-Qusayr in December 2012. Incendiary weapons contain flammable substances designed to set fire to objects or to cause burn injuries and death.

Syria's air force also repeatedly carried out indiscriminate, and in some cases deliberate, strikes against civilians, and its army has also struck populated areas with ballistic missiles. Human Rights Watch investigated nine apparent ballistic missile attacks in 2013 that killed at least 215 people, including 100 children. No military targets were struck in the attacks and in seven of nine cases investigated Human Rights Watch found no signs of any apparent military targets in the vicinity.

Executions by Government and Pro-government Forces

Syrian government and pro-government forces conducted several large-scale military operations across the country during which government forces and pro-government militias carried out mass killings.

On May 2-3, these forces killed at least 248 people, including 45 women and 43 children, in the towns of al-Bayda and Baniyas in Tartous governorate. The overwhelming majority were summarily executed after the end of military confrontations. The attacks were one of the deadliest instances of mass summary executions since the start of the conflict.

At least 147 bodies were found in the city of Aleppo's river between January and March. The location where the bodies were discovered and information about the victims' last known whereabouts indicate that the executions most likely took place in government-controlled areas, although the perpetrators or their motivation remains unknown.

Arbitrary Arrests, Enforced Disappearances, Torture, and Deaths in Custody

Since the beginning of the uprising security forces have subjected tens of thousands of people to arbitrary arrests, unlawful detentions, enforced disappearances, ill-treatment, and torture using an extensive network of detention facilities throughout Syria. Many detainees were young men in their 20s or 30s; but children, women, and elderly people were also detained.

Those arrested include peaceful protesters and activists involved in organizing, filming, and reporting on protests as well as journalists, humanitarian assistance providers, lawyers, and doctors. In some instances, activists reported that

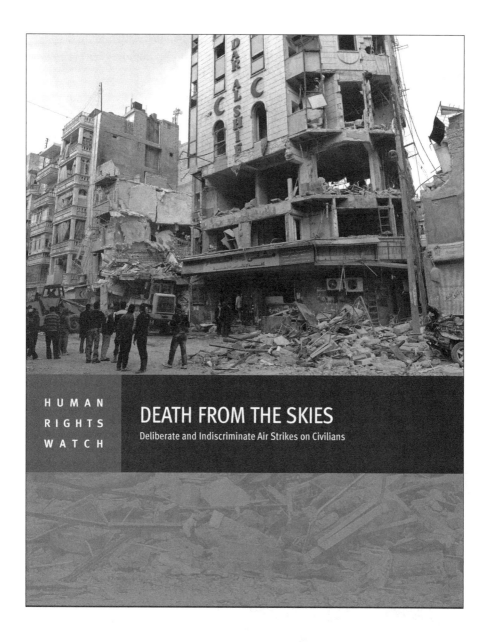

HUMAN
RIGHTS
WATCH

DEATH FROM THE SKIES
Deliberate and Indiscriminate Air Strikes on Civilians

security forces detained their family members, including children, to pressure them to turn themselves in. A large number of political activists remain in incommunicado detention while others have faced trial, including before military and counterterrorism courts, for exercising their rights.

On February 3, security officials arrested Mohammed Atfah, a Syrian Arab Red Crescent volunteer working with children in Homs, at a checkpoint. A detainee who was held with Mohammed and later released told his family that Mohammed's health had deteriorated so significantly in detention that he was no longer able to recognize people around him.

On March 13, security forces also arrested Nidal Nahlawi and his friends in Damascus while they were planning relief operations. Nidal has been accused of supporting terrorism under the overbroad July 2012 Counterterrorism Law.

He and other activists, including several members of the Syrian Center for Media and Freedom of Expression (SCM) are standing trial before a special counterterrorism court on the basis of this law. The court does not meet basic international fair trial standards. The charges are brought under the guise of countering violent militancy, but the allegations against the activists actually amount to such acts as distributing humanitarian aid and documenting human rights abuses.

Released detainees and defectors describe a range of torture methods used by Syrian security forces including prolonged beatings, often with batons and wires, use of painful stress positions, electrocution, sexual assault, the pulling of fingernails, and mock execution. During a visit to an abandoned state security detention facility in Raqqa in April 2013, Human Rights Watch found a *basat al-reeh* torture device—a cross-shaped contraption used to immobilize detainees during torture.

Several former detainees said they witnessed people dying from torture in detention. At least 490 detainees died in custody in 2013, according to local activists.

In February 2013, Human Rights Watch documented the death in detention of Omar Aziz, 64, a peaceful activist who had been helping local committees deliver aid. A second detainee Ayham Ghazzoul, 26, a human rights activist, and

HUMAN
RIGHTS
WATCH

"No One's Left"

Summary Executions by Syrian Forces in al-Bayda & Baniyas

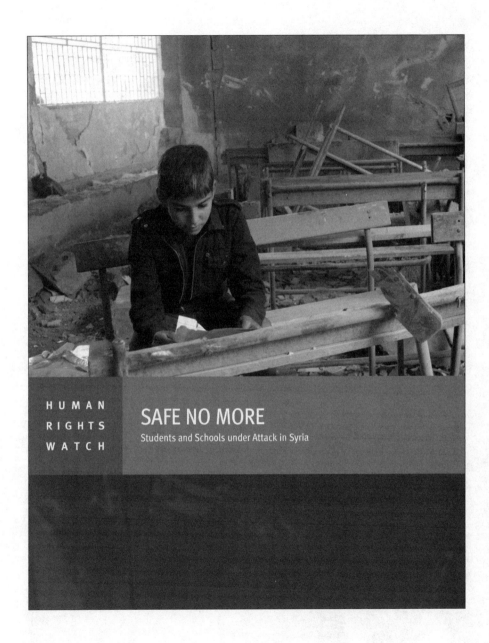

HUMAN
RIGHTS
WATCH

SAFE NO MORE
Students and Schools under Attack in Syria

and member of SCM, died in detention in November, a released detainee told his family.

Armed Opposition Abuses

Armed opposition groups have increasingly carried out serious abuses including indiscriminate attacks, extrajudicial executions, kidnapping, and torture. Foreign fighters and jihadist groups have been among the worst perpetrators of the abuses that Human Rights Watch has documented.

On August 4, a coalition of opposition groups led predominately by Islamist militant groups conducted an operation in the Latakia countryside in which some of the groups killed at least 190 civilians, including 57 women, at least 18 children, and 14 elderly men. Many of them were summarily executed. Armed opposition groups have been implicated in other indiscriminate attacks against the civilian population, including car bombings and mortar attacks on government-held civilian areas inside Syria as well as cross-border strikes on Shia villages in Lebanon.

Armed opposition groups fighting in Syria are also using children for combat and other military purposes, and have used schools as military bases, barracks, detention centers, and sniper posts, turning places of learning into military targets and putting students at risk.

Displacement Crisis

The UN Office for the Coordination of Humanitarian Affairs (OCHA) estimates that 4.25 million Syrians are internally displaced. In 2013, humanitarian aid agencies experienced significant challenges in getting assistance to the displaced and affected civilian population within Syria because of sieges imposed by both government and opposition fighters, the government's continuing refusal to allow assistance to come in across the border, and armed opposition groups' failure to guarantee security for humanitarian workers.

Attacks on healthcare workers and facilities have significantly eroded the country's ability to protect the right to health: 32 of the country's 88 public hospitals have closed and government forces have detained, tortured, and killed hundreds of health workers and patients, and have deliberately attacked vehicles carrying patients and supplies. A recent report of the UN Human Rights Council (UNHRC) concluded that "the denial of medical care as a weapon of war is a distinct and chilling reality of the war in Syria."

As of November 18, 2013, 2.23 million Syrians had registered or were pending registration as refugees with the UN Refugee Agency (UNHCR), the vast of majority of them in Lebanon, Jordan, Turkey, Iraq, and Egypt. In 2013 Iraq, Jordan, and Turkey denied entry to tens of thousands of Syrians, either by limiting daily numbers and the profile of those who could cross or by closing border crossings entirely and only sporadically allowing a limited number to cross. Syrians stranded as a result lived in poor conditions and were at risk of attacks by government forces.

All four neighboring countries accepting Syrian refugees have denied Syrians secure legal status. Israeli Defense Minister Ehud Barak said that Israel would prevent "waves of refugees" from fleeing Syria to the occupied Golan Heights.

On January 13, 2013, Egyptian airport officials deported two Syrians back to Syria, in violation of Egypt's non-refoulement obligations, and, on July 8, without warning, the Egyptian government changed its entry policy for Syrians by requiring them to obtain a visa and security clearance beforehand. On the same day, Egypt denied entry to 276 people arriving from Syria, including a plane forced to fly back to Syria. On July 19 and 20, Egyptian security forces arrested dozens of Syrian men and some boys at checkpoints on main roads in Cairo, many arbitrarily. The authorities deported at least 24 of them, including 7 boys, to neighboring countries.

Palestinians from Syria have faced additional obstacles. Since March, Jordan has routinely denied entry to Palestinian refugees from Syria. Egypt has also restricted entry to Palestinians from Syria starting in January. The Lebanese government also began on August 6 to bar most Palestinians from Syria from entering.

In 2013, the number of refugees from Syria attempting to reach Europe, including through dangerous smuggling routes, has increased. While some European Union countries offer them safety, in others, including Greece, they face detention and significant obstacles in getting protection.

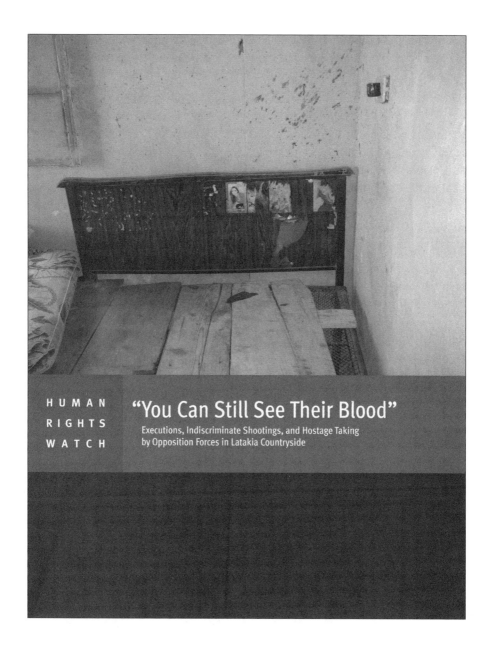

HUMAN
RIGHTS
WATCH

"You Can Still See Their Blood"

Executions, Indiscriminate Shootings, and Hostage Taking
by Opposition Forces in Latakia Countryside

UNHCR reported that over 75 percent of the registered Syrian refugees in neigh-boring countries are women and children who face particular vulnerabilities. Aid agencies report that domestic violence, sexual harassment, and exploitation have increased and social constraints and fear limit the mobility of refugee women, restricting their access to income-generating activities or health and other critical services.

At time of writing, UNHCR reports that only 62 percent of its appeal for the regional refugee response is funded, leaving a US$1.14 billion budget shortfall. As a result, UNHCR has cut assistance to refugees, including subsidization of health care and provision of basic goods.

Key International Actors

The UN Security Council (Security Council) remained deeply divided on Syria. The August 21 chemical weapons attack pushed the US and Russian govern-ments to negotiate a deal that resulted in a September 27 Security Council reso-lution requiring the Syrian government to destroy its chemical weapons program and cooperate with international inspectors. A presidential statement of the Security Council followed on October 2 calling for immediate action to ensure safe and unhindered humanitarian access throughout Syria, including across borders where appropriate.

Despite these developments, Russian and Chinese opposition precluded the Security Council from referring the situation to the International Criminal Court (ICC), obstructing accountability for violations in the conflict.

The General Assembly and the Human Rights Council passed resolutions on Syria with overwhelming majorities in 2013. The Human Rights Council extended until March 2014 the international commission of inquiry mandated to investi-gate violations and identify where possible those responsible. A total of 64 countries called on the Security Council to refer the situation in Syria to the ICC, including 6 Security Council members: France, the United Kingdom, Luxembourg, Argentina, Australia, and South Korea. France included an ICC referral in an early draft of the Security Council resolution on chemical weapons use, but this was later removed during negotiations over the text. Neither the United States nor China expressed support for a referral. Russia said an ICC referral would be "ill-timed and counterproductive."

Syrian opposition factions under the umbrella grouping, the National Coalition of Syrian Revolutionary and Opposition Forces continued to gain international support in 2013 and recognition as the legitimate representative of the Syrian people. Despite this however, the coalition has failed to create a unified political or military opposition. Armed opposition groups in Syria are receiving financial and military support from Saudi Arabia, Qatar, Turkey, and the US. The UK and France provide non-lethal aid to armed opposition groups.

The governments of Iran, Russia, and China continued to support the Syrian government either diplomatically or through financial and military support.

The European Union as a whole remained the second largest humanitarian donor for the Syrian crisis after the US. However, despite the EU's stated commitment to both the ICC and to justice for serious crimes, the EU high representative failed to ensure a strong collective EU voice and strategy that would advance the chances of bringing the crimes in Syria before the ICC. Twenty-seven EU member states—all but Sweden—joined a Swiss-led initiative calling on the Security Council to refer the situation in Syria to the ICC.

Tunisia

Tunisia's process of democratic transition continued, but at a slow pace. The National Constituent Assembly (NCA), elected in October 2011, continued to draft a new constitution but at this writing it had yet to be approved. The assassination by alleged Islamist militants of two leading leftist opposition politicians, Chokri Belaid and Mohamed Brahmi, on February 6 and July 25 respectively, caused widespread shock and sparked a political crisis that saw the NCA suspended for two months.

Since they overthrew the Ben Ali regime in 2011, Tunisians have enjoyed greater freedom of expression, assembly and association, including the freedom to form political parties. However, several factors have hampered the consolidation of rights' protections. These include the delay in adopting a new constitution consistent with international human rights law and standards, the retention of the former regime's repressive legal arsenal, and attempts by the executive branch to control media and prosecute speech offenses.

Human Rights in the Draft Constitution

The NCA issued a new draft constitution in June. Thought an improvement on the three previous drafts—providing safeguards for most civil, political, economic, social, and cultural rights—it was also deficient in several respects. In particular, it failed to include a clause directly incorporating human rights, as defined under customary international law and in international treaties that Tunisia has ratified, into Tunisian national law. In addition, the new draft contained only weak formulations of the principles of equality and non-discrimination before the law, and allowed for limitation of the rights to freedom of expression, assembly, association, movement, and access to information in overly broad terms, which could result in their arbitrary restriction. At time of writing, it remained unclear when the new constitution would be adopted.

Freedom of Expression and Media

The authorities decided in May 2013, after some delay, to implement decree-law 116 on audiovisual media. This required the creation of an Independent High Authority for Audiovisual Communication (HAICA) to regulate broadcast media.

Despite this, the executive branch continued unilaterally to appoint the heads of state radio and television broadcasters in contravention of international freedom of expression standards governing the independence of public service media.

In 2013, judicial authorities prosecuted many journalists, bloggers, artists, and intellectuals on account of their peaceful exercise of freedom of expression using penal code provisions criminalizing "defamation," "offenses against state agents," and "harming public order," all of which can result in prison terms. The NCA made no effort to abolish or suspend these Ben Ali era provisions, and the courts did not rule them inconsistent with international human rights law.

On March 8, authorities charged blogger Olfa Riahi with criminal defamation after she published information online about alleged misuse of public funds by former foreign minister Rafik Abdessalem. Her case was still under investigation at time of writing.

On August 30, a criminal court in Hammamet imposed prison terms on two Tunisian rappers, known by the names "Weld El 15" and "Klay BBJ," after convicting them in their absence of "insulting the police" and other charges. They had performed a song critical of police violence at a music festival. On October 17, an appeals court acquitted Klay BBJ and set him free after three weeks in prison. In March, Weld El 15 had released a video accompanying his song "Cops Are Dogs," which showed police assaulting people. For this, a criminal court in Manouba sentenced him to two years in prison, which the Appeals Court in Tunis reduced to a suspended six-month term on July 2.

On September 9, an investigative judge ordered the arrest and detention of police union leader Walid Zarrouk after he allegedly posted comments on a Facebook post criticizing politicized prosecutions. The same day, in separate cases, prosecutors summoned Zouhaer al-Jiss, a journalist, for moderating a radio program in which a participant criticized Tunisia's president, and Zied al-Heni, a journalist who had criticized the arrest of a cameraman who filmed an egg-throwing attack on the culture minister. Al-Heni was arrested that day and spent three days in jail before being released on bail.

617

Judicial Reform

In April, the NCA appointed a temporary high judicial council to supervise the appointment, promotion, transfer, and discipline of judges pending the adoption of a new constitution. This long awaited reform was intended to end or reduce the undue executive influence over the judiciary that, in October 2012, saw the Ministry of Justice arbitrarily dismiss 75 judges.

Women's Rights

Tunisia has long had a reputation as among the most progressive of Arab states with respect to women's rights. The new draft constitution reflects this, declaring that the state "guarantees the protection of women's rights and supports their gains," "guarantees equal opportunity between men and women to assume responsibilities," and "guarantees the elimination of all forms of violence against women." This is an improvement over previous constitutional drafts that invoked notions of "complementary" gender roles that risked diluting the principle of equality between men and women. However, the new draft constitution fails to fully embody the principle of equality between the sexes as it refers to equal opportunity in "assuming responsibilities," but not to the broader right to equality of opportunity in all political, economic, and other spheres.

Prosecution of Attacks by Fundamentalist Groups

In May, a Tunis court imposed two-year suspended prison sentences on 20 defendants it convicted of participating in an attack on the American Embassy on September 14, 2012, by thousands of people, mostly religious conservatives, protesting a movie made in the US that they deemed insulting to Islam. Four protesters died in the attack, in which protestors burned the American flag and a nearby American school, and destroyed cars and other property.

The authorities also accused Islamist religious conservatives of responsibility for the assassinations of Chokri Belaid and Mohamed Brahmi, and said that both men were shot with the same gun. Their murders sparked widespread protests. The authorities declared Ansar al-Sharia, an Islamist group, a "terrorist organization" and arrested dozens of suspected members. Two of the suspects alleged torture in prison.

HUMAN
RIGHTS
WATCH

CRACKS IN THE SYSTEM

Conditions of Pre-Charge Detainees in Tunisia

Abuses against Protesters

Tunisians now have more freedom to exercise their rights to peaceful demonstration since Ben Ali's ousting. However, police and other security forces continued to use excessive force against demonstrators in 2013. For example, on May 19, security forces fired live ammunition and birdshot at protestors during clashes in Intilaka and Cite Ettadhamen, Tunis neighborhoods, killing one person and injuring four others. Following the murder of Mohamed Brahmi, security forces used excessive force, including beatings and tear gas, to disperse protesters, killing one person and injuring others. The authorities failed to investigate and to hold the security forces accountable.

Accountability for Past Crimes

In June, the NCA began considering a draft transitional justice law, which proposes the creation of a Council of Truth and Dignity to uncover the truth about past rights abuses. At time of writing, the law had yet to be enacted.

Military courts have tried several groups of defendants accused of killing protesters during the revolution which toppled the former president. A military court also sentenced Ben Ali, who remains in Saudi Arabia, to life in prison for complicity in murder, after trying him in absentia, and jailed several former high-ranking officials.

These trials appeared to respect defendants' rights and enabled some victims to pursue justice, but several factors undermined their value towards achieving accountability, notably the authorities' failure to identify the direct perpetrators of killings and lack of an adequate legal framework to prosecute senior officers with command responsibility for crimes that their subordinates committed. The government's failure to press effectively for Ben Ali's extradition from Saudi Arabia also undermined accountability.

Although Ben Ali's security forces used torture extensively, the new authorities have failed in the almost three years since the overthrow of Ben Ali to investigate the majority of torture cases. In the one torture-related trial that has taken place, a court convicted former Interior Minister Abdallah Kallel and three security officials of "using violence against others either directly or through others," and sentenced them to two year prison terms. The case arose from the arrest and detention of 17 senior military officers in 1991 in connection with an alleged plot by the Islamist group Al-Nahdha against Ben Ali.

Key International Actors

The European Union provides funding support for judicial, security sector and other institutional reform. In October 2012, the EU approved €25 million (US$32 million) to support strengthening judicial independence and pledged a further €40 million ($51.2 million) in June 2013.

On September 13, following his visit to Tunisia, the special rapporteur on the promotion of truth, justice, reparation and guarantees of non-recurrence urged the government to adopt a comprehensive transitional justice program, and to enact legislation transferring jurisdiction over cases involving gross violations of human rights in which the military or security forces are implicated, from military courts to the ordinary civilian justice system.

United Arab Emirates

The United Arab Emirates (UAE) continues to crack down on freedom of expression and association. The authorities are arbitrarily detaining scores of individuals they suspect of links to domestic and international Islamist groups. A court convicted 69 dissidents in July after a manifestly unfair trial, in which evidence emerged of systematic torture at state security facilities. The UAE made no reforms to a system that facilitates the forced labor of migrant workers. Plans to ameliorate conditions for female domestic workers fall short of the standards outlined in the convention on domestic workers that the International Labour Organization (ILO) adopted in 2012.

Torture and Fair Trial

In July, the Federal Supreme Court sentenced 69 Emirati dissidents to prison terms of up to 10 years on charges of aiming to overthrow the government after a mass trial of a total of 94 defendants marred by violations of fair trial standards, including credible allegations that the defendants endured torture in pre-trial detention. The court acquitted 25 of the defendants.

Authorities held at least 64 of the detainees at undisclosed locations for up to a year before the trial began in March, and many of the detainees had no access to legal assistance until late February. Prior to the opening of the trial, security officials denied international observers entry to the UAE. Authorities prevented other observers who had been admitted to the country from entering the court, despite the fact that they had complied with the stipulated procedures.

At the first trial hearing, some of the defendants told the judge they had been seriously ill-treated during their months in detention. In June, rights groups received 22 statements written by some of the 94 people on trial that corroborated these claims. All but six of those who wrote statements said that officials subjected them to temperature extremes and interrogated them while they were blindfolded. Two said their interrogators threatened them with electrocution.

Other detainees in the UAE have also alleged that they endured ill-treatment that in some cases amounted to torture. Officials held Egyptian journalist Anas Fouda in custody for 35 days after state security officers detained him in July, and after his release, he said that officials kept him in solitary confinement, with extremes of temperature and harsh lighting that resulted in sleep deprivation. Saud Kulaib, an Emirati national, spent five months in incommunicado detention between December 29 and May 27. In addition to enduring solitary confinement, extremes of temperature, and sleep deprivation, he told family members and other inmates that officers beat him, sliced his hand open with a razor blade, threatened to pull out his fingernails, and told him that his wife was in detention and on hunger strike.

Fourteen Egyptians are at time of writing in Al Wathba jail after spending up to seven months in incommunicado detention before their transfer there in June. They did not have access to a lawyer until September 22 and their family members claim they had been subjected to physical and psychological torture in detention.

Freedom of Association and Expression

Those convicted in the mass trial all have ties to an Emirati Islamist group, al-Islah, that has advocated political reform in the UAE. The judgment in the case indicates that the judge convicted them solely on the basis of their exercise of their rights to freedom of association and expression. The bulk of the evidence in the 243-page judgment focuses on the peaceful political activities of the accused and their ties to al-Islah, which the judgment asserts is a branch of the Muslim Brotherhood.

The only evidence that suggests any intention to overthrow the government is a confession by one defendant, Ahmed al-Suweidi, whom authorities forcibly disappeared for five months after his arrest on March 26, 2012. In court, al-Suweidi denied all the charges. There is nothing in the judgment aside from al-Suweidi's disputed confession that suggests those convicted were doing anything other than expressing opinions in the context of an organization whose goal was political reform.

The authorities continue to arbitrarily detain individuals with suspected links to peaceful Islamist groups and to arrest and prosecute people for criticizing the government.

In April, an Abu Dhabi court sentenced Abdulla al-Hadidi to 10 months in prison for publishing false details of a public trial session via the Internet. Al-Hadidi had attended four court sessions of the UAE's mass trial and had posted comments about what he witnessed on social media sites. The court's judgment invoked the UAE federal decree on cybercrime, passed in November 2012. The decree provides for prison sentences for a range of nonviolent political activities carried out on or via the Internet, from criticism of the UAE's rulers to calling for unlicensed demonstrations. In July, the day after authorities arrested an Emirati national named Khalifa Rabia, a government-linked television channel aired a piece accusing him of "affiliation with secret cells" on the basis of an analysis of his Twitter account, which contained tweets in support of political detainees in the UAE. Rabia remained in detention at time of writing.

Authorities have not yet filed charges against the 14 Egyptians detained between November 21, 2012 and January 7, 2013, but local media alleged that the detained men had formed a covert Muslim Brotherhood cell attempting to establish a foothold in the UAE. According to their lawyer, only three of them have ever been members of the Muslim Brotherhood in Egypt. The detainees include doctors, engineers, and university professors, all of whom have lived and worked in the UAE for many years. Eight of the detainees have been in the UAE for between 20 and 30 years.

Migrant Workers

According to 2011 government statistics, foreigners account for more than 88.5 percent of UAE residents, many of them low-paid migrant workers from South Asia. Despite years of criticism, the UAE has not addressed shortcomings in its legal and regulatory framework that facilitate the exploitation and forced labor of these workers.

Recruiting agencies often charge workers fees of several thousand dollars and employers customarily confiscate the workers' passports for the duration of their stay in the UAE. The authorities have taken no steps to stop either of these illegal practices. Nor have they taken steps to reform the *kafala* (sponsorship) system that ties a migrant worker's legal residence to his or her employer, or "sponsor." Migrant workers have no right to organize or bargain collectively, and face penalties for going on strike. In May, hundreds of workers at a site in

Dubai went on strike demanding better pay and conditions. After the two-day strike, immigration officials issued at least 40 deportation orders.

UAE labor law excludes domestic workers, almost exclusively migrant women, denying them basic protections such as limits to hours of work and a weekly day off. A flawed 2012 draft law for domestic workers has yet to be adopted and a regional unified contract for domestic workers, expected to be approved in 2014, falls well short of the minimum standards outlined in the Domestic Workers Convention that the ILO adopted in 2011.

Women's Rights

In July, a Norwegian woman received a 16-month prison sentence for extramarital sex after she reported to the police that she had been raped. The police did not believe her claim that the sex was nonconsensual. The subsequent international outcry led to an official pardon and her release, but the case highlighted how women who report rape can be threatened with criminal charges instead, and as such exposed longstanding problems with procedures for victims of sexual violence.

Federal Law No. 28 of 2005 regulates matters of personal status in the UAE and some of its provisions discriminate against women. The law states that UAE women have the right to work "without being held disobedient" and the right to complete their education, but it also requires that a male guardian concludes a woman's marriage contract. *Talaq*, unilateral divorce, occurs by a declaration from the husband in the presence of a judge.

Despite the existence of shelters and hotlines to help protect women, domestic violence remains a pervasive problem. The penal code gives men the legal right to discipline their wives and children, including through the use of physical violence. The Federal Supreme Court has upheld a husband's right to "chastise" his wife and children with physical abuse.

Key International Actors

Influential allies such as the United States, France, and the United Kingdom, all of which are seeking multibillion-dollar fighter jet contracts with the UAE, have refrained from criticizing the UAE's crackdown on political dissent.

Yemen

The fragile transition government that succeeded President Ali Abdullah Saleh in 2012 following mass protests failed to address multiple human rights challenges. Conflict-related abuses, legally sanctioned discrimination against women, judicial executions of child offenders, and non-accountability for the previous government's human rights violations all persisted in 2013.

Five hundred and sixty five representatives of political parties, women, youth, and civil society launched a national dialogue process in March, which was slated to produce recommendations within six months to guide the subsequent constitutional drafting process regarding the nature of the state. At time of writing, the dialogue had yet to end because of delays caused by political maneuvering.

Clashes continued between state security forces and armed factions demanding greater autonomy in southern Yemen and between Salafist groups and armed tribesmen and Huthis in the north. The Yemeni government and the United States continued to engage in military operations with the Islamist armed group Al-Qaeda in the Arabian Peninsula (AQAP). On December 5, suicide bombing attacks both claimed and denied by AQAP against Yemen's Defense Ministry compound killed at least 52 people and injured another 161. The dead included at least seven foreign doctors and nurses working at the military hospital in the compound.

Yemen faces a growing humanitarian crisis, with nearly half the population lacking sufficient food, according to UN agencies.

Accountability

In 2012, Yemen's parliament granted Saleh and his aides immunity from prosecution, and the current president, Abdu Rabu Mansour Hadi, has not created mechanisms to provide accountability for past abuses.

In September 2012, President Hadi decreed that an independent commission of inquiry should be created to investigate alleged violations committed during the 2011 uprising and recommend accountability for perpetrators and redress for victims. Over one year later, he had still not nominated the commissioners.

Hadi presented a deeply flawed draft transitional justice law to parliament in January, but it has yet to be passed. The draft law does not grant victims judicial redress, but is merely a victim compensation scheme, limited in time to events of 2011.

The trial began in September 2012 of 78 defendants—but not the key suspects—for the deadliest attack of the uprising, in which pro-government gunmen killed 45 protesters and wounded 200 on March 18, 2011. It was marred by political interference, failure to follow leads that might have implicated government officials, and factual errors. In April 2013, a trial judge ordered prosecutors to reinvestigate former president Saleh and 11 top aides in connection with the incident.

Militant Attacks

AQAP carried out dozens of deadly bombings and other attacks on Yemeni security forces. The Islamist group held several foreigners for ransom, releasing most after weeks or months, but continued to detain Saudi diplomat Abdallah al-Khalidi, who was abducted in March 2012.

The US carried out at least 22 drone strikes on alleged AQAP members as of mid-September, according to the New America Foundation and the United Kingdom-based Bureau of Investigative Journalism. The strikes killed between 72 and 139 people, most of them alleged militants, but lack of access to most targeted areas and the unwillingness of the United States to provide information on attacks, prevented full inquiries, including regarding civilian casualties.

A Human Rights Watch investigation of six US targeted killing operations in Yemen—one in 2009 and the rest in 2012-13—found two attacks were unlawfully indiscriminate and four others raised serious laws-of-war concerns.

Unlawful Use of Mines

In May 2013, Human Rights Watch documented the use of antipersonnel landmines allegedly by the Republican Guards in Bani Jarmooz, an area northeast of the capital, Sanaa, in 2011. The mines have caused at least 1 death and 14 injuries of civilians, including 9 children.

Yemen is a state party to the Mine Ban Treaty, and at a meeting of the treaty in Geneva in May, renewed its commitment to the treaty, promised to investigate the allegations, and committed itself to addressing the issue by clearing the mines and assisting the victims.

HUMAN
RIGHTS
WATCH

"Look at Us with a Merciful Eye"
Juvenile Offenders Awaiting Execution in Yemen

The Ministry of Defense established a committee to investigate the allegations of landmine use and demine the area, but as of September the committee had yet to send an assessment team to the area.

Attacks on Health Workers

Health workers and facilities are struggling to protect themselves from armed groups. Medecins Sans Frontieres reported 18 different attacks against their staff in Amran in the past year, including shootings, threats, and physical attacks on health workers.

Children and Armed Conflict

In recent years, Human Rights Watch has documented cases of children participating in combat with both the First Armored Division and the Republican Guard. In June 2012, UNICEF Yemen reported several incidents of child recruitment by the Yemeni armed forces and by the armed group Ansar al-Sharia, an offshoot of AQAP. In September, the United Nations special rapporteur on children in armed conflict announced that the government had approved an action plan to end the recruitment and use of children in government armed forces.

In Aden, from February until June, the Southern Movement (or Hirak), an umbrella group seeking independence or greater autonomy for southern Yemen, prevented nearly 50,000 children from going to school on Wednesdays and Saturdays so that they could participate in a civil disobedience campaign. At least a dozen schools in Aden came under armed attack during the campaign from Hirak forces, some several times. In September, the civil disobedience campaign resumed, but campaigners agreed to exempt schools, allowing students to attend even on the weekly day of general strike.

Juvenile Death Penalty

Despite a 1994 law prohibiting death sentences for child offenders (anyone under 18 at the time of their crime), in the last five years Yemen has carried out multiple executions of individuals who may have been children at the time of their offense. At least 22 possible child offenders among convicted murderers remain on death row in Sanaa's Central Prison, and in prisons in Ibb, Taiz, Hodeida, and Aden.

Yemen's low rate of birth registration means that accused individuals often do not have birth certificates to establish their age. In addition, not all judges follow the law prohibiting death sentences for juvenile offenders.

In June 2013, Yemen's Justice Ministry established a committee of forensic medical experts to assess the age of young individuals accused of serious crimes whose age remains in doubt. The committee represented an effort to tackle the problem of death sentences for child offenders, but it relies solely on forensic medicine, which has a high margin of error, according to studies carried out by the Dutch government and the UK Royal College of Pediatrics and Child Health. Social evaluations, including a review of documents such as school registration as well as interviews with community members, remain necessary to supplement forensic evidence.

Women's and Girls' Rights

Women in Yemen face severe discrimination in law and in practice. Women cannot marry without the permission of their male guardians; they do not have equal rights to divorce, inheritance or child custody; and a lack of legal protection leaves them exposed to domestic and sexual violence.

Child marriage remains widespread with doctors and the media reporting the deaths of child brides as young as 8 years old following their wedding night or childbirth. Yemen has not legislated a minimum age of marriage.

The national dialogue presented an important opportunity to secure protection for women and girls' rights. The rights and freedoms committee within the national dialogue made positive recommendations on equality of men and women and non-discrimination, including a recommendation that the minimum age of marriage should be set at 18.

Attacks on Journalists

Since President Hadi took office, the authorities have eased formal controls on media, though legal restrictions remain. However there has been an increase in assaults on journalists and bloggers by the authorities and their supporters, and by militant groups, including Saleh loyalists, Huthis, and religious conservatives.

لا لقمع الحريات وتكميم
الأفواه

لا لسجن الصحفيين

لا للإختطاف والإخفاء
القسري

لا للتهديد

لا لإغلاق الصحف.

نعم لحرية التعبير
الصحافة .

HUMAN
RIGHTS
WATCH

"A Life-Threatening Career"
Attacks on Journalists under Yemen's New Government

In the first half of 2013, the Freedom Foundation, a Yemeni organization that monitors press freedom, recorded 144 attacks affecting 205 media members, including verbal harassment, confiscations, politicized prosecutions, enforced disappearances, and killings.

The government generally has not condemned these attacks, investigated them, held those responsible to account, or taken measures to protect journalists.

Key International Actors

In September 2013, the Friends of Yemen, a group of 39 countries and 8 international organizations, reiterated their joint pledge of US$7.8 billion that was made in 2012. Only 24 percent of the aid pledges had been dispersed by September 2013, according to the Yemeni government.

The US, the largest non-Arab donor, pledged $256 million in bilateral aid from January to September 2013. It reports having provided more than $221 million in humanitarian assistance since 2012, $100 million in development and economic aid, and approximately $247 million in counterterrorism and security assistance.

Since May 2012, US President Barack Obama has in place an executive order allowing the Treasury Department to freeze the US-based assets of anyone who "obstructs" implementation of the political transition, scheduled to end with the Yemeni presidential elections in 2014.

In September 2013, for the fifth consecutive year, Obama issued a full waiver allowing Yemen to receive military assistance, despite documented use of child soldiers by various forces, including government troops and pro-government militias.

In September 2013, the UN Human Rights Council passed resolution 24/32, which made reference to different human rights challenges, including child offenders facing the death penalty, child marriage, the protection of journalists, the need for investigations into past abuses, and the passage of a transitional justice law.

H U M A N
R I G H T S
W A T C H

AN OFFER YOU CAN'T REFUSE

How US Federal Prosecutors Force Drug Defendants to Plead Guilty

WORLD REPORT

2014

UNITED STATES
AND CANADA

Canada

Canada enjoys a global reputation as a defender of human rights at home and abroad that reflects a solid record on core civil and political rights protections, and a generally progressive approach to economic and social rights. Nonetheless, serious human rights concerns demand remedial action by federal and provincial governments, particularly with regard to the rights of the indigenous peoples of Canada, people impacted abroad by Canada's extractive industries, and ethnic and religious minorities in Quebec. Recent federal government actions undermining the ability of civil society organizations to engage in advocacy impede progress on a range of human rights issues.

Violence against Indigenous Women and Girls

In February 2013, the federal government established an all-party committee in Canada's House of Commons to hold hearings on the issue of missing and murdered indigenous women and to propose solutions to address root causes of violence. The committee made limited progress and was criticized by missing women advocates for lacking clear direction, prioritizing government witnesses over victims' family members, and failing to consider alternative, culturally sensitive methods of family and community participation.

The Native Women's Association of Canada has documented 582 cases of missing and murdered indigenous women and girls in Canada as of March 2010. Many of the killings and disappearances were between the 1960s and the 1990s, but 39 percent occurred after 2000. The number of cases is undoubtedly higher today, but comprehensive data is not available since the government cut funding for the organization's database, and police forces in Canada do not consistently collect race and ethnicity data.

In February, Royal Canadian Mounted Police (RCMP) Commissioner Bob Paulson told his officers via email, "Don't worry about it, I've got your back," in response to a 2013 Human Rights Watch report documenting the RCMP's failure in British Columbia (BC) to protect indigenous women and girls from violence, as well as abusive police behavior against indigenous women and girls, including excessive use of force, and physical and sexual assault. Canada has inadequate police complaint mechanisms and oversight procedures, including a lack of a

HUMAN
RIGHTS
WATCH

THOSE WHO TAKE US AWAY
Abusive Policing and Failures in Protection of Indigenous Women
and Girls in Northern British Columbia, Canada

mandate for independent civilian investigations into all reported incidents of serious police misconduct.

In February 2013, the federal government referred Human Rights Watch's report on police mistreatment of indigenous women and girls in BC to a complaints commission for investigation. The commission, while civilian led, often works closely with the police and does not have the power to issue binding recommendations on the RCMP. As of November, the commission's investigation was ongoing.

The federal government continues to reject calls for a national inquiry into the murders and disappearances sounded by the premiers of Canada's provinces and territories, the Assembly of First Nations, and many civil society organizations. Public national inquiries allow for impartial investigation into issues of national importance.

More than a dozen countries, including Switzerland and New Zealand, raised the issue of violence against indigenous women and girls in Canada during its second periodic review by the United Nations Human Rights Council in April 2013. Both the UN Committee on the Elimination of Discrimination against Women and the Inter-American Commission on Human Rights sent delegations to Canada to investigate the problem in 2013. After conducting his own visit in October 2013, UN Special Rapporteur on the Rights of Indigenous Peoples James Anaya endorsed the call for Canada to hold a national inquiry into the murders and disappearances of indigenous women.

Mining Industry Abuses

Canada is the mining industry's most important global hub, home to most of the world's mining and exploration companies. These firms have an enormous collective impact on the human rights of vulnerable communities worldwide

In 2013, Human Rights Watch documented allegations that Vancouver-based Nevsun Resources' flagship Bisha gold mine in Eritrea was partly built using forced labor deployed by local state-owned contractor, Segen Construction. In a statement, Nevsun expressed "regret if certain employees of Segen were conscripts" during the mine's construction, and insisted there were no ongoing abuses. However, it refused to sever ties with Segen.

In 2011, Human Rights Watch documented allegations that security guards employed by Canadian mining giant Barrick Gold had gang-raped women at a Papua New Guinea mine site and engaged in other abuses. The company has since taken steps to prevent further abuses and has promised to provide remediation to dozens of women who were victims of sexual violence. Some activists have criticized Barrick's plan because women who elect to accept the benefits will be required to sign legal waivers that they will not participate in any civil legal action against the company. However, if the plan's end results respect the rights of victims to prompt and appropriate redress, it could be a path-breaking example of how companies can move proactively to respond to serious abuses linked to their operations at home and abroad. The remediation scheme was scheduled to begin delivering compensation packages to victims in late 2013.

The Canadian government neither regulates nor monitors the human rights practices of Canadian mining companies when they go abroad. Its sole action on this front has been to establish in 2009 a corporate social responsibility counselor whose office is without oversight or investigatory powers.

Counterterrorism

Canadian citizen Omar Khadr, whom US forces captured on the battlefield in Afghanistan in July 2002 at the age of 15, was repatriated in 2012. Canada has continued to deny Khadr access to rehabilitation and reintegration services as required for former child soldiers. He remains incarcerated, serving an eight-year sentence under a plea agreement for murder in violation of the laws of war and material support for terrorism, entered in the military commission system in Guantanamo, a fundamentally flawed system with no provisions for adjudicating youth offenders. In June 2013, Khadr became eligible for parole after having served one-third of his sentence, or 32 months.

Indigenous Rights

Canada's federal government has apologized for the residential school system of the 1800s and 1900s. Approximately 150,000 indigenous children were removed from their families and communities and placed in the schools, where they were forbidden to speak their own languages or practice their culture. Many also suffered physical and sexual abuse. In 2013, information surfaced indicating that some children in residential schools in the 1940s and 50s were subjected to medical experimentation.

Indigenous groups have criticized Canada for failing to respect land agreements with indigenous communities or to consult adequately with them, including with regard to resource extraction plans on traditional lands. The government has to pay adequate attention to severe poverty, housing, water, sanitation, health care, and education problems in indigenous communities, particularly those in remote and rural areas.

Freedom of Religion

In September 2013, the provincial government of Quebec introduced a potentially discriminatory proposal that would impinge on freedom of religious expression by prohibiting government employees from displaying conspicuous religious symbols, which would include head scarves, but not small symbols, such as cross pendants. Women's centers in Quebec reported an increase in verbal and physical attacks on Muslim women after debate over the proposal began.

Asylum Seeker and Migrant Rights

In September 2013, more than 150 immigration detainees in a Toronto detention center launched a hunger strike to demand improved access to medical care and better conditions. In June 2012, Canada's parliament passed Bill C-31, which permits the government to designate a group of people arriving as an "irregular arrival," making them subject to mandatory detention with limited judicial review and risking the prolonged detention of refugees and children 16 and older.

C-31 created an administrative Refugee Appeal Division, but asylum seekers from 27 "designated countries" that have a history of respecting human rights are not allowed to appeal their denials to it, although the Federal Court may review their denials. C-31 also places a five-year ban on "irregular arrivals" from applying for permanent residence, negatively impacting the right of separated refugee families to reunite.

Civil Society

Civil society representatives and organizations across a range of fields report that government actions, including funding cuts, threatened revocation of non-profit status, and intrusive monitoring have had a chilling effect on dissent to the current federal government's policies.

In July 2013, Voices-Voix, a coalition of more than 200 national and local civil society organizations, expressed concern that the Prime Minister's Office had reportedly instructed government officials to compile "friend and enemy stake-holder" lists as part of the process of preparing briefing materials for new cabinet members.

In 2012, the natural resources minister accused environmental and other "radical groups" of trying to use money from "foreign special-interest groups" to undermine development in the country. His comments came a day before federal regulatory hearings began on whether to approve Enbridge's Northern Gateway pipeline that would deliver crude from Alberta's oilsands to Kitimat, BC, for shipment to Asia.

United States

The United States has a vibrant civil society and media that enjoy strong constitutional protections. Yet its rights record is marred by abuses related to criminal justice, immigration, national security, and drug policy. Within these areas, victims are often the most vulnerable members of society: racial and ethnic minorities, immigrants, children, the elderly, the poor, and prisoners.

Revelations in 2013 of extensive government surveillance and aggressive prosecutions of whistleblowers raised concerns about infringement of privacy rights and freedom of expression, generating a firestorm of international protest against US practices.

Federal policymakers proposed reforms to harmful longstanding immigration and sentencing laws and policies. The outcome of these initiatives was uncertain at time of writing.

A renewed commitment by President Barack Obama to close the Guantanamo Bay detention facility remained unfulfilled. Lack of transparency made it impossible to assess the implementation of promised reforms to the practice of "targeted killings" abroad, including through use of unmanned aerial drones; new information on individual strikes found instances of violations of international humanitarian and human rights law.

Harsh Sentencing

The US has the largest reported incarcerated population in the world, and by far the highest rate of imprisonment, holding 2.2 million people in adult prisons or jails as of year-end 2011.

Mass incarceration reflects three decades of harsh state and federal sentencing regimes, including increased use of life and life without parole sentences, high mandatory minimum sentences, and "three strikes" laws. The Sentencing Project reported that one in nine US prisoners are serving a life sentence.

The growing number of elderly prisoners poses a serious challenge to correctional authorities: as of 2011, the latest year for which complete numbers are available, 26,136 persons aged 65 and older were incarcerated in state and federal prisons, up 62 percent in five years.

In a positive step, the US Department of Justice in August announced revisions to its rules for reviewing requests for compassionate release of elderly or disabled prisoners, making more federal inmates eligible for this rarely used mechanism.

Also in August, US Attorney General Eric Holder instructed federal prosecutors to try to avoid charges carrying mandatory minimum sentences for certain low-level, nonviolent drug offenders. Though welcome, this policy change still leaves many drug offenders subject to disproportionately long mandatory sentences. Legislative efforts to grant judges more discretion in such cases are under debate.

In 2013, Maryland joined 17 other states and the District of Columbia in abolishing the death penalty, but 32 states still allow it. At time of writing, 34 people had been executed in the US in 2013. North Carolina repealed its 2009 Racial Justice Act, which allowed death row prisoners to appeal their sentences on the basis of racial discrimination.

Racial Disparities in Criminal Justice

Whites, African Americans, and Latinos have comparable rates of drug use but are arrested, prosecuted, and incarcerated for drug offenses at vastly different rates. For example, African Americans are nearly four times more likely to be arrested for marijuana possession than whites, even though their rates of marijuana use are roughly equivalent. While only 13 percent of the US population, African Americans represent 41 percent of state prisoners, and 44 percent of federal prisoners serving time for drug offenses.

Because they are disproportionately likely to have criminal records, members of racial and ethnic minorities are more likely than whites to experience stigma and legal discrimination in employment, housing, education, public benefits, jury service, and the right to vote.

In August, a federal court found that the "stop and frisk" policy of the New York City Police Department (NYPD) violated the rights of minorities. A disproportionate share of people "stopped and frisked" under the policy are African American or Latino, and the New York Civil Liberties Union reports that 89 percent of those stopped are innocent of any wrongdoing. The NYPD appealed the ruling.

Drug Policy Reform

In recent decades the US has spent hundreds of billions of dollars to arrest and incarcerate drug offenders in the US. Its heavy reliance on criminal laws for drug control has had serious human rights costs, including infringement of the autonomy and privacy rights of those who simply possess or use drugs.

In a welcome shift, the US Department of Justice announced in August that it would not interfere with states' legalization of marijuana so long as states comply with certain federal priorities, such as prohibiting sale of drugs to children or transport of drugs across state lines. It also noted that a robust state regulatory approach to marijuana may prevent organized crime from benefiting from the illicit marijuana trade.

Washington and Colorado moved forward with implementation of state ballot initiatives to legalize the recreational use of marijuana, as well as to regulate its production, sale, and distribution. Twenty other US states have legalized marijuana for medical purposes.

Prison Conditions

September 2013 marked the 10-year anniversary of the passage of the Prison Rape Elimination Act (PREA), which resulted in the development of national standards to detect, prevent, and punish prison rape. Implementation remains a challenge: approximately 4 percent of state and federal prison inmates and 3 percent of jail inmates report having experienced one or more incidents of sexual abuse in 2011-2012, and many incidents continue to go unreported. Transgender prisoners continue to experience high levels of violence in detention.

Many prisoners and jail inmates—including youth under age 18—are held in solitary confinement, often for weeks or months on end. In July, an estimated 30,000 inmates in California's prison system engaged in a hunger strike to protest conditions, including the use of solitary confinement. Prolonged solitary confinement is considered ill-treatment under international law and can amount to torture.

Poverty and Criminal Justice

Poor defendants across the country languish in pretrial detention because they are too poor to post bail. The most recent data indicates 60 percent of jail inmates—at a cost of $9 billion a year—are confined pending trial, often because they lack the financial resources to secure their release. In 2013, the chief judge of New York supported legislative reforms that would begin to reduce the pretrial incarceration of indigent defendants.

Extremely high court fees and surcharges are also increasingly common, as cash-strapped counties and municipalities often expect their courts to pay for themselves or even tap them as sources of public revenue. The impact on poor defendants is particularly harsh.

Practices that exacerbate and even punish economic hardship are increasingly common. In Arkansas, tenants who fall behind on their rent face criminal prosecution. In states across the US, courts put hundreds of thousands of misdemeanor offenders on probation with private, for-profit companies that charge local authorities nothing for their services but collect tens of millions of dollars in fees each year from the offenders they supervise.

In August, a decade after a group of inmates' families filed a petition challenging the exorbitant rates charged for interstate jail and prison phone calls, the Federal Communications Commission (FCC) voted to cap the cost of the calls.

In cities throughout the US, homeless people are targeted and arrested under laws that prohibit loitering, sitting, and occupying public space.

Youth in the Criminal Justice System

In nearly all US jurisdictions, substantial numbers of youth offenders are tried in adult court and sentenced to serve time in adult jails and prisons.

The widespread practice of sentencing youth offenders to life without the possibility of parole is changing as states grapple with how to comply with recent US Supreme Court decisions. Separate decisions have held that the sentence cannot ever be mandatory for youth offenders, nor can it be imposed on youth offenders convicted of non-homicide crimes. The Supreme Court has not yet abolished application of the sentence to juveniles, however, and youth offenders continue to receive life without parole sentences for homicide crimes. In 2012, Human Rights Watch reported that of 500 youth offenders serving life without parole, nearly every one reported physical violence or sexual abuse by inmates or corrections officers.

Youth are also sentenced to other extreme prison terms that are the functional equivalent of life without parole because the sentence exceeds an average lifespan. In September 2013, California passed a law creating a review process for youth sentenced to adult prison terms, requiring the parole board to provide a meaningful opportunity for release based on the diminished culpability of youth as compared to adults. In many cases this will mean earlier release.

Federal law requires jurisdictions to register juveniles convicted of certain sexual offenses on a national, publicly accessible online registry. Registration impacts youth offenders' access to education, housing, and employment.

The Rights of Noncitizens

There are approximately 25 million noncitizens in the US, nearly 12 million of whom are in the country without authorization.

The vast network of immigration detention centers in the US now holds about 400,000 noncitizens each year. At any given time, hundreds of detainees are held in solitary confinement. In September, US Immigration and Customs Enforcement (ICE) announced it would limit but not ban the use of solitary confinement.

The criminal prosecution of immigration offenses, which historically had been largely dealt with through deportation and other non-criminal sanctions, continues to increase. In 2012, immigration cases constituted 41 percent of all federal criminal cases; illegal reentry is now the most prosecuted federal crime. Many of those prosecuted have minor or no criminal history and have substantial ties to the US such as US citizen family members they were seeking to rejoin when arrested.

In 2013, after years of inaction, the US Congress began debating a major overhaul of the US immigration system. In June, the Senate passed a bill that would create a path to citizenship for millions of unauthorized immigrants and allow for greater consideration of the right to family unity in some deportation deci-

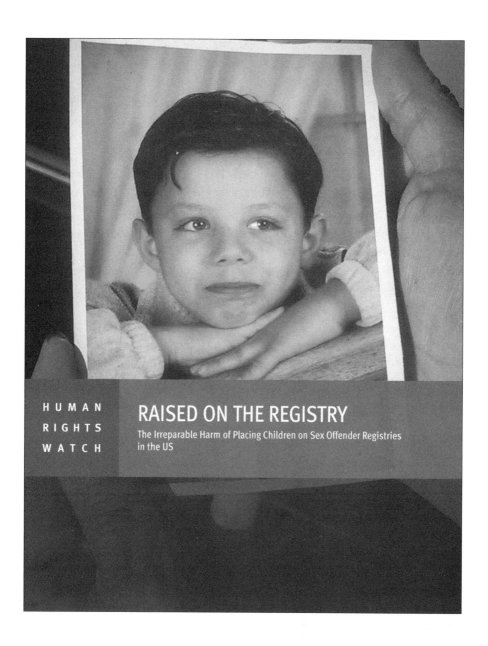

sions. If enacted into law, the bill would better align immigration enforcement and detention practices with human rights requirements, including eliminating a one-year filing deadline for asylum applicants, though it would continue to mandate the automatic deportation of noncitizens with criminal convictions, even for minor offenses. The bill calls for an additional $47 billion to be spent on enforcement efforts along the US-Mexico border, including a major increase in federal prosecutions of immigration offenses and substantial increases in penalties for illegal entry and reentry.

At time of writing, the House of Representatives had not made any serious progress on comprehensive immigration reform.

"Secure Communities" and other federal programs involving local law enforcement agencies continued to play an important role in deportations. The federal government has portrayed these programs as focused on dangerous criminals, but most immigrants deported through Secure Communities are non-criminal or lower level offenders. These programs also exacerbate distrust of police in immigrant communities.

Connecticut and California, along with the cities of Newark and New Orleans, have joined a growing number of states and localities that have placed limits on local law enforcement participation in Secure Communities, largely by declining to hold people without charge for federal immigration authorities if they have no or minor criminal history.

Labor Rights

Hundreds of thousands of children work on American farms. The 1938 Fair Labor Standards Act exempts child farmworkers from the minimum age and maximum hour requirements that apply to other working children. As a result, child farmworkers often work 10 or more hours a day and risk pesticide exposure, nicotine poisoning, heat illness, injuries, life-long disabilities, and death. Seventy-five percent of children under 16 who died from work-related injuries in 2012 worked in agriculture. Federal protections that do exist are often not enforced.

Congress has still not closed a legal loophole allowing children to do hazardous work in agriculture starting at age 16; hazardous work is prohibited in all other jobs until age 18.

Millions of US workers, including parents of infants, are harmed by weak or non-existent laws on paid leave, breastfeeding accommodation, and discrimination against workers with family responsibilities. Inadequate leave contributes to delaying babies' immunizations, postpartum depression, and other health problems, and causes mothers to stop breastfeeding early. In 2013, several federal bills were introduced to improve national work-family policies; Rhode Island joined California and New Jersey in establishing state paid family leave insurance; and several cities adopted paid sick day laws.

In September, the Obama administration issued a regulation ending the exclusion of certain homecare workers from minimum wage and hour protections. These workers, most of whom are women, including many immigrants and minorities, provide essential services to people with disabilities and the elderly.

Health Policy

Sixteen states have refused to expand Medicaid services under the Affordable Care Act, impeding the right to health for the poor, African Americans, and other groups with limited access to medical care.

HIV infections in the US continue to disproportionately affect minority communities, men who have sex with men, and transgender women. Many states continue to undermine human rights and public health through restrictions on sex education, inadequate legal protections for HIV-positive persons, resistance to harm-reduction programs such as syringe exchanges, and failure to fund HIV prevention and care. Harmful criminal justice measures include laws that target people living with HIV for enhanced penalties and police use of condom possession as evidence of prostitution.

The Rights of Women and Girls

In February, Congress renewed the Violence Against Women Act (VAWA), the primary federal law providing legal protection and services to victims of domestic and sexual violence and stalking. The new law includes enhanced protections for immigrant victims; lesbian, gay, bisexual, and transgender (LGBT) victims; and victims on tribal lands.

In January, a Human Rights Watch report detailed the inadequacy of police response to sexual assaults in the District of Columbia, leading to reforms in that police department's approach to these cases.

Emergency contraception became available without a doctor's prescription to customers of all ages in 2013. According to the Guttmacher Institute, states adopted 43 restrictions on access to abortion in the first half of 2013. These restrictions took a variety of forms, including requiring that abortion providers have admitting privileges at local hospitals, that patients undergo pre-abortion ultrasounds, and banning abortion after a specified number of weeks since the woman's last menstrual period.

In January 2013, the Department of Defense lifted a longstanding ban on women serving in direct combat roles.

Military women and men continue to face high levels of sexual violence. The government estimates that 26,000 sexual assaults took place in the military in 2012, and Defense Department data suggests that 62 percent of those who report such assaults experience retaliation.

Sexual Orientation and Gender Identity

In June, the US Supreme Court invalidated two of the most egregious anti-LGBT initiatives in the country. In *United States v. Windsor*, the court struck down section 3 of the 1996 Defense of Marriage Act (DOMA), which prohibited federal recognition of state-approved same-sex marriages. In *Hollingsworth v. Perry*, the court dismissed an appeal by proponents of Proposition 8, a 2008 California state referendum that would have revoked the right of same-sex couples to marry. The court has not yet ruled on the constitutionality of state laws that prohibit same-sex marriage.

Counterterrorism and Surveillance

The indefinite detention without charge or trial of detainees at Guantanamo Bay entered its twelfth year, with 162 detainees remaining at the facility. Eighty-two of them have been cleared for transfer to home or third countries by an inter-agency task force since 2009. Though President Barack Obama renewed his pledge to close the prison at Guantanamo in May, at time of writing his adminis-

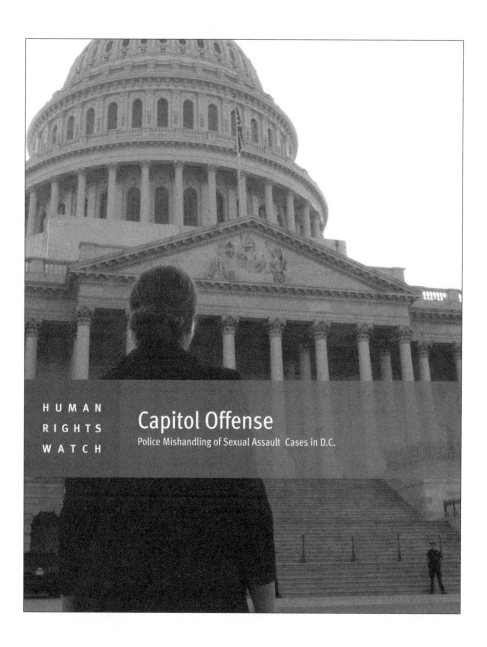

HUMAN
RIGHTS
WATCH

Capitol Offense
Police Mishandling of Sexual Assault Cases in D.C.

tration had only transferred eight detainees from the facility since 2011. Two of them were repatriated to Algeria in August, and two more were repatriated to Algeria in December.

Early in 2013, several detainees at Guantanamo began a hunger strike; at its peak, 106 reportedly participated in some fashion, with 45 being tube-fed twice a day. Medical and human rights groups wrote letters of protest noting that force-feeding of competent prisoners was a violation of medical ethics and human rights norms.

The administration continued to use fundamentally flawed military commissions at Guantanamo to prosecute detainees. Pre-trial hearings moved slowly in the only two active commission cases: one against five men accused of plotting the September 11, 2001, attacks and another against a man accused of plotting the bombing of the USS Cole in Yemen in October 2000. The commission's inability to establish rules protecting attorney-client access and communications, among other things, hampered progression of the cases. The prosecution has announced it intends to bring charges against only seven other Guantanamo detainees.

Long after the process was set to begin, the administration began reviewing the cases of Guantanamo detainees not slated for release or facing active charges, an important step towards closing the facility. But guidelines for the reviews fail to safeguard detainees' basic rights—including access to classified information where such information provides the basis for their detention, the right to be present throughout proceedings, and meaningful access to counsel.

In late 2012, the Senate Select Committee on Intelligence completed a comprehensive study of the CIA's post-September 11, 2001 secret detention and interrogation program, which ended in 2009. At time of writing, the report remained classified.

In May, President Obama announced a policy for targeted killings abroad requiring that the target be a continuing, imminent threat to US persons and that there should be near certainty that no civilians would be harmed in the strike. President Obama said the US government preference is to detain rather than kill. The full policy remains classified and no information on compliance has

has been provided. The administration has also not provided the full legal basis for its targeted killings under US and international law.

In August, Secretary of State John Kerry stated that drone strikes in Pakistan would end "very soon," though he provided no exact timeline.

Classified documents leaked to journalists by former National Security Agency (NSA) contractor Edward Snowden showed that the US has secretly used surveillance powers, granted by Congress to prevent terror attacks, to systematically capture huge streams of data, including emails, Internet searches, phone call information, and other records, from companies and communications nodes located both in the US and abroad, sometimes with the assistance of foreign governments. Most of what it intercepts comes from people not suspected of any wrongdoing, and the government retains substantial amounts of data for various periods of time. Judicial and congressional oversight of the surveillance is minimal and secretive.

People in the US have some legal protection of their privacy interest in the contents of their communications, but not in the "metadata" or details of communications usually shared with companies or other third parties (such as date, time, location, sender, and recipient). US officials assert that collection of communications does not invade privacy until the data is examined, or "queried." US law on surveillance offers little or no privacy protections for non-Americans outside the United States.

Disclosures in 2013 revealed that US officials may also be systematically undermining international encryption standards and security practices adopted by Internet companies, weakening the online security of all Internet users.

Prosecutors filed charges against Snowden under the Espionage Act. US law does not provide adequate legal protections or defenses for whistleblowers who disclose national security or intelligence information to the public, even on matters of pressing public importance. The Obama administration tried to block attempts by Snowden to obtain asylum in various countries. Snowden ultimately obtained temporary asylum in Russia.

In August, a US court martial sentenced Pfc. Chelsea (previously Bradley) Manning to 35 years in prison on Espionage Act and other charges for leaking hundreds of thousands of secret government records to Wikileaks for publication, including some that showed evidence of wrongdoing or possible war crimes. Before the trial, Manning had already pled guilty to charges amounting to 20 years' imprisonment.

US Foreign Policy

In January, US lawmakers discussed whether to send military assistance to Syrian opposition forces in that country's civil war. In February, the administration said that it would begin sending non-lethal aid, including food and medical supplies, to the opposition. In September, the US appeared ready to conduct strikes against Syria in response to the Syrian government's use of chemical weapons near Damascus that killed more than 300 people. Obama had previously indicated that use of chemical weapons in Syria constituted a "red line" that would prompt US action in the conflict.

Obama sought congressional authorization for US military engagement in Syria, but a United Nations Security Council-supported agreement to place Syria's chemical weapons under international control indefinitely delayed a congressional vote

Burma became an important part of Obama's "pivot" toward Asia, with Burma seeking to lessen its reliance on China. The US promoted greater political reform in the country and encouraged US investment in Burma, subject to human rights reporting requirements that went into effect in May. In September, the US restricted military assistance to Burma in light of child soldiers concerns.

Following the July overthrow of President Mohammed Morsi in Egypt, the US condemned the interim military government for declaring a state of emergency and for violations against civilians, including Muslim Brotherhood supporters. In October 2013, the US suspended some military and economic assistance but did so because the interim government was failing to move the country toward democracy, not because of the ongoing abuses or lack of accountability.

The US continued to play a pivotal role in mobilizing the UN Human Rights Council to respond to egregious human rights violations, including in Sri Lanka, Iran, and North Korea.

HUMAN
RIGHTS
WATCH

TOXIC TOIL

Child Labor and Mercury Exposure in Tanzania's Small-Scale Gold Mines

WORLD REPORT
2014

2013
HUMAN RIGHTS WATCH
PUBLICATIONS

The following is a list of Human Rights Watch reports published from mid-December 2012 to the end of November 2013. This list does not include press releases or other Human Rights Watch material released during the year

DECEMBER 2012

Under Siege: Indiscriminate Bombing and Abuses in Sudan's Southern Kordofan and Blue Nile States, 48 pp.

Waiting for Justice: Accountability before Guinea's Courts for the September 28, 2009 Stadium Massacre, Rapes, and Other Abuses, 58 pp.

Why They Left: Stories of Iranian Activists in Exile, 60 pp.

JANUARY 2013

Capitol Offense: Police Mishandling of Sexual Assault Cases in the District of Columbia, 196 pp.

Hear No Evil: Forced Labor and Corporate Responsibility in Eritrea's Mining Sector, 29 pp.

Race Against Time: The Need for Legal and Institutional Reforms Ahead of Zimbabwe's Elections, 28 pp.

Turned Away: Summary Returns of Unaccompanied Migrant Children and Adult Asylum Seekers from Italy to Greece, 45 pp.

FEBRUARY 2013

Breaking the Silence: Child Sexual Abuse in India, 82 pp.

High Stakes: Political Violence and the 2013 Elections in Kenya, 58 pp.

In Religion's Name: Abuses against Religious Minorities in Indonesia, 107 pp.

Mexico's Disappeared: The Enduring Cost of a Crisis Ignored, 176 pp.

Pay the Rent or Face Arrest: Abusive Impacts of Arkansas's Draconian Evictions Law, 44 pp.

Race to the Bottom: Exploitation of Migrant Workers in Advance of the 2014 Winter Olympic Games in Sochi, 142 pp.

Those Who Take Us Away: Abusive Policing and Failures in Protection of Indigenous Women and Girls in Northern British Columbia, Canada, 89 pp.

Unpunished Massacre: Yemen's Failed Response to the "Friday of Dignity" Killings, 69 pp.

"We Will Teach You a Lesson": Sexual Violence against Tamils by Sri Lankan Security Forces, 140 pp.

MARCH 2013

Guilty by Association: Human Rights Violations in the Enforcement of Cameroon's Anti-Homosexuality Law, 55 pp.

Hostages of the Gatekeepers: Abuses against Internally Displaced in Mogadishu, Somalia, 80 pp.

"Look at Us with a Merciful Eye": Juvenile Offenders Awaiting Execution in Yemen, 30 pp.

"This Old Man Can Feed Us, You Will Marry Him": Child and Forced Marriage in South Sudan, 95 pp.

APRIL 2013

"All You Can Do is Pray": Crimes Against Humanity and Ethnic Cleansing of Rohingya Muslims in Burma's Arakan State, 157 pp.

Death from the Skies: Deliberate and Indiscriminate Air Strikes on Civilians (Syria), 81 pp.

Laws of Attrition: Crackdown on Russia's Civil Society after Putin's Return to the Presidency, 76 pp.

One Billion Forgotten: Protecting the Human Rights of Persons with Disabilities, 23 pp.

Turning Rhetoric into Reality: Accountability for Serious International Crimes in Côte d'Ivoire, 73 pp.

MAY 2013

A Revolution for All: Women's Rights in the New Libya, 40 pp.

Raised on the Registry: The Irreparable Harm of Placing Children on Sex Offender Registries in the US, 110 pp.

Reforming Telecommunications in Burma: Human Rights and Responsible Investment in Mobile and the Internet, 24 pp.

"Swept Away": Abuses against Sex Workers in China, 51 pp.

Turning Migrants into Criminals: The Harmful Impact of US Border Prosecutions, 82 pp.

"What is a House without Food?": Mozambique's Coal Mining Boom and Resettlements, 122 pp.

Wrong Direction on Rights: Assessing the Impact of Hungary's New Constitution and Laws, 29 pp.

"You Are All Terrorists": Kenyan Police Abuse of Refugees in Nairobi, 68 pp.

JUNE 2013

Barely Surviving: Detention, Abuse, and Neglect of Migrant Children in Indonesia, 86 pp.

"Interfere, Restrict, Control": Restraints on Freedom of Association in Bahrain, 87 pp.

"It's Part of the Job": Ill-treatment and Torture of Vulnerable Groups in Lebanese Police Stations, 66 pp.

"Just Sign Here": Unfair Trials Based on Confessions to the Police in Morocco, 131 pp.

Safe No More: Students and Schools under Attack in Syria, 33 pp.

The Elephant in the Room: Reforming Zimbabwe's Security Sector Ahead of Elections, 37 pp.

"They Say We Should Be Grateful": Mass Rehousing and Relocation Programs in Tibetan Areas of China, 114 pp.

"Treat Us Like Human Beings": Discrimination against Sex Workers, Sexual and Gender Minorities, and People Who Use Drugs in Tanzania, 98 pp.

Unwelcome Guests: Greek Police Abuses of Migrants in Athens, 52 pp.

HUMAN
RIGHTS
WATCH

ABUSE-FREE DEVELOPMENT

How the World Bank Should Safeguard Against Human Rights Violations

"I Can Still Smell the Dead": The Forgotten Human Rights Crisis in the Central African Republic, 79 pp.

"No One's Left": Summary Executions by Syrian Forces in al-Bayda and Baniyas, 68 pp.

Rights Should Be Central to Post-2015 Development Agenda, 22 pp.

"Take That Filth Away": Police Abuses Against Street Vendors in Angola, 38 pp.

The Risk of Returning Home: Violence and Threats against Displaced People Reclaiming Land in Colombia, 184 pp.

"They Are Killing Us": Abuses Against Civilians in South Sudan's Pibor County, 45 pp.

Tightening the Screws: Azerbaijan's Crackdown on Civil Society and Dissent, 100 pp.

OCTOBER 2013

Abandoned in Agony: Cancer and the Struggle for Pain Treatment in Senegal, 85 pp.

"Between a Drone and Al-Qaeda": The Civilian Cost of US Targeted Killings in Yemen, 98 pp.

Claiming Rights: Domestic Workers' Movements and Global Advances for Labor Reform, 33 pp.

"Letting the Big Fish Swim": Failures to Prosecute High-Level Corruption in Uganda, 63 pp.

"That Land Is My Family's Wealth": Addressing Land Dispossession after Côte d'Ivoire's Post-Election Conflict, 111 pp.

"They Want a Confession": Torture and Ill-Treatment in Ethiopia's Maekelawi Police Station, 70 pp.

"You Can Still See Their Blood": Executions, Unlawful Killings, and Hostage Taking by Opposition Forces in Latakia Countryside, 105 pp.

NOVEMBER 2013

At Least Let Them Work: The Denial of Work Authorization and Assistance for Asylum Seekers in the United States, 56 pp.

Troubled Water: Burst Pipes, Contaminated Wells, and Open Defecation in Zimbabwe's Capital, 59 pp.

Unless Blood Flows: Lack of Protection from Domestic Violence in Hungary, 58 pp.

Unwelcome Guests: Iran's Violation of Afghan Refugee and Migrant Rights, 110 pp.

DECEMBER 2013

Challenging the Red Lines: Stories of Rights Activists in Saudi Arabia, 48 pp.

Cracks in the System: Conditions of Pre-Charge Detainees in Tunisia, 65 pp.

In Harm's Way: State Response to Sex Workers, Drug Users, and HIV in New Orleans, 66 pp.

"It's Nature, Not a Crime": Discriminatory Laws and LGBT People in Liberia, 34 pp.

"Leave Everything to God": Accountability for Inter-Communal Violence in Plateau and Kaduna States, Nigeria, 110 pp.

"They Came To Kill": Escalating Atrocities in the Central African Republic, 43 pp.

"They Treat Us Like Animals": Mistreatment of Drug Users and "Undesirables" in Cambodia's Drug Detention Centers, 55 pp.

All reports can be accessed online and ordered at www.hrw.org/en/publications.

Acknowledgments

A compilation of this magnitude requires contribution from a large number of people, including most of the Human Rights Watch staff. The contributors were:

Fred Abrahams, Brad Adams, Chris Albin-Lackey, Osamah Al-Fakih, Tamara Alrifai, Laetitia Bader, Pierre Bairin, Amanda Bailly, Jayshree Bajoria, Clive Baldwin, Heather Barr, Jo Becker, Rothna Begum, Daniel Bekele, Nicholas Bequelin, Eleanor Blatchley, Julia Bleckner, Carroll Bogert, Philippe Bolopion, Jackie Bornstein, Jana Boulus, Amy Braunschweiger, Valerie Brender, Sebastian Brett, Reed Brody, Jane Buchanan, Wolfgang Buettner, Joyce Bukuru, Maria Burnett, Inga Butefisch, Elizabeth Calvin, Teresa Cantero, Anna Chaplin, Grace Choi, Rashmi Chopra, Jane Cohen, Carlos Conde, Adam Coogle, Tanya Cooper, Eva Cosse, Zama Coursen-Neff, Emma Daly, Philippe Dam, Kiran D'Amico, Beneva Davies, Juliette Delay, Juliette de Rivero, Rachel Denber, Boris Dittrich, Corinne Dufka, Mariam Dwedar, Brahim Elansari, Sandy Elkhoury, Marianna Enamoneta, Jessica Evans, Elizabeth Evenson, Erin Evers, Lama Fakih, Jean-Marie Fardeau, Alice Farmer, Jamie Fellner, Bill Frelick, Elizabeth Fry, Lydia Gall, Arvind Ganesan, Meenakshi Ganguly, Leani Garcia, Liesl Gerntholtz, Neela Ghoshal, Allison Gill, Giorgi Gogia, Vugar Gojayev, Eric Goldstein, Steve Goose, Yulia Gorbunova, Jessie Graham, Laura Grant, Amna Guellali, Inara Gulpe-Laganovska, Eric Guttschuss, Danielle Haas, Charlene Harry, Andreas Harsono, Lane Hartill, Ali Dayan Hasan, Leslie Haskell, Jehanne Henry, Amy Herrman, Peggy Hicks, Felix Horne, Nadim Houry, Kyle Hunter, Peter Huvos, Claire Ivers, Shajia Jaffri, Balkees Jarrah, Rafael Jiménez, Danielle Johnson, Jeanne Jeong, Ahmed Kaaniche, Tiseke Kasambala, Aruna Kashyap, Elise Keppler, Amr Khairy, Viktoriya Kim, Phelim Kine, Juliane Kippenberg, Anna Kirey, Mariam Kirollos, Amanda Klasing, Adrian Klocke, George Kobakhidze, Maria Kunineva, Sharon Kwong, Lea Labaki, Leslie Lefkow, Izza Leghtas, Lotte Leicht, Iain Levine, Diederik Lohman, Tanya Lokshina, Hillary Margolis, Kaitlin Martin, Sarah Margon, Veronica Matushaj,

Dewa Mavhinga, Andrea Mazzarino, Maria McFarland, Nicholas McGeehan, Megan McLemore, Grace Meng, David Mepham, Lianna Merner, Wenzel Michalski, Darcy Milburn, Kathy Mills, Lisa Misol, Alba Morales, Heba Morayef, Stephanie Morin, Priyanka Motaparthy, Evita Mouawad, Lewis Mudge, Jim Murphy, Samer Muscati, Jenny Nilsson, Lisandra Novo, Agnes Odhiambo, Babatunde Olugboji, Shaivalini Parmar, Richard Pearshouse, Elaine Pearson, Rona Peligal, Camille Pendley, Sunai Phasuk, Jennifer Pierre, Laura Pitter, Dinah PoKempner, Tom Porteous, Andrea Prasow, Graeme Reid, Samantha Reiser, Meghan Rhoad, Sophie Richardson, Lisa Rimli, Mihra Rittmann, Phil Robertson, Kathy Rose, James Ross, Kenneth Roth, Hanan Salah, Katya Salmi, Faraz Sanei, Joseph Saunders, Ida Sawyer, Lea Scarpel, Max Schoening, Laura Schulke, Birgit Schwarz, Mausi Segun, Diana Semaan, Kriti Sharma, Ivy Shen, Bede Sheppard, Daniel Sheron, Robin Shulman, John Sifton, Gerry Simpson, Emma Sinclair-Webb, Param-Preet Singh, Jillian Slutzker, Paul Smith, Mickey Spiegel, Nik Steinberg, Hannah Stone, Joe Stork, Judith Sunderland, Steve Swerdlow, Veronika Szente-Goldston, Letta Tayler, Tamara Taraciuk Broner, Carina Tertsakian, Elena Testi, Tej Thapa, Storm Tiv, Annkatrin Tritschoks, Bill van Esveld, Gauri van Gulik, Nisha Varia, Jamie Vernaelde, José Miguel Vivanco, Janet Walsh, Maya Wang, Benjamin Ward, Matt Wells, Skye Wheeler, Sarah Leah Whitson, Daniel Wilkinson, Belkis Wille, Hugh Williamson, Cynthia Wong, Minky Worden, Marina Yalon, and Yasmin Yonis.

Senior Editor Danielle Haas edited the report with assistance from Deputy Program Directors Tom Porteous, Joseph Saunders, and Babatunde Olugboji. Publications Director Grace Choi and Graphic Designer Rafael Jiménez oversaw layout and production, in coordination with Creative Director Veronica Matushaj, Multimedia and Creative Services Officer Ivy Shen, Digital Director Stephen Northfield, Senior Online Editor Jim Murphy, and Publications Specialist Kathy Mills. Program Office Project Coordinator Marina Yalon coordinated editing and production.

This 24th World Report is dedicated to the memory of **Ernest Ulrich,** our dear colleague who died on November 26, 2013, at age 85. Ernest came to Human Rights Watch in 1997 after retiring from a successful career in business, and immediately began making unique and lasting contributions to the organization. From accomplishments as mundane as bringing new rigor to our negotiations with office supply companies to initiatives as grand as pushing us to open what became our Berlin office, Ernest always found no-nonsense ways to improve our work and lives. He came to the United States as a child fleeing Nazism, an experience that motivated him throughout his life. During the nearly 16 years he was with us, Ernest was a steadfast champion of international justice, of attacking corruption using human rights tools, and of the human rights cause in all its manifestations. And he was deeply beloved, someone sought out by staff at all levels for his warmth and wisdom, his gentleness and humility, and, always, his graciousness. He was also wonderful at the waltz. We miss him deeply.